THE AMERICAN PAINTINGS IN THE
PENNSYLVANIA ACADEMY OF THE FINE ARTS

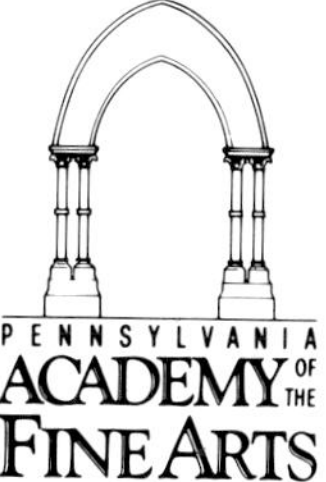

This project was jointly supported by grants from the following:

Pennsylvania Historical and Museum Commission
Henry Luce Foundation
Andrew W. Mellon Foundation

The American Paintings in the Pennsylvania Academy of the Fine Arts

AN ILLUSTRATED CHECKLIST

Compiled by Nancy Fresella-Lee
Edited by Jacolyn A. Mott

Pennsylvania Academy of the Fine Arts / Philadelphia
in association with the
University of Washington Press / Seattle and London

Designed by Klaus Gemming
Typeset by Finn Typographic Service
Printed and bound in the United States of America
by Rembrandt Press, a division of Corbett Press,
and Mueller Trade Bindery, respectively.

Library of Congress Cataloging-in-Publication Data

Fresella-Lee, Nancy, 1960–
The American paintings in the Pennsylvania
Academy of the Fine Arts: an illustrated checklist /
compiled by Nancy Fresella-Lee; [edited] by
Jacolyn A. Mott.
p. cm.
1. Painting, American—Catalogs.
2. Painting—Pennsylvania—Philadelphia
—Catalogs. 3. Pennsylvania Academy of
the Fine Arts—Catalogs. I. Mott, Jacolyn A.
II. Pennsylvania Academy of the Fine Arts.
III. Title.
ND205.F728 1989
759.13'074'74811—dc20 89-16205

ISBN 0-943836-11-5

CONTENTS

ACKNOWLEDGMENTS

The Pennsylvania Academy of the Fine Arts is deeply grateful to the Pennsylvania Historical and Museum Commission, the Henry Luce Foundation, and the Andrew W. Mellon Foundation for the generous grants that made possible not only the publication of this book but also the extensive research on which it is based. The resulting insights, reassessments, and new information will make the Pennsylvania Academy's paintings collection all the more useful to scholars and public alike. This project began under the leadership of Frank H. Goodyear, Jr., when he was curator; and the preliminary work was ably carried out by Steven Ediden. The bulk of responsibility, however, was borne by Nancy Fresella-Lee. She researched, made comparisons, and measured paintings; interviewed Academy faculty; wrote letters of inquiry to artists, artists' families, collectors, gallery owners, and scholars; and kept careful records. It is to her that the greatest measure of appreciation is due.

We are grateful to the many scholars who generously shared their knowledge. Principal among them are Robin Bolton-Smith, associate curator, National Museum of American Art, Smithsonian Institution; Rowland Elzea, associate director and chief curator, Delaware Art Museum, Wilmington; William Gerdts, professor of art history, Graduate School, City University of New York; Carol E. Hevner, research consultant, Peale Family Papers, Smithsonian Institution; Patricia Hills, professor of art history, Boston University; Dale Johnson, research consultant, Department of American Paintings and Sculpture, Metropolitan Museum of Art; Deborah Johnson, twentieth-century critic, Providence College, Rhode Island; Ellen Miles, curator, Department of Painting and Sculpture, National Portrait Gallery, Smithsonian Institution; Linda Simmons, assistant curator of collections, Corcoran Gallery of Art; Mark Thistlethwaite, associate professor of art history, Texas Christian University, Fort Worth; Carolyn J. Weekley, director, Abby Aldrich Rockefeller Folk Art Center, Williamsburg; and Barbara Wolanin, curator, United States Capitol. Kathleen Luhrs, editor, Department of American Paintings and Sculpture, Metropolitan Museum of Art, identified sitters, dated paintings, and suggested sources for further information. David Meschutt provided information on Alonzo Chappel; Phyllis Peet, on Emily Sartain; and Robert Torchia, on John Neagle. Tara Tappert identified many of the Beaux sketches as studies for major works. James Yarnall and Peter Y. Lee provided computer expertise.

A project of this scope necessarily involves most of the Pennsylvania Academy's staff–including former employees as well as current ones. They are all commended for their enthusiastic cooperation amid other pressing deadlines. Special thanks are due to Susan Danly, curator, who coordinated the efforts of the curatorial staff and provided valuable information and suggestions for further research. Thanks also to Kathleen A. Foster, adjunct curator; Mark Bockrath, paintings conservator; Marietta Bushnell, librarian; Cheryl A. Leibold, archivist; Gale Rawson, registrar; and Robert A. Harman, associate registrar. Intensive work on the project was done by Cynthia Haveson Veloric, research assistant; Ann Pryce, curatorial assistant; Timothy Gilfillan and the entire staff of preparators; Lynn Candido, student intern; and William Gremmel, computer keypunch operator.

The preparation of this catalogue was in the capable hands of Jacolyn A. Mott, editor in chief. Her contribution extended throughout the book from the editing of all text, to the visual appearance, to the index. Working closely with the compiler, the curator, and the designer, she gave cohesion to all the efforts. Klaus Gemming created an elegant design, which presents the many photographs with sensitive regard for their importance and relative size; he also coordinated the production of the book. Jean Wagner was tirelessly meticulous in proofreading under pressure.

Linda Bantel
Director of the Museum

A Rich Heritage

Any serious scholar studying the history of American art must visit the Pennsylvania Academy of the Fine Arts to see its rich collection and vast archives. The history of the Academy is the history not only of a museum but also of an art school, itself a major cultural force. The two components reflect over 180 years of teaching, collecting, exhibiting, and preserving.

The Pennsylvania Academy was established in 1805, when the nation was still young. The founders represented a unique collaboration of the artistic, civic, and mercantile interests of Philadelphia. They were inspired by the example of the Royal Academy in London. Philadelphia was the interim capital of the nation at the time, and it was felt that institutions like the Pennsylvania Academy would develop a cultural climate so captivating that Philadelphia might be made the permanent seat of government. While the strategy failed to prevent the move of the nation's capital to Washington, D.C., it brought about the creation, in the Pennsylvania Academy, of one of the most prestigious and long-lived institutions of its kind in America.

Since 1805, the Museum of the Pennsylvania Academy has amassed one of the most distinguished American art collections in the world, comprising almost 1,700 paintings, over 300 sculptures, and 12,000 works on paper. This catalogue is the first illustrated publication to list all the paintings. It is also the first of a series that will present the entire collection to the public and the scholarly community. The catalogue gives basic information on 1,679 works: 1,621 oils on canvas, 5 artist's palettes, 43 miniatures, and 10 miscellaneous objects, including tapestries by Alexander Calder and stained glass by John La Farge. Over 900 illustrations provide an armchair tour of the collection. It spans more than 250 years, beginning in the colonial period with a painting by Gustavus Hesselius of about 1720 and continuing with an early portrait by Benjamin West, a Pennsylvanian and the first American artist to achieve international recognition. Of the same period are two recently acquired pictures: an imposing portrait by Boston's John Singleton Copley and a monumental group portrait by the Pennsylvania-born artist Henry Benbridge.

The undisputed strength of the paintings collection, however, lies in the subsequent Federal period coincident with the Academy's founding. Few collections can boast the depth and quality represented in the portrait, history, genre, still-life, and landscape paintings of this era. Charles Willson Peale, an artist and natural scientist and a founder of the Pennsylvania Academy, is well represented, as are various members of his family. Sixty paintings by the Peales are in the collection. There are forty-five portraits by Thomas Sully; twenty-eight by Gilbert Stuart, including his regal Lansdowne portrait of George Washington; and excellent examples of the work of lesser-known artists, such as Jacob Eichholtz and John Neagle. The collection contains early genre paintings by John Lewis Krimmel, landscapes by Thomas Doughty, still lifes by James and Raphaelle Peale, and magnificent history paintings that have become icons of American art—for example, John Vanderlyn's *Ariadne Asleep on the Island of Naxos* and Benjamin West's *Death on the Pale Horse.* Such quality and diversity became possible only because most of these works were acquired during the nineteenth century when other American institutions were focusing on European works. The Pennsylvania Academy's collection is therefore an important reflection of the history of American art as well as a documentation of the patronage and artistic milieu of Philadelphia during the nineteenth century.

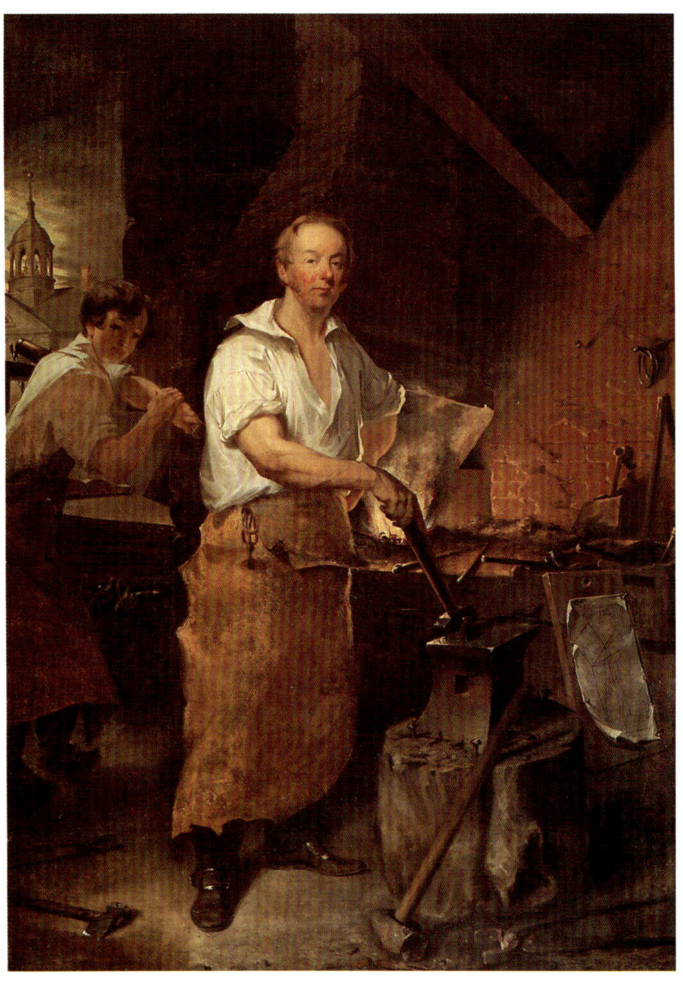

Pat Lyon at the Forge by John Neagle

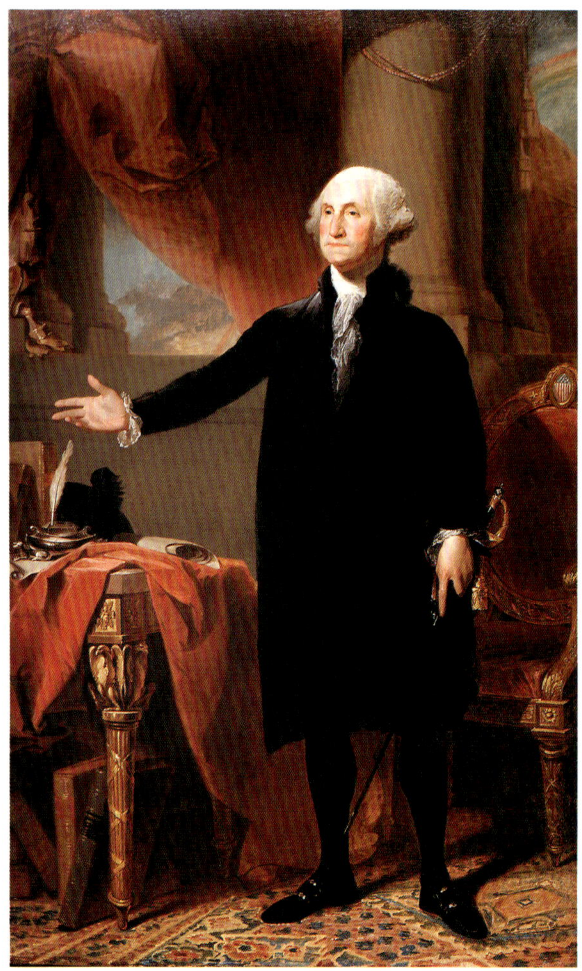

George Washington (The Lansdowne Portrait) by Gilbert Stuart

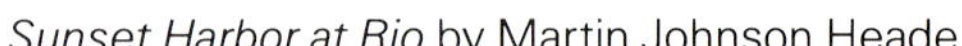

Sunset Harbor at Rio by Martin Johnson Heade

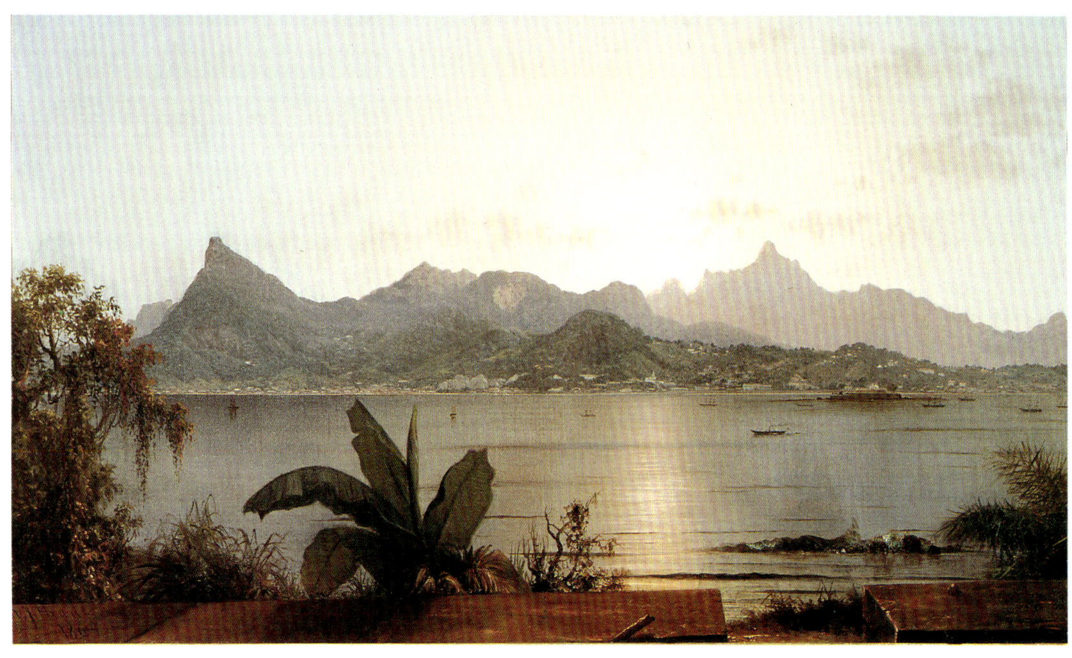

The characteristics that set apart the collection of the Pennsylvania Academy are not only its age and variety, which are indeed impressive, but also the fact that a continuous philosophy of buying works of living artists has been pursued. In this context, one can appreciate the collection's emphasis on portraits of the early nineteenth century. The popularity of portraiture at that time reflected a youthful obsession with self, related to the affluence and national pride of the post-revolutionary-war era.

As the nineteenth century progressed, the collection was shaped by Philadelphia's collectors, by the Academy's administration, and particularly by the artists who taught at the School and participated in the prestigious Pennsylvania Academy annual exhibitions. The emphasis on history painting that had defined the early decades of the nineteenth century set the stage for a century-long preoccupation with the figure. Figure drawing and the study of anatomy became the core of the School's curriculum and, in turn, defined the Museum's collecting preference. Landscape painting, which dominated mid-nineteenth-century painting in New York, was therefore of little interest to the academic taste of Philadelphia. Thus, it was not until the twentieth century that significant works by the artists of the Hudson River school entered the collection. They were donated by John Frederick Lewis, Jr. Among his gifts were Jasper F. Cropsey's *Landscape with Figures near Rome* and John Frederick Kensett's *Hill Valley, Sunrise*.

The period from 1890 to 1910, when American artists began working in a more international style, represents one of the high points of the Academy's collecting and exhibiting history. In 1892, for example, the sixty-second annual exhibition positioned the Pennsylvania Academy among the most progressive institutions in the country because it showcased a cross section of American artists, from Philadelphia, Boston, and New York, as well as

Sailing in the Mist by John H. Twachtman

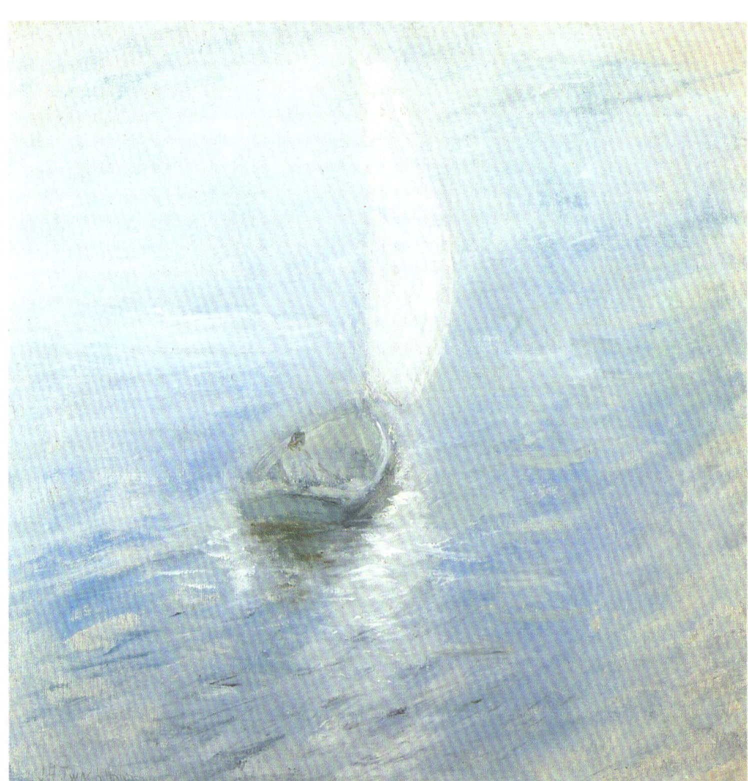

American artists working abroad, many in the new style of impressionism. For the first time, the jury included artists outside the Philadelphia area, such as Kenyon Cox, Abbott H. Thayer, and Will H. Low. The advertisement for the show heralded it as "The Dawn of New American Art: Impressionism!" It was from exhibits such as this that the Museum purchased works by some of the most extraordinary artists of the day: John H. Twachtman's *Sailing in the Mist,* Edmund C. Tarbell's *The Breakfast Room,* Childe Hassam's *Catboats, Newport,* Thomas Eakins's *The Cello Player,* and William Sergeant Kendall's *Beatrice.*

In the early twentieth century, the Museum gradually concentrated on artists with Academy affiliations, either as teachers or as students. In 1908, for example, the Academy hosted the landmark exhibition of The Eight, dubbed "The Ashcan School" by the press. They were a group of artists whose works had been rejected by the conservative jury of the National Academy of Design. Organized by Robert Henri for the Macbeth Gallery in New York, the exhibition featured five artists who had studied at the Pennsylvania Academy: Henri, John Sloan, William J. Glackens, George Luks, and Everett Shinn. As a result, this group is well represented in the Academy's collection. Academy faculty during this period are equally well represented. There are works by Arthur B. Carles, Jr.–who was perhaps Philadelphia's most important and influential twentieth-century painter working in the French modernist mode–and by Daniel Garber, Hobson Pittman, and Morris Blackburn, among many others. The philosophy of collecting works by Academy and Philadelphia artists served the Academy well when it and the city played a more central role in the art world. As that focus shifted away from Philadelphia, the notion became less viable. After World War II, for instance, abstract expressionism was considered the dominant style, and works by artists of the New York School were shown in the Academy's annual exhibitions. Nonetheless, the Museum continued to collect realism, and the School held fast to a strongly academic curriculum. There were, however, occasional courageous acquisitions, such as Conrad Marca-Relli's cubistic abstraction *The Hurdle,* purchased in 1960, and Richard Diebenkorn's *Interior with Doorway,* purchased in 1964.

No discussion of the collection would be complete without mention of the Academy's most famous alumnus and teacher, Thomas Eakins. During his lifetime and immediately thereafter, significant portraits by Eakins, such as *Walt Whitman* and *The Cello Player,* were bought for the collection. Then, in 1985, the Academy was able to buy a treasure trove of inestimable value to Eakins scholars. Although Susan Macdowell Eakins, the artist's widow, had given the bulk of his major works to the Philadelphia Museum of Art, one important cache of Eakins material–the Charles Bregler collection–remained in private hands. Charles Bregler, a long-time friend and student of Eakins, had assembled 160 oil sketches, 1,500 photographs, 883 drawings (many unpublished), and more than 1,000 letters and other manuscripts. With the purchase of this collection from Bregler's widow, Mary, the Pennsylvania Academy became a major center for the study of Thomas Eakins. (The Bregler materials, including the paintings, are in the process of being catalogued for a forthcoming publication.)

The Academy has concentrated holdings of several artists' works: for example, sixty-two paintings by Charles Lewis Fussell, an Academy student and lifelong friend of Eakins, and forty-one paintings by Thomas P. Anshutz, one of Eakins's star pupils and later an Academy teacher. Cecilia Beaux studied at the Academy from 1877 to 1879, when Eakins was a teacher of drawing and painting. The Academy bought its first Beaux painting, *New England Woman,* in 1896. Since then, due to the generosity of her descendants, the Beaux collection has expanded to include nine more major oils, forty oil sketches, and a vast body of manuscript material.

When the Pennsylvania Academy's annual exhibitions were discontinued in 1969, a lull in collecting occurred that lasted nearly a decade. In 1976, the Academy completely renovated its magnificent main building, designed a century earlier by Frank Furness and George Hewitt. Once this National Historic Landmark had been restored to its Victorian splendor, the Academy again turned its attention to building the collection. A philosophy was formulated that focused on contemporary American realism, in keeping with the figurative tradition represented in the Museum's collection and stressed in the School's curriculum. As a result, important realist works by Alex Katz, Philip Pearlstein, Alfred Leslie, James Robert Valerio, Neil G. Welliver, William Bailey, Rackstraw Downes, and Lennart Anderson were acquired. More recently, the Academy has reaffirmed its role as a national museum of American art and expanded the scope of the collection by including a broader representation of American art, both stylistically and regionally. Recent acquisitions include major paintings by Katherine Porter, Gregory Amenoff, Jacob Lawrence, Robert Motherwell, Irving Petlin, Red Grooms, and Jack Tworkov. These last two artists were subjects of major retrospectives organized by the Academy.

The Pennsylvania Academy's collection has grown and evolved in a variety of ways. In the early nineteenth century, it was not uncommon for the board of directors to raise money for purchases through public subscriptions. Twice, they mortgaged the building to acquire important paintings: Washington Allston's *The Dead Man Restored to Life by Touching the Bones of the Prophet Elisha* and Benjamin West's *Death on the Pale Horse*. By the third quarter of the century, generous benefactors began to establish funds expressly for the purchase of works of art. The first was provided by Henry D. Gilpin, who was president of the Academy from 1852 to 1859. A second was endowed by another board member, Joseph E. Temple, for the purchase of works from the annual exhibitions. Since the discontinuance of the annuals in 1969, the Temple fund has been used to buy works by living American artists. In 1911 another purchase fund for works from the annual exhibitions was established by the bequest of John Lambert, a former Academy student. He designated it to "help younger artists who have not yet made a standard reputation." This fund, like the Temple fund, is now used to acquire contemporary art. In fact, the John Lambert Fund has been the principal vehicle in shaping the contemporary portion of the Academy's collection. There are over 400 Lambert fund acquisitions, making them the largest group within the paintings collection. Most recently, this fund has been used to buy work exhibited in the Morris Gallery, a space in the Museum devoted to emerging artists with a Philadelphia connection. The newest acquisitions fund is named after Henry S. McNeil, who was active on the board of directors from 1971 until his death in 1983 and served as its president from 1977 to 1980. Aware of the Academy's pressing need for money to buy works of art that address some of the historical gaps in the collection, he bequeathed an endowment for that purpose. His family has added to it over the years until it is now one of the major funds for that formerly neglected category of acquisitions. The Academy had long felt the lack of a painting by John Singleton Copley, who influenced Charles Willson Peale in the formative years of the latter's career. Therefore, in 1984, the first purchase made through the McNeil fund was Copley's *Robert "King" Hooper*. It was followed in 1987 by the purchase of another colonial painting, *The Gordon Family* by Henry Benbridge.

Donations of large collections of objects, particularly in the nineteenth century, provided the core of the Pennsylvania Academy's collection. Joseph Harrison, Jr., who had earned his fortune building locomotives for the Russian railroad, bought a number of important paintings from the sale of Charles Willson Peale's museum in 1854. The following year, Harrison became a member of the Pennsylvania Academy's board of directors, on which he

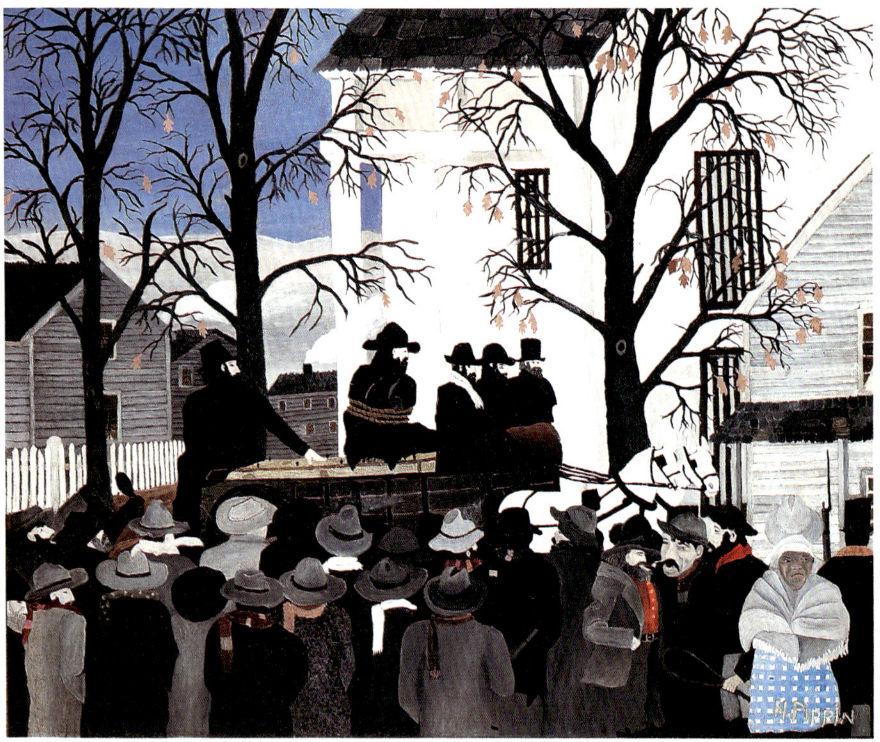

John Brown Going to His Hanging by Horace Pippin

Jefferson Market by John Sloan

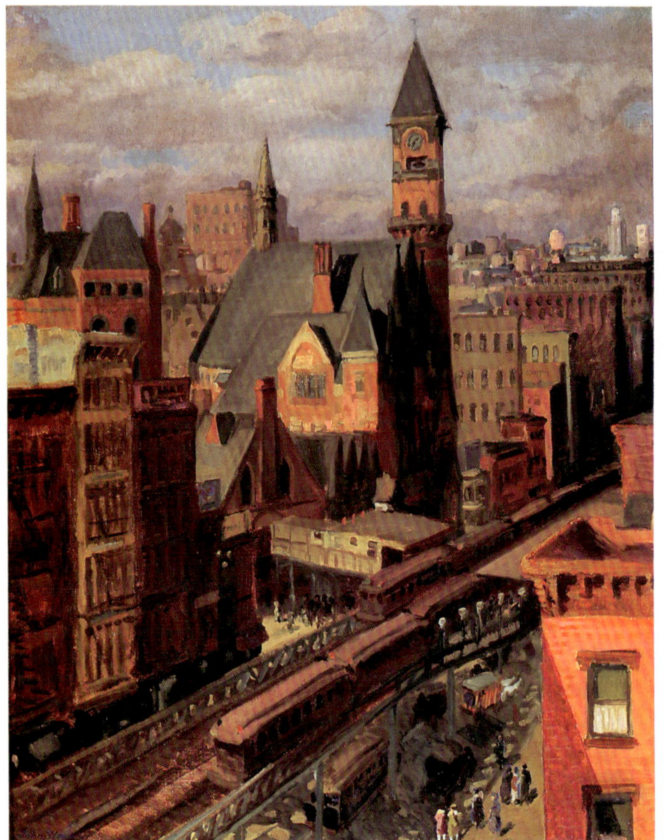

Interior with Doorway by Richard Diebenkorn

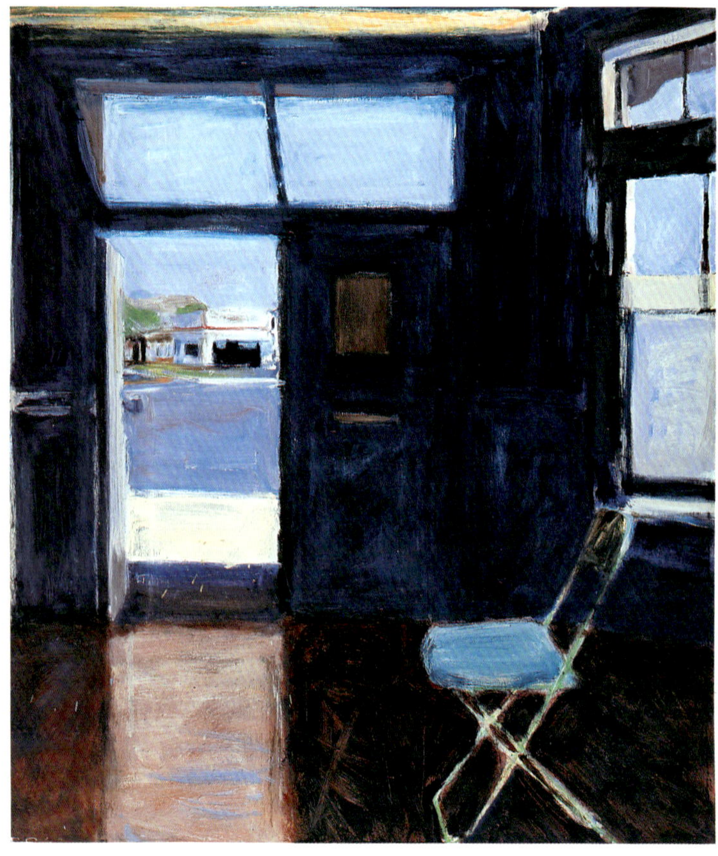

served until 1870. The first gift from his collection was given in 1878 when Harrison's widow, Sarah, presented the Academy with eleven paintings. Among them were many that have since become the most widely recognized works in the Academy's collection. They include Charles Willson Peale's *The Artist in His Museum,* John Vanderlyn's *Ariadne Asleep on the Island of Naxos,* and Benjamin West's *Penn's Treaty with the Indians* and *Christ Rejected.* The second installment came in 1912 as a bequest from Sarah Harrison of six more works from her husband's collection. Among them were Charles Willson Peale's portraits of Benjamin Franklin and George Washington, and Rembrandt Peale's *George Washington, Patriae Pater.*

Edward L. Carey, an eminent publisher, was elected the Academy's fourth president on June 2, 1845, but died only two weeks later. He had befriended many American artists and

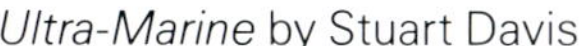

Ultra-Marine by Stuart Davis

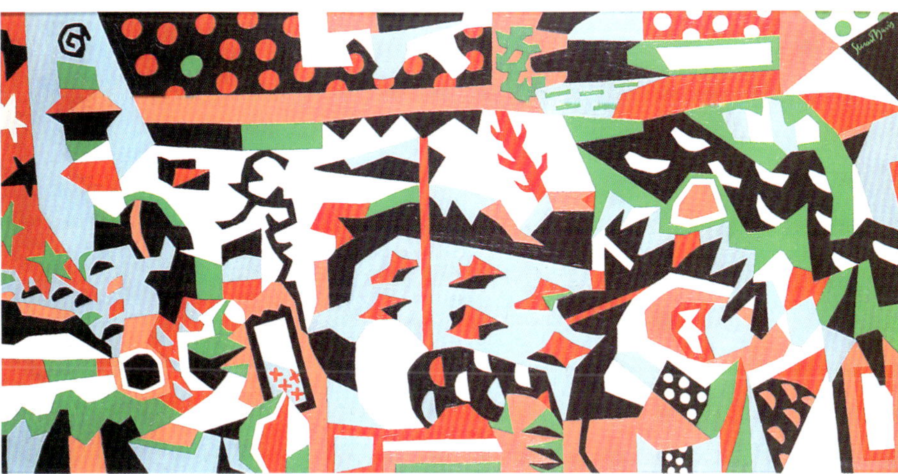

Night by Alex Katz

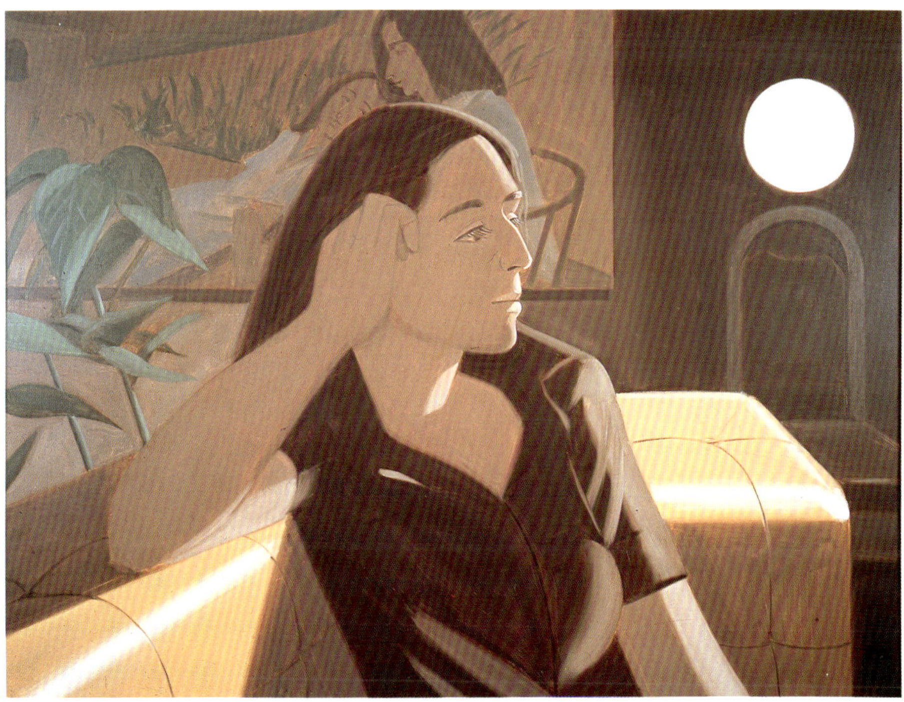

commissioned from them such works as Daniel Huntington's *Christiana and Her Family Passing through the Valley of the Shadow of Death,* Henry Inman's *Mumble-the-Peg,* and William Sidney Mount's *The Painter's Triumph.* Carey left his collection to his brother, Henry, and their sister, Maria. Then, in 1879, Henry, who had also acquired Maria's share upon her death in 1863, bequeathed the whole collection to the Academy.

Henry C. Gibson was a nineteenth-century collector whose fortune was founded on his family's distillery and wine-importing business. A patron of many Philadelphia institutions, he served on the board of directors of the Pennsylvania Academy from 1870 until his death in 1891 and was vice president during his last year. He bequeathed 102 objects to the Academy, mostly by nineteenth-century European artists. The Museum's redefining of its mission so as to focus on American art has entailed the deaccessioning of European works that are without legal restrictions, including those of the Gibson collection. The income from the sale of these paintings has been placed in a fund bearing the name of the original donor. The Henry C. Gibson Fund is restricted to the purchase of American art of the nineteenth century, the same period as his original collection. In 1985, the Gibson fund was used to buy *Sunset Harbor at Rio* by Martin Johnson Heade, the first work by this Pennsylvania-born artist to enter the collection. Two years later, *De Soto Raising the Cross on the Banks of the Mississippi,* an important, recently rediscovered, early history painting by Peter Frederick Rothermel, was acquired. From 1843 until his death in 1895, Rothermel exhibited and taught at the Academy and at various times was active on the board of directors. Altogether there are now thirteen of his works in the Academy's collection, including three from the Gibson bequest.

Fortunately, donors in the twentieth century have perpetuated the tradition of generosity. For example, John Frederick Lewis, the president of the Pennsylvania Academy from 1907 to 1932 and an avid collector of American portraits of the eighteenth and nineteenth centuries, gave many paintings during his lifetime. In 1933 in his memory, Anne H. Baker Lewis, his widow, gave over 100 more. Included in these gifts were Benjamin West's early portrait *Elizabeth Peel,* James Peale's *The Artist and His Family,* Sarah Miriam Peale's *Anna Maria Smyth,* and self-portraits by Adolph Ulric Wertmüller, Charles Loring Elliot, William Sidney Mount, and Emanuel Leutze. In 1979, the Academy received a bequest from David J. Grossman of seven paintings by Horace Pippin, a self-taught artist born in Pennsylvania. The Academy had already acquired *John Brown Going to His Hanging,* and the Grossman bequest made the institution a major repository for Pippin's work.

The past has given the Pennsylvania Academy a rich heritage—together with a grave responsibility to maintain the standards of the generous donors and perceptive administrators who handed down that legacy. We must build on its strengths while dealing effectively with the economic realities of the present day. Continual refining of our collecting philosophy will be necessary so that it reflects the Academy's ongoing commitment to its traditional goals: to support living American artists and to play both a regional and a national role in contemporary art.

Linda Bantel
and Nancy Fresella-Lee

READER'S GUIDE TO THE CATALOGUE

The purpose of this catalogue is to provide scholars, students, and the public in general with an illustrated checklist of the American paintings acquired through 1987 by the Pennsylvania Academy of the Fine Arts. Not included are the paintings and sketches in Charles Bregler's Thomas Eakins Collection, which are being catalogued, conserved, and photographed for publication in a separate catalogue of that important collection. In addition to its paintings, the Pennsylvania Academy has large collections of sculpture and works on paper (including watercolors). Catalogues of these objects are also being prepared.

The entire paintings collection has been reevaluated for this checklist. All the objects have been freshly examined and their histories reviewed, especially as recorded in the files of the Museum's registrar and the archives. Correspondence with artists, artists' families and descendants, scholars, and donors has elicited valuable new information.

Organization The catalogue is divided into four parts: oil paintings, palettes, miniatures, and miscellaneous works. Each is arranged alphabetically by artist. There are cross-references when artists have used more than one name; the main reference is the name most often used professionally. Furthermore, there are cross-references from the paintings section to the others for artists who are represented by works in more than one medium; in that event, not only the name but also the entry number or numbers are given. Unidentified artists are grouped at the end of each section.

Uncertain Authorship *Attributed to* indicates that there is strong scholarly opinion in favor of assigning the work to the hand of a given artist but insufficient documentary evidence to be conclusive. *Formerly attributed to* designates an attribution that appeared in previous records or publications by the Pennsylvania Academy but for which there is now sufficient documentation or scholarly opinion to warrant deattribution or reattribution to another artist.

Artists' Life Dates Dates in parentheses after an artist's name are those of birth and death. If only one is known, it is identified by *b.* or *d.* preceding the date. When an artist is known to be living, the birth date is followed by a dash and a blank space.

Nationality Almost all the paintings are by Americans or by artists who worked mainly in the United States. A few Europeans who painted American subjects are included; their nationalities are given before the life dates and are enclosed in the same parentheses.

Sequence of the Artwork The works of each artist are arranged alphabetically by title, and portraits are alphabetized by surname. Sitters' names with particles, such as *de* and *von*, are treated according to the preference of the individual or the usage established by tradition (e.g., *Baron Frederick William von Steuben* is alphabetized by *S*). When several works bear identical titles, the dated ones are given first, in chronological order, the undated follow in order of their accession numbers (found in the last line of each entry). *Formerly* preceding a title indicates that the painting was so called in previous records or publications by the Pennsylvania Academy but new evidence warrants a change in title.

Order within the Entries The information about each work is arranged as follows: title, date, medium and support, dimensions, signature and inscriptions, credit and accession number. In the case of portraits, a great effort has been made to provide the sitters' names and life dates. When the identification is uncertain, a question mark follows the title. *After* indicates that the painting is a copy of a work by another artist whose name is then given; when known, the date of the original is also supplied.

Date of work The date a work was executed appears after the title and is separated from it by a comma rather than being enclosed in parentheses (as life dates are). Many dates have been assigned, based on such criteria as documentary evidence, style, and, in the case of portraits, the age of the sitter. Inclusive dates (e.g., 1811–13) signify that the work was in progress during that span of time; they do not express uncertainty. Dates that are approximate are preceded by *ca.* Sometimes, although the date of execution is not known, there is evidence in the records of the Pennsylvania Academy or in an early publication that a work was in existence by a certain time (e.g., it may have been shown in one of the Academy's annual exhibitions). In this case, *by* precedes the date.

Measurements Dimensions are given first in inches, then in centimeters. Height precedes width. Supports are understood to be rectangular except when characterized as *oval*, which is always used to indicate the shape of the support rather than the painted area.

Inscriptions The artist's signature and any inscriptions on the painting are noted. The terms *signed, inscribed, and/or dated* indicate handwriting that, in the compiler's opinion, belongs to the artist; whereas *annotated* signals writing that has not been identified.

Credit and accession number The last line gives the source of the work, usually the donor of purchase funds or of the art itself. The accession number tells the year the Academy acquired the work (the first four digits) and the sequence in which it was accepted (e.g., *1938.15* denotes the fifteenth work to be received in 1938). Added digits indicate the sequence of the work within an acquisition composed of a number of works.

Related Works Related works–such as preliminary studies and finished paintings, also originals and copies–are cross-referenced.

Illustrations More than half the collection is illustrated. A catalogue number accompanies each photograph to relate it to the appropriate entry.

Index The index lists artists, works, and sitters. The numbers refer to catalogue entries rather than pages. Many of the artists are represented not only by their own works but also by portraits painted by their colleagues. Because the index consolidates all the information on a particular artist, these portraits can be readily discovered.

Catalogue

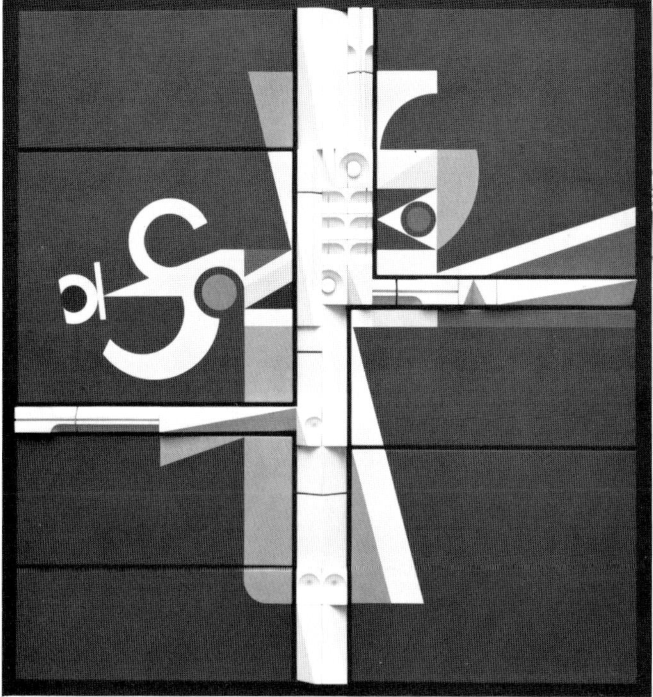

8

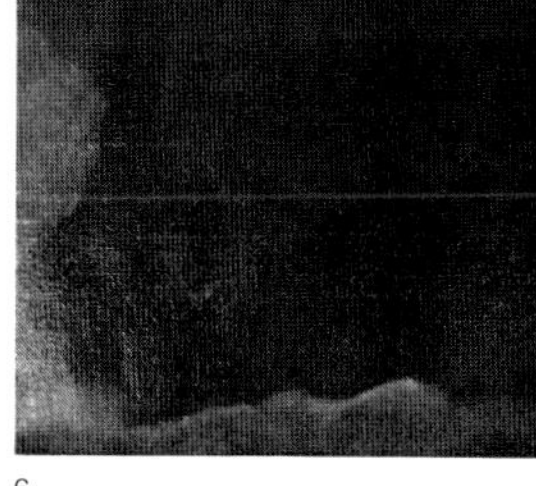

6

May Todd Aaron (1879–1968)

1 *Gangway*, 1931
Oil on canvas
20 1/16 x 24 3/16 in. (51 x 61.4 cm.)
Signed and dated at lower left: MAYTODDAA 7 '31
John Lambert Fund, 1932.2

Eleanor Plaisted Abbott (Mrs. Yarnall Abbott, 1875–1935)

2 *Allegro* (formerly *The Dance*), 1896–97
Oil on canvas
Approx. 80 x 102 in. (203 x 259 cm.)
Signed at lower right: ELEANOR/PLAISTED
Commissioned by the Pennsylvania Academy, 1897.9.6

Yarnall Abbott (1870–1938)

3 *August, Lanesville*, 1935
Oil on canvas
40 1/4 x 50 3/16 in. (102.2 x 127.5 cm.)
Signed at lower left: Yarnall/Abbott; inscribed, signed, and dated on back: August, Lanesville/ Yarnall Abbott'35
Gift of Marjorie Abbott Harvey, 1938.15

Katherine Langhorne Adams (ca. 1882–1977)

4 *Man and Beast*, 1934
Oil on canvas
26 1/16 x 32 in. (66.2 x 81.3 cm.)
Signed and dated on back: Signed:/ K.Langhorne- 1934
John Lambert Fund, 1934.1

Clifford Isaac Addams (1876–1942)

5 *Decoration*; on back, *Landscape* (sketch), ca. 1912
Oil on canvas
18 3/8 x 29 3/4 in. (46.7 x 75.6 cm.)
Signed at upper left: CIA [monogram]
Annotated on stretcher: Clifford Addams
John Lambert Fund, 1913.2

6 *Portrait of the Artist's Wife* (Inez Bate Addams), 1906
Oil on canvas
78 1/2 x 35 3/16 in. (199.4 x 89.4 cm.)
Signed and dated at lower right: ADDAMS'06
Henry D. Gilpin Fund, 1913.1

David Adickes (1927–)

7 *Still Life with Melon*, 1957
Oil and silver leaf on masonite
12 1/16 x 15 15/16 in. (30.6 x 40.5 cm.)
John Lambert Fund, 1958.1

Abe Ajay (1919–)

8 *Relief Painting #1274*, 1974
Polyester resin and acrylic on canvas, mounted on wood
44 1/2 x 44 1/2 x 2 1/2 in. (113.5 x 113.5 x 6.4 cm.)
Signed and dated at lower right: AJAY 74
Gift of Will Barnet, 1976.20

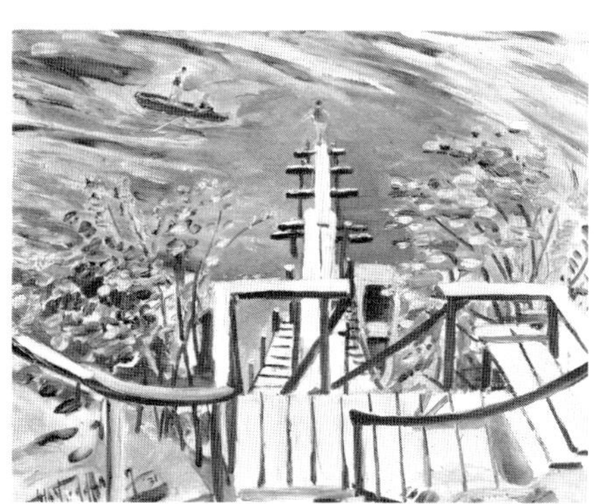

1

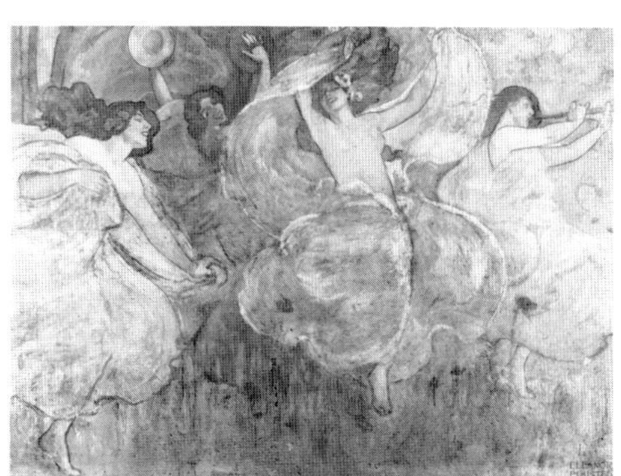

2

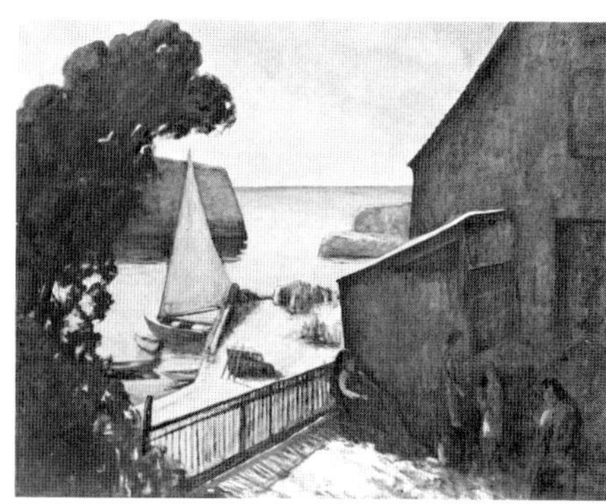

3

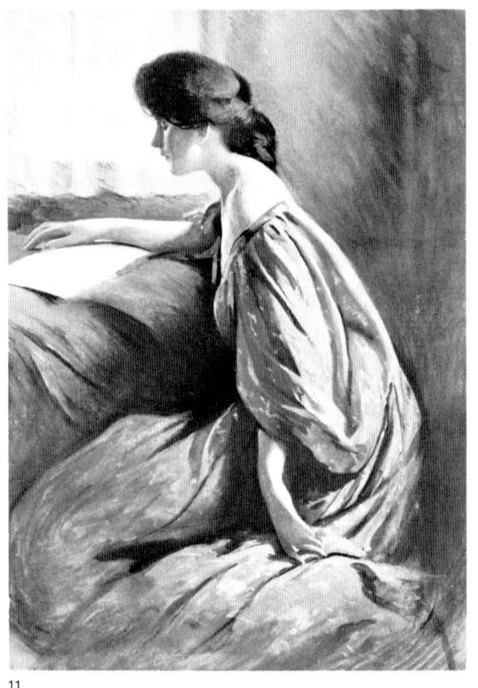
11

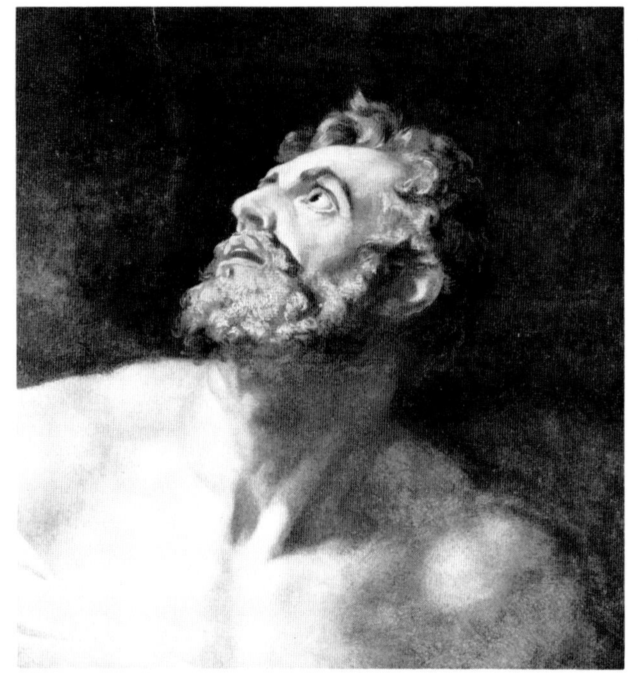
13

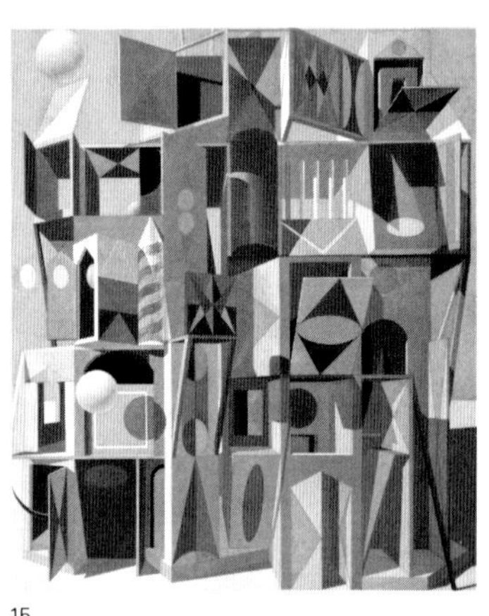
15

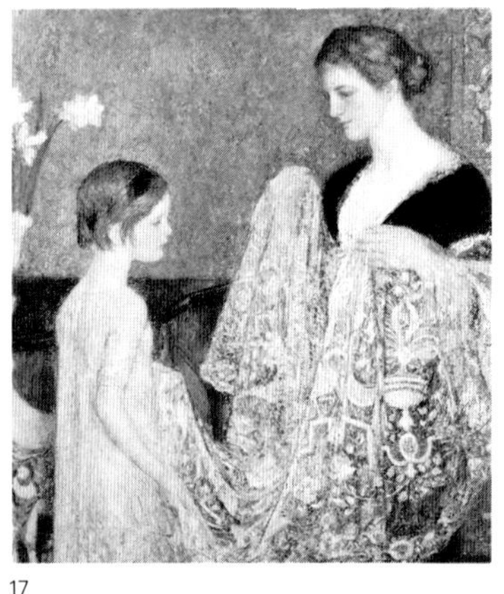
17

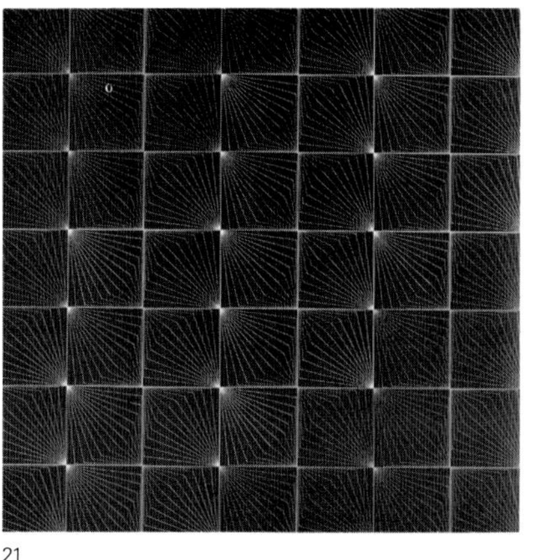
21

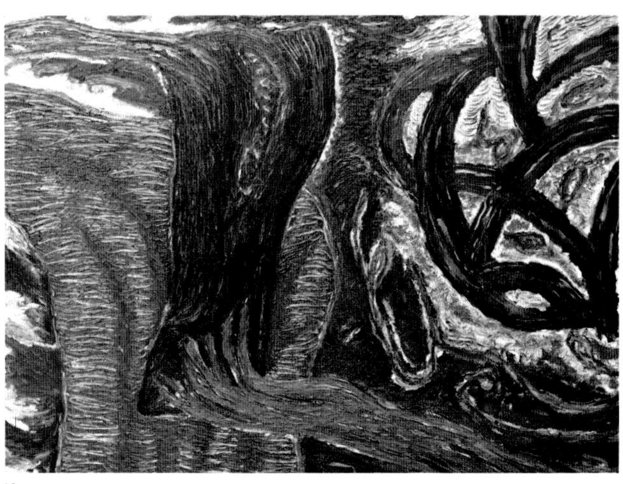
16

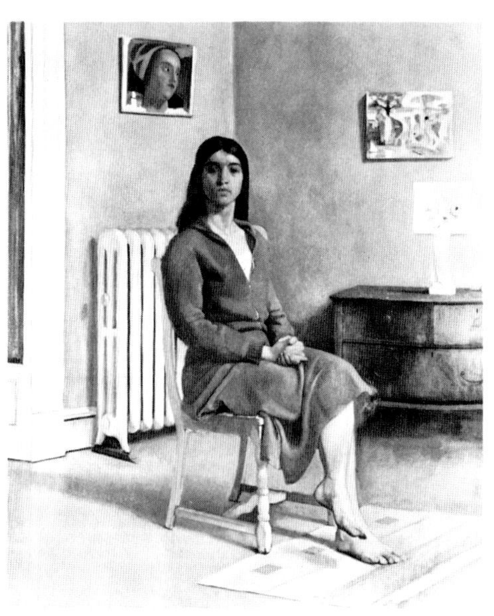
18

Adam Emory Albright (1862 – 1957)

9 *Quoits*, 1908
Oil on canvas
20¼ x 26³⁄₁₆ in. (51.4 x 66.5 cm.)
Signed at lower right: ADAM EMORY ALBRIGHT
Gift of Ivan LeLorraine Albright, 1966.11.1

10 *Supper Call on the Farm*, 1908
Oil on canvas
30⁵⁄₁₆ x 24⅛ in. (77 x 61.3 cm.)
Signed at lower right: ADAM EMORY ALBRIGHT
Gift of Ivan LeLorraine Albright, 1966.11.2

Malvin Marr Albright. *See* Zsissly.

John White Alexander (1856 – 1915)

11 *A Quiet Hour*, ca. 1901
Oil on canvas
48⅜ x 35⅝ in. (122.9 x 90.5 cm.)
Signed at lower left: John W Alexander -
Joseph E. Temple Fund, 1904.6

Washington Allston (1779 – 1843)

12 *The Dead Man Restored to Life by Touching the Bones of the Prophet Elisha*, 1811 – 13
Oil on canvas
156 x 122 in. (396.2 x 309.9 cm.)
Pennsylvania Academy purchase, by subscription, 1816.1

13 *Head of Saint Peter: Study for "The Angel Releasing Saint Peter from Prison,"* 1814 – 15
Oil on academy board
25½ x 24⅛ in. (64.8 x 61.3 cm.)
Annotated on masonite backing: St. Peter; a study for one/of the heads in a large Picture,/ painted for Sir George Beaumont;/the subject the Angel liberating/St. Peter from prison./ W. ALLSTON A.R.A. pinx.
Gift of Eleanor A. Bliss, 1980.11

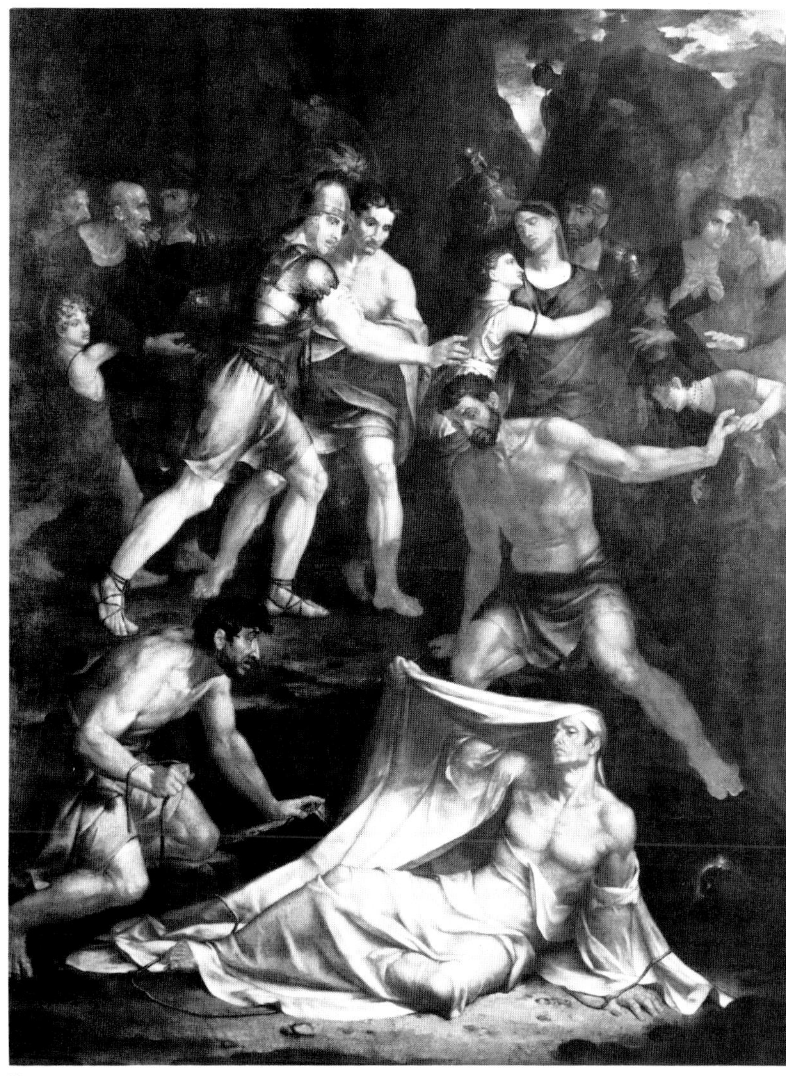

12

Vahan Amadouni (1933 –)

14 *Still Life*, 1952
Oil on canvas
10⁹⁄₁₆ x 13¾ in. (26.8 x 34.9 cm.)
Signed and dated at lower right: V.Amadouni-/ 52.
Gift of James P. and Ruth Marshall Magill, 1957.15.1

Joseph Amarotico (1931 – 1985)

15 *Synopsis*, 1968
Acrylic on masonite
29¹¹⁄₁₆ x 25¹¹⁄₁₆ in. (75.4 x 65.2 cm.)
Signed and dated at lower right: Amarotico - 68
John Lambert Fund, 1968.18

Gregory Amenoff (1948 –)

16 *Gordian Knot II*, 1986
Oil on canvas
92 x 125 in. (233.7 x 317.5 cm.)
Signed, dated, and inscribed on back: Gregory Amenoff/June/1986/92 x 125/GORDIAN KNOT II
Lewis S. Ware Fund, 1986.47

Karl Anderson (1874 – 1956)

17 *The Heirloom* (Helen E. Buell Anderson, the artist's wife, d. 1950, and Alice Melissa Anderson, his daughter, 1906–1946); on back, *Figure Study*, ca. 1915
Oil on canvas
40 x 35⅛ in. (101.6 x 89.2 cm.)
Signed at lower right: KARL ANDERSON
Joseph E. Temple Fund, 1916.9

Lennart Anderson (1928 –)

18 *Portrait of Barbara S.* (Barbara Stenglein), 1976 – 77
Oil on canvas
72⅛ x 60¼ in. (183.2 x 153 cm.)
Gift of the Pennsylvania Academy Women's Committee, Balis and Co., Mrs. E. R. Detchon, Jr., Mrs. Kenneth W. Gemmill, J. Welles Henderson, The Blanche P. Levi Foundation, L'Oréal Corp., Dr. Charles W. Nichols, David N. Pincus, Marion B. Stroud, Mr. and Mrs. Stanley C. Tuttleman, Mrs. Bernice McIlhenny Wintersteen, and public subscription, 1982.3

Edna Andrade (1917 –)

19 *Diptych – Space Cage – A*, 1966
Acrylic on linen
60 x 60 in. (152.4 x 152.4 cm.)
Signed at lower left: EA [monogram]; signed and inscribed on back: EDNA ANDRADE "SPACE CAGE - A"
Gift of Howard A. Wolf, 1977.11a

20 *Diptych – Space Cage – B*, 1966
Acrylic on linen
60 x 40 in. (152.4 x 101.6 cm.)
Signed at lower right: EA [monogram]; signed and inscribed on back: EDNA ANDRADE "SPACE CAGE - B"
Gift of Howard A. Wolf, 1977.11b

21 *Dynamite*, 1976
Acrylic on canvas
42 x 42 in. (106.6 x 106.6 cm.)
Signed at lower left: EA [monogram]
Signed on stretcher: EDNA ANDRADE
Gift of Mr. and Mrs. Robert E. A. Petersen, 1986.39.1

22 *Space Frame – D*, 1966 – 67
Oil on canvas
50 x 50⅛ in. (127 x 127.3 cm.)
Signed at lower right: EA [monogram]; inscribed and signed on back: "SPACE FRAME - D" EDNA ANDRADE (OIL PAINTING)
John Lambert Fund, 1968.1

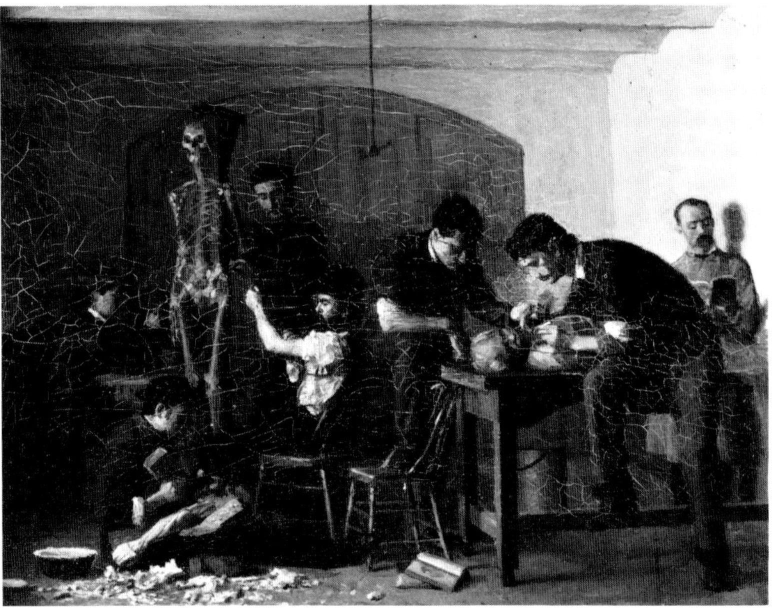

23

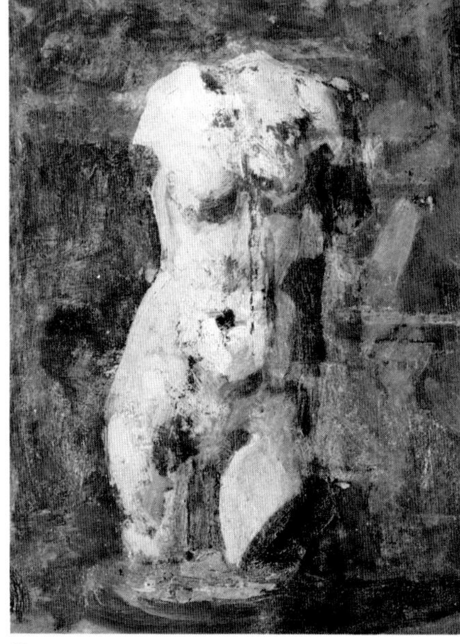

30

Thomas P. Anshutz (1851–1912)

23 *Dissecting Room* (illustration for William C. Brownell, "The Art Schools of Philadelphia," *Scribner's Monthly* 18, Sept. 1879, pp. 737–50), ca. 1879
Oil on cardboard (grisaille)
10 x 12½ in. (25.4 x 31.8 cm.)
Gift of the artist, 1879.1

24 *Helen W. Henderson* (1874–1956)
Oil on canvas
36 x 26¹⁄₁₆ in. (91.4 x 66.2 cm.)
Bequest of Helen W. Henderson, 1956.11.1

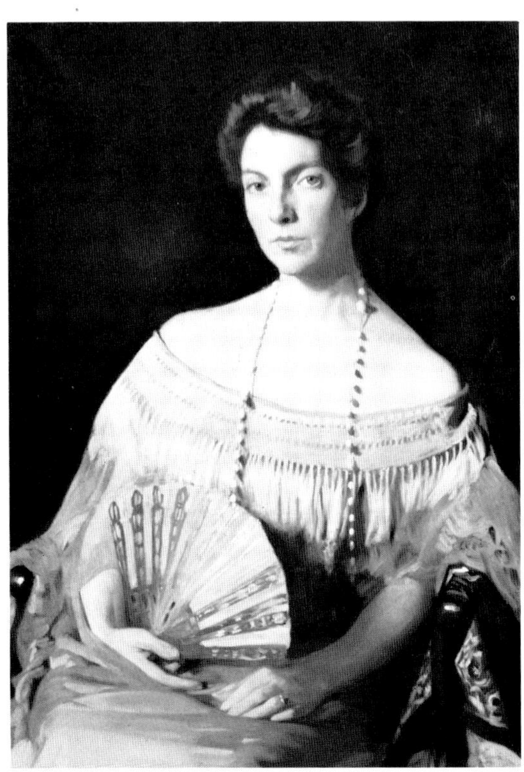

24

25 *In a Garret*, 1891
Oil on canvas
10¹⁄₁₆ x 16¹⁄₁₆ in. (25.6 x 40.8 cm.)
Signed at lower left: Thos. Anshutz
Gift of the pupils of the artist in the Pennsylvania Academy School, 1897.7

26 *The Incense Burner* (Rebecca H. Whelan), ca. 1905
Oil on canvas
64 x 40 in. (162.6 x 101.6 cm.)
Signed at lower left: Thomas Anshutz-
Henry D. Gilpin Fund, 1940.11

27 *A Studio Study*, ca. 1891
Oil on canvas
22¹⁄₁₆ x 36⅛ in. (56 x 91.8 cm.)
Bequest of Helen W. Henderson, 1956.11.3

28 *The Tanagra* (Rebecca H. Whelan), by 1909
Oil on canvas
80 x 40 in. (203.2 x 101.6 cm.)
Signed at lower right: Thos. Anshutz
Gift of friends and admirers of the artist, 1912.1

The following thirty-five oil sketches by Thomas P. Anshutz were given to the Pennsylvania Academy in 1971 by the artist's daughter-in-law:

29 *Boat in Water*
Oil on academy board
7½ x 9⅞ in. (19.1 x 25.1 cm.)
Gift of Mrs. Edward R. Anshutz, 1971.8.35

30 *Female Torso*, ca. 1891
Oil on cardboard
10¼ x 8 in. (26 x 20.3 cm.)
Gift of Mrs. Edward R. Anshutz, 1971.8.27

31 *Landscape*, ca. 1885
Oil on cardboard
4¹⁵⁄₁₆ x 6⅞ in. (12.5 x 17.5 cm.)
Gift of Mrs. Edward R. Anshutz, 1971.8.18

32 *Landscape*
Oil on academy board
7⁹⁄₁₆ x 9¹⁵⁄₁₆ in. (19.2 x 25.2 cm.)
Gift of Mrs. Edward R. Anshutz, 1971.8.10

33 *Landscape*; on back, *Landscape*
Oil on academy board
7⁹⁄₁₆ x 10 in. (19.2 x 25.4 cm.)
Gift of Mrs. Edward R. Anshutz, 1971.8.11

34 *Landscape*
Oil on academy board
7½ x 9¹⁵⁄₁₆ in. (19.1 x 25.2 cm.)
Gift of Mrs. Edward R. Anshutz, 1971.8.14

35 *Landscape*
Oil on cardboard

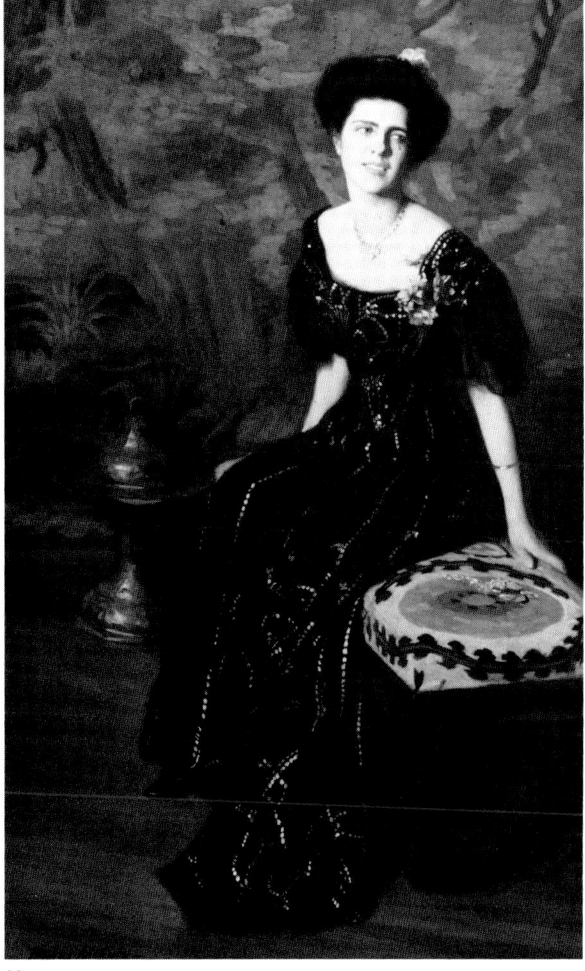

26

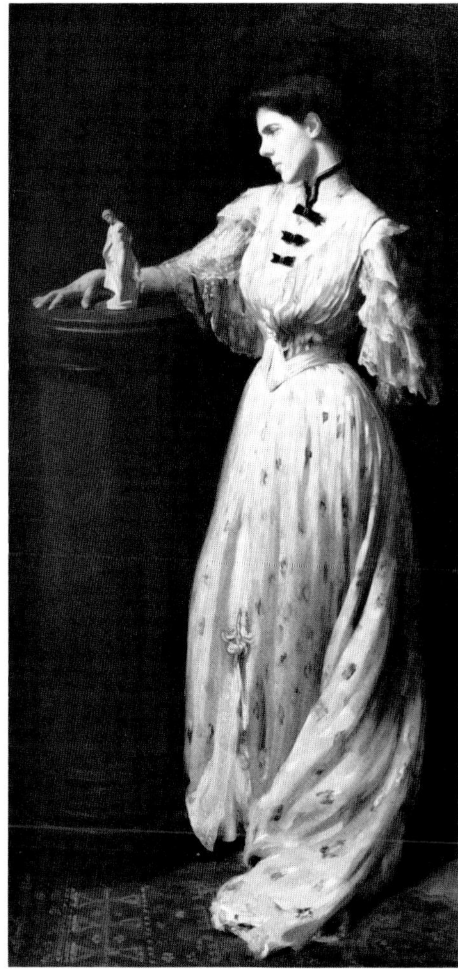

28

8¼ x 5¼ in. (21 x 13.3 cm.)
Gift of Mrs. Edward R. Anshutz, 1971.8.16

36 *Landscape*
Oil on cardboard
5⅛ x 8 9/16 in. (13 x 21.8 cm.)
Gift of Mrs. Edward R. Anshutz, 1971.8.21

37 *Landscape*
Oil on cardboard
8 13/16 x 5 7/16 in. (22.4 x 13.8 cm.)
Gift of Mrs. Edward R. Anshutz, 1971.8.22

38 *Landscape*; on back, *Figure in Red Seated in Front of a Tree*
Oil on academy board
7 9/16 x 9 15/16 in. (19.2 x 25.2 cm.)
Gift of Mrs. Edward R. Anshutz, 1971.8.29

39 *Landscape*
Oil on academy board
7 9/16 x 10 in. (19.2 x 25.4 cm.)
Gift of Mrs. Edward R. Anshutz, 1971.8.32

40 *Landscape*
Oil on academy board
7 9/16 x 9 15/16 in. (19.2 x 25.2 cm.)
Gift of Mrs. Edward R. Anshutz, 1971.8.33

41 *Landscape*; on back, *Building*
Oil on academy board
7½ x 9⅞ in. (19.1 x 25.1 cm.)
Gift of Mrs. Edward R. Anshutz, 1971.8.36

42 *Landscape*; on back, *Landscape*
Oil on academy board
7 9/16 x 9 15/16 in. (19.2 x 25.2 cm.)
Gift of Mrs. Edward R. Anshutz, 1971.8.37

43 *Landscape in Winter*
Oil on academy board
9⅝ x 7½ in. (24.5 x 19.1 cm.)
Gift of Mrs. Edward R. Anshutz, 1971.8.15

44 *Landscape with Buildings*
Oil on canvas
21 x 15 in. (53.3 x 38.1 cm.)
Gift of Mrs. Edward R. Anshutz, 1971.8.5

45 *Landscape with Buildings*
Oil on academy board
7 9/16 x 9 15/16 in. (19.2 x 25.2 cm.)
Gift of Mrs. Edward R. Anshutz, 1971.8.26

46 *Landscape with House*
Oil on academy board
7 9/16 x 9 15/16 in. (19.2 x 25.2 cm.)
Gift of Mrs. Edward R. Anshutz, 1971.8.31

47 *Landscape with Road*; on back, *Landscape with Building*
Oil on academy board
7 9/16 x 9 15/16 in. (19.2 x 25.2 cm.)
Gift of Mrs. Edward R. Anshutz, 1971.8.30

48 *Landscape with Tree*, ca. 1885
Oil on cardboard
5 13/16 x 8 1/16 in. (14.8 x 20.5 cm.)
Gift of Mrs. Edward R. Anshutz, 1971.8.19

49 *Landscape with Tree, Building, and Water*
Oil on canvas
13 x 9 in. (33 x 22.9 cm.)
Gift of Mrs. Edward R. Anshutz, 1971.8.8

50 *Landscape with Trees*
Oil on cardboard
5 11/16 x 8 in. (14.4 x 20.3 cm.)
Gift of Mrs. Edward R. Anshutz, 1971.8.20

51 *Landscape with Trees*; on back, *Landscape*
Oil on academy board
9 15/16 x 7 9/16 in. (25.2 x 19.2 cm.)
Gift of Mrs. Edward R. Anshutz, 1971.8.28

52 *Landscape with Trees and House*; on back, *Landscape with Tree and Building*
Oil on academy board
7 9/16 x 9 15/16 in. (19.2 x 25.2 cm.)
Gift of Mrs. Edward R. Anshutz, 1971.8.13

53 *Landscape with White Building*; on back, *Landscape*
Oil on academy board
7 1/2 x 9 13/16 in. (19.1 x 24.9 cm.)
Gift of Mrs. Edward R. Anshutz, 1971.8.34

54 *Man Dressed as a Matador*; on back, *Landscape with Buildings*
Oil on academy board
9 7/8 x 7 7/16 in. (25.1 x 18.9 cm.)
Gift of Mrs. Edward R. Anshutz, 1971.8.12

55 *Marine View*
Oil on canvas
17 1/2 x 28 1/2 in. (44.5 x 72.4 cm.)
Gift of Mrs. Edward R. Anshutz, 1971.8.4

56 *Mother and Child*, ca. 1900
Oil on cardboard
10 1/4 x 8 in. (26 x 20.3 cm.)
Gift of Mrs. Edward R. Anshutz, 1971.8.24

57 *Seated Figure*
Oil on academy board
8 x 5 15/16 in. (20.3 x 15.1 cm.)
Gift of Mrs. Edward R. Anshutz, 1971.8.17

58 *Seated Woman and Boy*; on back, *Landscape with Buildings*
Oil on academy board
9 15/16 x 7 1/2 in. (25.2 x 19.1 cm.)
Gift of Mrs. Edward R. Anshutz, 1971.8.25

59 *Shore Scene*; on back, *Landscape*
Oil on academy board
7 1/2 x 9 13/16 in. (19.1 x 24.9 cm.)
Gift of Mrs. Edward R. Anshutz, 1971.8.23

60 *Study of Model*
Oil on canvas
19 15/16 x 14 1/16 in. (50.6 x 35.7 cm.)
Gift of Mrs. Edward R. Anshutz, 1971.8.6

61 *Study of Model*
Oil on canvas
19 15/16 x 13 13/16 in. (50.6 x 35.1 cm.)
Gift of Mrs. Edward R. Anshutz, 1971.8.7

62 *Unidentified Man*
Oil on canvas
35 x 25 1/2 in. (88.9 x 64.8 cm.)
Gift of Mrs. Edward R. Anshutz, 1971.8.2

63 *Unidentified Man*
Oil on canvas
23 3/4 x 19 1/2 in. (60.3 x 49.5 cm.)
Gift of Mrs. Edward R. Anshutz, 1971.8.3

Richard J. Anuszkiewicz (1930–)

64 *Systematic Whole*, 1966
Acrylic and tape on canvas
60 1/4 x 60 1/4 in. (153 x 153 cm.)
Signed and dated on back: ©1966/143/RICHARD ANUSZKIEWICZ/1966
John Lambert Fund, 1968.2

Anna Margaretta Archambault
See cat. nos. 1627–30.

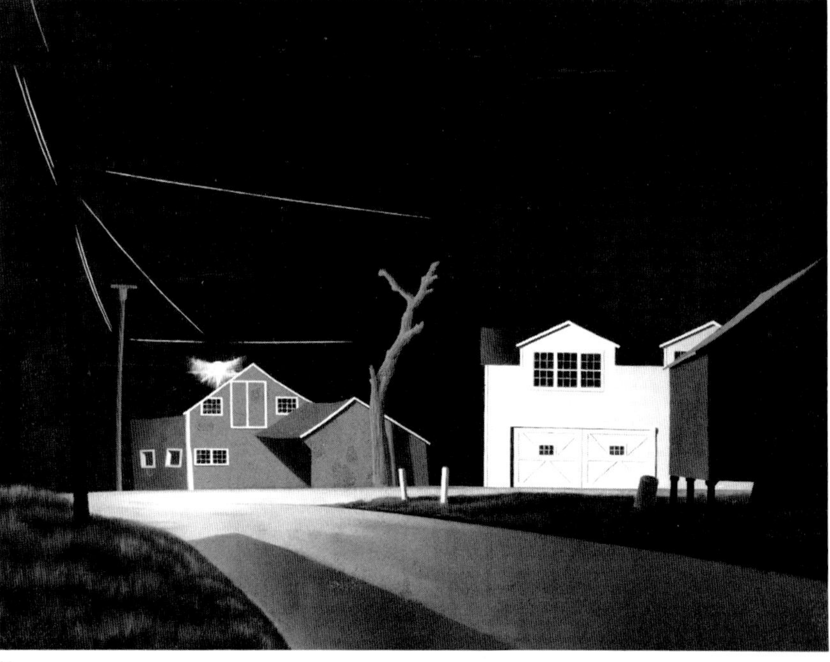
68

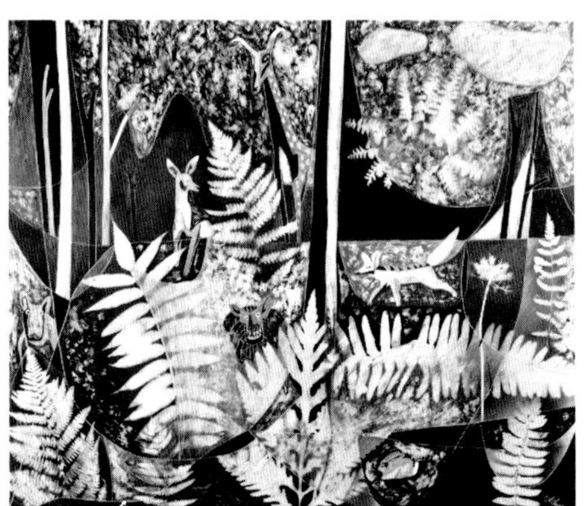
66

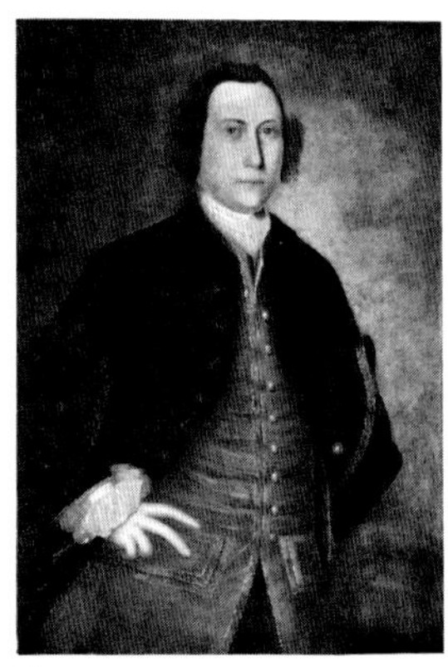
72

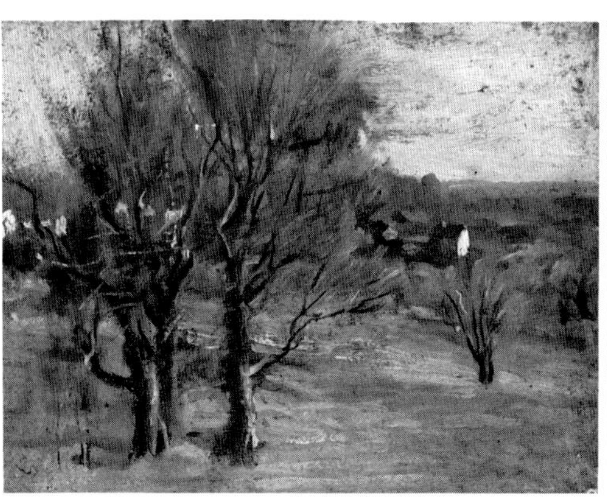
52

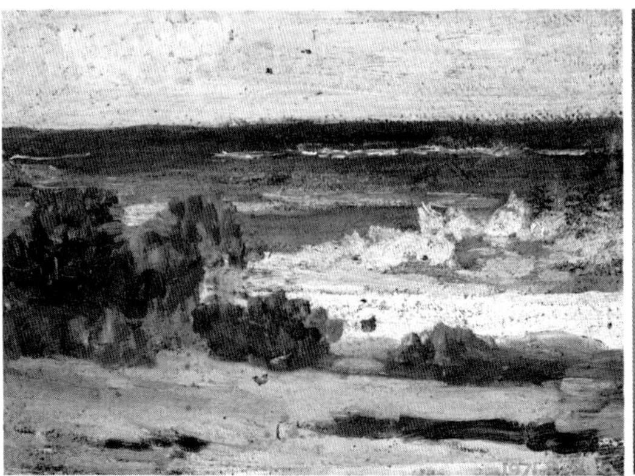
59

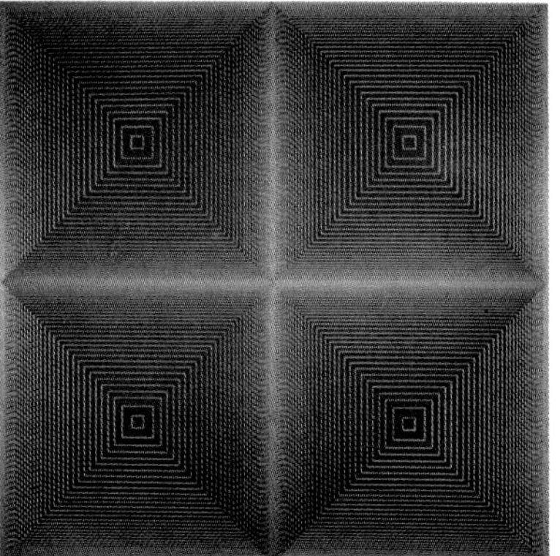
64

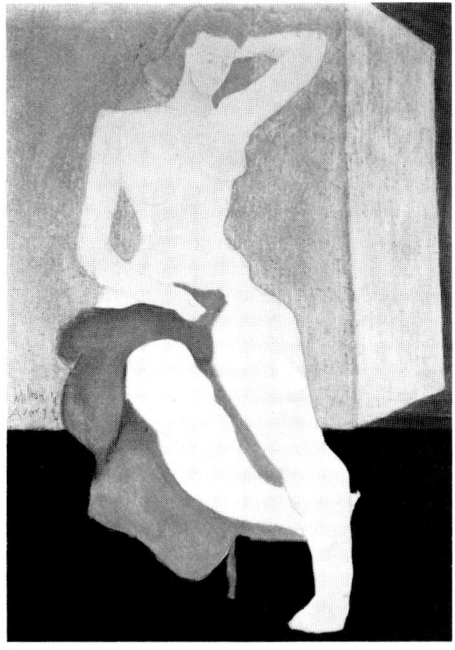

70

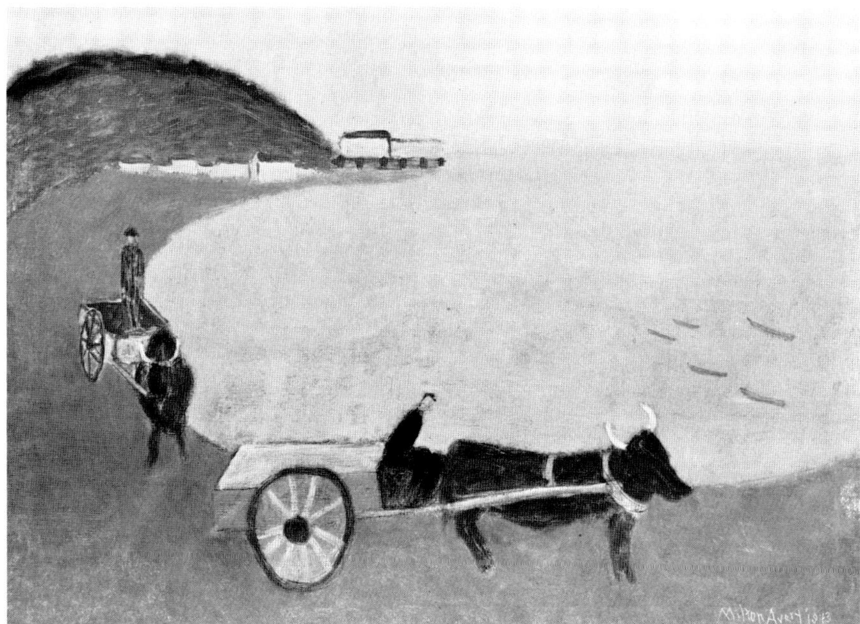

71

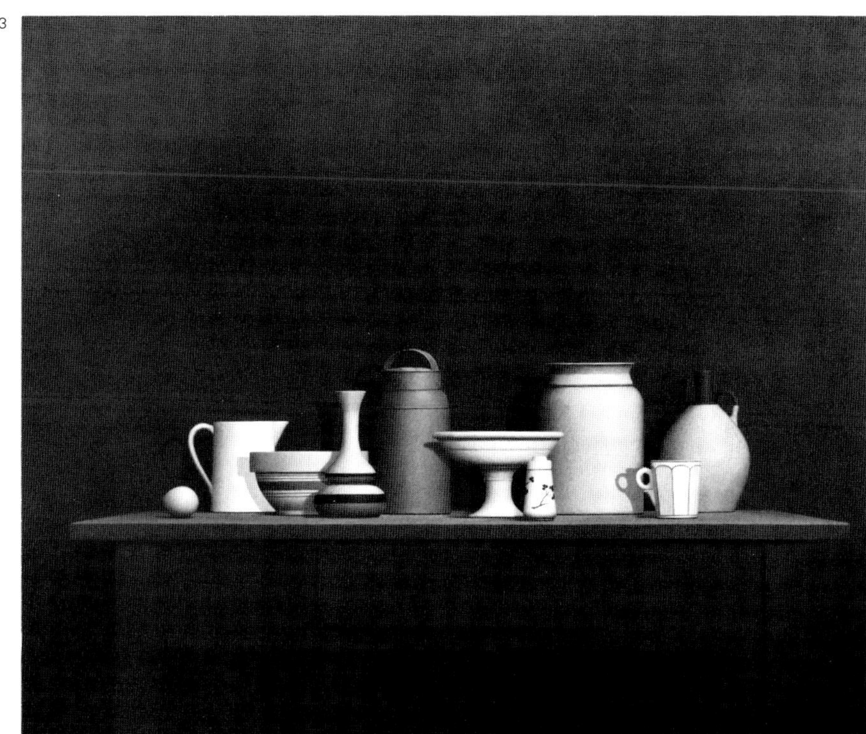

73

Carolyn Faught Armstrong (b. 1910)

65 *Three Flowers*; on back, *Unidentified Woman* (sketch), 1939
Oil on masonite
23$^{15}/_{16}$ x 21$^{15}/_{16}$ in. (60.8 x 55.7 cm.)
Signed and dated at lower left: CAROLYN F. ARMSTRONG/'39
John Lambert Fund, 1940.1

John C. Atherton (1900–1952)

66 *The Magic Forest*, 1945
Gouache on gessoed board ("Renaissance Panel")
24$^{3}/_{8}$ x 30 in. (61.9 x 76.2 cm.)
Signed at lower right: Atherton
Annotated on frame: JOHN ATHERTON-"THE MAGIC FOREST" 1945
Henry D. Gilpin Fund, 1946.2

Robert Atwood (b. 1892)

67 *Mid-Winter*, 1928
Oil on canvas
30$^{1}/_{16}$ x 36$^{1}/_{16}$ in. (76.4 x 91.6 cm.)
Signed and dated at lower right: ROBERT ATWOOD/ 1928.
John Lambert Fund, 1929.1

George Copeland Ault (1891–1948)

68 *Black Night: Russell's Corners*, 1943
Oil on canvas
18 x 24$^{1}/_{16}$ in. (45.7 x 61.1 cm.)
Signed and dated at lower left: G. C. Ault '43.
John Lambert Fund, 1946.3

Darrel Austin (1907–)

69 *The Sorceress*, 1948
Oil on canvas
47$^{15}/_{16}$ x 14$^{15}/_{16}$ in. (121.8 x 37.9 cm.)
Signed and dated at lower right: Darrel Austin 1948
Joseph E. Temple Fund, 1950.1

Milton Avery (1885–1965)

70 *Nude with Blue Cloth*, 1944
Oil on canvas board
30$^{1}/_{2}$ x 22$^{3}/_{4}$ in. (77.5 x 57.8 cm.)
Signed and dated at left center: Milton/Avery/ 1/9/4/4
Bequest of Mrs. Martha G. Speiser in memory of her husband, Maurice J. Speiser, 1968.19

71 *Oxcart–Blue Sea*, 1943
Oil on canvas
32$^{1}/_{8}$ x 44 in. (81.6 x 111.8 cm.)
Signed and dated at lower right: Milton Avery 1943
Gift of Mrs. Herbert Cameron Morris, 1952.16

Attributed to **Joseph Badger** (1708–1765)

72 *Lawrence Washington* (?) (1718–1752)
Oil on canvas
40$^{3}/_{8}$ x 29$^{3}/_{8}$ in. (102.6 x 74.6 cm.)
Gift of Mrs. John Frederick Lewis (The John Frederick Lewis Memorial Collection), 1933.10.1

Mrs. Bernard Badura. *See* Faye Swengel.

William Bailey (1930–)

73 *Monte Migiana Still Life*, 1979
Oil on linen
54$^{1}/_{4}$ x 60$^{3}/_{16}$ in. (137.8 x 152.9 cm.)

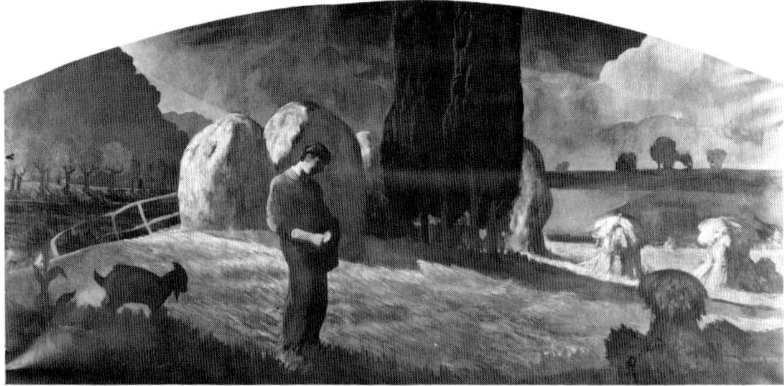
74

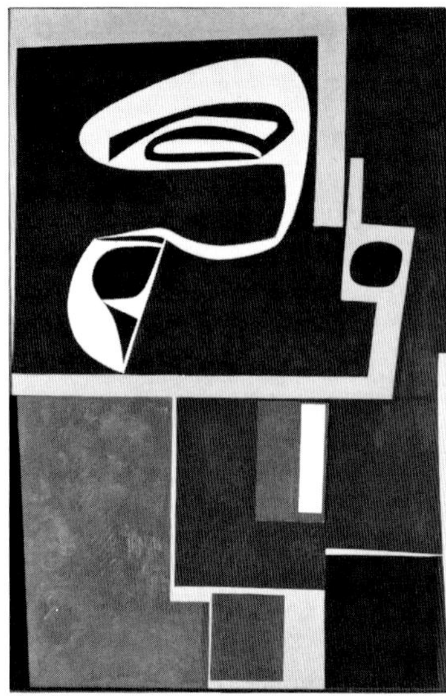
76

Signed and dated on back: Bailey '1979
Funds provided by the National Endowment for the Arts, the Contemporary Arts Fund, Mrs. Bernice McIlhenny Wintersteen, Pennsylvania Academy Women's Committee, Marion B. Stroud, Mrs. H. Gates Lloyd, and Theodore T. Newbold, 1980.2

Frank Baisden (b. 1904)

74 *Harvest Evening*, 1924
Oil on canvas
Approx. 80 x 167 in. (203 x 424 cm.)
Signed and dated at lower right: FRANK-BAISDEN-1924
Commissioned by the Pennsylvania Academy, 1925.14

Esther Baldwin. *See* Esther Williams.

John Bannon (1933–)

75 *Still Life*, 1957
Oil on masonite
12 x 15¹⁵⁄₁₆ in. (30.5 x 40.5 cm.)
Signed and dated at lower right: bannon 1957
John Lambert Fund, 1958.2

Alice Barber. *See* Alice Barber Stephens.

Will Barnet (1911–)

76 *Whiplash*, 1959
Oil on canvas
62¼ x 41⅛ in. (158.1 x 104.5 cm.)
Signed at lower right: Will Barnet
Signed and dated on stretcher: Will Barnet 1959
John Lambert Fund, 1962.3

Herbert Barnett (1910–1972)

77 *Landscape*, ca. 1937
Oil on canvas
25 x 30 in. (63.5 x 76.2 cm.)
Signed at lower left: HERBERT BARNETT
John Lambert Fund, 1938.7

William Barnett (1919–)

78 *Cool Flowers*, 1951
Oil on canvas
15¹¹⁄₁₆ x 20³⁄₁₆ in. (39.8 x 51.3 cm.)
Signed at lower right: WILLIAM BARNETT
John Lambert Fund, 1951.2

79 *Interior*, 1956
Oil on canvas
25 x 34¹³⁄₁₆ in. (63.5 x 88.4 cm.)
Signed at lower right: William Barnett
John Lambert Fund, 1958.3

John Dobson Barrow (1823–1907)

80 *June Morning*, ca. 1863
Oil on wood
8⅞ x 14 in. (22.5 x 35.6 cm.)
Gift of Mr. and Mrs. Theodore T. Newbold, 1980.31

Evelyn Bartlett (1887–)

81 *Smelts*, 1934
Oil on canvas
13⅛ x 20¹⁄₁₆ in. (33.3 x 51 cm.)
Signed and dated at lower right: Evelyn Bartlett'34
John Lambert Fund, 1937.1

Kenneth Bates (1895–1973)

82 *Boundaries*, ca. 1927
Oil on canvas
36 x 48 in. (91.4 x 121.9 cm.)
John Lambert Fund, 1928.2

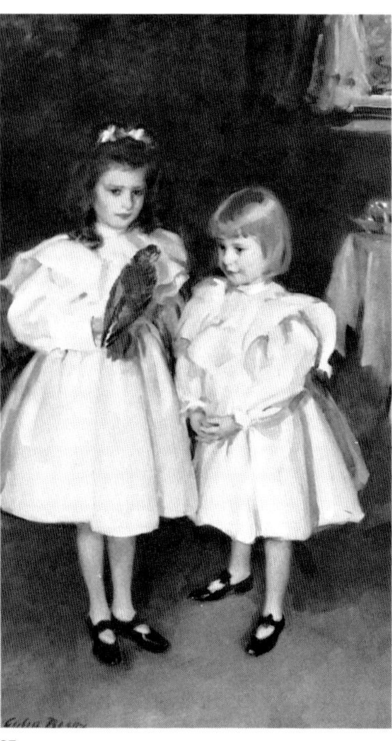
87

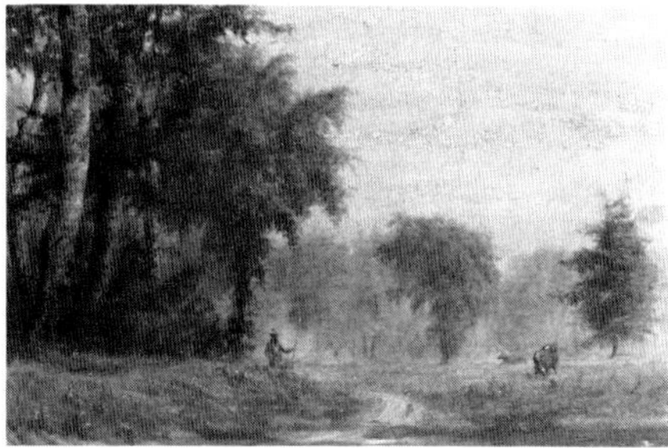
80

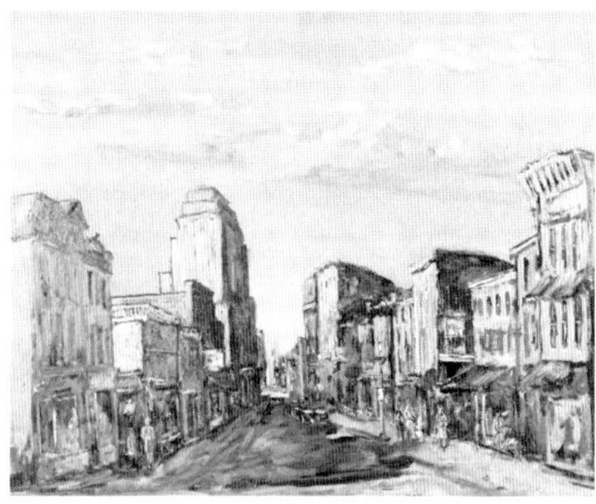
83

Walter Emerson Baum (1884–1956)

83 *Quaint Street*, 1951
Oil and egg tempera on masonite
33⅝ x 41¾ in. (85.4 x 106 cm.)
Signed and dated at lower right: W E Baum/1951; inscribed and signed on back: QUAINT STREET/BAUM
Gift of George P. Orr, 1952.17

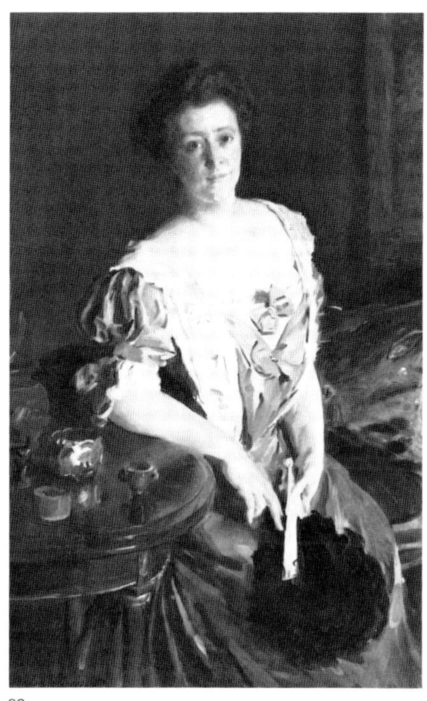

88

Cecilia Beaux (1855–1942)

84 *Travis Cochran*, 1897
Oil on canvas
34 x 24⅛ in. (86.4 x 61.3 cm.)
Signed at lower left: Cecilia Beaux
Bequest of Fanny Travis Cochran, 1977.13

85 *Mary Rodman Fox*, 1892
Oil on canvas
27¹⁄₁₆ x 22 in. (68.7 x 55.9 cm.)
Signed at lower left: Cecilia Beaux
Gift of Mrs. Edward M. Cheston, 1968.16

86 *The Reverend Matthew Blackburne Grier* (1820–1899), 1892
Oil on canvas, mounted on wood
49⅝ x 39⅜ in. (126.1 x 100 cm.)
Signed and dated at lower left: Cecilia Beaux./92
Gift of Anne Farr Bartol, 1961.10

87 *Gertrude and Elizabeth Henry*, 1898–99
Oil on canvas
64 x 37¼ in. (162.6 x 94.6 cm.)
Signed at lower left: Cecilia Beaux
Funds provided by the descendants and relatives of Gertrude and Elizabeth Henry and by the Pennsylvania Academy, 1986.9

88 *Mrs. John Frederick Lewis* (née Anne H. R. Baker), 1906
Oil on canvas
46½ x 29¹⁵⁄₁₆ in. (118.1 x 76 cm.)
Signed at lower left: CECILIA BEAUX
Gift of Alfred Baker Lewis, 1974.13

89 *A Little Girl* (Fanny Travis Cochran, 1876–1977), 1887
Oil on canvas
36 x 29³⁄₁₆ in. (91.4 x 74.1 cm.)
Signed at upper left: E. C. Beaux
Gift of Fanny Travis Cochran, 1955.12
See also cat. no. 120.

90 *Mother and Daughter* (Mrs. Clement Acton Griscom, 1850–1925, and Frances C. Griscom, 1879–1974), 1898
Oil on canvas
83 x 44 in. (210.8 x 111.8 cm.)
Signed at lower left: Cecilia Beaux-
Gift of Frances C. Griscom, 1950.15

91 *Clement B. Newbold* (d. 1926), 1912
Oil on canvas
47⅜ x 35 in. (120.3 x 88.9 cm.)
Signed at upper left: Cecilia Beaux-
Gift of Clement B. Newbold, 1973.25.1

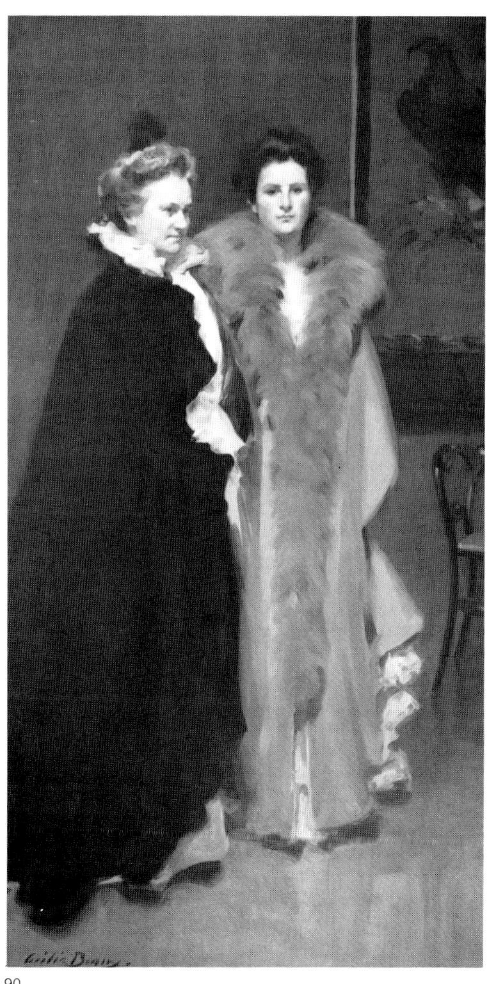

90

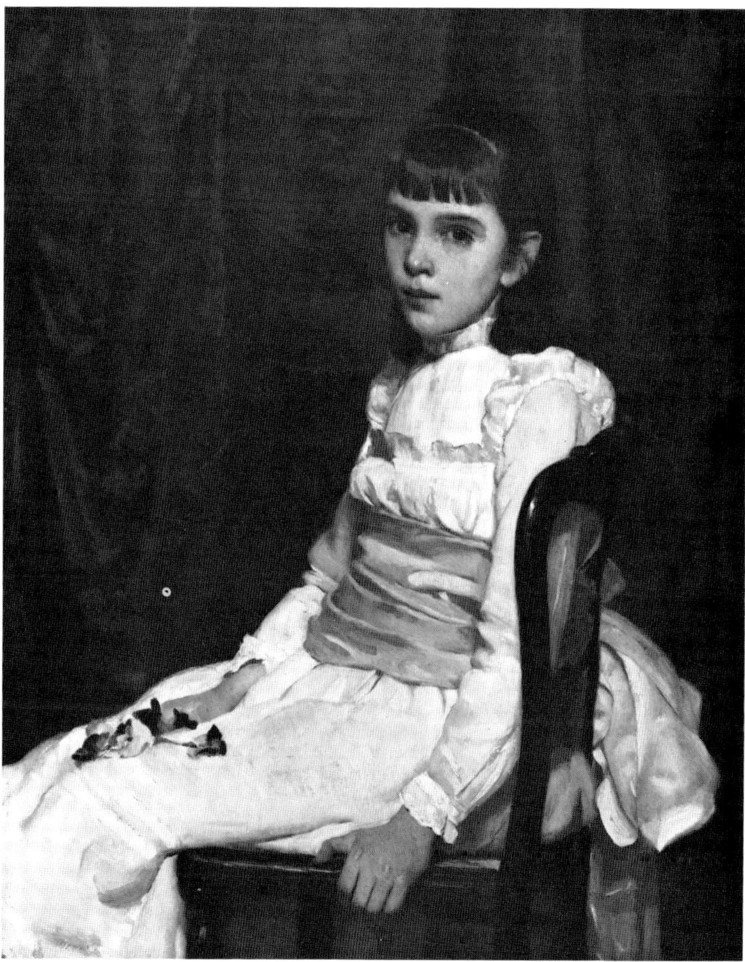

89

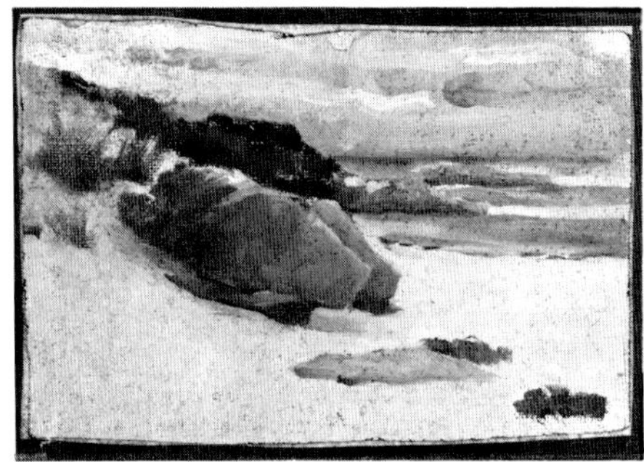
94

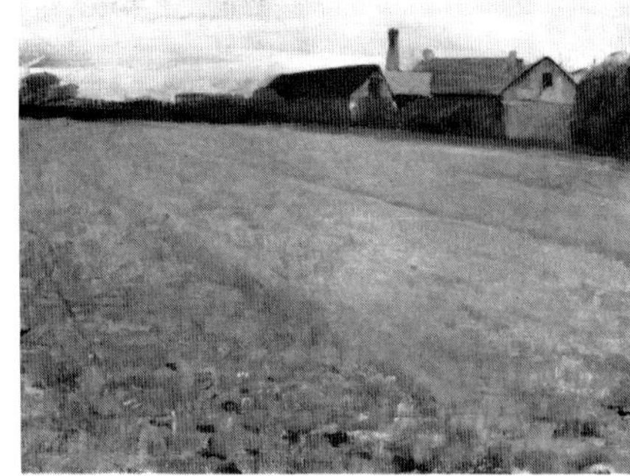
104

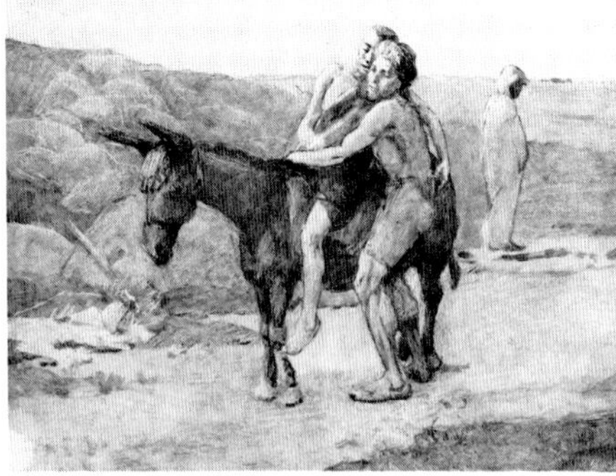
98

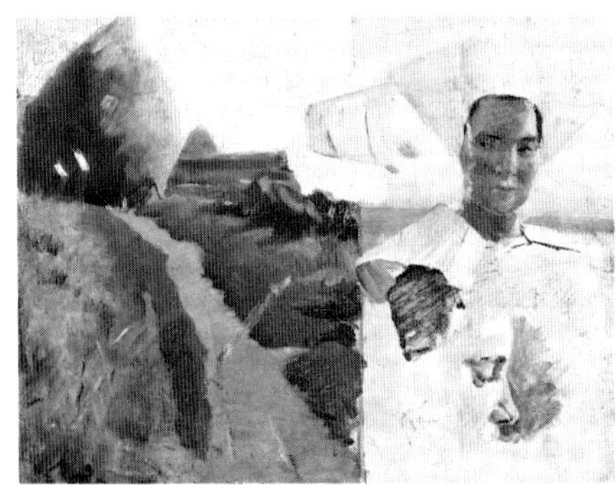
105

92 *Mrs. Clement B. Newbold* (née Mary Scott), 1896
Oil on canvas
78½ x 48 in. (199.4 x 121.9 cm.)
Signed at lower right: Cecilia Beaux
Gift of Clement B. Newbold, 1973.25.2

93 *New England Woman* (Mrs. Jedediah H. Richards, née Julia Leavitt, 1840–1915), 1895
Oil on canvas
43 x 24¼ in. (109.2 x 61.6 cm.)
Signed at lower left: Cecilia Beaux
Joseph E. Temple Fund, 1896.1

The following forty oil sketches by Cecilia Beaux were given to the Pennsylvania Academy in 1950 by the artist's nephew:

94 *Beach Haven, New Jersey*, 1889–90
Oil on canvas
6¹⁄₁₆ x 8⁹⁄₁₆ in. (15.4 x 21.8 cm.)
Gift of Henry Sandwith Drinker, 1950.17.19

95 *A Breton Woman and Other Studies*, 1888
Oil on canvas
15 x 10⅝ in. (38.1 x 27 cm.)
Gift of Henry Sandwith Drinker, 1950.17.9

96 *Bust of a Woman*
Oil on wood (artist's palette)
9⁵⁄₁₆ x 8¹¹⁄₁₆ in. (23.7 x 22.1 cm.), irregular
Gift of Henry Sandwith Drinker, 1950.17.34

97 *A Country Woman, Concarneau, France*, 1888
Oil on canvas
14¹⁄₁₆ x 8⅝ in. (35.7 x 21.9 cm.)
Gift of Henry Sandwith Drinker, 1950.17.32

98 *The Good Samaritan*, 1888
Oil on cardboard (grisaille)
10½ x 13⅝ in. (26.7 x 34.6 cm.)
Signed, inscribed, and dated at lower right: E.C.B-Paris 88-
Gift of Henry Sandwith Drinker, 1950.17.12

99 *Head of a French Peasant Woman*, 1888
Oil on cardboard
12¹³⁄₁₆ x 9½ in. (32.5 x 24.1 cm.)
Signed on back: Beau[x].
Gift of Henry Sandwith Drinker, 1950.17.33

100 *Head of a French Peasant Woman*
Oil on cardboard
16¹⁄₁₆ x 12⅞ in. (40.8 x 32.7 cm.)
Signed on back: Beaux.
Gift of Henry Sandwith Drinker, 1950.17.14

101 *Head of a Woman*, ca. 1888
Oil on canvas
16 x 12⅞ in. (40.6 x 32.7 cm.)
Signed on back: Beaux
Gift of Henry Sandwith Drinker, 1950.17.4

102 *Head of a Woman*
Oil on cardboard
16¹⁄₁₆ x 12¹⁵⁄₁₆ in. (40.8 x 32.9 cm.)
Gift of Henry Sandwith Drinker, 1950.17.13

103 *Landscape*, 1880s
Oil on cardboard
6¹³⁄₁₆ x 9¼ in. (17.3 x 23.5 cm.)
Gift of Henry Sandwith Drinker, 1950.17.28

104 *Landscape with Farm Building, Concarneau, France*, 1888
Oil on canvas
11¹⁄₁₆ x 14³⁄₁₆ in. (28.1 x 36 cm.)
Gift of Henry Sandwith Drinker, 1950.17.31

105 *Landscape with Haystack and Breton Woman, Concarneau, France*, 1888
Oil on canvas
13¾ x 17¹¹⁄₁₆ in. (34.9 x 44.9 cm.)
Gift of Henry Sandwith Drinker, 1950.17.3

106 *Landscape with Pack Mule*, ca. 1885
Oil on canvas
11¹³⁄₁₆ x 7¹⁵⁄₁₆ in. (30 x 20.2 cm.)
Gift of Henry Sandwith Drinker, 1950.17.29

107 *Landscape with Trees*, 1888–89
Oil on cardboard
9³⁄₁₆ x 5½ in. (23.3 x 14 cm.)
Gift of Henry Sandwith Drinker, 1950.17.27

108 *Landscape with Villa and Fountain*, 1896
Oil on canvas
14³⁄₁₆ x 10¹³⁄₁₆ in. (36 x 27.5 cm.)
Gift of Henry Sandwith Drinker, 1950.17.2

109 *The Last Supper*, 1888–89
Oil and graphite on cardboard (monochrome)

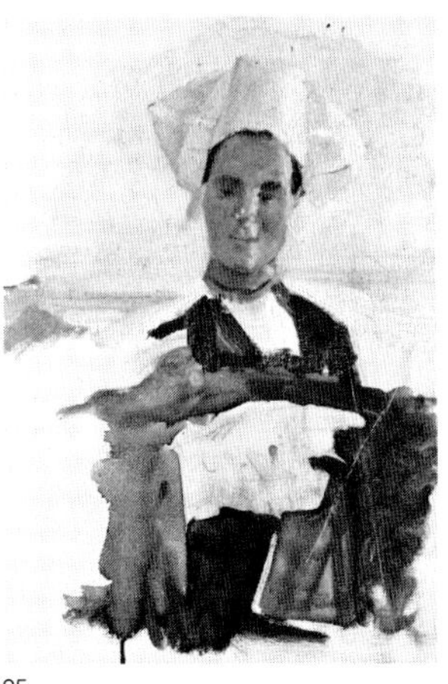
95

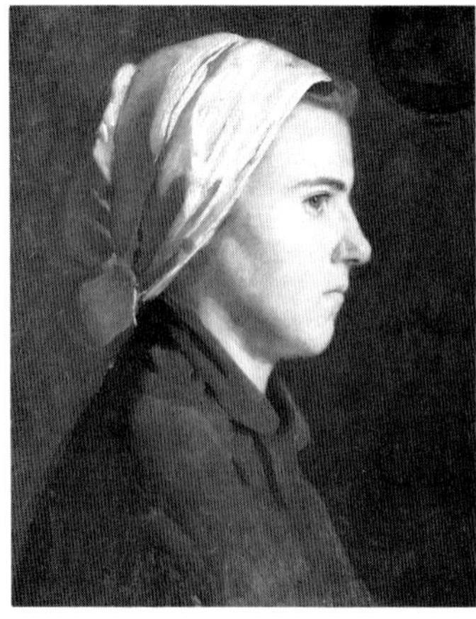
97

100

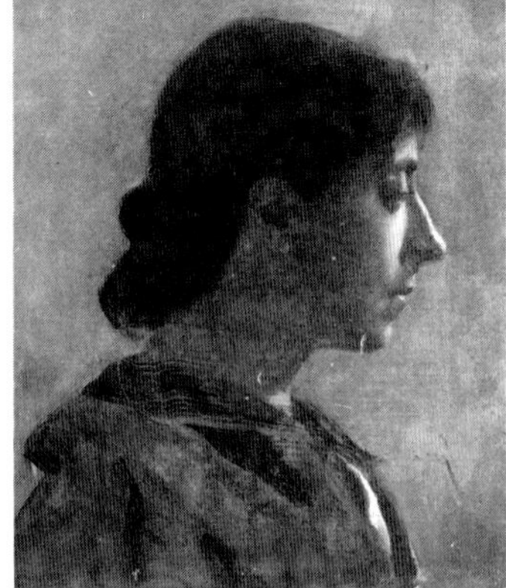
101

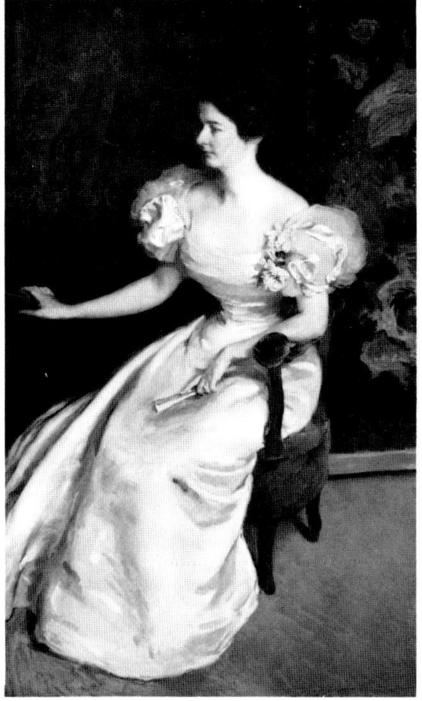

92

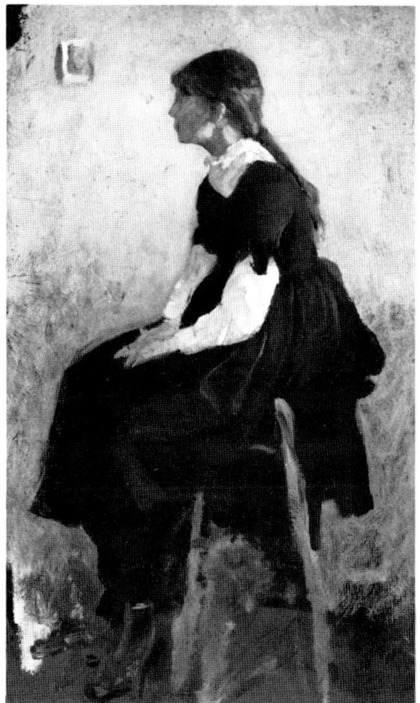

113

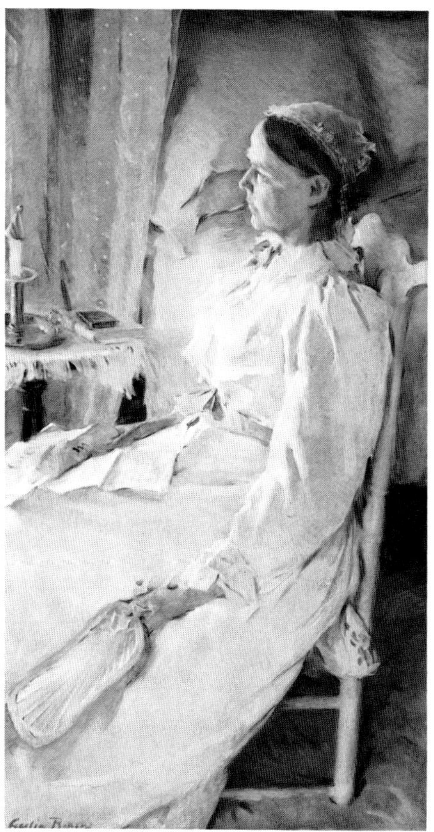

93

13⅜ x 10⁵⁄₁₆ in. (34 x 26.2 cm.)
Gift of Henry Sandwith Drinker, 1950.17.1

110 *Man before Classical Temple*, 1910s
Oil on cardboard
11¾ x 9 in. (29.8 x 22.9 cm.)
Gift of Henry Sandwith Drinker, 1950.17.30

111 *Replica of "Miss Agnes Irwin"* (1841–1914), 1933–34
Oil on canvas
45 x 35 in. (114.3 x 88.9 cm.)
Gift of Henry Sandwith Drinker, 1950.17.52

112 *Seaside Inlet, Concarneau, France*, ca. 1888
Oil on cardboard
5⅞ x 9¼ in. (14.9 x 23.5 cm.)
Gift of Henry Sandwith Drinker, 1950.17.26

113 *Seated Girl in a Long Black Dress*; on back, *Figure in Biblical Dress*, ca. 1885
Oil on cardboard
19⅝ x 12¼ in. (49.8 x 31.1 cm.)
Gift of Henry Sandwith Drinker, 1950.17.5

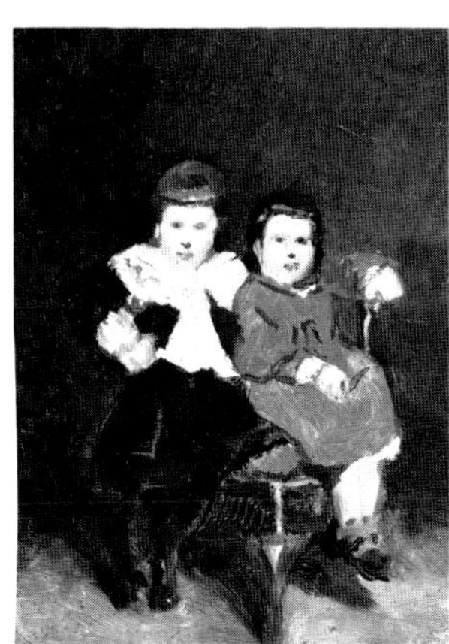

125

114 *Seated Man, Seated Woman*; on back, *Blue Dress*
Oil on cardboard
5¾ x 9¹⁄₁₆ in. (14.6 x 23 cm.)
Gift of Henry Sandwith Drinker, 1950.17.23

115 *Seated Woman*
Oil on cardboard
6¹¹⁄₁₆ x 5⁷⁄₁₆ in. (17 x 13.8 cm.)
Gift of Henry Sandwith Drinker, 1950.17.16

116 *Seated Woman*
Oil on cardboard
8½ x 5½ in. (21.6 x 14 cm.)
Gift of Henry Sandwith Drinker, 1950.17.20

117 *Sketch of Ernesta Drinker* (1892–1981), ca. 1907
Oil on canvas
25¾ x 20 in. (65.4 x 50.8 cm.)
Gift of Henry Sandwith Drinker, 1950.17.49

118 *Sketch of Mrs. Howard Wurts Page*, ca. 1887
Oil on cardboard
4¹³⁄₁₆ x 3¾ in. (12.2 x 9.5 cm.)
Inscribed on back: Mrs. Howard/W Page
Gift of Henry Sandwith Drinker, 1950.17.17

119 *Sketch of William Foster Biddle* (1834–1910), ca. 1890
Oil on wood
9³⁄₁₆ x 5⁹⁄₁₆ in. (23.3 x 14.1 cm.)
Gift of Henry Sandwith Drinker, 1950.17.24

120 *Study for "A Little Girl,"* 1887
Oil on cardboard
5⁷⁄₁₆ x 4⅝ in. (13.8 x 11.7 cm.)
Gift of Henry Sandwith Drinker, 1950.17.22
See also cat. no. 89.

121 *Study for "Charles Sumner Bird and His Sister Edith Bird Bass,"* 1905
Oil on cardboard
10⅝ x 4⁹⁄₁₆ in. (27 x 11.6 cm.)
Gift of Henry Sandwith Drinker, 1950.17.18

122 *Study for "Ernesta Drinker,"* 1914
Oil on cardboard
10 x 7¼ in. (25.4 x 18.4 cm.)
Gift of Henry Sandwith Drinker, 1950.17.54

123 *Study for "Ernesta with Nurse"* (Ernesta Drinker), ca. 1894
Oil on cardboard
8¹¹⁄₁₆ x 6⁵⁄₁₆ in. (22.1 x 16 cm.)
Gift of Henry Sandwith Drinker, 1950.17.55

124 *Study for "Ethel Burnham,"* 1889
Oil on cardboard
9¼ x 5⅝ in. (23.5 x 14.3 cm.)
Gift of Henry Sandwith Drinker, 1950.17.21

125 *Study for "Harold and Mildred Colton,"* ca. 1886
Oil on cardboard
8¼ x 6 in. (21 x 15.2 cm.)
Gift of Henry Sandwith Drinker, 1950.17.25

126 *Study for "Henry Sandwith Drinker III"* (1880–1965), ca. 1924
Oil on wood
14 x 10¾ in. (35.6 x 27.3 cm.)
Gift of Henry Sandwith Drinker, 1950.17.10

127 *Study for "Les Derniers Jours d'Enfance"*; on back, *Profile of a Young Man*, ca. 1883
Oil on cardboard
15¼ x 13¼ in. (38.7 x 33.7 cm.)
Gift of Henry Sandwith Drinker, 1950.17.11

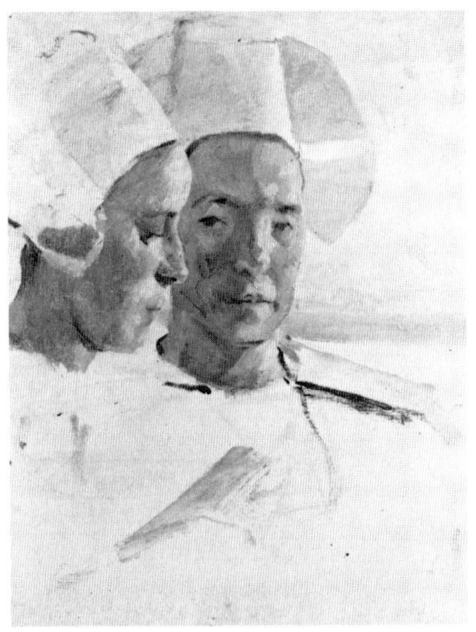

128

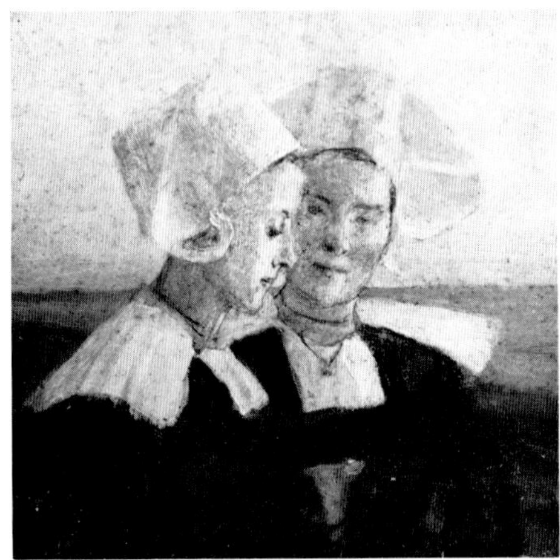

129

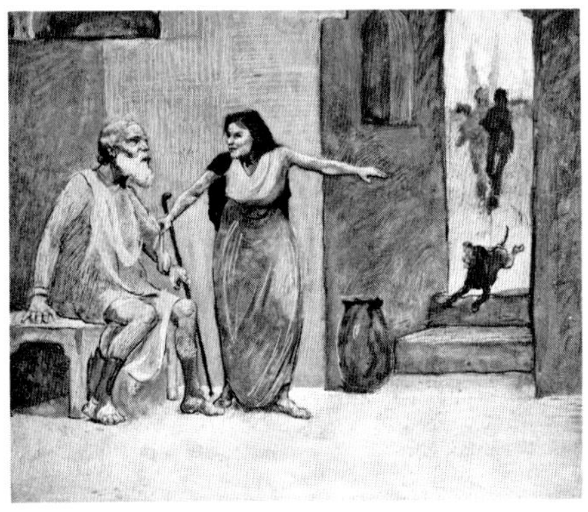

131

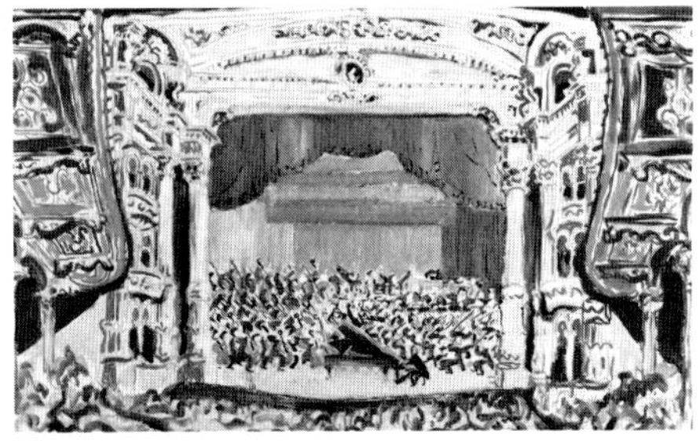

141

133

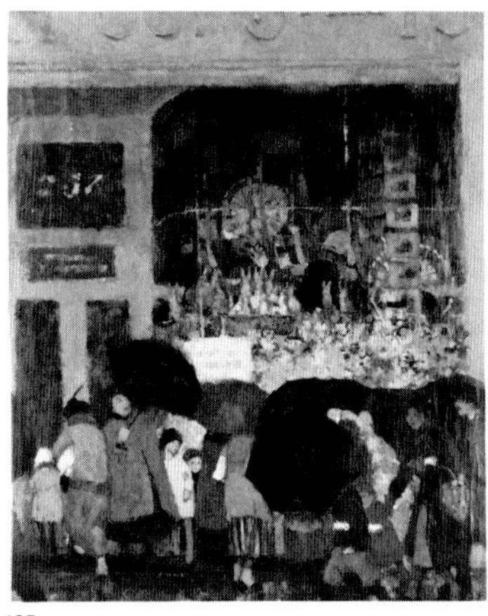

135

128 *Study of Two Breton Women, Concarneau, France* (probably for *Twilight Confidences*), 1888
Oil on canvas
13 11/16 x 10 5/8 in. (34.8 x 27 cm.)
Gift of Henry Sandwith Drinker, 1950.17.7

129 *Study of Two Breton Women, Concarneau, France* (probably for *Twilight Confidences*), 1888
Oil on cardboard (grisaille)
5 1/2 x 5 7/8 in. (14 x 14.9 cm.)
Gift of Henry Sandwith Drinker, 1950.17.15

130 *Supper at Emmaus*, 1888
Oil on cardboard (grisaille)
9 3/8 x 11 1/2 in. (23.8 x 29.2 cm.)
Inscribed, signed, and dated at lower left: à monsieur Julian/souvenir respectueuse [*sic*]/ de son eleve - Cecilia Beaux/Paris 1888 [scratched out]; signed at lower right: Beaux
Gift of Henry Sandwith Drinker, 1950.17.56

131 *Tobias Returning to His Family*, ca. 1888
Oil on cardboard (grisaille)
12 7/8 x 15 1/4 in. (32.7 x 38.7 cm.)
Gift of Henry Sandwith Drinker, 1950.17.8

132 *Two Women by a Fireplace*, ca. 1885
Oil on canvas
10 1/16 x 7 1/8 in. (25.6 x 18.1 cm.)
Gift of Henry Sandwith Drinker, 1950.17.6

133 *A Young Woman*, ca. 1895
Oil on canvas
29 9/16 x 22 1/16 in. (75.1 x 56 cm.)
Gift of Henry Sandwith Drinker, 1950.17.50

John Bekavac (1933–)

134 *White House*, 1961
Oil on canvas
10 1/16 x 18 1/4 in. (25.6 x 46.4 cm.)
Annotated on stretcher: (Bekavac)
John Lambert Fund, 1962.4

Hilda Belcher (1881–1963)

135 *The Easter Window*, ca. 1920
Oil on canvas
36 x 30 in. (91.4 x 76.2 cm.)
John Lambert Fund, 1921.2

George Bellows (1882–1925)

136 *Hunter and Mountains*, 1920
Oil on wood
18 x 22 in. (45.7 x 55.9 cm.)
Signed at lower right: Geo Bellows; inscribed on back: HUNTER AND MOUNTAINS.
Gift of Mr. and Mrs. Daniel W. Dietrich II, 1978.17.2

137 *North River*, 1908
Oil on canvas
32 7/8 x 43 in. (83.5 x 109.2 cm.)
Signed at lower left: G. Bellows
Joseph E. Temple Fund, 1909.2

138 *Up the Gorge*, 1913
Oil on wood
14 3/4 x 19 1/8 in. (37.5 x 48.6 cm.)
Signed at lower left: Geo Bellows-; signed and inscribed on back: ROY B/GEO BELLOWS/146 E 19 N.Y./A DRAMATIC PLACE [crossed out]/"UP THE GORGE"/A 172
Gift of Mr. and Mrs. Daniel W. Dietrich II, 1978.17.1

Henry Benbridge (1743–1812)

139 *The Gordon Family* (Thomas Gordon, the artist's stepfather, 1712–1772; possibly Ann, b. 1756, and Dolley Gordon; Mary Clark Benbridge Gordon, the artist's mother, possibly with Frances Gordon, b. 1761; and Thomas, b. 1758, or James Gordon), ca. 1762

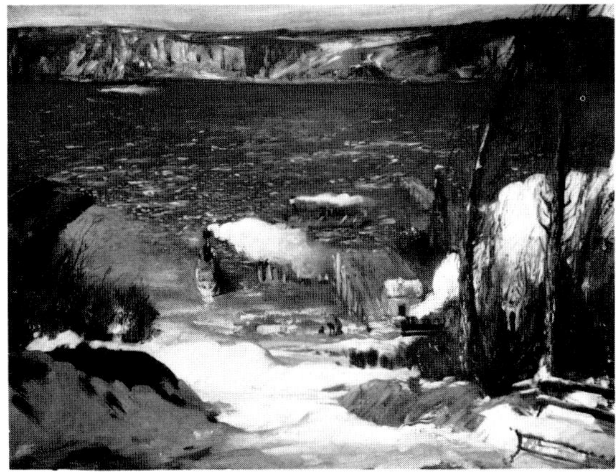

137

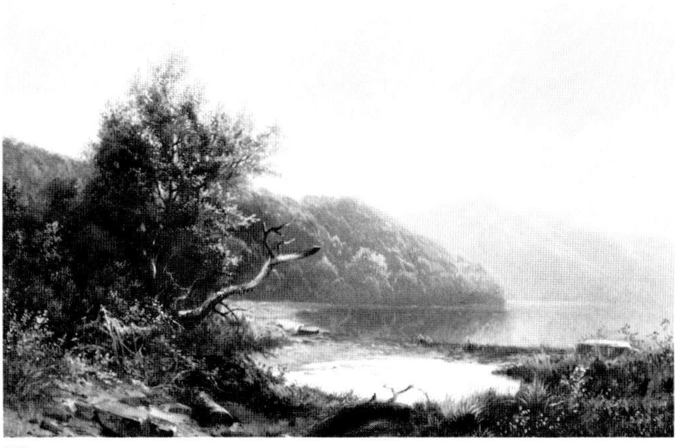

143

Oil on canvas
66 x 78 in. (167.6 x 198.1 cm.)
Henry S. McNeil Fund, 1987.8

Alfred Bendiner (1899–1964)

140 *Approach to Modern Art*, 1948
Oil on masonite
20 x 24$\frac{1}{16}$ in. (50.8 x 61.1 cm.)
Signed at lower right: A. Bendiner
Gift of the artist, 1949.1

141 *Philadelphia Orchestra, Academy of Music*, 1952
Oil on canvas
15 x 25$\frac{1}{8}$ in. (38.1 x 63.8 cm.)
Signed at lower right: Alfred Bendiner; inscribed and dated on back: approved sketch for Mural–Gimbel Brothers Competition June 1952/interior of the Academy of Music–Philadelphia Phila Orchestra playing Ormandy Conducting/Rachmaninoff soloist
Gift of James P. and Ruth Marshall Magill, 1957.15.3

George Frederick Bensell (1837–1879)

142 *Landscape #1 (Autumn)*
Oil on canvas
16 x 24 in. (40.6 x 61 cm.)
Signed at lower left: G. F. Bensell.
Source unknown, 1944.15.1

143 *Landscape #2 (Summer)*
Oil on canvas
16 x 24 in. (40.6 x 61 cm.)
Signed at lower left: G. F. Bensell.
Source unknown, 1944.15.2

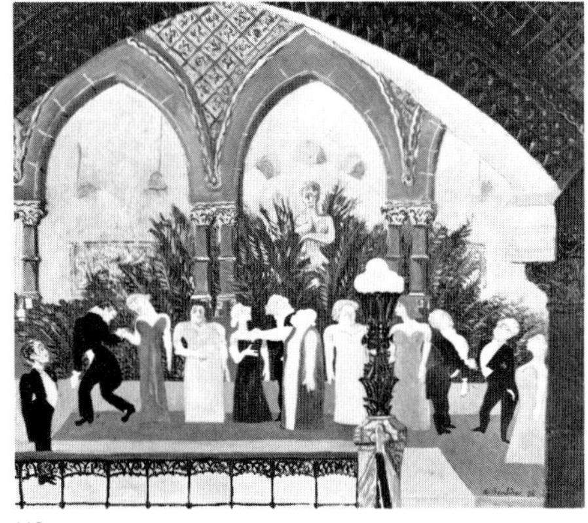

140

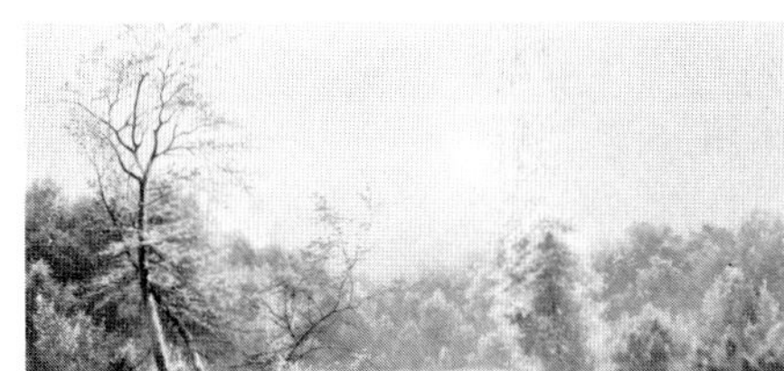

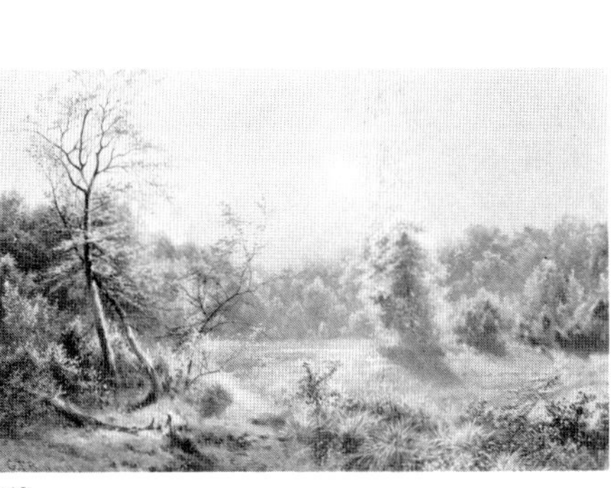

142

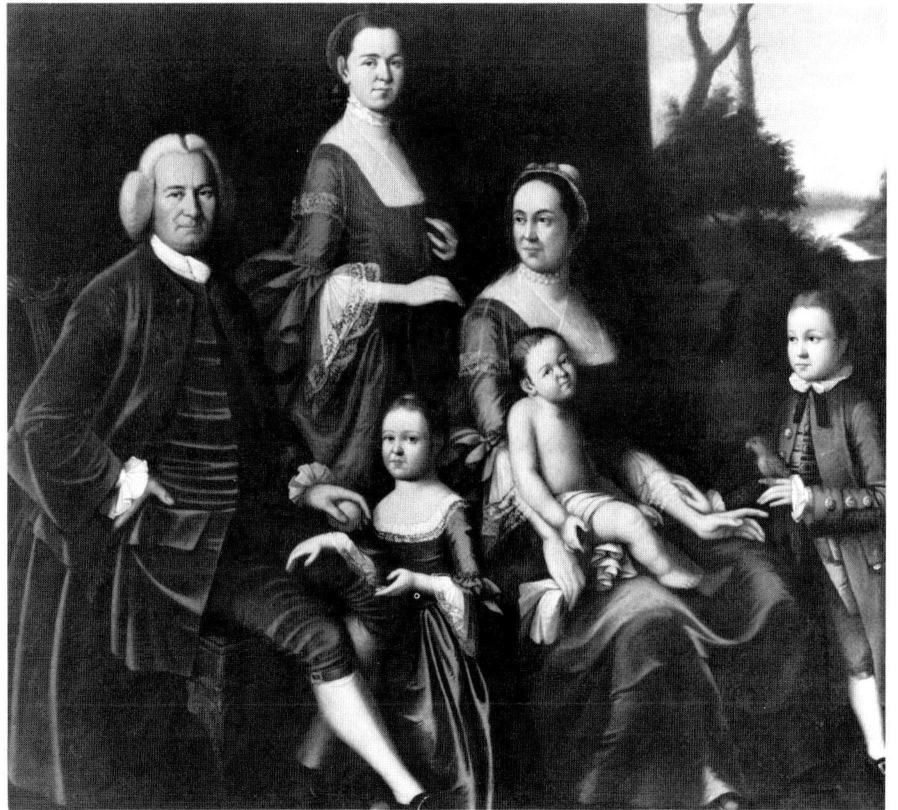

139

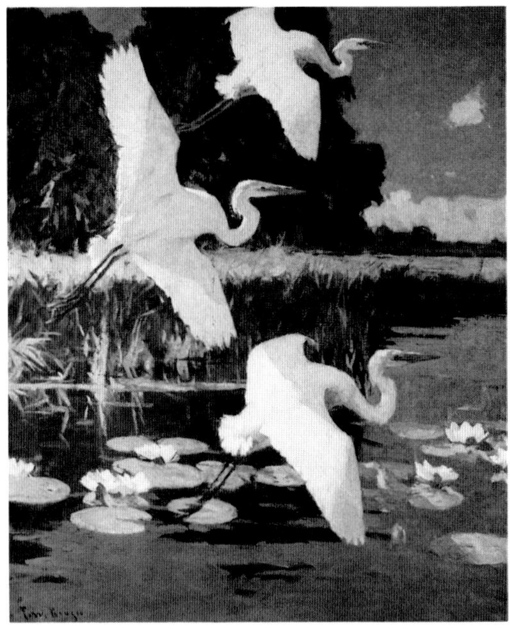
144

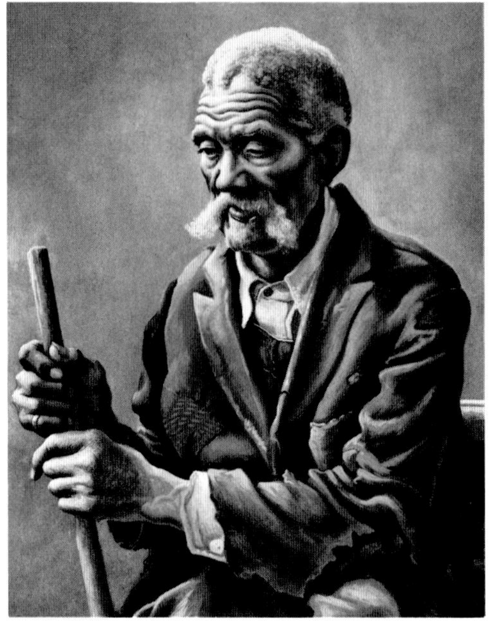
145

Frank W. Benson (1862–1951)

144 *Great White Herons*, 1933
Oil on canvas
44 x 36⅛ in. (111.8 x 91.8 cm.)
Signed and dated at lower left: F. W. Benson/'33
Joseph E. Temple Fund, 1934.2

Thomas Hart Benton (1889–1975)

145 *Aaron*, 1941
Oil and egg tempera on canvas, mounted on plywood
30⁵⁄₁₆ x 24⁵⁄₁₆ in. (77 x 61.8 cm.)
Signed at lower left: Benton
Joseph E. Temple Fund, 1943.3

Morris Berd (1914–)

146 *Home #3*, 1953–54
Oil on canvas
31¹⁵⁄₁₆ x 39¹⁵⁄₁₆ in. (81.1 x 101.4 cm.)
Signed at lower right: Berd
John Lambert Fund, 1954.4

Charles F. Berger (active 1841–1890)

147 *Henry Clay* (1777–1852)
(after John Neagle, 1843)
Oil on canvas
49¾ x 27¾ in. (126.4 x 70.5 cm.)
Signed at lower left: C. F. Berger.
Gift of Mrs. John Frederick Lewis (The John Frederick Lewis Memorial Collection), 1933.10.2

Eugene Berman (1899–1972)

148 *The Lions of the Arsenal– Venice*, 1954
Oil on canvas
25 x 17¹⁵⁄₁₆ in. (63.5 x 45.6 cm.)
Signed and dated at lower left: E. B/19 54; signed, inscribed, and dated on back: E.B./ New York. June–July 1954./The Lions of the Arsenal./Venice.
Henry D. Gilpin Fund, 1958.4

Helen Murrin Berry (b. 1900)

149 *Unloading Herring*, ca. 1935
Oil on canvas
20 x 24 in. (50.8 x 61 cm.)
Signed at lower left: HELEN BERRY; signed and inscribed on back: H. M. BERRY/6133 MORTON ST/UNLOADING HERRING
John Lambert Fund, 1936.2

Murray Percival Bewley (1884–1964)

150 *Convalescent*, ca. 1917
Oil on canvas
25 x 30⅛ in. (63.5 x 76.5 cm.)
Signed at upper right: M BEWLEY
John Lambert Fund, 1918.7

Edward Biberman (1904–1986)

151 *Girl with Flower*, 1928
Oil on canvas
28¹³⁄₁₆ x 23⁹⁄₁₆ in. (73.2 x 59.8 cm.)
Signed and dated at lower right: Biberman/1928
John Lambert Fund, 1931.1

George Biddle (1885–1973)

152 *Girl's Head*, 1931
Oil on canvas
12⅞ x 11⁷⁄₁₆ in. (32.7 x 29.1 cm.)
Signed and dated at lower left: Biddle-1931.;

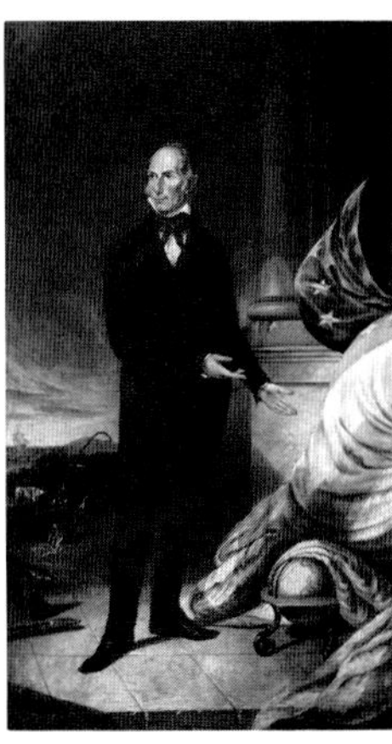
147

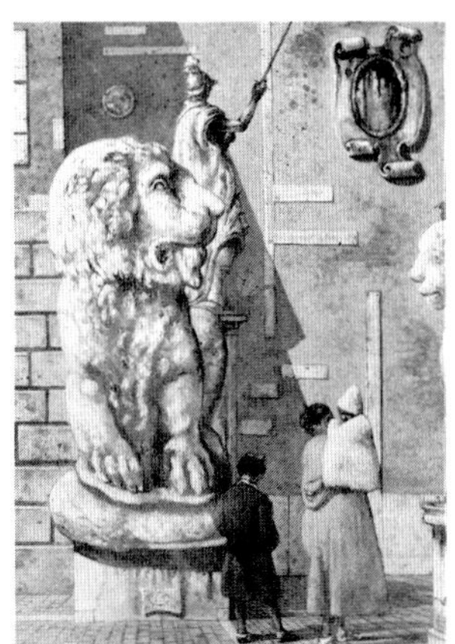
148

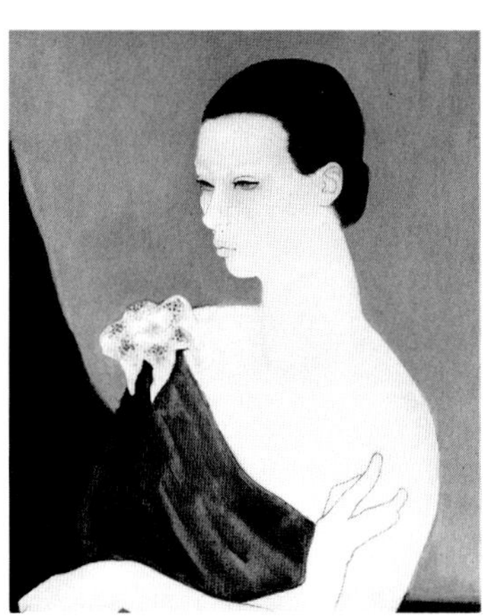
151

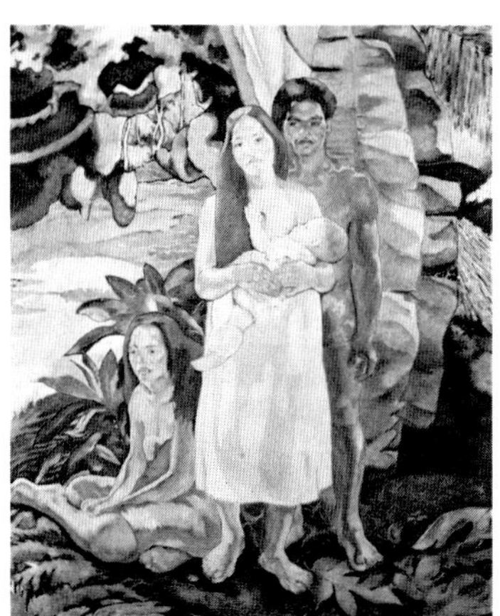
153

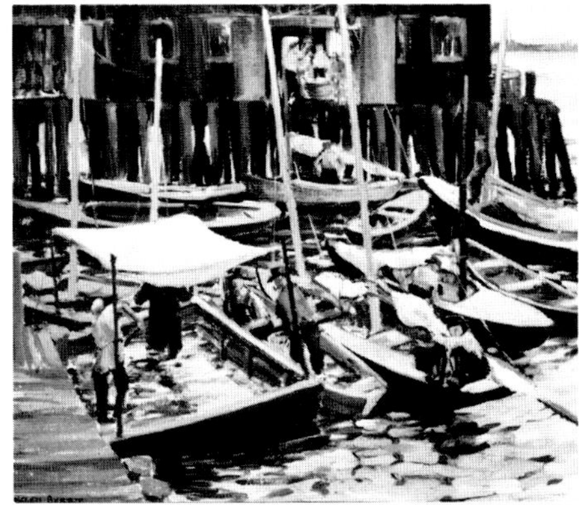

149

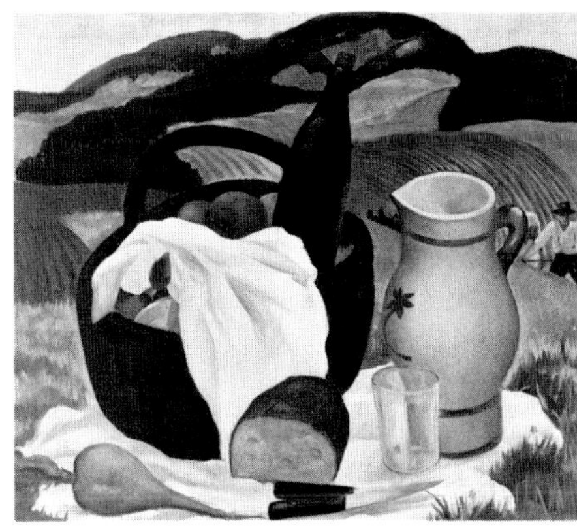

154

inscribed and signed on back: 244/Biddle/9-12
Gift of Mrs. Thomas E. Drake (The Margaretta S. Hinchman Collection), 1955.15.1

153 *Tahitians*, ca. 1920
Oil on canvas
60 x 50$\frac{1}{16}$ in. (152.4 x 127.2 cm.)
John Lambert Fund, 1921.3

Carl F. Binder (b. 1887)

154 *The Lunch Basket*, 1927
Oil on canvas
24 x 28 in. (61 x 71.1 cm.)
Signed and dated at lower right: C. F. Binder. 1927.
John Lambert Fund, 1928.3

Thomas Birch (1779–1851)

155 *Between the Rocks*
Oil on canvas
17½ x 25½ in. (44.5 x 64.8 cm.)
Collections Fund, 1962.20.1

156 *Fairmount Water Works*, 1821
Oil on canvas
20⅛ x 30$\frac{1}{16}$ in. (51.1 x 76.4 cm.)
Signed and dated at lower left: T.Birch/1821
Bequest of Charles Graff, 1845.1

157 *Perry's Victory on Lake Erie*, ca. 1814
Oil on canvas
66 x 96½ in. (167.6 x 245.1 cm.)
Gift of Mrs. Charles H. A. Esling, 1912.15

William Russell Birch. *See* cat. nos. 1631–32.

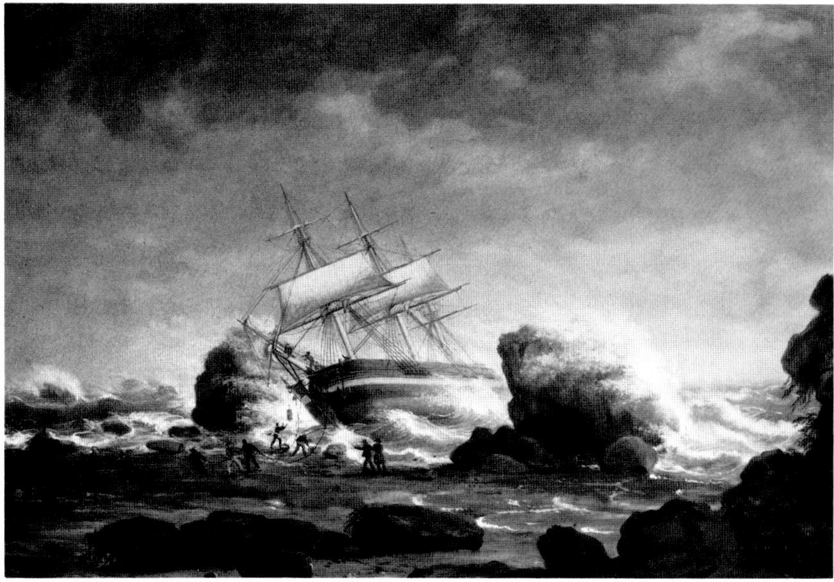

155

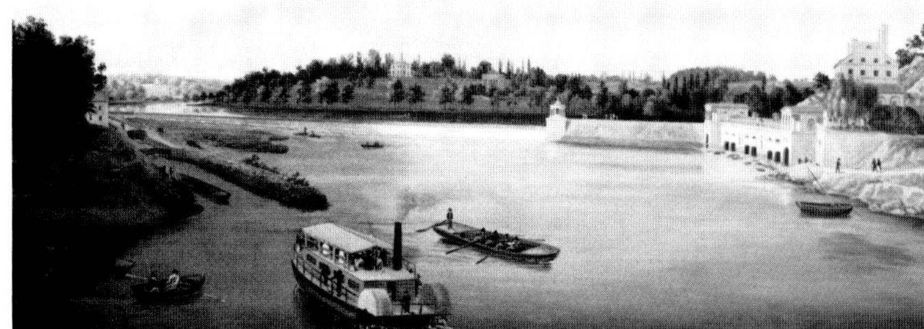

156

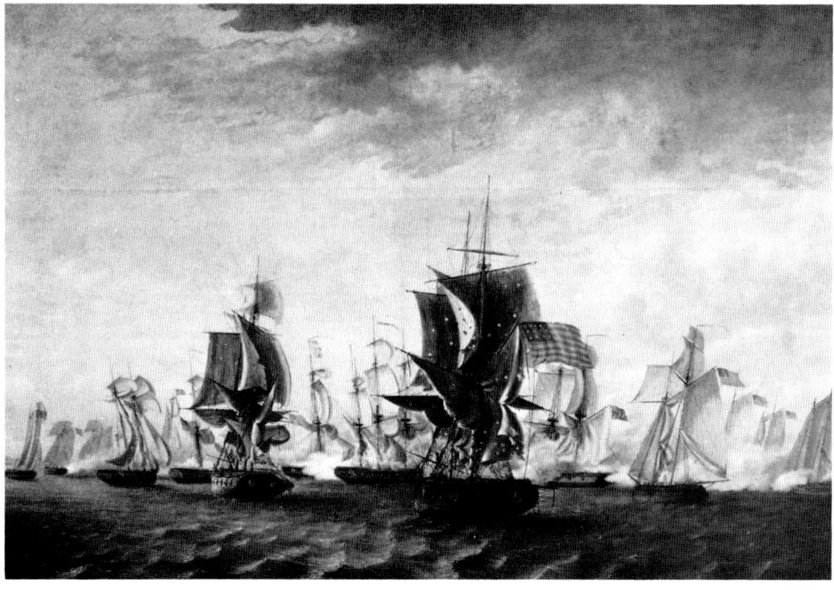

157

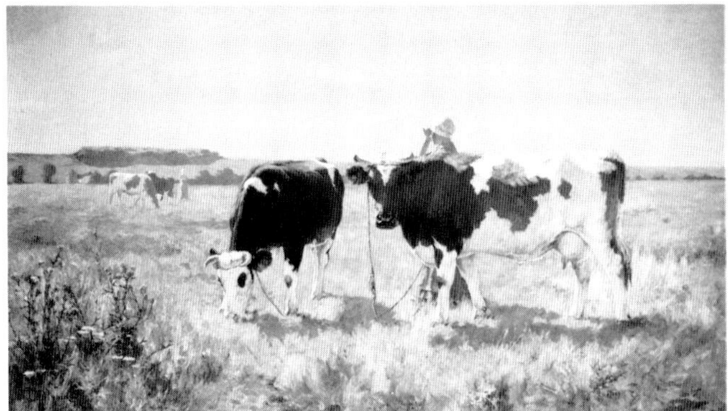

158

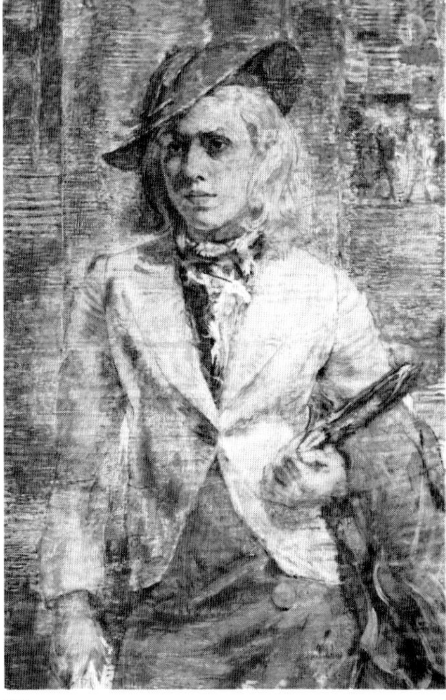

159

Henry Singlewood Bisbing (1849–1933)

158 *In the Meadow*, 1888
Oil on canvas
79 x 138 in. (200.7 x 350.5 cm.)
Signed and dated at lower left: HS [monogram] Bisbing/'88
Gift of Colonel Thomas Fitzgerald, 1891.1

Isabel Bishop (1902–1988)

159 *Young Woman*, 1937
Oil and egg tempera on masonite
30 x 21¼ in. (76.2 x 54 cm.)
Signed at upper left: Isabel Bishop
Henry D. Gilpin Fund, 1938.2

Henry Collins Bispham (1841–1882)

160 *The Bull*, 1867
Oil on canvas
49⅛ x 62⅛ in. (124.8 x 157.8 cm.)
Signed, inscribed, and dated at lower right: H. C. Bispham N.Y./1867
Gift of Frank Pleasanton, 1923.1

Edna Bistline (1914–)

161 *A Perry County Landscape*, 1944
Oil on canvas
24³⁄₁₆ x 31¹⁵⁄₁₆ in. (61.4 x 81.1 cm.)
Signed at lower right: Edna Bistline
John Lambert Fund, 1945.1

Morris Blackburn (1902–1979)

162 *Appalachian Spring I*, 1946–47
Oil on canvas
24½ x 32⅛ in. (62.2 x 81.6 cm.)
Signed at lower right: Morris Blackburn
Joseph E. Temple Fund, 1987.33

163 *Jersey Shore*, 1948
Oil and egg tempera on canvas
25¼ x 30¹⁄₁₆ in. (64.1 x 76.4 cm.)
Signed at lower right: Morris Blackburn
John Lambert Fund, 1949.2

164 *Taxco*, 1958–59
Oil and egg tempera on canvas
30³⁄₁₆ x 36¹⁄₁₆ in. (76.7 x 91.6 cm.)
Signed at lower right: Morris Blackburn
Anonymous gift, 1959.9

Morris Blackman (1930–)

165 *Shrine of the Primaries: Karnak*, 1969–70
Acrylic on masonite
48 x 49½ in. (121.9 x 125.7 cm.)
Signed and dated at lower right: MB [monogram] 69–70; inscribed on back: Shrine of the/ Primaries: Karnak/48" x 49½"
Gift of Mrs. William Clarke Mason, by exchange, 1971.2

Sarah Blakeslee (Mrs. Francis Speight, 1912–)

166 *Along the River*, 1938
Oil on canvas
30½ x 40⅜ in. (77.5 x 102.6 cm.)
Signed at lower left: SARAH BLAKESLEE
Inscribed and signed on stretcher: ALONG THE RIVER/BY SARAH BLAKESLEE
John Lambert Fund, 1941.1

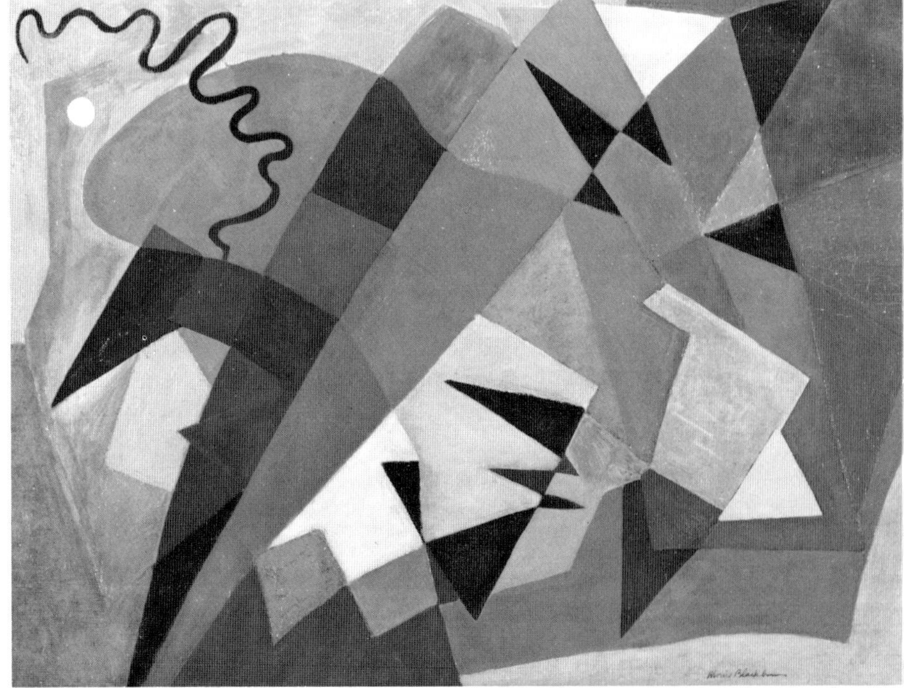

162

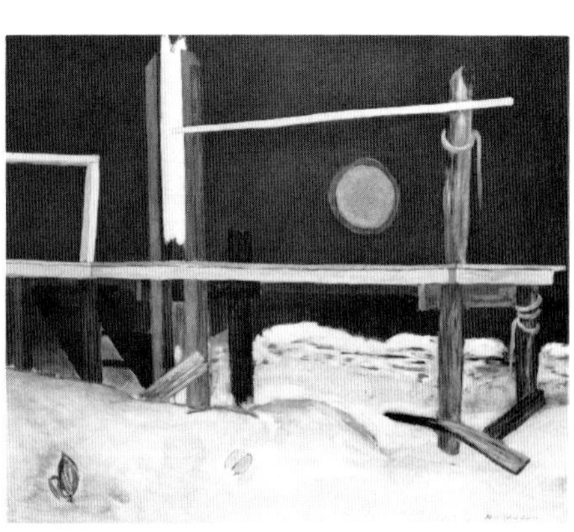

163

Al Blaustein (1924–)

167 *Golden City II*, 1958
Oil and graphite on masonite
36 x 48 in. (91.4 x 121.9 cm.)
Signed at lower right: Al Blaustein
John Lambert Fund, 1960.1

168 *The Search*, 1960 or 1961
Oil and graphite on canvas
30 1/16 x 19 in. (76.4 x 48.3 cm.)
Signed at lower right: Al Blaustein
Gift of Dr. and Mrs. Matthew T. Moore, 1967.13

Julius T. Bloch (1888–1966)

169 *Agriculture*, 1912
Oil on canvas
Approx. 80 x 167 in. (203 x 424 cm.)
Signed and dated at lower right: Julius T Bloch/ 191[2]
Commissioned by the Pennsylvania Academy, 1912.16.1
See also cat. no. 172.

170 *Lynching*, 1936
Oil over egg tempera on gessoed board ("Renaissance Panel")
25 1/16 x 16 in. (63.7 x 40.6 cm.)
Signed at lower left: Bloch .
Gift of the Free Library of Philadelphia, 1958.5

171 *Horace Pippin* (1888–1946), 1943
Oil on canvas
24 x 20 1/16 in. (61 x 51 cm.)
Signed and dated at upper right: Julius Bloch/ 1943
Bequest of the artist in memory of Emma and Nathan Bloch, 1967.8.2

172 *Study for "Agriculture,"* 1912
Oil on canvas
17 13/16 x 34 1/16 in. (45.2 x 86.5 cm.)
Signed at upper left: Julius T Bloch; dated at upper right: 1912
Bequest of the artist, 1967.8.1
See also cat. no. 169.

173 *Tulips and Anemones*, 1927
Oil on canvas
20 1/16 x 24 in. (51 x 61 cm.)
Signed at lower left: Julius T Bloch
John Lambert Fund, 1927.1

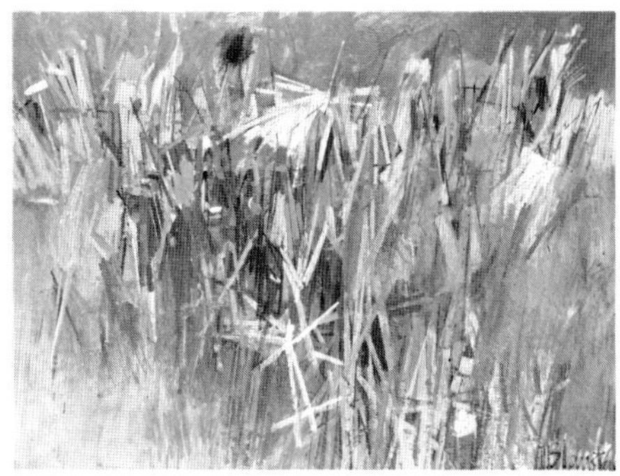
167

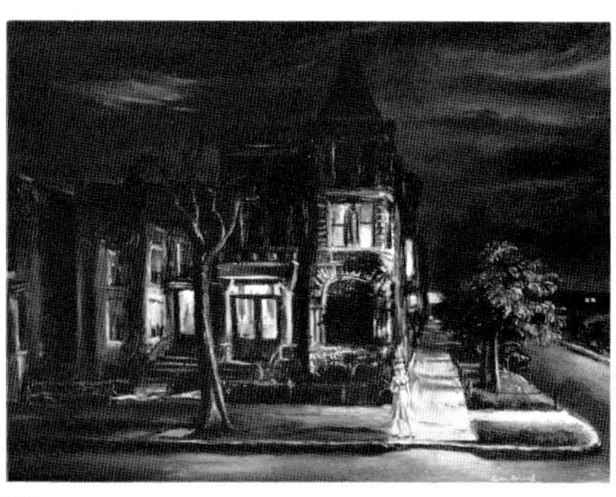
176

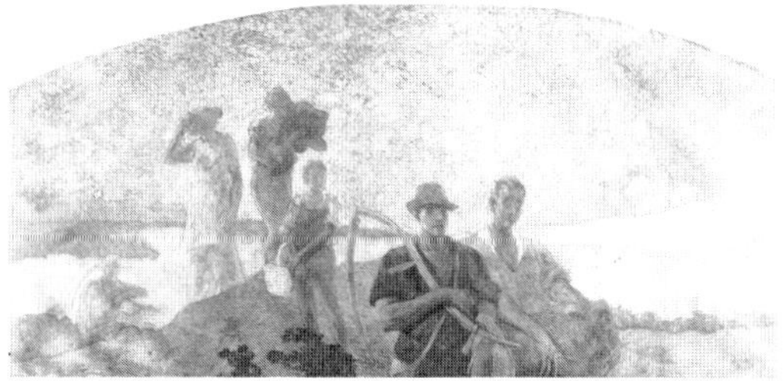
169

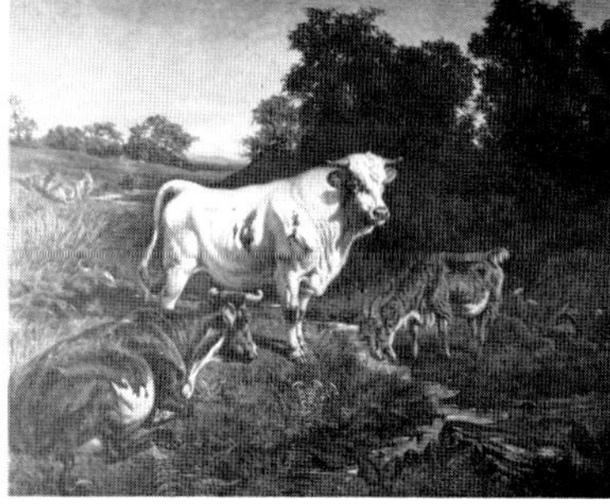
160

174 *Ephraim Wilson*, 1945
Oil on canvas
36 1/16 x 30 1/16 in. (91.6 x 76.4 cm.)
Signed at lower right: Julius Bloch
Gift of R. Sturgis Ingersoll, 1951.29

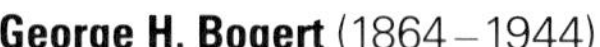

George H. Bogert (1864–1944)

175 *After Sunset: Longpré*, by 1894
Oil on wood
22 x 29 3/8 in. (55.9 x 74.6 cm.)
Gift of George A. Hearn, 1894.8

Aaron Bohrod (1907–)

176 *Oakdale Avenue at Night*, 1942
Oil on masonite
21 x 28 in. (53.3 x 71.1 cm.)
Signed at lower right: Aaron Bohrod; inscribed on back: OAKDALE AVENUE AT NIGHT/42/Photo
Henry D. Gilpin Fund, 1943.4

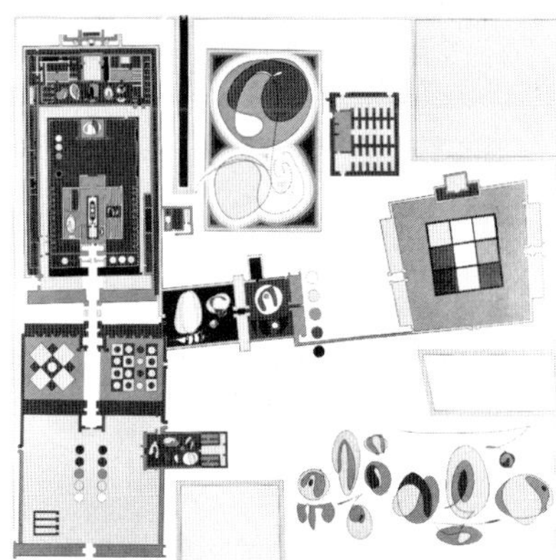
165

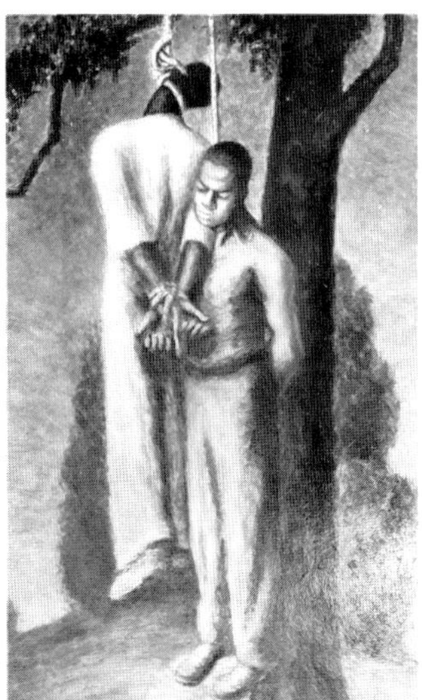
170

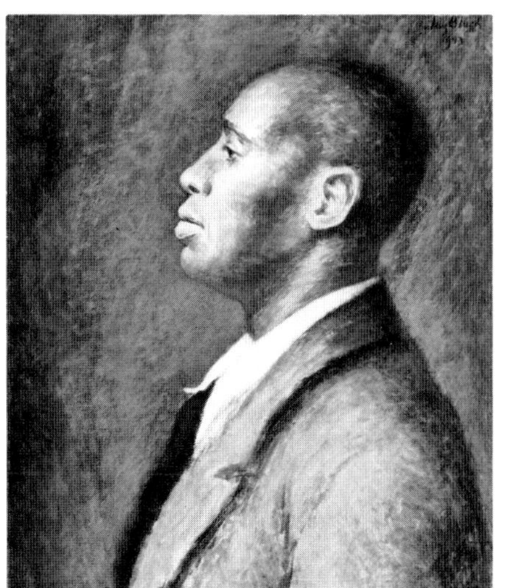
171

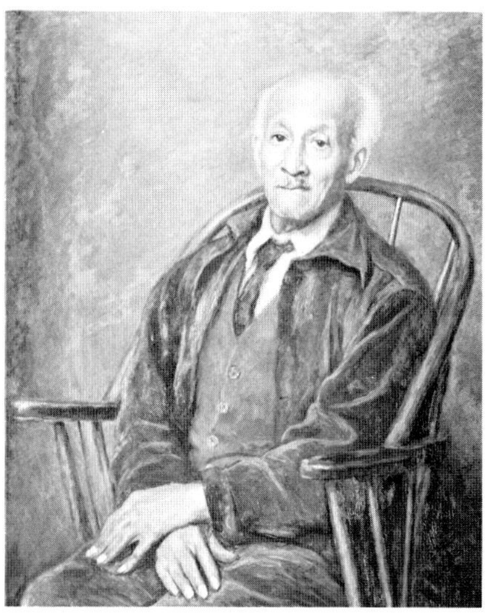
174

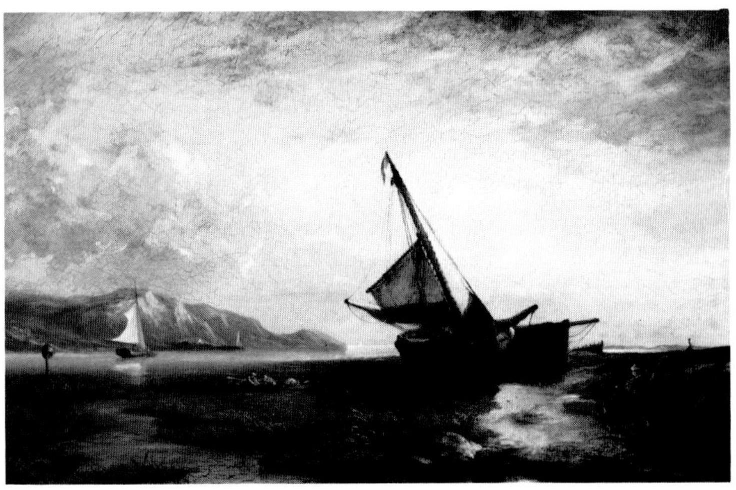

177

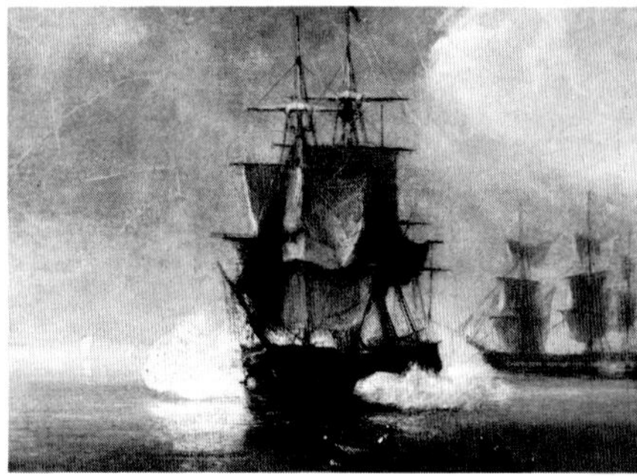

179

George R. Bonfield (1805–1898)

177 *Entrance to a River* (formerly *Wreck on Shore, Morning*), 1886
Oil on canvas
$23\frac{1}{4}$ x $36\frac{1}{16}$ in. (59.1 x 91.6 cm.)
Signed at lower left: G. R. Bonfield; inscribed, signed, and dated on back: Entrance to a River./Evening. Low tide./G. R. Bonfield. Pinxt/ 1886.
General Fund, 1893.3.2

178 *Marine View*, by 1893
Oil on academy board
$11\frac{1}{2}$ x $17\frac{1}{4}$ in. (29.2 x 43.8 cm.)
Signed twice, at lower left and right: G. R. Bonfield
General Fund, 1893.3.1

179 *View of a Sea Battle*, 1872
Oil on canvas, mounted on masonite
9 x 12 in. (22.9 x 30.5 cm.)
Annotated on canvas swatch glued to back: G. Bonfield/1872
Gift of Dr. Frederick M. Chacker, 1971.13.1

Elisabeth Fearn Bonsall (1861–1956)

180 *Hot Milk*, 1896
Oil on canvas
18 x $32\frac{1}{4}$ in. (45.7 x 81.9 cm.)
Signed and dated at lower left: E. F. Bonsall 1896
Joseph E. Temple Fund, 1897.4

Jack Bookbinder (1911–)

181 *The Gaiety Theatre, Philadelphia*, 1952
Oil on canvas
$27\frac{15}{16}$ x $37\frac{1}{16}$ in. (71 x 94.1 cm.)
Signed and dated at lower right: bookbinder '52
Inscribed and signed on frame: Gaiety Theatre/ Jack Bookbinder/Phila. Pa.
John Lambert Fund, 1953.15

182 *The White Gate*, 1957
Oil on canvas
12 x $17\frac{1}{16}$ in. (30.5 x 43.3 cm.)
Signed and dated at lower right: bookbinder '57
Inscribed and signed on frame: "The White Gate"/-Jack Bookbinder
Gift of Mrs. Samuel W. Levitties, 1959.12

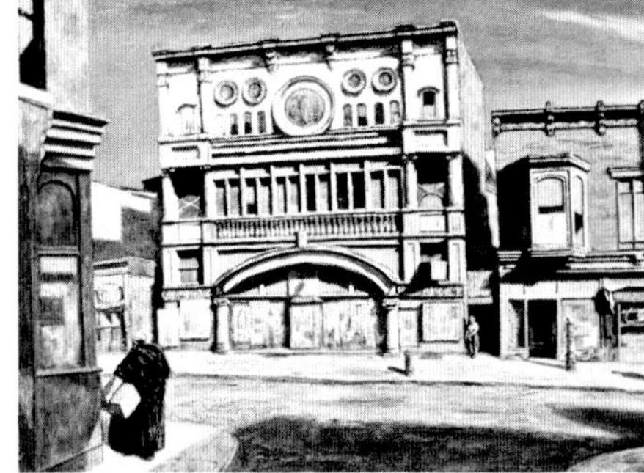

181

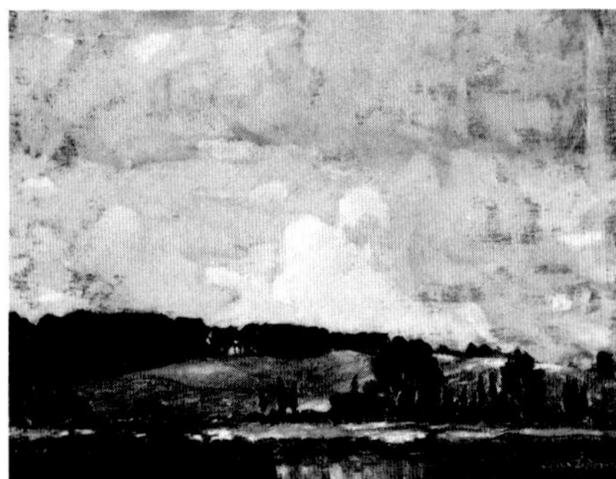

188

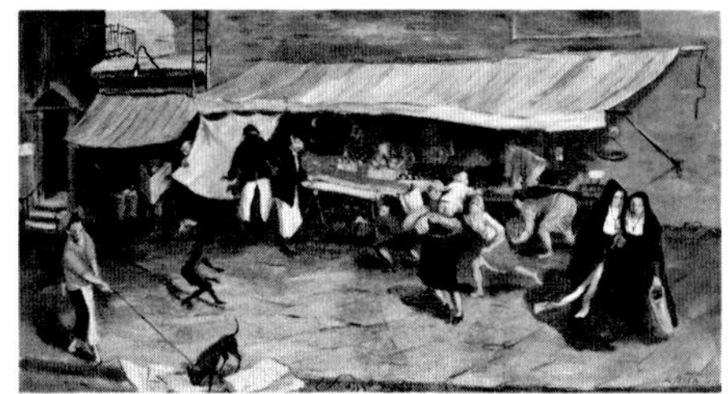

189

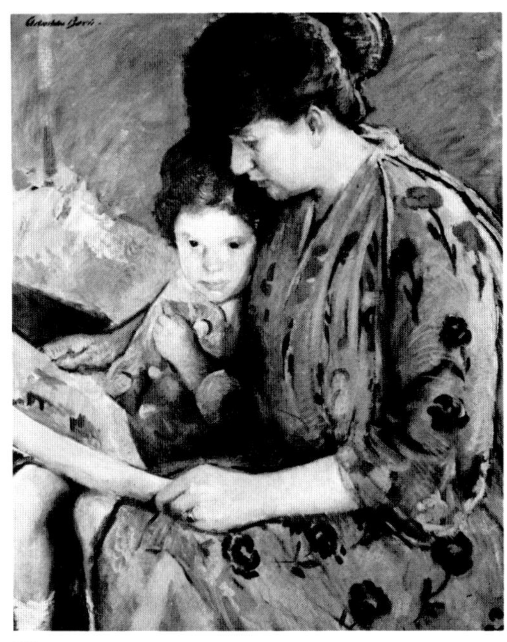

185

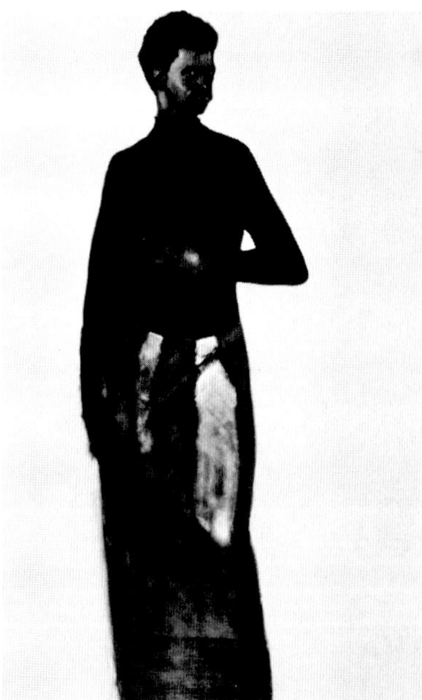

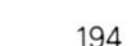

194

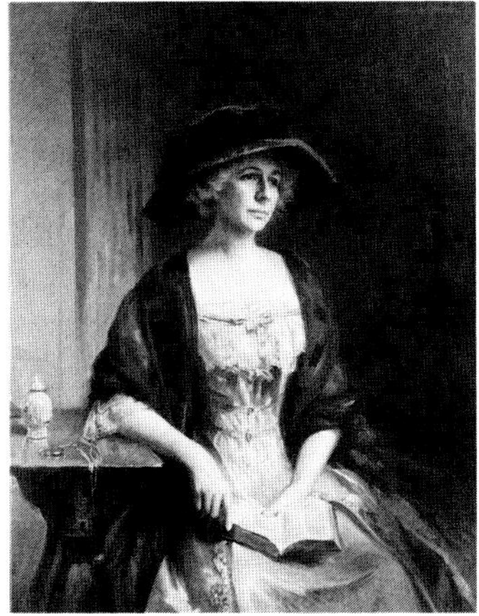
184

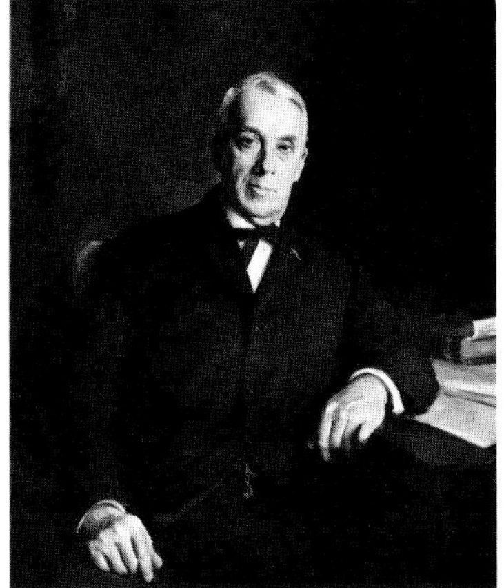
187

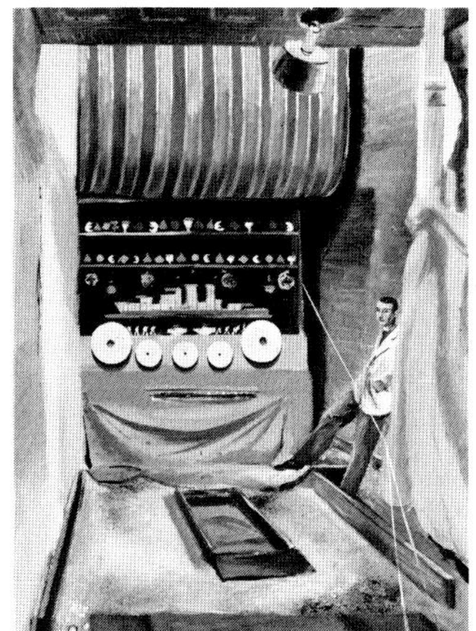
191

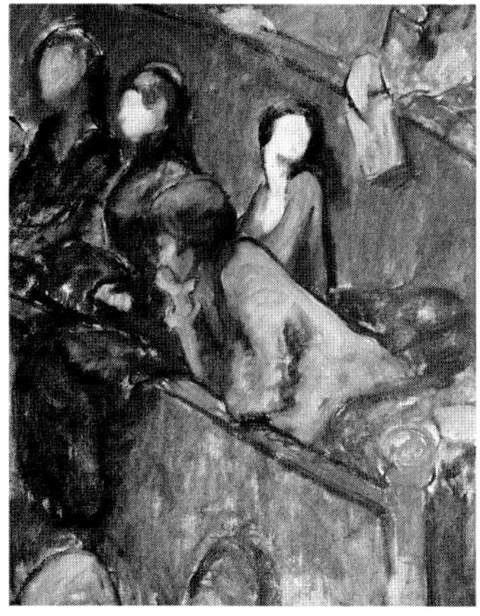
193

Cameron Booth (1892–1980)

183 *Horses*, 1924
Oil on canvas
42 1/16 x 54 1/8 in. (106.8 x 137.5 cm.)
Signed and dated at lower left: Cameron Booth 1924
John Lambert Fund, 1925.2

Adolphe Borie (1877–1934)

184 *Elizabeth Matthews Jayne* (Mrs. Henry La Barre Jayne), 1913
Oil on canvas
46 1/8 x 36 1/8 in. (117.2 x 91.8 cm.)
Signed and dated at upper right: Adolphe Borie -1913
Gift of Horace H. F. Jayne, 1963.6

185 *The Picture Book*, 1918
Oil on canvas
30 x 25 in. (76.2 x 63.5 cm.)
Signed at upper left: Adolphe Borie-
Henry D. Gilpin Fund, 1941.15

186 *Vase of Flowers*, 1925
Oil on canvas
20 3/16 x 16 in. (51.3 x 40.6 cm.)
Signed at upper left: Adolphe Borie
Gift of James P. and Ruth Marshall Magill, 1957.15.4

187 *Samuel Matthews Vauclain* (1856–1940), 1920
Oil on canvas
43 x 36 in. (109.2 x 91.4 cm.)
Signed and dated at upper left: Adolphe Borie 1920.
Gift of the Baldwin Locomotive Works, 1925.11.1

Lester D. Boronda (1886–1953)

188 *Whisper Low*, ca. 1918
Oil on canvas
25 1/16 x 29 15/16 in. (63.7 x 76 cm.)
Signed at lower right: Lester D Boronda
John Lambert Fund, 1919.2

Louis Bosa (1905–1981)

189 *Sidewalk Market*, 1941
Oil on canvas
20 3/16 x 36 3/16 in. (51.3 x 91.9 cm.)
Signed and dated at lower right: L. BOSA 1941
Joseph E. Temple Fund, 1950.22

190 *Skating in the Park*, ca. 1942
Oil on masonite
10 1/16 x 15 7/8 in. (25.6 x 40.3 cm.)
Signed at lower right: L. BOSA
John Lambert Fund, 1943.5

Louis Bouché (1896–1969)

191 *Shooting Gallery*, 1940
Oil on canvas
40 1/16 x 30 1/16 in. (101.8 x 76.4 cm.)
Signed and dated at lower center: LOUIS BOUCHÉ/ 1940
John Lambert Fund, 1941.2

Ted Bradley

192 *The Shawl*, 1945
Oil on canvas
33 1/16 x 28 in. (84 x 71.1 cm.)
Signed and dated at lower right: TED BRADLEY 1945
John Lambert Fund, 1946.4

Delphine Bradt (b. 1898)

193 *Music*, ca. 1919
Oil on canvas
20 x 16 in. (50.8 x 40.6 cm.)
John Lambert Fund, 1920.3

James Sherman Brantley (1945–)

194 *Brother James* (self-portrait), 1968
Oil on canvas
60 7/16 x 40 1/4 in. (153.5 x 102.2 cm.)
Signed and dated at upper left: Brantley/68
Gift of the artist, 1970.1

Ross Eugene Braught (b. 1898)

195 *Dead Chestnut*, 1927
Oil on canvas
54 x 60 1/8 in. (137.2 x 152.7 cm.)
Signed and dated at lower left: Ross Braught 1927
Joseph E. Temple Fund, 1928.4

196 *In the Valley*, 1922
Oil on canvas
46 1/2 x 50 1/2 in. (118.1 x 128.3 cm.)
Signed and dated at lower right: Ross E. Braught/1922.
John Lambert Fund, 1923.3

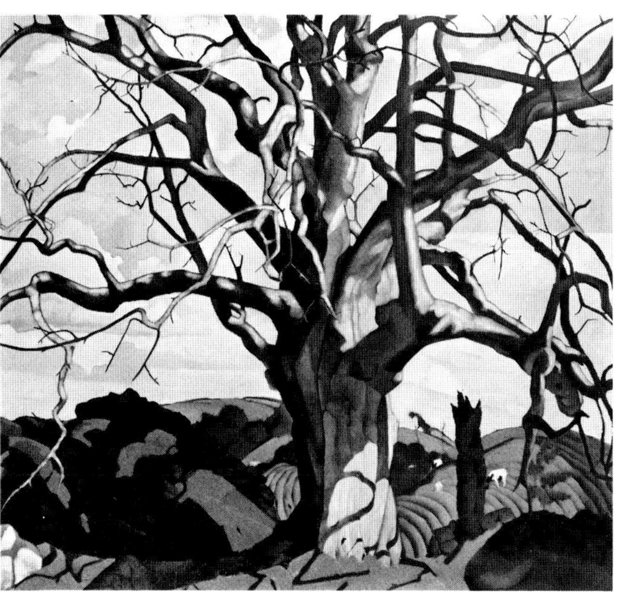
195

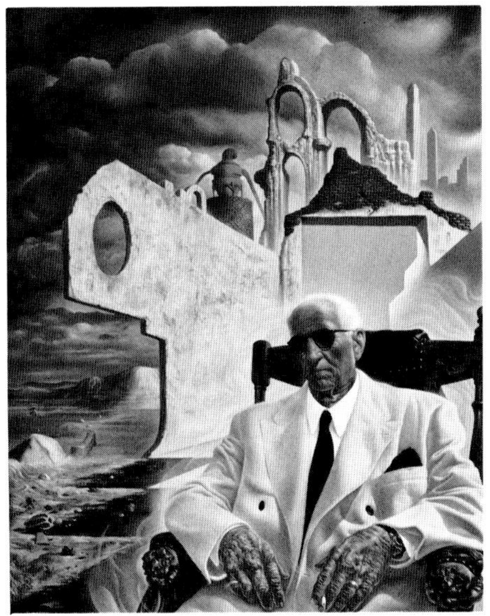

197

Robert Braun (b. 1921)

197 *Transient*, 1948
Oil on canvas
20 x 16 in. (50.8 x 40.6 cm.)
Signed at lower left: R-H-BRAUN
John Lambert Fund, 1949.3

Hugh H. Breckenridge (1870–1937)

198 *The Pestilence* (formerly *War*), by 1918
Oil on canvas
65 3/16 x 80 1/4 in. (165.6 x 203.8 cm.)
Signed at lower left: Hugh H. Breckenridge.
Gift of the artist, 1928.10

199 *Philadelphia*, by 1917
Oil on canvas
37 x 43 in. (94 x 109.2 cm.)
Signed at lower right: Hugh H. Breckenridge
Gift of Mrs. Hugh H. Breckenridge in memory of the artist, 1938.14

200 *The Tree of Life*, by 1929
Oil on canvas
37 x 43 in. (94 x 109.2 cm.)
Signed at lower left: Hugh H. Breckenridge
Gift of the Fellowship of the Pennsylvania Academy, 1934.14

201 *The Village Stream*, ca. 1924
Oil on canvas
28 7/8 x 36 1/8 in. (73.3 x 91.8 cm.)
Signed at lower left: Hugh H. Breckenridge
Joseph E. Temple Fund, 1925.9

Raymond Breinin (1910–)

202 *Dr. Jean Piccard* (1884–1963), 1946
Oil on canvas
48 1/8 x 37 1/8 in. (122.2 x 94.3 cm.)
Signed and dated at lower left: Breinin/'46
Joseph E. Temple Fund, 1948.2

James Brewton (1930–1967)

203 *The Suicide of Judas*, 1959
Egg tempera, oil, and charcoal on cardboard
47 1/2 x 47 3/4 in. (120.7 x 121.3 cm.)
Signed at upper right: Brewton
John Lambert Fund, 1960.3

Alexander Brook (1898–1980)

204 *Fall*, 1936
Oil on canvas
12 x 16 in. (30.5 x 40.6 cm.)
Signed at lower right: A. Brook; dated on back: 1936
Annotated on stretcher: 172-Fall Brook 14
Gift of Mrs. Herbert Cameron Morris, 1958.22.1

205 *Girl in White*, 1947
Casein emulsion and oil on canvas
33 15/16 x 25 15/16 in. (86.2 x 65.9 cm.)
Signed at lower right: A. Brook
Henry D. Gilpin Fund, 1950.3

206 *Girl Reading*, mid-1930s
Oil on canvas
35 15/16 x 30 in. (91.3 x 76.2 cm.)
Signed at lower right: A. Brook
Gift of Mrs. Herbert Cameron Morris, 1956.4

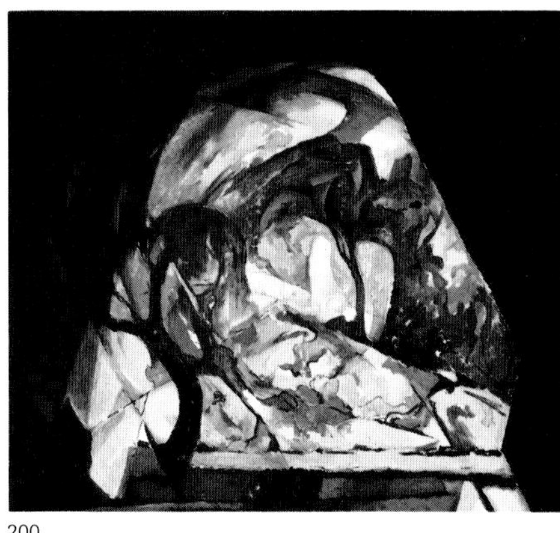

200

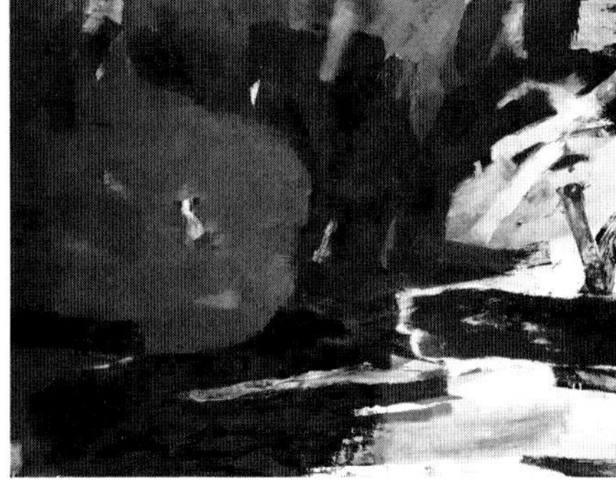

207

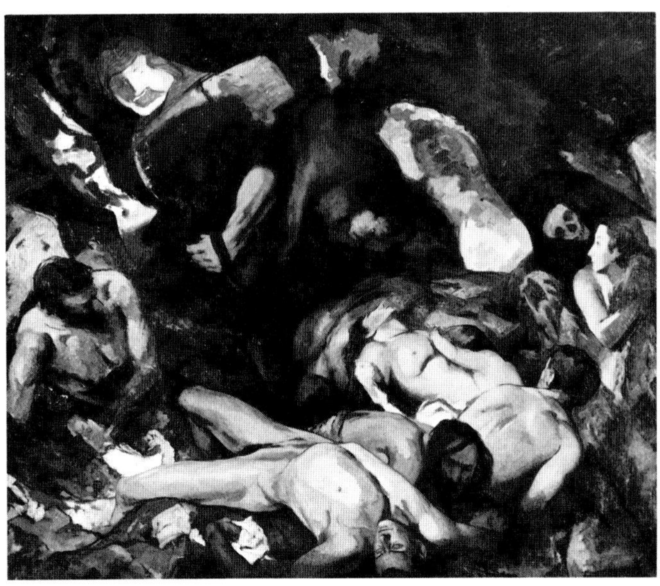

198

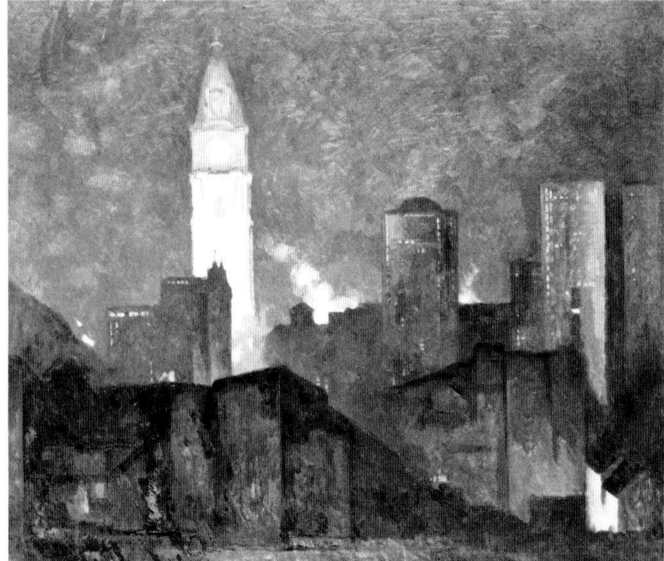

199

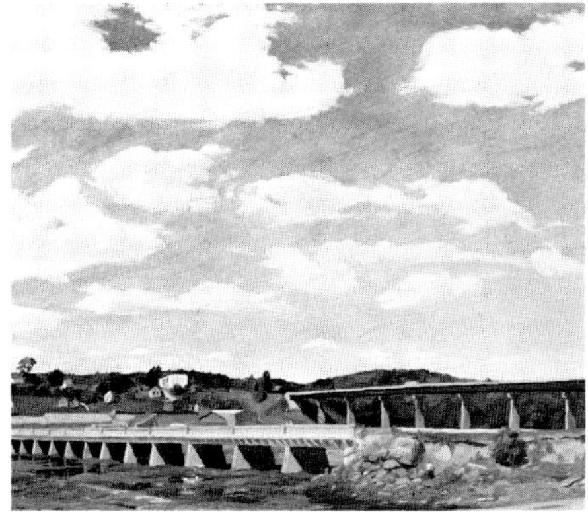
209

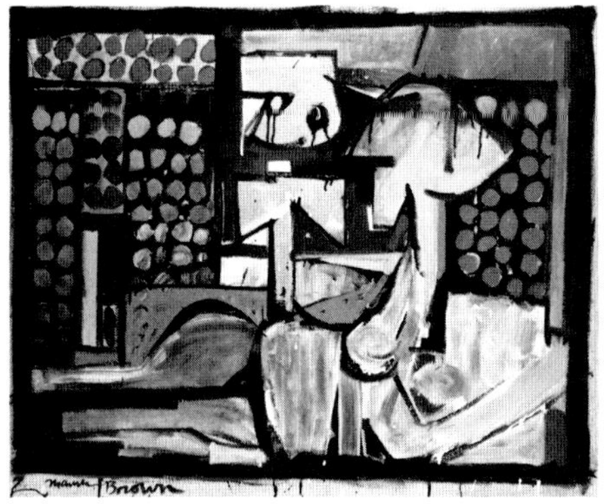
212

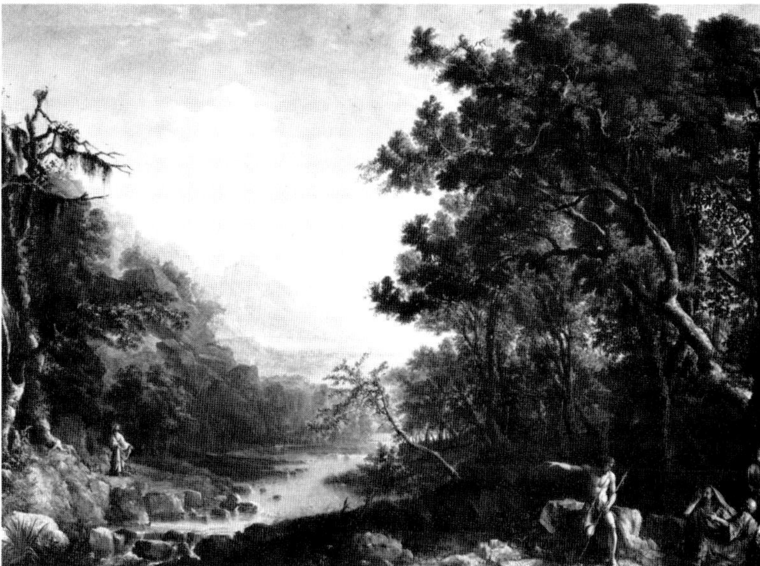
210

James Brooks (1906–)

207 *Mohan*, 1960
Oil and acrylic on canvas
51⅞ x 65⅞ in. (131.8 x 167.3 cm.)
Signed twice, at lower left and right: J. Brooks; inscribed and signed on back: "MOHAN"/51x66/ James Brooks
Gift of the Ford Foundation, 1962.5.1

Carlyle Brown (1919–1963)

208 *Table with Fish and Scales*, 1950
Oil on canvas
40 x 48⅛ in. (101.6 x 122.2 cm.)
Signed and dated at upper right: CARLYLE BROWN '50
Henry D. Gilpin Fund, 1954.5

Charles Van Dyck Brown. *See* cat. no. 1633.

Emily S. Brown (1943–)

209 *Both Bridges, Belfast, Maine*, 1981
Oil on canvas
15$\frac{1}{16}$ x 17$\frac{1}{16}$ in. (38.3 x 43.3 cm.)
Signed and dated at lower left: ESB 81
Gift of Dr. Elizabeth B. Brown, 1982.19

George Loring Brown (1814–1889)

210 *Saint John the Baptist in the Wilderness*, 1845–46
Oil on canvas
58$\frac{11}{16}$ x 81 in. (149.1 x 205.7 cm.)
Signed, inscribed, and dated at lower right: G. L. Brown./Florence/1845–6
Henry D. Gilpin Fund with contributions from members of the Peale Club, 1969.24

Horace Brown (1876–1949)

211 *Wind and Clouds*, ca. 1925
Oil on canvas
27 x 34 in. (68.6 x 86.4 cm.)
Signed at lower right: Horace Brown-
John Lambert Fund, 1926.1

John Henry Brown. *See* cat. nos. 1634–38.

Maurice Brown (b. 1932)

212 *Room*, 1959
Oil on canvas
32$\frac{5}{16}$ x 39$\frac{1}{16}$ in. (82.1 x 99.2 cm.)
Signed at lower left: Maurice Brown
John Lambert Fund, 1960.4

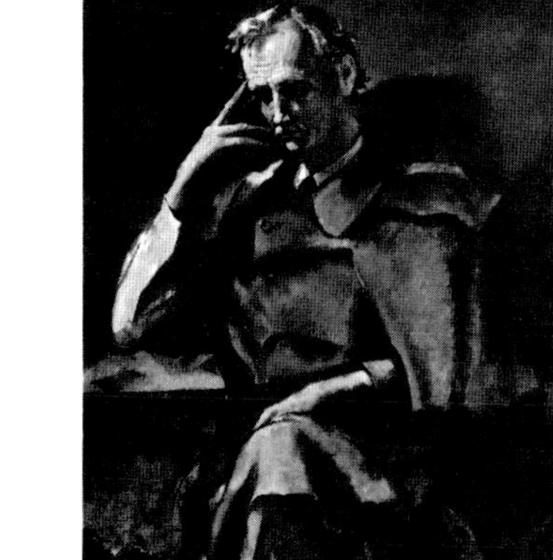
202

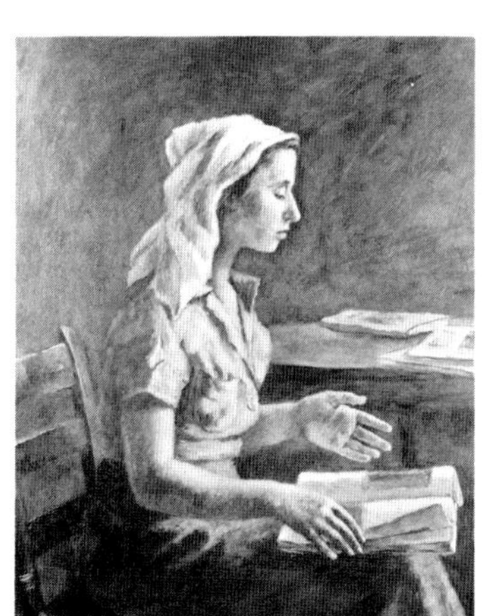
206

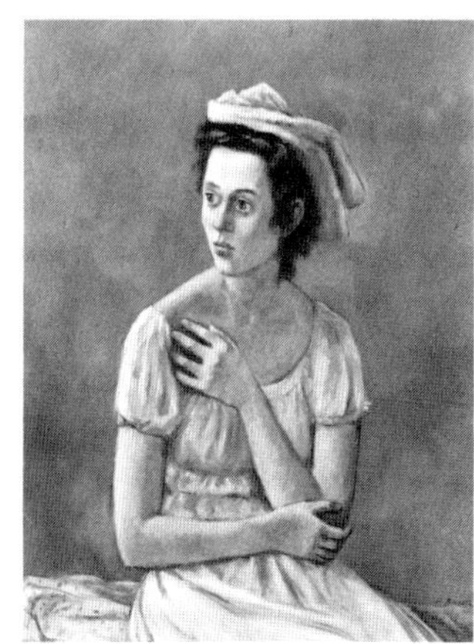
205

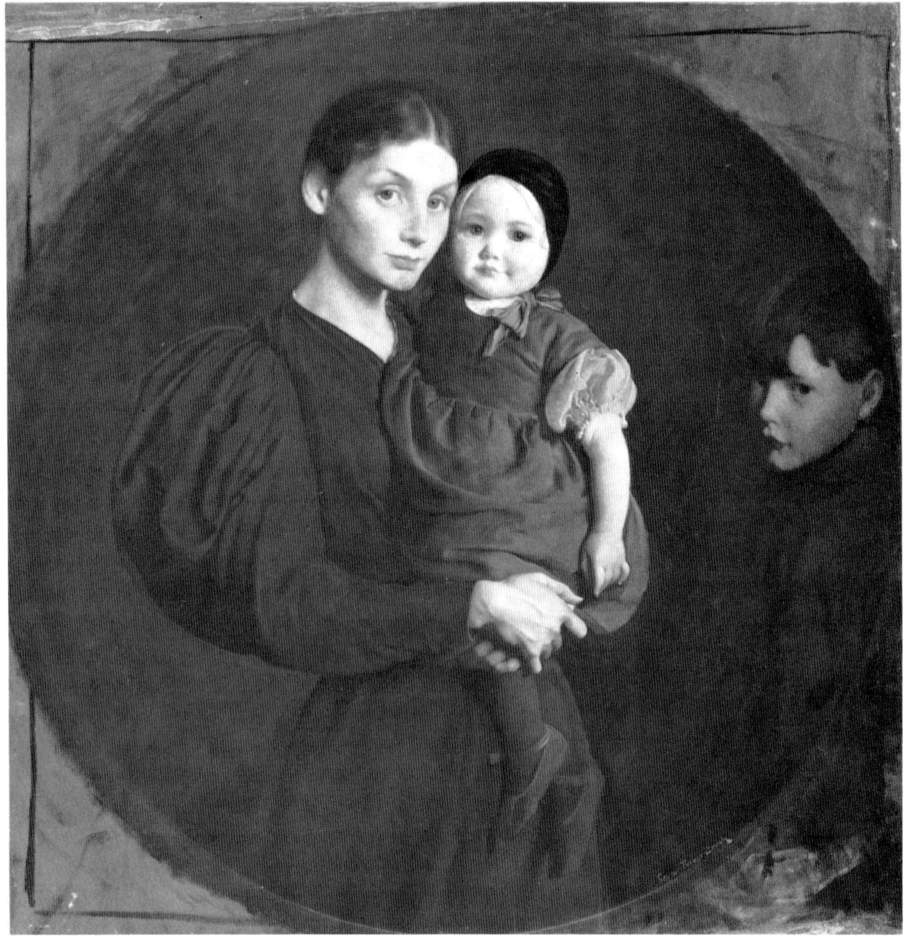
215

William Mason Brown (1828–1898)

213 *Fruit and Art Objects*, ca. 1888
Oil on canvas
22 1/16 x 16 3/16 in. (56 x 41.1 cm.)
Signed at lower right: WMBrown [initials in monogram]
Joseph E. Temple Fund, 1889.1

Byron Browne (1907–1961)

214 *Still Life*, 1953
Oil on linen
48 x 38 1/8 in. (121.9 x 96.8 cm.)
Signed and dated at lower right: Byron Browne/1953; signed, dated, and inscribed on back: Byron Browne/1953/STILL-LIFE/38 x 48/N.Y.C
John Lambert Fund, 1954.7

George de Forest Brush (1855–1941)

215 *Mother and Child* (Mary "Mittie" Taylor Whelpley Brush, the artist's wife, ca. 1866–1949, and Nancy, b. 1890, with Gerome, b. 1888), ca. 1897
Oil on canvas
39 1/4 in. diam. (99.7 cm.)
Signed at lower right: Geo De Forest Brush
Joseph E. Temple Fund, 1898.2

Everett L. Bryant (1864–1946)

216 *Asters*, ca. 1912
Oil on canvas
18 15/16 x 15 11/16 in. (48.1 x 39.8 cm.)
Signed at lower left: E L Bryant
John Lambert Fund, 1913.4

Maude Drein Bryant (Mrs. Everett L. Bryant, 1880–1946)

217 *Calendulas and Asters*, ca. 1913
Oil on canvas
25 1/8 x 30 1/4 in. (63.8 x 76.8 cm.)
Signed at lower right: Maude Drein
John Lambert Fund, 1914.3

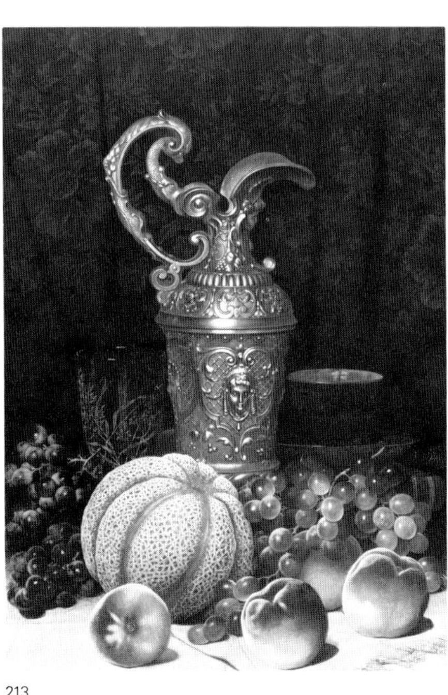
213

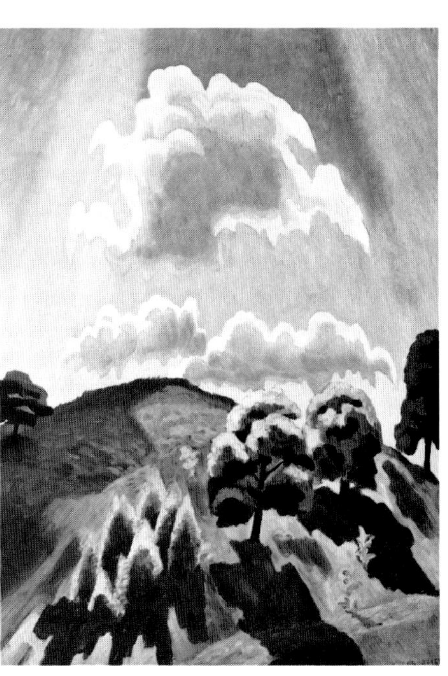
219

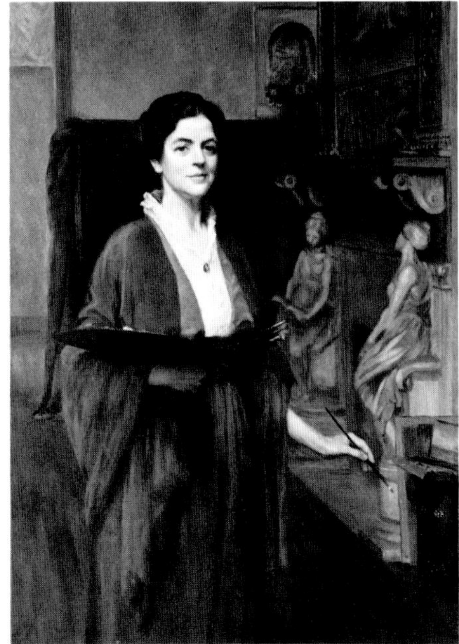
221

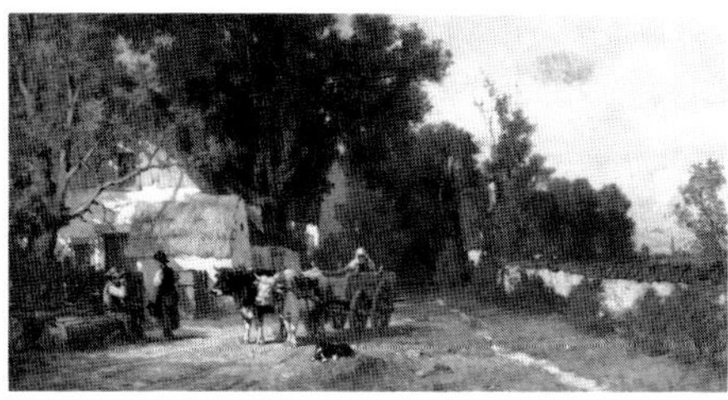

218

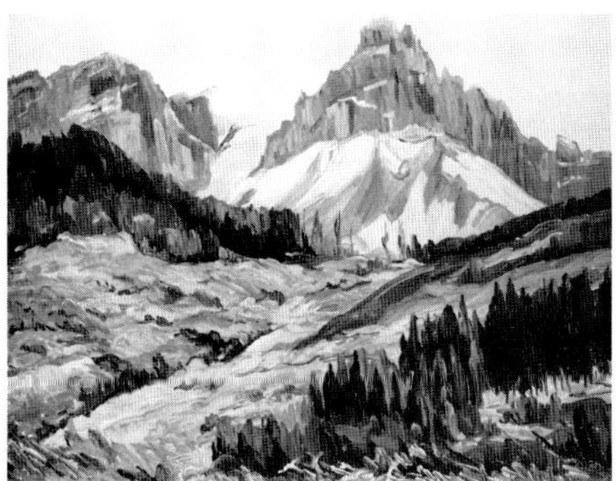

222

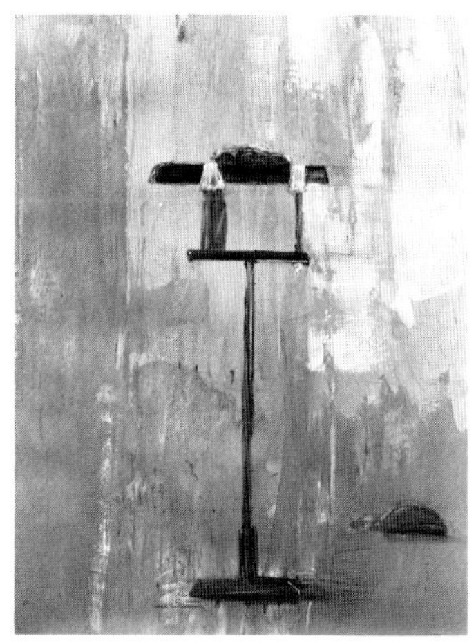

224

Andrew Fisher Bunner (1841–1897)

218 *A Country Road in Germany*, 1875
Oil on canvas
12 3/4 x 24 9/16 in. (32.4 x 62.4 cm.)
Signed, inscribed, and dated at lower left: A. F. BUNNER/München 1875; inscribed, signed, and dated on back: "A Country Road in Germany"/ A.F. Bunner/MUNICH.1875
Bequest of Harrison Earl, 1894.6.1

Charles Burchfield (1893–1967)

219 *Hill Top at High Noon*, 1925
Oil on cardboard
31 x 22 in. (78.7 x 55.9 cm.)
Signed and dated at lower right: C.BURCHFIELD/1925
John Lambert Fund, 1928.5

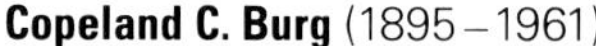

Copeland C. Burg (1895–1961)

220 *Black Boats*, ca. 1938
Oil on canvas
24 x 28 in. (61 x 71.1 cm.)
Signed at lower left: Copeland Burg
John Lambert Fund, 1939.2

Margaret Lesley Bush-Brown (1857–1944)

221 *Self-Portrait*, 1914
Oil on canvas
56 1/2 x 42 1/2 in. (143.5 x 108 cm.)
Signed and dated at lower left: M. Lesley Bush-Brown 1914
Gift of the artist, 1927.10

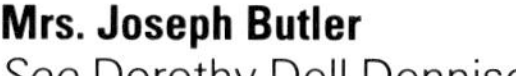

Mrs. Joseph Butler
See Dorothy Dell Dennison.

Mary Butler (1865–1946)

222 *Cathedral Crag, Yoho Road*, ca. 1935
Oil on canvas
27 15/16 x 36 in. (71 x 91.4 cm.)
Signed at lower right: MARY BUTLER; signed and inscribed on back: MARY BUTLER/PHILA/CATHEDRAL CRAG/YOHO ROAD
Gift of the Fellowship of the Pennsylvania Academy, 1936.20

223 *Flood Tide*, ca. 1924
Oil on canvas
23 15/16 x 32 in. (60.8 x 81.3 cm.)
Signed at lower right: MARY BUTLER.
John Lambert Fund, 1925.3

Michael J. Byron (1954–)

224 *Funeral Pyre*, 1983
Oil on plaster on wood
48 x 36 in. (121.9 x 91.4 cm.)
Signed on back: M J Byron
Contemporary Arts Fund, 1984.2

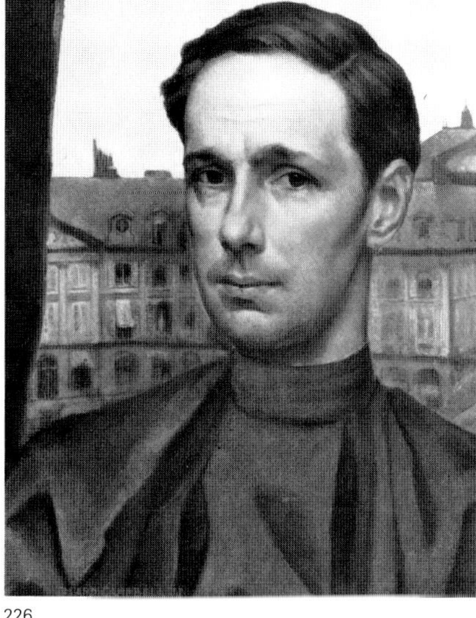

226

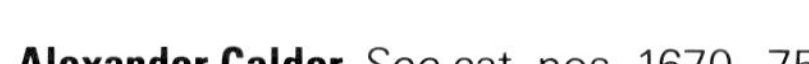

Alexander Calder. *See* cat. nos. 1670–75.

Kenneth Callahan (1906–1986)

225 *The Tides*, 1948–49
Oil on gessoed plywood
23 11/16 x 31 9/16 in. (60.2 x 80.2 cm.)
Signed at lower right: KENNETH/CALLAHAN
John Lambert Fund, 1950.4

Orland Campbell (1890–1972)

226 *Holland Robinson* (ca. 1901–ca. 1960), 1933
Oil on canvas
18 3/16 x 15 1/8 in. (46.2 x 38.4 cm.)
Signed and dated at lower left: ORLAND CAMPBELL '33
Gift of Mrs. Elizabeth de C. Wilson, 1981.10

Gertrude Rowan Capolino (1899–1946)

227 *Parkway*, ca. 1932
Oil on canvas
24 x 30 1/2 in. (61 x 77.5 cm.)
John Lambert Fund, 1933.1

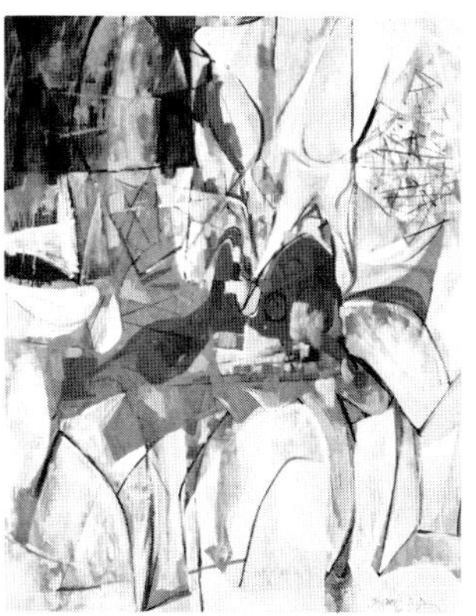

214

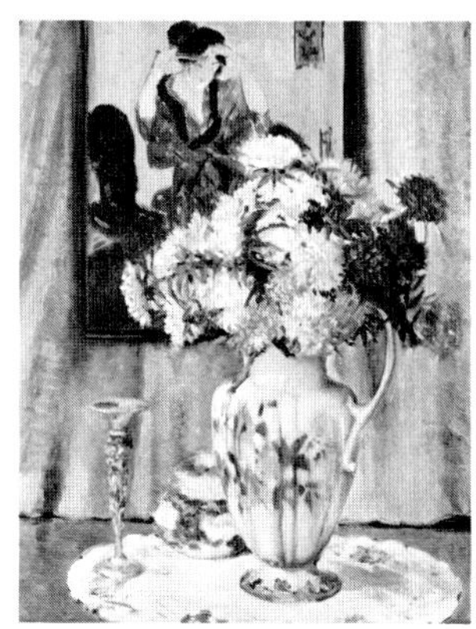

216

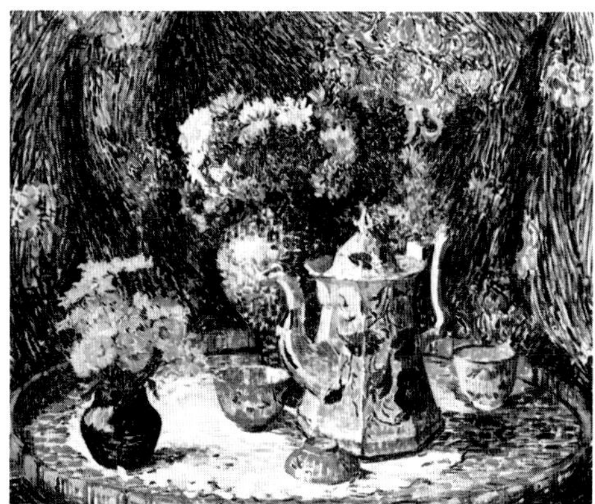

217

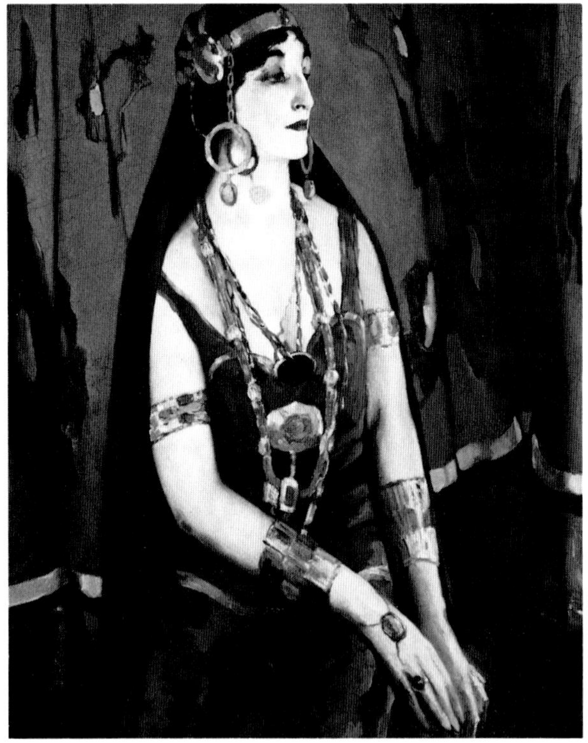

228

238

Arthur B. Carles, Jr. (1882–1952)

228 *An Actress as Cleopatra* (Mercedes de Cordoba, the artist's wife), 1914
Oil on canvas
30$\frac{3}{16}$ x 25$\frac{1}{8}$ in. (76.7 x 63.8 cm.)
Signed at lower right: A. CARLES
John Lambert Fund, 1915.3

229 *Bouquet*, 1932
Oil on canvas
34 x 40$\frac{1}{2}$ in. (86.4 x 102.9 cm.)
Bequest of Mrs. Bernice McIlhenny Wintersteen, 1986.31.3

230 *Composition No. 6*, 1936
Oil on canvas
40$\frac{3}{4}$ x 51$\frac{1}{4}$ in. (103.5 x 130.2 cm.)
Gift of Joseph Wood, Jr., 1957.25

231 *Corner of the Studio*, ca. 1930
Oil on canvas
51$\frac{7}{16}$ x 40$\frac{3}{4}$ in. (130.7 x 103.5 cm.)
Signed on back: carles
Gift of Dr. and Mrs. David Wood, 1978.1

232 *Floral Fragment*, 1914
Oil on canvas
18 x 18 in. (45.7 x 45.7 cm.)
Gift of Dr. David W. Wood, 1983.22

233 *Flowers in Glass Jar*, ca. 1930
Oil on canvas
22$\frac{1}{8}$ x 18$\frac{1}{8}$ in. (56.2 x 46 cm.)
Signed at lower right: CARLES
Gift of Mrs. Thomas E. Drake (The Margaretta S. Hinchman Collection), 1956.5.2

234 *The Philadelphia Orchestra*, ca. 1925
Oil on canvas
26$\frac{1}{16}$ x 31$\frac{3}{16}$ in. (66.2 x 79.2 cm.)
Gift of Thomas A. Greene, 1953.10

235 *Study for "Helen Taylor,"* ca. 1931
Oil on canvas
50$\frac{1}{4}$ x 38 in. (127.6 x 96.5 cm.)
Gift of Dr. and Mrs. Norman H. Taylor, 1960.14.2
See also cat. no. 236.

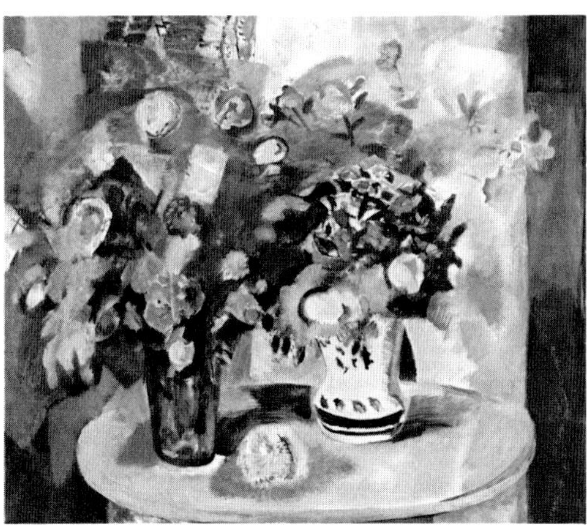

229

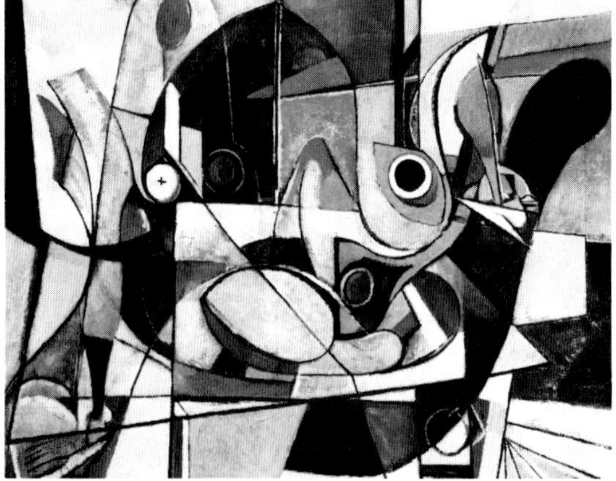

230

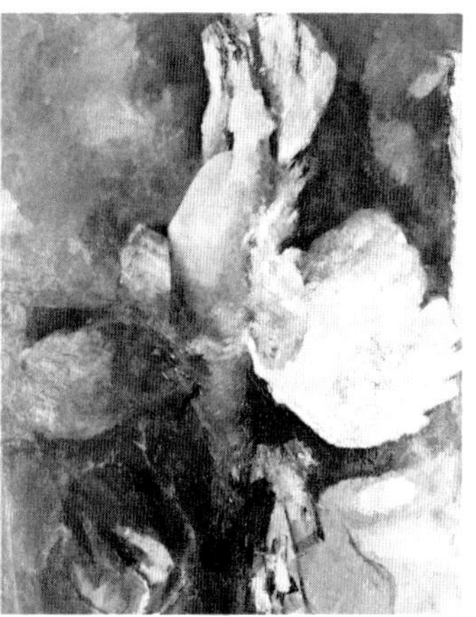

237

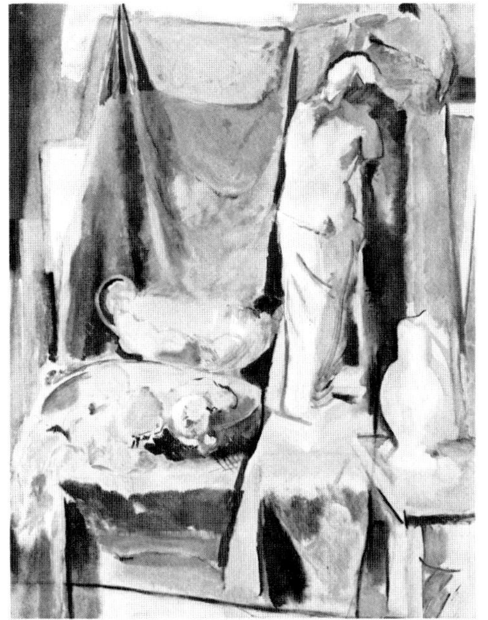
231

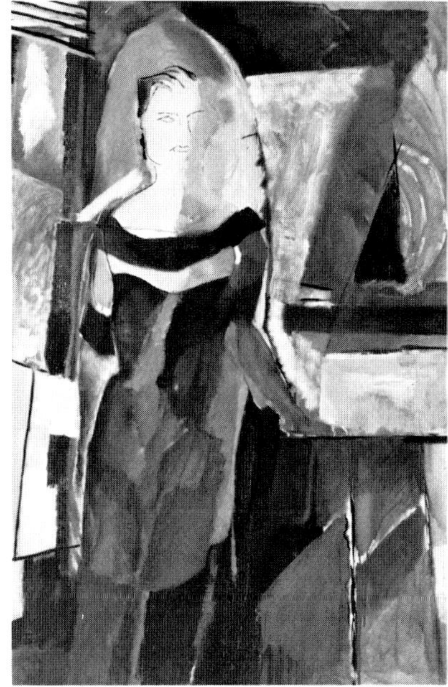
236

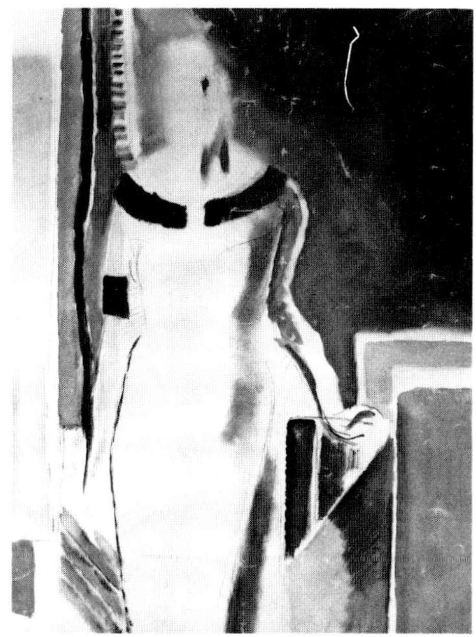
235

236 *Helen Taylor* (Mrs. Norman H. Taylor), 1931
Oil on canvas
65¼ x 43¼ in. (165.7 x 109.9 cm.)
Gift of Dr. and Mrs. Norman H. Taylor, 1960.14.1
See also cat. no. 235.

237 *The Turkey*, 1927
Oil on canvas
57½ x 45 in. (146.1 x 114.3 cm.)
Inscribed on stretcher: carles-14 N East
Gift of the Board of Directors, 1960.15

238 *White Callas*, 1925–27
Oil on canvas
50¾ x 37¾ in. (128.9 x 95.9 cm.)
Signed at lower right: CARLES
Gift of Harry G. Sundheim, Jr., 1958.25.1

Sara Carles (1894–1965)

239 *In White*, ca. 1923
Oil on canvas
30¹⁄₁₆ x 25¹⁄₁₆ in. (76.4 x 63.7 cm.)
John Lambert Fund, 1924.1

Emil Carlsen (1853–1932)

240 *Summer Clouds*, ca. 1912
Oil on canvas
39⅛ x 44¹⁵⁄₁₆ in. (99.4 x 114.1 cm.)
Signed at lower right: Emil Carlsen.
Joseph E. Temple Fund, 1913.5

Fred Green Carpenter (b. 1882)

241 *Rose Color, Scarlet, and Black*, 1912
Oil on canvas
29 x 24 in. (73.7 x 61 cm.)
Signed and dated at lower left: F.G. CARPENTER. 1912
John Lambert Fund, 1914.4

Donald Carrick (1929–)

242 *Santorini Churches*, 1956
Oil on canvas
37⅜ x 39¼ in. (94.9 x 99.7 cm.)
Signed and dated at lower right: CARRICK-56-
Annotated on stretcher: SANTORINI CHURCHES/ CARRICK
John Lambert Fund, 1958.6

John Carroll (1892–1959)

243 *Agatha*, ca. 1923
Oil on canvas
33¹⁵⁄₁₆ x 36¹⁄₁₆ in. (86.2 x 91.6 cm.)
Signed at lower right: John Carroll
Annotated on stretcher: Agata [*sic*]
John Lambert Fund, 1924.2

244 *The Christening*, 1935
Oil on canvas
24⅛ x 18⅛ in. (61.3 x 46 cm.)
Signed and dated at lower left: John Carroll 35
Annotated on stretcher: The Christening
Gift of Mrs. Herbert Cameron Morris, 1968.20

Norman Carton (1908–1980)

245 *Three Gifts*, 1948
Oil on canvas
32¹⁄₁₆ x 24 in. (81.4 x 61 cm.)
Signed and dated at lower left: CARTON/48; inscribed and signed on back: TITLE. THREE GIFTS/ ARTIST: NORMAN CARTON/721 SANSOM ST./PHILA. 6, PA.
John Lambert Fund, 1949.4

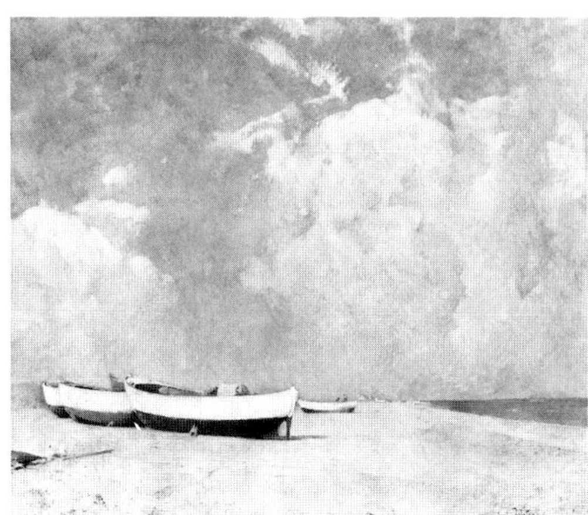
240

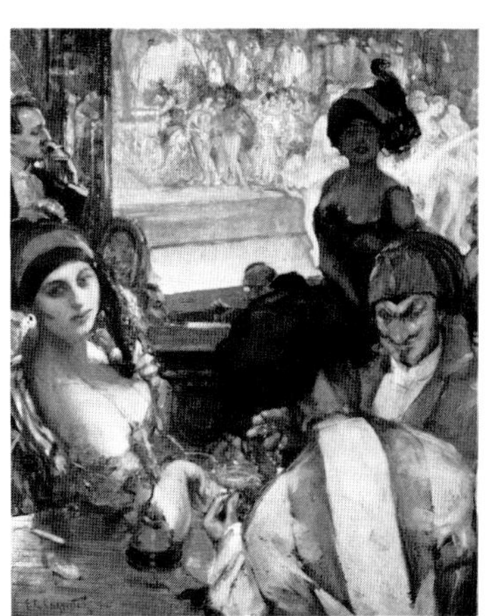
241

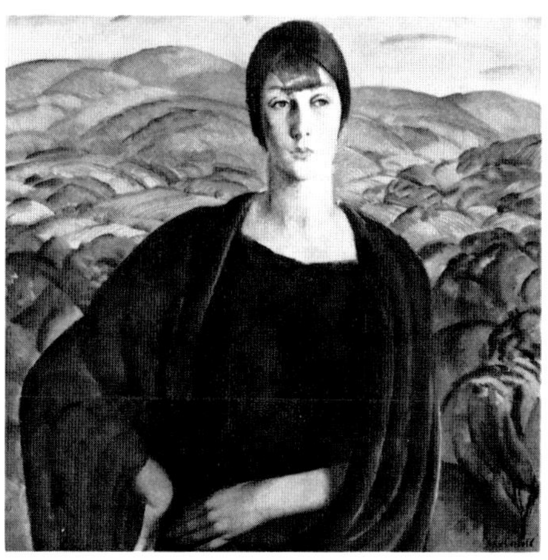
243

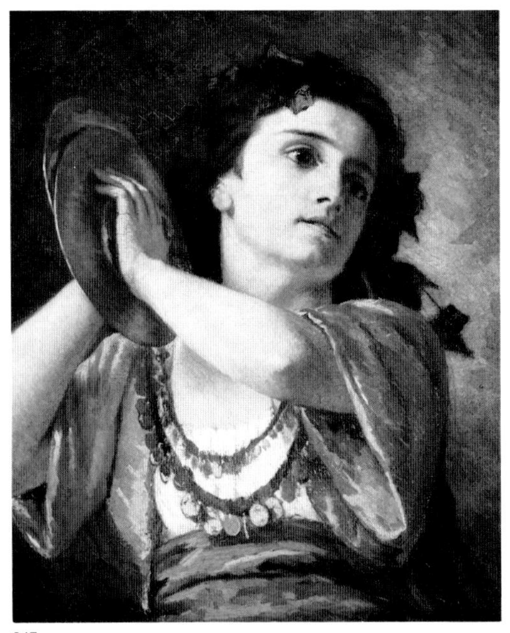

247

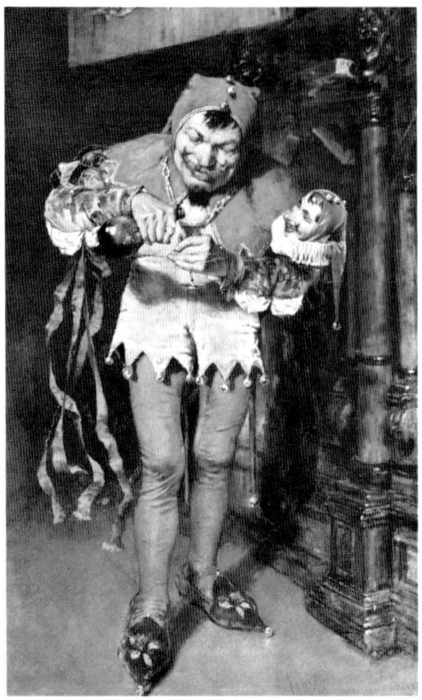

257

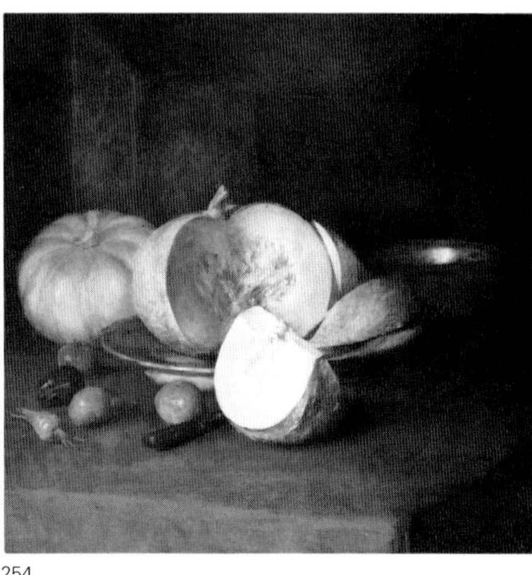

254

Solomon Nunes Carvalho (1815–1897)

246 *John C. Frémont* (1813–1890), ca. 1856
(formerly attributed to unidentified artist)
Oil on canvas
30⅛ x 25 in. (76.5 x 63.5 cm.)
Incorrectly inscribed at lower left: Thos Sully-Pinxt
Gift of Mrs. John Frederick Lewis (The John Frederick Lewis Memorial Collection), 1933.10.85

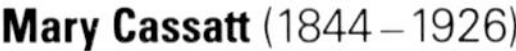

Mary Cassatt (1844–1926)

247 *Bacchante*, 1872
Oil on canvas
24 x 19¹⁵⁄₁₆ in. (61 x 50.6 cm.)
Signed, inscribed, and dated at lower left: Mary/Stevenson Cassatt/Parma 1872
Gift of John Frederick Lewis, 1932.13.1

Federico Castellon (1914–1971)

248 *Fallen Angels in a Hostile World*, ca. 1942
Oil on canvas
15¹⁄₁₆ x 18³⁄₁₆ in. (38.3 x 46.2 cm.)
Signed at lower left: CASTELLON
John Lambert Fund, 1943.6

George Catlin (1796–1872)

249 *James Madison* (1751–1836), ca. 1830
Oil on wood
33¹⁄₁₆ x 25⁹⁄₁₆ in. (84 x 64.9 cm.)
Gift of Mrs. John Frederick Lewis (The John Frederick Lewis Memorial Collection), 1933.10.3

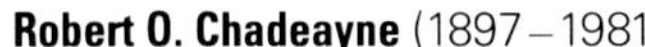

Robert O. Chadeayne (1897–1981)

250 *Backyards*, ca. 1919
Oil on canvas
24¹⁄₁₆ x 30⅛ in. (61.1 x 76.5 cm.)
Signed at lower right: R O CHADEAYNE
John Lambert Fund, 1920.4

Christine Chambers (active 1924–1933)

251 *Flower Study*, ca. 1933
Oil on canvas
20 x 16¹⁄₁₆ in. (50.8 x 40.8 cm.)
John Lambert Fund, 1934.3

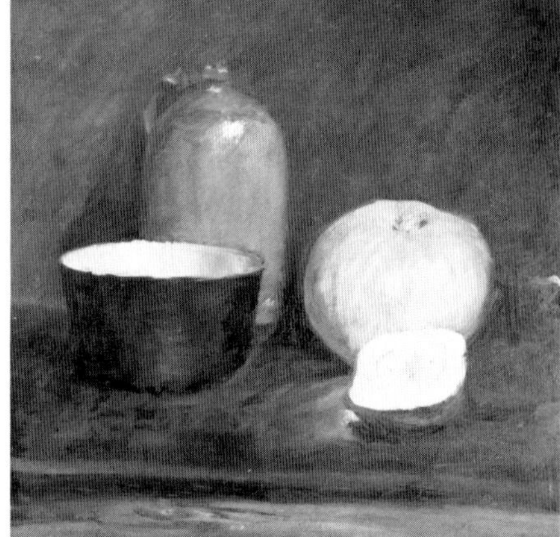

261

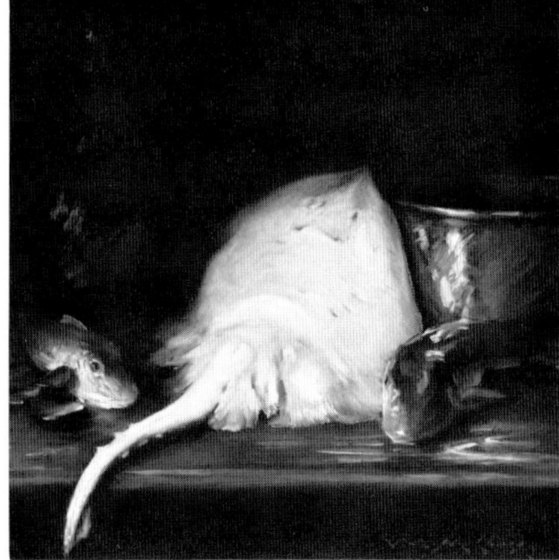

262

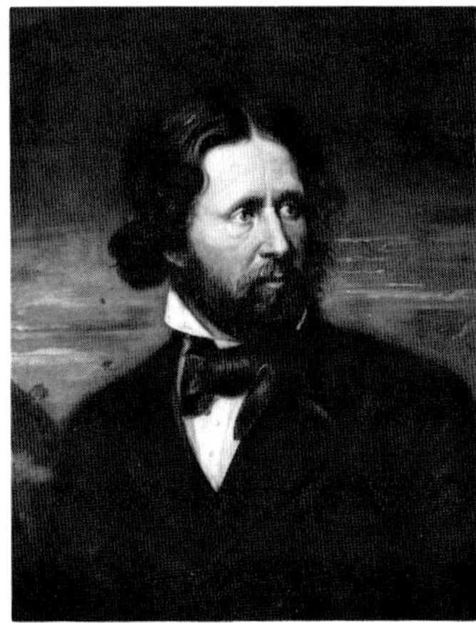

246

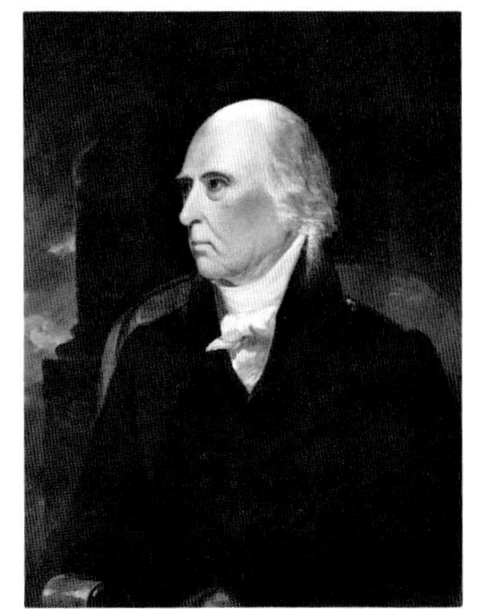

249

Mrs. Francis Taylor Chambers
See Jean Knox.

Francis Chapin (1899–1965)

252 *Gray River*, ca. 1938
Oil on canvas
34³⁄₁₆ x 44¼ in. (86.8 x 112.4 cm.)
Signed at lower right: F. Chapin
John Lambert Fund, 1939.3

James Ormsbee Chapin (1877–1975)

253 *George Marvin and His Daughter Edith*, 1926
Oil on canvas
38¼ x 44 in. (97.2 x 111.8 cm.)
Signed and dated at lower left: JAMES CHAPIN '26
Joseph E. Temple Fund, 1940.9

William Merritt Chase (1849–1916)

254 *Autumn Still Life*
Oil on canvas
40¼ x 40⅜ in. (102.2 x 102.6 cm.)
Signed at right center: Wm M Chase.
Gift of Joseph Nash Field in memory of his wife, Frances Field, 1955.5

255 *Female Figure Study (front view)*
Oil on canvas
46¹⁄₁₆ x 23⅞ in. (117 x 60.6 cm.)
Inscribed and signed on back: 3. Hour. Sketch/ By/Wm. M. Chase
Source unknown (probably a gift of the artist), 1909.13.1

256 *Female Figure Study (side view)*
Oil on canvas
40 x 22 in. (101.6 x 55.9 cm.)
Inscribed and signed on back: 3. Hour. Sketch./ By/Wm. M. Chase
Source unknown (probably a gift of the artist), 1909.13.2

257 *"Keying Up"–The Court Jester*, 1875
Oil on canvas
39¾ x 25 in. (101 x 63.5 cm.)
Signed, inscribed, and dated at lower right: Will. M. Chase/Will. M. Chase. Munich. 1875.
Gift of the Chapellier Galleries, 1969.37

258 *August B. Loeb* (1841–1915), 1905
Oil on canvas
36 x 29 in. (91.4 x 73.7 cm.)
Signed at lower left: Wm. M. Chase.; inscribed, signed, and dated on back (before lining): August B. Loeb Esq./ Painted by Wm. M. Chase./Philadelphia April 20 to 30/1905
Gift of Mrs. Bella Loeb Selig, 1954.9

259 *Portrait of Mrs. C. (Lady with a White Shawl)*, 1893
Oil on canvas
75 x 52 in. (190.5 x 132.1 cm.)
Signed at lower left: Wm. M. Chase.
Joseph E. Temple Fund, 1895.1

260 *Mrs. Charles Scott*
Oil on canvas
50¹⁄₁₆ x 36 in. (127.1 x 91.4 cm.)
Signed at lower right: Wm. M. Chase
Gift of the Misses Scott, 1935.1

261 *Still Life*
Oil on canvas
36 x 36 in. (91.4 x 91.4 cm.)
Inscribed and signed on back: 3. Hour. Sketch/ By/W. M. Chase
Source unknown (probably a gift of the artist), 1909.13.3

262 *Still Life, Fish*, ca. 1903
Oil on canvas
28 x 32 in. (71.1 x 81.3 cm.)
Signed at lower right: Wm. M. Chase.
Joseph E. Temple Fund, 1904.1

See also palette, cat. no. 1622.

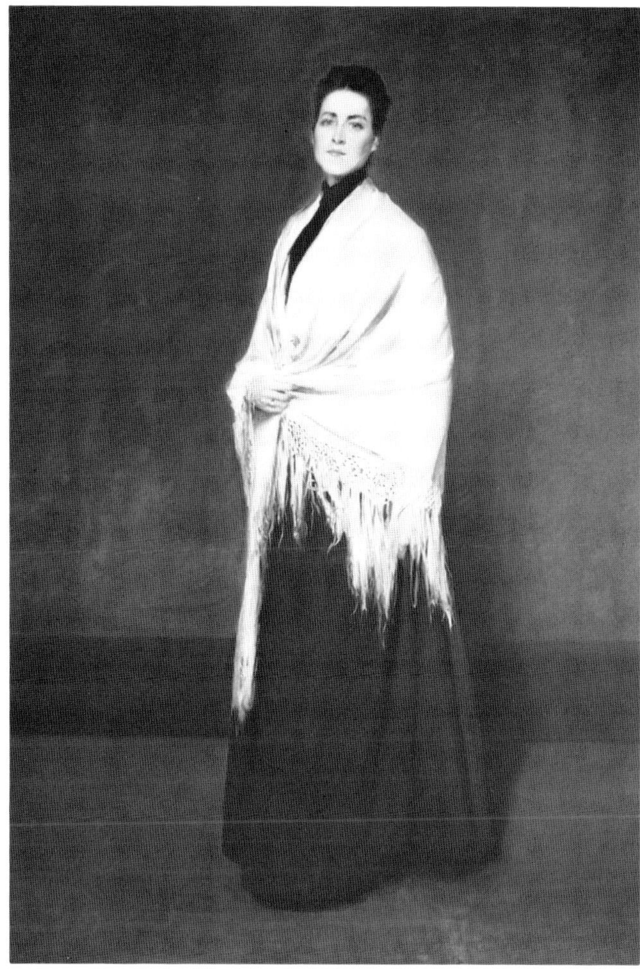

259

Judy Chicago. *See* cat. no. 1676.

Margaret Chrystie (1895–1960)

263 *Avian Tragedy*, ca. 1940
Oil on canvas
18¹⁵⁄₁₆ x 24 in. (48.1 x 61 cm.)
John Lambert Fund, 1941.3

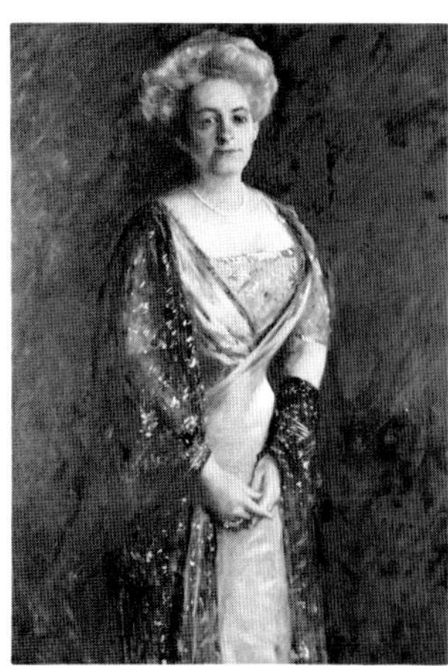

260

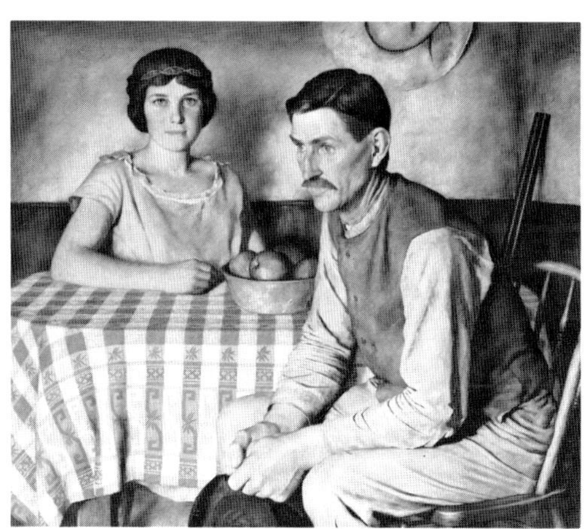

253

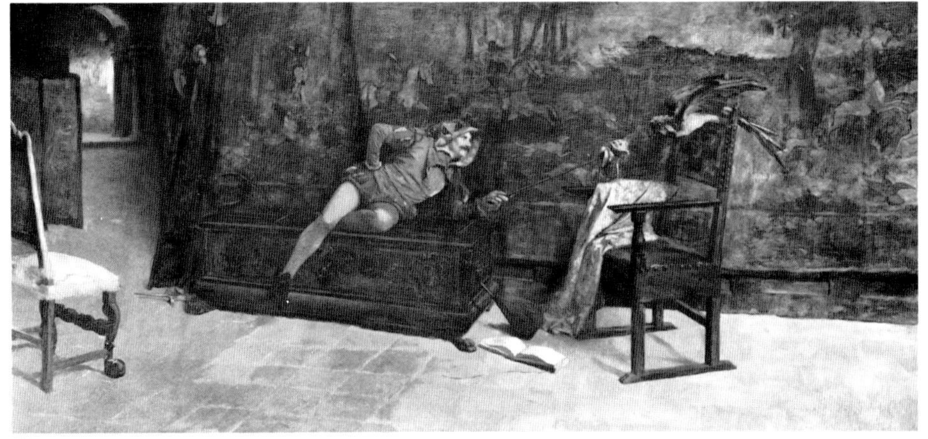
265

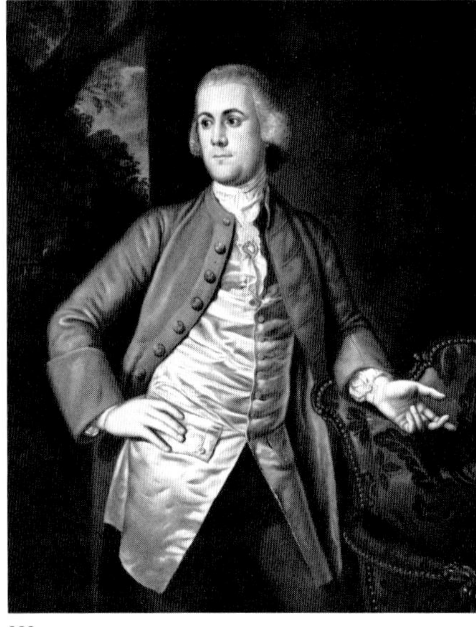
267

266

Nicolai S. Cikovsky (1894–1984)

264 *The Harbor*, ca. 1932
Oil on canvas
20 x 28 in. (50.8 x 71.1 cm.)
Signed at lower right: N. Cikovsky.
John Lambert Fund, 1933.2

Thomas Shields Clarke (1860–1920)

265 *Fool's Fool*, 1887
Oil on canvas
39½ x 83 in. (100.3 x 210.8 cm.)
Signed, inscribed, and dated at lower right: Thos. Shields Clarke/Florence, Feb/'87
Gift of Charles J. Clarke, 1888.1

James Claypoole, Jr. (ca. 1743–before 1815)

266 *Joseph Pemberton* (1745–1782), ca. 1767
Oil on canvas
50½ x 41 in. (128.3 x 104.1 cm.)
Gift of Henry R. Pemberton, 1967.15

267 *Mrs. Joseph Pemberton* (née Ann Galloway, 1750–1798), ca. 1767
Oil on canvas
50½ x 40½ in. (128.3 x 102.9 cm.)
Gift of Henry R. Pemberton, 1968.6

James G. Clonney (1812–1867)

268 *Militia Training*, 1841
Oil on canvas
28 x 40 in. (71.1 x 101.6 cm.)
Signed and dated at lower right: James G. Clonney/1841.
Bequest of Henry C. Carey (The Carey Collection), 1879.8.1

Charles Cohill (ca. 1812–after 1860)

269 *General George Cadwalader* (1804–1879), 1847
Oil on canvas
35⅞ x 29 in. (91.1 x 73.7 cm.)
Signed and dated at lower left: C. COHILL 1847
Gift of Mrs. John Frederick Lewis (The John Frederick Lewis Memorial Collection), 1933.10.6

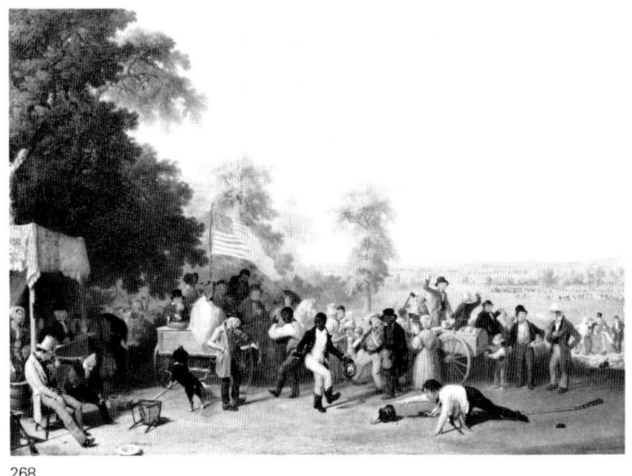
268

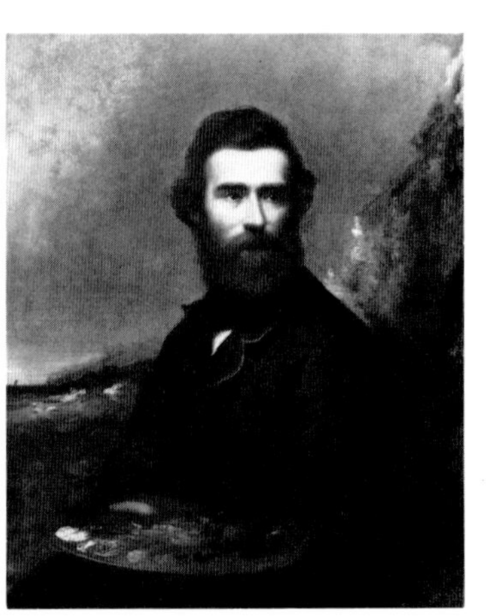
274

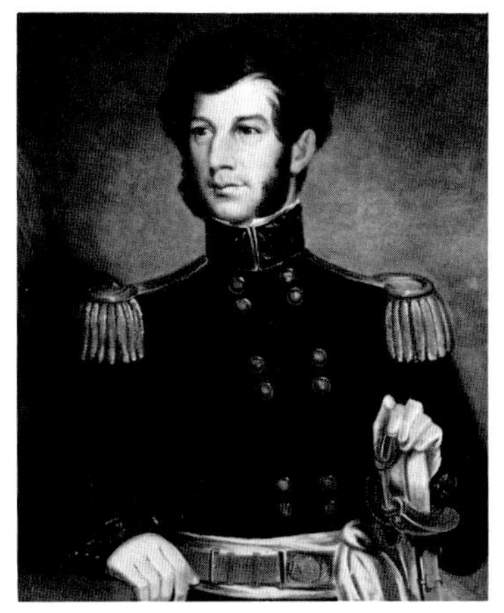
269

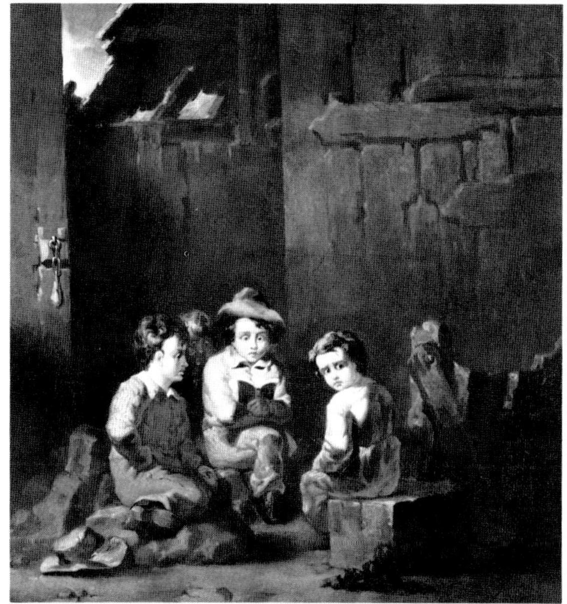

272

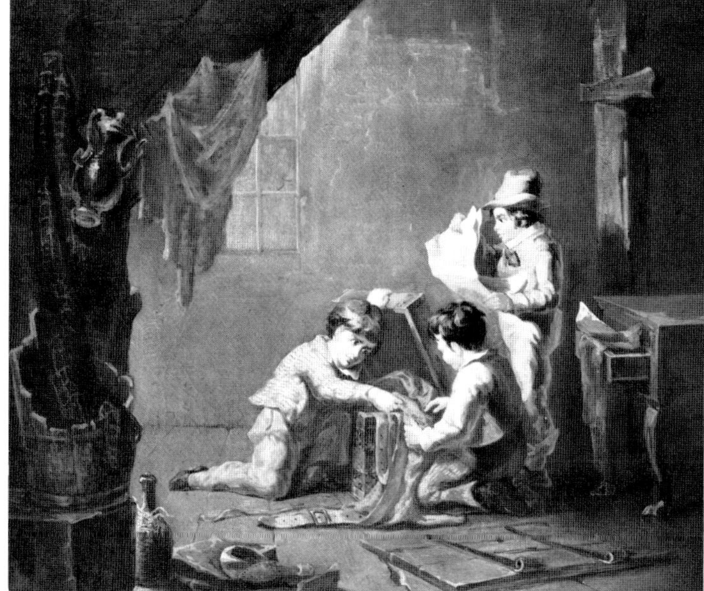

273

Charles T. Coiner (1898–)

270 *The Branch*, 1948
Oil on canvas
19⅞ x 28⅛ in. (50.5 x 71.4 cm.)
Signed and dated at lower right: C. Coiner 48
John Lambert Fund, 1951.3

271 *From the Brake*, ca. 1931
Oil on canvas
35 x 44$\frac{1}{16}$ in. (88.9 x 111.9 cm.)
Signed at lower left: C. Coiner
John Lambert Fund, 1932.4

Constance Coleman
See Constance Coleman Richardson.

Mrs. Stewart Colin
See Alice Turner Mumford.

George H. Comegys (active 1836–1845)

272 *The Ghost Story*, by 1840
Oil on canvas
17$\frac{9}{16}$ x 16$\frac{13}{16}$ in. (44.6 x 42.7 cm.)
Bequest of Henry C. Carey (The Carey Collection), 1879.8.2

273 *The Little Plunderers*, ca. 1845
Oil on canvas
17⅛ x 20¼ in. (43.5 x 51.4 cm.)
Bequest of Henry C. Carey (The Carey Collection), 1879.8.3

George W. Conarroe (1803–1882)

274 *James Hamilton* (1819–1878), 1866
Oil on canvas
36 x 29 in. (91.4 x 73.7 cm.)
Signed and dated at lower right: [Conar]roe/[illegible] 1866
Gift of John Frederick Lewis, 1928.8.2

John Ramsey Conner (1869–1952)

275 *The Fisherman*, ca. 1913
Oil on canvas
36$\frac{1}{16}$ x 26$\frac{15}{16}$ in. (91.6 x 68.4 cm.)
Signed at lower right: J. R. CONNER
John Lambert Fund, 1914.5

George Constant (1892–1978)

276 *Sea, Sun, and Sky*, 1955
Oil on canvas
53 x 72⅝ in. (134.6 x 184.5 cm.)
Signed at lower right: G CONSTANT
Gift of the Shilling Fund, 1956.15

Colin Campbell Cooper (1856–1937)

277 *Lower Broadway in Wartime*, 1917
Oil on canvas
57½ x 35¼ in. (146.1 x 89.5 cm.)
Signed and dated at lower left: Colin Campbell Cooper 1917
Joseph E. Temple Fund, 1918.2

Henry Cooper (b. 1905)

278 *The Rolling Chair*, ca. 1933
Oil on canvas
16$\frac{1}{16}$ x 20$\frac{1}{16}$ in. (40.8 x 51 cm.)
Signed at lower right: h. cooper
John Lambert Fund, 1934.4

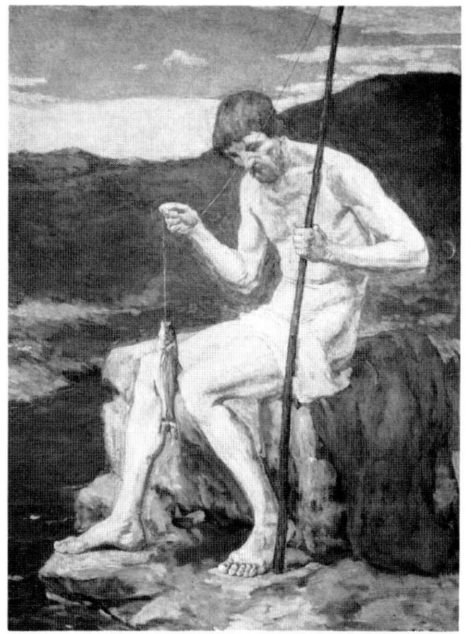

275

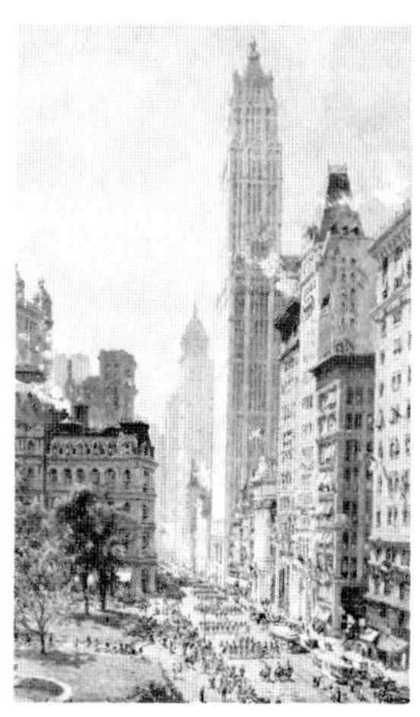

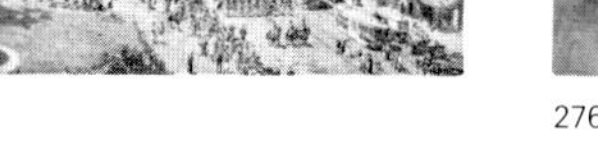

277

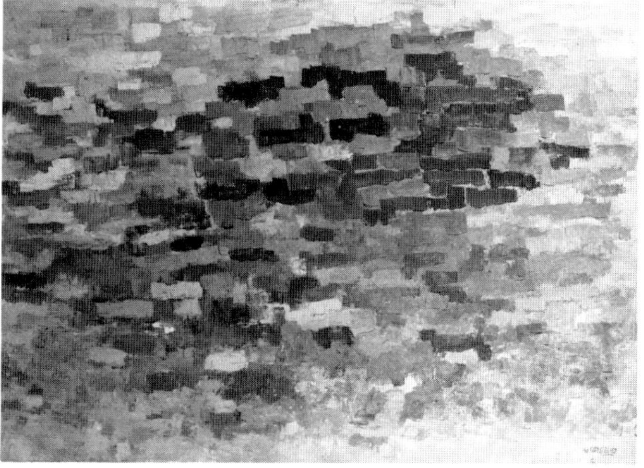

276

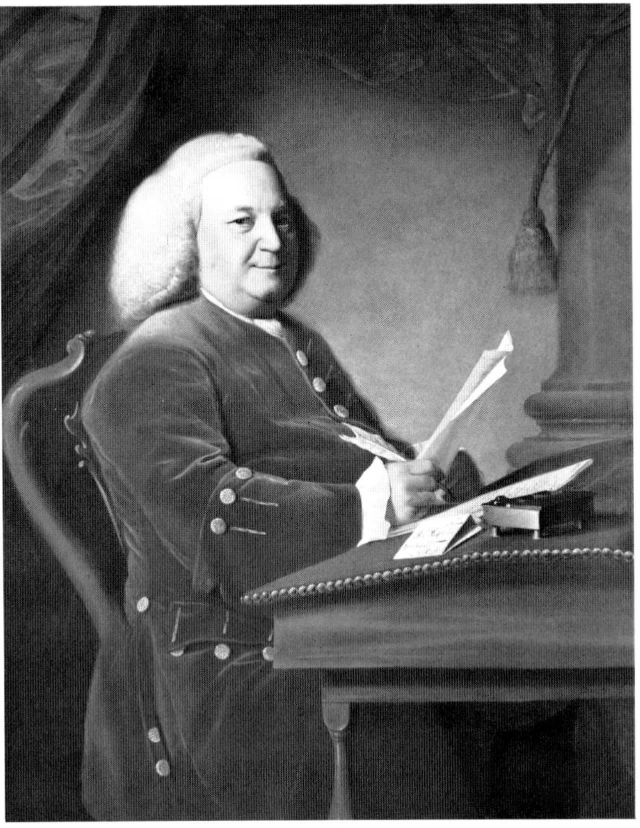
279

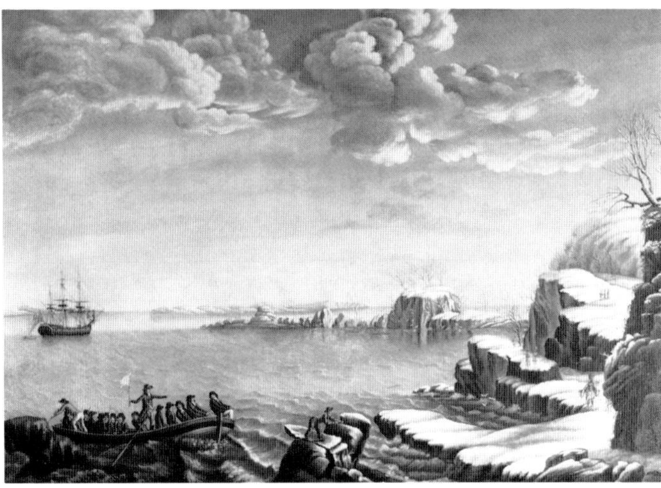
281

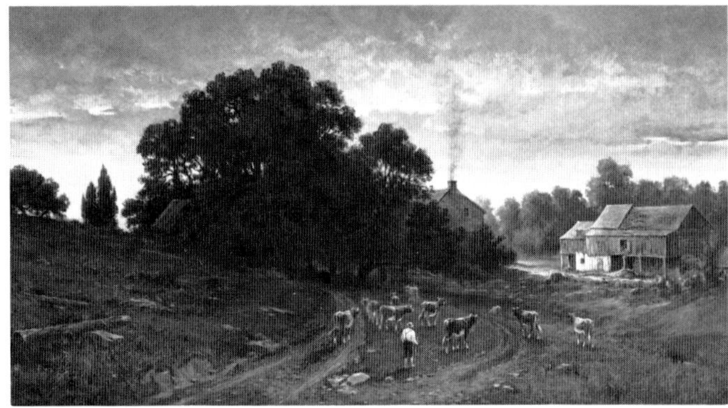
285

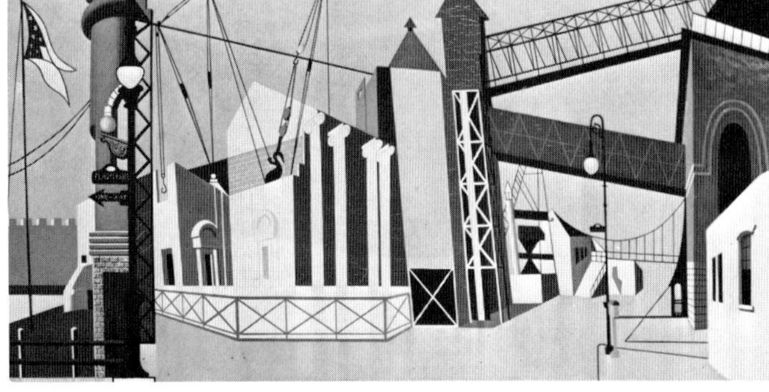
292

John Singleton Copley (1738–1815)

279 *Robert "King" Hooper* (1709–1790), 1767
Oil on canvas
50 x 39¾ in. (127 x 101 cm.)
Signed, dated, and inscribed at lower right: JSC [monogram] p. 1767. Bos.n; inscribed on folded letter: To-/Robt Hooper Esq/in-/ Marblehead/New England
The Henry S. McNeil Collection. Given in loving memory of her husband by Lois F. McNeil and in honor of their parents by Barbara and Henry A. Jordan, Marjorie M. Findlay, and Robert D. McNeil, 1984.13

Jon Corbino (1905–1964)

280 *Bathers' Picnic*, 1936
Oil on canvas
36 x 41 15/16 in. (91.4 x 106.5 cm.)
Signed at lower right: Jon Corbino
Annotated on stretcher: Bathers Picnic
Henry D. Gilpin Fund, 1938.3

Michele Felice Cornè (1752–1845)

281 *The Landing of the Pilgrims*, ca. 1807
Oil on canvas
36 9/16 x 52⅛ in. (92.9 x 132.4 cm.)
Gift of Mrs. Henry S. McNeil in loving memory of her husband, Henry S. McNeil, 1985.46

Russell Cowles (1887–1979)

282 *The Prodigal Son*, 1948
Oil on canvas
66 1/16 x 62⅞ in. (167.8 x 159.7 cm.)
Signed at lower right: Cowles
Joseph E. Temple Fund, 1951.4

Elizabeth Kitchenman Coyne (1892–1971)

283 *Landscape, Nantucket*, 1936
Oil on canvas
30 x 36 1/16 in. (76.2 x 91.6 cm.)
Signed at lower right: Coyne
John Lambert Fund, by exchange, 1936.3

Robert C. Craig

284 *An Autumn Morning in Fairmount Park*, 1870
Oil on canvas
13 1/16 x 22⅛ in. (33.2 x 56.2 cm.)
Inscribed, signed, and dated on back: "An Autumn Morning in Fairmount Park"/To Lotta/ by Robert Craig/Philadelphia 1870
Gift of Alfred G. B. Steel, 1933.11

Thomas Bigelow Craig (1849–1924)

285 *Evening*, 1886–87
Oil on canvas
33⅜ x 68¼ in. (84.8 x 173.3 cm.)
Signed and dated at lower right: Thos. B. Craig. 1887; inscribed, signed, and dated on back: Evening/Painted by Thos. B. Craig. 1886–87
Gift of the artist, 1887.3

William Emlen Cresson (1843–1868)

286 *The Enchanted Princess*, 1866
Oil on canvas
14 x 12⅛ in. (35.6 x 30.8 cm.)
Signed and dated at lower left: CRESSON/1866
Bequest of Priscilla P. Cresson, 1902.1.2

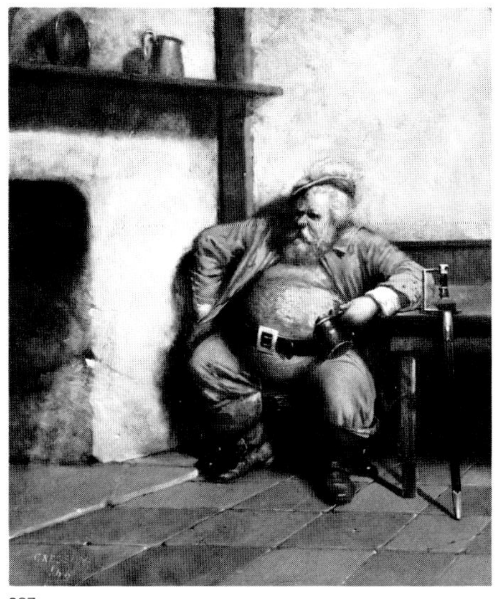
287

287 *Falstaff*, 1866
Oil on canvas
14 1/8 x 12 1/4 in. (35.9 x 31.1 cm.)
Signed and dated at lower left: CRESSON./66
Bequest of Priscilla P. Cresson, 1902.1.3

288 *Indian Character*, ca. 1865
Oil on canvas
9 7/16 x 7 1/16 in. (24 x 17.9 cm.)
Signed at lower right: W. E. CRESSON
Gift of Mrs. Joseph Bancroft, 1939.20

289 *A Monk*, 1865
Oil on canvas

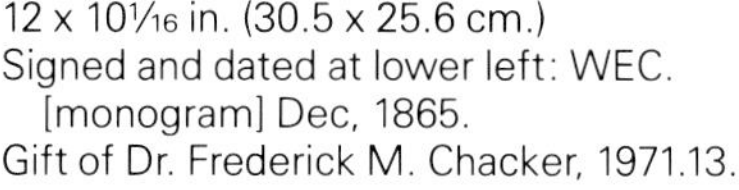
12 x 10 1/16 in. (30.5 x 25.6 cm.)
Signed and dated at lower left: WEC.
[monogram] Dec, 1865.
Gift of Dr. Frederick M. Chacker, 1971.13.3

290 *An Old Woman*, 1867
Oil on canvas
11 15/16 x 10 in. (30.3 x 25.4 cm.)
Signed and dated at lower left: Cresson 1867
Gift of Dr. Frederick M. Chacker, 1971.13.2

291 *Unidentified Man*, 1865
Oil on canvas
9 15/16 x 10 in. (25.3 x 25.4 cm.)
Signed and dated at lower right: Cresson/1865
Source unknown, 1944.18

H. Francis Criss (1901 – 1973)

292 *Rhapsody in Steel*, 1939
Oil on canvas
21 15/16 x 42 in. (55.7 x 106.7 cm.)
Signed and dated at right center: CRISS-39
Gift of friends of the artist, 1952.19

Jasper F. Cropsey (1823 – 1900)

293 *Landscape with Figures near Rome*, 1847
Oil on canvas
27 5/16 x 40 3/16 in. (69.4 x 102.1 cm.)
Signed, inscribed, and dated at lower left:
J. F. CROPSEY/Roma/1847
Gift of John Frederick Lewis, Jr., 1954.22.1

294 *Mount Washington from Lake Sebago, Maine*, 1867
Oil on canvas
10 1/16 x 18 1/8 in. (25.6 x 46 cm.)
Signed and dated at lower right: J. F. Cropsey
1867
Gift of Mr. and Mrs. Edward Kesler, 1975.20.5

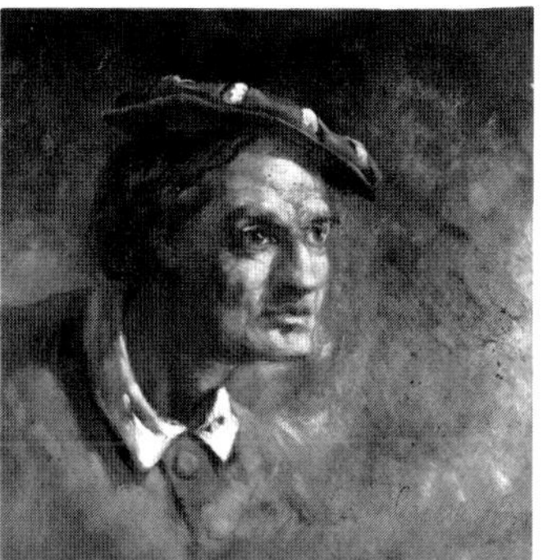
291

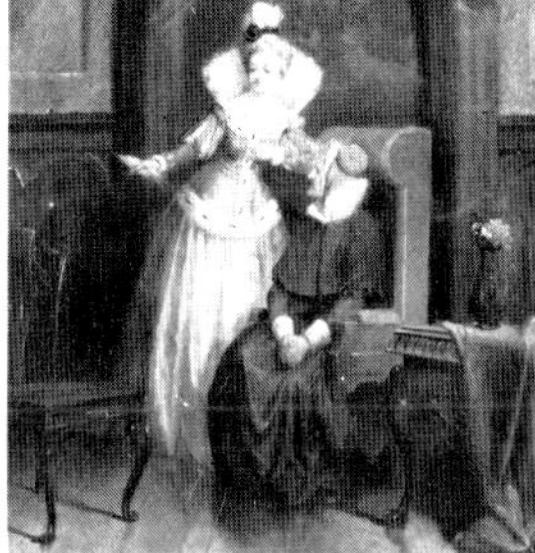
286

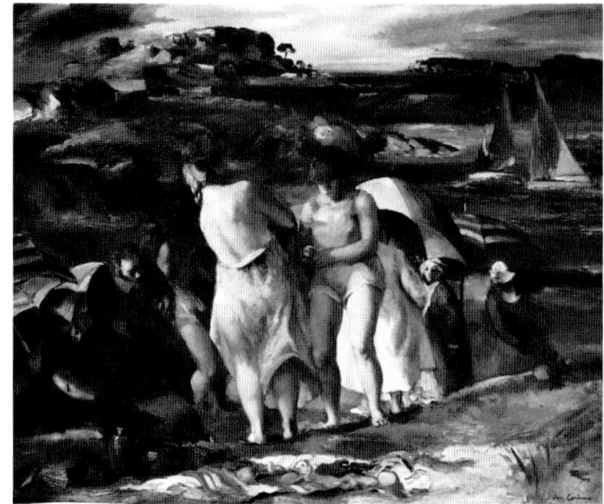
280

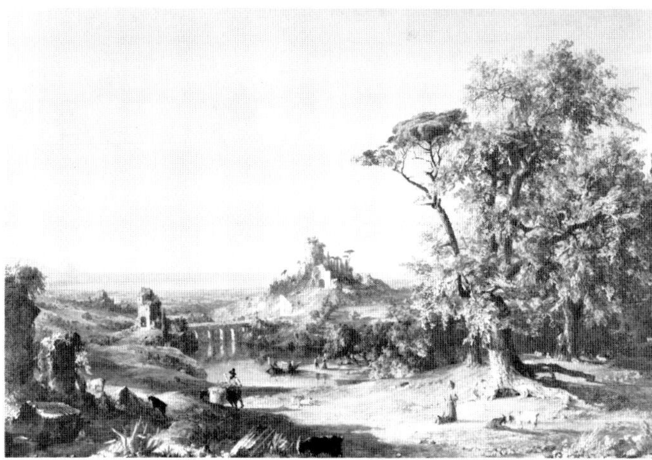
293

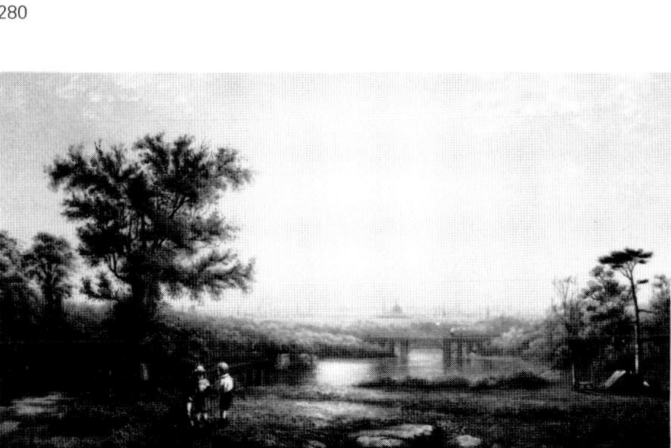
284

294

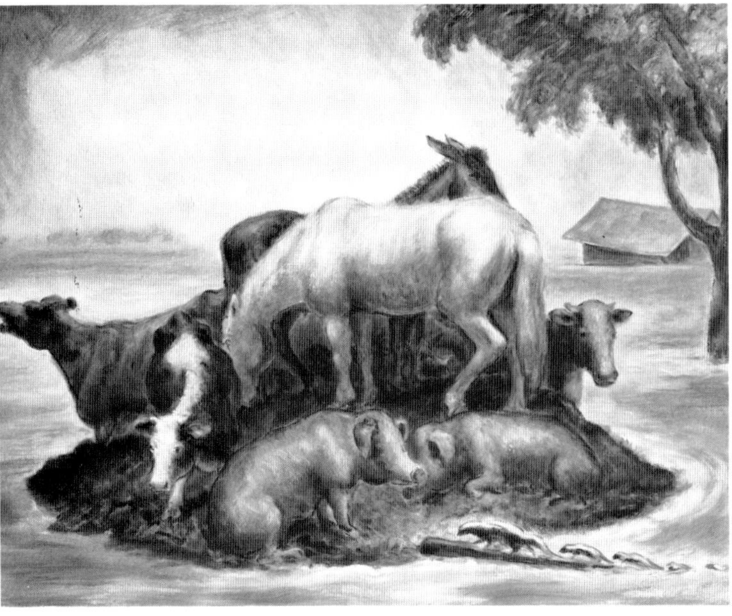

297

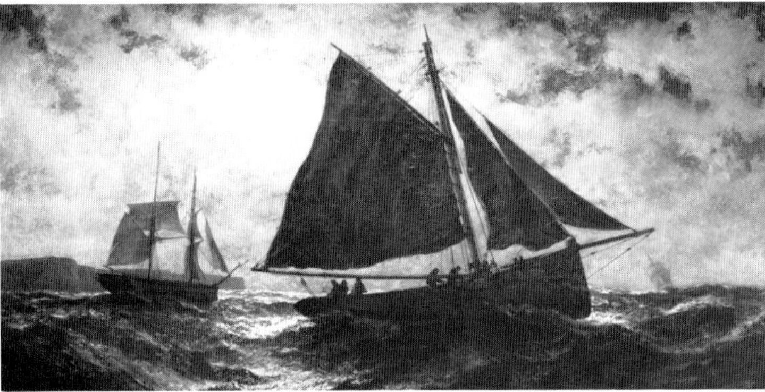

299

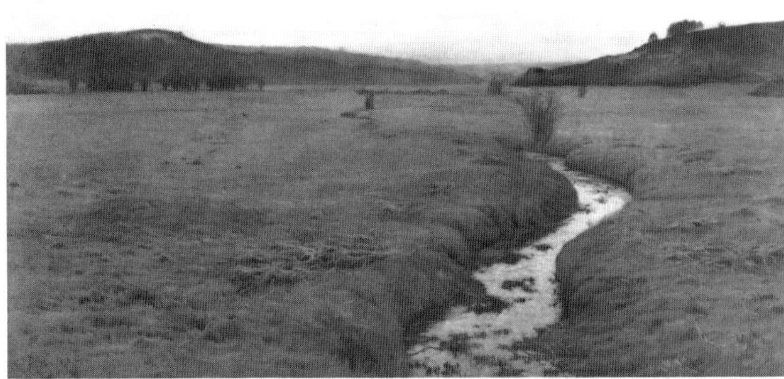

307

Lucius Crowell (1911 – 1988)

295 *Fisherman at San Felice, Circeo*, 1957
Oil on canvas
16 x 19 15/16 in. (40.6 x 50.6 cm.)
Signed at lower right: L. CROWELL
John Lambert Fund, 1958.8

Charles C. Curran (1861 – 1942)

296 *A Breezy Day*, 1887
Oil on canvas
11 15/16 x 20 in. (30.3 x 50.8 cm.)
Signed and dated at lower right: CHAS. C. CURRAN. 1887.
Henry D. Gilpin Fund, 1899.1

John Steuart Curry (1897 – 1946)

297 *Sanctuary*, 1935
Oil on canvas, mounted on masonite
24 1/8 x 30 7/16 in. (61.3 x 77.3 cm.)
Signed and dated at lower left: JOHN STEUART CURRY/1935
Collections Fund, 1954.1

Stefano Cusumano (1912 – 1975)

298 *Tulips in Stone Vase*, 1947
Oil on canvas
34 x 28 in. (86.4 x 71.1 cm.)
Signed and dated at upper right: S.Cusumano/ 1947
Inscribed, dated, and signed on stretcher: "TULIPS IN STONE VASE" 1947/S. Cusumano
Gift of Dr. and Mrs. Matthew T. Moore, 1969.18.1

William P. W. Dana (1833 – 1927)

299 *Off the French Coast, Moonlight*, by 1881
Oil on canvas
42 1/8 x 84 3/8 in. (107 x 214.3 cm.)
Gift of Atherton Blight, 1882.3

George Daniell (1911 –)

300 *Oregon Rocks*, 1946
Oil on canvas
26 1/16 x 36 in. (66.2 x 91.4 cm.)
Signed at lower right: DANIELL
John Lambert Fund, 1947.1

Fred Danziger (1946 –)

301 *Endgame*, ca. 1972
Acrylic on canvas
51 1/4 x 48 1/2 in. (130.2 x 123.2 cm.)
Signed at lower left: DANZIGER
Gift of Mr. and Mrs. Sydney Dorr, 1974.14

Jane Cooper Sully Darley (1807 – 1877)

302 *Detail of "Madonna della Sedia,"* 1826 (after Thomas Sully, after Raphael)
Oil on canvas
19 1/8 x 15 1/8 in. (48.6 x 38.4 cm.)
Signed, inscribed, and dated at lower right: Jane Sully after TS 1826
Bequest of Harriet P. Smith, 1905.11.2

303 *Fancy Head*, 1840
Oil on canvas
20 x 17 1/4 in. (50.8 x 43.8 cm.)
Signed and dated on back (before lining): Jane C Darley/Pinxt/1840
Gift of the artist, 1877.2

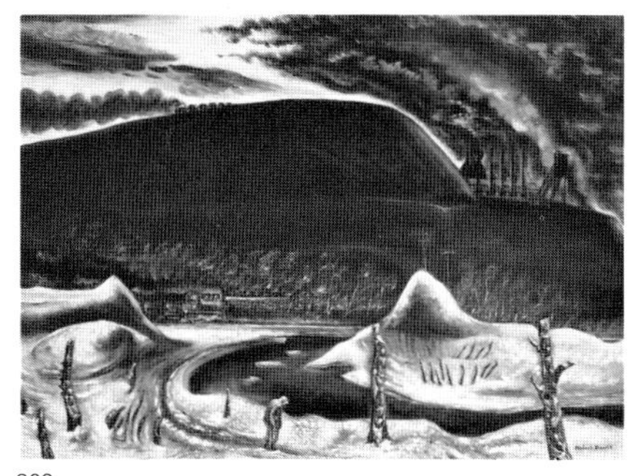
309

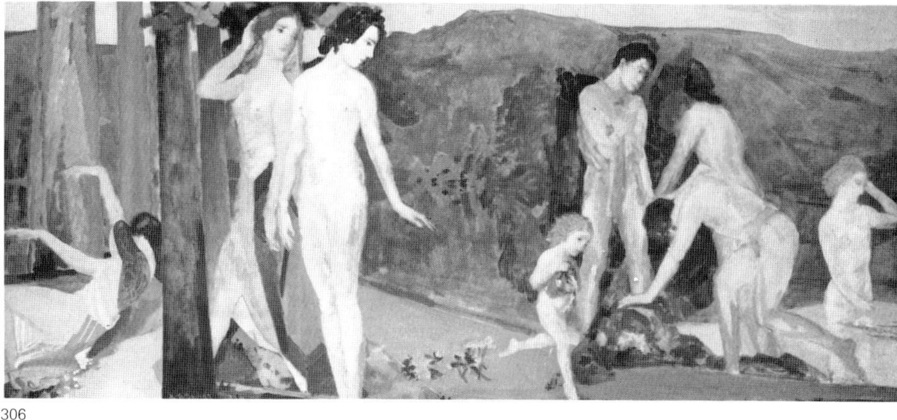
306

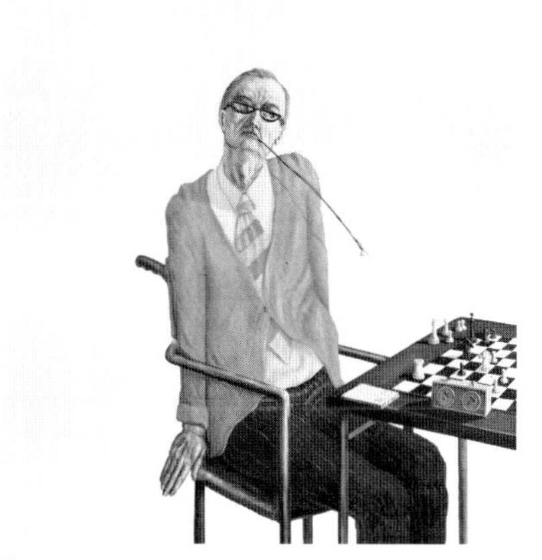
301

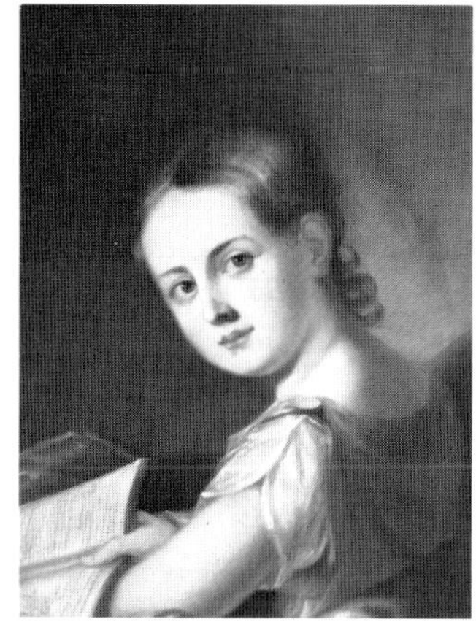
304

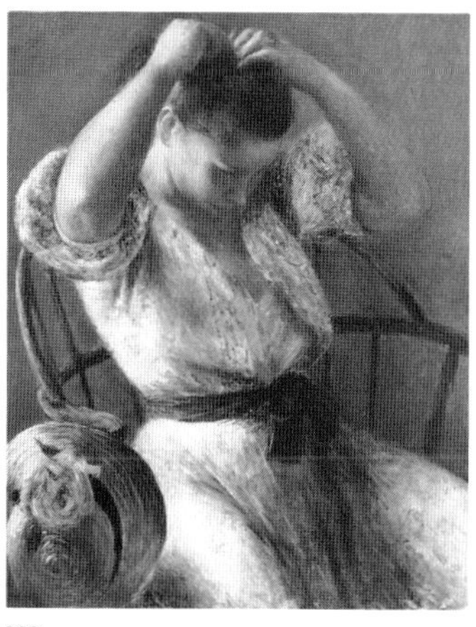
308

304 *Clementia Somers* (1814–1888), ca. 1825
Oil on canvas
19⅛ x 15⁵⁄₁₆ in. (48.6 x 38.9 cm.)
Bequest of Harriet P. Smith, 1905.11.1

305 *Henry Toland*, 1830
Oil on canvas
19⅛ x 15¹⁄₁₆ in. (48.6 x 38.3 cm.)
Signed and dated at lower right:
Jane C. Sully 1830
Gift of Washington S. Toland, 1897.6

Arthur B. Davies (1862–1928)

306 *Isle of Destiny*, ca. 1910
Oil on canvas, mounted on wood
18¹⁄₁₆ x 40¼ in. (45.9 x 102.2 cm.)
Signed at lower left: A. B. DAVIES
Annotated on stretcher: Teneya Lake [crossed out]/Discoveries [crossed out]/ Isle of Destiny
Gift of Mr. and Mrs. Alfred G. B. Steel, 1943.17

Charles H. Davis (1856–1933)

307 *The Brook*, 1890
Oil on canvas, mounted on wood
71 x 114½ in. (180.3 x 290.8 cm.)
Signed and dated at lower left: C.H.DAVIS. 1890-
Joseph E. Temple Fund, 1891.2

Gladys Rockmore Davis (1901–1967)

308 *Seated Figure*, ca. 1937
Oil on canvas
30¹⁄₁₆ x 25 in. (76.4 x 63.5 cm.)
John Lambert Fund, 1938.8

Hubert Davis (b. 1902)

309 *Spring in the Coal Regions*, 1944
Oil on canvas
26 x 36 in. (66 x 91.4 cm.)
Signed at lower left: Hubert Davis
John Lambert Fund, 1945.2

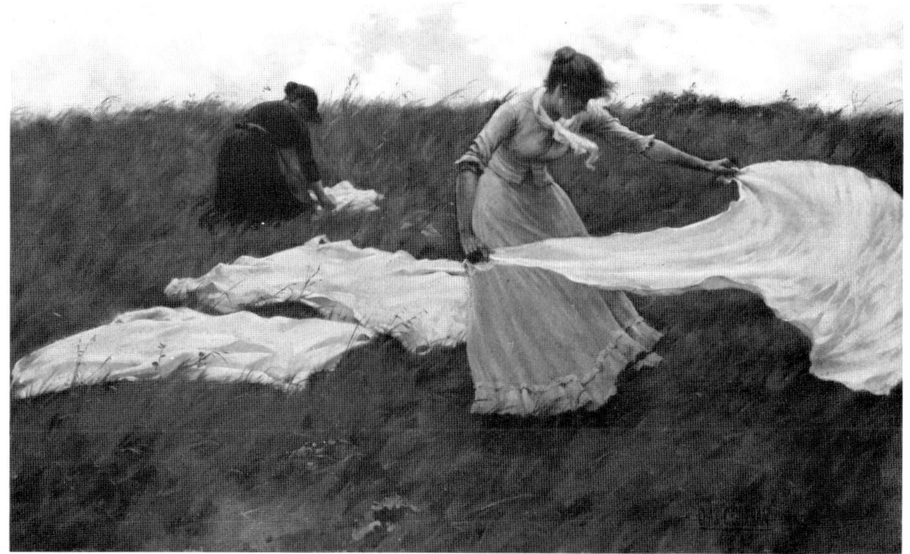
296

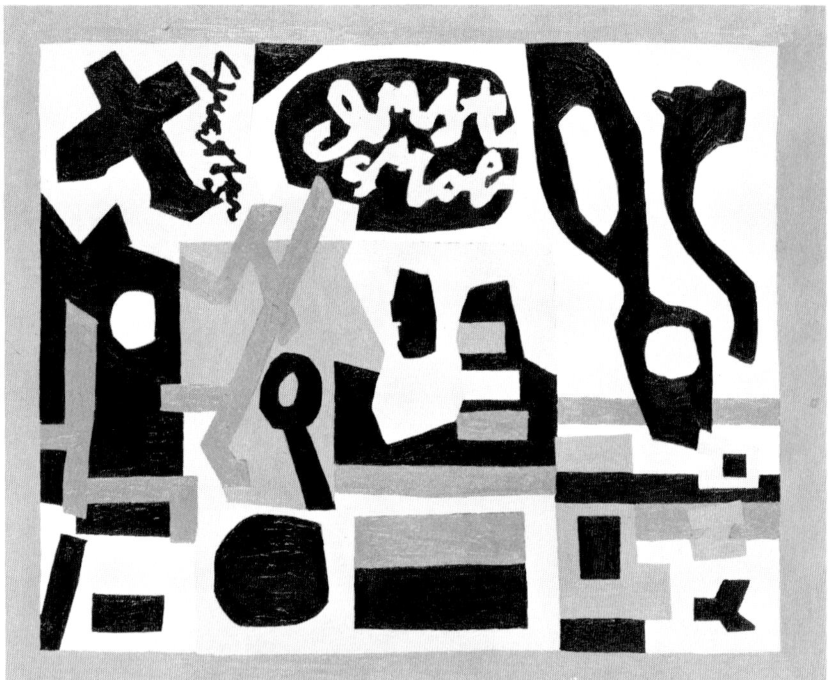

310

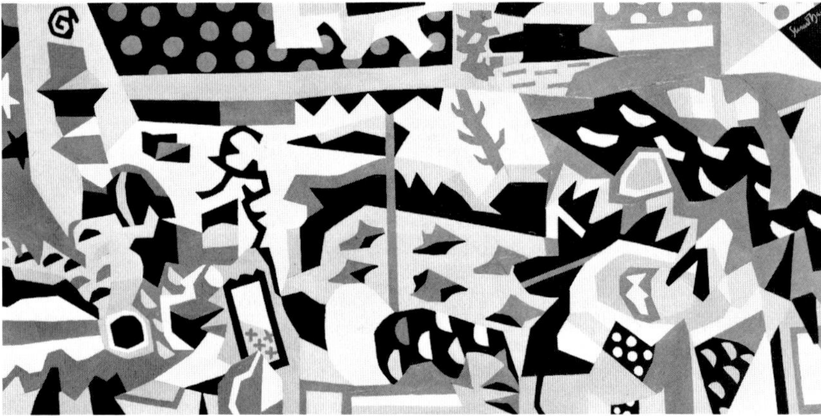

312

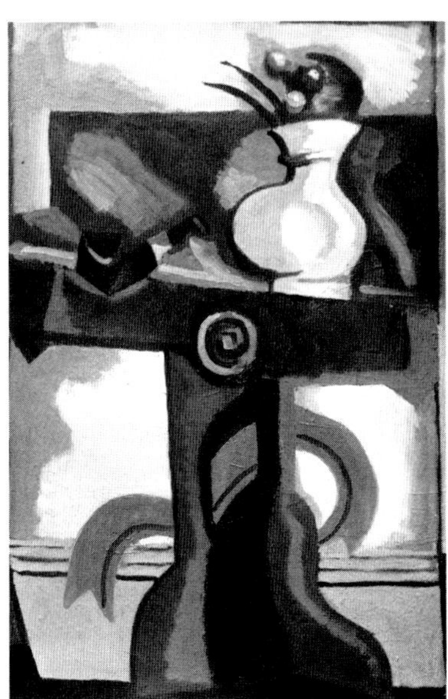

311

Stuart Davis (1894–1964)

310 *Letter and His Ecol*, 1962
Oil on canvas
24 x 30 in. (61 x 76.2 cm.)
Signed at upper left: Stuart Davis
John Lambert Fund, 1964.2

311 *Table with Pipe*, 1922
Oil on canvas
$32\frac{1}{8}$ x $22\frac{1}{8}$ in. (81.6 x 56.2 cm.)
John Lambert Fund, 1930.1

312 *Ultra-Marine*, 1943
Oil on canvas
20 x $40\frac{1}{8}$ in. (50.8 x 101.9 cm.)
Signed at upper right: Stuart Davis
Joseph E. Temple Fund, 1952.11

Larry Day (1921–)

313 *Construction Site*, 1979
Oil on canvas
$54\frac{1}{8}$ x $60\frac{5}{16}$ in. (137.5 x 153.2 cm.)
Gift of Mr. and Mrs. B. Herbert Lee, 1984.18

Joseph R. De Camp (1858–1923)

314 *Dr. Horace Howard Furness* (1833–1912), 1906
Oil on canvas
$36\frac{7}{16}$ x $33\frac{1}{2}$ in. (92.6 x 85.1 cm.)
Signed and dated at lower right: Joseph-DeCamp-06; inscribed, dated, and signed on back: HORACE HOWARD FURNESS-/-1906-/JOSEPH-DE-CAMP/PINXIT
Commissioned by the Pennsylvania Academy, 1906.6

315 *The Little Hotel*, 1903
Oil on canvas
20 x $24\frac{1}{16}$ in. (50.8 x 61.1 cm.)
Signed and dated at lower left: JOSEPH-DE-CAMP-1903
Joseph E. Temple Fund, 1904.2

316 *Fairman Rogers* (1833–1900)
Oil on canvas
$43\frac{1}{4}$ x $32\frac{1}{4}$ in. (109.9 x 81.9 cm.)
Signed and inscribed at lower left: Joseph de CAMP/After Photo
Bequest of Dr. Horace Howard Furness, Jr., 1930.8

Arthur De Costa (1921–)

317 *Seven Pears*, 1960
Oil on canvas
$9\frac{15}{16}$ x $12\frac{1}{16}$ in. (25.2 x 30.6 cm.)
Signed at lower left: DECOSTA
John Lambert Fund, 1962.6

Adolf A. Dehn (1895–1968)

318 *Jungle in Venezuela*, 1946
Oil on watercolor paper, mounted on cardboard
$21\frac{13}{16}$ x $29\frac{3}{4}$ in. (55.4 x 75.6 cm.)
Signed and dated at lower right: Adolf Dehn 1946; signed, dated, and inscribed on back: Adolf Dehn 1946/230 East 15 str./New York City 3/"Jungle in Venezuela"
Collections Fund, 1950.23.1

Frank Standish Deigendish

319 *William Morris Hunt* (1824–1879), ca. 1875
Oil on canvas
$24\frac{3}{16}$ x $21\frac{11}{16}$ in. (61.4 x 55.1 cm.)
Signed at upper right: FD [monogram]
Gift of Mrs. John Frederick Lewis (The John Frederick Lewis Memorial Collection), 1933.10.7

David K. DeLong (1930–)

320 Interior, 1953
Oil on canvas
$41\frac{15}{16}$ x $24\frac{15}{16}$ in. (106.5 x 63.3 cm.)
Signed and dated at lower left: DELONG/53; inscribed, signed, and dated on back: WAX MED. OVER N. YEL. UNDER PAINTING WT. ½ D ½ T. + 5. T. LO = Var./D.K.D. '53'
John Lambert Fund, 1954.10

Irene Denney

321 *The Five-and-Ten*, ca. 1937
Oil on canvas
$26\frac{1}{8}$ x $32\frac{1}{16}$ in. (66.4 x 81.4 cm.)
Signed at lower left: I. DENNEY
John Lambert Fund, 1938.9

Dorothy Dell Dennison (Mrs. Joseph Butler, 1908–)

322 *Comestibles*, 1952
Oil on canvas
$16\frac{1}{8}$ x $30\frac{1}{16}$ in. (41 x 76.4 cm.)
Signed at lower right: Dennison
Collections Fund, 1956.17

Murray Dessner (1934–)

323 *Lady Locks (Marian)*, 1972
Acrylic on canvas
$100\frac{1}{4}$ x 114 in. (254.6 x 289.6 cm.)
Signed and dated on back: M D 72
Gift of Mrs. Avery B. Clark and Benjamin D. Bernstein, 1972.20

Charles Melville Dewey (1849–1937)

324 *Old Fields*, ca. 1904
Oil on canvas

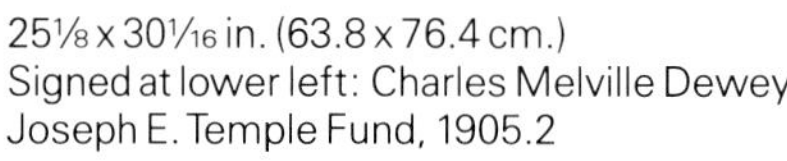

$25\frac{1}{8}$ x $30\frac{1}{16}$ in. (63.8 x 76.4 cm.)
Signed at lower left: Charles Melville Dewey
Joseph E. Temple Fund, 1905.2

Daniel Dickinson. *See* cat. no. 1639.

Edwin W. Dickinson (1891–1978)

325 *Andrée's Balloon*, 1928
Oil on canvas
$30\frac{1}{4}$ x $25\frac{3}{16}$ in. (76.8 x 64 cm.)
Dated and signed at lower left: 1928 E W Dickinson [incised]; signed on back: E.W.DICKINSON.
Funds provided by the National Endowment for the Arts, Sponsors of the Fine Arts Ball and Discotheque, and Daniel W. Dietrich Foundation, 1978.6

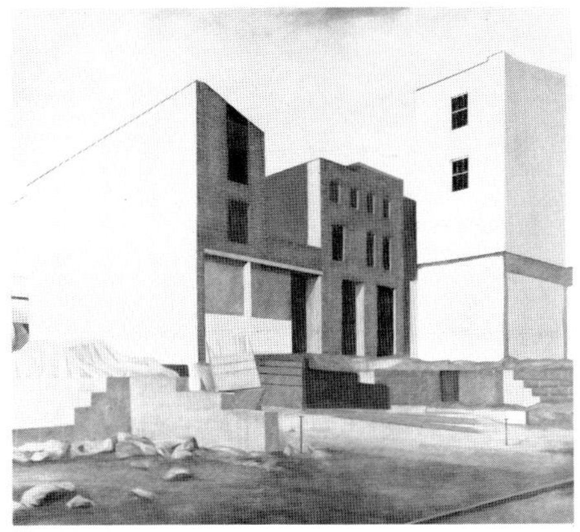

313

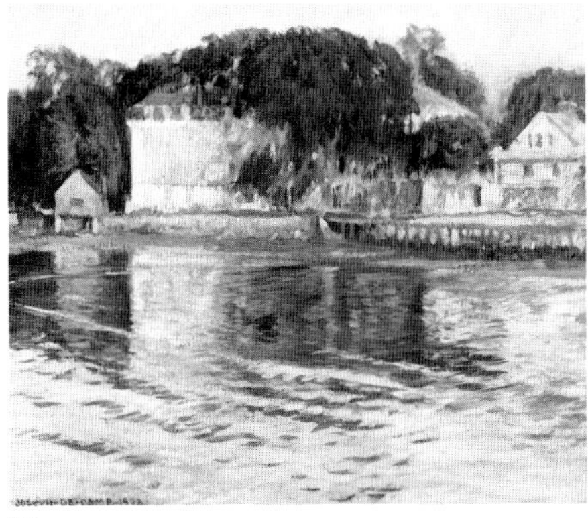

315

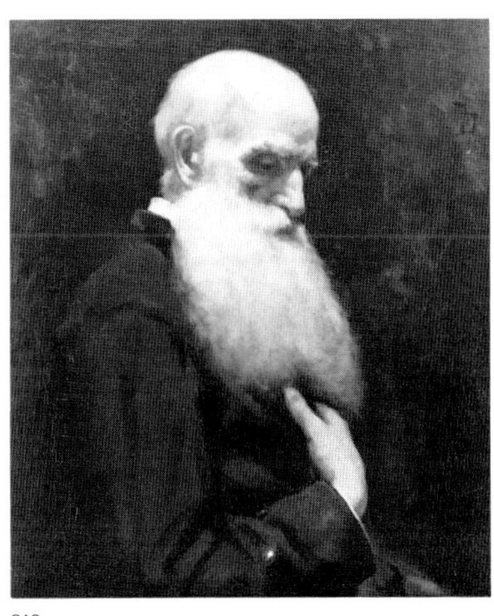

319

323

317

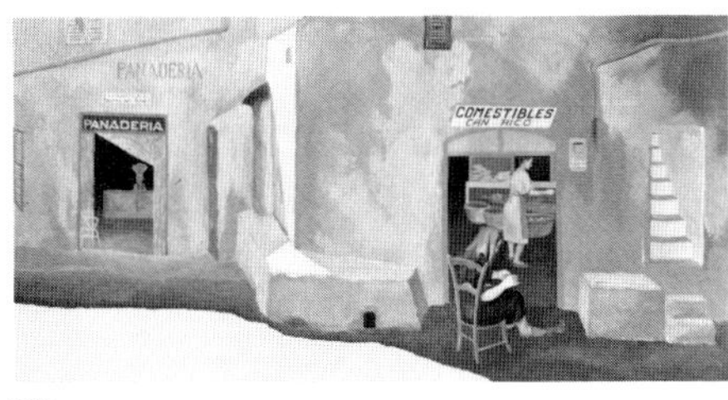

322

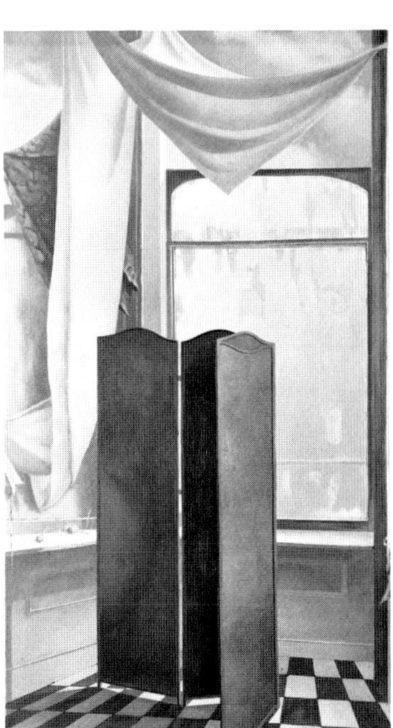

320

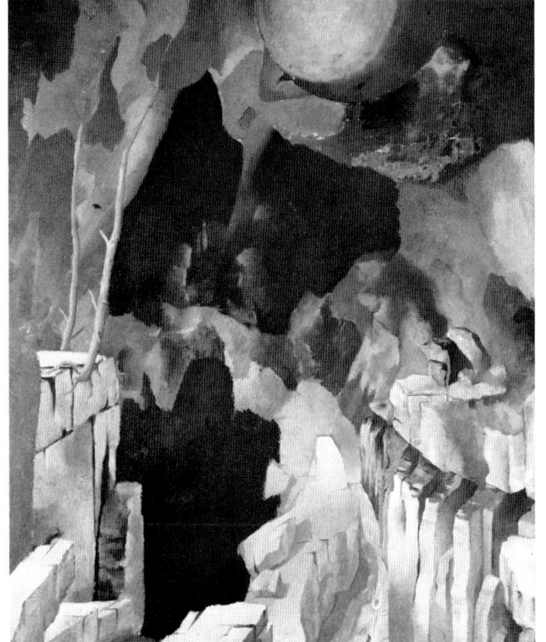

325

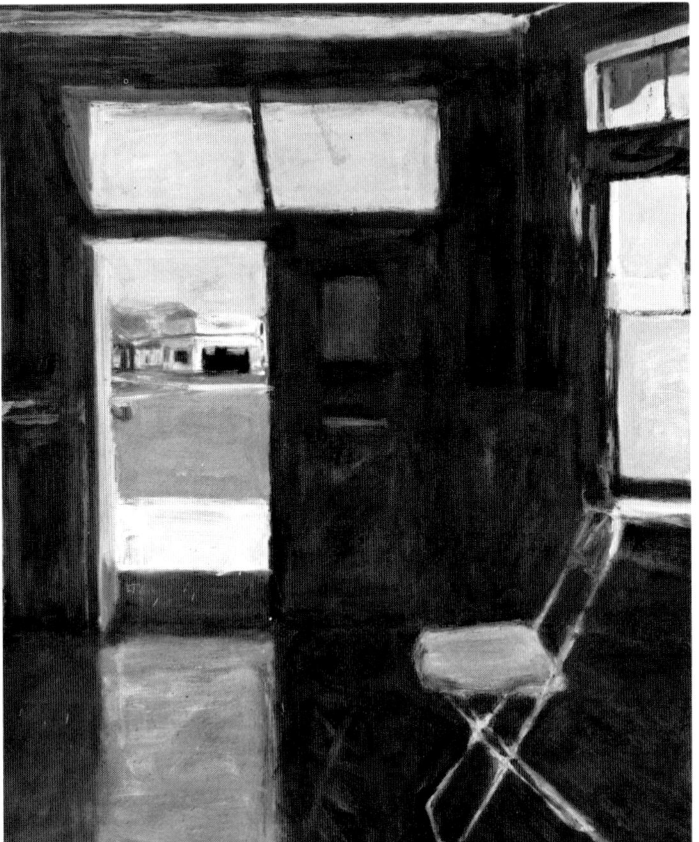

327

Preston Dickinson (1891–1930)

326 *Still Life*, ca. 1924
Oil on canvas
34 x $21\frac{15}{16}$ in. (86.4 x 55.7 cm.)
Signed at lower right: Dickinson
John Lambert Fund, 1925.4

Richard Diebenkorn (1922–)

327 *Interior with Doorway*, 1962
Oil on canvas
$70\frac{5}{16}$ x 60 in. (178.6 x 152.4 cm.)
Signed and dated at lower left: RD 62;
signed, inscribed, and dated on back:
R. DIEBENKORN/INTERIOR–WITH DOORWAY/1962
Henry D. Gilpin Fund, 1964.3

Frederick Dielman (1847–1935)

328 *A Study (Mrs. Frederick Dielman)*, 1888
Oil on composition board
$12\frac{3}{16}$ x $9\frac{13}{16}$ in. (31 x 24.9 cm.)
Signed and dated at lower left: Frederick Dielman 88
Gift of Charles Coleman Sellers, 1973.26.1

Harvey Dinnerstein (1928–)

329 *Noah Wolf*, ca. 1949
Oil on canvas
$45\frac{13}{16}$ x $26\frac{1}{8}$ in. (116.4 x 66.4 cm.)
Signed at lower left: H.Dinnerstein
John Lambert Fund, 1950.6

Ken Dirsa (1948–)

330 *Sky and Sea*, 1986
Oil on canvas
$54\frac{1}{8}$ x $60\frac{1}{8}$ in. (137.5 x 152.7 cm.)
Inscribed, signed, and dated on back: © Kenneth Dirsa 86
Pennsylvania Academy Purchase Prize from the 1986 Annual Fellowship Exhibition, 1986.48

Lamar Dodd (1909–)

331 *Across the Bosphorus*, 1957
Oil on canvas
$30\frac{1}{4}$ x $42\frac{1}{4}$ in. (76.8 x 107.3 cm.)
Signed and dated at lower right: Lamar Dodd '57
Henry D. Gilpin Fund, 1958.9

John Wood Dodge (1807–1893)

332 *Henry Clay* (1777–1852), ca. 1840
Oil on canvas
$30\frac{1}{2}$ x $25\frac{1}{2}$ in. (77.5 x 64.8 cm.)
Gift of John Frederick Lewis, 1923.8.15

Ellen Donovan (b. 1903)

333 *The Village*, ca. 1930
Oil on canvas
20 x $24\frac{1}{16}$ in. (50.8 x 61.1 cm.)
Signed at lower left: Ellen Donovan
John Lambert Fund, 1931.2

Emilie Zeckwer Dooner (1877–1973)

334 *Dutch Woman and Child*, 1904
Oil on canvas
$16\frac{3}{16}$ x $10\frac{11}{16}$ in. (41.1 x 27.1 cm.)
Signed and dated at lower right: E. Zeckwer 1904
Signed, inscribed, and dated on stretcher: Emilie Zeckwer/St Brioc Aug. 1904
Gift of Vera White, 1960.18.7

Thomas Doughty (1793–1856)

335 *Landscape with Curving River*, ca. 1823
Oil on canvas
$18\frac{9}{16}$ x $27\frac{1}{2}$ in. (47.1 x 69.9 cm.)
Signed at lower right: DOUGHTY
Bequest of Henry C. Carey (The Carey Collection), 1879.8.5

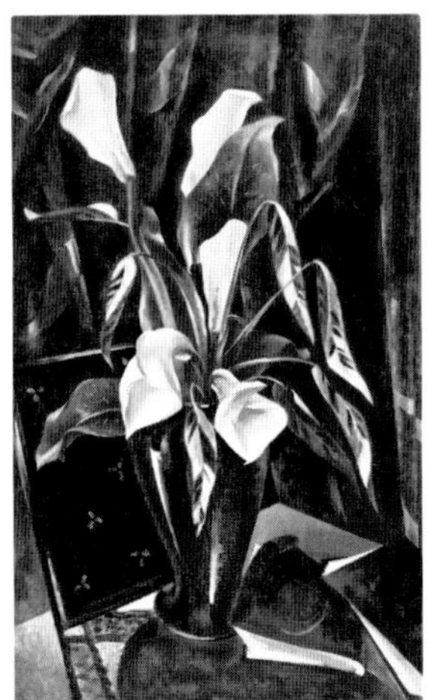

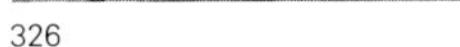

326

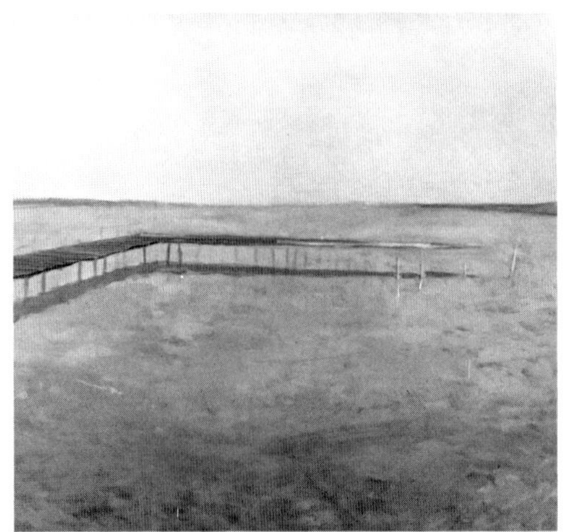

330

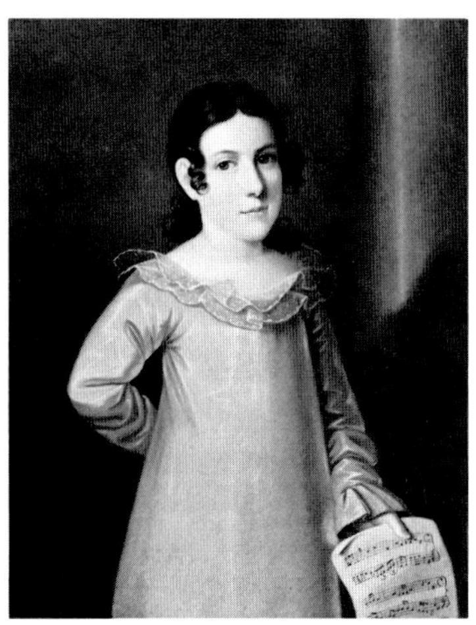

344

336 *Landscape with Pool*, ca. 1823
Oil on canvas
18⁵⁄₁₆ x 25 in. (46.5 x 63.5 cm.)
Bequest of Henry C. Carey (The Carey Collection), 1879.8.6

337 *Morning among the Hills*, 1829–30
Oil on canvas
15¼ x 21¹⁄₁₆ in. (38.7 x 53.5 cm.)
Signed and dated at lower right: TDOUGHTY./ 1829.30
Bequest of Henry C. Carey (The Carey Collection), 1879.8.4

338 *View near Hartford, Connecticut*, 1828
Oil on canvas
16¾ x 24⅛ in. (42.5 x 61.3 cm.)
Annotated on back (before lining): View near Hartford Conn./painted by T Doughty 1828
Gift of Cephas G. Childs, 1828.1

339 *View on the Susquehanna near Harrisburg*, ca. 1830
Oil on canvas
18⁹⁄₁₆ x 27⁹⁄₁₆ in. (47.1 x 70 cm.)
Source unknown, 1844.1

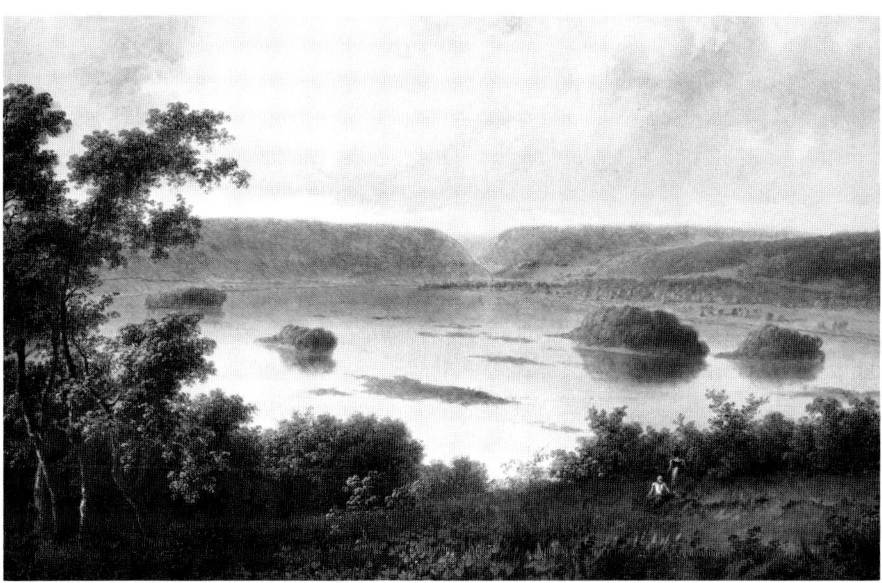
339

Rackstraw Downes (1939–)

340 *Behind the Store at Prospect*, 1979–80
Oil on canvas
18¾ x 46¹¹⁄₁₆ in. (47.6 x 118.6 cm.)
Signed at lower right: RD
Signed, inscribed, and dated on stretcher: RACKSTRAW DOWNES "BEHIND THE STORE AT PROSPECT" (TO WILLARD ROBISON) O/C 1979–80 18¾ x 46¾"
Funds provided by the National Endowment for the Arts and the Contemporary Arts Fund, 1981.5

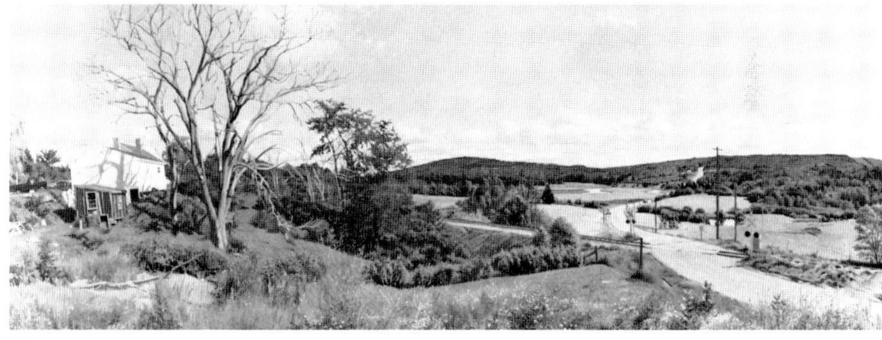
340

Stella Drabkin (1906–1971)

341 *Mother and Child*, ca. 1946
Oil on canvas
16¹³⁄₁₆ x 14¼ in. (42.7 x 36.2 cm.)
Signed at lower right: STELLA DRABKIN
John Lambert Fund, 1947.2

Maude Drein. *See* Maude Drein Bryant.

Jessie Drew-Bear (1879–1962)

342 *Turkey Knob Farm*, 1949
Oil on canvas
21¹⁄₁₆ x 26 in. (53.5 x 66 cm.)
Signed and dated at lower right: DREW-BEAR. 1949.
John Lambert Fund, 1950.7

Werner Drewes (1899–1985)

343 *Red House, New Hope*, 1932
Oil on composition board
18 x 23⅞ in. (45.7 x 60.6 cm.)
Dated at lower right: 3 0 2; dated on back: 3 0 2
Inscribed and signed on stretcher: red house at the canal - (NEW HOPE)/W. Drewes/507 E. 55th N. York
John Lambert Fund, 1933.3

Francis Martin Drexel (1792–1863)

344 *Unidentified Girl*, 1818
Oil on canvas
30⅛ x 24¼ in. (76.5 x 61.6 cm.)
Signed and dated on back: F.M.Drexel, Pinxit 1818
Gift of John Frederick Lewis, 1923.8.19

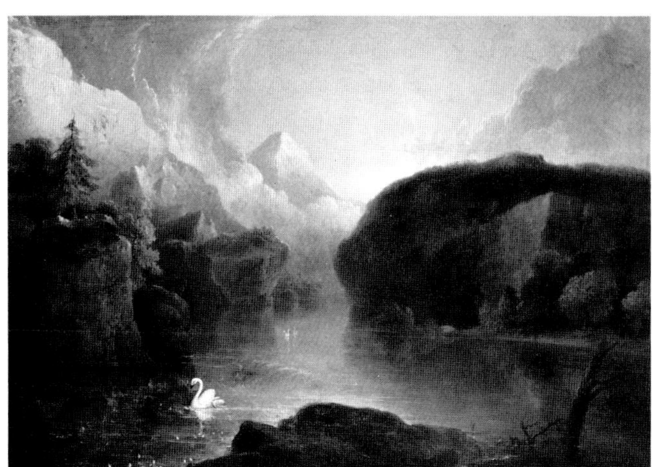
337

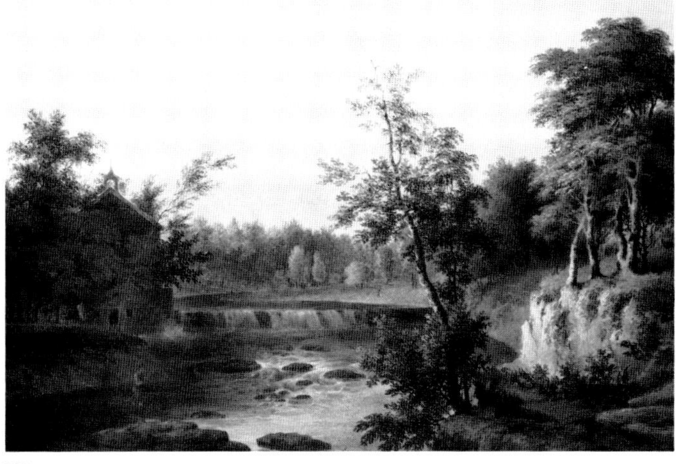
338

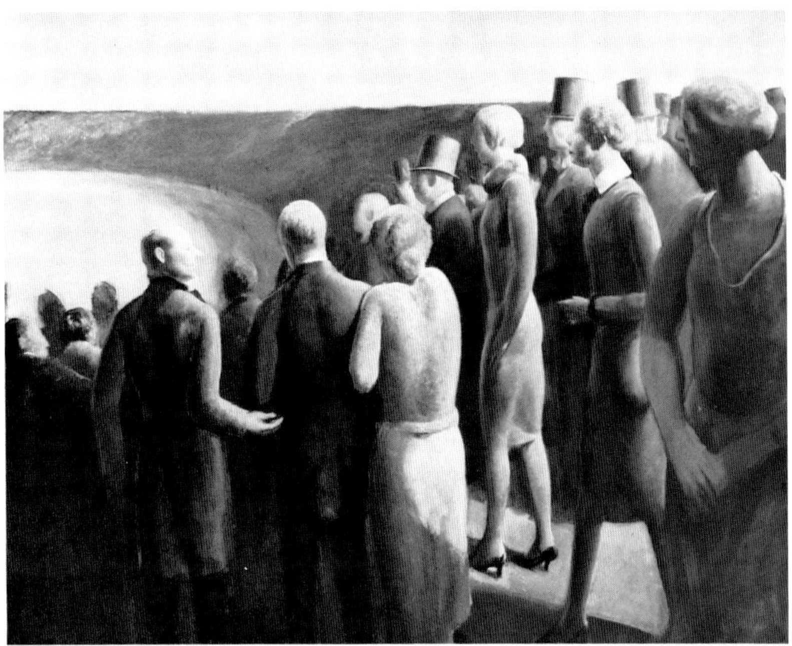
348

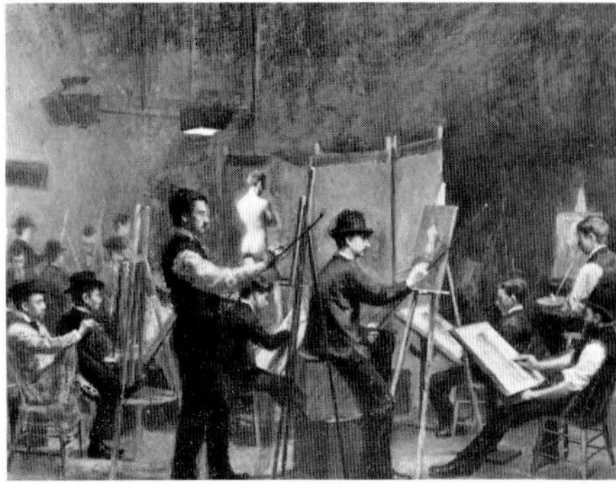
352

Eistein Olaf Drogseth (1874–1948)

345 *Winter in Norway*, ca. 1917
Oil on cardboard
18³⁄₁₆ x 24½ in. (46.2 x 62.2 cm.)
Signed at lower left: E. DROGSETH.
John Lambert Fund, 1918.8

Ralph Dubin (1918–)

346 *Across the Tracks*, 1952
Oil on canvas
36 x 30 in. (91.4 x 76.2 cm.)
Signed at lower left: Ralph DUBIN
John Lambert Fund, 1953.1

Guy Pène du Bois (1884–1958)

347 *Club Meeting*, 1936
Oil on canvas
24⅛ x 20¹⁄₁₆ in. (61.3 x 51 cm.)
Signed and dated at lower right: Guy Pène du Bois '36
Henry D. Gilpin Fund, 1939.4

348 *People*, 1927
Oil on canvas
45⅛ x 57⅞ in. (114.6 x 147 cm.)
Signed and dated at lower left: Guy Pene du Bois 27.
Joseph E. Temple Fund, 1943.12

Samuel F. DuBois (1805–1889)

349 *Dr. Samuel Moore*, 1848
Oil on canvas
29¾ x 25 in. (75.6 x 63.5 cm.)
Annotated on back: Dr Samuel Moore/by Samuel F DuBois 1848.
Gift of Elinor Ewing Curwen and Alice Osborne McKeen, 1973.7.2

350 *Mrs. Samuel Moore (née Mary Patterson)*, 1848
Oil on canvas
30¹⁄₁₆ x 25¹⁄₁₆ in. (76.4 x 63.7 cm.)
Annotated on back: Mary Patterson Moore/ Daughter of Robert Patterson PhD. & Amie [*sic*] Ewing Patterson/Wife of Dr Samuel Moore/Painted by Samuel F. DuBois 1848
Gift of Elinor Ewing Curwen and Alice Osborne McKeen, 1973.7.1

351 *Amy Ewing Patterson* (Mrs. Robert Patterson)
Oil on canvas
30 x 25½ in. (76.2 x 64.8 cm.)
Gift of Elinor Ewing Curwen and Alice Osborne McKeen, 1973.7.3

Walter M. Dunk (b. 1855)

352 *Men's Life Class* (illustration for William C. Brownell, "The Art Schools of Philadelphia," *Scribner's Monthly* 18, Sept. 1879, pp. 737-50), ca. 1879
Oil on cardboard (grisaille)
10¼ x 12¾ in. (26 x 32.4 cm.)
Gift of the artist, 1879.3

Attributed to **William Dunlap** (1766–1839)

353 *Charles Brockden Brown* (?) (1791–1810)
Oil on wood
23¹⁵⁄₁₆ x 19¼ in. (60.8 x 48.9 cm.)
Gift of Mrs. John Frederick Lewis (The John Frederick Lewis Memorial Collection), 1933.10.8

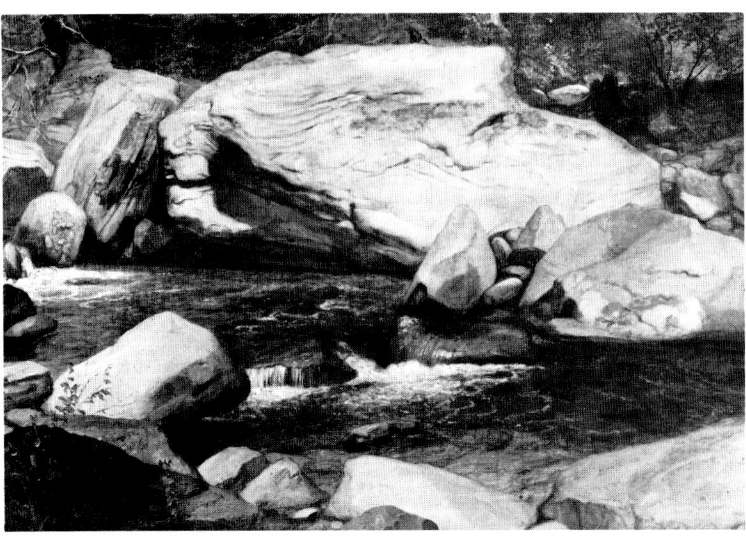
356

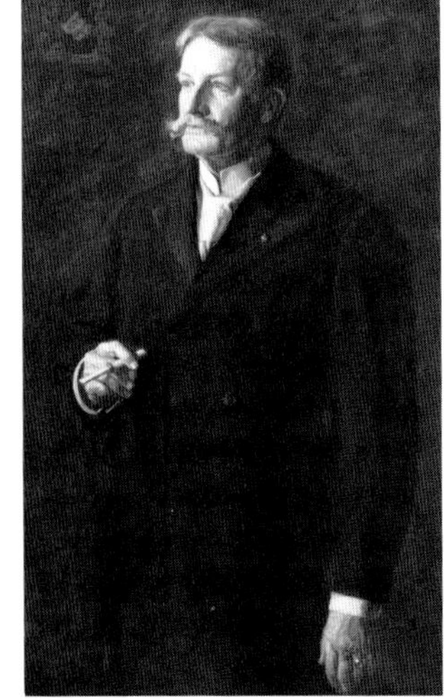
360

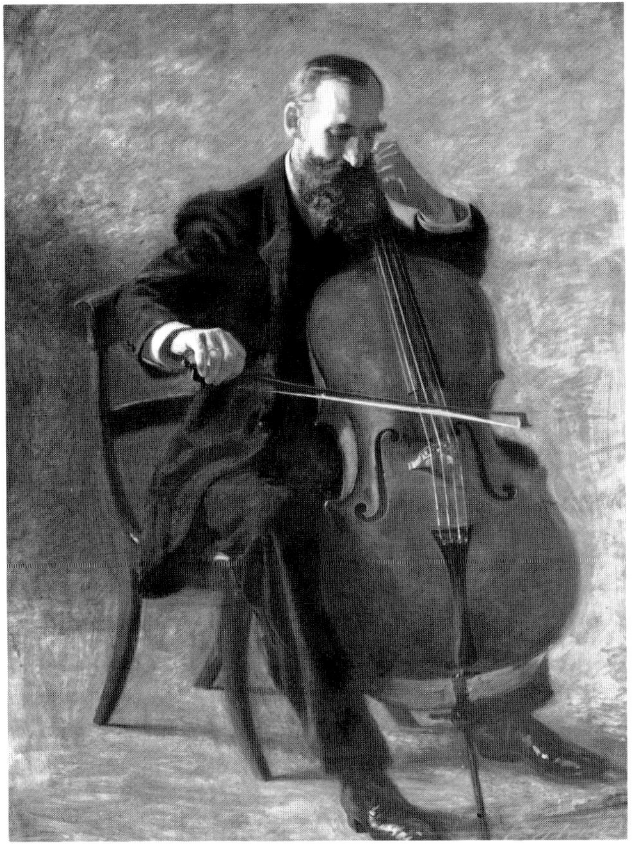

359

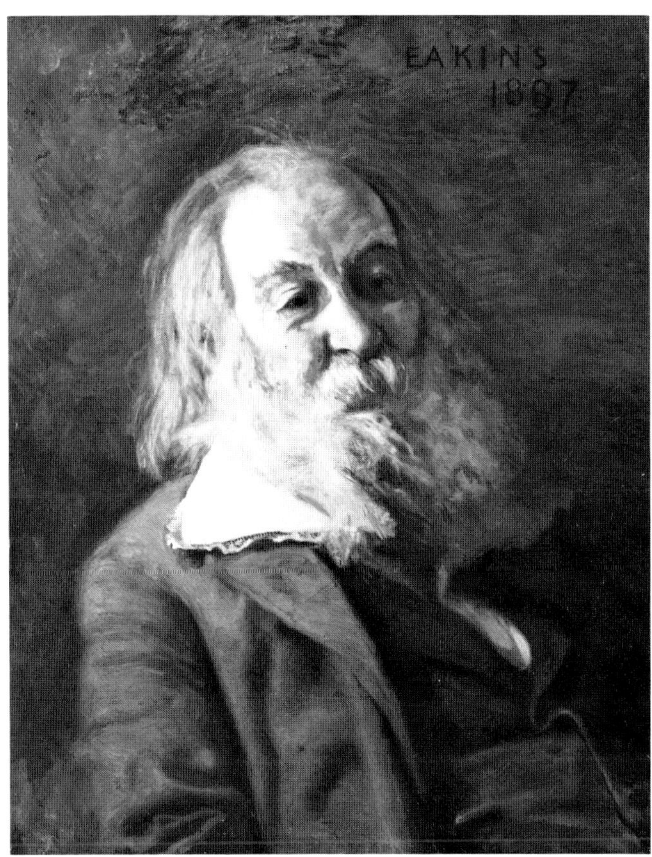

362

354 *Unidentified Man*
Oil on canvas
30$\frac{1}{16}$ x 25$\frac{1}{16}$ in. (76.4 x 63.7 cm.)
Gift of John Frederick Lewis, 1923.8.1

355 *Unidentified Man*
Oil on canvas
30$\frac{1}{16}$ x 25$\frac{1}{16}$ in. (76.4 x 63.7 cm.)
Gift of John Frederick Lewis, 1932.13.2

Asher B. Durand (1796–1886)

356 *Landscape: Creek and Rocks*, 1850s
Oil on canvas
16$\frac{15}{16}$ x 24 in. (43 x 61 cm.)
Gift of Charles Henry Hart, 1915.9

Frank Duveneck (1848–1919)

357 *The Turkish Page*, 1876
Oil on canvas
42 x 58$\frac{1}{4}$ in. (106.7 x 148 cm.)
Signed, inscribed, and dated at lower left: F. Duveneck. Munich.1876
Joseph E. Temple Fund, 1894.1

Herrmann Dyer (Mrs. Briggs Dyer, b. 1916)

358 *Little Landscape*, ca. 1941
Oil on canvas
20 x 42 in. (50.8 x 106.7 cm.)
Signed at lower right: Herrmann Dyer
John Lambert Fund, 1942.2

Thomas Eakins (1844–1916)

359 *The Cello Player* (Rudolph Hennig, 1845–1904), 1896
Oil on canvas
64$\frac{1}{4}$ x 48$\frac{1}{8}$ in. (163.2 x 122.2 cm.)
Signed and dated at lower right: Eakins/96
Joseph E. Temple Fund, 1897.3

360 *Charles Edmund Dana* (1843–1914), ca. 1902
Oil on canvas
50$\frac{1}{4}$ x 30$\frac{1}{8}$ in. (127.6 x 76.5 cm.)
Gift of Charles Edmund Dana, 1913.16

361 *Delaware River Study*, ca. 1881
Oil on board
4$\frac{1}{4}$ x 7$\frac{1}{2}$ in. (10.8 x 19.1 cm.)
Gift of Mrs. Charles Bregler, 1966.14

362 *Walt Whitman* (1819–1892), 1888
Oil on canvas
30$\frac{1}{8}$ x 24$\frac{1}{4}$ in. (76.5 x 61.6 cm.)
Signed and incorrectly dated at upper right: EAKINS/1887.
General Fund, 1917.1

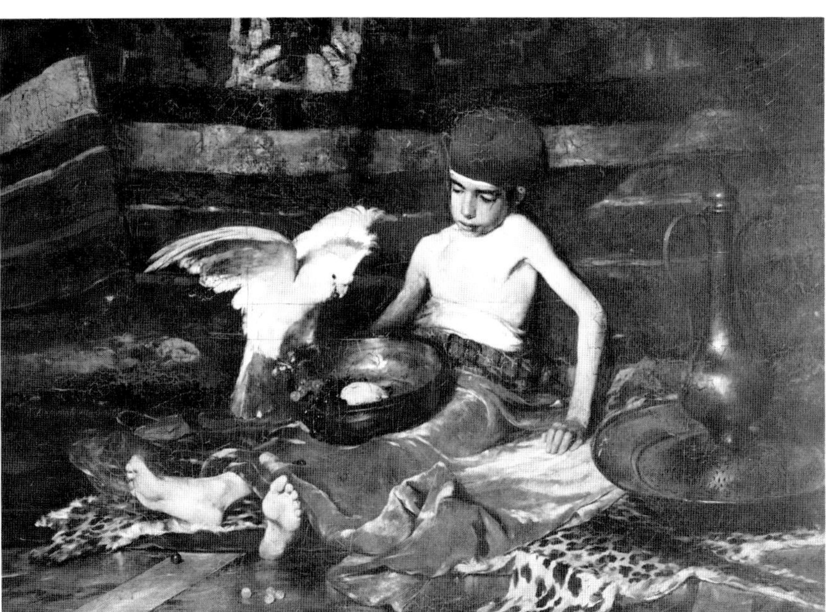

357

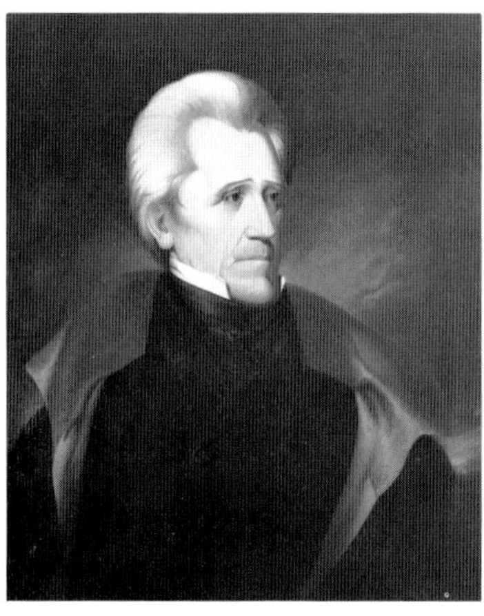
363

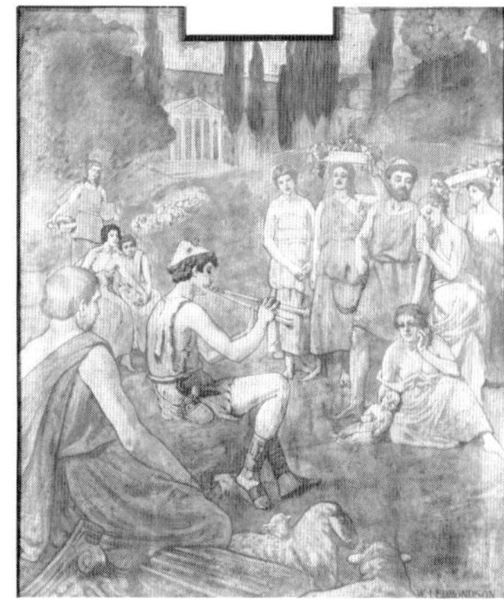
365

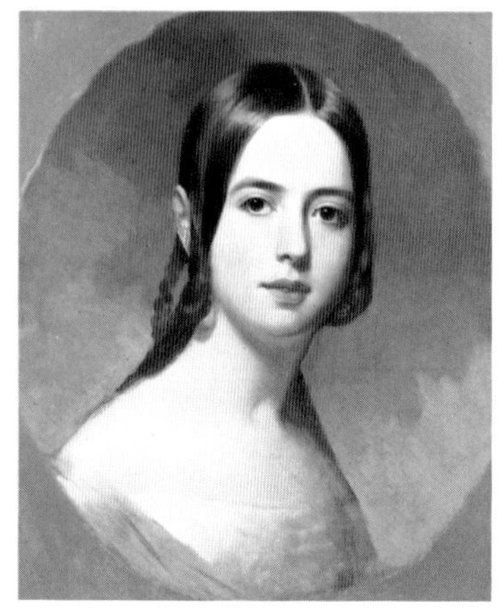
370

Ralph E. W. Earl (ca. 1785–1838)

363 *Andrew Jackson* (1767–1845), ca. 1835
Oil on canvas
29 15/16 x 24 7/8 in. (76 x 63.2 cm.)
Gift of Mrs. John Frederick Lewis (The John Frederick Lewis Memorial Collection), 1933.10.9

William J. Edmondson (1868–1966)

364 *Clio* (formerly *Literature*), 1896–97
Oil on canvas
Approx. 66 x 42 in. (167 x 106 cm.)
Signed at lower right: W.J./EDMOND-/SON
Commissioned by the Pennsylvania Academy, 1897.9.1

365 *Pastoral Music* (formerly *The Shepherd's Song*), 1896–97
Oil on canvas
Approx. 66 x 66 in. (167 x 167 cm.)
Signed at lower right: W.J.EDMONDSON
Commissioned by the Pennsylvania Academy, 1897.9.2

Jacob Eichholtz (1776–1842)

366 *Conestoga Creek and Lancaster*, 1833
Oil on canvas
20 1/4 x 30 1/4 in. (51.4 x 76.8 cm.)
Signed and dated at lower right: J.Eichholtz/1833.
Gift of Mrs. James H. Beal, 1961.8.10

367 *Edward Eichholtz* (1819–1821), 1821
Oil on canvas
44 x 35 in. (111.8 x 88.9 cm.)
Gift of Katharine Todd Eichholtz, 1954.3

368 *Henry Clay Eichholtz* (1830–1918), ca. 1831
Oil on wood
4 1/2 x 3 3/4 in. (11.4 x 9.5 cm.)
Gift of Mrs. James H. Beal, 1961.8.8

369 *Mrs. Jacob Eichholtz* (née Catherine Trissler, 1791–1867), 1818
Oil on wood
10 x 7 3/4 in. (25.4 x 19.7 cm.)
Annotated on back: Pinxit 1818
Gift of Mrs. James H. Beal, 1961.8.2

370 *Rebecca Trissler Eichholtz* (1828–1888), ca. 1841
Oil on canvas
20 x 16 in. (50.8 x 40.6 cm.)
Gift of Mrs. James H. Beal, 1961.8.3

371 *Rubens Mayor Eichholtz* (1810–1841); on back, *Head of a Prophet*, ca. 1813
Oil on wood
8 1/2 x 6 1/8 in. (21.6 x 15.6 cm.)
Gift of Mrs. James H. Beal, 1961.8.4

372 *Mrs. Elizabeth Wurtz Elder and Her Three Children* (Mrs. Elder, d. 1852; William Smith Elder; Rebekah Heaton Elder; and Henry Lentz Elder), 1825
Oil on canvas
42 1/2 x 47 1/2 in. (108 x 120.7 cm.)
Signed and dated on back: J. Eichholtz 1825
Bequest of Mrs. Blanche Elder Howell, 1923.12

373 *Mrs. Walter Franklin* (née Ann Emlen, 1784–1852), ca. 1814
Oil on canvas
28 3/4 x 23 1/2 in. (73 x 59.7 cm.)
Gift of Mrs. John Frederick Lewis (The John Frederick Lewis Memorial Collection), 1934.12

374 *The Reverend John Gottlieb Ernestus Heckewelder* (1743–1823), 1823
Oil on canvas
29 15/16 x 25 in. (76 x 63.5 cm.)
Signed and dated at right center: JE [monogram] 1823; annotated on back: This Portrait of/Rev John Heckewelder,/was/Painted at Bethlehem, Pa./In August 1822 By/-Jacob Eicholtz [*sic*]/Presented to The Pa Aca'my/of the Fine Arts By/William L. Elkins/of Phil. Pa/Feb'y 1st 1893; and in another hand: John Heckewelder./Jacob Eicholtz [*sic*] fecit./Bethlehem. August 1823.
Gift of William L. Elkins, 1893.2

375 *John Frederick Lewis* (1791–1858), 1827
Oil on canvas
36 1/4 x 28 in. (92.1 x 71.1 cm.)
Gift of Mrs. John Frederick Lewis (The John Frederick Lewis Memorial Collection), 1933.10.12

376 *Mrs. John Frederick Lewis* (née Elizabeth Mower, 1788–1865), 1827
Oil on canvas
36 x 28 1/2 in. (91.4 x 72.4 cm.)
Gift of Mrs. John Frederick Lewis (The John Frederick Lewis Memorial Collection), 1933.10.11

377 *Susan Earl Miller (1807–1837)*, 1825
Oil on canvas
24 x 19 3/4 in. (61 x 50.2 cm.), oval
Bequest of Harrison Earl, 1894.6.2

378 *Mathias Musser* (1785–1833), ca. 1806
Oil on wood
9 x 7 in. (22.9 x 17.8 cm.)

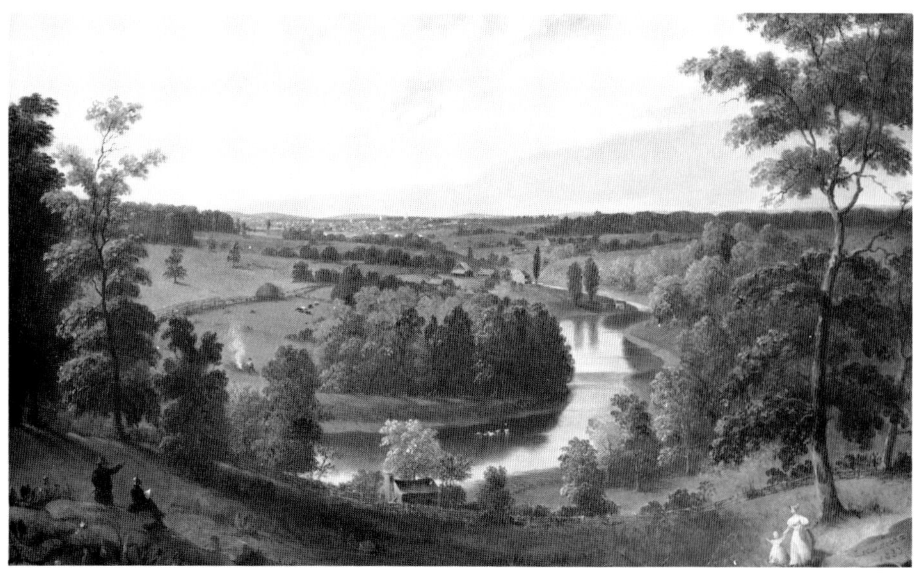
366

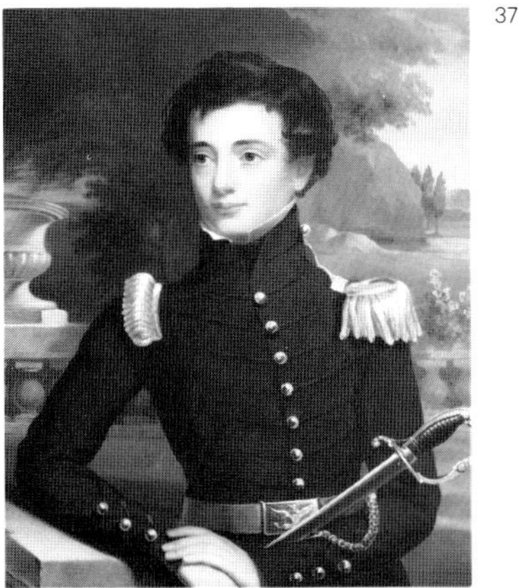
379

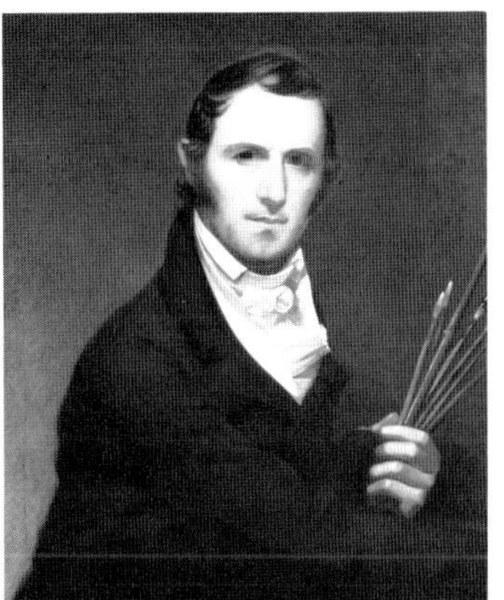
382

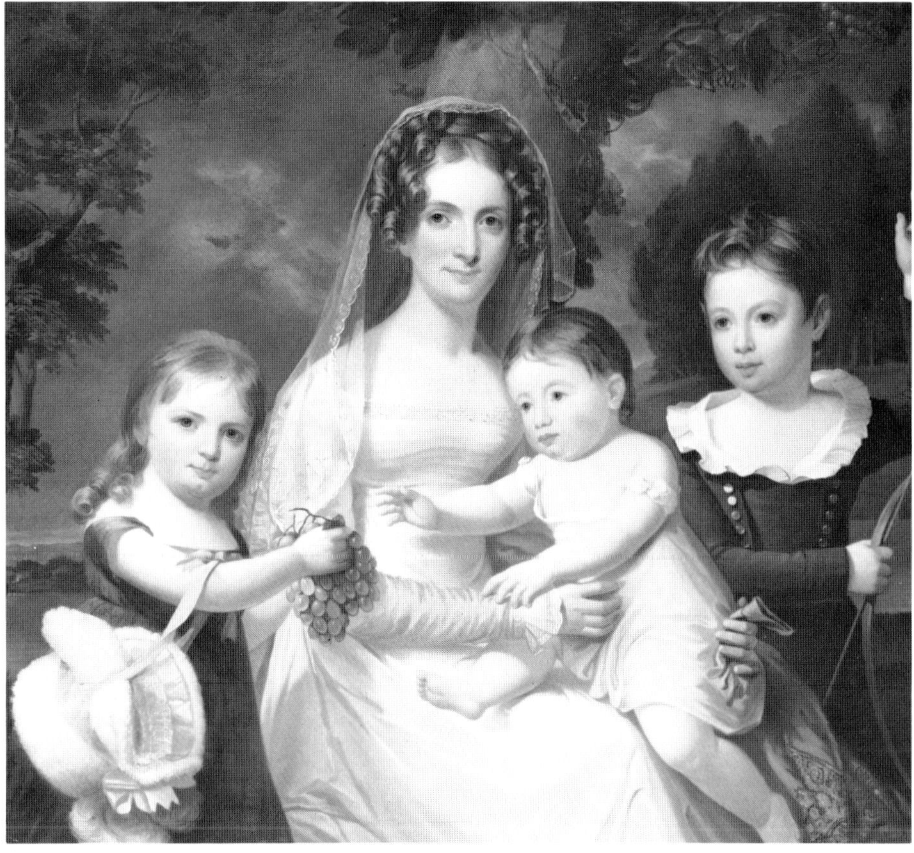
372

Signed and inscribed on back: J. Eichholtz/
Pinxit/Lanc-.
Gift of Mrs. James H. Beal, 1961.8.5

379 *Admiral David Dixon Porter* (1813–1891), 1829
Oil on canvas
$30\frac{1}{8}$ x $24\frac{15}{16}$ in. (76.5 x 63.3 cm.)
Annotated on back (before lining): Painted by/ Eichholtz/Philadelphia/1829
Gift of Mrs. John Frederick Lewis (The John Frederick Lewis Memorial Collection), 1933.10.14

380 *Eliza Schaum* (later Mrs. Frederick Augustus Hall Muhlenberg, 1798–1826), 1816
Oil on canvas
$29\frac{1}{4}$ x $24\frac{11}{16}$ in. (74.3 x 62.7 cm.)
Gift of Mrs. James H. Beal, 1961.8.6

381 *Self-Portrait*, ca. 1809
Oil on wood
$4\frac{3}{8}$ x $3\frac{1}{4}$ in. (11.1 x 8.3 cm.), oval
Gift of Mrs. James H. Beal, 1961.8.1

382 *Self-Portrait*, ca. 1810
Oil on canvas
29 x $23\frac{7}{8}$ in. (73.7 x 60.6 cm.)
Gift of Mrs. James H. Beal, 1961.8.7

383 *Self-Portrait*, 1834
Oil on canvas
$28\frac{7}{8}$ x $23\frac{7}{8}$ in. (73.3 x 60.6 cm.)
Inscribed, signed, and dated on back (before lining): Presented to my Sister Catharine Leman during her life which I hope may be long by Jacob Eichholtz, 1841 in his 58th year.
Gift of Mrs. James H. Beal, 1961.8.9

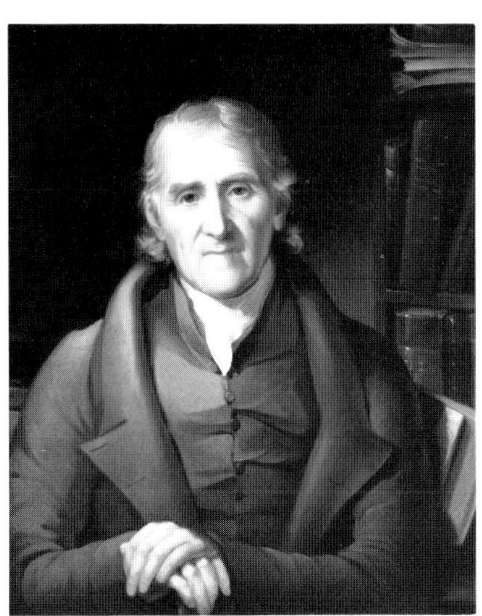
374

376

383

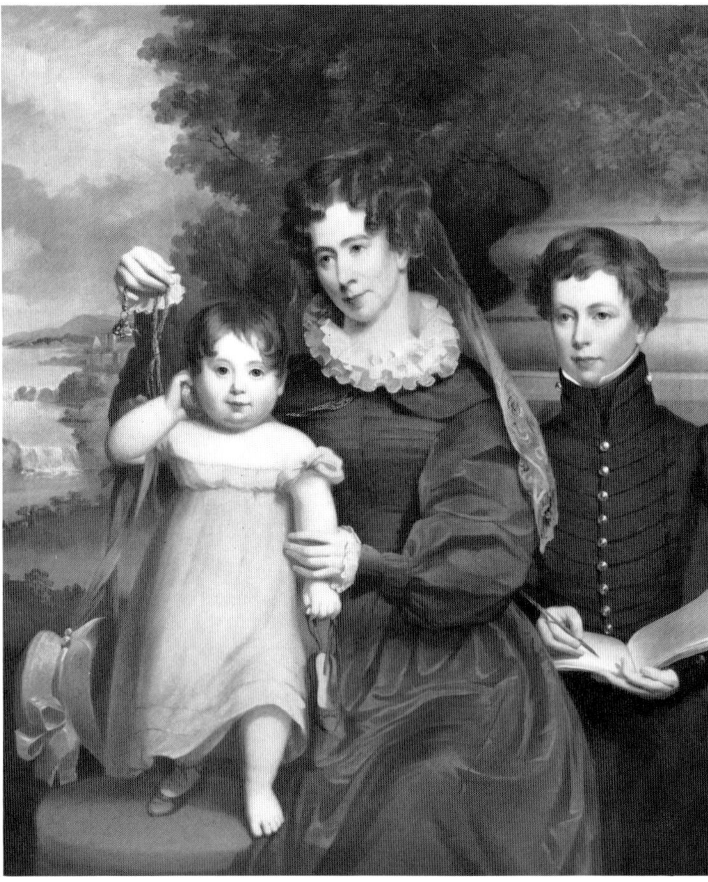

384

384 *Mrs. Victor René Value, Her Daughter Victoria Matilda, and Her Stepson Jesse René* (Mrs. Value, née Ann Lane Bean, 1790–after 1859; Victoria, 1828–1900; and Jesse, 1816–1891), ca. 1830
Oil on canvas
52⅞ x 45 in. (134.2 x 114.3 cm.)
Gift of Mrs. Charles E. Dunbar, 1986.40

385 *Unidentified Man* (formerly *Oliver Hazard Perry*), ca. 1814
Oil on canvas
29⁵⁄₁₆ x 24¼ in. (74.5 x 61.6 cm.)
Gift of Mrs. John Frederick Lewis (The John Frederick Lewis Memorial Collection), 1933.10.15

386 *Unidentified Man* (formerly *Jacob Eichholtz*), 1815–20
Oil on canvas
29¹⁄₁₆ x 24 in. (73.8 x 61 cm.)
Henry D. Gilpin Fund, 1916.1

387 *Unidentified Man* (formerly *John Howard Payne*), 1815–20
Oil on canvas
29⅛ x 23¹⁵⁄₁₆ in. (74 x 60.8 cm.)
Gift of Mrs. John Frederick Lewis (The John Frederick Lewis Memorial Collection), 1933.10.16

388 *Unidentified Man*, ca. 1820
Oil on canvas, mounted on wood
29⅛ x 24⅛ in. (74 x 61.3 cm.)
Gift of Mrs. John Frederick Lewis (The John Frederick Lewis Memorial Collection), 1933.10.13

389 *Unidentified Man*, ca. 1825
Oil on canvas
29⁹⁄₁₆ x 24½ in. (75.1 x 62.2 cm.)
Gift of Mrs. John Frederick Lewis (The John Frederick Lewis Memorial Collection), 1933.10.10

Louis M. Eilshemius (1864–1941)

390 *Autumn Bathers*, ca. 1915
Oil on masonite
19½ x 29¾ in. (49.5 x 75.6 cm.)
Signed at lower left: Eilshemius
Gift of Mr. and Mrs. Lawrence M. C. Smith, 1952.24

Charles Loring Elliott (1812–1868)

391 *Robert Havell, Jr.* (1793–1878), probably 1851–52
Oil on canvas
29¾ x 24⅞ in. (75.6 x 63.2 cm.)
Gift of Charles Henry Hart, 1884.4

392 *Self-Portrait*, ca. 1845
Oil on canvas, mounted on masonite
24⅝ x 19¹¹⁄₁₆ in. (62.5 x 50 cm.)
Gift of Mrs. John Frederick Lewis (The John Frederick Lewis Memorial Collection), 1933.10.17

Attributed to **Henri Elouis** (French, 1755–1840)

393 *Martha Washington* (1731–1802), ca. 1793
Oil on canvas
23⅞ x 19⁵⁄₁₆ in. (60.6 x 49.1 cm.)
Bequest of Mrs. John Frederick Lewis, 1939.17.3

Edith Emerson (1888–1981)

394 *Violet Oakley* (1874–1961), ca. 1935, unfinished
Oil on canvas
43⅝ x 31¼ in. (110.8 x 79.4 cm.)
Signed at upper right: Edith/Emerson
Gift of the artist, 1969.33

Jimmy Ernst (1920–1984)

395 *Warning*, 1960
Oil on canvas
40¹⁄₁₆ x 50¹⁄₁₆ in. (101.8 x 127.2 cm.)
Signed and dated at lower right: Jimmy Ernst 60
Gift of Mrs. Herbert Cameron Morris, 1969.11

J. Richards Essig (b. 1902)

396 *Frank T. Howard* (d. 1982), 1971
Oil on canvas
30⅞ x 28¹⁄₁₆ in. (78.4 x 71.3 cm.)
Signed and dated at lower right: Essig-1971
Henry D. Gilpin Fund, 1971.19

Florence Este (1860–1926)

397 *Brittany Pines*, 1905
Oil on canvas
116 x 258 in. (294.6 x 655.3 cm.)
Signed and dated at lower right: Fl.Este.1905
Gift of the artist, 1905.10

Stephen M. Etnier (1903–1984)

398 *Café Tables, Haiti*, 1936
Oil on canvas
25 x 30¹⁄₁₆ in. (63.5 x 76.4 cm.)
Signed at lower left: Stephen Etnier
Signed and inscribed on stretcher: STEPHEN ETNIER/CAFE TABLES
Joseph E. Temple Fund, 1939.5

Emlen P. Etting (1905–)

399 *Still Life*, ca. 1935
Oil on canvas
18⅛ x 25¾ in. (46 x 65.4 cm.)
Signed at upper right: etting
John Lambert Fund, 1936.4

Philip Evergood (1901–1973)

400 *Threshold to Success*, 1955–57
Oil on gessoed celotex board
67½ x 36¼ in. (171.5 x 92.1 cm.)
Signed at lower right: Philip Evergood; signed and inscribed on back: PHILIP EVERGOOD/TITLE: "THRESHOLD TO/SUCCESS"/MEDIUM: OIL ON GESSOED CELOTEX/BOARD
Joseph E. Temple Fund, 1958.10

Thomas Ewing (1935–)

401 *Two/Four, Atlantic City*, 1965
Oil, cement, and stones on masonite
36¼ x 40⅛ in. (92.1 x 101.9 cm.)
Inscribed, signed, and dated on back: "4/6"/T. Ewing/July/1965
John Lambert Fund, 1966.3

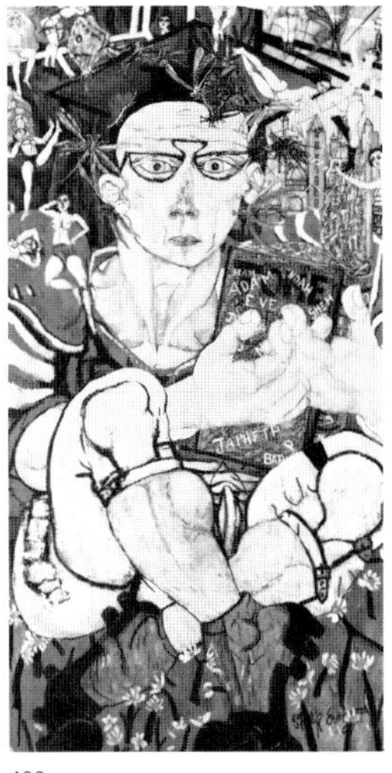
400

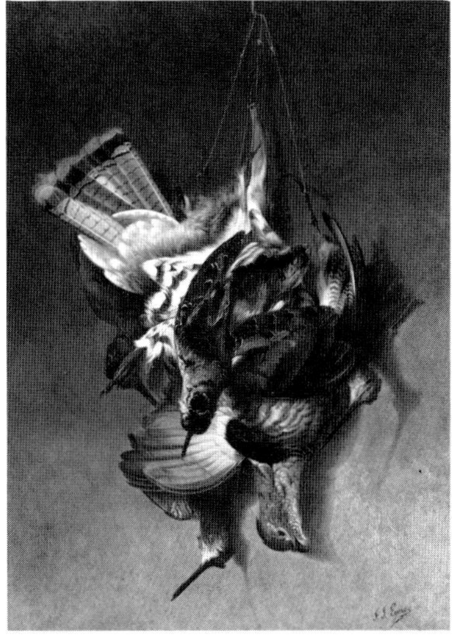
402

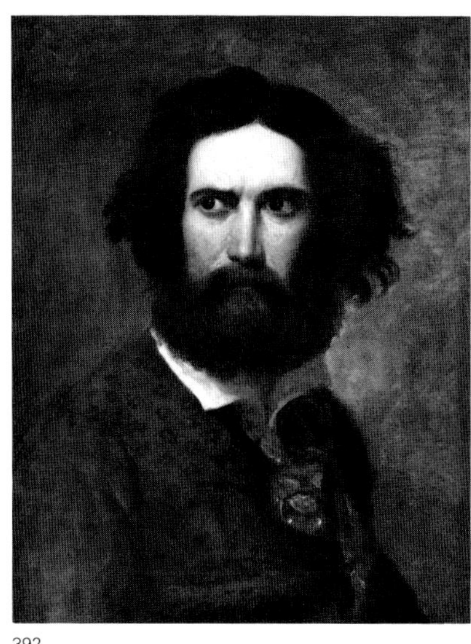
392

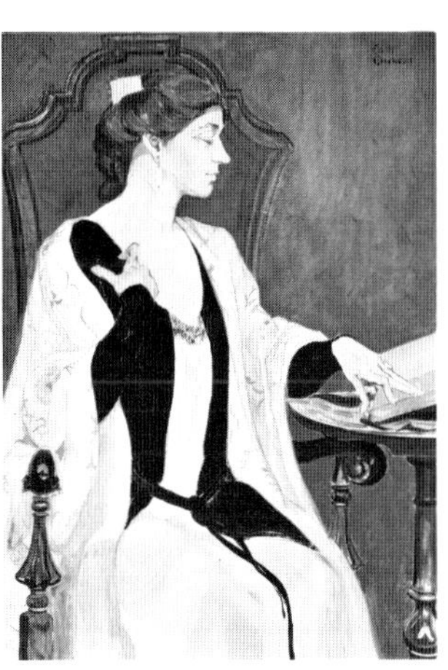
394

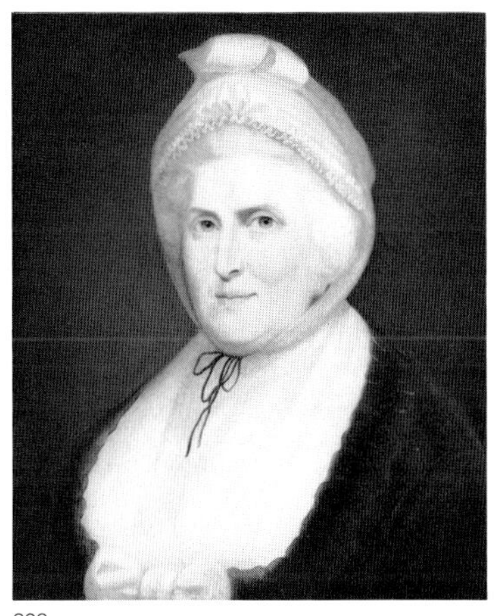
393

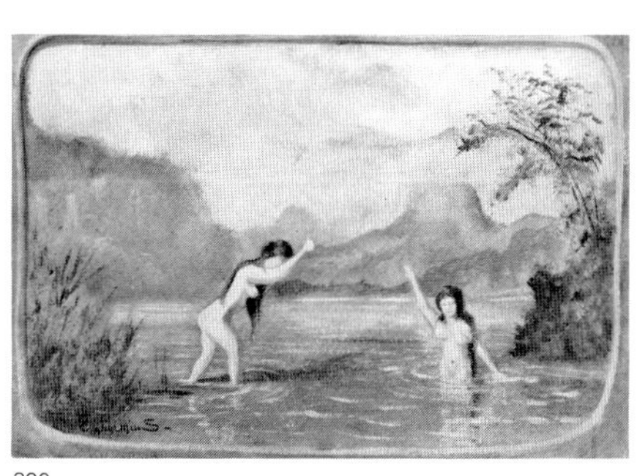
390

John J. Eyers

402 *Game*, by 1868
Oil on canvas
27³⁄₁₆ x 20¹⁄₁₆ in. (69.1 x 51 cm.)
Signed at lower right: J.J. Eyers
Source unknown (ca. 1868), 1944.19

William H. Fairfax (d. by 1840)

403 *Robert Beverley Randolph* (1791–1869), ca. 1835
Oil on canvas
14³⁄₁₆ x 11 in. (36 x 27.9 cm.)
Gift of Mrs. John Frederick Lewis (The John Frederick Lewis Memorial Collection), 1933.10.18

Richard Blossom Farley (1875–1954)

404 *Morning Mists*, 1913
Oil on canvas
25 x 32 in. (63.5 x 81.3 cm.)
Dated and signed at lower left: 1913/Farley
John Lambert Fund, 1913.6

405 *New Jersey Beach*, 1911
Oil on plywood
6³⁄₁₆ x 9³⁄₈ in. (15.7 x 23.8 cm.)
Signed and dated at lower left: RBF [monogram]/1911; inscribed and signed on back: A mon ami/S.S.White 3rd./avec compliments &/Richard Blossom Farley.
Gift of Vera White, 1956.3.1.

406 *Studio Corner*, by 1904
Oil on canvas
19 x 15¹⁵⁄₁₆ in. (48.3 x 40.5 cm.)
Signed at lower left: R B. Farley; signed and inscribed on back: R. B. Farley/1305 Arch St./Phila. Pa.
Gift of Vera White, 1960.18.1

Jerry Farnsworth (1895–1982)

407 *Three Churches*, ca. 1928
Oil on canvas, mounted on cardboard
68¹⁄₄ x 38 in. (173.4 x 96.5 cm.)
Signed at lower right: Jerry Farnsworth
John Lambert Fund, 1929.2

Mrs. Jerry Farnsworth
See Helen Alton Sawyer.

Katherine Levin Farrell (1857–1950)

408 *Monomoy*, ca. 1931
Oil on canvas
22 x 26¹⁄₁₆ in. (55.9 x 66.2 cm.)
Signed at lower right: Katherine L. Farrell
John Lambert Fund, 1932.5

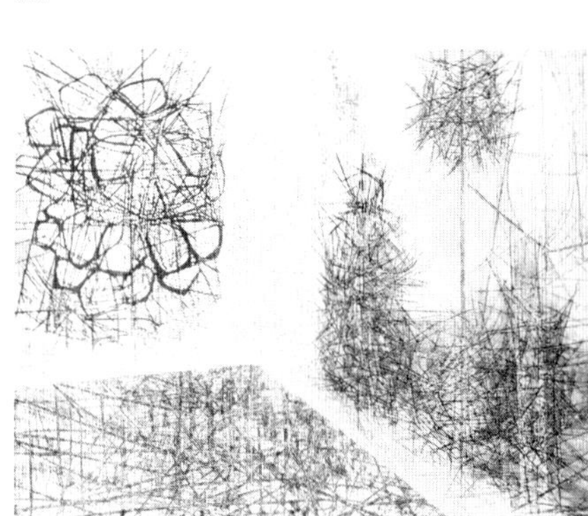
395

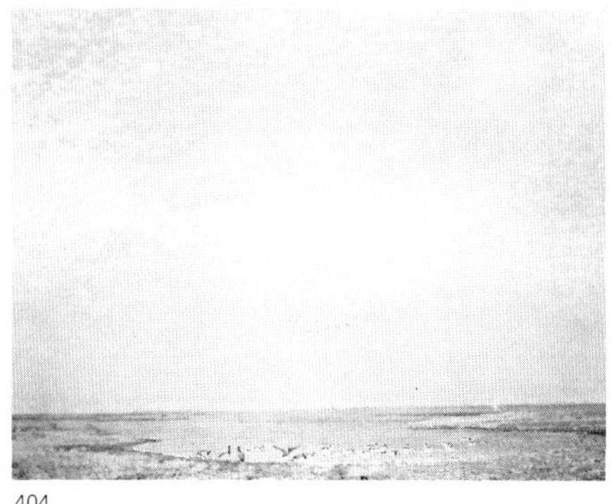
404

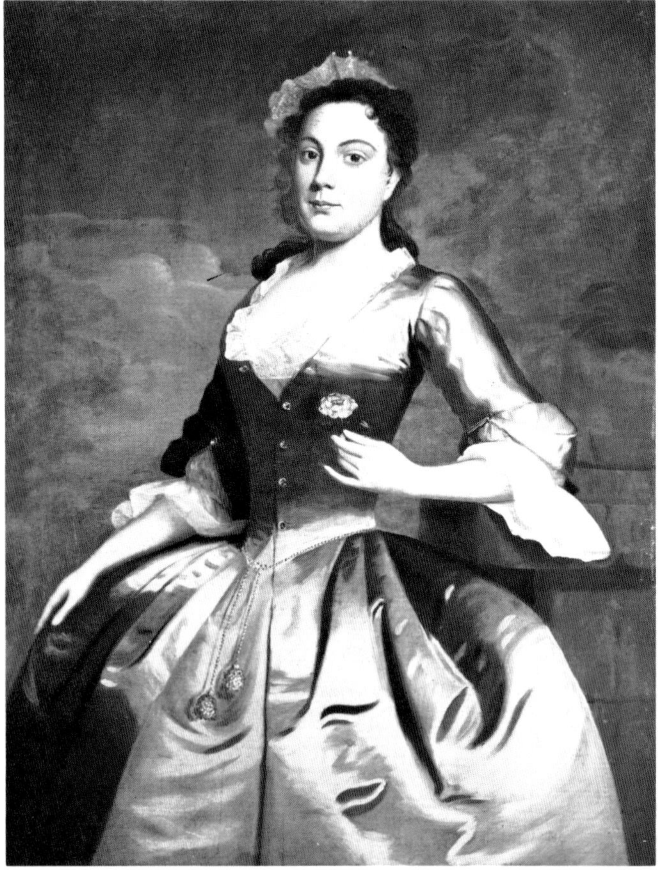

410

Lyonel Feininger (1871–1956)

409 *Possendorf*, 1929
Oil on canvas
30⅝ x 38⅝ in. (77.8 x 98.1 cm.)
Signed and dated at lower right: Feininger/29; signed, dated, and inscribed on back: Lyonel Feininger 1929 "village church in Possendorf['']
Henry D. Gilpin Fund, 1951.5

Robert Feke (ca. 1707–ca. 1751)

410 *Mary McCall* (1725–1799), ca. 1746
Oil on canvas
50¼ x 40¼ in. (127.6 x 102.2 cm.)
Bequest of Helen Ross Scheetz, 1891.3

T. J. Fenimore (1842–1873)

411 *Schuylkill River*
Oil on canvas
12⅜ x 22⅜ in. (31.4 x 56.8 cm.)
Signed at lower left: T.J.Fenimore; inscribed, signed, and dated on back: Schuylkill River./ T.JFenimore./18[68?]
Gift of Mr. and Mrs. J. Welles Henderson, 1976.24.2

Nancy Maybin Ferguson (1872–1967)

412 *Mrs. Smith in Her Rocking Chair Watches the People Pass By*, by 1960
Oil on masonite
35½ x 47½ in. (90.2 x 120.6 cm.)
Signed at lower right: N M F
Bequest of Frank M. Ferguson, 1970.23

413 *On a Saturday Afternoon*, ca. 1915
Oil on canvas
32 x 40 in. (81.3 x 101.6 cm.)
Signed at lower right: N M F; and on back: NANCY M. FERGUSON.
John Lambert Fund, 1916.3

William H. Ferguson (1905–1985)

414 *The Water Towers*, 1928
Oil on canvas
25 x 36¹⁄₁₆ in. (63.5 x 91.6 cm.)
Signed and dated at lower right: William H Ferguson 1928
John Lambert Fund, 1933.4

Michael Fioriglio (1916–)

415 *Springtime Notes*, ca. 1938
Oil on canvas
16⅛ x 20¹⁄₁₆ in. (41 x 51 cm.)
Annotated on back: Mike
John Lambert Fund, 1939.6

Gertrude Fiske (1879–1961)

416 *Sunday Afternoon*, ca. 1925
Oil on canvas
46⅛ x 48¼ in. (117.2 x 122.6 cm.)
Signed at lower left: Gertrude Fiske
Joseph E. Temple Fund, 1926.2

Helen Fleck. *See* Helen Fleck Seyffert.

Arthur L. Flory (1914–1972)

417 *The Weirs*, 1951
Oil on canvas
30 x 35¹⁵⁄₁₆ in. (76.2 x 91.3 cm.)
Signed and dated at lower right: arthur Flory '51
John Lambert Fund, 1953.3

John Fulton Folinsbee (1892–1972)

418 *Dark Hollow*, 1945
Oil on canvas
34⅛ x 50⅛ in. (86.7 x 127.3 cm.)
Signed at lower right: John Folinsbee-
Joseph E. Temple Fund, 1946.5

John Formicola (1941–)

419 *Shimmering Black*, 1969
Acrylic on canvas
14¹⁄₁₆ x 12 in. (35.7 x 30.5 cm.)
Signed and dated on back: formicola/-69-/Aug
Inscribed on masonite key: SHIMMERING/BLACK
Gift of Benjamin D. Bernstein, 1974.7.2

420 *Untitled*, 1970
Acrylic on canvas
54⅛ x 40⅛ in. (137.5 x 101.9 cm.)
Signed, dated, and inscribed on back: formicola/ -70-/Oct./u.Acrylic
Gift of Benjamin D. Bernstein, 1974.7.1

James W. Fosburgh (1910–1978)

421 *Brook Trout*, 1940
Oil on canvas
13⅝ x 20¹⁄₁₆ in. (34.6 x 51 cm.)
Signed and dated at upper left: J.W.F. '40
John Lambert Fund, 1941.4

Josef Foshko (1889–1969)

422 *Newsboy*, ca. 1941
Oil on canvas
28 x 23¹⁄₁₆ in. (71.1 x 58.6 cm.)
Signed at lower right: FOSHKO
John Lambert Fund, 1942.3

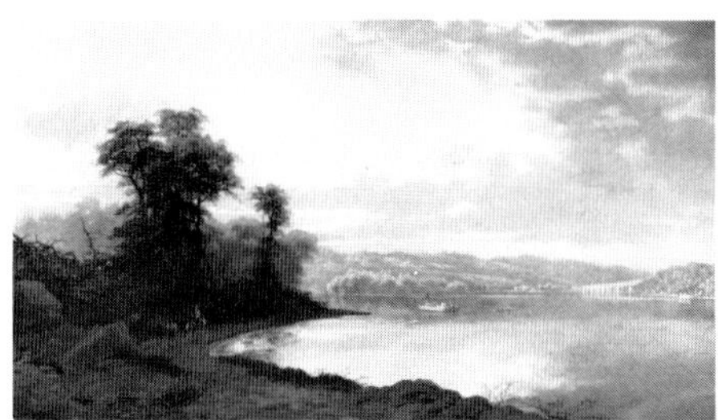

411

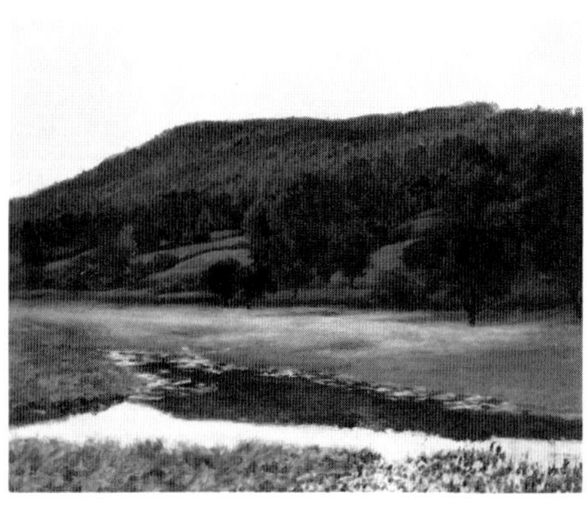

423

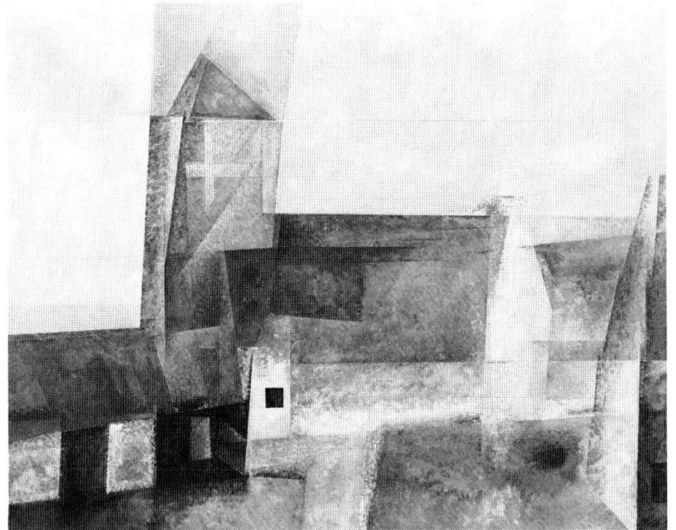
400

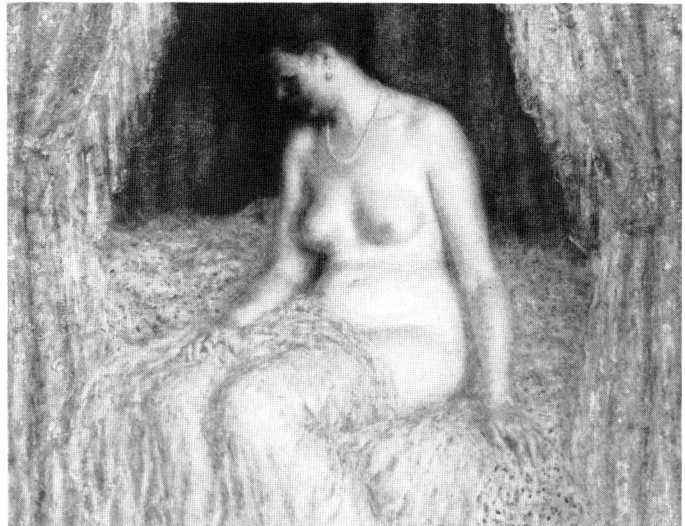
429

Ben Foster (1852–1926)

423 *A Hill: Early Twilight*, ca. 1902
Oil on canvas
30¼ x 36⅛ in. (76.8 x 91.8 cm.)
Joseph E. Temple Fund, 1903.2

John F. Francis (1810–1885)

424 *Jane Aldricks Johnson*, 1839
Oil on canvas
30³⁄₁₆ x 25⅛ in. (76.7 x 63.8 cm.)
Signed and dated on back: Jno F Francis/Pinxit/ Dec 1839
Bequest of Fannie Aldricks Schugert, 1918.14

Attributed to **Oliver S. Frazer** (1808–1864)

425 *George Cadwalader* (1804–1879), probably 1847
Oil on canvas
36³⁄₁₆ x 29¼ in. (91.9 x 74.3 cm.)
Signed and dated on back (before lining): O. S. F. 47
Gift of John Frederick Lewis, 1923.8.2

F. Lyder Fredrickson (b. 1905)

426 *Winter, Long Island City*, ca. 1940
Oil on canvas
24 x 32 in. (61 x 81.3 cm.)
Signed at lower left: LYDER/FREDRICKSON
John Lambert Fund, 1941.5

Maurice Freedman (1904–1984)

427 *Longitude 72–Latitude 42*, 1933
Oil on canvas
21³⁄₁₆ x 25⁷⁄₁₆ in. (53.8 x 64.6 cm.)
Signed and dated at lower right: Maurice Freedman 33
John Lambert Fund, 1934.5

Robert Matthew Freimark (1922–)

428 *Mexican Arena*, 1952
Oil on cardboard
21½ x 43⁹⁄₁₆ in. (54.6 x 110.7 cm.)
Dated and signed at lower left: 1952Freimark; inscribed and dated on back: MEXICAN ARENA-1952
John Lambert Fund, 1953.4

Frederick Carl Frieseke (1874–1939)

429 *Seated Nude*, 1920
Oil on canvas
39½ x 52⅛ in. (100.3 x 132.4 cm.)
Signed and dated at lower left: F.C. Frieseke 1920
Joseph E. Temple Fund, 1937.2

Paul Froelich (1898–1968)

430 *Corn, Wind, and Snow*, 1957
Oil, egg tempera, and charcoal on canvas
38⅛ x 56 in. (96.8 x 142.2 cm.)
Signed at lower left: froelich
John Lambert Fund, 1958.12

431 *Man in Blue*, ca. 1944
Oil on canvas
25 x 20 in. (63.5 x 50.8 cm.)
Signed at lower left: Froelich
John Lambert Fund, 1945.3

Maurice Fromkes (1872–1931)

432 *Gothic Madonna*
Oil on canvas
43⅜ x 37 in. (110.2 x 94 cm.)
Signed and dated at upper right: M. FROMKES/19[?]
Bequest of Eva Halle Fromkes, 1963.3

James Frothingham (1786–1864)

433 *Ann Trusell*
Oil on canvas
33⅜ x 26¹⁵⁄₁₆ in. (84.8 x 68.4 cm.)
Gift of Mrs. Thomas H. Lineaweaver, 1965.5

434 *Unidentified Man* (formerly *Gilbert Stuart*)
Oil on canvas
30⅛ x 24¹⁄₁₆ in. (76.5 x 61.1 cm.)
Gift of John Frederick Lewis, 1921.1

Lily Furedi (b. 1901)

435 *Forlorn*, ca. 1930
Oil on canvas
24 x 20 in. (61 x 50.8 cm.)
Signed at lower left: L Furedi.
John Lambert Fund, 1931.3

William Henry Furness, Jr. (1828–1867)

436 *Ralph Waldo Emerson* (1803–1882), ca. 1867, unfinished
Oil on canvas
45¾ x 36³⁄₁₆ in. (116.2 x 91.9 cm.)
Gift of Horace Howard Furness, 1899.8

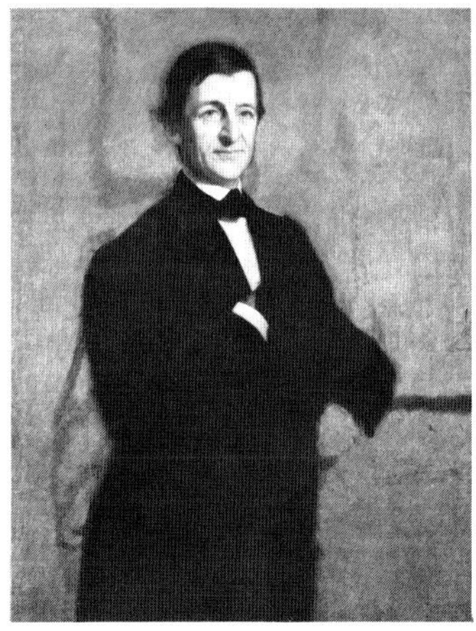
436

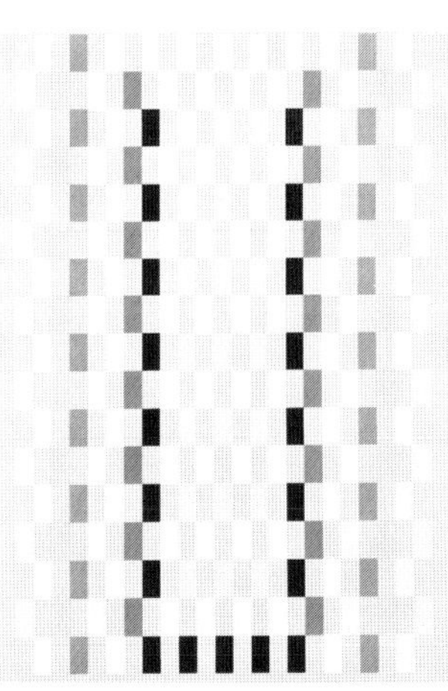
420

Charles Lewis Fussell (1840–1909)

437 *Academy Students Dissecting a Horse* (illustration for William C. Brownell, "The Art Schools of Philadelphia," *Scribner's Monthly* 18, Sept. 1879, pp.737-50), ca. 1879
Oil on cardboard (grisaille)
7⅜ x 10¼ in. (18.7 x 26 cm.)
Gift of the artist, 1879.4

438 *Landscape*, 1897
Oil on canvas
36³⁄₁₆ x 29⅛ in. (91.9 x 74 cm.)
Signed and dated at lower left: C.L.FUSSELL/1897.
Gift of Mrs. Morris H. Fussell, 1973.13

439 *Landscape*, 1906
Oil on canvas
17¼ x 14 in. (43.8 x 35.6 cm.)
Signed and dated at lower right: C. L. Fussell/ 1906
Gift of Mrs. Morris H. Fussell, 1976.11.2

All but one of the following fifty-nine oil sketches by Charles Lewis Fussell were given to the Pennsylvania Academy as a group in 1973:

440 *Beached Boat and Lobster Traps*, 1893
Oil on canvas
12¹⁄₁₆ x 17¹⁵⁄₁₆ in. (30.6 x 45.6 cm.)
Signed and dated at lower left: C.L. FUSSELL/1893
Gift of the T. Carrick Jordan Fund through Bertram L. O'Neill, Henry S. McNeil, and Mrs. Edward B. Leisenring, Jr., 1973.12.1

441 *Beached Boat, Evening*
Oil on canvas
10⅛ x 6⅞ in. (25.7 x 17.5 cm.)
Gift of the T. Carrick Jordan Fund through Bertram L. O'Neill, Henry S. McNeil, and Mrs. Edward B. Leisenring, Jr., 1973.12.5

442 *Canarsie, Long Island*, probably 1882
Oil on canvas
10⅞ x 8⅜ in. (27.6 x 21.3 cm.)
Signed and inscribed at lower left: C.L. FUSSELL/ CANARSIE
Gift of the T. Carrick Jordan Fund through Bertram L. O'Neill, Henry S. McNeil, and Mrs. Edward B. Leisenring, Jr., 1973.12.17

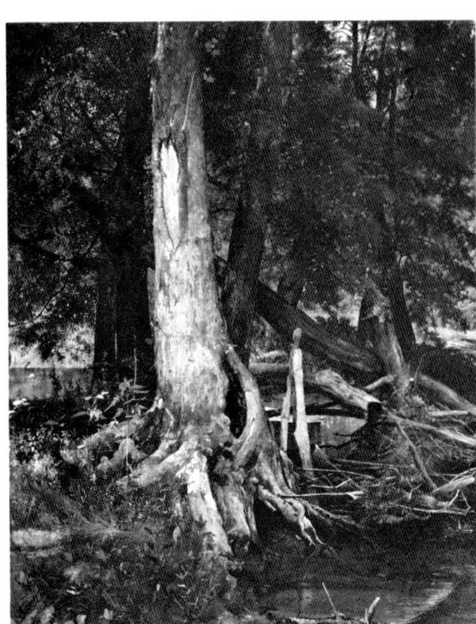
438

443 *Collins*, ca. 1900
Oil on canvas, mounted on cardboard
10⁹⁄₁₆ x 10¹⁵⁄₁₆ in. (26.8 x 27.8 cm.)
Signed and inscribed at lower left: C.L. FUSSELL/ COLLINS
Gift of the T. Carrick Jordan Fund through Bertram L. O'Neill, Henry S. McNeil, and Mrs. Edward B. Leisenring, Jr., 1973.12.56

444 *Coney Island*, probably 1882
Oil on canvas
10⅛ x 17¹³⁄₁₆ in. (25.7 x 45.2 cm.)
Gift of the T. Carrick Jordan Fund through Bertram L. O'Neill, Henry S. McNeil, and Mrs. Edward B. Leisenring, Jr., 1973.12.2

445 *Crow Hill*
Oil on canvas
6 x 9⁷⁄₁₆ in. (15.2 x 24 cm.)
Signed and inscribed at lower right: C L FUSSELL/ CROWHILL
Gift of the T. Carrick Jordan Fund through Bertram L. O'Neill, Henry S. McNeil, and Mrs. Edward B. Leisenring, Jr., 1973.12.29

446 *Crow Hill*
Oil on canvas
7⁹⁄₁₆ x 9⁵⁄₁₆ in. (19.1 x 23.7 cm.)
Signed and inscribed at lower left: C.L. FUSSELL/ CROWHILL
Gift of the T. Carrick Jordan Fund through Bertram L. O'Neill, Henry S. McNeil, and Mrs. Edward B. Leisenring, Jr., 1973.12.30

447 *Crow Hill*
Oil on canvas
3¹⁵⁄₁₆ x 7⁷⁄₁₆ in. (10 x 18.9 cm.)
Signed and inscribed at lower left: FUSSELL/ CROWHILL
Gift of the T. Carrick Jordan Fund through Bertram L. O'Neill, Henry S. McNeil, and Mrs. Edward B. Leisenring, Jr., 1973.12.31

448 *Crow Hill*
Oil on canvas
4⁷⁄₁₆ x 8⁹⁄₁₆ in. (11.3 x 21.8 cm.)
Signed and inscribed at lower left: C.L. FUSSELL/ CROWHILL
Gift of the T. Carrick Jordan Fund through Bertram L. O'Neill, Henry S. McNeil, and Mrs. Edward B. Leisenring, Jr., 1973.12.32

449 *Crow Hill*
Oil on canvas
4⅜ x 8¹⁄₁₆ in. (11.1 x 20.5 cm.)
Signed and inscribed at lower left: C.L.FUSSELL/ CROWHILL
Gift of the T. Carrick Jordan Fund through Bertram L. O'Neill, Henry S. McNeil, and Mrs. Edward B. Leisenring, Jr., 1973.12.44

450 *Crow Hill*
Oil on canvas
8⅝ x 11⅞ in. (21.9 x 30.2 cm.)
Signed and inscribed at lower right: C.L.FUSSELL/ CROWHILL
Gift of the T. Carrick Jordan Fund through Bertram L. O'Neill, Henry S. McNeil, and Mrs. Edward B. Leisenring, Jr., 1973.12.45

451 *East Hampton*, probably 1882
Oil on canvas
8⅞ x 12 in. (22.5 x 30.5 cm.)
Signed and inscribed at lower right: C. L. FUSSELL/ EASTHAMPTON
Gift of the T. Carrick Jordan Fund through Bertram L. O'Neill, Henry S. McNeil, and Mrs. Edward B. Leisenring, Jr., 1973.12.3

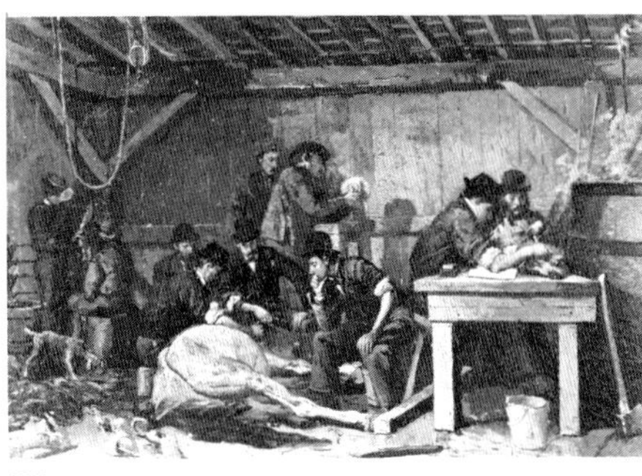
437

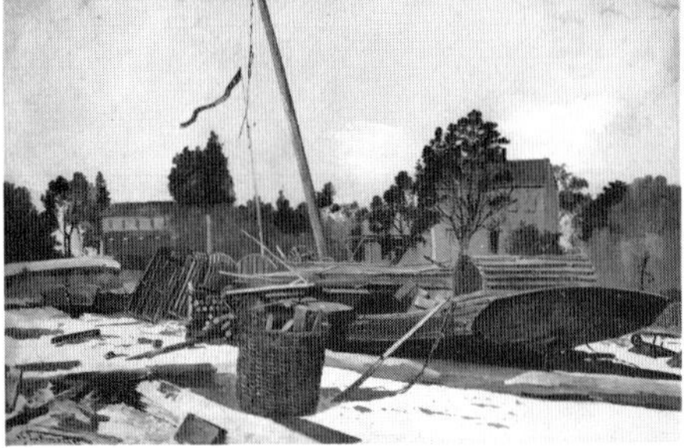
440

452 *East Hampton*, probably 1882
Oil on canvas
11⅞ x 9 in. (30.2 x 22.9 cm.)
Signed and inscribed at lower left: FUSSELL/ EASTHAMPTON
Gift of the T. Carrick Jordan Fund through Bertram L. O'Neill, Henry S. McNeil, and Mrs. Edward B. Leisenring, Jr., 1973.12.28

453 *Evening Landscape*, 1880s
Oil on composition board (grisaille)
6 x 7 in. (15.2 x 17.8 cm.)
Gift of the T. Carrick Jordan Fund through Bertram L. O'Neill, Henry S. McNeil, and Mrs. Edward B. Leisenring, Jr., 1973.12.6

454 *Flatbush*
Oil on canvas
6⁹⁄₁₆ x 9¼ in. (16.7 x 23.5 cm.)
Signed at lower left: C.L. FUSSELL; inscribed on back: Flatbush
Gift of the T. Carrick Jordan Fund through Bertram L. O'Neill, Henry S. McNeil, and Mrs. Edward B. Leisenring, Jr., 1973.12.9

455 *Flatbush*
Oil on canvas
7¹⁵⁄₁₆ x 11⅜ in. (20.1 x 28.9 cm.)
Signed and inscribed at lower left: C. L. FUSSELL/ FLATBUSH
Gift of the T. Carrick Jordan Fund through Bertram L. O'Neill, Henry S. McNeil, and Mrs. Edward B. Leisenring, Jr., 1973.12.25

456 *Flatbush*
Oil on canvas
11⅜ x 7½ in. (28.9 x 19.1 cm.)
Signed and inscribed at lower left: C.L. FUSSELL/ FLATBUSH
Gift of the T. Carrick Jordan Fund through Bertram L. O'Neill, Henry S. McNeil, and Mrs. Edward B. Leisenring, Jr., 1973.12.26

457 *Flatbush*
Oil on canvas
7½ x 10¹³⁄₁₆ in. (19.1 x 27.5 cm.)

Signed and inscribed at lower left: C.L.FUSSELL/ FLATBUSH
Gift of the T. Carrick Jordan Fund through Bertram L. O'Neill, Henry S. McNeil, and Mrs. Edward B. Leisenring, Jr., 1973.12.27

458 *Flatbush*
Oil on canvas
8 1/16 x 11 1/4 in. (20.5 x 28.6 cm.)
Signed and inscribed at lower right: C.L.FUSSELL/ FLATBUSH
Gift of Mrs. Morris H. Fussell, 1976.11.1

459 *Fort Hamilton*, ca. 1890
Oil on canvas
8 15/16 x 12 3/8 in. (22.7 x 31.4 cm.)
Inscribed at lower right: FT HAMILTON
Gift of the T. Carrick Jordan Fund through Bertram L. O'Neill, Henry S. McNeil, and Mrs. Edward B. Leisenring, Jr., 1973.12.40

460 *Fort Hamilton*, ca. 1890
Oil on canvas
4 11/16 x 9 in. (11.9 x 22.9 cm.)
Signed and inscribed at lower left: C.L.FUSSELL/ FT HAMILTON
Gift of the T. Carrick Jordan Fund through Bertram L. O'Neill, Henry S. McNeil, and Mrs. Edward B. Leisenring, Jr., 1973.12.41

461 *Fort Hamilton*, ca. 1890
Oil on canvas
5 5/8 x 8 3/4 in. (14.3 x 22.2 cm.)
Signed and inscribed at lower left: C.L.FUSSELL/ FT HAMILTON
Gift of the T. Carrick Jordan Fund through Bertram L. O'Neill, Henry S. McNeil, and Mrs. Edward B. Leisenring, Jr., 1973.12.42

462 *Landscape*, 1880s
Oil on composition board (grisaille)
12 5/16 x 6 1/16 in. (31.3 x 15.4 cm.)
Gift of the T. Carrick Jordan Fund through Bertram L. O'Neill, Henry S. McNeil, and Mrs. Edward B. Leisenring, Jr., 1973.12.33

463 *Landscape*, ca. 1900
Oil on canvas
9 9/16 x 8 7/16 in. (24.3 x 21.4 cm.)
Gift of the T. Carrick Jordan Fund through Bertram L. O'Neill, Henry S. McNeil, and Mrs. Edward B. Leisenring, Jr., 1973.12.8

464 *Landscape*, ca. 1900
Oil on canvas
9 5/8 x 12 in. (24.4 x 30.5 cm.)
Gift of the T. Carrick Jordan Fund through Bertram L. O'Neill, Henry S. McNeil, and Mrs. Edward B. Leisenring, Jr., 1973.12.10

465 *Landscape*, ca. 1900
Oil on canvas
19 1/2 x 12 in. (49.5 x 30.5 cm.)
Gift of the T. Carrick Jordan Fund through Bertram L. O'Neill, Henry S. McNeil, and Mrs. Edward B. Leisenring, Jr., 1973.12.12

466 *Landscape*, ca. 1900
Oil on canvas
9 5/16 x 12 in. (23.7 x 30.5 cm.)
Gift of the T. Carrick Jordan Fund through Bertram L. O'Neill, Henry S. McNeil, and Mrs. Edward B. Leisenring, Jr., 1973.12.48

467 *Landscape*, ca. 1900
Oil on canvas
8 1/2 x 12 9/16 in. (21.6 x 31.9 cm.)
Gift of the T. Carrick Jordan Fund through Bertram L. O'Neill, Henry S. McNeil, and Mrs. Edward B. Leisenring, Jr., 1973.12.49

468 *Landscape*, ca. 1900
Oil on canvas
9 x 12 1/8 in. (22.9 x 30.8 cm.)
Gift of the T. Carrick Jordan Fund through Bertram L. O'Neill, Henry S. McNeil, and Mrs. Edward B. Leisenring, Jr., 1973.12.51

469 *Landscape*, ca. 1900
Oil on canvas
10 x 13 in. (25.4 x 33 cm.)
Gift of the T. Carrick Jordan Fund through Bertram L. O'Neill, Henry S. McNeil, and Mrs. Edward B. Leisenring, Jr., 1973.12.52

470 *Landscape*
Oil on canvas
12 3/8 x 8 13/16 in. (31.4 x 22.4 cm.)
Gift of the T. Carrick Jordan Fund through Bertram L. O'Neill, Henry S. McNeil, and Mrs. Edward B. Leisenring, Jr., 1973.12.11

471 *Landscape*
Oil on canvas
4 1/2 x 9 1/8 in. (11.4 x 23.2 cm.)
Gift of the T. Carrick Jordan Fund through Bertram L. O'Neill, Henry S. McNeil, and Mrs. Edward B. Leisenring, Jr., 1973.12.13

472 *Landscape*
Oil on canvas
6 5/16 x 9 in. (16 x 22.9 cm.)
Gift of the T. Carrick Jordan Fund through Bertram L. O'Neill, Henry S. McNeil, and Mrs. Edward B. Leisenring, Jr., 1973.12.53

473 *Landscape with Barn and Pond*, ca. 1880
Oil on canvas
9 1/4 x 12 15/16 in. (23.5 x 32.9 cm.)
Gift of the T. Carrick Jordan Fund through Bertram L. O'Neill, Henry S. McNeil, and Mrs. Edward B. Leisenring, Jr., 1973.12.55

474 *Landscape with Children on Bridge*
Oil on canvas
11 1/8 x 8 5/8 in. (28.3 x 21.9 cm.)
Gift of the T. Carrick Jordan Fund through Bertram L. O'Neill, Henry S. McNeil, and Mrs. Edward B. Leisenring, Jr., 1973.12.43

475 *Landscape with Cows*, ca. 1900
Oil on canvas
12 7/8 x 9 7/8 in. (32.7 x 25.1 cm.)
Gift of the T. Carrick Jordan Fund through Bertram L. O'Neill, Henry S. McNeil, and Mrs. Edward B. Leisenring, Jr., 1973.12.47

476 *Landscape with Cows*, ca. 1900
Oil on canvas
8 x 12 in. (20.3 x 30.5 cm.)
Gift of the T. Carrick Jordan Fund through Bertram L. O'Neill, Henry S. McNeil, and Mrs. Edward B. Leisenring, Jr., 1973.12.50

477 *Landscape with Cows and Barn*, ca. 1900
Oil on canvas
11 1/2 x 8 1/2 in. (29.2 x 21.6 cm.)
Gift of the T. Carrick Jordan Fund through Bertram L. O'Neill, Henry S. McNeil, and Mrs. Edward B. Leisenring, Jr., 1973.12.46

478 *Landscape with Cows and Fence*, ca. 1900
Oil on canvas
5 1/4 x 9 in. (13.3 x 22.9 cm.)
Gift of the T. Carrick Jordan Fund through Bertram L. O'Neill, Henry S. McNeil, and Mrs. Edward B. Leisenring, Jr., 1973.12.7

479 *Landscape with Two Bathers*, ca. 1900
Oil on canvas
7 7/16 x 9 in. (18.9 x 22.9 cm.)
Gift of the T. Carrick Jordan Fund through Bertram L. O'Neill, Henry S. McNeil, and Mrs. Edward B. Leisenring, Jr., 1973.12.14

480 *Newtown*
Oil on canvas
3 1/8 x 4 7/16 in. (7.9 x 11.3 cm.)
Signed and inscribed at lower left: FUSSELL/ NEWTOWN
Gift of the T. Carrick Jordan Fund through

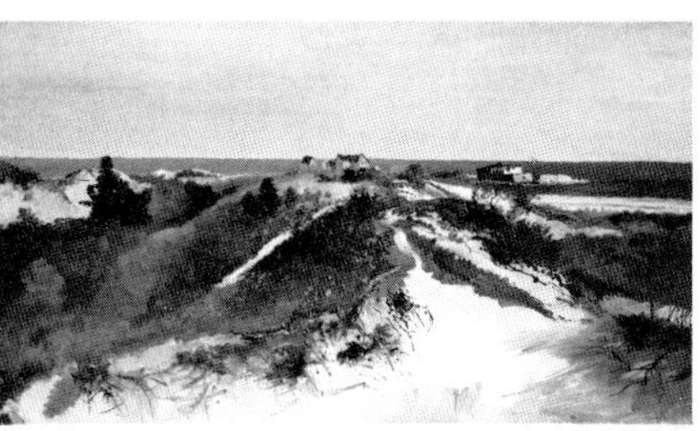
444

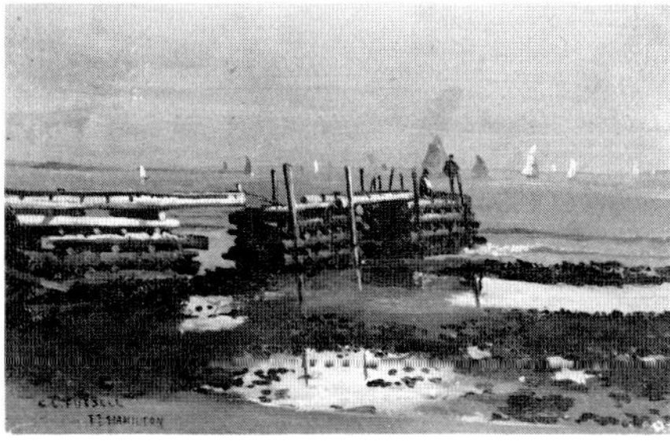
461

441

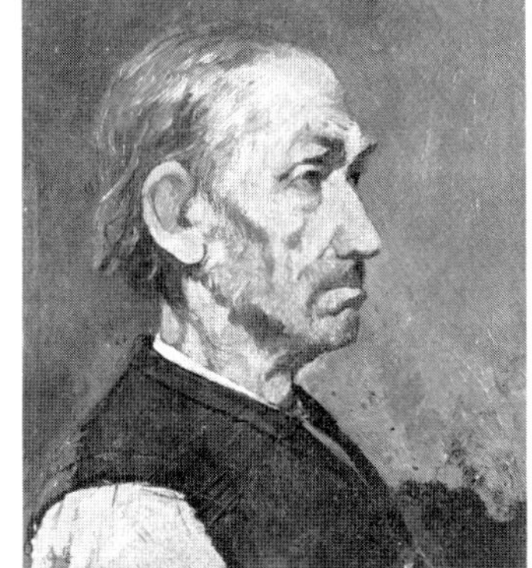
443

Bertram L. O'Neill, Henry S. McNeil, and Mrs. Edward B. Leisenring, Jr., 1973.12.36

481 *Newtown*
Oil on canvas
5 11/16 x 9 3/8 in. (14.4 x 23.8 cm.)
Signed and inscribed at lower left:
C.L.FUSSELL/NEWTOWN
Gift of the T. Carrick Jordan Fund through Bertram L. O'Neill, Henry S. McNeil, and Mrs. Edward B. Leisenring, Jr., 1973.12.37

482 *Newtown Creek*
Oil on canvas
5 7/16 x 8 5/8 in. (13.8 x 21.9 cm.)
Signed and inscribed at lower left:
C.L.FUSSELL/NEWTOWN CRK.
Gift of the T. Carrick Jordan Fund through Bertram L. O'Neill, Henry S. McNeil, and Mrs. Edward B. Leisenring, Jr., 1973.12.38

483 *Newtown Creek*
Oil on canvas
4 15/16 x 8 5/8 in. (12.5 x 21.9 cm.)
Signed and inscribed at lower left:
CL. FUSSELL/NEWTOWN CREEK
Gift of the T. Carrick Jordan Fund through Bertram L. O'Neill, Henry S. McNeil, and Mrs. Edward B. Leisenring, Jr., 1973.12.39

484 *North Beach*
Oil on canvas
7 3/16 x 9 3/8 in. (18.3 x 23.8 cm.)
Signed and inscribed at lower left:
C.L.FUSSELL/NORTH BEACH
Gift of the T. Carrick Jordan Fund through Bertram L. O'Neill, Henry S. McNeil, and Mrs. Edward B. Leisenring, Jr., 1973.12.19

485 *Old Mill*
Oil on canvas
8 7/8 x 6 3/4 in. (22.5 x 17.1 cm.)
Signed and inscribed at lower right:
C.L. FUSSELL/OLD MILL
Gift of the T. Carrick Jordan Fund through Bertram L. O'Neill, Henry S. McNeil and Mrs. Edward B. Leisenring, Jr., 1973.12.34

486 *Old Mill*
Oil on canvas
5 3/4 x 9 13/16 in. (14.6 x 24.9 cm.)
Signed and inscribed at lower left:
C. L. FUSSELL/OLD MILL
Gift of the T. Carrick Jordan Fund through Bertram L. O'Neill, Henry S. McNeil, and Mrs. Edward B. Leisenring, Jr., 1973.12.35

487 *Rockaway, Long Island*, probably 1891
Oil on canvas
11 11/16 x 8 13/16 in. (29.7 x 22.4 cm.)
Signed and inscribed at lower left:
FUSSELL/ROCKAWAY
Gift of the T. Carrick Jordan Fund through Bertram L. O'Neill, Henry S. McNeil, and Mrs. Edward B. Leisenring, Jr., 1973.12.21

488 *Rockaway, Long Island*, probably 1891
Oil on canvas
5 13/16 x 9 3/8 in. (14.8 x 23.8 cm.)
Signed and inscribed at lower right: FUSSELL/ROCKAWAY
Gift of the T. Carrick Jordan Fund through Bertram L. O'Neill, Henry S. McNeil, and Mrs. Edward B. Leisenring, Jr., 1973.12.22

489 *Rockaway, Long Island*, 1891
Oil on canvas
7 1/4 x 9 11/16 in. (18.4 x 24.6 cm.)
Signed, dated, and inscribed at lower left:
C.L.FUSSELL/1891 ROCKAWAY
Gift of the T. Carrick Jordan Fund through Bertram L. O'Neill, Henry S. McNeil, and Mrs. Edward B. Leisenring, Jr., 1973.12.23

490 *Rockaway, Long Island*, 1891
Oil on canvas
9 x 5 15/16 in. (22.9 x 15.1 cm.)
Signed and inscribed at lower left:
C.L.FUSSELL/ROCKAWAY
Gift of the T. Carrick Jordan Fund through Bertram L. O'Neill, Henry S. McNeil, and Mrs. Edward B. Leisenring, Jr., 1973.12.24

491 *Sea Cliff, Long Island*, probably 1882
Oil on canvas
8 3/4 x 11 7/16 in. (22.2 x 29.1 cm.)
Signed and inscribed at lower left:
C.L.FUSSELL/SEA CLIFF
Gift of the T. Carrick Jordan Fund through Bertram L. O'Neill, Henry S. McNeil, and Mrs. Edward B. Leisenring, Jr., 1973.12.16

492 *Sea Cliff, Long Island*, probably 1882
Oil on composition board (grisaille)
6 x 12 in. (15.2 x 30.5 cm.)
Inscribed on back: Sea Cliff, L.I.
Gift of the T. Carrick Jordan Fund through Bertram L. O'Neill, Henry S. McNeil, and Mrs. Edward B. Leisenring, Jr., 1973.12.57

493 *Seascape*, ca. 1890
Oil on canvas
6 1/4 x 9 in. (15.9 x 22.9 cm.)
Gift of the T. Carrick Jordan Fund through Bertram L. O'Neill, Henry S. McNeil, and Mrs. Edward B. Leisenring, Jr., 1973.12.54

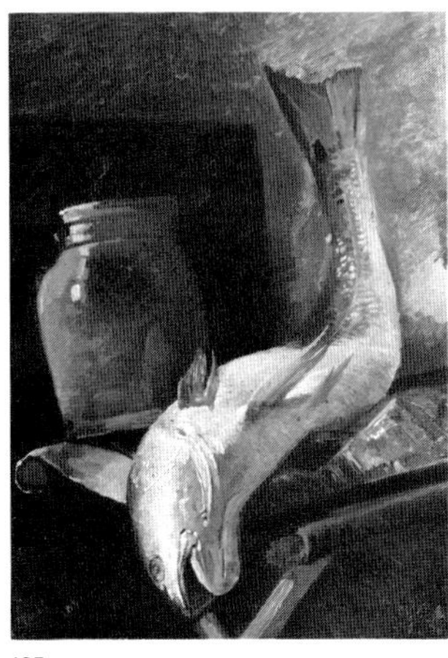
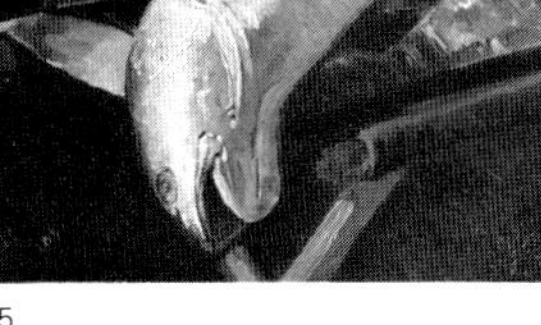
495

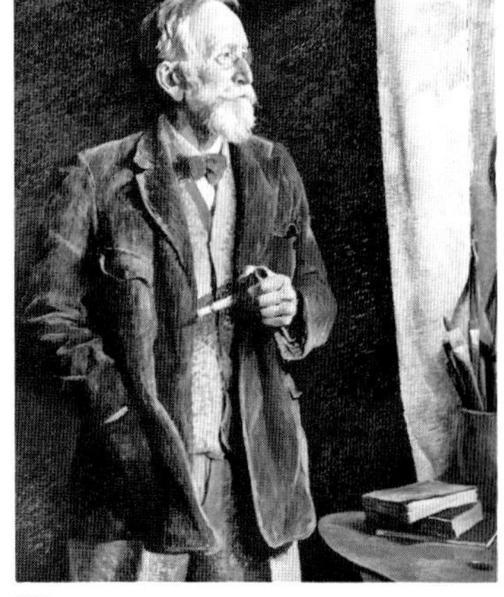
503

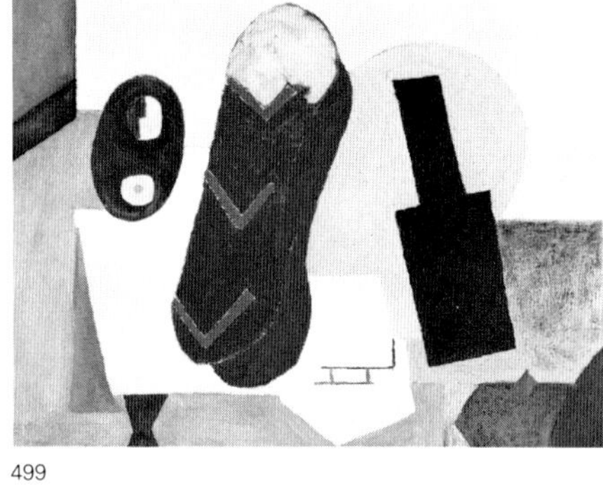
499

494 *Sheepshead Bay*, ca. 1890
Oil on canvas
4 15/16 x 8 11/16 in. (12.5 x 22.1 cm.)
Signed and inscribed at lower left:
C.L.FUSSELL/SHEEPSHEAD BAY
Gift of the T. Carrick Jordan Fund through Bertram L. O'Neill, Henry S. McNeil, and Mrs. Edward B. Leisenring, Jr., 1973.12.20

495 *Still Life: Fish*, 1891
Oil on canvas
17 7/8 x 12 15/16 in. (45.4 x 32.9 cm.)
Signed and dated at lower left: FUSSELL/1891
Gift of the T. Carrick Jordan Fund through Bertram L. O'Neill, Henry S. McNeil, and Mrs. Edward B. Leisenring, Jr., 1973.12.4

496 *Tomb of William Cullen Bryant, Roslyn, Long Island*
Oil on canvas
12 1/16 x 8 7/16 in. (30.6 x 21.4 cm.)
Signed and inscribed at lower left:
C L FUSSELL/TOMB OF Wm CULLEN BRYANT/ROSLYN
Gift of the T. Carrick Jordan Fund through Bertram L. O'Neill, Henry S. McNeil, and Mrs. Edward B. Leisenring, Jr., 1973.12.18

497 *Tree Study*, ca. 1900
Oil on canvas
8 7/8 x 7 1/8 in. (22.5 x 18.1 cm.)
Gift of the T. Carrick Jordan Fund through Bertram L. O'Neill, Henry S. McNeil, and Mrs. Edward B. Leisenring, Jr., 1973.12.15

498 *Unidentified Man*, 1879
Oil on canvas, mounted on primed artist's board
Canvas: 8 1/8 x 6 3/8 in. (20.6 x 16.2 cm.); board: 8 1/2 x 6 1/2 in. (21.6 x 16.5 cm.)
Signed and dated at lower right: CL/FUSSELL/1879
Gift of the T. Carrick Jordan Fund through Bertram L. O'Neill, Henry S. McNeil, and Mrs. Edward B. Leisenring, Jr., 1973.12.58

Albert Eugene Gallatin (1881–1952)

499 *Untitled*, 1936
Oil on canvas
10 x 12 in. (25.4 x 30.5 cm.)
Signed and dated on back: Gallatin May 1936
Anonymous gift, 1986.19

Roy C. Gamble (1887–1972)

500 *The Old Courtyard*, ca. 1915
Oil on canvas
13 x 17 in. (33 x 43.2 cm.)
John Lambert Fund, 1916.4

Daniel Garber (1880–1958)

501 *The Aged Sycamore*, 1902
Oil on canvas
$41\frac{3}{16} \times 30\frac{3}{16}$ in. (104.6 x 76.7 cm.)
Signed at lower right: DANIEL GARBER
Gift of Arthur Block, 1945.21

502 *Battersea Bridge*, 1905
Oil on cardboard
$9\frac{11}{16} \times 13$ in. (24.6 x 33 cm.)
Annotated on torn label on back: [B]ATTERSEA BRIDGE. NEW./NO 136 IN THE RECORD/[P]AINTED SEPTEMBER 1905/SIZE 9 1/2 x 13
Gift of Vera White, 1956.3.2

503 *William Langson Lathrop* (1859–1938), 1935
Oil on canvas
$50 \times 41\frac{7}{8}$ in. (127 x 106.3 cm.)
Signed at upper right: Daniel Garber
Joseph E. Temple Fund, 1936.5

504 *Lowry's Hill*, 1922
Oil on canvas
50 x 61 in. (127 x 154.9 cm.)
Gift of the Locust Club, Philadelphia, 1955.1.1

505 *Mother and Son* (the artist's wife, Mary "May" Garber, 1876–1968, and John Garber, 1910–), 1933
Oil on canvas
$80\frac{1}{8} \times 70\frac{1}{4}$ in. (203.5 x 178.4 cm.)
Signed at lower left: Daniel Garber
Gift of the artist, 1953.20

506 *Night Life*; on back, *Landscape*, ca. 1900
Oil on canvas
$29\frac{15}{16} \times 17$ in. (76 x 43.2 cm.)
Signed and inscribed on back: DANIEL GARBER/NIGHT LIFE
Source unknown, 1945.23

507 *George Washington Norris*, 1930s
Oil on canvas
$30\frac{1}{2} \times 25$ in. (77.5 x 63.5 cm.)
Signed at upper right: Daniel Garber
Gift of William Jordan, 1979.11

508 *Quarry*, 1917
Oil on canvas
50 x 60 in. (127 x 152.4 cm.)
Signed at lower right: DANIEL GARBER
Joseph E. Temple Fund, 1918.3

509 *Reading Room*, 1922
Oil on composition board
18 x 20 in. (45.7 x 50.8 cm.)
Signed at lower right: Daniel Garber; inscribed and signed on back: Reading Room/by/Daniel Garber/RECORD BOOK PAGE 25 LINE 7
Gift of John Franklin Garber and Mrs. Tanis Page, 1974.30.2

510 *Saint James's Park, London*, 1905
Oil on canvas
$15\frac{1}{2} \times 11\frac{15}{16}$ in. (39.4 x 30.3 cm.)
Signed at lower left: DANIEL GARBER
Gift of Vera White, 1960.18.2

505

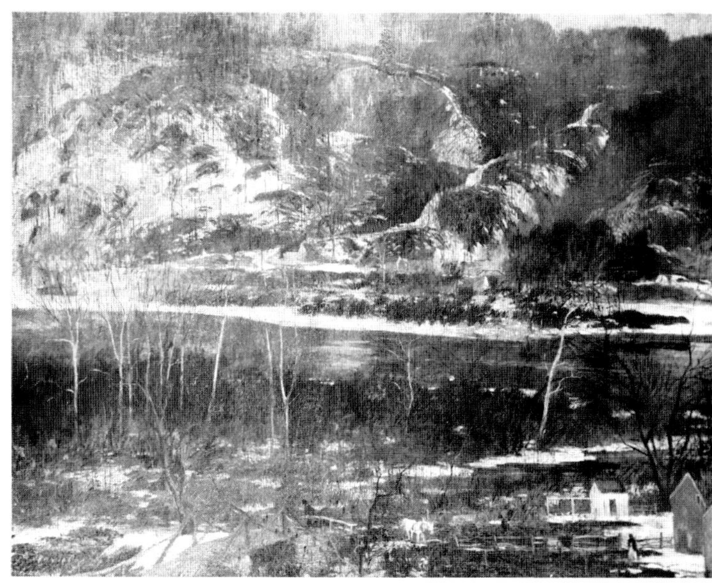

504

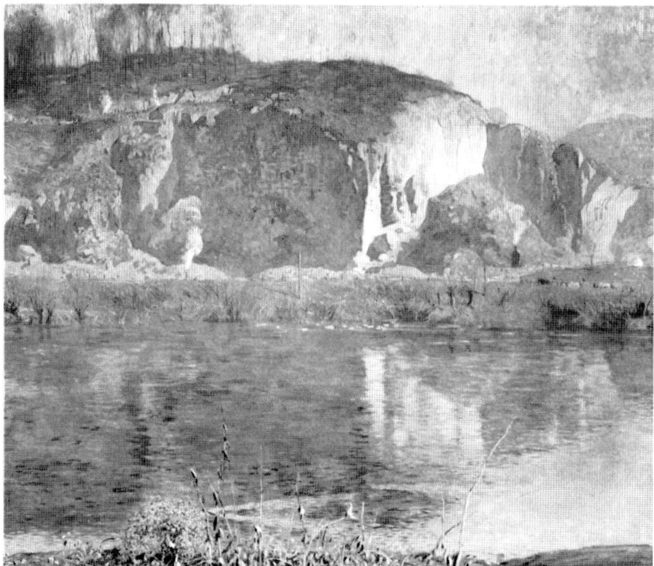

508

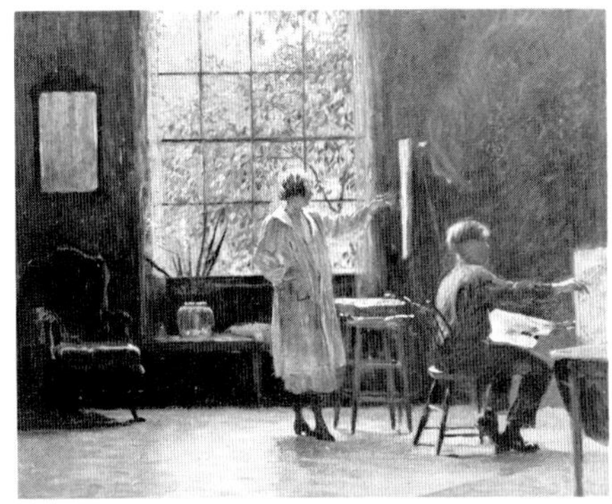

511

511 *Students of Painting*, 1923
Oil on composition board
18 x $21\frac{15}{16}$ in. (45.7 x 55.7 cm.)
Signed at lower left: Daniel Garber;
inscribed and signed on back: Students of Painting/by/Daniel Garber
Gift of John Franklin Garber and Mrs. Tanis Page, 1974.30.1

512 *Sun in Summer* (formerly *Old Elms*), 1919
Oil on canvas
$52\frac{1}{4}$ x 56 in. (132.7 x 142.2 cm.)
Signed at lower left: DANIEL GARBER
Annotated on stretcher label: Sun in Summer/by/Daniel Garber
Gift of the artist, 1945.14.2

Charles S. Garner, Jr. (1890–1933)

513 *Old Garden*, ca. 1922
Oil on canvas
$25\frac{5}{8}$ x $31\frac{15}{16}$ in. (65.1 x 81.1 cm.)
Signed at lower right: GA[RNER]
Annotated on stretcher: CHAS S GARNER
John Lambert Fund, 1923.4

Priscilla Longshore Garrett (1907–)

514 *Quartet*, 1942
Oil on canvas
$24\frac{3}{16}$ x $18\frac{1}{8}$ in. (61.4 x 46 cm.)
Signed and dated at lower left: Priscilla Longshore Garrett Nov 1942
Gift of Helen Morgan Brooks, 1986.24

515 *Three Old Trees*, ca. 1933
Oil on canvas
$30\frac{1}{16}$ x 26 in. (76.4 x 66 cm.)
Signed at lower left: Priscilla Longshore Garret[t]
John Lambert Fund, 1934.6

Lee Gatch (1902–1968)

516 *White Horse*, ca. 1943
Oil on canvas
$17\frac{3}{4}$ x 32 in. (45.1 x 81.3 cm.)
Signed at lower right: GATCH
John Lambert Fund, 1944.1

Thomas Gaughan (1923–)

517 *Fruit on Table*, 1953
Oil on canvas
$8\frac{1}{8}$ x $14\frac{1}{16}$ in. (20.6 x 35.7 cm.)
Signed and dated at lower right: Gaughan53
Gift of James P. and Ruth Marshall Magill, 1957.15.9

518 *Manayunk*, 1954
Oil on canvas
$40\frac{1}{16}$ x $26\frac{1}{16}$ in. (101.8 x 66.2 cm.)
Signed and dated at lower right: gaughan54
Gift of James P. and Ruth Marshall Magill, 1957.15.10

Arrah Lee Gaul (1888–1980)

519 *A Corner of Ravello*, 1914
Oil on canvas
$30\frac{3}{16}$ x $25\frac{3}{16}$ in. (76.7 x 64 cm.)
Signed and dated at lower left: Arrah Lee Gaul -1914
Bequest of Ida Budd, 1935.2.1

Walter Gay (1856–1937)

520 *Chez Helleu*, ca. 1902
Oil on cardboard
$21\frac{5}{8}$ x 18 in. (54.9 x 45.7 cm.)
Signed at lower right: Walter Gay
Joseph E. Temple Fund, 1903.3.1

521 *La Console*, ca. 1902
Oil on cardboard
$21\frac{5}{8}$ x 18 in. (54.9 x 45.7 cm.)
Signed at lower left: Walter Gay
Joseph E. Temple Fund, 1903.3.2

522 *Interior of Artist's Apartment in Paris*, after 1910
Oil on canvas
$28\frac{3}{4}$ x $23\frac{3}{4}$ in. (73 x 60.3 cm.)
Gift of James P. and Ruth Marshall Magill, 1954.24.1

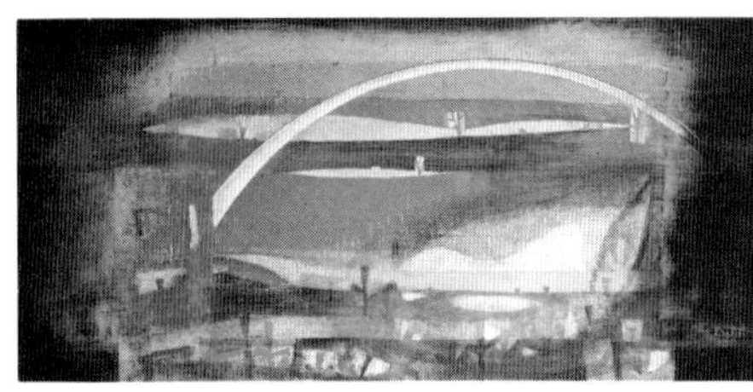

516

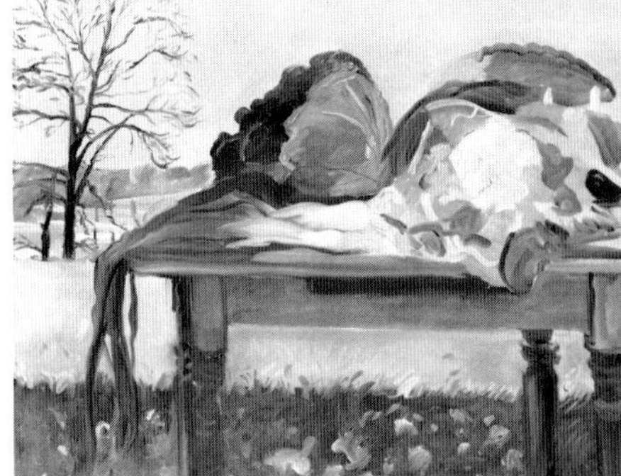

526

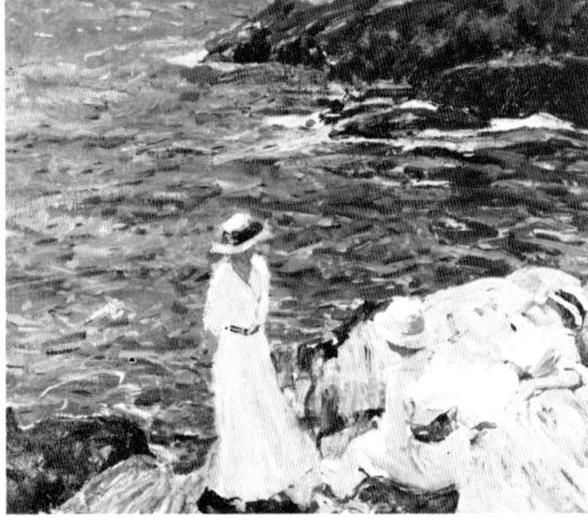

529

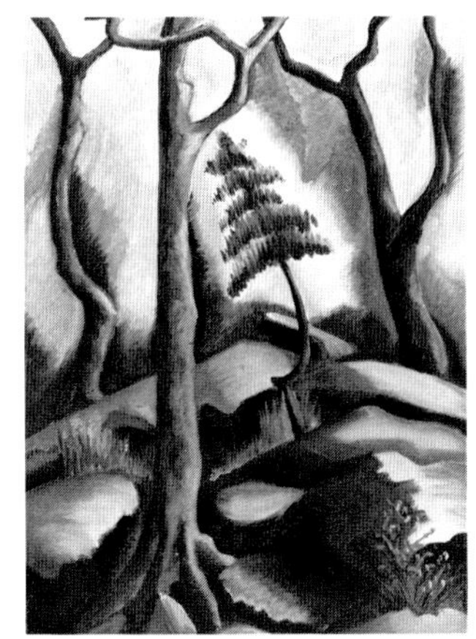

514

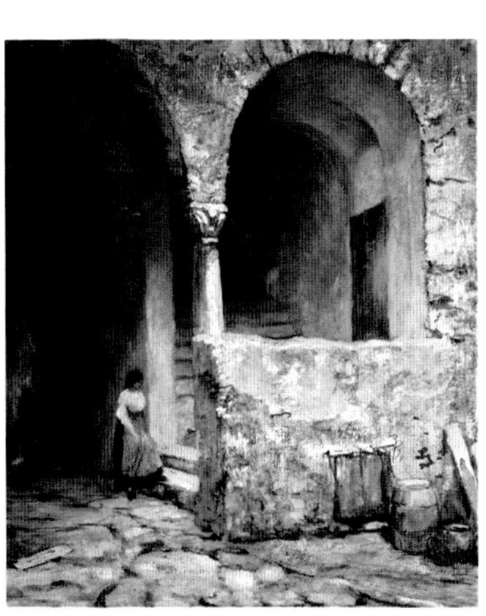

519

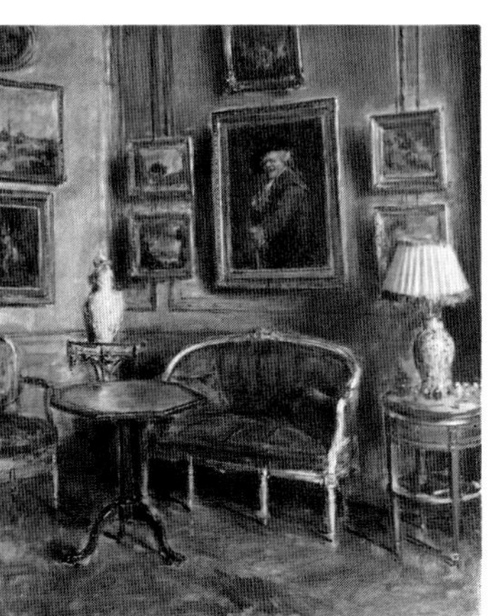

522

523 *Interior of the Bedroom of the Château du Bréau*, ca. 1912
Oil on canvas
$21\frac{3}{8}$ x $25\frac{13}{16}$ in. (54.3 x 65.6 cm.)
Signed at lower left: Walter Gay
Gift of James P. and Ruth Marshall Magill, 1954.24.2

Aaron Gelman (b. 1899)

524 *Across Gowanus Canal*, ca. 1943
Oil on canvas
$16\frac{1}{16}$ x $23\frac{15}{16}$ in. (40.8 x 60.8 cm.)
Signed at lower left: GELMAN
Annotated on stretcher: THE GOWANUS CANAL/ AARON GELMAN
John Lambert Fund, 1944.2

Grace Thorp Gemberling (b. 1903)

525 *Lilies*, ca. 1935
Oil on canvas
$24\frac{1}{8}$ x $22\frac{1}{8}$ in. (61.3 x 56.2 cm.)
Inscribed and signed on stretcher: "LILIES"/ Grace Thorp Gemberling
John Lambert Fund, 1936.6

Paul Georges (1923–   )

526 *Backyard, Bridgehampton*, 1974
Oil on canvas
$39\frac{7}{8}$ x $52\frac{1}{8}$ in. (101.3 x 132.4 cm.)
Signed and dated at lower right: [illegible] 74
Gift of Mr. and Mrs. Arie Ilton, 1981.3

Margaret Ralston Gest (1900–1965)

527 *Farm Pattern*, ca. 1931
Oil on canvas
$30\frac{1}{16}$ x $40\frac{1}{8}$ in. (76.4 x 101.9 cm.)
Signed at lower left: GEST
John Lambert Fund, 1932.6

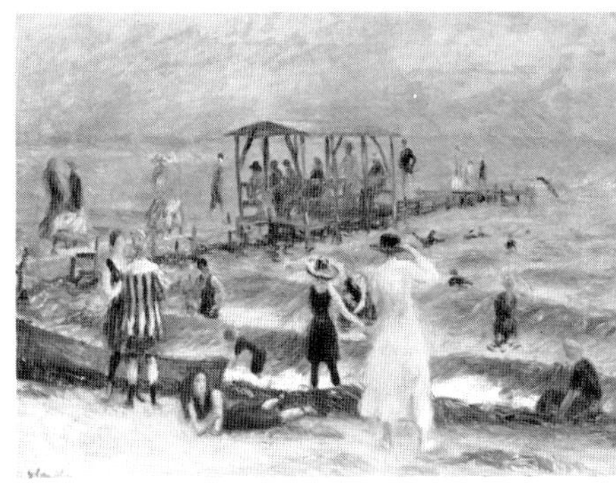

532

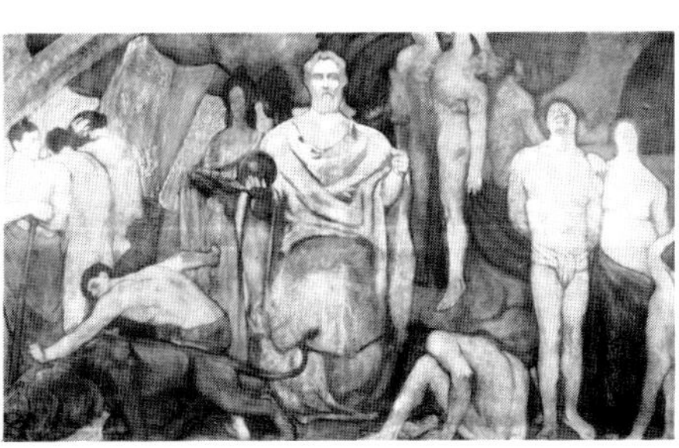

533

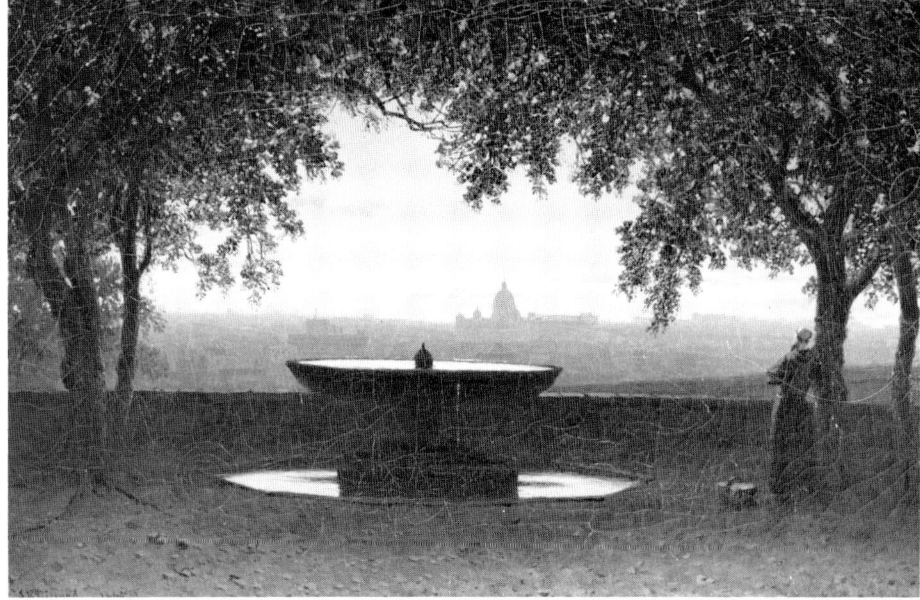

528

Sanford Robinson Gifford (1823–1880)

528 *Saint Peter's from Pincian Hill*, 1865
Oil on canvas
$9\frac{13}{16}$ x $15\frac{9}{16}$ in. (24.9 x 39.5 cm.)
Signed and dated at lower left: SRGifford 1865
Gift of Mr. and Mrs. Edward Kesler, 1975.20.3

Howard E. Giles (1876–1955)

529 *Holidays*, ca. 1915
Oil on composition board
$24\frac{15}{16}$ x $29\frac{15}{16}$ in. (63.3 x 76 cm.)
Signed at lower center: H. Giles.
John Lambert Fund, 1916.5

Sue May Gill (Mrs. Paul Gill, 1890–   )

530 *Alfred G. B. Steel* (1886–1949), 1934 or 1935
Oil on canvas
38 x 30 in. (96.5 x 76.2 cm.)
Signed at lower right: Sue May Gill
Gift of Mrs. Henry V. Greenough, 1956.6

Stephen H. Gimber (1810–1862)

531 *Ship Captain's Wife*
Oil on canvas
$21\frac{9}{16}$ x $17\frac{5}{8}$ in. (54.8 x 44.8 cm.)
Signed at lower right: SHG [monogram]
Gift of Frances C. Griscom, 1970.27

William J. Glackens (1870–1938)

532 *At the Beach*, 1917
Oil on canvas
$18\frac{1}{8}$ x $24\frac{1}{16}$ in. (46 x 61.1 cm.)
Signed at lower left: W. Glackens; inscribed and dated at lower right: TO THE AMERICAN [Red Cross] 1917
Edward H. Coates Fund, 1952.6.1

533 *Science* (formerly *Justice*), 1896–97
Oil on canvas
$77\frac{1}{2}$ x $127\frac{1}{2}$ in. (196.9 x 323.9 cm.)
Signed at lower left: W.J.GLACKENS
Commissioned by the Pennsylvania Academy, 1897.9.4

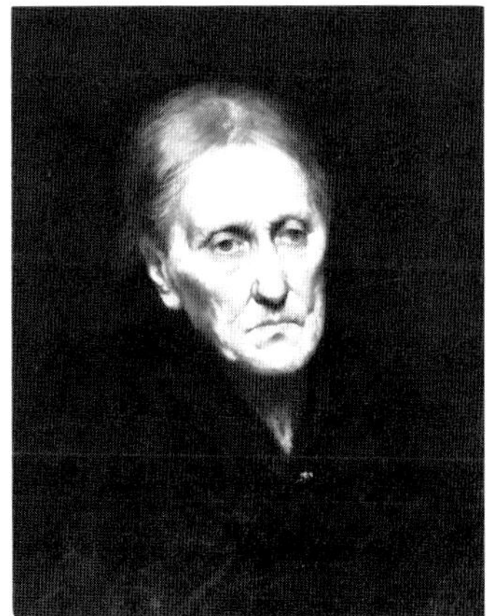

531

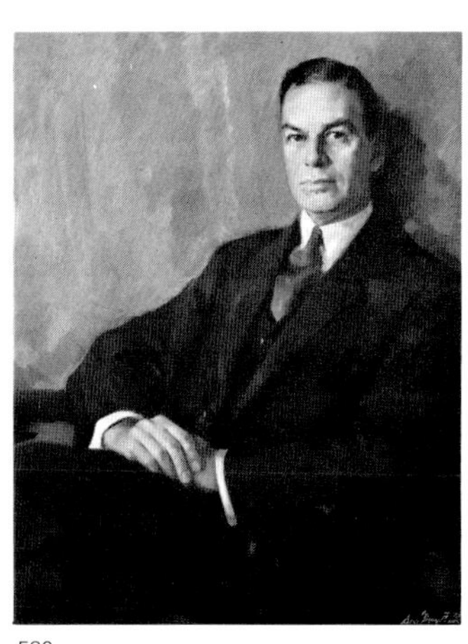

530

534 *The Soda Fountain*, 1935
Oil on canvas
48 x 36 in. (121.9 x 91.4 cm.)
Signed and dated at lower right: W. Glackens/35
Joseph E. Temple and Henry D. Gilpin funds, 1955.3

535 *Woman in Red Dress*, ca. 1918
Oil on canvas
13 x 10 in. (33 x 25.4 cm.)
Signed at lower left: W.G.
Gift of Margot Newman Stickley in memory of her parents, Philip and Helen S. Newman, 1987.18.2

Raphael Gleitsmann (1910–)

536 *From the Wheatfield*, 1940
Oil on cardboard
15⅞ x 20¹⁄₁₆ in. (40.3 x 51 cm.)
Signed at lower right: Raphael Gleitsman[n]
John Lambert Fund, 1945.4

Albert Gold (1916–)

537 *Nicetown*, 1949
Oil on masonite
32⅞ x 45⅜ in. (83.5 x 115.3 cm.)
Signed at lower right: Albert Gold
John Lambert Fund, 1950.8

Leon Goldin (1923–)

538 *Staten Island, Winter*, 1960
Oil on canvas
37¾ x 77¼ in. (95.9 x 196.2 cm.)
Signed and dated at lower right: goldin 60
Annotated on stretcher: STATEN ISLAND 1960
John Lambert Fund, 1962.7

Xavier Gonzalez (1898–)

539 *Landscape in Construction*, ca. 1955
Oil and egg tempera on paper, mounted on pressed wood
36 x 50 in. (91.4 x 127 cm.)
Signed at lower right: XavierGonzalez
Gift of the American Academy of Arts and Letters (The Childe Hassam Fund), 1957.18

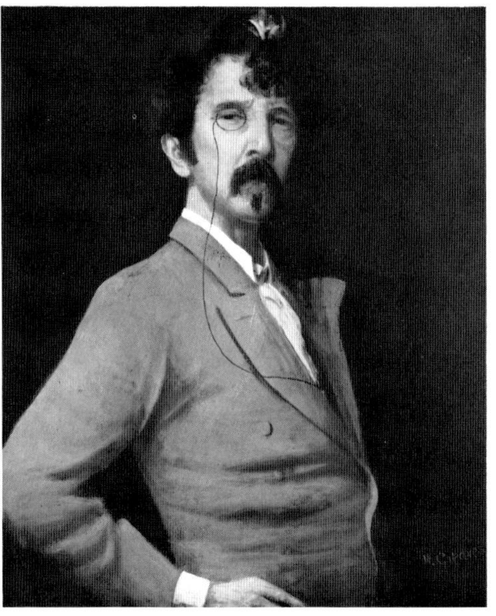
548

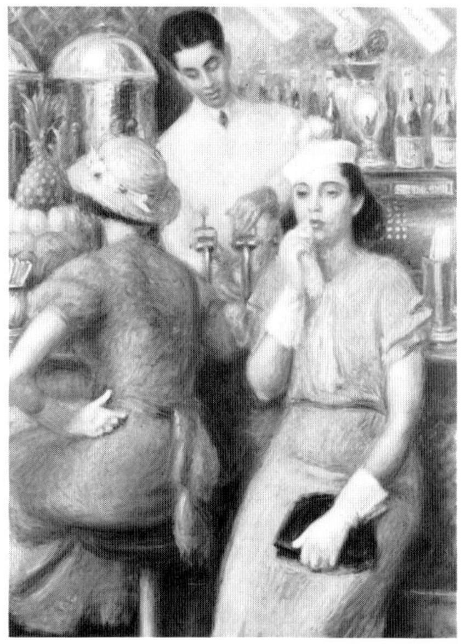
534

Sidney Goodman (1936–)

540 *Nude on a Red Table*, 1977–80
Oil on canvas
53½ x 77¾ in. (135.9 x 197.5 cm.)
Signed and dated at lower right: GOODMAN 77–80
Funds provided by the National Endowment for the Arts, the Contemporary Arts Fund, and Mrs. H. Gates Lloyd, 1980.20

Paul Gorka (1931–)

541 *The Circle of the Sphere*, 1965
Oil on canvas
50 x 60 in. (127 x 152.4 cm.)
Signed at lower left: Paul Gorka
John Lambert Fund, 1966.4

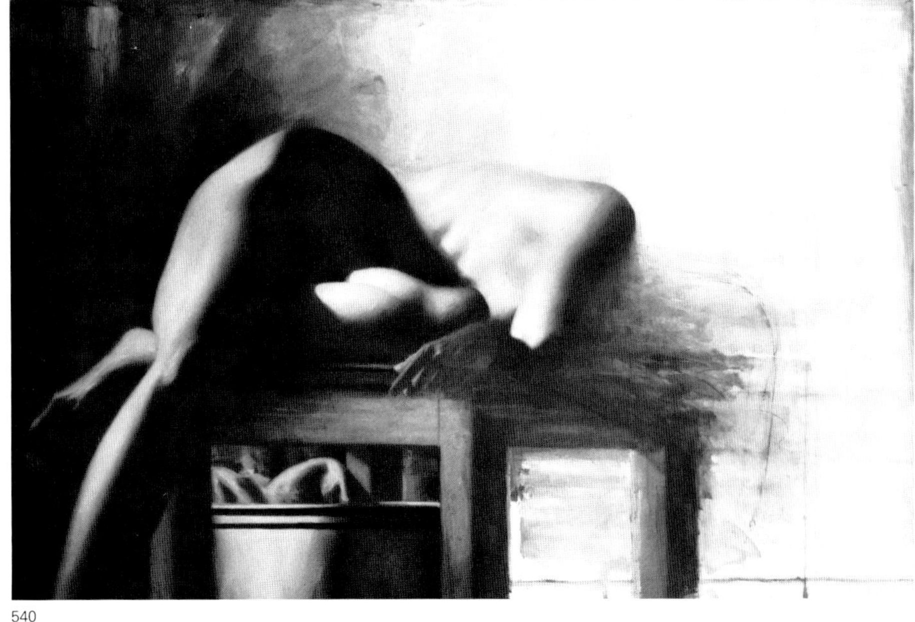
540

Dolya Goutman (1915–)

542 *Bryn Mawr Landscape*, 1956
Oil on canvas
24 x 30¹⁄₁₆ in. (61 x 76.4 cm.)
Signed at lower right: GOUTMAN
Gift of Benjamin D. Bernstein, 1959.10.1

William Graham (1832–1911)

543 *Outside the Porta del Popolo, Rome*, 1874–75
Oil on canvas
12⅛ x 16⁹⁄₁₆ in. (30.8 x 42.1 cm.)
Signed, inscribed, and dated at lower left: W.GRAHAM ROME 1874–75
Gift of Mr. and Mrs. John White Field, 1887.1.4

Catharine Harley Grant (1897–1954)

544 *The Villa Maria*, 1946
Oil on canvas
18⅛ x 24⅛ in. (46 x 61.3 cm.)
Signed and dated at lower right: CATHARINE GRANT-1946
John Lambert Fund, 1949.5

Frederick G. Gray

545 *Grandmother's Dressing Gown*, 1912
Oil on canvas
24¹⁄₁₆ x 18¹⁄₁₆ in. (61.1 x 45.9 cm.)
Signed and dated at lower right: Fred G. Gray -'12
John Lambert Fund, 1913.7

Henry Peters Gray (1819–1877)

546 *Cupid Begging His Arrow*, 1844
Oil on canvas
30³⁄₁₆ x 25⅛ in. (76.7 x 63.8 cm.)
Signed and dated at lower right: Gray '44
Bequest of Henry C. Carey (The Carey Collection), 1879.8.7

Sante Graziani (1920–)

547 *Peale's Staircase*, 1965
Acrylic on canvas
46 x 46 in. (116.8 x 116.8 cm.)

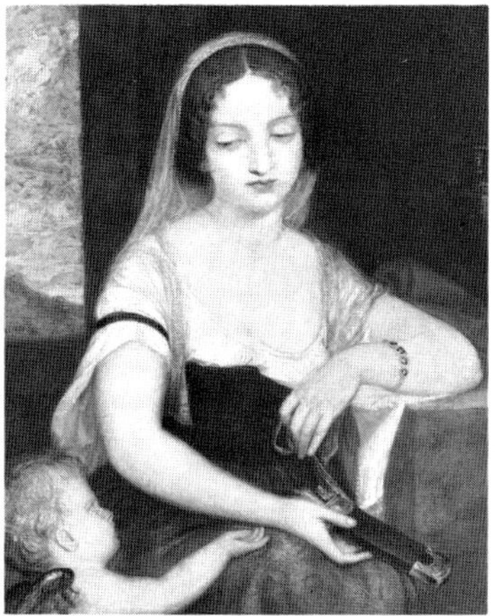
546

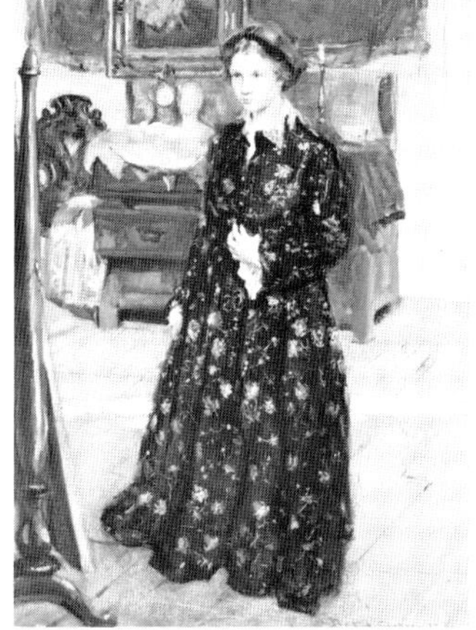
545

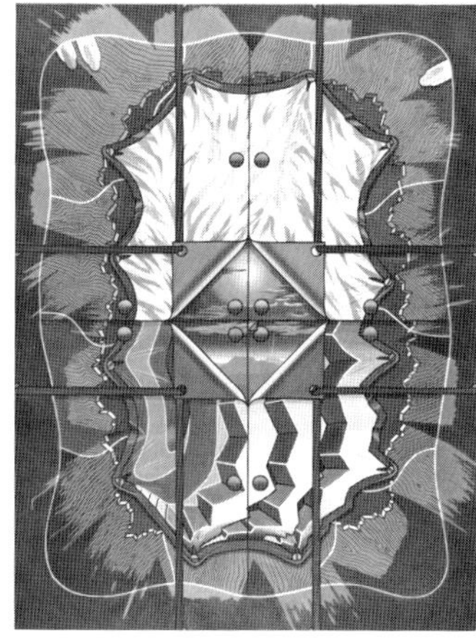
549

Signed at lower right: Sante Graziani
Gift of Mr. and Mrs. Meyer P. Potamkin, 1977.4

Walter Greaves (English, 1841–1930)

548 *James Abbott McNeill Whistler (1834–1903)*, 1871
Oil on canvas
$30\frac{1}{8}$ x 25 in. (76.5 x 63.5 cm.)
Signed and dated at lower right: W. Greaves/ 1871
Henry D. Gilpin Fund, 1914.17

Art Green (1941–)

549 *Deceptive Practices*, 1974
Oil on canvas
$49\frac{13}{16}$ x $38\frac{9}{16}$ in. (126.5 x 97.9 cm.)
Signed and dated on back: Art Green/1974
Inscribed, dated, and signed on stretcher: "Deceptive Practices" 1974 Art Green Vancouver BC OIL
Gift of James Arthur Varchmin, 1986.49.3

Balcomb Greene (1904–)

550 *Carnival of Sails*, ca. 1971
Oil on canvas
60 x 56 in. (152.4 x 142.2 cm.)
Signed at lower right: Balcomb/Greene
Inscribed and signed on stretcher: Carnival of sails 60-56 716 Balcomb Greene
Gift of the American Academy of Arts and Letters (The Childe Hassam Fund), 1974.4

Marion Greenwood (1909–1970)

551 *Slaughterhouse*, 1942
Oil on canvas board
16 x $11\frac{15}{16}$ in. (40.6 x 30.3 cm.)
Signed at lower right: Marion Greenwood; inscribed, signed, and dated on back: "IN THE SLAUGHTER/HOUSE"/MARION GREENWOOD/ AUGUST 1942
John Lambert Fund, 1945.5

Eliot Gregory. *See* cat. no. 1640.

Jack J. Greitzer (1910–)

552 *Still Life*, 1931
Oil on canvas
$20\frac{3}{16}$ x 16 in. (51.3 x 40.6 cm.)
Signed and dated at lower right: J. J. GREITZER/1931
John Lambert Fund, 1932.7

June Gertrude Groff (1903–1974)

553 *Straw Flowers*; on back, *Female Portrait Sketch*, ca. 1935
Oil on canvas
$19\frac{15}{16}$ x $16\frac{1}{4}$ in. (50.6 x 41.3 cm.)
John Lambert Fund, 1936.7

Red Grooms (1937–)

554 *A Room in Connecticut*, 1984
Oil on canvas and acrylic on Plexiglas with aluminum frame
72 x 96 in. (182.9 x 243.8 cm.)
Signed and dated at lower left: Red Grooms '84
John Lambert Fund, 1985.4

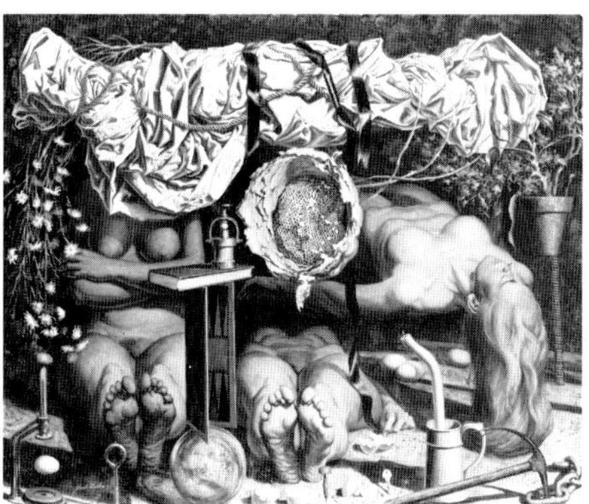
541

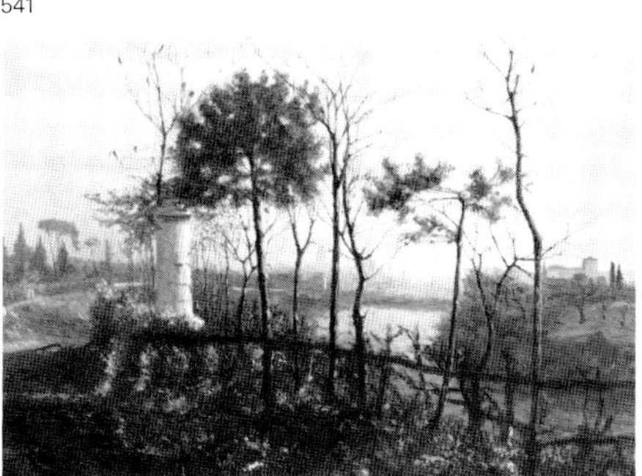
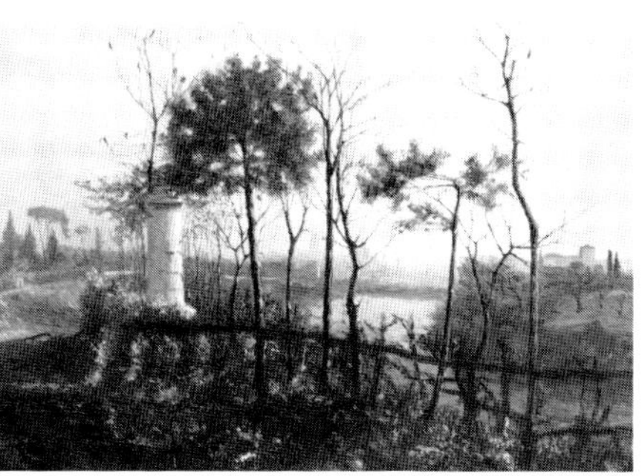
543

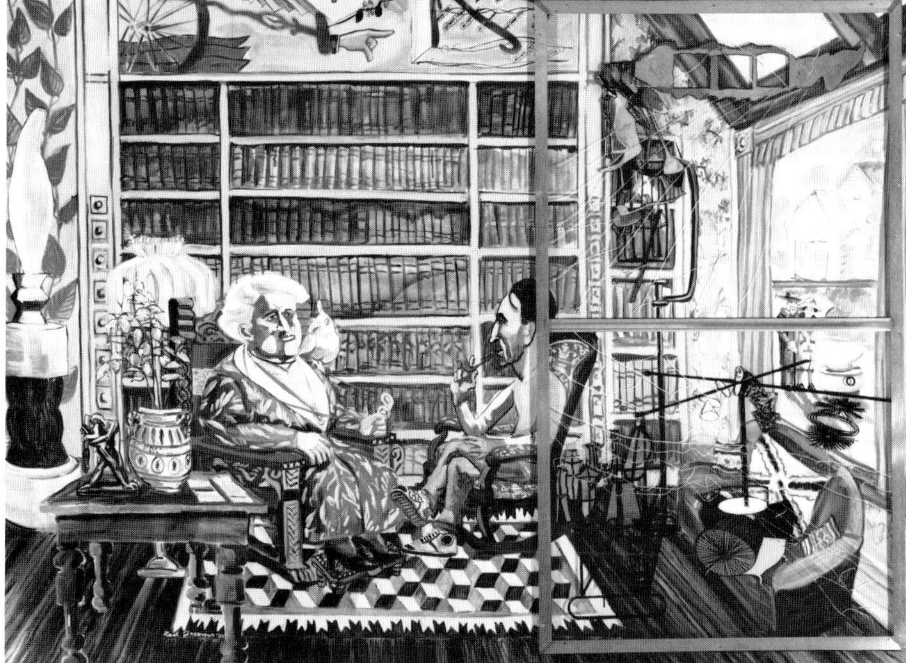
554

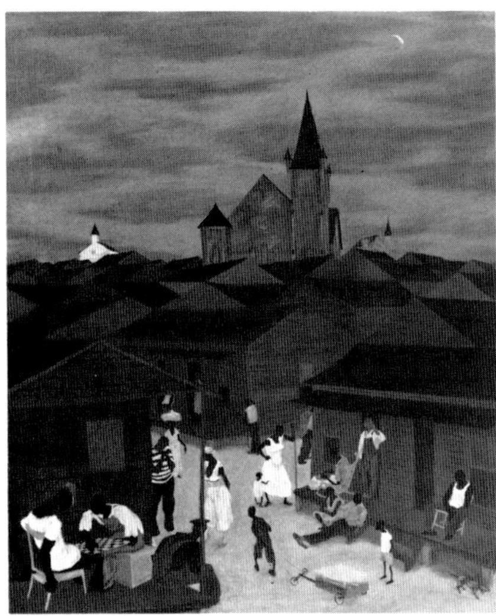

563

566

William Gropper (1897–1977)

555 *Upper House*, 1944
Oil on canvas
18 x $25\frac{15}{16}$ in. (45.7 x 65.9 cm.)
Signed at lower right: GROPPER-
Henry D. Gilpin Fund, 1945.6

Helen Omansky Gross (Mrs. Norman Gross, b. 1918)

556 *Busy Corner*, ca. 1943
Oil on canvas
$19\frac{15}{16}$ x $26\frac{1}{4}$ in. (50.6 x 66.7 cm.)
Signed at lower left: Om [ansky]; and on back: Omansky
John Lambert Fund, 1944.9

Frederick W. Gruger (1871–1953)

557 *Military Music* (formerly *Jeanne d'Arc*), 1896–97
Oil on canvas
Approx. 78 x 73 in. (198 x 185 cm.)
Signed at lower left: F.W.GRUGER
Commissioned by the Pennsylvania Academy, 1897.9.4

Joseph P. Gualtieri (1916–)

558 *City Patterns*, 1950
Oil on canvas
$36\frac{1}{16}$ x $27\frac{15}{16}$ in. (91.6 x 71 cm.)
Signed at lower right: Gualtieri
John Lambert Fund, 1951.6

559 *Roberto*, 1946
Oil on canvas
$21\frac{1}{16}$ x $17\frac{1}{16}$ in. (53.5 x 43.3 cm.)
Signed at lower left: Gualtieri
John Lambert Fund, 1948.3

Salvatore Anthony Guarino (b. 1883)

560 *The Exhibition*, ca. 1917
Oil on canvas
24 x 24 in. (61 x 61 cm.)
John Lambert Fund, 1918.9

José Guerrero (1914–)

561 *Reds and Browns*, ca. 1960
Oil on canvas
$51\frac{1}{8}$ x $60\frac{1}{8}$ in. (129.9 x 152.7 cm.)
Signed at upper left: José Guerrero
Gift of Mrs. Herbert Cameron Morris, 1966.7

Blanchard Gummo (1906–1986)

562 *Ruined House*, ca. 1943
Oil on canvas
$15\frac{3}{16}$ x 20 in. (38.6 x 50.8 cm.)
Signed at lower right: GUMMO
John Lambert Fund, 1944.3

Robert Gwathmey (1903–1988)

563 *Street Scene*, 1938
Oil on canvas
$36\frac{3}{16}$ x $30\frac{1}{16}$ in. (91.9 x 76.4 cm.)
Signed at upper left: Gwathmey
Joseph E. Temple Fund, 1942.4

Philip B. Hahs (1853–1882)

564 *Old Timers*, 1882
Oil on canvas
$15\frac{7}{8}$ x $11\frac{15}{16}$ in. (40.3 x 30.3 cm.)
Signed and dated at lower left: Philip B Hahs 1882/Hahs 1882; inscribed, signed, and dated on back: "Old Timers"/Philip B Hahs/ 1882
Gift of Mrs. Charles B. Hahs, 1895.2.1

565 *Study of an Old Man*, 1882
Oil on canvas
16 x $11\frac{15}{16}$ in. (40.6 x 30.3 cm.)
Signed and dated at lower right: Philip B Hahs 1882; inscribed, signed, and dated on back: Study of an/Old Man/Philip B Hahs/1882
Gift of Mrs. Charles B. Hahs, 1884.2.2

Lilian Westcott Hale (Mrs. Philip Leslie Hale, 1880–1963)

566 *Portrait* (Miss Foley), ca. 1918
Oil on canvas
36 x $30\frac{3}{16}$ in. (91.4 x 76.7 cm.)
Signed at upper right: Lilian Westcott Hale
John Lambert Fund, 1919.3

Philip Leslie Hale (1865–1931)

567 *Conversation Piece*, by 1908
Oil on canvas
$30\frac{1}{2}$ x $20\frac{1}{2}$ in. (77.5 x 52.1 cm.)
Signed at lower right: PHILIP L HALE [partially rubbed out]
Gift of Mr. and Mrs. Stuart P. Feld, 1976.17

568 *The Crimson Rambler*, ca. 1908
Oil on canvas

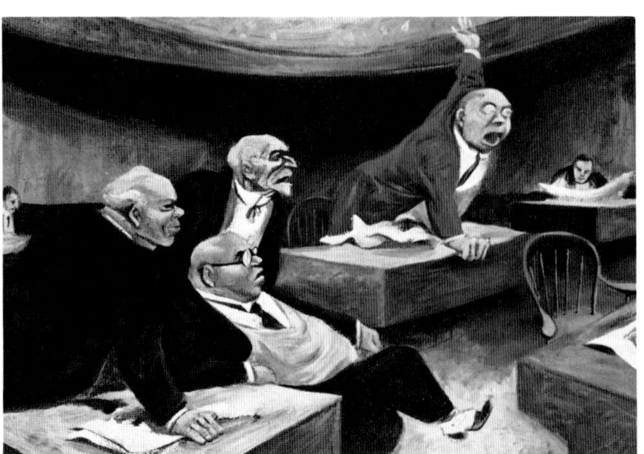

555

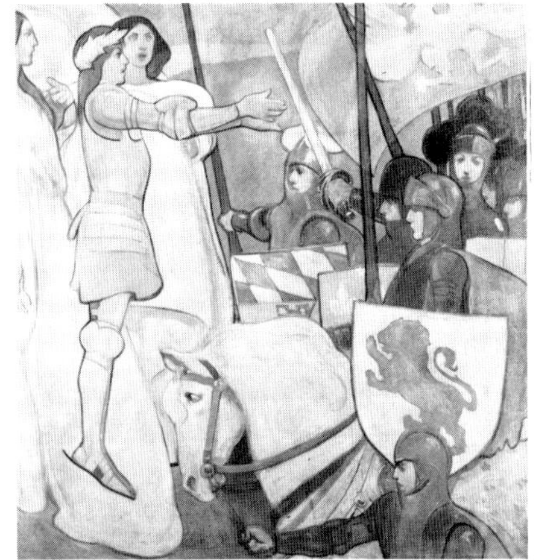

557

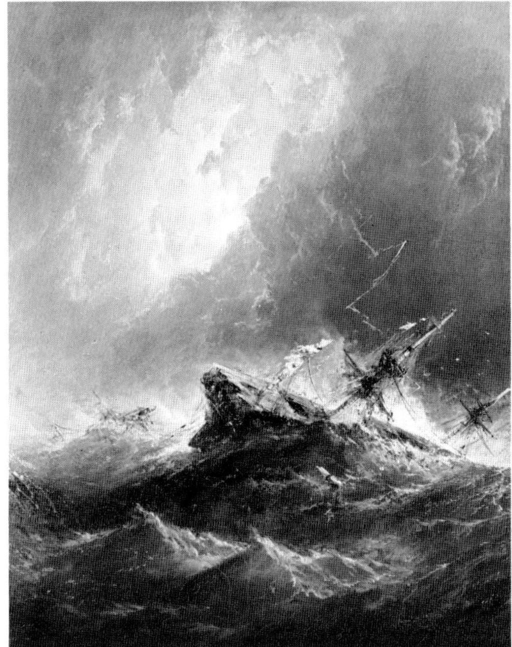

572

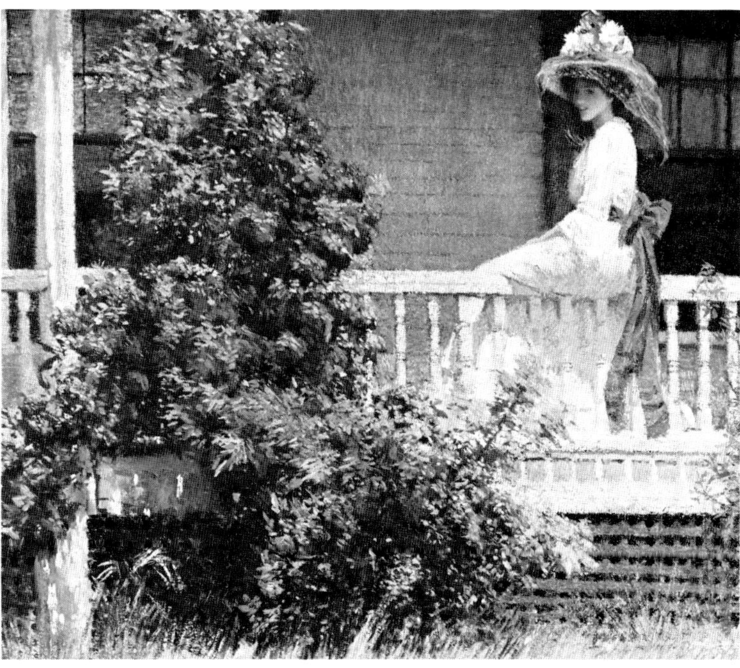

568

25¼ x 30 3/16 in. (64.1 x 76.7 cm.)
Joseph E. Temple Fund, 1909.12

William Weeks Hall (1899–1958)

569 *Still Life*, ca. 1919
Oil on canvas
24⅛ x 21 in. (61.3 x 53.3 cm.)
John Lambert Fund, 1920.5

Samuel Halpert (1884–1930)

570 *The Seine, Paris*, 1911
Oil on canvas
25½ x 31 11/16 in. (64.8 x 80.5 cm.)
Signed and dated at lower left: S.HALPERT–11
John Lambert Fund, 1917.3

James Hamilton (1819–1878)

571 *The Ancient Mariner*, 1863
Oil on canvas
47 x 72⅛ in. (119.4 x 183.2 cm.)
Signed at lower right: Jas. Hamilton; signed, inscribed, and dated on back: Ja Hamilton/ Philada 1863/"Day after day, day after day/ We stuck–nor breath nor motion/As idle as a painted ship/Upon a painted ccean."/Rime of the Ancient/Mariner
Gift of Edward H. Coates, 1894.2

572 *Old Ironsides*, 1863
Oil on canvas
60⅜ x 48 in. (153.4 x 121.9 cm.)
Signed and dated at lower right: J Hamilton/ 1863; inscribed, signed, and dated on back: Old Ironsides/Jas Hamilton/Philada 1863/ "O better that her shattered hulk/Should sink beneath the wave; Her thunders shook the mighty deep,/And there should be her grave;/ Nail to the mast her holy flag./Set every threadbare sail,/And give her to the god of storms–/The lightning and the gale!"/ O. W. Holmes
Gift of Caroline Gibson Taitt, 1885.1

James A. Hamilton III (1931–)

573 *South Street Market*, 1955
Oil on canvas
33 13/16 x 46 in. (85.9 x 116.8 cm.)
Signed at lower right: J A HAMILTON III
Gift of Louis C. Sunstein, 1955.8.1

John McLure Hamilton (1853–1936)

574 *Charles E. Dana* [1843–1914], *Henry J. Thouron* [1851–1915], *John M. Hamilton* [1853–1936], *and Herbert Welsh* [1851–1941]
Oil on canvas
33⅞ x 49⅛ in. (86 x 124.8 cm.)
Gift of Charles Morris Young, 1936.21

575 *The Right Hon. William Ewart Gladstone at Downing Street* (1809–1898), 1893
Oil on canvas
31¼ x 35⅛ in. (79.4 x 89.2 cm.)
Signed, inscribed, and dated at upper left: J. McLure Hamilton./Downing Street 1893
Henry D. Gilpin Fund, 1894.3

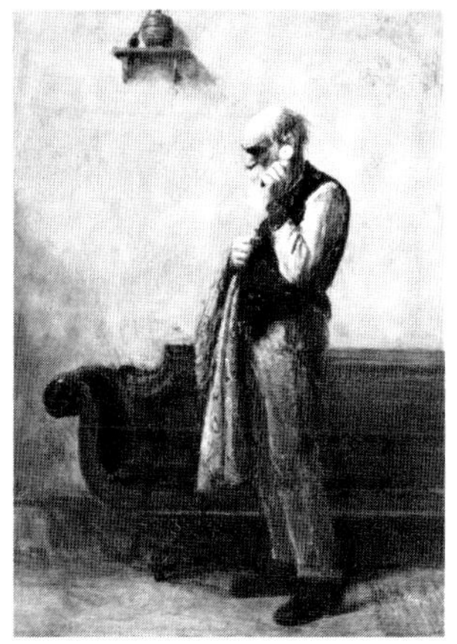

564

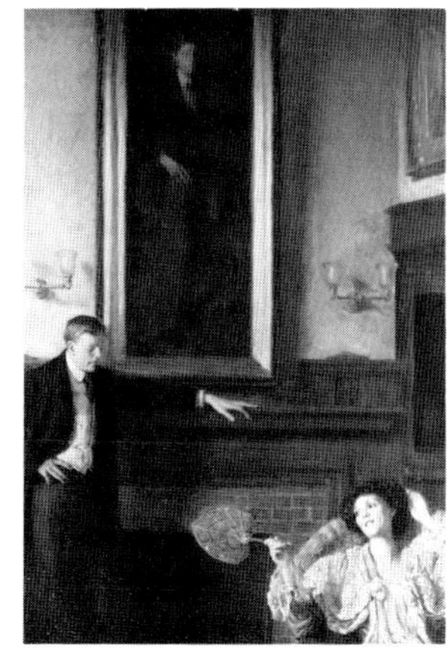

567

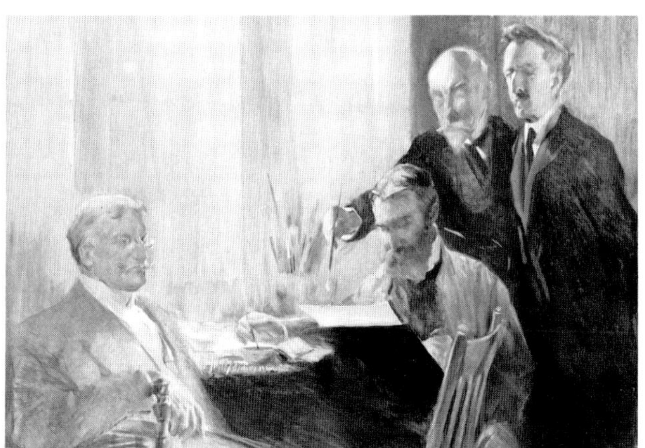

574

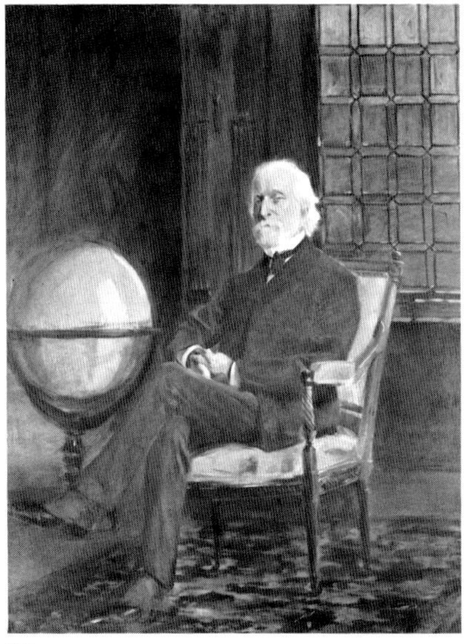
578

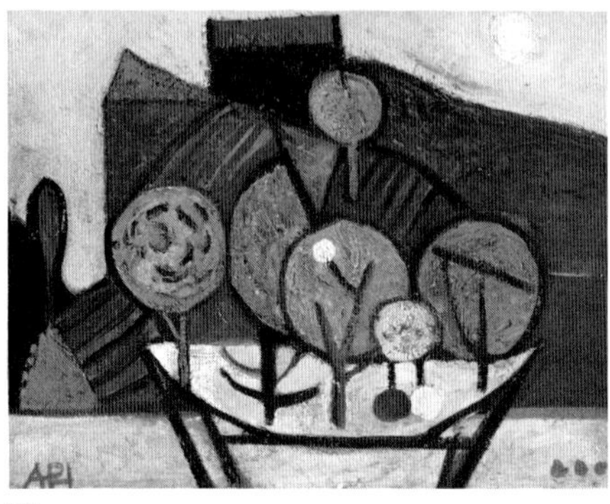
591

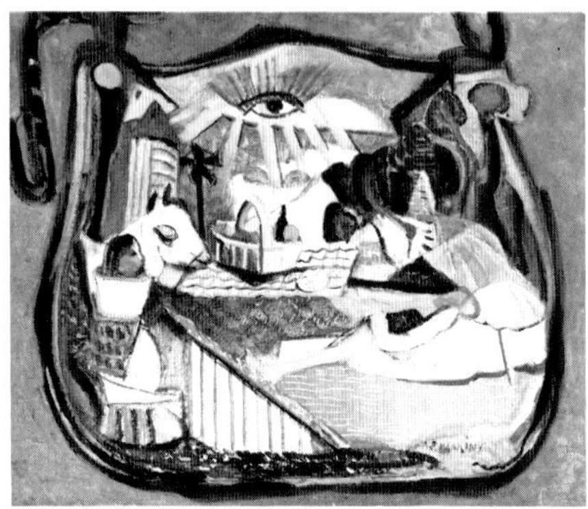
593

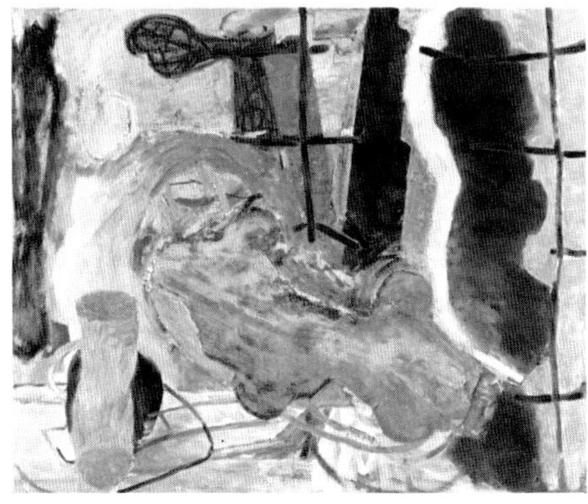
600

576 *George Meredith* (1828–1909), ca. 1911
Oil on canvas
29⅛ x 38⅛ in. (74 x 96.8 cm.)
Signed at lower left: Hamilton
Henry D. Gilpin Fund, 1912.5

577 *Anna Lea Merritt* (1844–1930), 1920s
Oil on canvas
24 x 18 in. (61 x 45.7 cm.)
Gift of Arthur H. Lea, 1936.23.1

578 *William Trost Richards* (1833–1905), by 1906
Oil on canvas
46¼ x 36⅛ in. (117.5 x 91.8 cm.)
Signed at lower right: Hamilton
Pennsylvania Academy purchase, 1929.9

579 *Tears*, 1879
Oil on wood
7¾ x 4¹⁵⁄₁₆ in. (19.7 x 12.5 cm.)
Signed and dated at upper right: Hamilton/1879.
Gift of Mr. and Mrs. John McLure Hamilton, 1936.24

580 *Henry Joseph Thouron* (1851–1915), by 1900
Oil on canvas
23¹⁵⁄₁₆ x 18¹⁄₁₆ in. (60.8 x 45.9 cm.)
Gift of the artist, 1914.1

581 *Hon. Richard Vaux* (1816–1895), by 1895
Oil on canvas
28 x 36 in. (71.1 x 91.4 cm.)
Gift of Alexander Biddle, John Cadwalader, Anthony J. Antelo, George C. Thomas, William L. Elkins, Charles C. Harrison, George H. McFadden, John H. Converse, and Edward H. Coates, 1895.7

James A. Hanes (1924–)

582 *View of Philadelphia*, ca. 1949
Oil on canvas
23⅞ x 28 in. (60.6 x 71.1 cm.)
Signed on back: Hanes
John Lambert Fund, 1950.9

Abraham Peter Hankins (1900–1963)

583 *Barnyard*, 1950
Oil on canvas
22¹⁄₁₆ x 34 in. (56 x 86.4 cm.)
Signed at lower center: Hankins; signed and inscribed on back: A. P. Hankins/130 S 17st Phila. Pa.
Gift of Dr. and Mrs. Matthew T. Moore, 1969.18.2

584 *Boat*
Oil on canvas
21 x 23 in. (53.3 x 58.4 cm.)
Bequest of Mrs. Abraham Peter Hankins, 1968.11.11

585 *The Chase*
Oil on canvas
20¾ x 22⅜ in. (52.7 x 56.8 cm.)
Signed at lower center: APH [monogram]; signed on back: A.P.Hankins
Bequest of Mrs. Abraham Peter Hankins, 1968.11.1

586 *Composition*, 1947
Oil on cardboard
9¹⁵⁄₁₆ x 8¹⁄₁₆ in. (25.2 x 20.5 cm.)
Signed at lower right: AP.Hankins; dated at lower center: 1947
Bequest of Mrs. Abraham Peter Hankins, 1968.11.2

587 *The Enchanted Forest*
Oil on canvas
29⅞ x 23¹⁵⁄₁₆ in. (75.9 x 60.8 cm.)
Signed at upper center: Hankins
Signed and inscribed on stretcher: A.P. HANKINS THE ENCHANTED FOREST
Gift of friends of the artist, 1964.9

588 *Golden Spot*, 1956
Oil on canvas
24⅞ x 16⅝ in. (63.2 x 42.2 cm.)
Signed at upper right: Hankins
Annotated on stretcher: #153 16 x 36 GOLDEN SPOT–1956
Bequest of Mrs. Abraham Peter Hankins, 1968.11.3

589 *Monhegan #1*
Oil on canvas board
16 x 20 in. (40.6 x 50.8 cm.)
Signed at lower right: Hankins
Bequest of Mrs. Abraham Peter Hankins, 1968.11.4

590 *Night Festivities*
Oil on canvas
20 x 22 in. (50.8 x 55.9 cm.)
Signed at lower center: A.P.Hankins
Bequest of Mrs. Abraham Peter Hankins, 1968.11.5

591 *Orange Grove*
Oil on canvas
10½ x 13⅝ in. (26.7 x 34.6 cm.)
Signed at lower left: APH [monogram]; inscribed and signed on back: 10½ x 13½ ORANGE GROVE #389/A.P.HANKINS
Bequest of Mrs. Abraham Peter Hankins, 1968.11.6

592 *Picnic in the Country*
Oil on canvas
13⅛ x 18 in. (33.3 x 45.7 cm.)
Signed at lower left: Hankins
Annotated on stretcher: #A6 13 x 18 PICNIC IN THE COUNTRY-AP.HANKINS
Bequest of Mrs. Abraham Peter Hankins, 1968.11.7

593 *Pocket Full of Dreams*
Oil on canvas
18⅛ x 22⅛ in. (46 x 56.2 cm.)
Signed at lower right: A.P.HANKINS
Bequest of Mrs. Abraham Peter Hankins, 1968.11.8

594 *Scared Cat*, ca. 1950
Oil on canvas
20 x 15 in. (50.8 x 38.1 cm.)
Signed at lower left: Hankins
Bequest of Mrs. Abraham Peter Hankins, 1968.11.9

595 *Still Life*
Oil on canvas, mounted on wood and then on plywood
6⁵⁄₁₆ x 7¾ in. (16 x 19.7 cm.)
Signed at upper right: APH/Hankin[s]
Bequest of Mrs. Abraham Peter Hankins, 1968.11.10

596 *Terminal Market*, 1950
Oil on canvas
25¹⁵⁄₁₆ x 36 in. (65.9 x 91.4 cm.)
Signed at lower center: Hankins; dated on back: 1950
Inscribed on stretcher: STAMATO–MEAT MARKET
John Lambert Fund, 1951.7

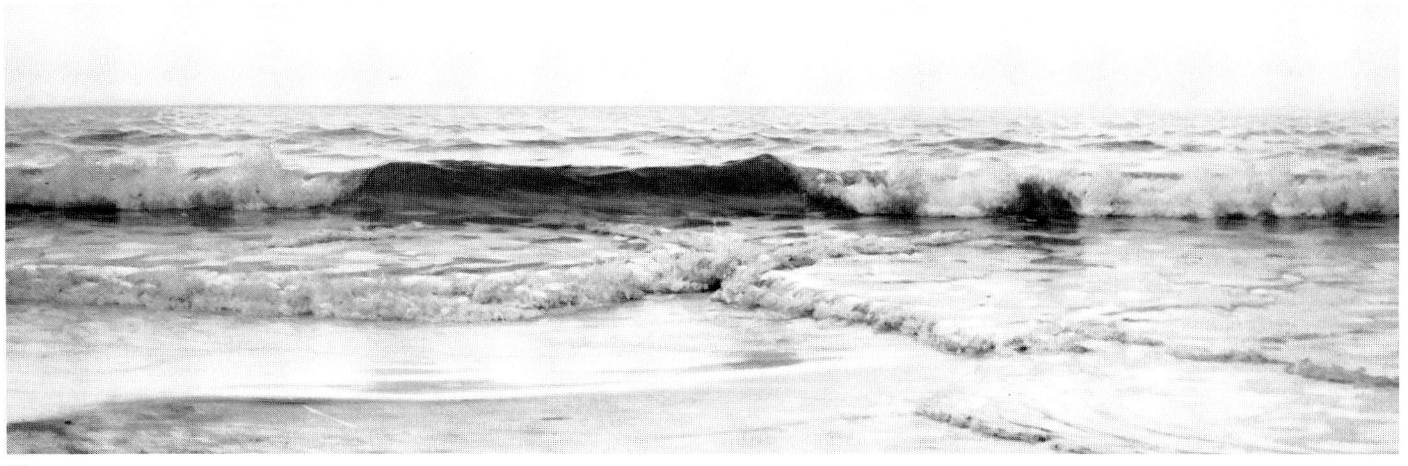
610

John G. Hanlen (1922–)

597 *Escape*, 1948
Oil on canvas
18⅜ x 23⅞ in. (46.7 x 60.6 cm.)
Signed at lower right: Hanlen
John Lambert Fund, 1949.6

598 *Untitled*, ca. 1975
Acrylic, fabric, paper towel, and cigarette foil on masonite
36 x 48 in. (91.4 x 121.9 cm.)
Signed at lower right: Hanlen; and on back: HANLEN
Gift of the artist, 1984.7.2

599 *Winter Thaw*, 1962
Acrylic on masonite
72 x 48 in. (182.9 x 121.9 cm.)
Signed at upper left: Hanlen
Gift of the artist, 1984.7.1

David Hannah (1937–)

600 *You Should Have More Courage. I Want to Be Chinese*, 1985
Oil on canvas
90 x 114 in. (228.6 x 289.6 cm.)
Inscribed, dated, and signed on back: "YOU SHOULD HAVE MORE/COURAGE. I WANT TO/BE CHINESE." 1985/David Hannah
John Lambert Fund, 1986.37

Chester Harding (1792–1866)

601 *William Lorman* (1764–ca. 1843), ca. 1820
Oil on canvas
30$\frac{1}{16}$ x 25$\frac{1}{16}$ in. (76.4 x 63.7 cm.)
Bequest of Mrs. Eleanor F. T. Conner, 1921.10.2

602 *Mrs. William Lorman* (née Mary Fulford, b. 1770), ca. 1820
Oil on canvas
30 x 24⅞ in. (76.2 x 63.2 cm.)
Bequest of Mrs. Eleanor F. T. Conner, 1921.10.1

603 *Colonel James Madison Thompson* (1811–1884)
Oil on canvas
49⅛ x 39 in. (124.8 x 99.1 cm.)
Gift of the Reverend S. Tagart Steele, Jr., 1962.21

604 *Unidentified Man*
Oil on canvas
30$\frac{3}{16}$ x 25 in. (76.7 x 63.5 cm.)
Gift of Mrs. John Frederick Lewis (The John Frederick Lewis Memorial Collection), 1933.10.19

George M. Harding (1882–1959)

605 *Earthquake at Rabaul*, 1947
Oil and egg tempera on canvas
40$\frac{3}{16}$ x 30$\frac{1}{16}$ in. (102.1 x 76.4 cm.)
Signed and dated at upper left: GEORGE HARDING/1947
Joseph E. Temple Fund, 1948.4

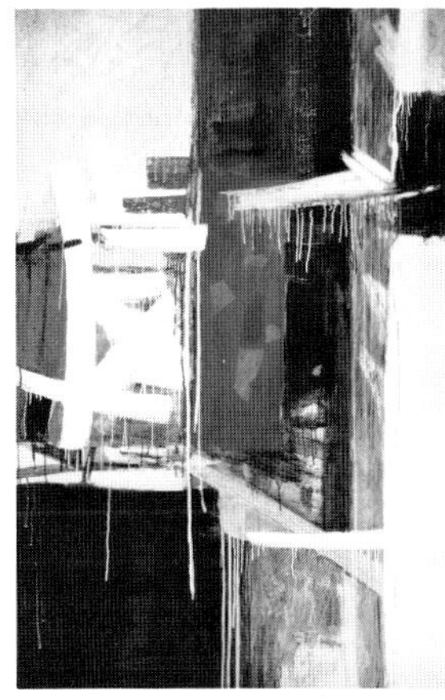
599

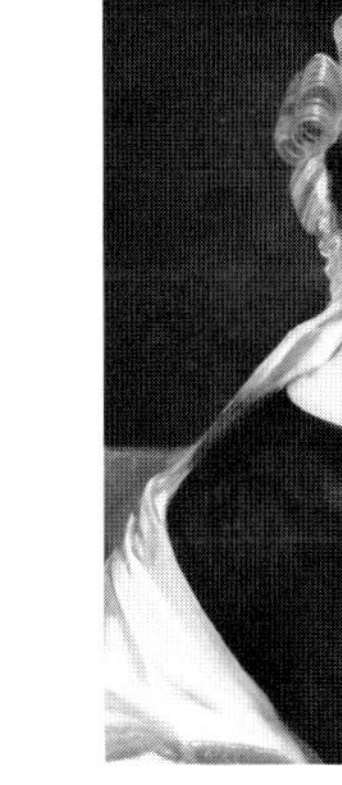
602

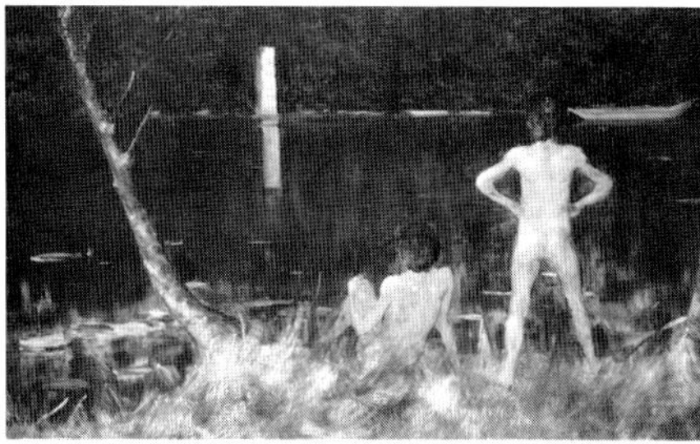
609

606 *Labrador Woman with Young Geese*, 1957
Egg tempera on masonite
60 x 27¾ in. (152.4 x 70.5 cm.)
Signed and dated at lower right: GEO HARDING/57
Collections Fund, 1957.23

Channing Hare (1899–1976)

607 *Anita*, 1948
Oil on canvas
44 x 30 in. (111.8 x 76.2 cm.)
Signed and dated at lower left: Channing Hare/ 1948
Annotated on stretcher: ANITA CHANNING HARE
Anonymous gift, 1949.16

Frederick W. Härer (1879–1948)

608 *Borinquena*, ca. 1916
Oil on canvas
28 x 22 in. (71.1 x 55.9 cm.)
Signed at upper right: F. W. HÄRER
John Lambert Fund, 1917.4

Alexander Harrison (1853–1930)

609 *Boys Bathing*, ca. 1866
Oil on canvas
39$\frac{11}{16}$ x 63⅛ in. (100.8 x 160.3 cm.)
Gift of Desna and Herman Goldman, 1984.35

610 *The Wave*, ca. 1885
Oil on canvas
39¼ x 118 in. (99.7 x 299.7 cm.)
Signed at lower left: Alex Harrison
Joseph E. Temple Fund, 1891.5

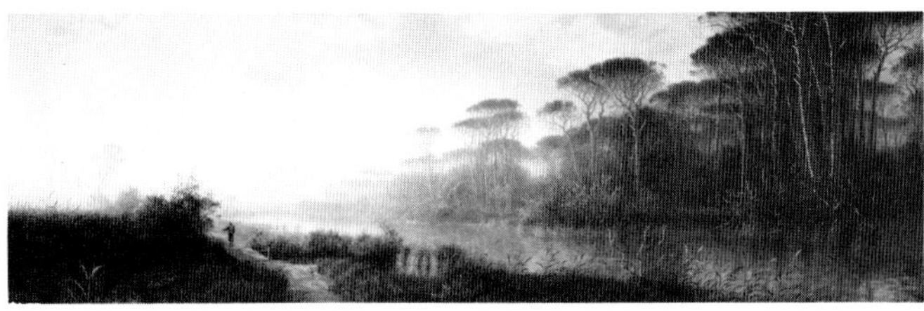
614

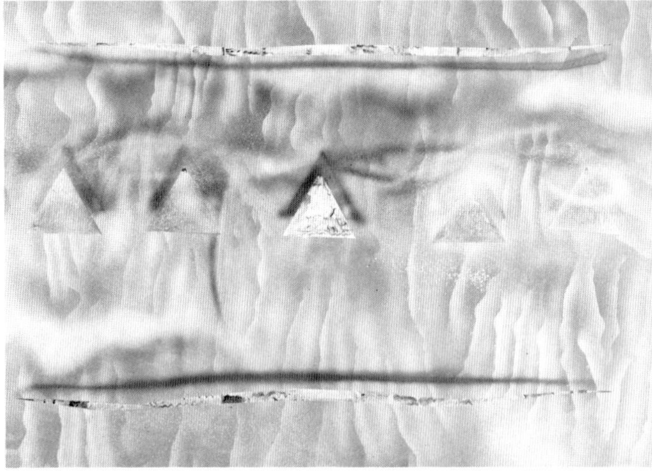
618

Birge Harrison (1854–1929)

611 *Glimpse of the Saint Lawrence*, 1904
Oil on canvas
24 1/16 x 30 in. (61.1 x 76.2 cm.)
Signed at lower right: Birge Harrison
Henry D. Gilpin Fund, 1904.3

612 *A Provençal Coopering Shop*, ca. 1889
Oil on canvas (grisaille)
14 7/8 x 17 7/8 in. (37.8 x 45.4 cm.)
Signed at lower right: B. H; inscribed on back: A Provencal coopering shop
Gift of Mrs. R. J. Carson, Jr., 1979.4.2

613 *A Street in Tarascon*, 1889
Oil on canvas (grisaille)
14 7/8 x 17 15/16 in. (37.8 x 45.6 cm.)
Signed and dated at lower left: B Harrison./89; inscribed on back: A street in Tarrascon [*sic*]
Gift of Mrs. R. J. Carson, Jr., 1979.4.1

William Stanley Haseltine (1835–1900)

614 *Landscape*
Oil on canvas
19 1/8 x 57 in. (48.6 x 144.8 cm.)
Signed at lower left: WSH
Gift of Mrs. Helen Haseltine Plowden, 1961.4

Childe Hassam (1859–1935)

615 *Cat Boats, Newport*, 1901
Oil on canvas
24 1/8 x 26 1/8 in. (61.3 x 66.4 cm.)
Signed and dated at lower right: Childe HASSAM 1901
Joseph E. Temple Fund, 1902.2

616 *Looking over Frenchman's Bay at Green Mountain*, 1896
Oil on canvas
26 7/16 x 36 1/8 in. (67.2 x 91.8 cm.)
Signed and dated at lower right: Childe Hassam. 1896
Gift of Orton P. Jackson in memory of Emily Penrose Jackson, 1983.7

John Woodsum Hatch (1919–)

617 *Outer Isles—Isles of Shoals*, 1970
Acrylic on gessoed masonite, overlaid with various papers in collage, watercolor, and inks
32 x 40 1/16 in. (81.3 x 101.8 cm.)
Signed and dated at lower right: John W. Hatch 1970
Joseph E. Temple Fund, 1970.20

James Havard (1937–)

618 *Stumickosucks (The Buffalo Bull's Back Fat)*, 1973
Acrylic on canvas
84 x 120 in. (213.4 x 304.8 cm.)
Signed and dated on back: Havard '73
Gift of Mrs. Avery B. Clark, 1973.9

Carolyn Haywood (1898–)

619 *Portrait*, 1922
Oil on canvas
24 3/16 x 19 15/16 in. (61.4 x 50.6 cm.)
Signed and dated at upper left: CAROLYN/HAYWOOD/1922
John Lambert Fund, 1923.5

Martin Johnson Heade (1819–1904)

620 *Sunset Harbor at Rio*, 1864
Oil on canvas
20 1/8 x 35 in. (51.1 x 88.9 cm.)
Signed and dated at lower left: M. J. Heade/1864
Henry C. Gibson Fund, 1985.10

George P. A. Healy (1813–1894)

621 *Self-Portrait*, 1881
Oil on canvas
20 x 17 1/8 in. (50.8 x 43.5 cm.)
Signed and dated at lower left: G.P.A.Healy./1881.
Gift of John Frederick Lewis, 1928.8.3

622 *Daniel Webster* (1782–1852), 1852
Oil on canvas
30 3/16 x 25 1/8 in. (76.7 x 63.8 cm.)
Signed and dated at right center: G.P.A.Healy/1852.
Gift of Mrs. John Frederick Lewis (The John Frederick Lewis Memorial Collection), 1933.10.20

Ann Heebner. *See* Ann Heebner McDonald.

John Edward Heliker (1909–)

623 *Dark Sky*, 1946
Oil on masonite
15 7/8 x 19 15/16 in. (40.3 x 50.6 cm.)
Signed at lower right: HELIKER
John Lambert Fund, 1947.4

Helen West Heller (ca. 1872–1955)

624 *Wild Ducks*
Oil on cardboard
29 15/16 x 24 3/16 in. (76 x 61.4 cm.)
Signed at lower left: Helen West Heller
Gift of Carl Zigrosser, 1955.13.1

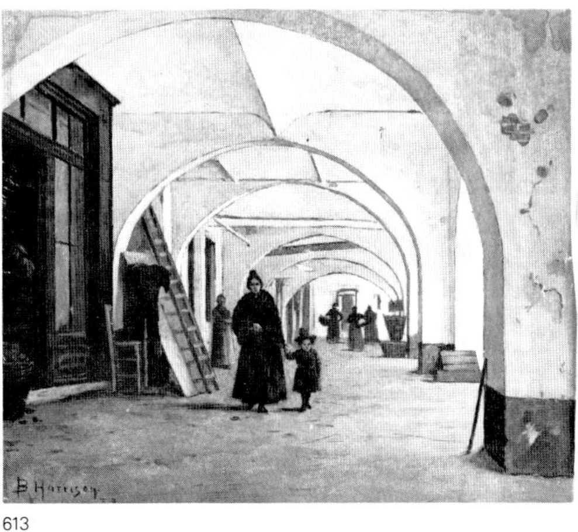
613

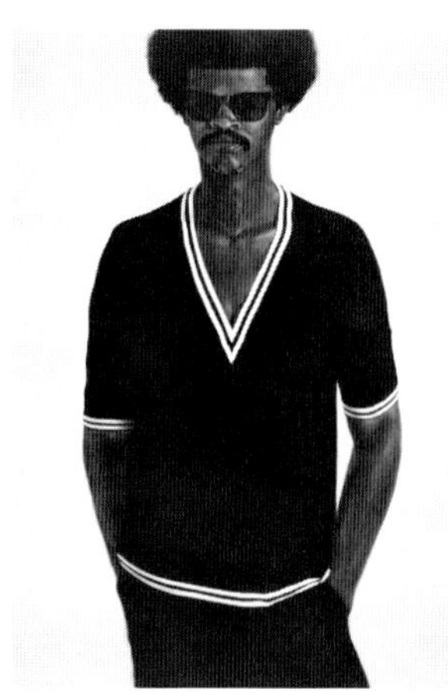
625

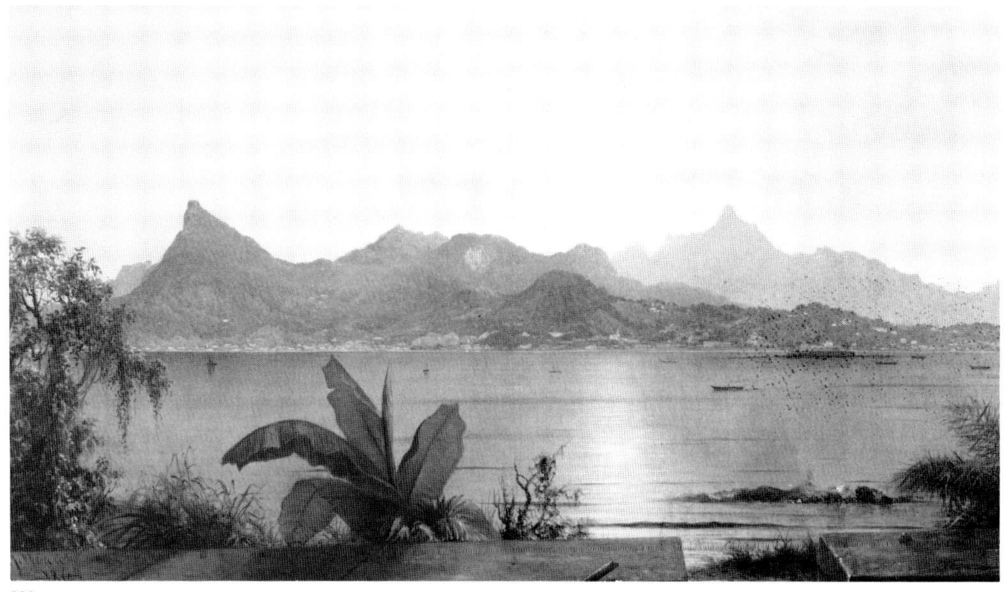

620

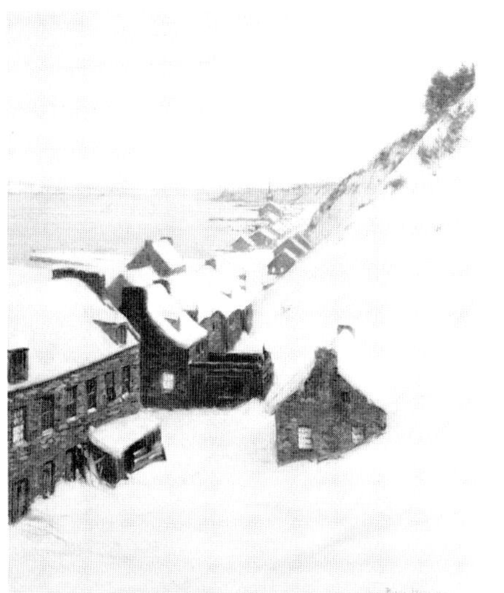

611

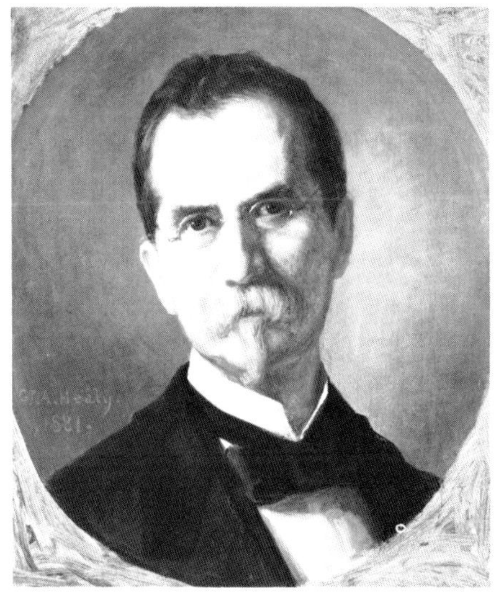

621

Barkley L. Hendricks (1945–)

625 *J. S. B. III* (James Sherman Brantley, 1945–), 1968
Oil on canvas
48 x 34⅜ in. (121.9 x 87.3 cm.)
Annotated on stretcher: 8/15/68
Gift of Mr. and Mrs. Richardson Dilworth, 1969.17

Ernest Martin Hennings (1886–1956)

626 *Announcements*, ca. 1924
Oil on canvas
43³⁄₁₆ x 45 in. (109.7 x 114.3 cm.)
Signed at lower right: E.Martin/Hennings
Joseph E. Temple Fund, 1925.10

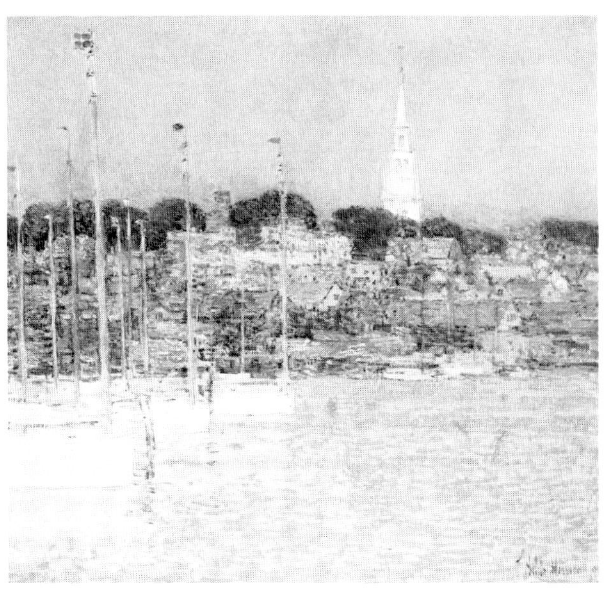

615

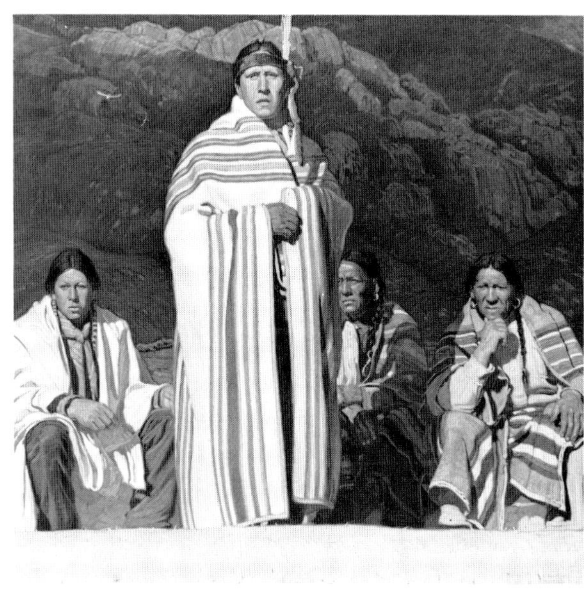

626

Robert Henri (1865–1929)

627 *Girl with Fan*, ca. 1911
Oil on canvas
72 x 49$\frac{1}{4}$ in. (182.9 x 125.1 cm.)
Signed at lower left: Robert Henri; signed and inscribed on back: Robert Henri/$\frac{213}{F}$
Joseph E. Temple Fund, 1912.3

628 *Ruth St. Denis in the Peacock Dance* (1878–1968), 1919
Oil on canvas
85 x 49 in. (215.9 x 124.5 cm.)
Signed at lower right: ROBERT HENRI; signed and inscribed on back: 256 Robert Henri/Portrait of Ruth St.Denis/in the Peacock Dance
Gift of the Sameric Corporation in memory of Eric Shapiro, 1976.1

629 *Wee Maureen*, 1926
Oil on canvas
24 x 20 in. (61 x 50.8 cm.)
Signed at lower right: ROBERT HENRI; inscribed and signed on back: "WEE MAUREEN"/$\frac{N}{60}$ Robert Henri
Gift of Mrs. Herbert Cameron Morris, 1962.17.1

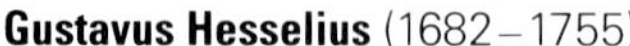

Gustavus Hesselius (1682–1755)

630 *Bacchanalian Revel*, ca. 1720
Oil on canvas
24$\frac{7}{16}$ x 32$\frac{7}{16}$ in. (62.1 x 82.4 cm.)
Joseph E. Temple Fund, 1949.14

Attributed to **Gustavus Hesselius**

631 *The Holy Family*
Oil on canvas
40 x 50$\frac{3}{16}$ in. (101.6 x 127.5 cm.)
Gift of John Frederick Lewis, 1930.7

Louise Lyons Heustis (1865–1951)

632 *John H. Gibbon, Jr., and His Sister Marjorie Young Gibbon* (John, age 7; Marjorie, age 6), 1908
Oil on canvas
60 x 40$\frac{1}{8}$ in. (152.4 x 101.9 cm.)
Signed and dated at lower right: Louise Heustis/1908–
Gift of Mr. and Mrs. Winthrop Battles, 1977.19

Madeline Hewes (ca. 1905–1969)

633 *Florida Chain Gang*, 1948
Oil on masonite
16$\frac{1}{16}$ x 20$\frac{1}{16}$ in. (40.8 x 51 cm.)
Signed at lower right: Hewes
John Lambert Fund, 1952.5

William Keesey Hewitt (1817–1893)

634 *Mrs. Margaret Myers* (née Dover)
Oil on canvas
30 x 25$\frac{1}{8}$ in. (76.2 x 63.8 cm.)
Gift of Agnes T. Myers, 1923.11

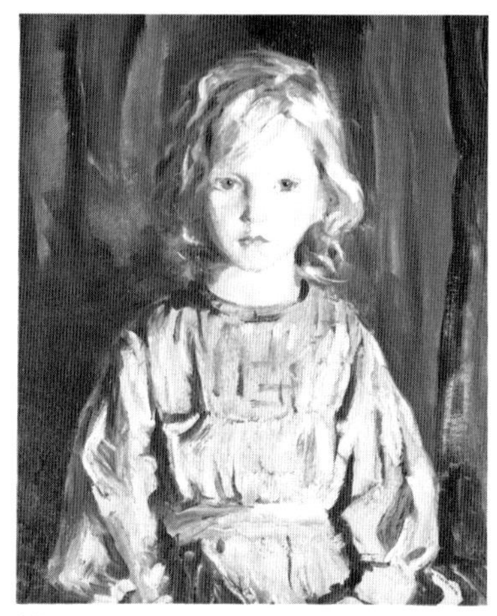

629

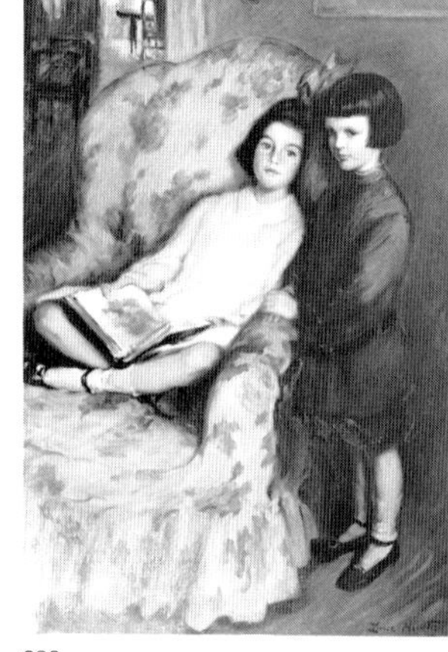

632

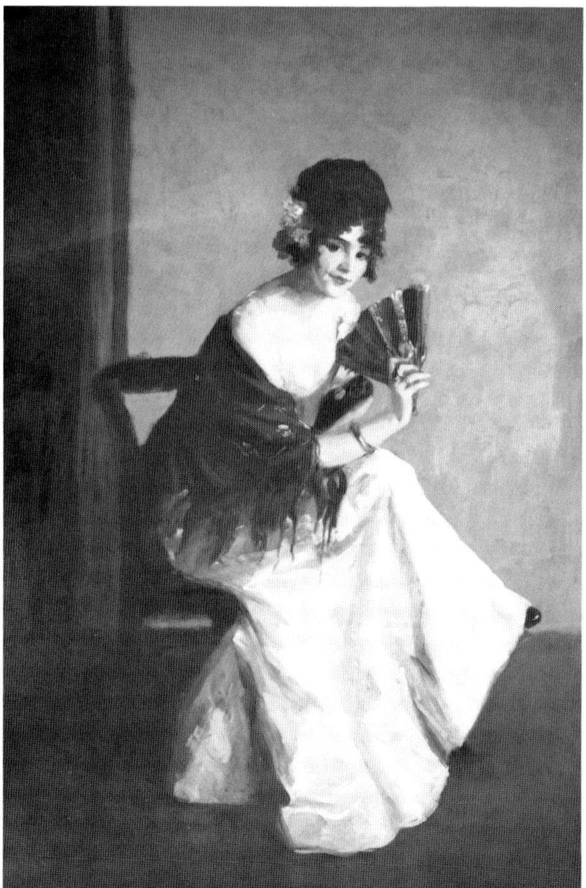

627

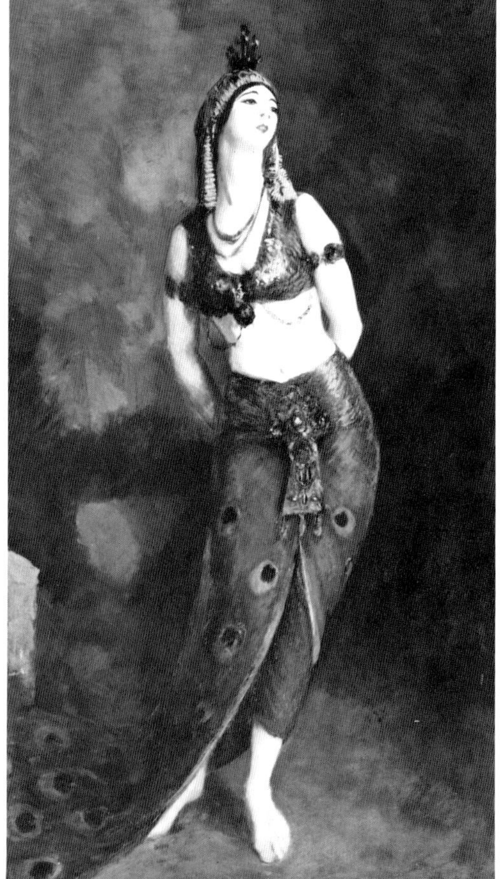

628

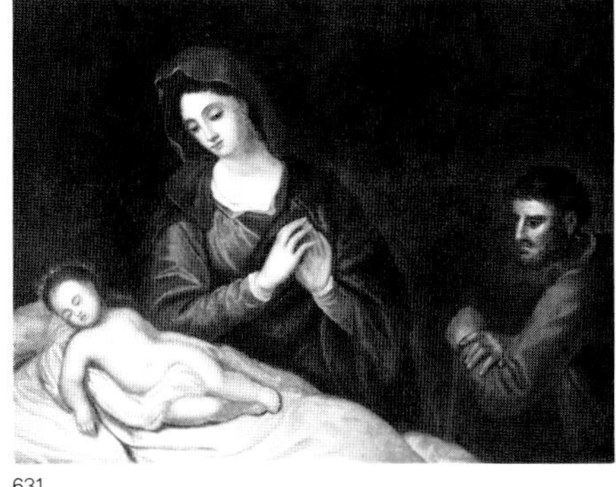

631

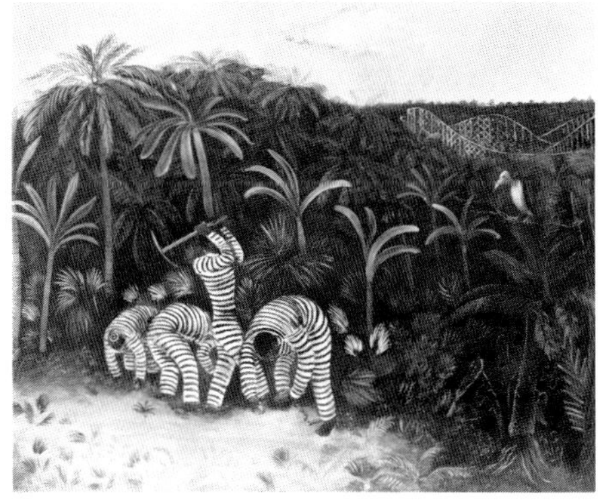

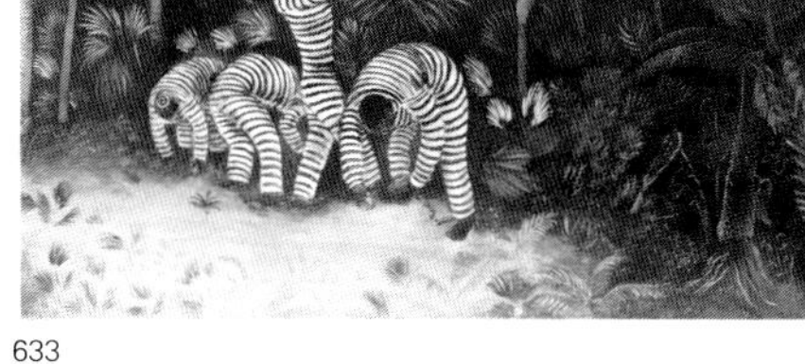

633

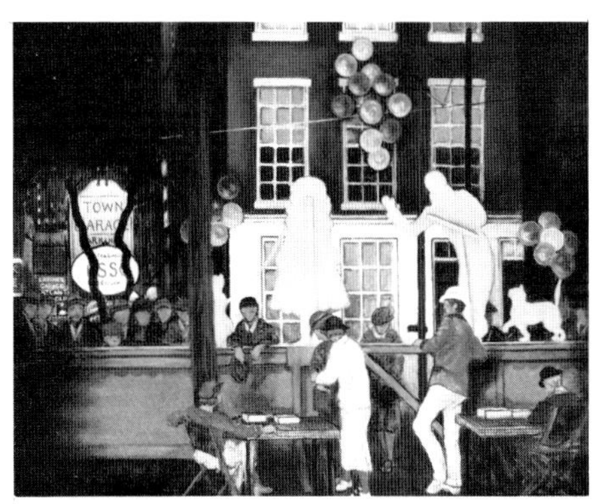

640

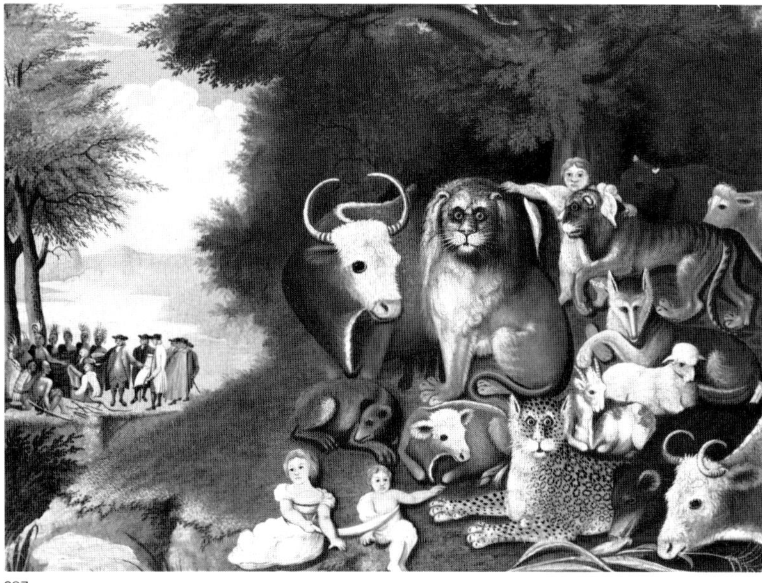

637

635 *Unidentified Man*
Oil on canvas
30 x 25$\frac{1}{16}$ in. (76.2 x 63.7 cm.)
Gift of Mrs. John Frederick Lewis (The John Frederick Lewis Memorial Collection), 1933.10.21

Aldro T. Hibbard (1886–1972)

636 *West River, Vermont*, 1934
Oil on canvas
40 x 50 in. (101.6 x 127 cm.)
Signed and dated at lower left: A. T. Hibbard 1934
Joseph E. Temple Fund, 1936.9

Edward Hicks (1780–1849)

637 *The Peaceable Kingdom*, ca. 1833
Oil on canvas
17$\frac{7}{8}$ x 23$\frac{15}{16}$ in. (45.4 x 60.8 cm.)
John S. Phillips bequest, by exchange (acquired from the Philadelphia Museum of Art, originally the 1950 bequest of Lisa Norris Elkins), 1985.17

Richard C. Hickson (b. 1914)

638 *Still Life*, ca. 1937
Oil on canvas
22$\frac{3}{16}$ x 32 in. (56.4 x 81.3 cm.)
John Lambert Fund, 1938.10

Victor Higgins (1884–1949)

639 *The Widower*, ca. 1923
Oil on canvas
57$\frac{1}{8}$ x 60$\frac{1}{4}$ in. (145.1 x 153 cm.)
Signed at lower left: VICTOR HIGGINS-
Joseph E. Temple Fund, 1924.4

Margaretta S. Hinchman (1876–1955)

640 *Lark in Latimer Street: Looking Out #2*, ca. 1935
Oil on composition board
15$\frac{13}{16}$ x 19$\frac{5}{8}$ in. (40.2 x 49.8 cm.)
Signed at lower left: Margaretta S. Hinchman
John Lambert Fund, 1936.10

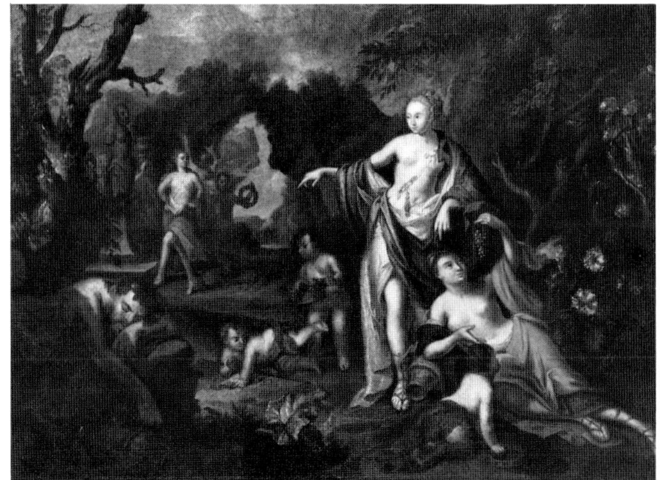

630

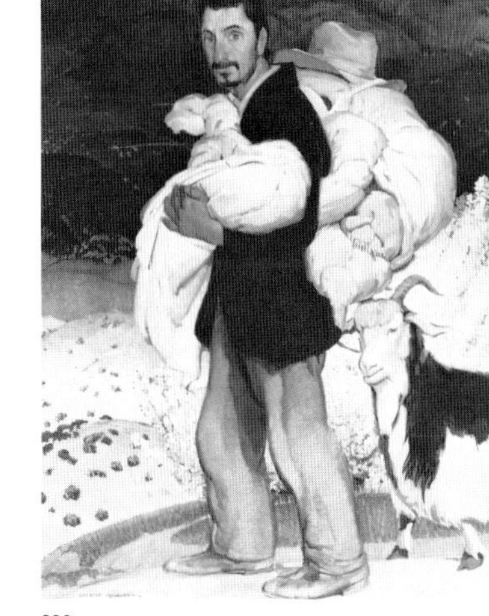

639

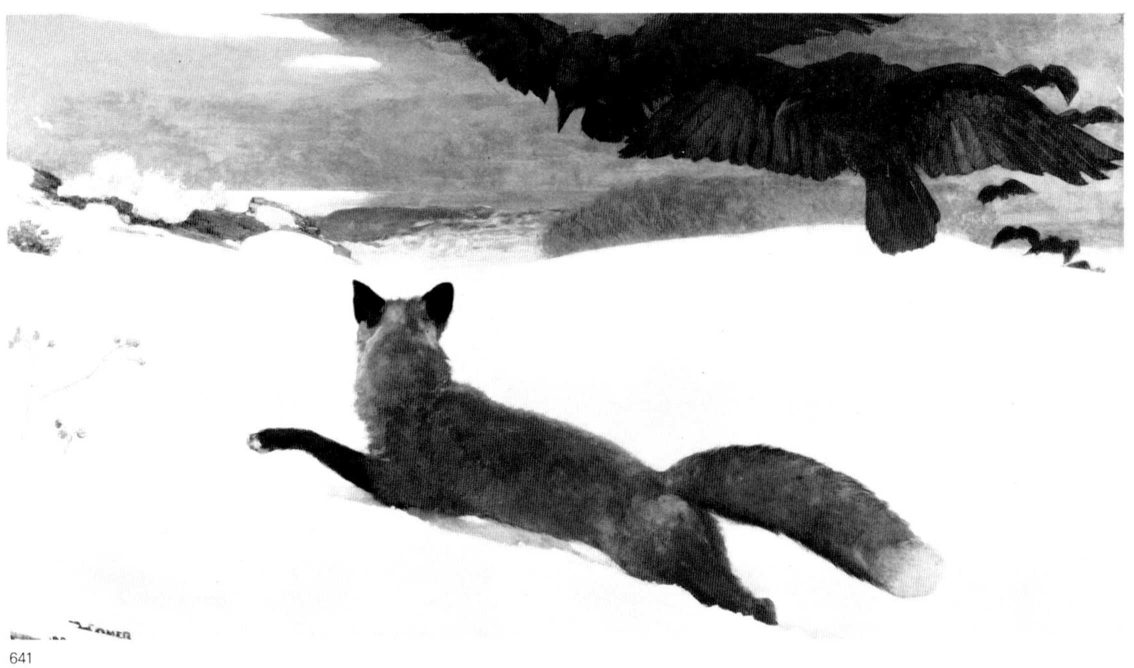
641

Winslow Homer (1836–1910)

641 *Fox Hunt*, 1893
Oil on canvas
38 x 68½ in. (96.5 x 174 cm.)
Signed and dated at lower left: HOMER/1893
Joseph E. Temple Fund, 1894.4

Edward Hopper (1882–1967)

642 *Apartment Houses*, 1923
Oil on canvas
24 x 28¹⁵⁄₁₆ in. (61 x 73.5 cm.)
Signed at lower right: EDWARD HOPPER
John Lambert Fund, 1925.5

643 *East Wind over Weehawken*, 1934
Oil on canvas
34 x 50¼ in. (86.4 x 127.6 cm.)
Signed at lower right: E. HOPPER
Collections Fund, 1952.12

Frank Horowitz (b. 1889)

644 *Still Life*, ca. 1926
Oil on canvas
20¹⁄₁₆ x 15¹⁵⁄₁₆ in. (51 x 40.5 cm.)
Annotated on back: Austin [upside down]
John Lambert Fund, 1927.2

Earle Horter (1881–1941)

645 *Toledo* (also called *Thames Bridge*), ca. 1923
Oil on canvas
20¹⁄₁₆ x 24¹⁄₁₆ in. (51 x 61.1 cm.)
John Lambert Fund, 1924.5

Helen Lloyd Horter (Mrs. Earle Horter, 1903–1981, formerly married to Leon Kelly)

646 *Autumn in Rockport*, ca. 1934
Oil on canvas
20¹⁄₁₆ x 22⅛ in. (51 x 56.2 cm.)
Signed at lower right: Helen Horter
John Lambert Fund, 1935.7

Thomas Hovenden (1840–1895)

647 *The Favorite Falcon* (formerly *The Falcon*), 1879
Oil on canvas
53⅝ x 38¾ in. (136.2 x 98.4 cm.)
Signed and dated at lower right: Hovenden 1879
Gift of Mrs. Edward H. Coates (The Edward H. Coates Memorial Collection), 1923.9.1

648 *Peonies*, 1886
Oil on canvas
20 x 24⅛ in. (50.8 x 61.3 cm.)
Signed at lower left: TH [monogram]; dated at lower right: 1886.
Gift of Mrs. Edward H. Coates (The Edward H. Coates Memorial Collection), 1923.9.2

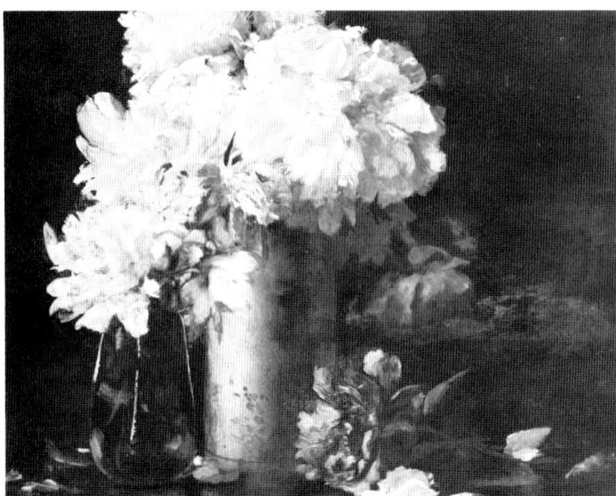

648

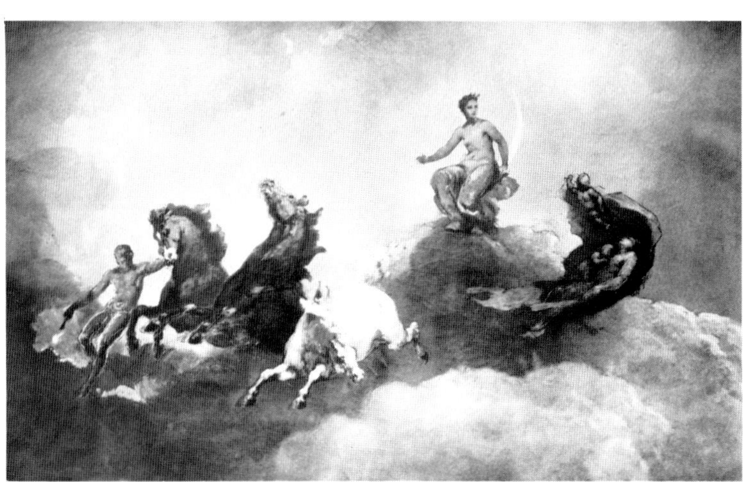
651

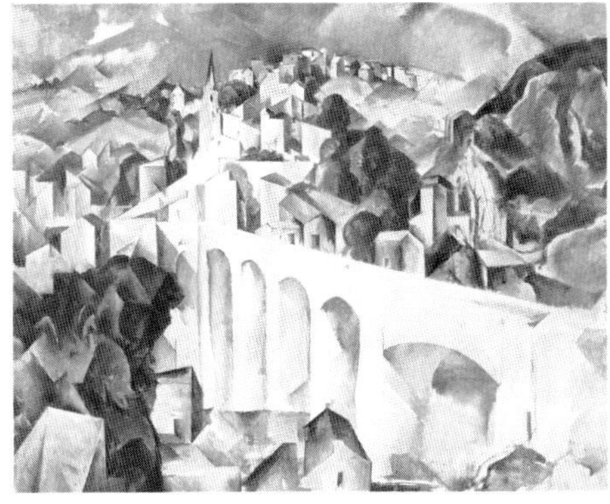
645

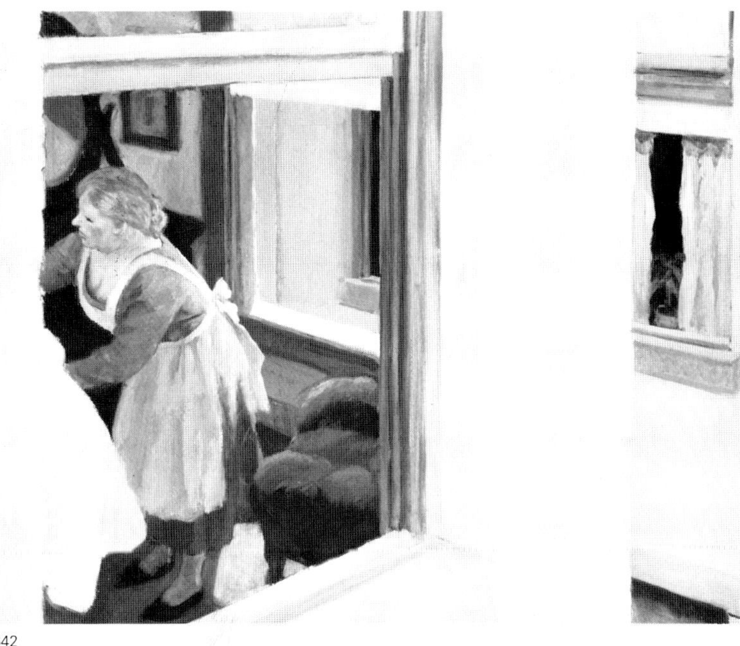
642

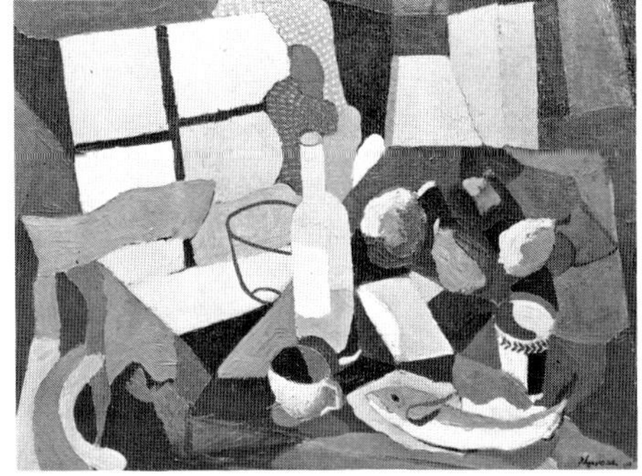
649

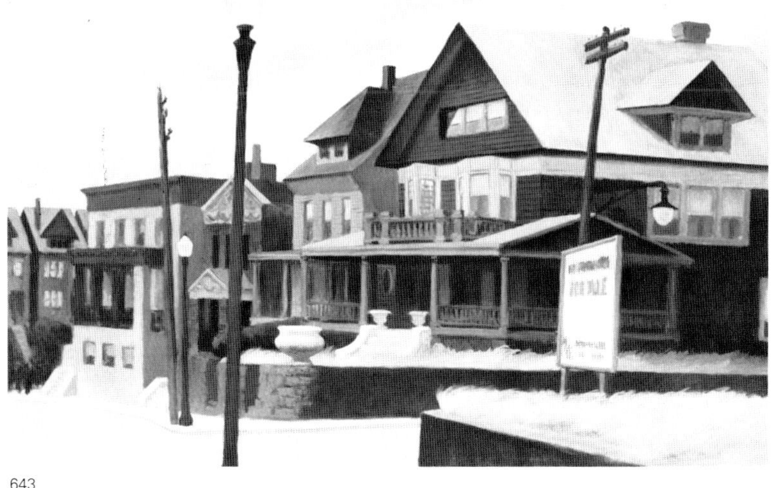
643

Humbert L. Howard (1915–)

649 *The Yellow Cup*, 1949–50
Oil on canvas
24 x 32⅛ in. (61 x 81.6 cm.)
Signed and dated at lower right: Howard 49; inscribed, signed, and dated on back: "The Yellow Cup"/Humbert Howard 1950 [painted over "49"]
John Lambert Fund, 1951.8

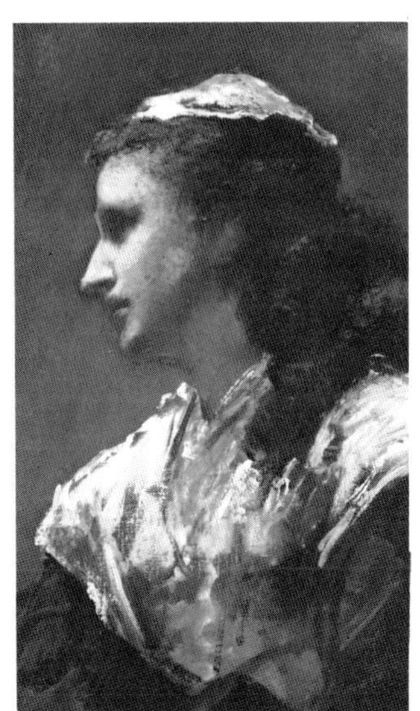
650

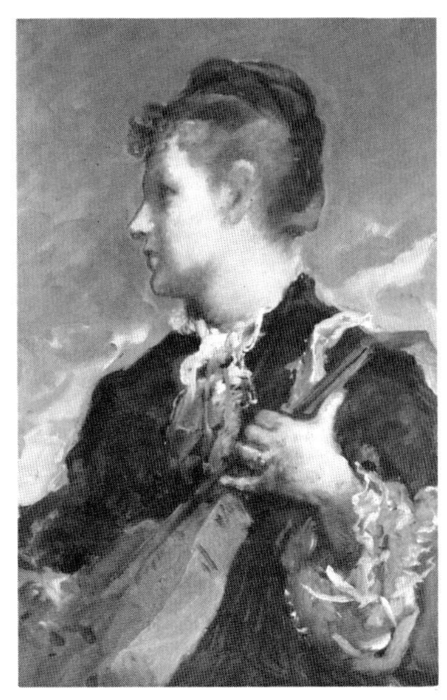
652

William Morris Hunt (1824–1879)

650 *Priscilla* (formerly *Girl with White Cap*), ca. 1873
Oil on canvas
24 x 14⅛ in. (61 x 35.9 cm.)
Henry D. Gilpin Fund, 1898.3.2

651 *Study for "The Flight of Night,"* 1878
Oil and chalk on canvas
62 x 99 in. (157.5 x 251.5 cm.)
Henry D. Gilpin Fund, 1898.3.1

652 *A Young Woman with a Guitar*, ca. 1875
Oil on canvas
30¼ x 20¼ in. (76.8 x 51.4 cm.)
Gift of Edith Howe DeWolf, Rhoda Howe Low, Grace Howe Jordan, and Amy Howe Steel in memory of their parents, Dr. and Mrs. Herbert M. Howe, and their grandparents Mr. and Mrs. J. Gillingham Fell, 1924.7.3

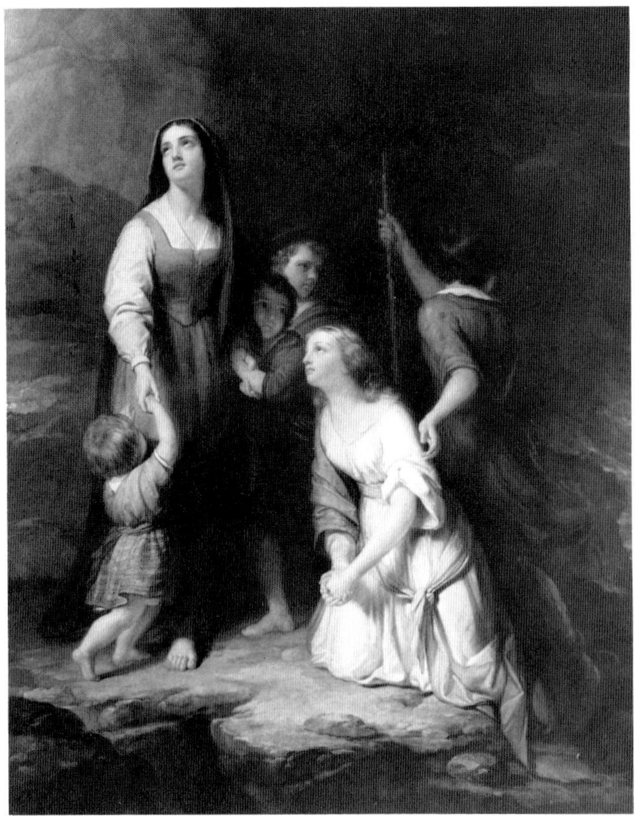
653

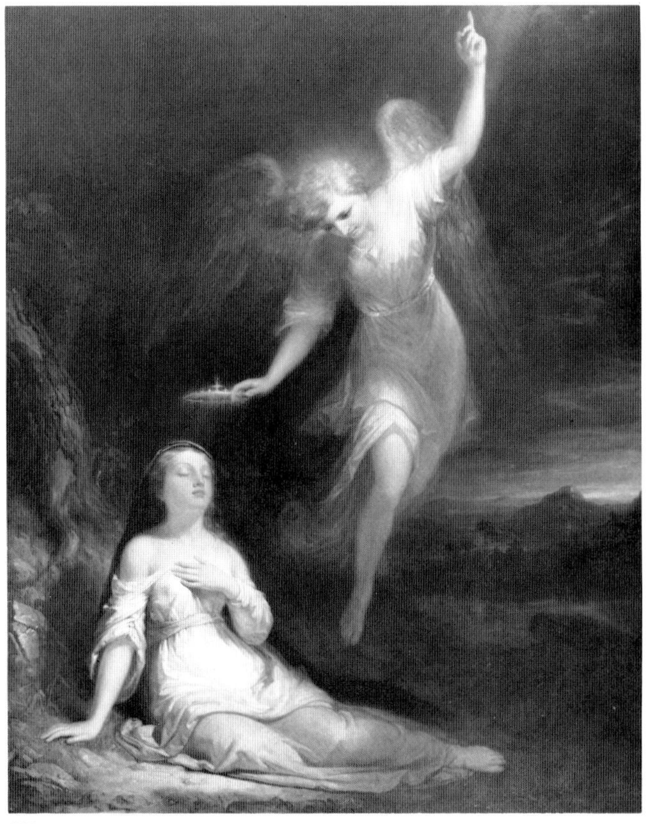
655

Daniel Huntington (1816–1906)

653 *Christiana and Her Family Passing through the Valley of the Shadow of Death*, 1842–44
Oil on canvas
92¼ x 74 in. (234.3 x 188 cm.)
Bequest of Henry C. Carey (The Carey Collection), 1879.8.8

654 *Albert Gallatin* (1761–1849), ca. 1841
Oil on canvas
30³⁄₁₆ x 25¹⁄₁₆ in. (76.7 x 63.7 cm.)
Signed at lower right: D.Huntington
Gift of Mrs. John Frederick Lewis (The John Frederick Lewis Memorial Collection), 1933.10.22

655 *Mercy's Dream*, 1841
Oil on canvas
84½ x 66½ in. (214.6 x 168.9 cm.)
Signed and dated at lower left: D. Huntington./ 1841
Bequest of Henry C. Carey (The Carey Collection), 1879.8.10

656 *Venetian Girl* (formerly *Florentine Girl*), ca. 1840
(after his *Florentine Girl*, 1839)
Oil on canvas
34¼ x 27⅛ in. (87 x 68.9 cm.)
Bequest of Henry C. Carey (The Carey Collection), 1879.8.9

Margaret Wendell Huntington (1867–1955)

657 *Cornwall Cliffs*, ca. 1918
Oil on canvas
23¹⁵⁄₁₆ x 30 in. (60.8 x 76.2 cm.)
John Lambert Fund, 1919.4

Peter Hurd (1904–1984)

658 *The New Mill*, ca. 1935
Egg tempera on gessoed board
21½ x 17½ in. (54.6 x 44.5 cm.)
Gift of Mrs. Thomas E. Drake (The Margaretta S. Hinchman Collection), 1955.15.7

John Eddy Hutchins (b. 1891)

659 *Bedroom*, ca. 1928
Oil on canvas
30 x 36 in. (76.2 x 91.4 cm.)
John Lambert Fund, 1929.3

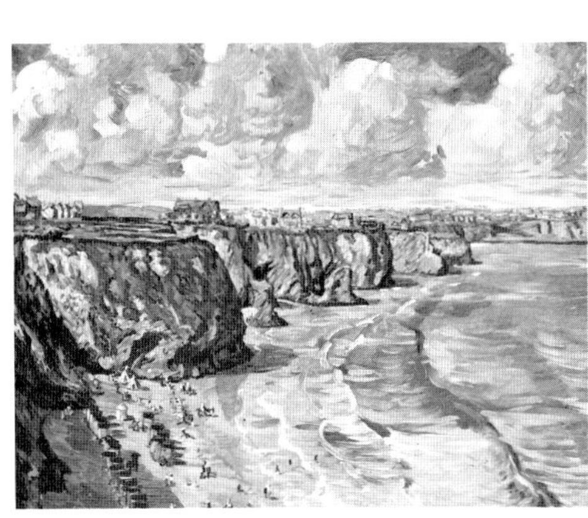
657

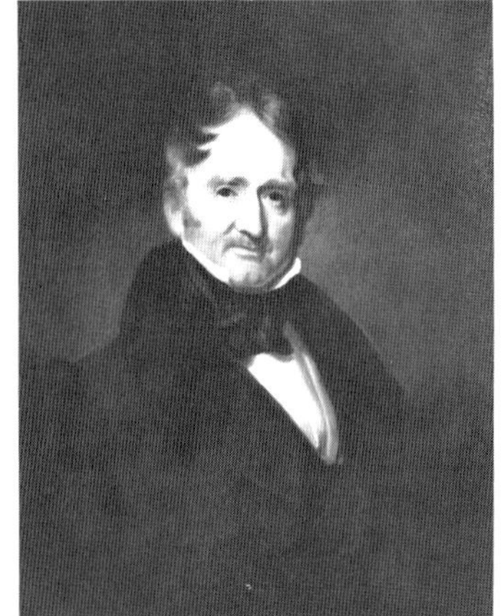
663

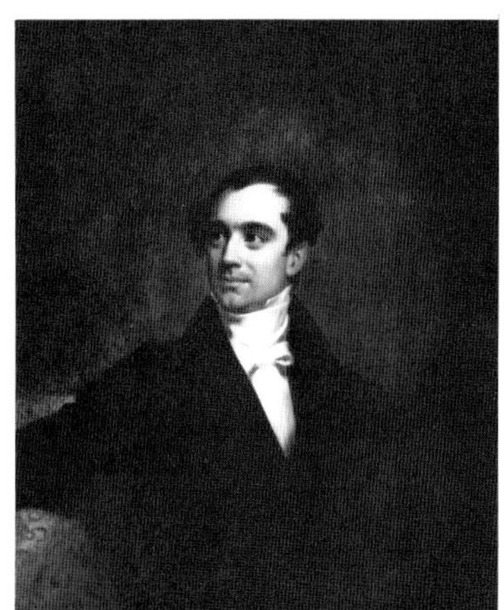
664

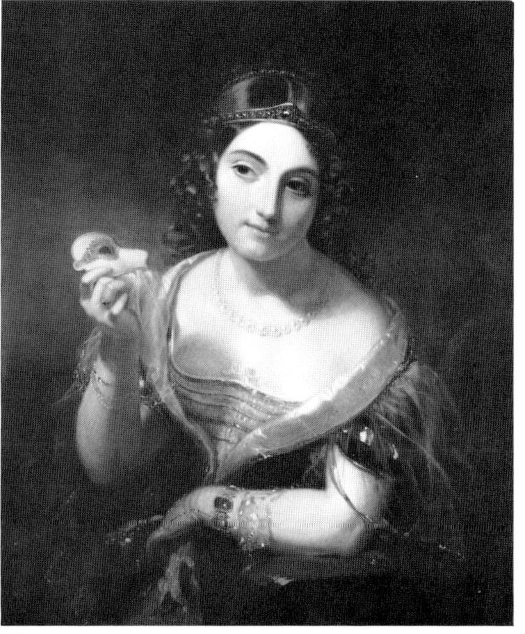

665

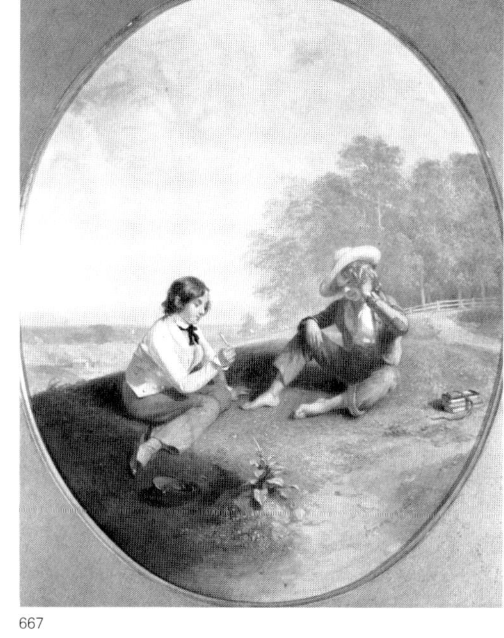

667

Anna Warren Ingersoll (1887–1980)

660 *Black Afternoon*, ca. 1934
Oil on canvas
25 x 36⅛ in. (63.5 x 91.8 cm.)
Signed at upper right: ingersoll
John Lambert Fund, 1935.8

Henry Inman (1801–1846)

661 *David Paul Brown* (1795–1872), ca. 1832
Oil on canvas
36⅜ x 28 in. (92.4 x 71.1 cm.)
Gift of Eva Brown, 1896.4

662 *Caleb Cope* (1797–1888), 1841
Oil on canvas
36⅛ x 28⅛ in. (91.8 x 71.4 cm.)
Inscribed on letter held by sitter: To/Caleb Cop[e]/[illegible]
Gift of Caleb Cope, 1862.1

663 *Robert Gilmor II* (1774–1848), ca. 1833
(formerly attributed to John Wesley Jarvis)
Oil on canvas
30⅛ x 25⅛ in. (76.5 x 63.8 cm.)
Gift of John Frederick Lewis, 1922.1.2

664 *Henry Dilworth Gilpin* (1801–1860), ca. 1834
Oil on canvas
36$^{13}/_{16}$ x 30½ in. (93.5 x 77.5 cm.)
Gift of Miss I. L. Gilpin, 1876.5

665 *Lady with a Mask*, 1841
Oil on canvas
30⅛ x 25⅛ in. (76.5 x 63.8 cm.)
Signed at lower right: H. Inman; annotated on lining since removed: The Lady with a Mask/ H.Inman Pinxt/N.York. 1841.
Bequest of Henry C. Carey (The Carey Collection), 1879.8.11

666 *Lord Thomas Babington Macaulay* (1800–1859), 1844
Oil on canvas
30⅜ x 25¼ in. (77.2 x 64.1 cm.)
Bequest of Henry C. Carey (The Carey Collection), 1879.8.12

667 *Mumble-the-Peg*, 1842
Oil on canvas
24⅛ x 20$^{1}/_{16}$ in. (61.3 x 51 cm.)
Signed and dated at lower right: Inman.1842.
Bequest of Henry C. Carey (The Carey Collection), 1879.8.13

668 *Henry Pratt* (1761–1838), ca. 1830
Oil on canvas
36¼ x 29¼ in. (92.1 x 74.3 cm.)
Gift of Mrs. J. Dundas Lippincott, 1905.7

669 *Self-Portrait*, 1834
Oil on canvas
12$^{1}/_{16}$ x 10$^{1}/_{16}$ in. (30.6 x 25.6 cm.)
Said to be inscribed and dated on back (before lining): sketch by H. Inman of himself at 33, June, 1834
Bequest of Cephas G. Childs, 1871.1.1

670 *Thomas Sully* (1783–1872), 1837
Oil on academy board
23$^{15}/_{16}$ x 19$^{13}/_{16}$ in. (60.7 x 50.3 cm.)
Gift of Blanche Sully, 1891.6

671 *Unidentified Man*, 1833
(formerly attributed to John Neagle)
Oil on canvas
30$^{1}/_{16}$ x 24$^{13}/_{16}$ in. (76.4 x 63 cm.)
Signed and dated at lower right: H. Inman/1833
Gift of Mrs. John Frederick Lewis (The John Frederick Lewis Memorial Collection), 1933.10.28

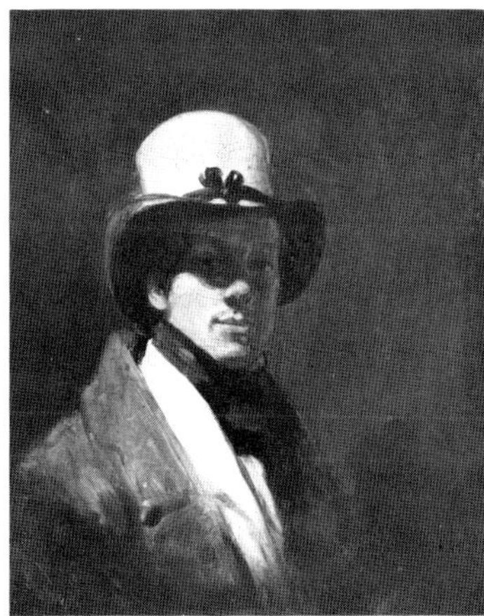

669

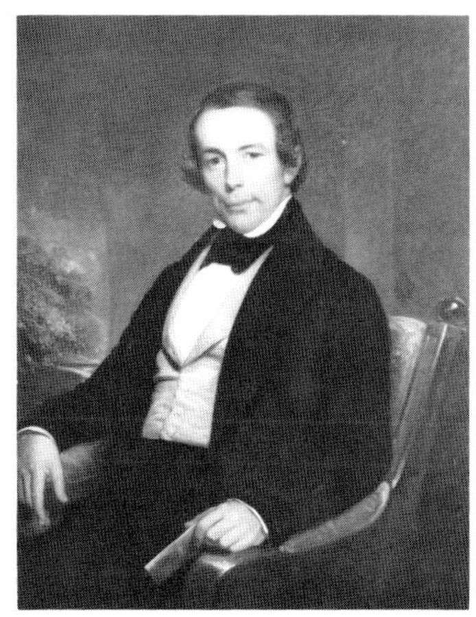

662

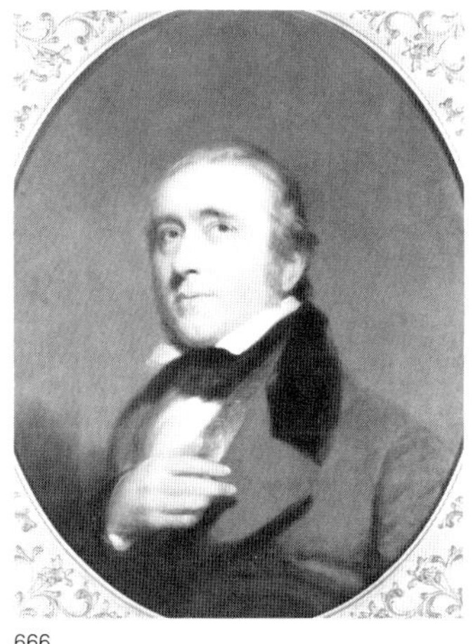

666

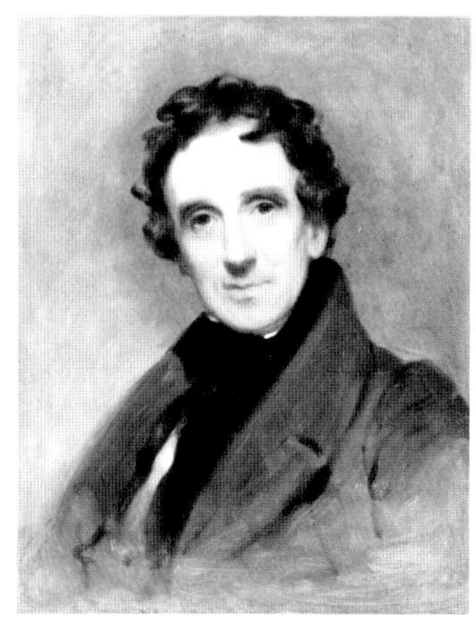

670

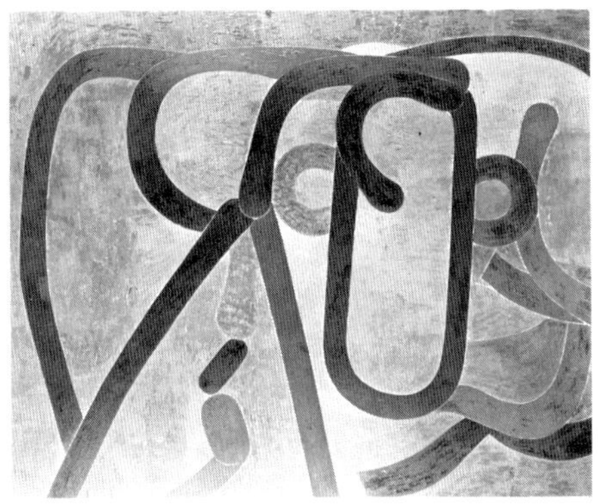

675

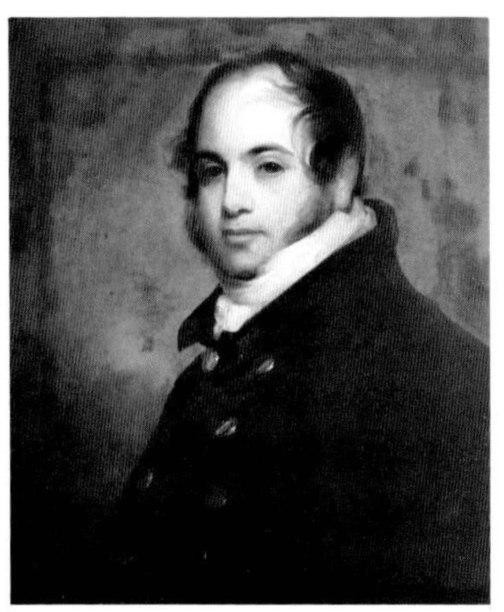

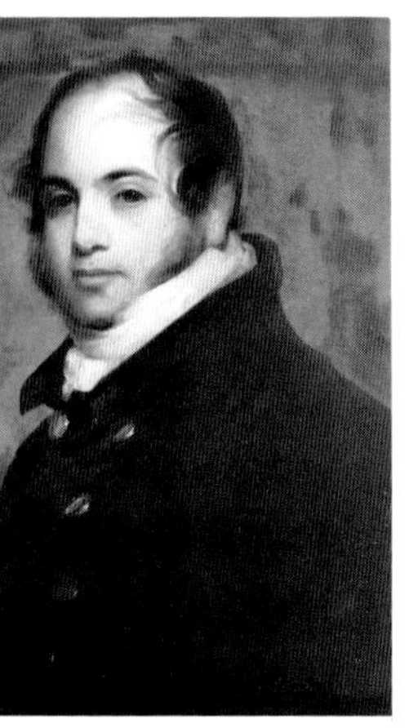

683

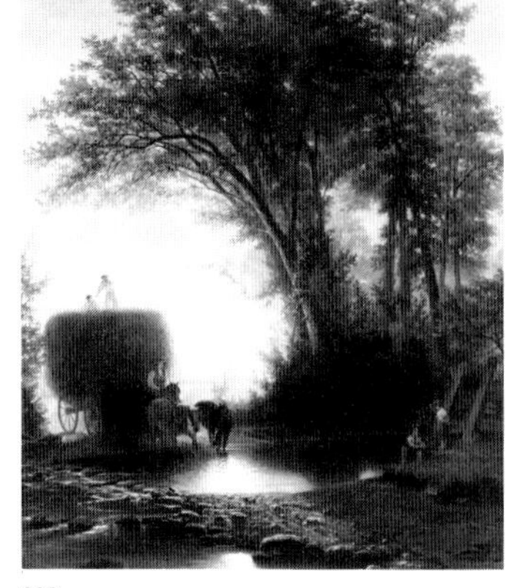

686

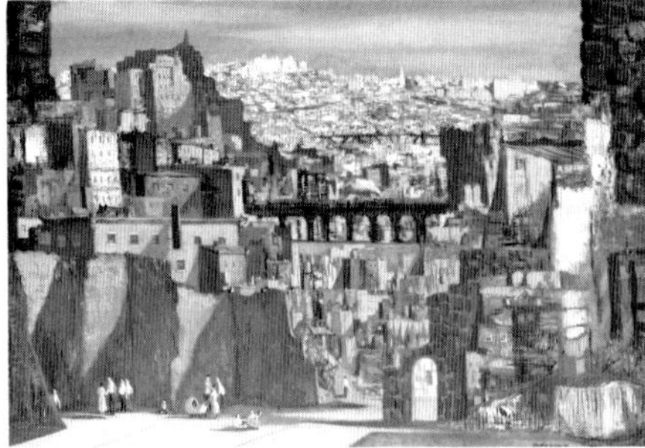

676

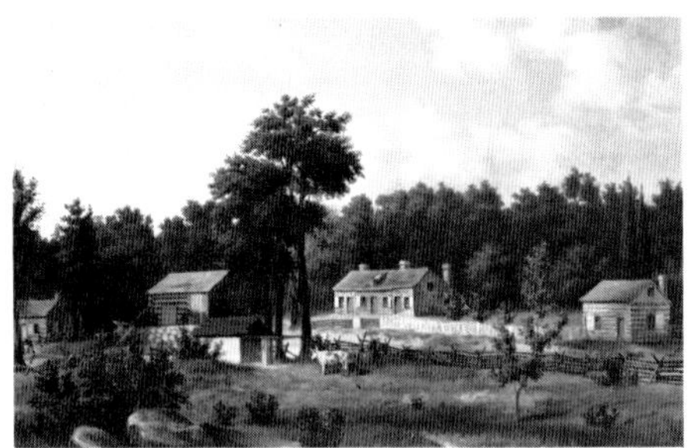

687

George Inness (1825–1894)

672 *Apple Blossom Time*, 1883
Oil on canvas
27 1/8 x 22 1/8 in. (68.9 x 56.2 cm.)
Signed and dated at lower right: G Inness 1883
Bequest of J. Mitchell Elliot, 1952.22.2

673 *Woodland Scene*, 1891
Oil on canvas
30 x 45 in. (76.2 x 114.3 cm.)
Signed and dated at lower right: G.Inness 1891
Gift of John Frederick Lewis, Jr., 1954.22.3

Eric Isenburger (1902–)

674 *Central Park in Winter*, 1942
Oil on canvas
30 1/4 x 36 3/16 in. (76.8 x 91.9 cm.)
Signed at lower left: isenburger; signed, dated, and inscribed on back: ERIC ISENBURGER 1942: CENTRAL PARK
John Lambert Fund, 1944.4

Miyoko Ito (1918–1983)

675 *Act Three by the Sea*, 1959
Oil on canvas
50 1/8 x 60 1/8 in. (127.3 x 152.7 cm.)
Henry D. Gilpin Fund, 1960.5

Martin Jackson (1919–1986)

676 *Place of Echoes*, 1948
Oil on canvas
21 7/8 x 31 15/16 in. (55.6 x 81.1 cm.)
Signed and dated at lower right: Martin Jackson 48
John Lambert Fund, 1949.7

677 *View to the East*, 1947
Oil on canvas
22 x 33 15/16 in. (55.9 x 86.2 cm.)
Signed at lower left: Martin Jackson
John Lambert Fund, 1948.6

Norman Jacobsen (b. 1884)

678 *Balinese Girl*, ca. 1930
Oil on masonite
24 1/8 x 18 3/16 in. (61.3 x 46.2 cm.)
Signed at lower left: Jacobsen
John Lambert Fund, 1931.4

Nora Jaffe (1928–)

679 *Lovescape I*, 1962
Oil on canvas
72 x 90 in. (182.9 x 228.6 cm.)

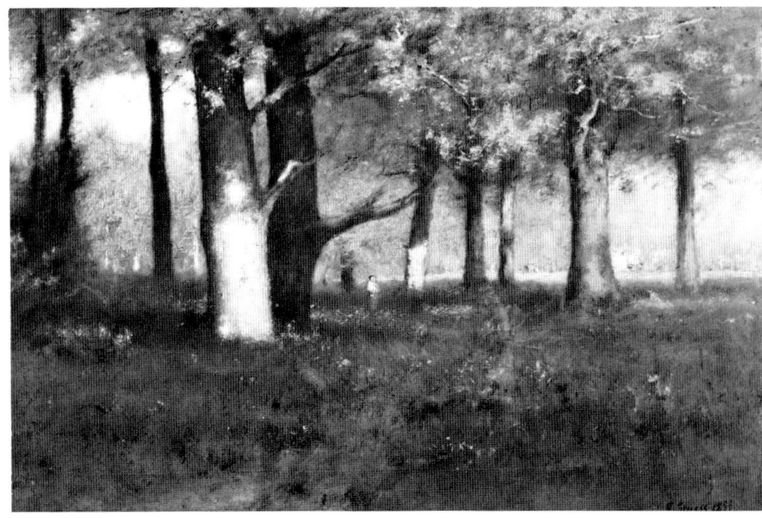

673

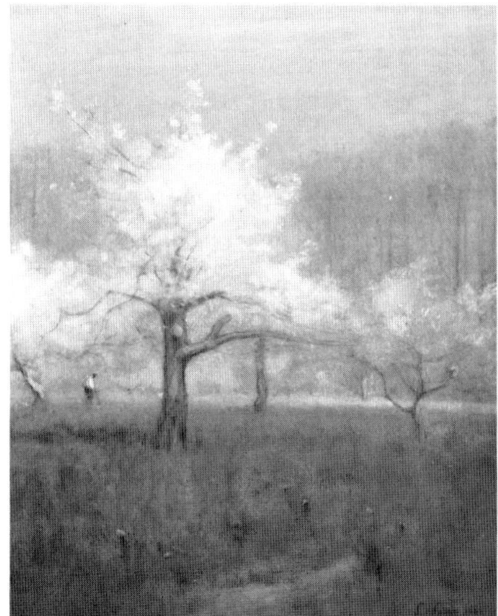

672

Signed and dated at lower right: Jaffe 1962
Inscribed and signed on canvas folded over stretcher: LOVESCAPE II [*sic*] NORA JAFFE
Gift of Mrs. Mary Venelia McNab, 1964.7

John Wesley Jarvis (1780–1840)

680 *William Harris Crawford* (1772–1834), ca. 1823
Oil on canvas
30 7/16 x 25 1/8 in. (77.3 x 63.8 cm.)
Gift of Charles Roberts, 1899.6

681 *Dr. David Hosack* (?) (1769–1835)
Oil on canvas
29 7/8 x 24 11/16 in. (75.9 x 62.7 cm.)
Gift of Mrs. John Frederick Lewis (The John Frederick Lewis Memorial Collection), 1933.10.29

682 *Commodore John B. Nicolson* (1783–1846), ca. 1815
Oil on wood
29 15/16 x 22 7/16 in. (76 x 57 cm.)
Gift of Mrs. John Frederick Lewis (The John Frederick Lewis Memorial Collection), 1933.10.32

683 *Commodore Oliver Hazard Perry* (?) (1785–1820)
Oil on canvas
25 3/16 x 22 1/16 in. (64 x 56 cm.)
Gift of Mrs. John Frederick Lewis (The John Frederick Lewis Memorial Collection), 1933.10.34

William Jennys (active 1793–1807)

684 *Colonel Constant Storrs* (1752–1828), 1802
Oil on canvas
29 7/8 x 24 11/16 in. (75.9 x 62.7 cm.)
Inscribed, signed, and dated on back: Col. Constant Storrs AE. 50/Wm Jennys Pinxt. June 23 1802
Gift of John Frederick Lewis, 1923.8.16

685 *Mrs. Constant Storrs* (née Lucinda Howe, 1758–1830), probably 1802
Oil on canvas
29 7/8 x 24 11/16 in. (75.9 x 62.7 cm.)
Gift of John Frederick Lewis, 1923.8.17

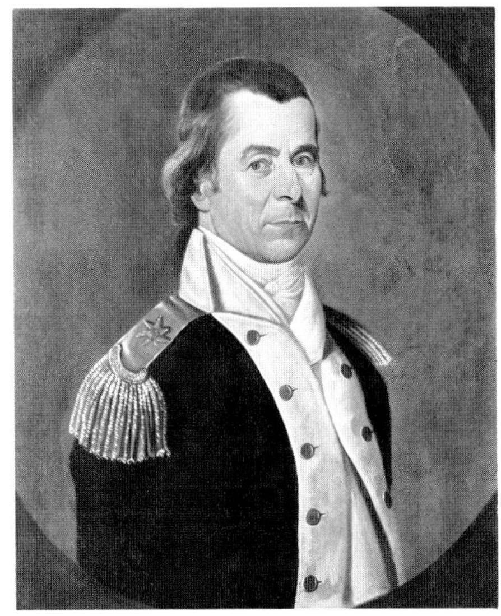
684

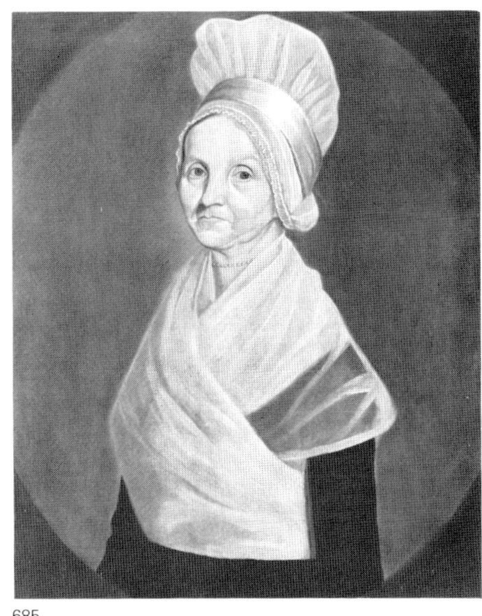
685

J. John

686 *Landscape with Figures*, 1866
Oil on canvas
46 3/16 x 36 1/8 in. (117.3 x 91.8 cm.)
Signed and dated at lower center: J.John 1866
Gift of Mrs. J. Maurice Gray, 1962.23.1

Attributed to **Joseph John** (1833–1877)

687 *Homestead of James and Margaret Green, Springfield Township, Bucks County, Pennsylvania*, ca. 1850
Oil on canvas
20 3/16 x 30 3/16 in. (51.3 x 76.7 cm.)
Gift of Mrs. Harry M. Bell, 1980.10

David Johnson (1827–1908)

688 *William Sidney Mount* (1807–1868), 1850 (after Charles Loring Elliott, 1848)
Oil on canvas
30 3/16 x 25 3/16 in. (76.7 x 64 cm.)
Inscribed, signed, and dated on back (before lining): Portrait of WmS. Mount/ D.Johnson./1850
Henry D. Gilpin Fund, 1916.10

689 *Mount Marcy, New York*, ca. 1865
Oil on canvas
16 1/16 x 30 1/16 in. (40.8 x 76.4 cm.)
Gift of Mr. and Mrs. Edward Kesler, 1975.20.6

690 *General Winfield Scott* (1786–1866), 1861
(after photograph by Brady studio)
Oil on canvas
36 1/8 x 29 1/8 in. (91.8 x 74 cm.)
Signed and dated at lower left: D. Johnson/ 1861.; annotated on lining: D.Johnson./ Sept 1861.
Gift of Mrs. John Frederick Lewis (The John Frederick Lewis Memorial Collection), 1933.10.35

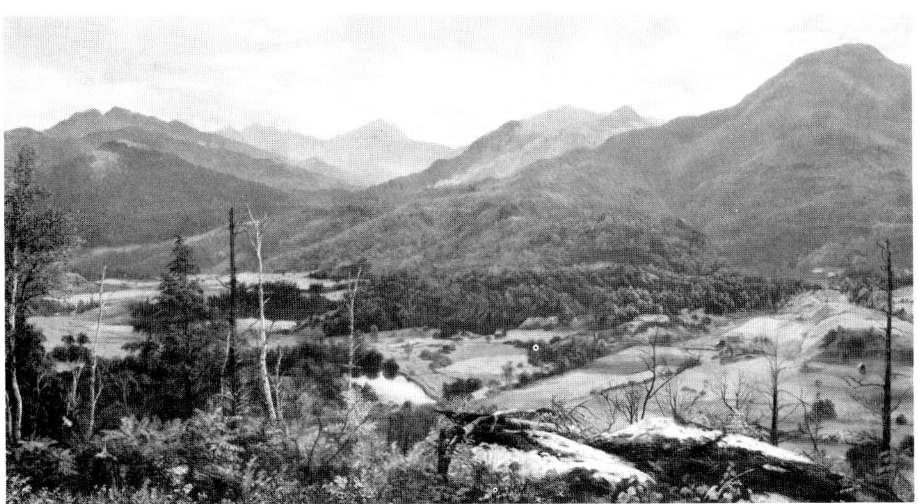
689

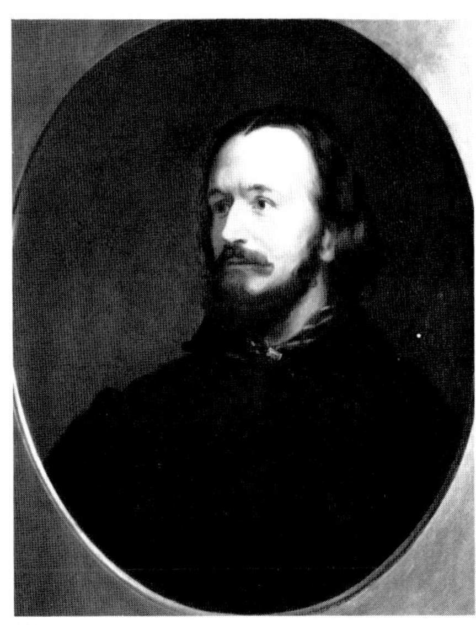
688

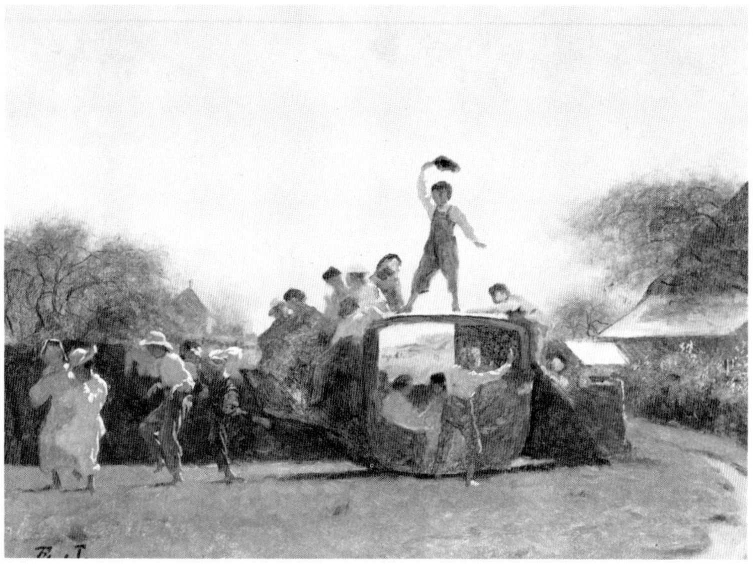
692

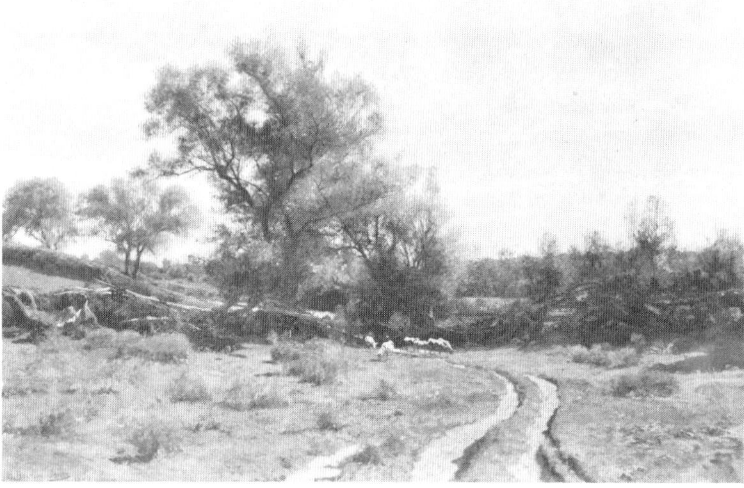
696

Eastman Johnson (1824–1906)

691 *Sanford Robinson Gifford* (1823–1880), ca. 1880
Oil on academy board
27³⁄₁₆ x 22¼ in. (69.1 x 56.5 cm.)
Signed at lower right: E.J.
Gift of John Frederick Lewis, 1920.10.2

692 *Study for "The Old Stage Coach,"* 1871
Oil on canvas
13¾ x 18 in. (34.9 x 45.7 cm.)
Signed at lower left: E.J.
Partial gift and bequest of Mrs. Bernice McIlhenny Wintersteen, 1977.24.1

Attributed to **Joshua Johnson** (active 1796–1824)

693 *Unidentified Man*, ca. 1810
Oil on canvas
26⅛ x 22¹⁄₁₆ in. (66.4 x 56 cm.)
Gift of Mrs. Edgar L. Smith, 1980.5.2

694 *Unidentified Woman*, ca. 1810
Oil on canvas
30½ x 24 in. (77.5 x 61 cm.)
Gift of Mrs. Edgar L. Smith, 1980.5.1

Thomas Murphy Johnston (1834–1869)

695 *Unidentified Boy*, 1867
Oil on wood
18 x 14⅞ in. (45.7 x 37.8 cm.)
Signed and dated at lower left: TM JOHNSTON/1867
Gift of Caroline Gibson Taitt, 1910.2.3

Hugh Bolton Jones (1848–1927)

696 *Sheep Pasture*, 1882
Oil on canvas
21⅛ x 31½ in. (53.7 x 80 cm.)
Signed and dated at lower left: H.BOLTON JONES/1882
Bequest of Harrison Earl, 1894.6.3

Matthew Harris Jouett (1788–1827)

697 *Peter Grayson*, 1827, unfinished
Oil on canvas
30 x 25 in. (76.2 x 63.5 cm.)
Gift of Mrs. Sarah B. Menefee, 1897.1

Attributed to **Matthew Harris Jouett**

698 *Charles Foster Lyon* (d. 1837)
Oil on canvas
35 x 27⁵⁄₁₆ in. (88.9 x 69.4 cm.)
Gift of Mrs. John Frederick Lewis (The John Frederick Lewis Memorial Collection), 1933.10.36

699 *Unidentified Man*
(possibly after Gilbert Stuart)
Oil on canvas
29 x 24 in. (73.7 x 61 cm.)
Gift of Mrs. John Frederick Lewis (The John Frederick Lewis Memorial Collection), 1933.10.37

Tom Judd (1952–)

700 *Time Hasn't Guessed*, 1983
Oil and graphite on canvas
91⅛ x 96⅛ in. (231.4 x 244.1 cm.)
Signed and dated at lower left: Tom Judd '83; inscribed, signed, and dated on back: "TIME HASN'T GUESSED"/(OIL ON CANVAS)/ Tom Judd-'83
John Lambert Fund, 1984.9

Ben Kamihira (1925–)

701 *Anne Baker Lewis* (later Mrs. Paul Stoudt, 1928–), ca. 1956
Oil on canvas
44¼ x 36¼ in. (112.4 x 92.1 cm.)
Signed at lower right: KAMIHIRA
Gift of Mrs. Paul Stoudt, 1968.13

702 *Promenade;* on back, *Landscape with Farm* (sketch), 1952
Oil on canvas
18 x 24⅛ in. (45.7 x 61.3 cm.)
Signed and dated at lower right: KAMIHIRA 52
Gift of the Fellowship of the Pennsylvania Academy, 1952.14

703 *Still Life: Fruit and Vegetables*, 1954
Oil on masonite
17¾ x 27¹³⁄₁₆ in. (45.1 x 70.6 cm.)
Signed and dated at lower left: KAMIHIRA 1954
Gift of James P. and Ruth Marshall Magill, 1957.15.14

704 *Twin Bridges, Schuylkill*, 1953
Oil on canvas
18 x 29¹⁄₁₆ in. (45.7 x 73.8 cm.)
Dated and signed at lower left: '53 KAMIHIRA
Gift of James P. and Ruth Marshall Magill, 1957.15.15

A. John Kammer (1932–)

705 *Antique Shop*, 1956
Oil on cardboard
20³⁄₁₆ x 20³⁄₁₆ in. (51.3 x 51.3 cm.)
Gift of James P. and Ruth Marshall Magill, 1957.15.50

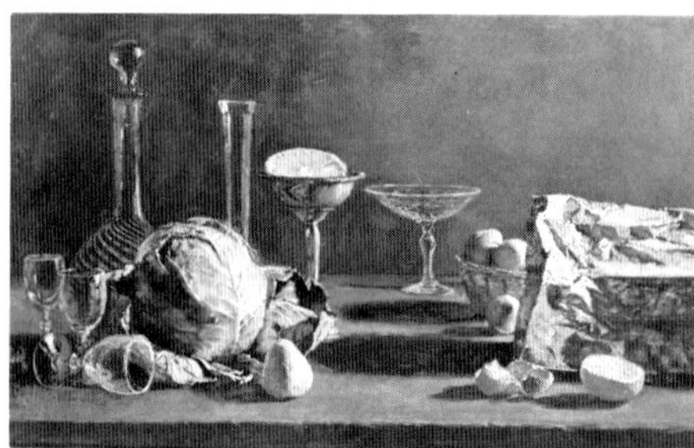
703

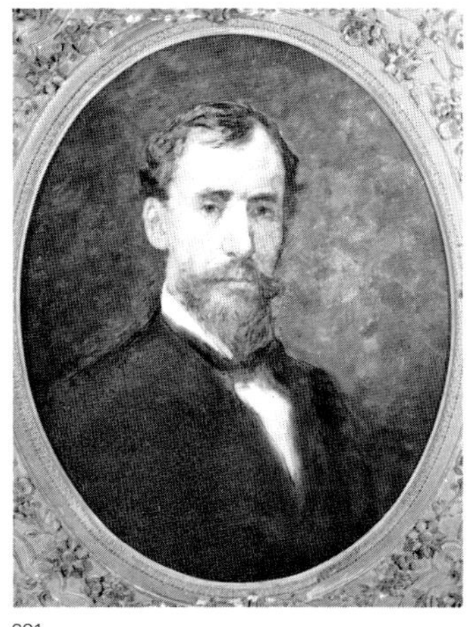
691

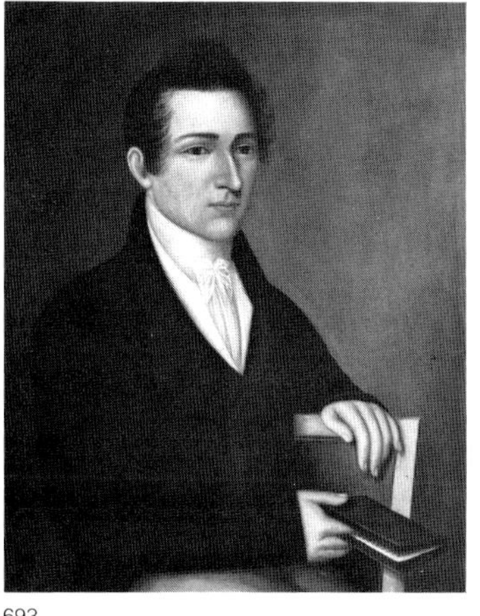
693

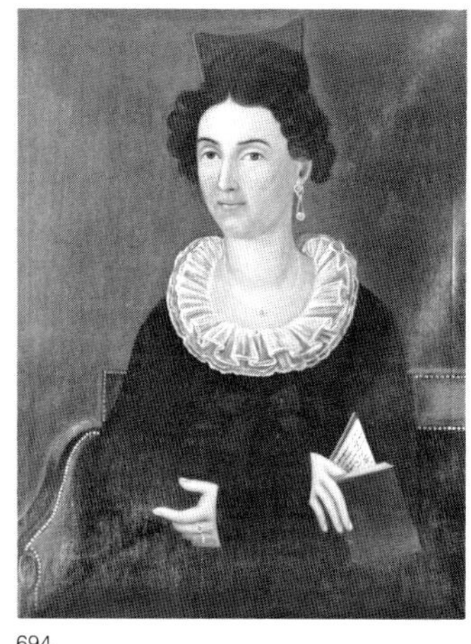
694

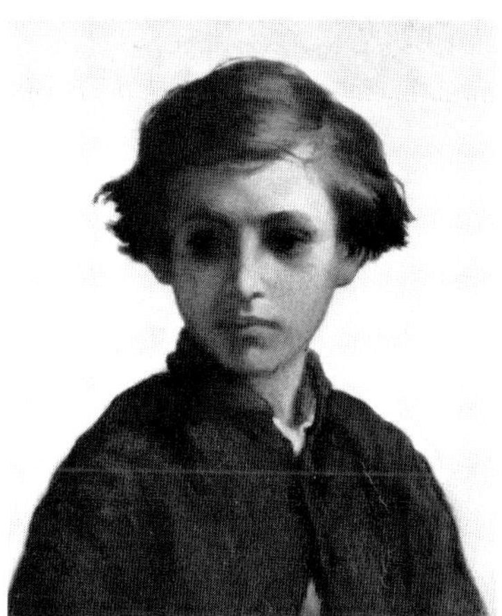
695

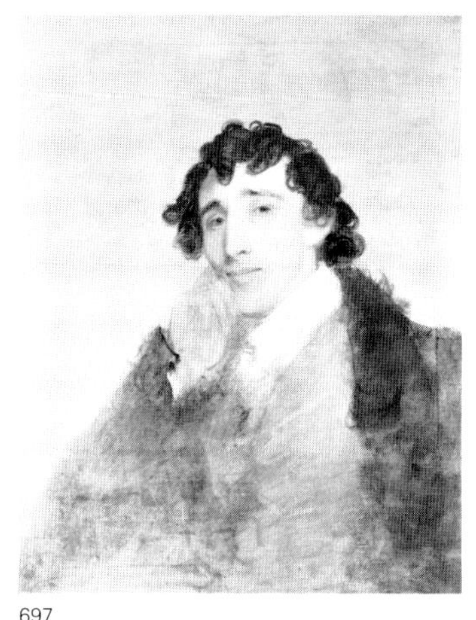
697

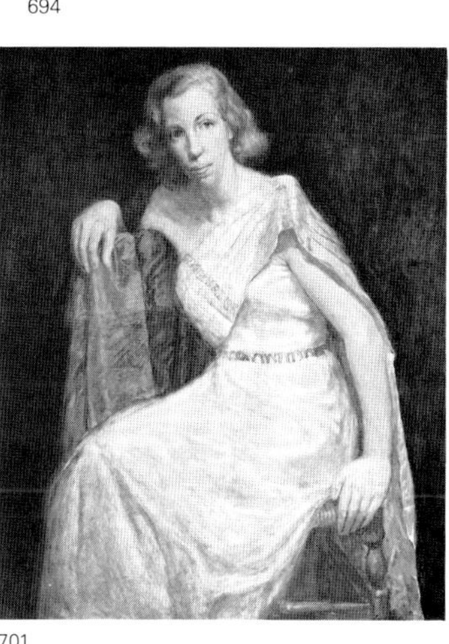
701

Morris Kantor (1896–1974)

706 *Lighthouse*, 1938
Oil on canvas
27 15/16 x 36 in. (71 x 91.4 cm.)
Signed and dated at upper left: M. Kantor/1938
Inscribed and signed on stretcher: Lighthouse Morris Kantor 136
Henry D. Gilpin Fund, 1940.4

707 *Sailing*, 1929
Oil on canvas
20 3/16 x 22 1/4 in. (51.3 x 56.5 cm.)
Signed and dated at lower left: M. Kantor/1929
John Lambert Fund, 1930.2

708 *Trees*, 1938
Oil on canvas
28 x 22 1/16 in. (71.1 x 56 cm.)
Signed and dated at lower left: M.Kantor/1938
Gift of Mrs. Thomas E. Drake (The Margaretta S. Hinchman Collection), 1956.5.3

Paula Kapp (1900–1974)

709 *Cape Cod Bouquet*, 1952
Oil on canvas
36 x 24 1/16 in. (91.4 x 61.1 cm.)
Signed at upper left: Paula Kapp
John Lambert Fund, 1954.11

Bernard Karfiol (1886–1952)

710 *Leah M. Rothner*, 1945
Oil on canvas
34 1/4 x 26 1/4 in. (87 x 66.7 cm.)
Signed at lower left: B.Karfiol
Dated on stretcher: March/1945
Gift of Dr. Jacoby T. Rothner, 1980.1

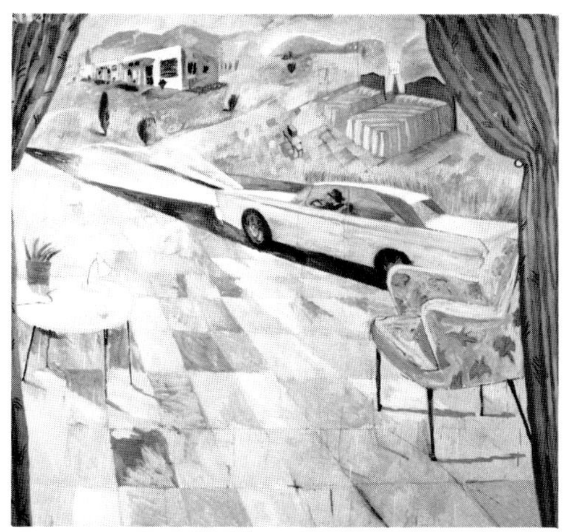
700

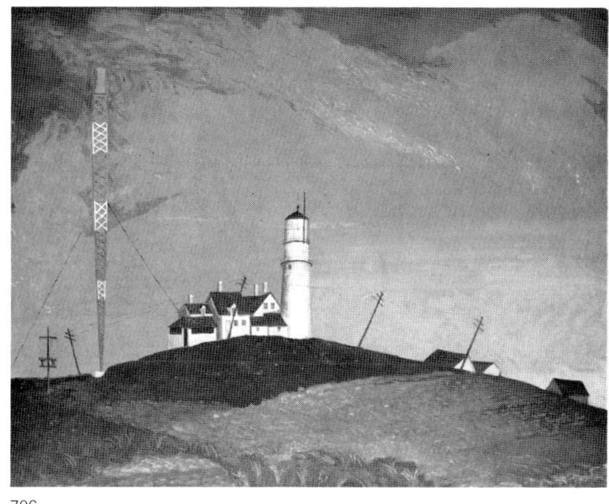
706

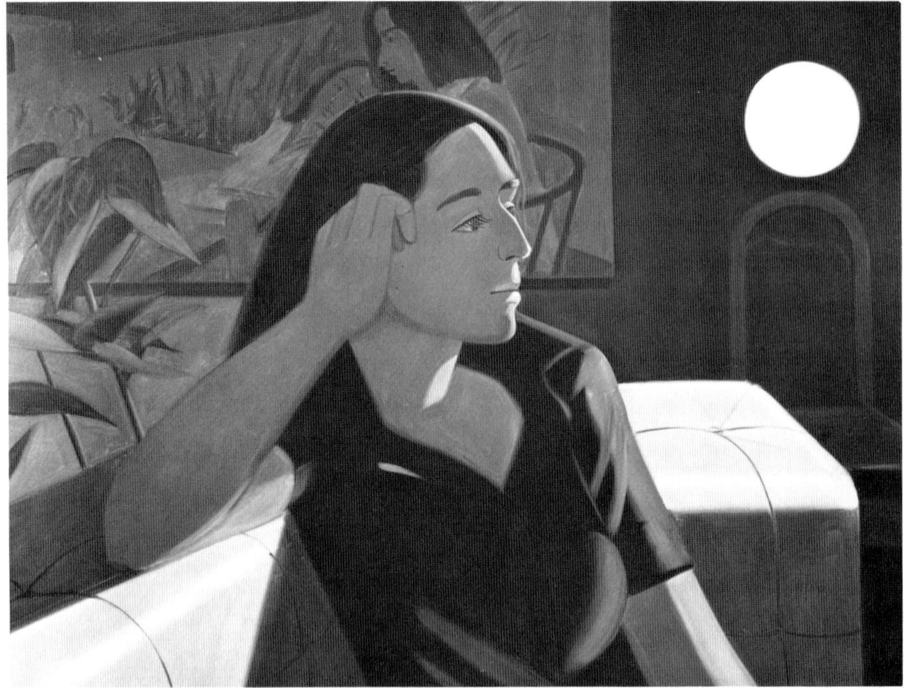

712

Leon Karp (1903–1951)

711 *Portrait of My Wife*, 1938
Oil on canvas
36 x 30⅛ in. (91.4 x 76.5 cm.)
Signed at lower right: Leon Karp
Joseph E. Temple Fund, 1939.8

Alex Katz (1927–)

712 *Night*, 1976
Oil on canvas
72⅛ x 96 in. (183.2 x 243.8 cm.)
Funds provided by the National Endowment for the Arts and the Contemporary Arts Fund, 1981.13

Theodor Kaufmann (German, 1814–1896)

713 *Admiral David G. Farragut* (?) (1801–1870)
Oil on canvas
26½ x 22½ in. (67.3 x 57.2 cm.), oval
Gift of Mrs. John Frederick Lewis (The John Frederick Lewis Memorial Collection), 1933.10.38

Hilde B. Kayn (1903–1950)

714 *The Healer*, 1943
Oil and egg tempera on gessoed masonite
20 x 30 in. (50.8 x 76.2 cm.)
Signed at lower right: H B. Kayn
Inscribed on stretcher: THE HEALER
Gift of Howard A. Wolf, 1953.16

Susette Schultz Keast (1892–1932)

715 *The Inner Harbor*, 1922
Oil on canvas
28 x 34$\frac{1}{16}$ in. (71.1 x 86.5 cm.)
Signed and dated at lower right: SUSETTE S. KEAST.22
John Lambert Fund, 1923.6

Esther Kee (Mrs. William G. Temple, 1914–)

716 *Valley Green Road*, ca. 1935
Oil on canvas
18$\frac{13}{16}$ x 22⅛ in. (47.8 x 56.2 cm.)
Signed at lower left: Kee
John Lambert Fund, 1936.1

Burton R. Keeler (b. 1886)

717 *Landscape Painting*, ca. 1912
Oil on canvas
Approx. 80 x 167 in. (203 x 424 cm.)
Signed at lower left: BURTON KEELER
Commissioned by the Pennsylvania Academy, 1912.16.2

Paul F. Keene, Jr. (1920–)

718 *Chicken Women*, 1953
Encaustic on cardboard
21¼ x 11 in. (54 x 27.9 cm.)
Signed and dated at lower right: Keene/53
Gift of Benjamin D. Bernstein, 1959.10.2

Russell Keeter (1935–)

719 *Human Elements*, 1964
Acrylic on canvas
51⅞ x 57 in. (131.8 x 144.8 cm.)
Signed at upper right: Russell KEETER
John Lambert Fund, 1966.5

James P. Kelly (1854–1893)

720 *Bearded Man in Bowler Hat*, 1891
Oil on canvas
25 x 20⅜ in. (63.5 x 51.8 cm.)
Signed and dated on back: Jam P. Kelly. 91./[?]; and: EK./By/J.P.Kelly '91
Gift of Mrs. John Sloan, 1972.12.2

721 *The Modeling Class* (illustration for William C. Brownell, "The Art Schools of Philadelphia," *Scribner's Monthly* 18, Sept. 1879, pp. 737-50), ca. 1879
Oil on cardboard (grisaille)
10¼ x 12¾ in. (26 x 32.4 cm.)
Gift of the artist, 1879.5

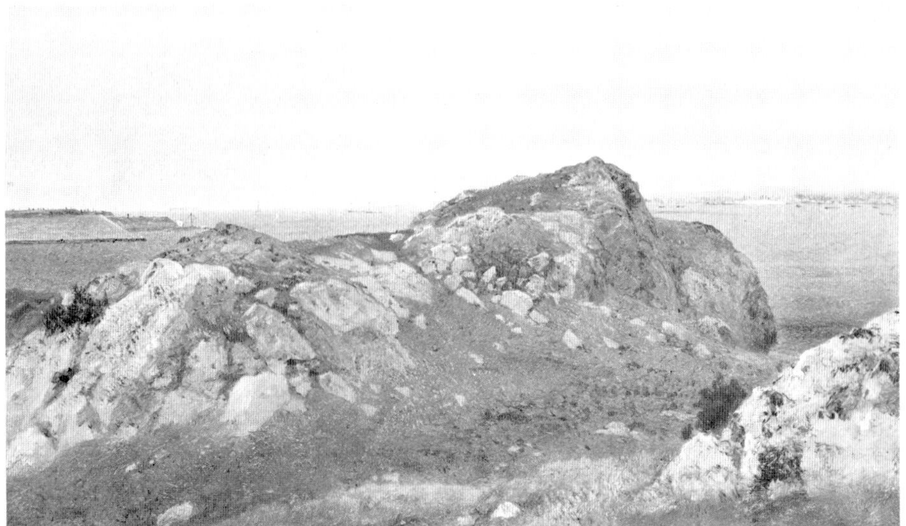

725

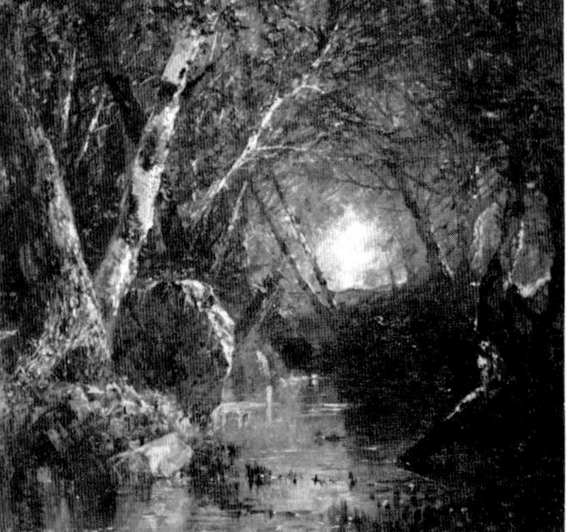

727

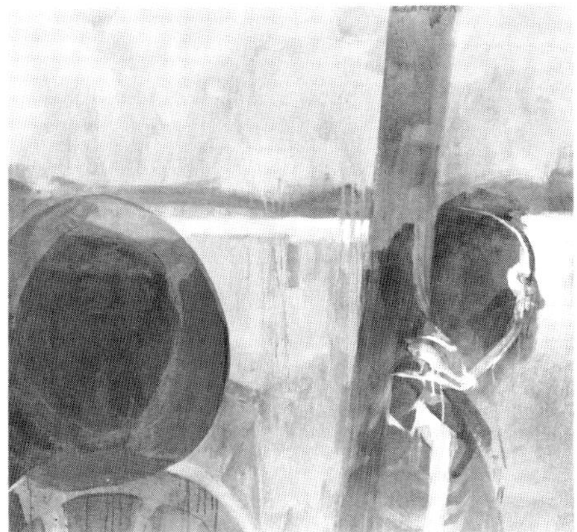

719

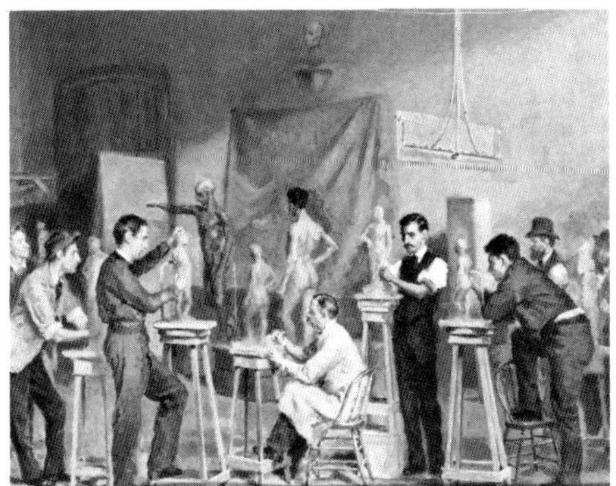

721

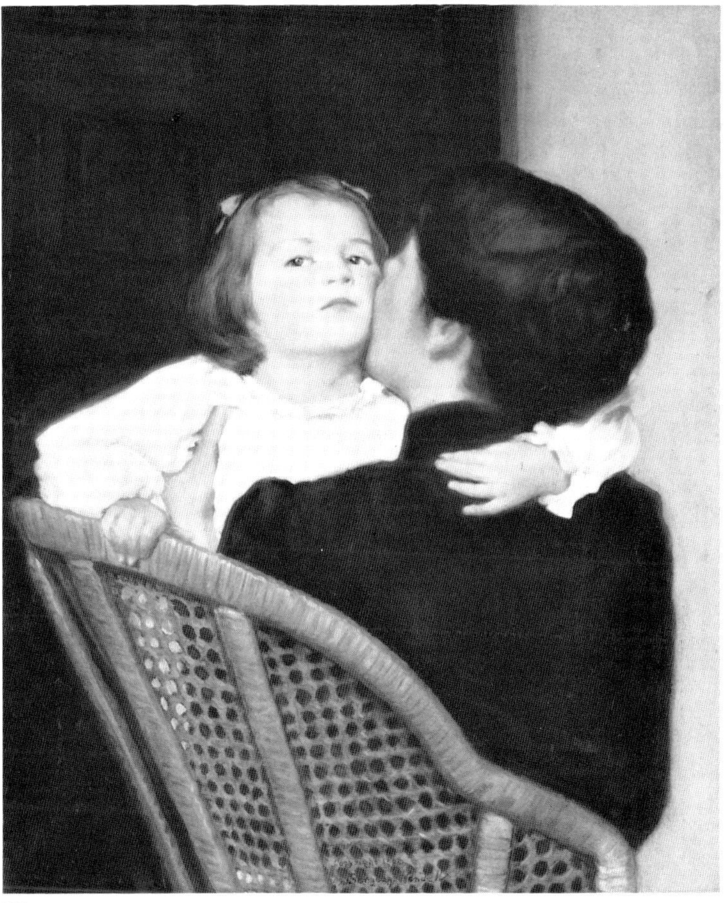

723

Leon Kelly (1901–1982)

722 *Henriette as My Model* (Henriette Kelly, the artist's first wife), 1929
Oil on canvas
28⅛ x 36$^{1}/_{16}$ in. (71.4 x 91.6 cm.)
Signed at upper left: Leon Kelly
Gift of Bernard Davis, 1950.20.1

Mrs. Leon Kelly. *See* Helen Lloyd Horter.

William Sergeant Kendall (1869–1938)

723 *Beatrice*, 1906
Oil on canvas
30 x 25$^{1}/_{16}$ in. (76.2 x 63.7 cm.)
Signed, dated, and inscribed at lower left: Sergeant Kendall/copyright 1906; annotated at lower center: Copyright 1906/by Sergeant Kendell [*sic*]; and annotated at lower left: ND
Joseph E. Temple Fund, 1907.1

Fay Kennedy (ca. 1895–1955)

724 *The White House*, ca. 1933
Oil on canvas
22$^{3}/_{16}$ x 30$^{3}/_{16}$ in. (56.4 x 76.7 cm.)
Signed at lower right: FAY KENNEDY
Gift of Carl Zigrosser, 1955.13.2

John Frederick Kensett (1816–1872)

725 *At Newport, Rhode Island*, ca. 1855
Oil on canvas
12 x 20 in. (30.5 x 50.8 cm.)
Gift of Mr. and Mrs. Edward Kesler, 1975.20.4

726 *Hill Valley, Sunrise*, 1851
Oil on canvas
18⅛ x 22¼ in. (46 x 56.5 cm.)
Signed and dated at lower left: JFK/51
Gift of John Frederick Lewis, Jr., 1954.22.2

727 *Landscape*, 1854
Oil on canvas, mounted on cardboard
17 x 14$^{3}/_{16}$ in. (43.2 x 36 cm.)
Signed and dated at lower left: JF.K./54
Gift of Mr. and Mrs. J. Welles Henderson, 1976.24.3

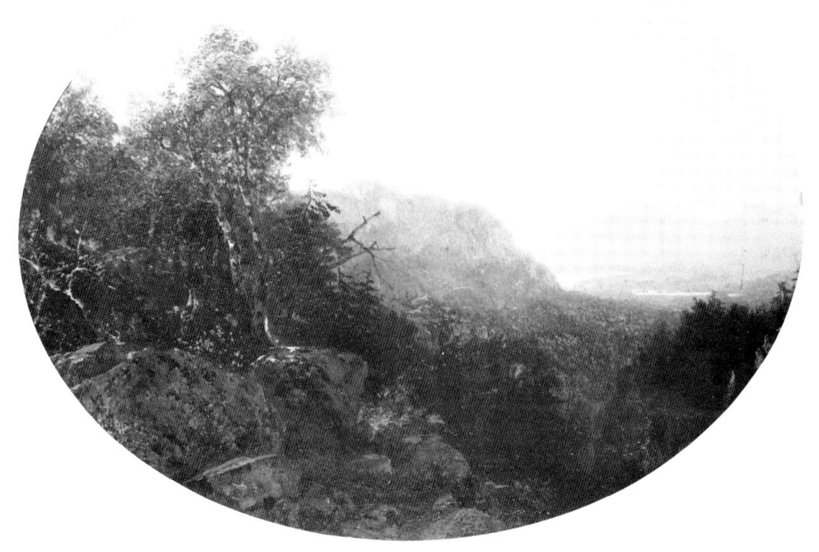

726

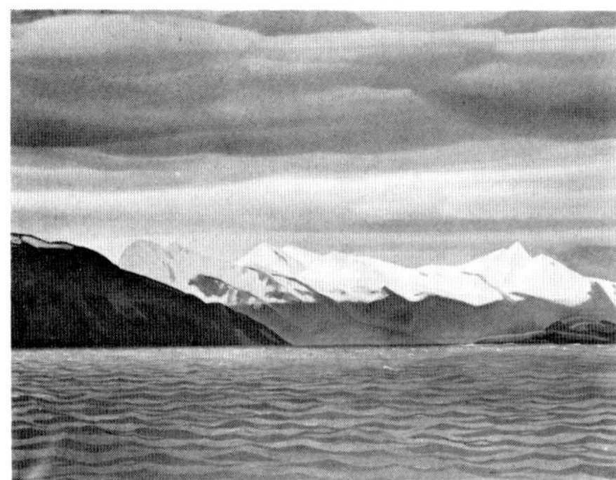

728

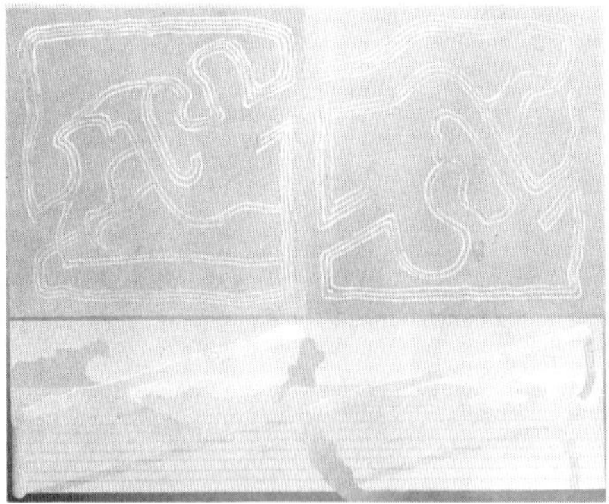

729

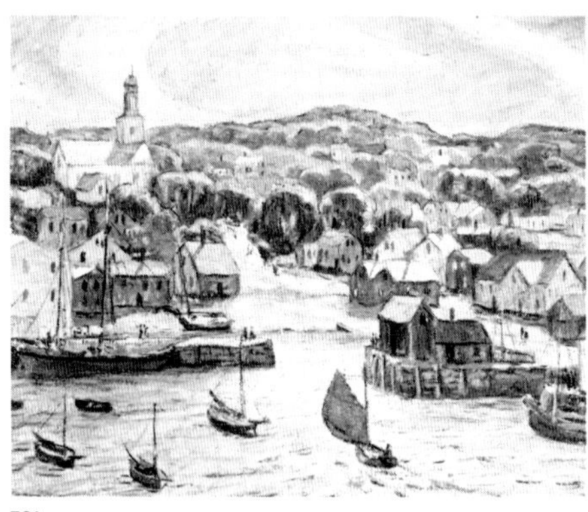

731

Rockwell Kent (1882–1971)

728 *Seascape*, 1933–35
Oil on canvas
$34\frac{1}{8}$ x 44 in. (86.7 x 111.8 cm.)
Signed and dated at lower right: Rockwell-Kent 1933–5.
Gift of Erhard Weyhe, 1952.1

Robert Keyser (1924–   )

729 *The Click of Recognition*, 1971
Oil on canvas
$27\frac{15}{16}$ x $34\frac{15}{16}$ in. (71 x 88.7 cm.)
Gift of Frederick McBrien, 1981.4

Joseph Bartholomew Kidd (Scottish, 1808–1889)

730 *The House Wren*, ca. 1832
(commissioned by John James Audubon, after his watercolor)
Oil on academy board
$18\frac{7}{8}$ x $11\frac{11}{16}$ in. (47.9 x 29.7 cm.)
Annotated on back: GR Audubon/from Mrs JJA./1863.
Collections Fund, 1951.27

Frank Howard Kidder (b. 1886)

731 *A Fishing Port*, ca. 1920
Oil on canvas, mounted on cardboard
16 x $20\frac{3}{16}$ in. (40.6 x 51.3 cm.)
Signed at lower left: F.H.KIDDER
John Lambert Fund, 1921.4

William Kienbusch (1914–1980)

732 *Coast Rocks, Flint Island*, 1958
Casein on paper, mounted on matboard
$26\frac{3}{4}$ x 37 in. (67.9 x 94 cm.)
Signed and dated at lower left: Kienbusch 58
John Lambert Fund, 1960.6

Richard M. Kimbel (1865–1942)

733 *The Old Antique Shop*, ca. 1920
Oil on canvas
23 x 26 in. (58.4 x 66 cm.)
Signed at lower left: Richard M. Kimbel.
John Lambert Fund, 1921.5

Alice Riddle Kindler (Mrs. Hans Kindler, 1892–1980)

734 *Dried Flowers*, ca. 1930
Oil on canvas

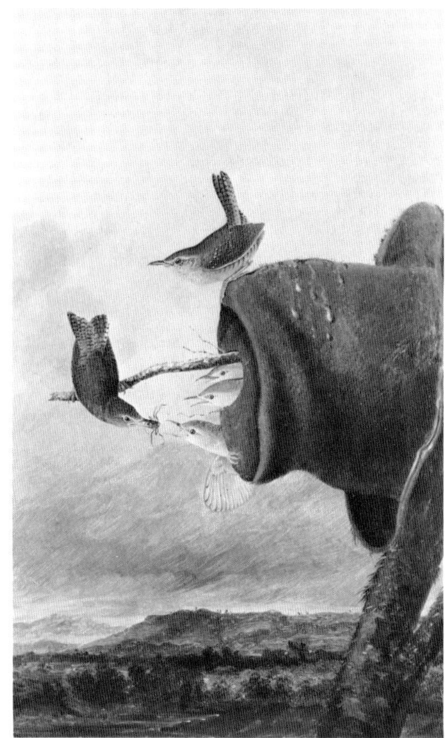

730

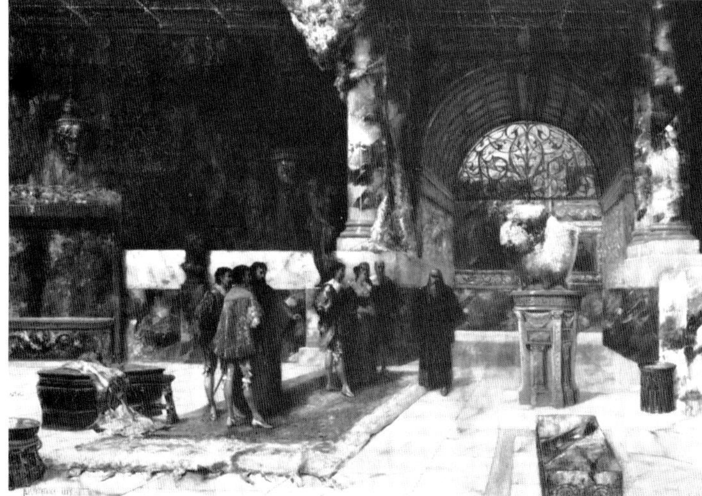

735

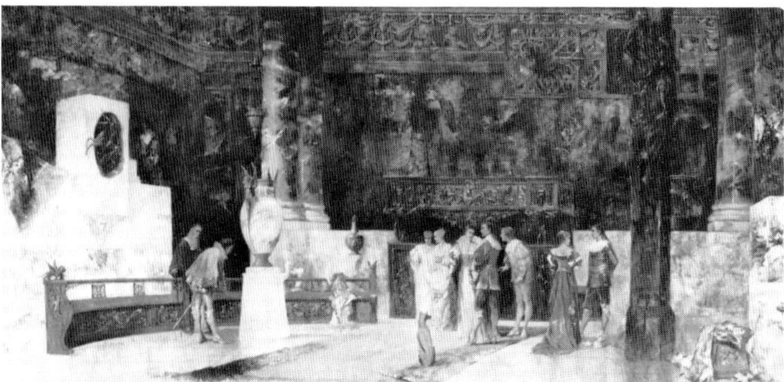

736

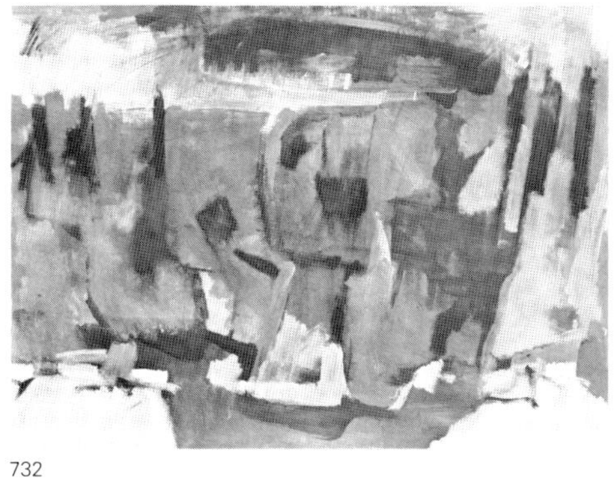

732

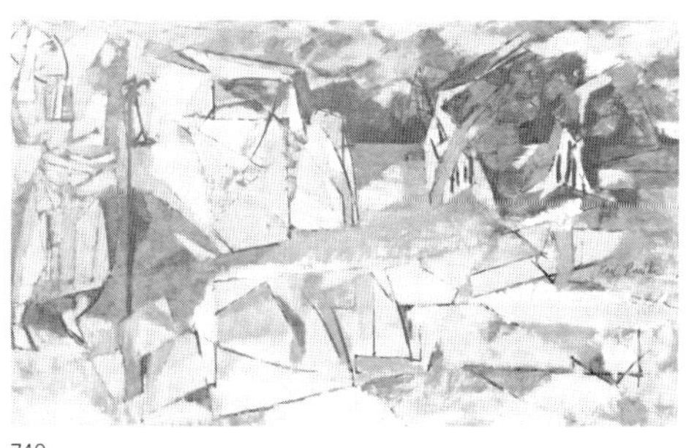

740

738

36½ x 28⅞ in. (92.7 x 73.3 cm.)
Signed at lower left: RIDDLE
John Lambert Fund, 1931.5

Frank LeBrun Kirkpatrick (1853–1917)

735 *In the Museum*, 1883
Oil on canvas
26⅛ x 36½ in. (66.4 x 92.7 cm.)
Signed and dated at lower left: FL:KIRKPATRICK -1883-
Joseph E. Temple Fund, 1884.5

736 *Venetian Palace*, 1883
Oil on canvas
29 x 60 in. (73.7 x 152.4 cm.)
Signed and dated at lower left: FL:KIRKPATRICK -1883-
Annotated on lining: The following inscription appears on the back/of the original canvas: / KIRK-PXXXII
Gift of Mr. and Mrs. Walter H. Rubin in memory of Abraham Rubin, 1978.14

T. Kitagawa (1942–)

737 *Seated Nude*, 1962
Oil on canvas
28 x $21\frac{15}{16}$ in. (71.1 x 55.7 cm.)
Dated and signed at lower right: 1962./[signed in Japanese]/KITAGAWA
Gift of Mrs. Herbert Cameron Morris, 1967.7

Anna Elizabeth Klumpke (1856–1942)

738 *In the Wash-House*, 1888
Oil on canvas, mounted on wood
79 x 67 in. (200.7 x 170.2 cm.)

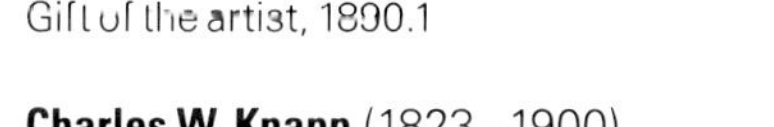

Signed, inscribed, and dated at lower right: A.E. Klumpke/Paris 1888
Gift of the artist, 1890.1

Charles W. Knapp (1823–1900)

739 *Delaware Valley near Milford*, by 1885
Oil on canvas
$30\frac{3}{16}$ x 50⅛ in. (76.7 x 127.3 cm.)
Signed at lower right: C.W.Knapp
Source unknown (ca. 1885), 1944.21

Karl Knaths (1891–1971)

740 *Number Nine—Eliphaz*, 1948
Oil on canvas
36¼ x 60½ in. (92.1 x 153.7 cm.)
Signed at right center: Karl Knaths
Joseph E. Temple Fund, 1951.9

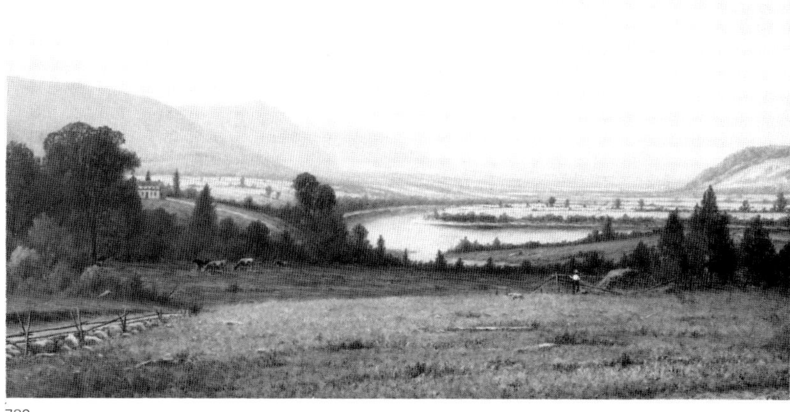

739

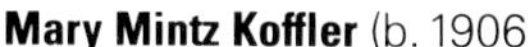

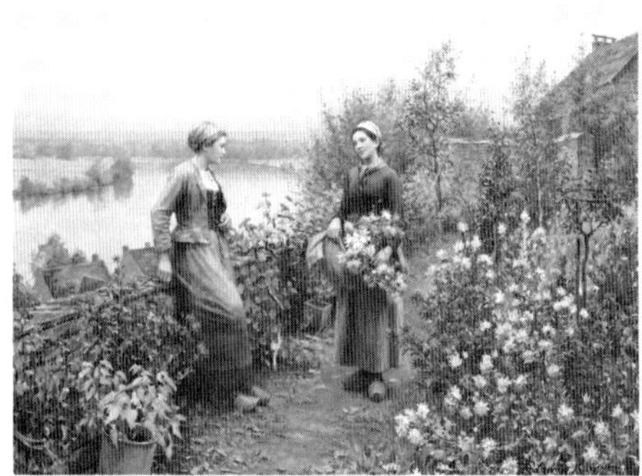

741

745

Daniel Ridgway Knight (1839–1924)

741 *The Gossips*, probably 1885
Oil on canvas
29 1/4 x 36 7/16 in. (74.3 x 92.6 cm.)
Signed and inscribed at lower right: Ridgway Knight/Paris.
Gift of Mr. and Mrs. Thomas Moyer in memory of his parents, Mr. and Mrs. Allen B. Moyer, 1977.7

742 *Hailing the Ferry*, 1888
Oil on canvas
64 1/2 x 83 1/8 in. (163.8 x 211.1 cm.)
Signed, inscribed, and dated at lower right: Ridgway Knight/Paris 1888
Gift of John H. Converse, 1891.7

Robert L. Knipschild (1927–)

743 *Composition—October 1950*, 1950
Encaustic on canvas
10 7/8 x 27 15/16 in. (27.6 x 71 cm.)
Signed and dated at lower right: Knipschild 50
John Lambert Fund, 1951.10

Jean Knox (Mrs. Francis Taylor Chambers, 1898–1972)

744 *Still Life*, ca. 1919
Oil on canvas
20 15/16 x 17 1/4 in. (53.2 x 43.8 cm.)
Signed at lower right: KNOX
John Lambert Fund, 1920.6

Robert Koehler (1850–1917)

745 *A Holiday Occupation*, 1881
Oil on canvas
37 7/16 x 32 3/4 in. (95.1 x 83.2 cm.)
Signed, inscribed, and dated at upper right: Rob. Koehler/Munich. 1881
Gift of Joseph E. Temple, 1882.2

Mary Mintz Koffler (b. 1906)

746 *Old Man's Park, Houston Street*, ca. 1957
Oil on canvas
25 1/8 x 30 in. (63.8 x 76.2 cm.)
Signed at lower right: MARY MINTZ KOFFLER
John Lambert Fund, 1958.13

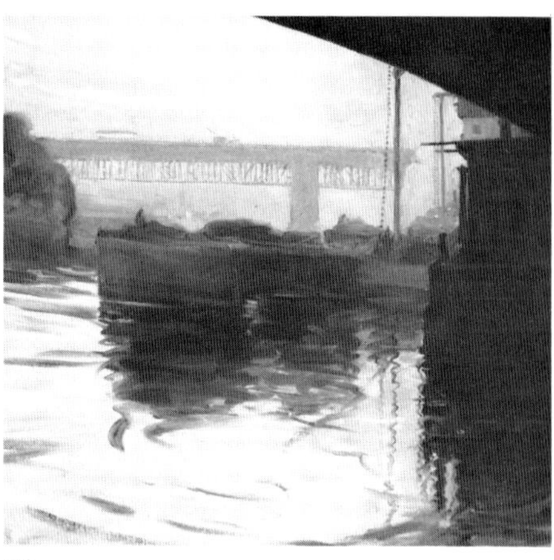

749

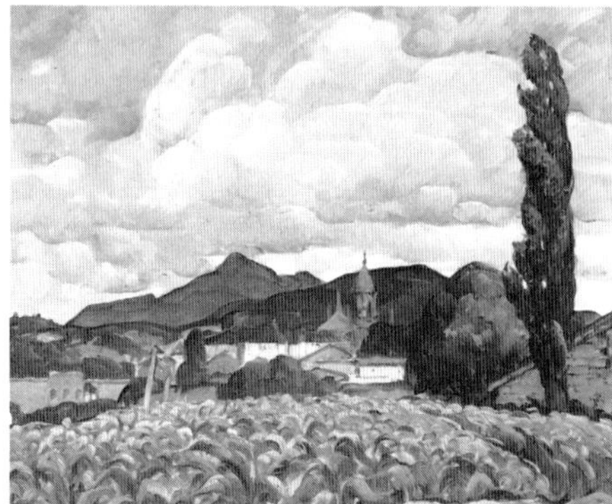

753

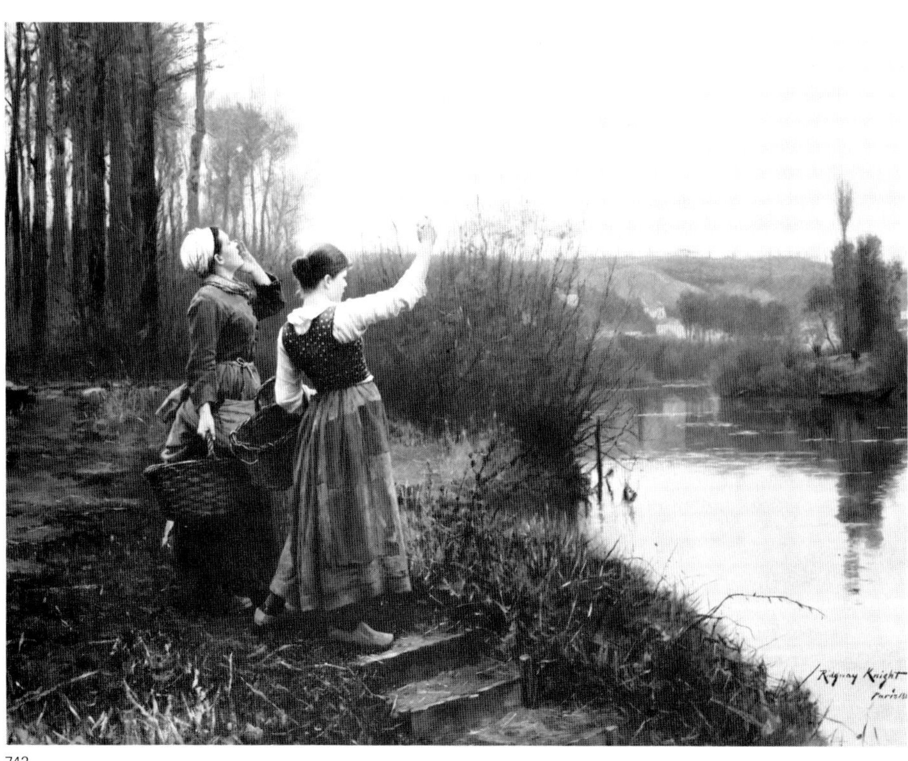

742

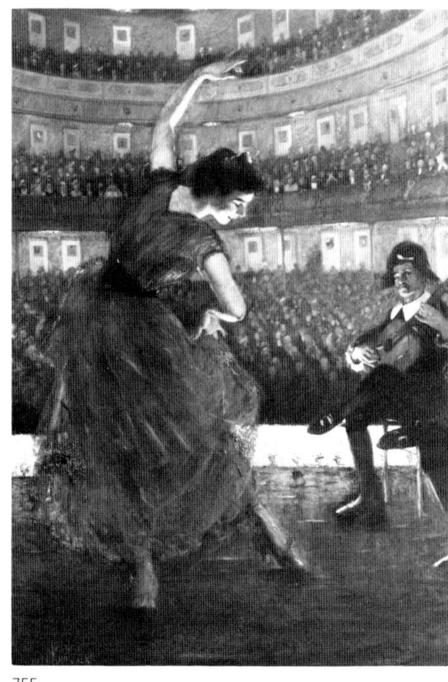

755

Irma Kohn (1883–1974)

747 *Fete Day, 1917,* 1917
Oil on canvas
20¹⁄₁₆ x 16 in. (51 x 40.6 cm.)
Signed at lower right: -IRMA KOHN.
John Lambert Fund, 1918.10

Benjamin D. Kopman (1887–1965)

748 *Portrait of a Young Man* (self-portrait), ca. 1916
Oil on canvas
24⅛ x 20⅛ in. (61.3 x 51.1 cm.)
Signed at upper right: Benj. D. Kopman
John Lambert Fund, 1917.8

David E. Kornhauser (1884–1944)

749 *Along the Schuylkill River,* 1913
Oil on canvas, mounted on wood
38⅜ x 40¼ in. (97.5 x 102.2 cm.)
Signed and dated at lower right: D. E. KORNHAUSER/-13
John Lambert Fund, 1913.8

Frederick W. Kost (1861–1923)

750 *On Saint John's River, New Brunswick,* ca. 1893
Oil on canvas
12¹⁄₁₆ x 20⅛ in. (30.6 x 51.1 cm.)
Signed at lower left: Fredck W. Kost.
Bequest of Harrison Earl, 1894.6.4

John Lewis Krimmel (1786–1821)

751 *Country Wedding, Bishop White Officiating,* probably 1814
Oil on canvas
16³⁄₁₆ x 22⅛ in. (41.1 x 56.2 cm.)
Inscribed on picture above mantel: MARIAGE; inscribed on book: ALMA[NAC]/1814
Gift of Paul Beck, Jr., 1842.2.1

752 *Fourth of July in Centre Square,* by 1812
Oil on canvas
22¾ x 29 in. (57.8 x 73.7 cm.)
Pennsylvania Academy purchase (from the estate of Paul Beck, Jr.), 1845.3.1

Leon Kroll (1884–1974)

753 *Basque Landscape,* 1914
Oil on canvas
26³⁄₁₆ x 32⅛ in. (66.5 x 81.6 cm.)
Signed and dated at lower right: Kroll 1914
John Lambert Fund, 1915.4

754 *Viette* (Geneviève Domec Kroll, the artist's wife, d. 1987), 1925
Oil on canvas
18⅛ x 15¹⁄₁₆ in. (46 x 38.3 cm.)
Signed and dated at upper right: Leon Kroll 1925
Gift of Mrs. Thomas E. Drake (The Margaretta S. Hinchman Collection), 1955.15.8

Louis Kronberg (1872–1965)

755 *Behind the Footlights,* 1892
Oil on canvas, mounted on wood
84 x 60 in. (213.4 x 152.4 cm.)
Signed and dated at lower left: Louis Kronberg/ 1892
Gift of Clarence H. Clark, 1897.8

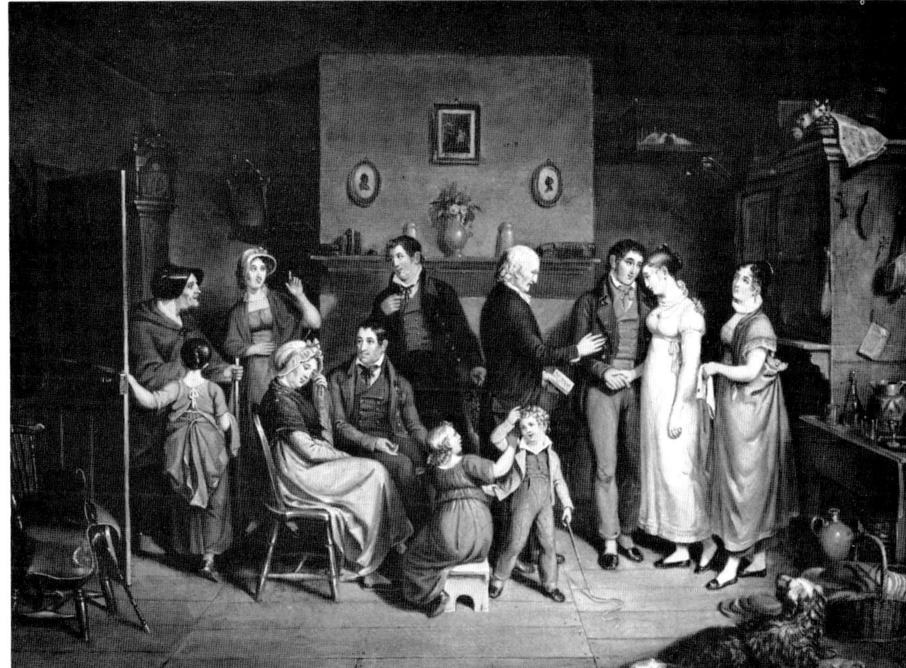

751

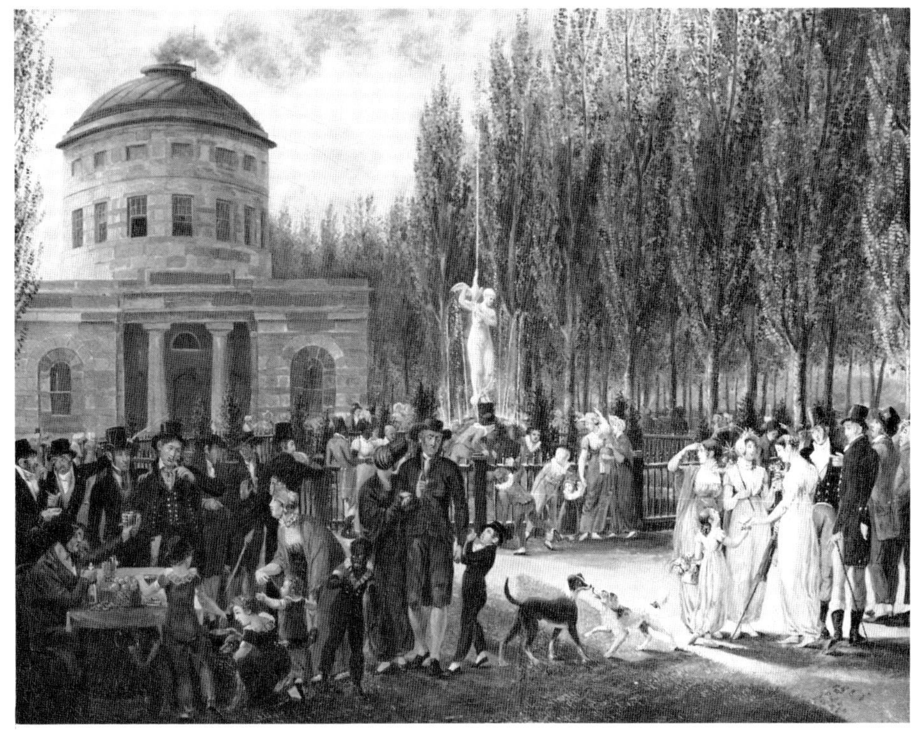

752

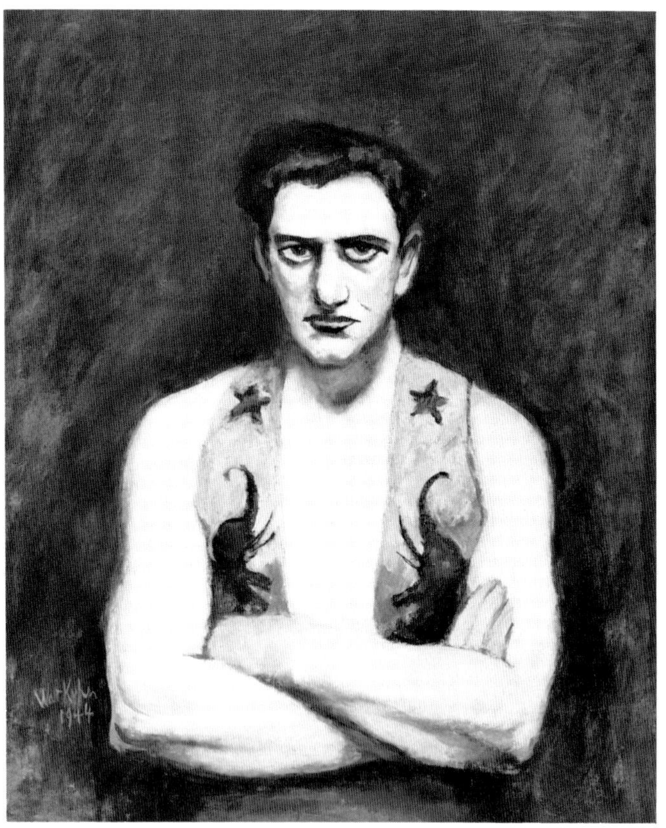

756

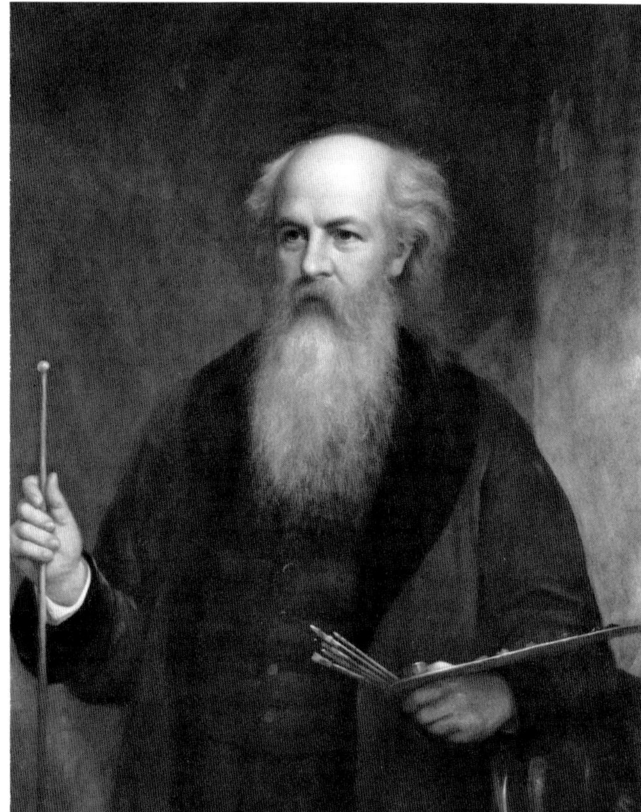

764

Walt Kuhn (1877–1949)

756 *Clown with Folded Arms*, 1944
Oil on canvas
30 x 25⅛ in. (76.2 x 63.8 cm.)
Signed and dated at lower left: Walt Kuhn/1944
Joseph E. Temple Fund, 1945.8

Doris Kunzie. *See* Doris Kunzie Weidner.

Laura D. S. Ladd (1863–1943)

757 *Petunias*, ca. 1935
Oil on canvas board
15$^{15}/_{16}$ x 18 in. (40.5 x 45.7 cm.)
Signed at upper left: Laura D. S. Ladd
John Lambert Fund, 1936.12

John La Farge. *See* cat. nos. 1677–78.

Richard Francis Lahey (1893–1979)

758 *Down by the River*, ca. 1926
Oil on wood
16$^{3}/_{16}$ x 24¼ in. (41.1 x 61.6 cm.)
Signed at upper left and on back: Richard Lahey.
John Lambert Fund, 1927.3

James R. Lambdin (1807–1889)

759 *John Quincy Adams* (1767–1848), ca. 1845
Oil on canvas
30¼ x 25⅛ in. (76.8 x 63.8 cm.)
Inscribed and signed on back: John Quincy Adams/by J R Lambdin
Gift of Mrs. John Frederick Lewis (The John Frederick Lewis Memorial Collection), 1933.10.41

760 *Oliver Ellsworth* (1745–1807), 1878 (after John Trumbull, 1792)
Oil on canvas
30$^{3}/_{16}$ x 25⅛ in. (76.7 x 63.8 cm.)
Inscribed, signed, and dated on back: Oliver Ellsworth/Ch Justice of Supreme Court/of US 1796–1801./from an original miniature/by Tr[u]mbull in Yale College./J R Lambdin,/1878.
Gift of Mrs. John Frederick Lewis (The John Frederick Lewis Memorial Collection), 1933.10.42

761 *General Ulysses Simpson Grant* (1822–1885), ca. 1865
Oil on canvas
36⅛ x 29$^{3}/_{16}$ in. (91.8 x 74.1 cm.)
Gift of Mrs. John Frederick Lewis (The John Frederick Lewis Memorial Collection), 1933.10.43

762 *General Andrew Jackson* (1767–1845), 1845
Oil on canvas
30½ x 25¼ in. (77.5 x 64.1 cm.)
Inscribed, signed, and dated on back: Andrew Jackson/by J R Lambdin/1845.
Gift of Mrs. John Frederick Lewis (The John Frederick Lewis Memorial Collection), 1933.10.44

763 *Franklin Pierce* (1804–1869), ca. 1855
Oil on canvas
30$^{3}/_{16}$ x 25$^{3}/_{16}$ in. (76.7 x 64 cm.)
Gift of Dr. Alfred C. Lambdin, 1908.5

764 *Self-Portrait*, ca. 1880
Oil on canvas
42½ x 34 in. (108 x 86.4 cm.)
Signed at lower left: J R L./1 [illegible]
Gift of Dr. Alfred C. Lambdin on behalf of the artist's family, 1891.8

Gertrude A. Lambert (b. 1885)

765 *The Little Market, Baveno* (sketch), 1913
Oil on canvas, mounted on cardboard
13½ x 11$^{7}/_{16}$ in. (34.3 x 29.1 cm.)
Signed and dated at upper left: G.A. Lambert/1913.
John Lambert Fund, 1914.7

766 *Poetry*, ca. 1912
Oil on canvas
Approx. 80 x 167 in. (203 x 424 cm.)
Commissioned by the Pennsylvania Academy, 1912.16.3

John Lambert (1861–1907)

767 *The Actor*, 1904
Oil on canvas
30 x 24$^{15}/_{16}$ in. (76.2 x 63.3 cm.)
Signed at upper left: John Lambert; dated at upper right: Nov. 1904
Bequest of the artist, 1908.1

768 *Cecilia Beaux* (1855–1942), ca. 1905
Oil on canvas
29$^{15}/_{16}$ x 24¾ in. (76 x 62.9 cm.)
Signed at upper left: John Lambert.
Gift of Henry Sandwith Drinker, 1950.17.53

769 *Miss Constance Biddle* (1882–1952), ca. 1900
Oil on canvas
58⅛ x 40¼ in. (147.6 x 102.2 cm.)
Signed at upper left: John Lambert.
Gift of Mr. and Mrs. H. Gates Lloyd, 1977.10

770 *Mrs. Samuel M. Fox* (1822–1903), 1901
Oil on canvas
$34\frac{3}{4} \times 28\frac{1}{16}$ in. (88.3 x 71.3 cm.)
Signed at upper left: John Lambert.; dated at upper right: 1901.
Gift of William Logan Fox, 1965.7

771 *Peasant Girl*, 1891
Oil on canvas
$31\frac{13}{16} \times 17\frac{11}{16}$ in. (80.8 x 44.9 cm.)
Inscribed, signed, and dated at lower right: To my friend-/Henry McCarter/John Lambert Jr.'91
Gift of Francis Cadwalader, 1963.4

772 *Sketch of an Unidentified Man*
Oil on wood
$14 \times 10\frac{1}{2}$ in. (35.6 x 26.7 cm.)
Gift of Joseph M. Fox, 1974.22

Annie Traquair Lang (1885–1918)

773 *J. Liberty Tadd* (1863–1917)
Oil on canvas
$50\frac{1}{8} \times 36$ in. (127.3 x 91.4 cm.)
Signed at lower left: A.TRAQUAIR LANG
Source unknown, 1944.22

Louis Lang (1814–1893)

774 *Mrs. T. Steiner*, 1839
Oil on canvas
$34 \times 26\frac{15}{16}$ in. (86.4 x 68.4 cm.)
Inscribed, signed, and dated on back: Mrs. T. Steiner/Painted by Louis Lang/Phild 1839.
Gift of Mrs. John Frederick Lewis (The John Frederick Lewis Memorial Collection), 1933.10.45

Katherine Langhorne
See Katherine Langhorne Adams.

Martyl Suzanne Schweig Langsdorf
See Martyl.

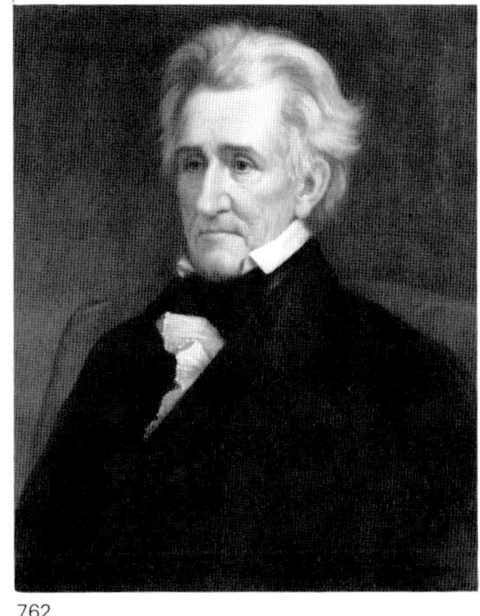

762

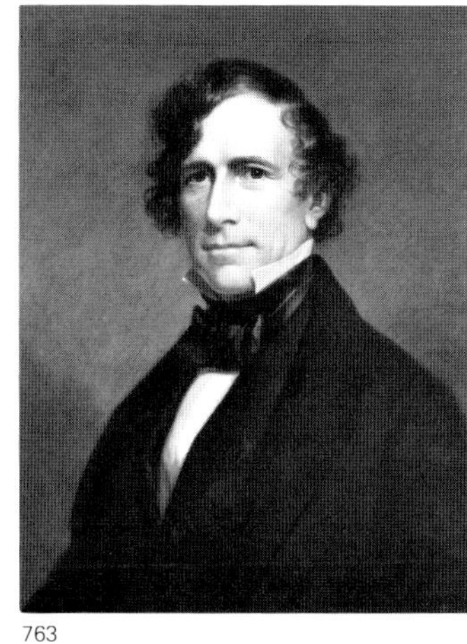
763

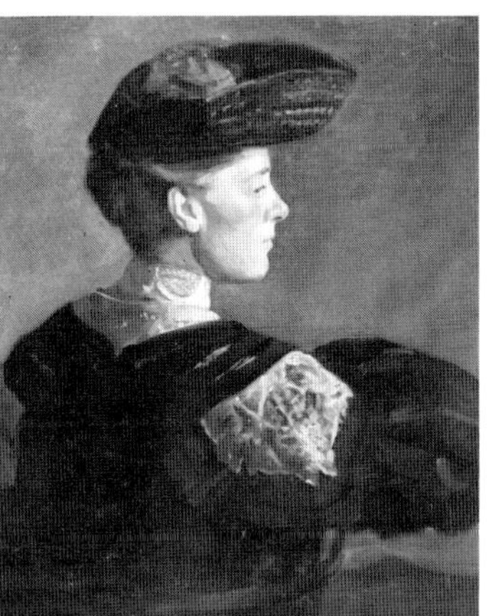

768

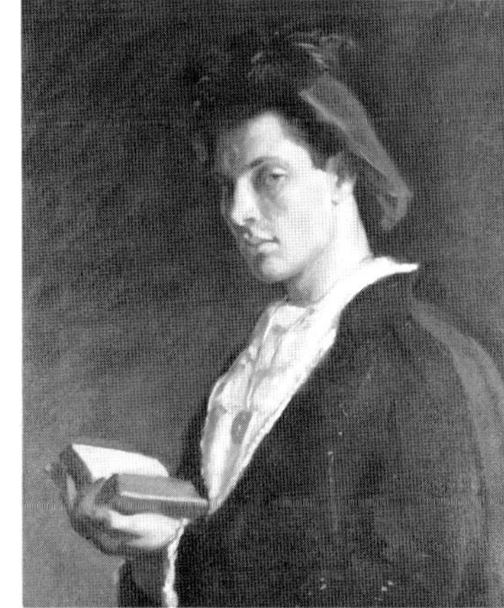

767

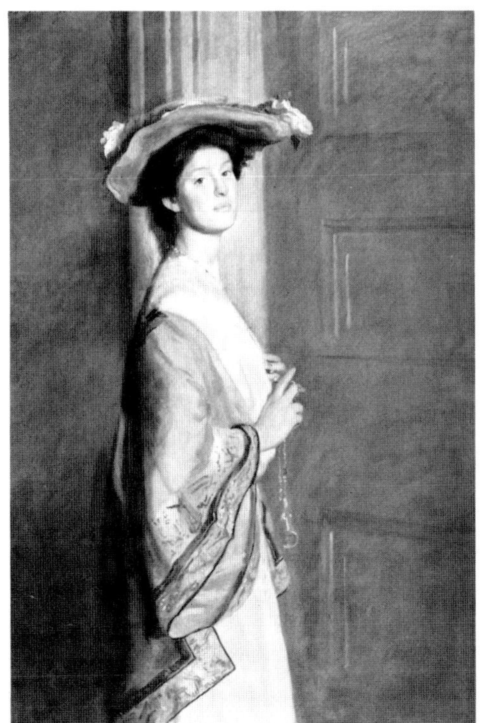

769

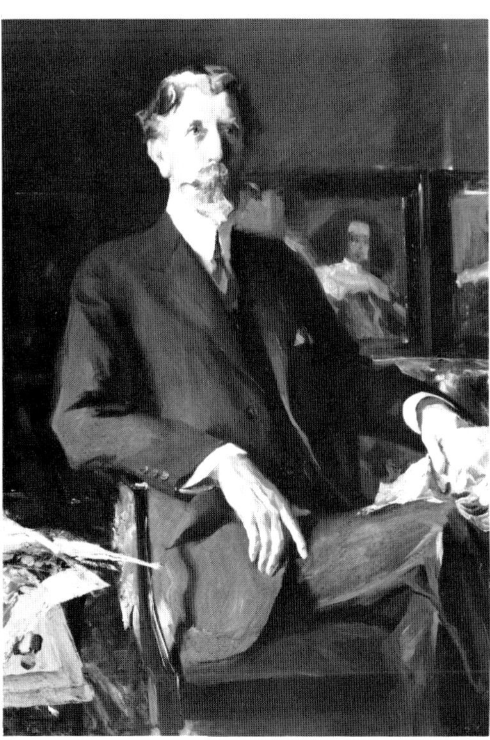
773

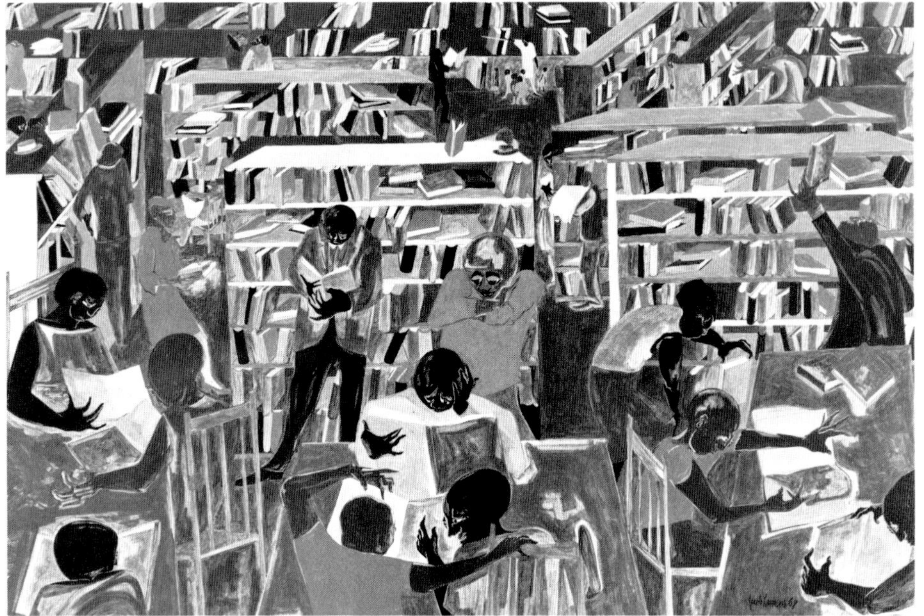
777

Philip Alexius de Laszlo de Lombos (English, 1869–1937)

775 *General John Joseph Pershing* (1860–1948), 1921
Oil on canvas
58¼ x 40¼ in. (148 x 102.2 cm.)
Signed, inscribed, and dated at lower right: de Laszlo/Washington 1921 July
Gift of George McFadden, 1923.10

William L. Lathrop (1859–1938)

776 *The Pool*, by 1919
Oil on canvas
19⅛ x 25⅛ in. (48.6 x 63.8 cm.)
Signed at lower right: W L LATHR [rubbed out]
Annotated on stretcher: The Pool
Henry D. Gilpin Fund, 1942.15

Jacob Lawrence (1917–)

777 *Dream Series #5: The Library*, 1967
Tempera on board
24 x 35⅞ in. (61 x 91.1 cm.)
Signed and dated at lower right: Jacob Lawrence 67
Funds provided by the National Endowment for the Arts, the Collectors' Circle, and the Henry D. Gilpin and John Lambert funds, 1987.34

Ernest Lawson (1873–1939)

778 *The Broken Fence: Spring Flood*
Oil on canvas
30³⁄₁₆ x 24¹⁄₁₆ in. (76.7 x 61.1 cm.)
Signed at lower left: E LAWSON
Gift of Bertha Schwacke, 1937.15.1

779 *Fort George Hill, Morning*, by 1911
Oil on canvas
25³⁄₁₆ x 30 in. (64 x 76.2 cm.)
Signed at lower left: E. LAWSON
Gift of Bertha Schwacke, 1937.15.2

780 *Peggy's Cove, Nova Scotia*, probably 1924
Oil on canvas
25³⁄₁₆ x 30¹⁄₁₆ in. (64 x 76.4 cm.)
Signed at lower right: E. LAWSON
Joseph E. Temple Fund, 1935.4

Rico Lebrun (1900–1964)

781 *Buchenwald Cart*, 1955
Oil on canvas
82½ x 122 in. (209.6 x 309.8 cm.)
Signed and dated at lower left: R. L. '55
John Lambert Fund, 1956.1

782 *The Listening Dead*, 1957–58
Oil on cardboard
96 x 48 in. (243.8 x 121.9 cm.)
Signed and dated at lower left: Lebrun 57; inscribed, signed, and dated on back: Listening Dead./Lebrun, 1957–58
Gift of the Ford Foundation, 1962.5.2

James Lechay (1907–)

783 *The River*, ca. 1941
Oil on canvas
24 x 32 in. (61 x 81.3 cm.)
Signed at lower left: James Lechay; inscribed and signed on back: "THE RIVER"/JAMES LECHAY/ 567-6th AVE/N.Y.C.
John Lambert Fund, 1942.6

Henry Leith-Ross (1886–1973)

784 *Flag Station*, 1945
Oil on canvas
15¹⁄₁₆ x 34¹⁄₁₆ in. (38.3 x 86.5 cm.)
Signed at lower left: Leith-Ross ©; inscribed on back: Reproduction Rights Reserved by the Artist
John Lambert Fund, 1946.6

Alfred Leslie (1927–)

785 *James Tate and Liselotte Tate* (James, b. 1941; Liselotte, b. 1946), 1976
Oil on canvas
84 x 60⅝ in. (213.4 x 154 cm.)
Signed, inscribed, and dated at lower left: Alfred Leslie copyright © 1976; dated, signed, and inscribed on back: 1976 Alfred Leslie/7 x 5 OIL & LINEN; inscribed on canvas folded over stretcher: JAMES TATE AND LISELOTTE TATE
Funds provided by the Crag Burn Fund, Marion B. Stroud, and an anonymous donor, 1977.3

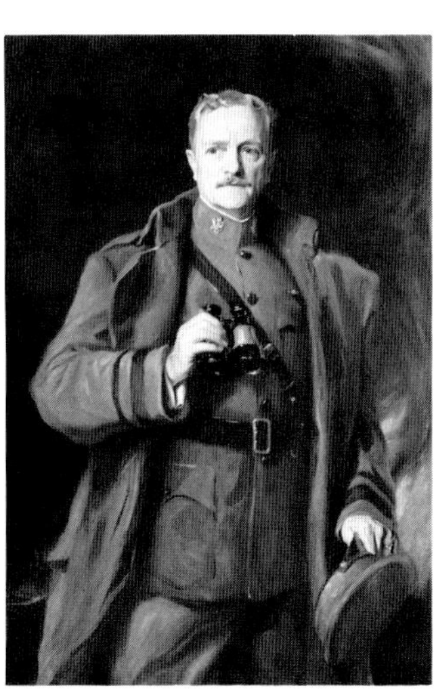
775

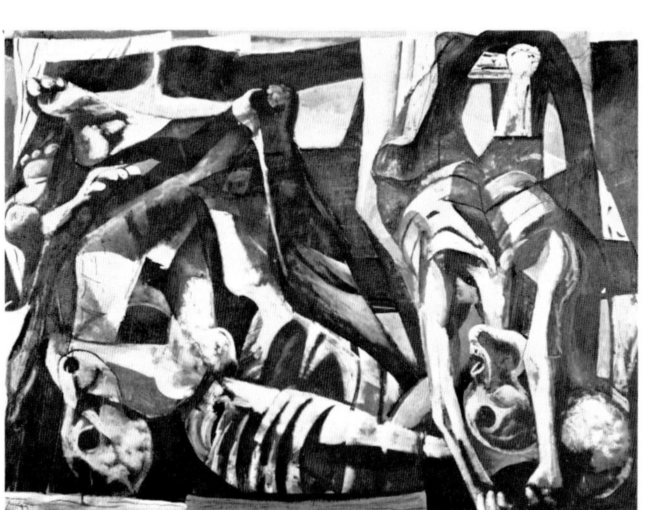
781

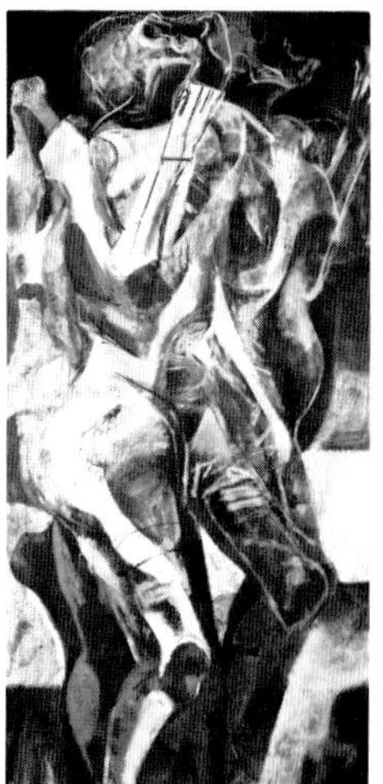
782

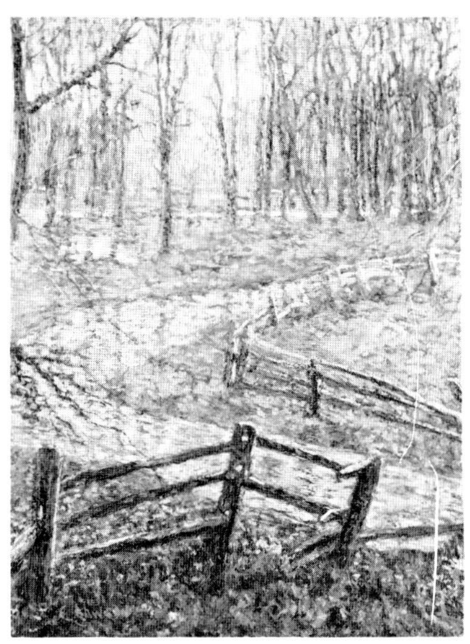
778

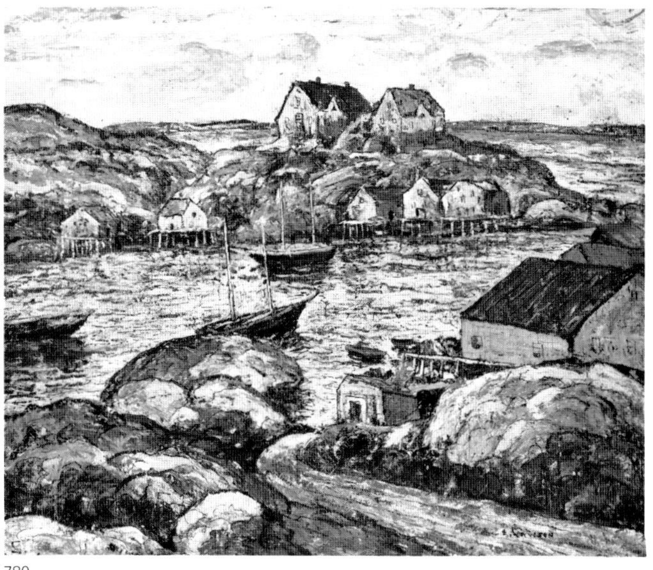
780

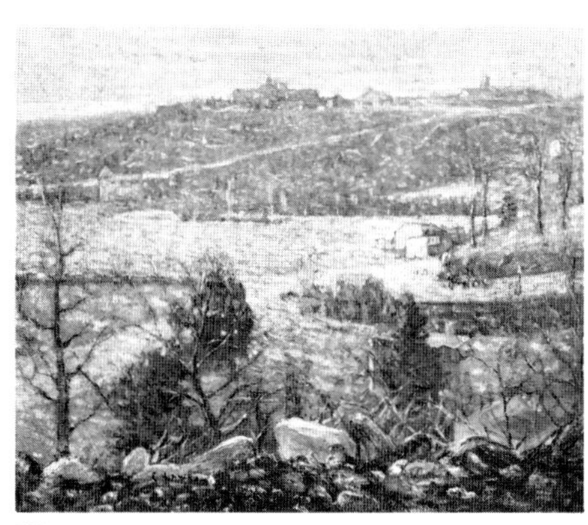
779

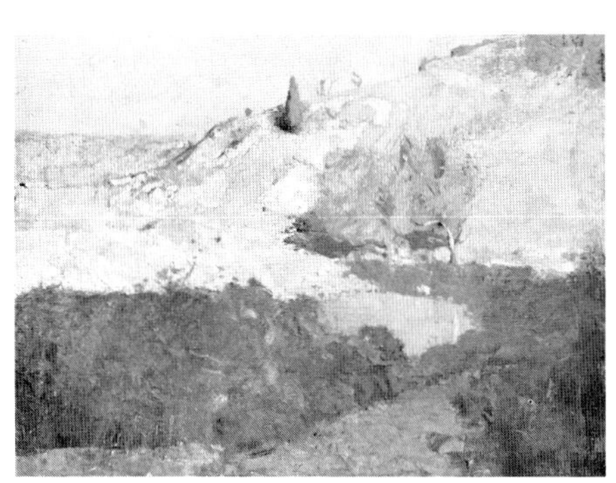
776

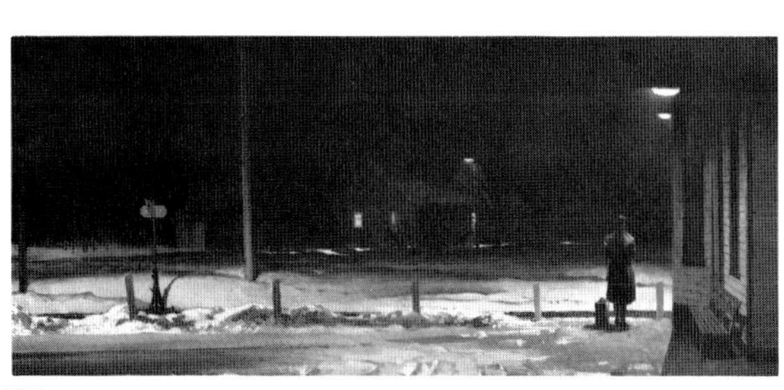
784

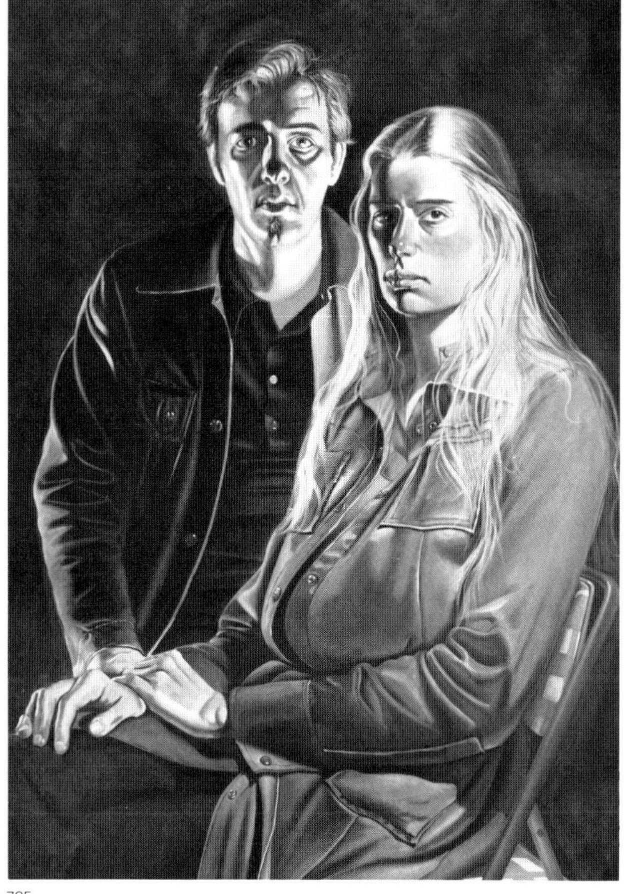
785

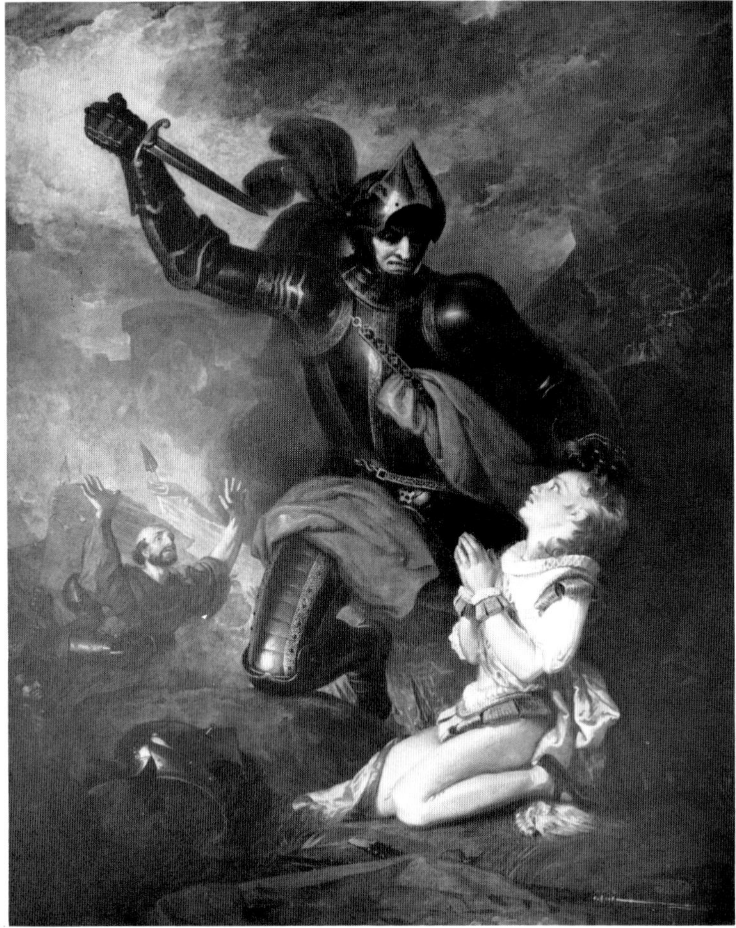
788

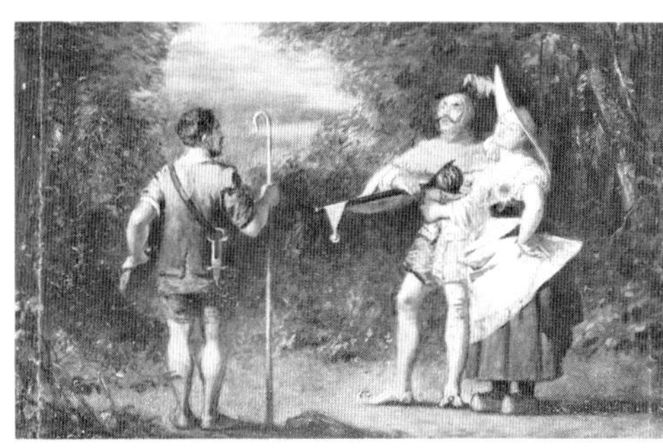
791

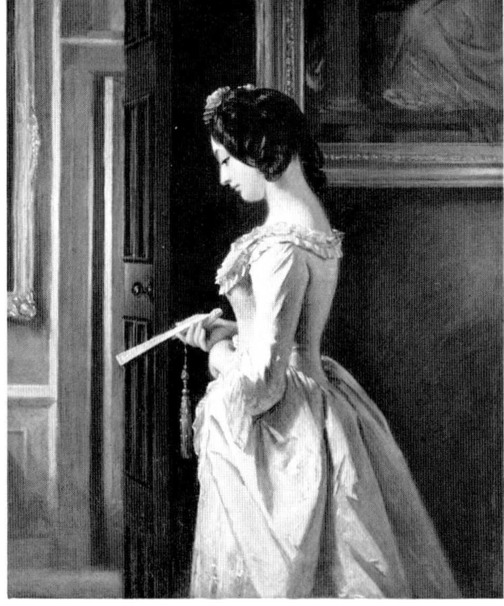
792

Charles R. Leslie (1794–1859)

786 *Henry C. Carey* (1793–1879), by 1826
Oil on wood
9 x 6⅞ in. (22.9 x 17.5 cm.)
Bequest of Henry C. Carey (The Carey Collection),1879.8.14

787 *Earl of Egremont* (1751–1837); on back, *Scene with a Man and Woman*, 1826–37
Oil on wood
9¹⁄₁₆ x 6⅞ in. (23 x 17.5 cm.)
Gift of Samuel P. Avery, 1898.12

788 *The Murder of Rutland by Lord Clifford*, 1815
Oil on canvas
96¾ x 79½ in. (245.7 x 202 cm.)
Signed and dated at lower right: C R LESLIE/1815
Gift of the Leslie family, 1831.1

789 *Olivia in "Twelfth Night,"* possibly 1855
Oil on wood
12 x 10 in. (30.5 x 25.4 cm.)
Bequest of Henry C. Carey (The Carey Collection), 1879.8.15

790 *John Swaine* (1775–1860), 1845
Oil on wood
11¹⁵⁄₁₆ x 9¹³⁄₁₆ in. (30.3 x 24.9 cm.)
Annotated on back (possibly by John Sartain): Portrait of John Swaine. (see Allitone's Bio. Dic.)/Painted for John Sartain. 1845 by Chas R. Leslie. R. A.
Bequest of Dr. Paul J. Sartain, 1945.18.1

791 *Touchstone, Audrey, and the Clown in "As You Like It,"* ca. 1831
Oil on paper, mounted on wood
11⅛ x 15¾ in. (28.3 x 40 cm.)
Bequest of Henry C. Carey (The Carey Collection), 1879.8.16

792 *Sophia Western*, 1849
Oil on canvas
16⅞ x 14⁷⁄₁₆ in. (42.9 x 36.7 cm.)
Gift of Samuel P. Avery, 1898.1.1

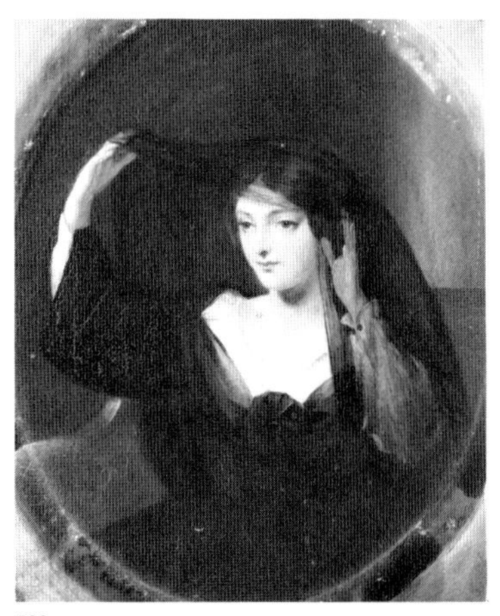

789

William Lester (1910–)

793 *Melons on a Red Floor*, 1951
Oil on masonite
20¹¹⁄₁₆ x 28¾ in. (52.5 x 73 cm.)
Inscribed, signed, and dated on back: "MELONS ON A RED FLOOR"/WM. LESTER - 1951
John Lambert Fund, 1952.7

Emanuel Leutze (1816–1868)

794 *The Poet's Dream*, by 1840
Oil on canvas

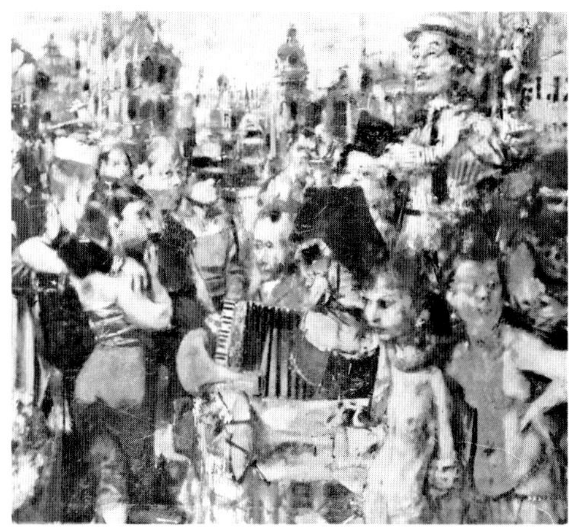
802

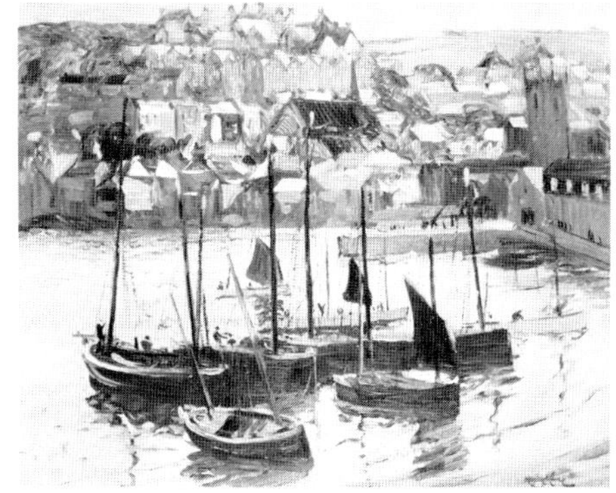

797

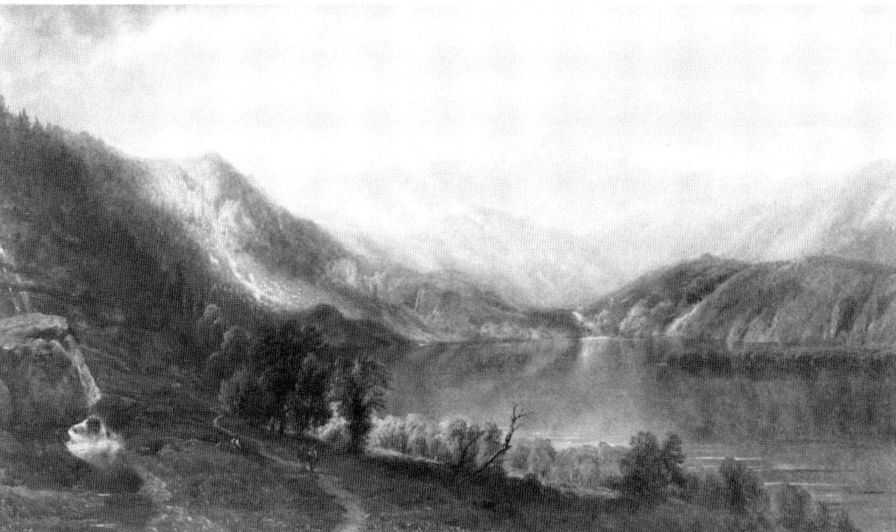

803

30⁵⁄₁₆ x 25¼ in. (77 x 64.1 cm.), oval
Bequest of Henry C. Carey (The Carey Collection), 1879.8.17

795 *Self-Portrait*, ca. 1865
Oil on canvas
28⅞ x 23⅝ in. (73.3 x 60 cm.)
Annotated on lining: Self Portrait/E. Leutze.
Gift of John Frederick Lewis, 1928.8.1

Hayley Lever (1876–1958)

796 *Cornwall, Evening Glow*, 1902
Oil on canvas
14¹⁄₁₆ x 18 in. (35.7 x 45.7 cm.)
Signed and dated at lower right: R.Hayley LEVER O[2]/R HAYLEY LEVER; inscribed on back: CORNWALL/EVENING/GLOW
Gift of Vera White, 1960.18.3

797 *Sunshine on Saint Ives, Cornwall*, ca. 1913
Oil on canvas
24 x 30 in. (61 x 76.2 cm.)
Signed at lower right: Hayley Lever
John Lambert Fund, 1914.8

Milton Levey (1923–1972)

798 *Hot Cat*, 1950
Oil on canvas
19¾ x 28³⁄₁₆ in. (50.2 x 71.6 cm.)
Signed at lower right: Milton Levey
John Lambert Fund, 1951.11

Julian E. Levi (1900–1982)

799 *Lime Kiln*, 1944–45
Oil on canvas
24¹⁵⁄₁₆ x 20 in. (63.3 x 50.8 cm.)
Signed at lower right: Julian Levi; dated on back: 1944.
Joseph E. Temple Fund, 1946.7

800 *Orpheus in the Studio*, ca. 1962
Oil on canvas
72 x 50 in. (182.9 x 127 cm.)
Signed at upper left: Julian Levi
Gift of Mrs. Herbert Cameron Morris, 1964.8

801 *Still Life*, ca. 1926
Oil on canvas
30¹⁄₁₆ x 22 in. (76.4 x 55.9 cm.)
John Lambert Fund, 1927.4

Jack Levine (1915–)

802 *Medicine Show*, 1955
Oil on canvas
40⅛ x 45¼ in. (101.9 x 114.9 cm.)
Signed at lower left: JLevine
Henry D. Gilpin and John Lambert funds, 1956.2

Edmund Darch Lewis (1835–1910)

803 *Lake Willoughby*, 1867
Oil on canvas
46 x 80 in. (116.8 x 203.2 cm.)
Signed and dated at lower left: Edmund D Lewis 1867
Gift of Mr. and Mrs. William W. Jeanes, 1974.3

Alice Whitten Lindborg (Mrs. Carl Lindborg, 1912–)

804 *South Street Corner*, ca. 1938
Oil on canvas
28⅜ x 24¼ in. (72.1 x 61.6 cm.)
Signed at lower left: Alice Whitten Lindborg
John Lambert Fund, 1939.15

Tod Lindenmuth (1885–1976)

805 *The Red Sail*, ca. 1926
Oil on canvas, mounted on wood
25³⁄₁₆ x 30⅛ in. (64 x 76.5 cm.)
Signed at lower right: TOD LINDENMUTH
John Lambert Fund, 1927.5

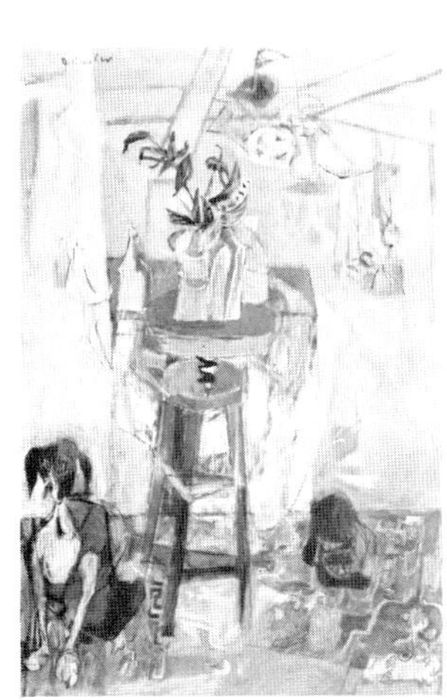

800

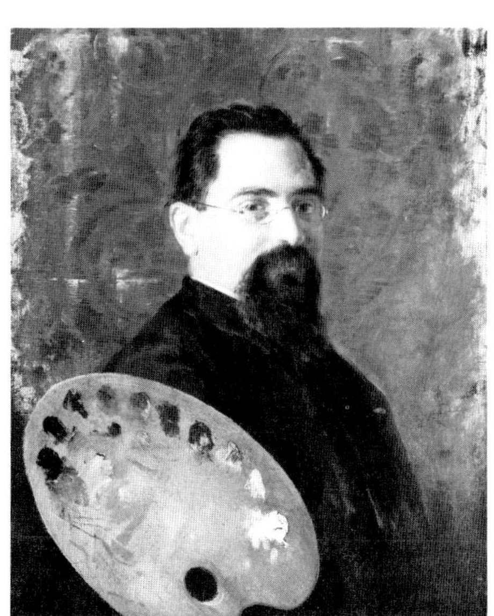

795

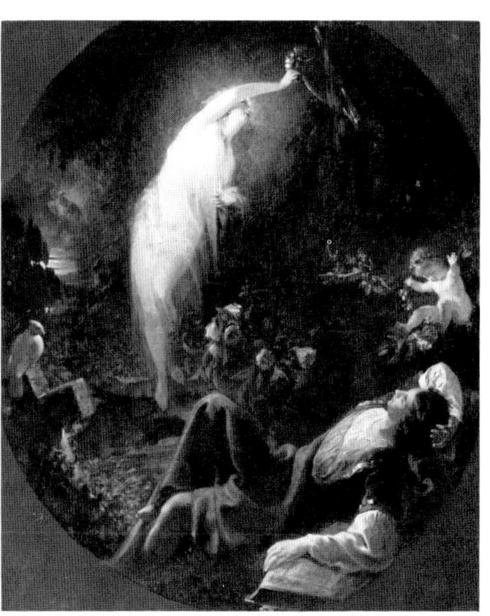

794

Charles Linford (1846–1897)

806 *Lowland Woods: Morning*, 1889
Oil on linen
40 x 30 in. (101.6 x 76.2 cm.)
Signed and dated at lower left: C. LINFORD. 1889.
Joseph E. Temple Fund, 1889.2

Frank B. A. Linton (1871–1943)

807 *Samuel Meyers*, by 1912
Oil on canvas
24 x 20 in. (61 x 50.8 cm.)
Signed at lower left: Frank B. A. Linton
Gift of Mrs. Rose Cheraskin in memory of her brother Harry Rubin, 1969.21.1

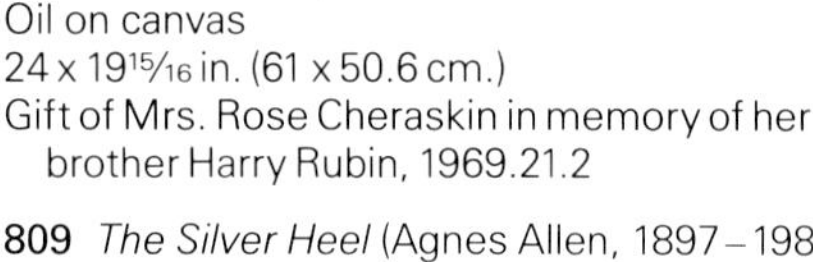

808 *Self-Portrait*, ca. 1935
Oil on canvas
24 x $19\frac{15}{16}$ in. (61 x 50.6 cm.)
Gift of Mrs. Rose Cheraskin in memory of her brother Harry Rubin, 1969.21.2

809 *The Silver Heel* (Agnes Allen, 1897–1988), 1923
Oil on canvas
84 x 46 in. (213.4 x 116.8 cm.)
Gift of Agnes Allen, 1973.14

William Henry Lippincott (1849–1920)

810 *Childish Thoughts*, 1895
Oil on canvas
$32\frac{1}{4}$ x $45\frac{11}{16}$ in. (81.9 x 116.1 cm.)
Inscribed, dated, and signed at lower right: copyright 1895 by Wm H. Lippincott.
Gift of Mary H. Rice, 1976.3

811 *Infantry in Arms*, 1887
Oil on canvas
32 x $53\frac{1}{4}$ in. (81.3 x 135.3 cm.)
Inscribed, dated, and signed at lower left: COPYRIGHT N.Y. 1887 BY W.H. LIPPINCOTT.; signed and dated at lower right: Wm. H. LIPPINCOTT. 1887.
Gift of Homer F. Emens and Francis C. Jones, 1922.10

Helen Sharpless Lloyd
See Helen Lloyd Horter.

De Witt M. Lockman (1870–1957)

812 *The Blue and Gold Kimono;* on back, *Sketch of Model Used in "The Blue and Gold Kimono,"* ca. 1917
Oil on canvas
$50\frac{1}{2}$ x $40\frac{1}{2}$ in. (128.3 x 102.9 cm.)
Signed at lower left: De Witt M Lockman
Joseph E. Temple Fund, 1918.4

Clinton Benedict Lockwood (b. 1907)

813 *The Waif*, ca. 1931
Oil on canvas
$24\frac{1}{8}$ x $20\frac{1}{16}$ in. (61.3 x 51 cm.)
Annotated on stretcher: "THE WAIF"/BY/CLINTON/LOCKWOOD
John Lambert Fund, 1932.8

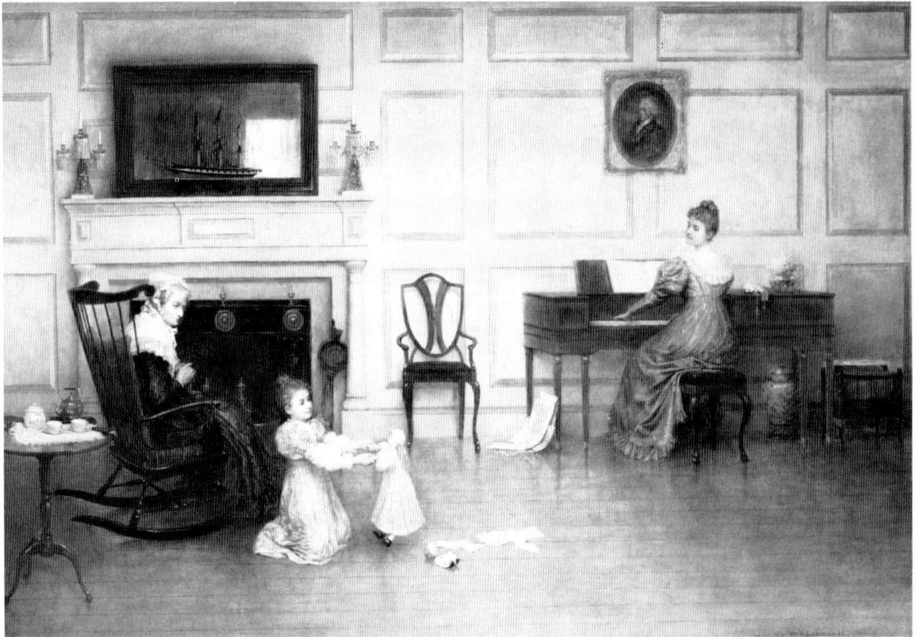

810

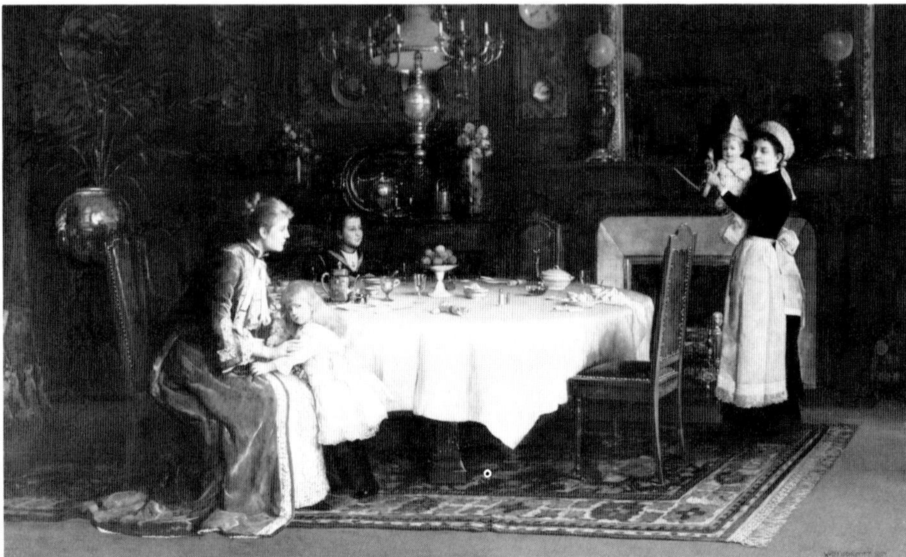

811

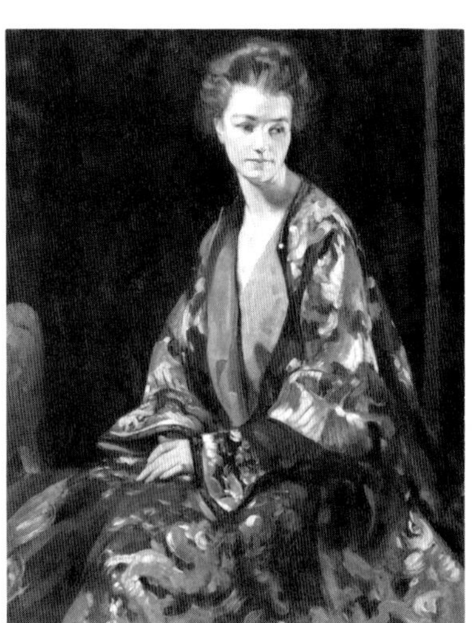

812

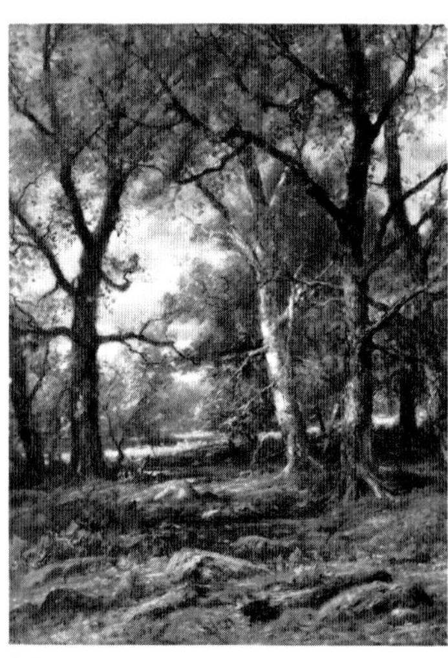

806

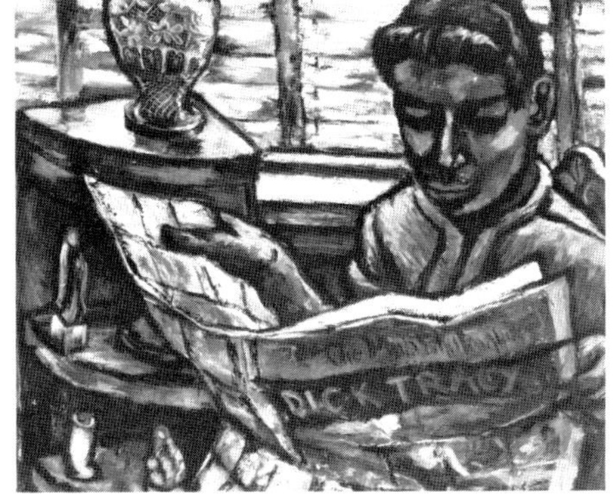

817

Ward Lockwood (1894–1963)

814 *Southwest #17: Prismatic*
Oil on canvas
47 7/8 x 29 7/8 in. (121.6 x 75.9 cm.)
Signed at lower right: LOCKWOOD
Bequest of Mrs. Clyde Bonbrake Lockwood, 1971.10

815 *Taos Plaza in Snow*, ca. 1933
Oil on canvas
30 1/16 x 40 1/16 in. (76.4 x 101.8 cm.)
Signed at lower right: LOCKWOOD
John Lambert Fund, 1934.8

Edward L. Loper (1916–)

816 *Landscape*, ca. 1944
Oil on canvas
23 15/16 x 29 15/16 in. (60.8 x 76 cm.)
Signed at lower left: Edw. L. Loper
John Lambert Fund, 1945.7

817 *Sunday Afternoon*, 1948
Oil on canvas
20 x 24 in. (50.8 x 61 cm.)
Signed at lower right: Edw L. Loper
Annotated on stretcher: Sunday Afternoon/1948
Gift of Dr. George J. Roth, 1970.34

Luigi Lucioni (1901–1988)

818 *Rose Hobart*, 1934
Oil on canvas

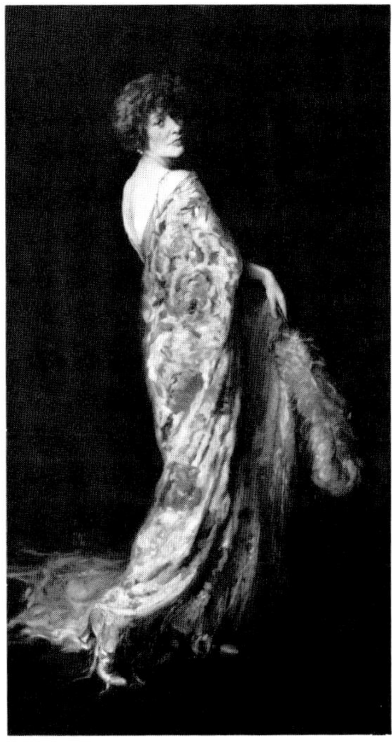

809

30 3/16 x 24 in. (76.7 x 61 cm.)
Signed and dated at lower left: Luigi Lucioni 1934
Joseph E. Temple Fund, 1935.6

Jimmy C. Lueders (1927–)

819 *Chess Players, Philadelphia*, 1952
Oil on masonite
10 x 14 in. (25.4 x 35.6 cm.)
Signed at lower right: Lueders; signed and inscribed on back: JC.LUEDERS/928 SPRUCE ST/PHILA PENNA
Gift of James P. and Ruth Marshall Magill, 1957.15.17

820 *Composition*, 1964
Acrylic on canvas
22 3/16 x 25 in. (56.4 x 63.5 cm.)

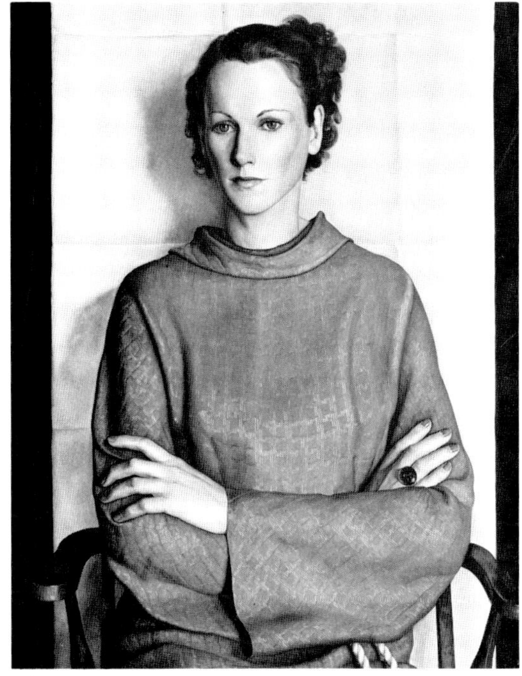

818

Signed at lower left: Lueders
John Lambert Fund, 1964.5

821 *Couple Playing Chess by Window*, 1952
Oil on cardboard
15 1/16 x 19 3/4 in. (38.3 x 50.2 cm.)
Gift of James P. and Ruth Marshall Magill, 1957.15.18

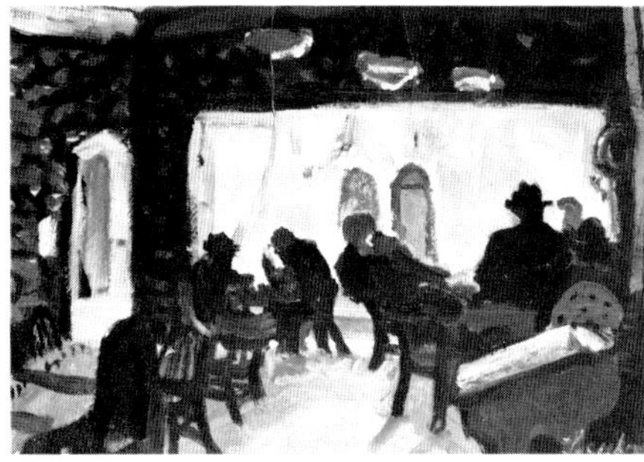
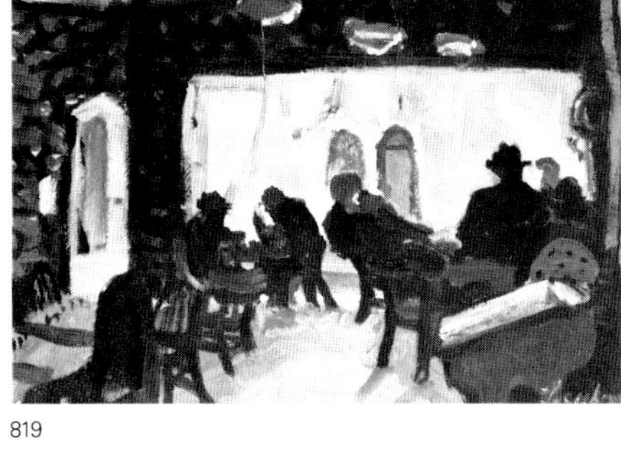

819

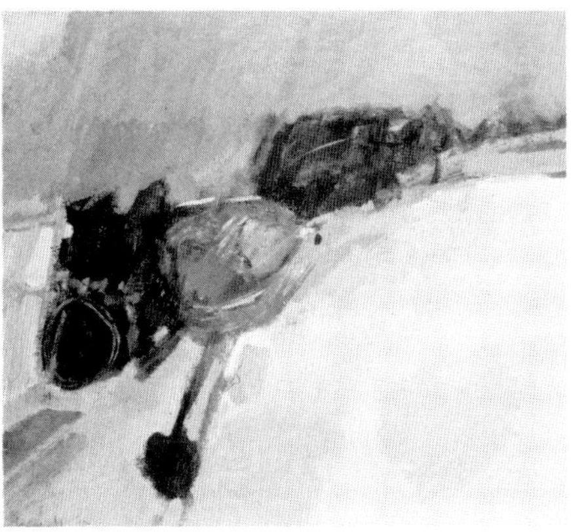

820

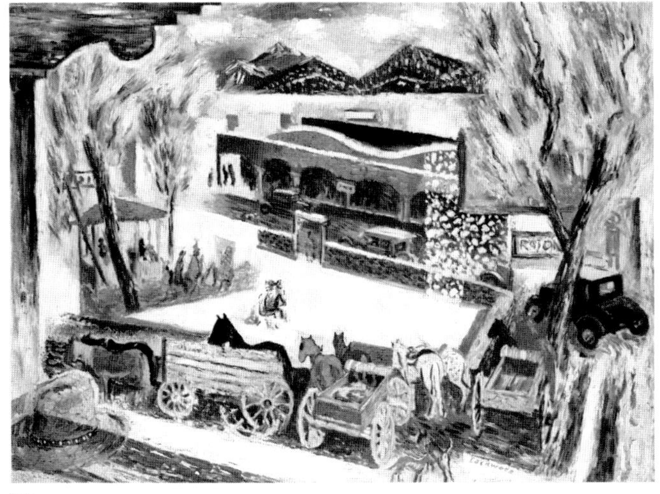

815

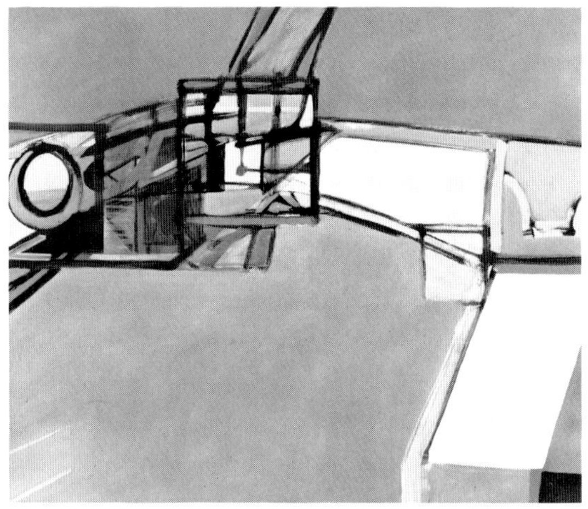
825

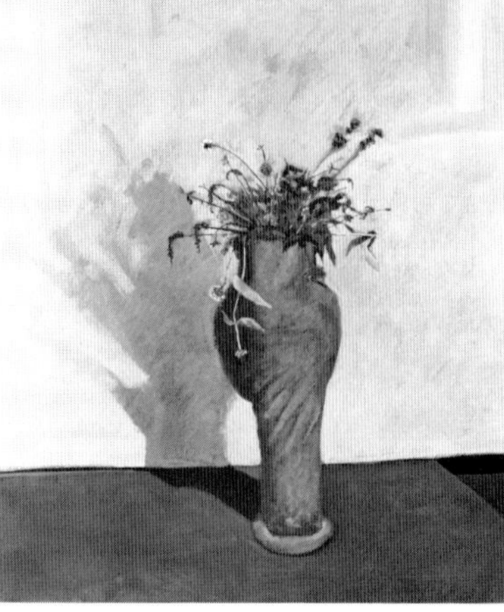
826

822 *Interior of Subway Car*, 1952
Oil on wood
10¹⁄₁₆ x 12¹⁄₁₆ in. (25.6 x 30.6 cm.)
Signed at lower left: Lueders; signed and inscribed on back: LUEDERS/928 Spruce St. [painted over]/Phila Pa-
Gift of James P. and Ruth Marshall Magill, 1957.15.19

823 *Saint John's*, 1952
Oil on canvas
26⅛ x 24¹⁄₁₆ in. (66.4 x 61.1 cm.)
Gift of Mr. and Mrs. Meyer P. Potamkin, 1984.39

824 *Space Composition*, 1967
Acrylic on canvas
96³⁄₁₆ x 84³⁄₁₆ in. (244.3 x 213.8 cm.)
Signed at lower left: Lueders
John Lambert Fund, 1967.3

825 *Space Composition XVIII*, 1969
Acrylic on canvas
60 x 72¹⁄₁₆ in. (152.4 x 183 cm.)
Dated and signed at lower right: 69/Lueders [incised in paint]
Gift of Mr. and Mrs. Robert M. Golder, 1986.26

826 *Winter Bouquet*, 1982
Acrylic on canvas
35⅞ x 30¹⁄₁₆ in. (91.1 x 76.4 cm.)
Signed and dated at lower right: Lueders 82
Pennsylvania Academy Purchase Prize from the 1983 Annual Fellowship Exhibition, Contemporary Arts Fund, 1983.18

George Luks (1867–1933)

827 *Polish Dancer*, ca. 1927
Oil on canvas, mounted on masonite
66⁵⁄₁₆ x 48 in. (168.4 x 121.9 cm.)
Gift of the Locust Club, Philadelphia, 1955.1.2

Dora C. Lust (b. 1890)

828 *Still Life*, ca. 1930
Oil on canvas
19¹³⁄₁₆ x 24¹⁄₁₆ in. (50.3 x 61.1 cm.)
John Lambert Fund, 1931.6

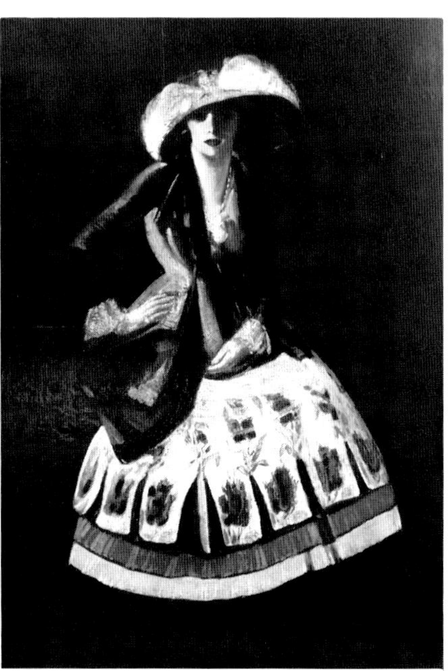
827

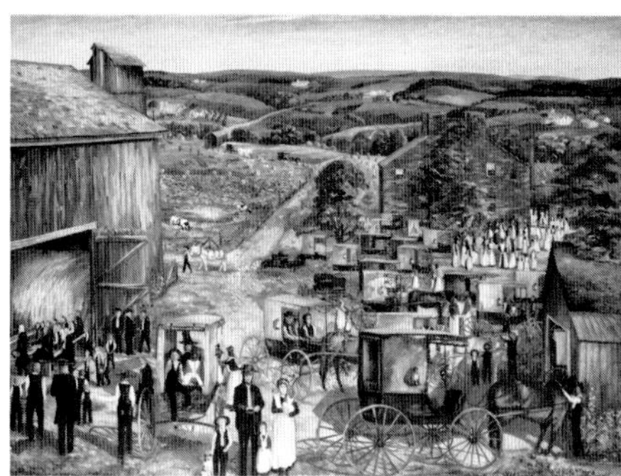
829

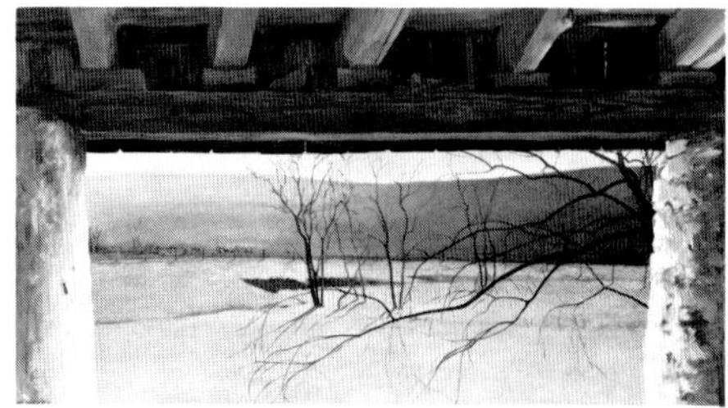
842

Charles Ford McCall (b. 1889)

829 *God's Day*, 1948
Oil on canvas
36½ x 47¹⁄₁₆ in. (92.7 x 119.5 cm.)
Signed and dated at lower right: CF McCall/1948
Gift of the artist, 1951.23

Virginia Armitage McCall (b. 1906)

830 *Assisi*, 1951
Oil on canvas
7 x 9¼ in. (17.8 x 23.5 cm.)
Signed at lower right: McCall
Gift of James P. and Ruth Marshall Magill, 1957.15.20

831 *Feast of the Pardon of Saint Francis, Assisi*, 1951
Oil and egg tempera on academy board
18 x 23 in. (45.7 x 58.4 cm.)
Signed at lower right: McCall
Gift of James P. and Ruth Marshall Magill, 1957.15.21

832 *Waldron Academy, Overbrook*, ca. 1931
Oil on canvas
25 x 30 in. (63.5 x 76.2 cm.)
Signed at lower left: McCall; and on back: VIRGINIA 'ARMITAGE' McCALL
John Lambert Fund, 1932.9

Henry McCarter (1864–1942)

833 *Coal Mine*, 1939
Oil on canvas
30⅛ x 36⅛ in. (76.5 x 91.8 cm.)
Gift of the estate of the artist, 1944.11.1

834 *An Eastern Legend, Arabesque*, by 1914
Oil on canvas
60 x 32¼ in. (152.4 x 81.9 cm.)
Gift of the estate of the artist, 1944.11.2

835 *Flower Still Life*
Oil on canvas
35¹⁵⁄₁₆ x 29¹⁵⁄₁₆ in. (91.3 x 76 cm.)
Signed at lower left: HENRY/McCARTER
Gift of Mrs. George Roberts, 1975.4

836 *The Fountain*, by 1931
Oil on canvas
72½ x 42¹⁄₁₆ in. (184.2 x 106.8 cm.)
Signed at lower left: HENRY McCARTER; inscribed and signed on back: "The Fountain"/Henry McCarter/1462 Spruce
Bequest of R. Sturgis Ingersoll, 1975.25

837 *Interior*, by 1932
Oil on canvas
40⅛ x 36⁵⁄₁₆ in. (101.9 x 92.2 cm.)
Signed at lower right: HENRY/McCARTER; inscribed and signed on back: "Interior"/HMcCarter
Gift of Mrs. Thomas E. Drake (The Margaretta S. Hinchman Collection), 1955.15.10

838 *Moby Dick*, by 1927
Oil on canvas
34¹¹⁄₁₆ x 42 in. (88.1 x 106.7 cm.)
Signed at lower right: HENRY McCARTER
Gift of Mrs. Morris Wenger, 1956.9

839 *Old Grindstone*, ca. 1933
Oil on canvas
30⅜ x 32¼ in. (77.2 x 81.9 cm.)
Signed at lower left: HENRY McCARTER
Joseph E. Temple Fund, 1934.9

840 *Pennsylvania's Broad Acres*, ca. 1937
Oil on canvas

42¼ x 48⅛ in. (107.3 x 122.2 cm.)
John Lambert Fund, 1938.11

841 *Symphony*, by 1915
Oil on canvas
103⅜ x 100⅜ in. (262.6 x 255 cm.)
Inscribed and signed on back: "Symphony"/by Henry McCarter [illegible]
Gift of Mrs. Henry Clifford, 1944.33

John W. McCoy (1910–1989)

842 *Craige's Meadow*, 1948
Oil and casein on masonite
22³⁄₁₆ x 40³⁄₁₆ in. (56.4 x 102.1 cm.)
Signed at lower left: J. W. McCoy
John Lambert Fund, 1950.10

Frances McCreery

843 *Fishing Village*, ca. 1916
Oil on burlap, mounted on canvas and then on board
29 x 27¾ in. (73.7 x 70.5 cm.)
Signed on back: McCreery
John Lambert Fund, 1917.5

Ann Heebner McDonald (Mrs. Ellice McDonald, d. 1958)

844 *Round Table*, ca. 1919
Oil on canvas
20⅛ x 23¹⁵⁄₁₆ in. (51.1 x 60.8 cm.)
Signed at lower right: Anne Heebner
John Lambert Fund, 1920.7

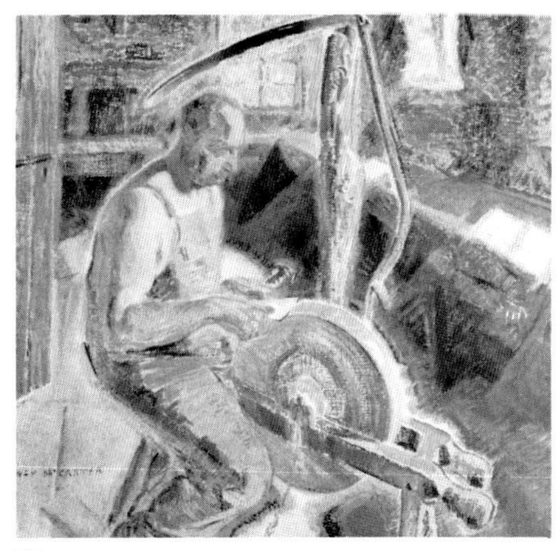

839

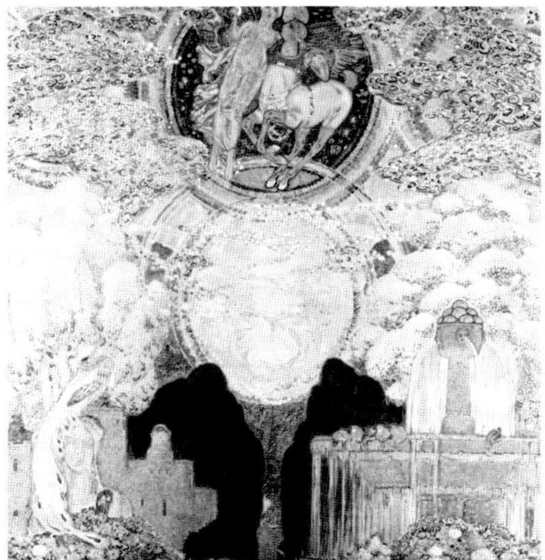

841

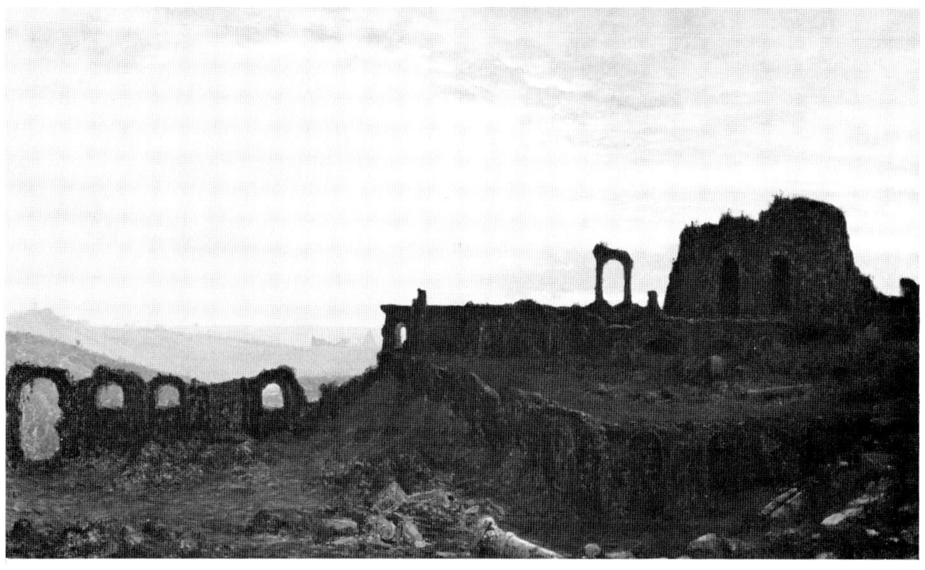

845

Jervis McEntee (1828–1891)

845 *The Ruins of Caesar's Palace*, ca. 1868
Oil on canvas
24¼ x 40⅛ in. (61.6 x 101.9 cm.)
Funds provided by the Fine Arts Ball and Discotheque, courtesy of the Pennsylvania Academy Women's Committee, 1978.9

Walter MacEwen (1860–1943)

846 *Miss Phyllis*, ca. 1909
Oil on canvas
48¹⁄₁₆ x 36 in. (122.1 x 91.4 cm.)
Signed at lower left: MACEWEN-
Joseph E. Temple Fund, 1910.1

Henry Lee McFee (1886–1953)

847 *Acorn Squash*, ca. 1942
Oil on canvas
24 x 30⅛ in. (61 x 76.5 cm.)
Signed at lower left: McFEE
Joseph E. Temple Fund, 1943.9

848 *Petunias*
Oil on canvas
20¹⁄₁₆ x 16¹⁄₁₆ in. (51 x 40.8 cm.)
Signed at lower left: McFee
Gift of Mrs. Herbert Cameron Morris, 1958.22.2

James McGarrell (1930–)

849 *Tour*, 1962
Oil on linen
68⅛ x 75¼ in. (173 x 191.1 cm.)
Gift of the Ford Foundation, 1964.1.5

William Erno Mackey (b. 1919)

850 *Blue and Still Life*, 1938
Oil on canvas
19¹⁵⁄₁₆ x 17 in. (50.6 x 43.2 cm.)
Signed and dated at lower left: William Mackey/ 1938 [incised in paint]
John Lambert Fund, 1939.9

Jeanne H. McLavy

851 *Intersection*, ca. 1943
Oil on canvas
24⅛ x 28⅛ in. (61.3 x 71.4 cm.)
Signed on back: McLavy
John Lambert Fund, 1944.8

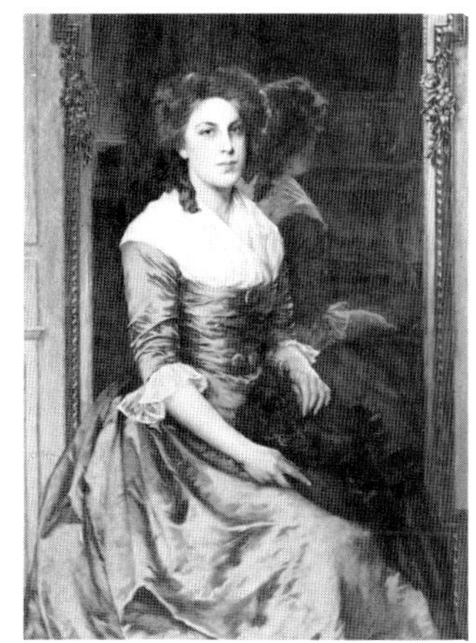

846

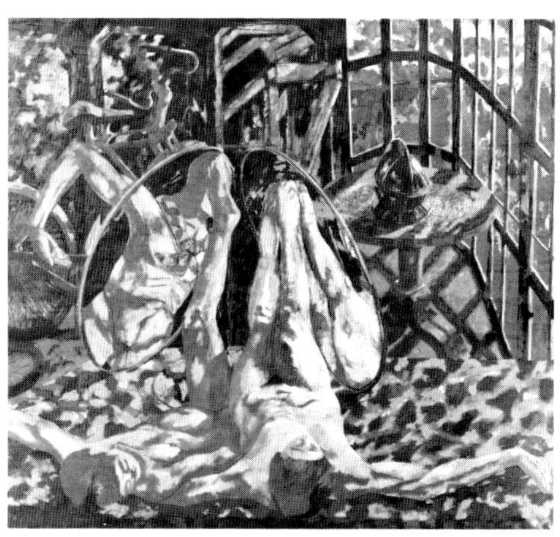

849

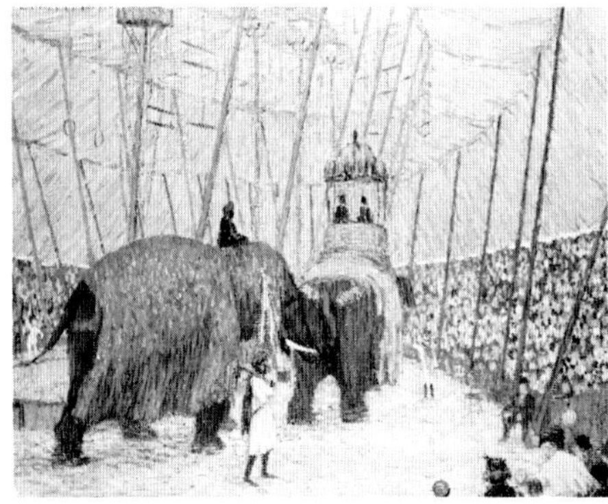
853

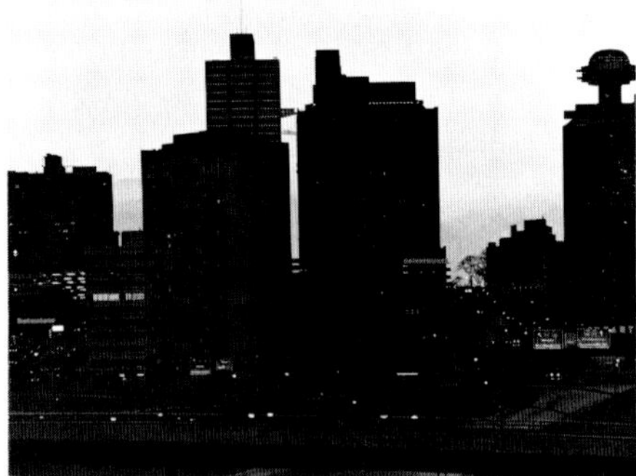
855

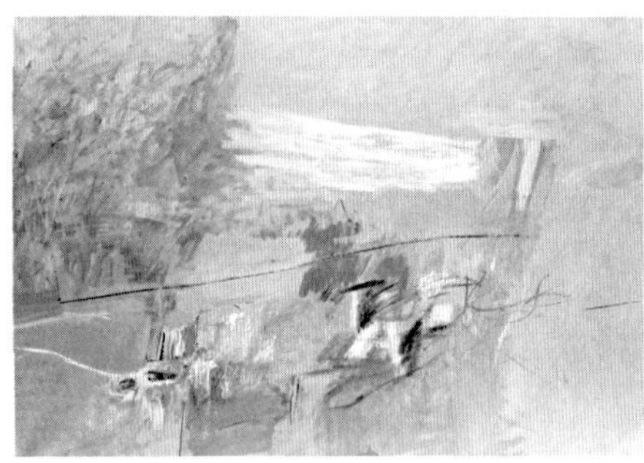
857

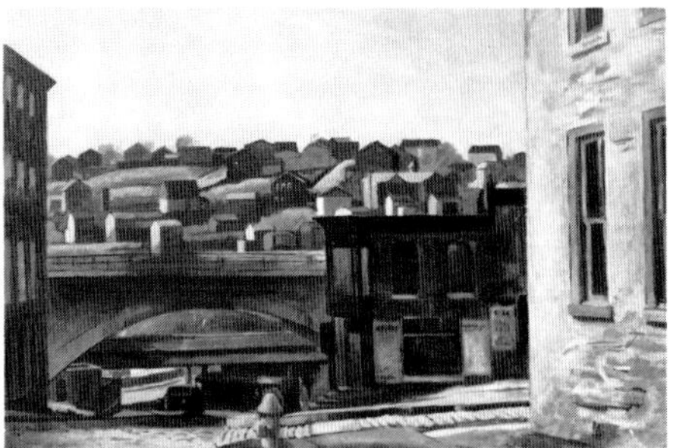
864

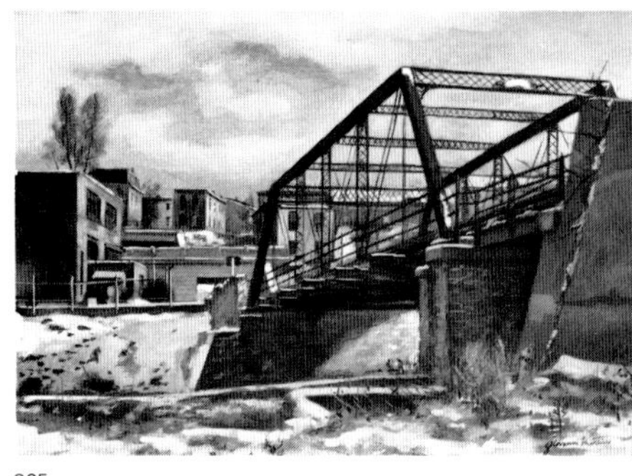
865

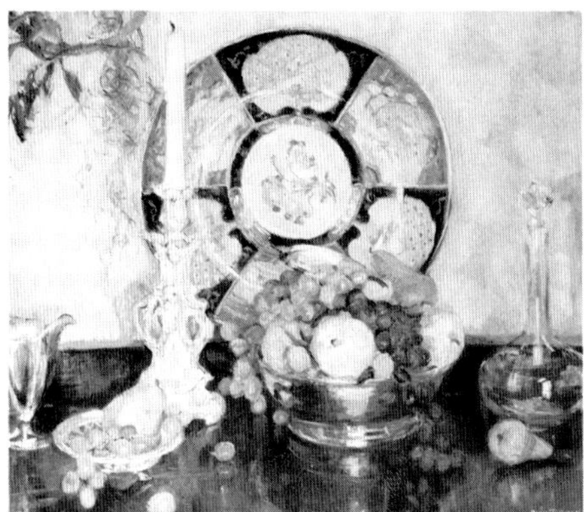
868

Leo Manso (1914–)

857 *Grey Sun*, 1961
Oil on canvas
50¾ x 72⅜ in. (128.9 x 183.9 cm.)
Signed at upper left: Manso
Joseph E. Temple Fund, 1962.8

Conrad Marca-Relli (1913–)

858 *The Hurdle*, 1959
Oil and canvas on canvas
56¼ x 76¾ in. (142.9 x 194.9 cm.)
Signed at lower left: MARCA-RELLI
John Lambert Fund, 1960.7

Edward D. Marchant (1806–1887)

859 *General Ulysses Simpson Grant (1822–1887)*, 1878
Oil on canvas
30⅛ x 25¹/₁₆ in. (76.5 x 63.7 cm.)
Signed and dated at lower left: E.D.Marchant./1878
Gift of Mrs. John Frederick Lewis (The John Frederick Lewis Memorial Collection), 1933.10.46

Reginald Marsh (1898–1954)

860 *End of 14th Street Crosstown Line*, 1936
Oil on wood
24 x 36⅛ in. (61 x 91.8 cm.)
Signed and dated at lower right: REGINALD/MARSH'36
Henry D. Gilpin Fund, 1942.7

861 *Five Women* (sketch)
Oil on cardboard
11⅛ x 16 in. (28.3 x 40.6 cm.)
Bequest of Felicia Meyer Marsh, 1979.8.2

862 *Woman in Red Skirt*, 1949; on back, *Woman in Red Blouse*, 1953
Oil on board
12 x 9 in. (30.5 x 22.9 cm.)
Signed and dated at lower right: Marsh 49; signed and dated on back: Marsh 1953.
Bequest of Felicia Meyer Marsh, 1979.8.1

Mrs. Donald J. McLean
See Doris Lucile Porter.

Edith McMurtrie (1883–1947)

852 *Building;* on back, *Desert Landscape*
Oil on canvas board
16 x 12 in. (40.6 x 30.5 cm.)
Signed at lower right and on back: Edith McMurtrie
Bequest of the artist, 1948.7

853 *The Circus*, ca. 1920
Oil on canvas
25⅜ x 30³/₁₆ in. (64.5 x 76.7 cm.)
Signed at upper left: Edith McMurtrie
John Lambert Fund, 1921.6

George Herbert Macrum (b. 1888)

854 *The Pile Driver*, 1912
Oil on canvas
20¼ x 24⅛ in. (51.4 x 61.3 cm.)
Signed and dated at lower left: G.H.Macrum/1912
John Lambert Fund, 1914.9

Noel Mahaffey (1944–)

855 *Atlanta, Georgia*, 1971
Acrylic on canvas
42⅜ x 54⁵/₁₆ in. (107.6 x 138 cm.)
Gift of Mr. and Mrs. Sydney Lewis, 1971.20

Edward Greene Malbone
See cat. nos. 1641–42.

Peppino Mangravite (1896–1978)

856 *Girl Combing Her Hair*, 1933
Oil on canvas
38³/₁₆ x 28¹¹/₁₆ in. (97 x 72.9 cm.)
Signed and dated at lower left: Mangravite/1933; signed and inscribed on back: P. Mangravite/Saint Paul/Alpes Maritimes/France
Joseph E. Temple Fund, 1937.3

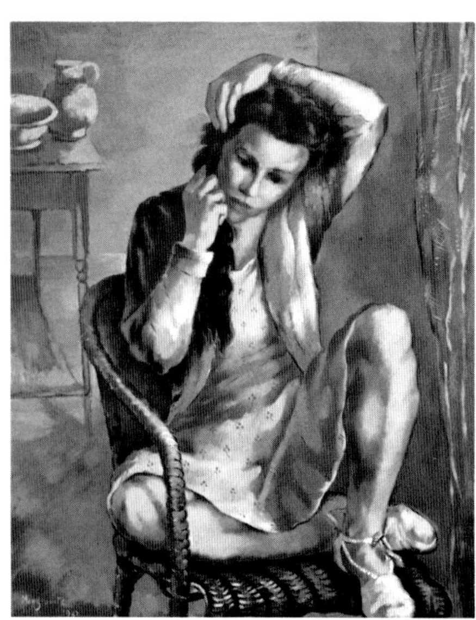
856

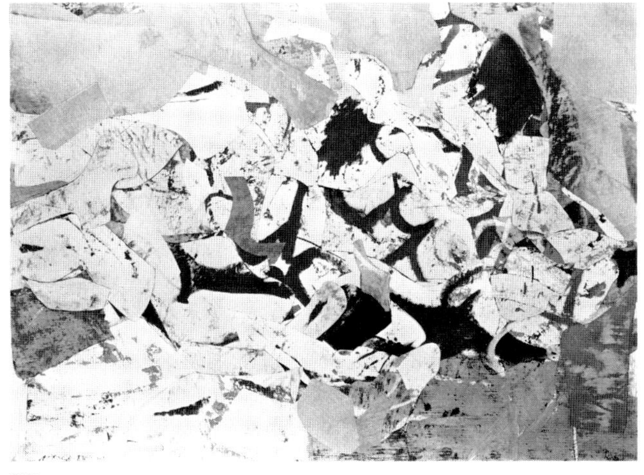
858

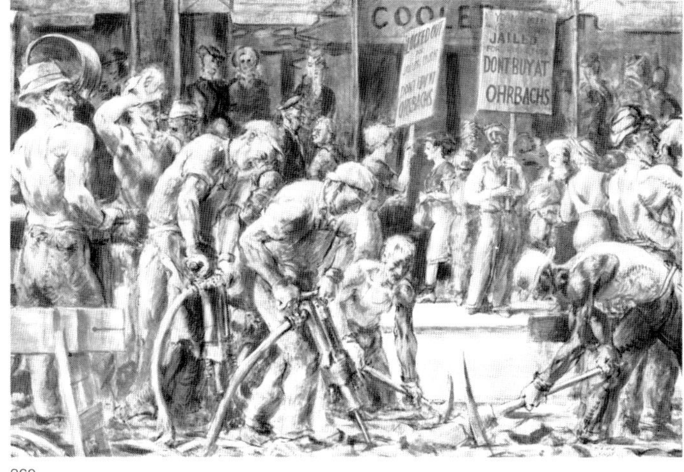

860

David Martin (Scottish, 1736–1798)

863 *Benjamin Franklin* (1706–1790), 1767
Oil on canvas
49$\frac{1}{2}$ x 39$\frac{1}{2}$ in. (125.8 x 100.4 cm.)
Gift of Maria McKean Allen and Phebe Warren Downes through the bequest of their mother, Elizabeth Wharton McKean, 1943.16.1

Antonio P. Martino (1902–1988)

864 *Leverington Avenue*, ca. 1937
Oil on canvas
30 x 45$\frac{1}{8}$ in. (76.2 x 114.6 cm.)
Signed at lower left: A. P. Martino
Henry D. Gilpin Fund, 1938.5

Giovanni Martino (1908–)

865 *Canal Bridge*, 1946
Egg tempera on cardboard
11$\frac{11}{16}$ x 16$\frac{1}{8}$ in. (29.7 x 41 cm.)
Signed at lower right: Giovanni Martino
John Lambert Fund, 1947.7

Martyl (Martyl Suzanne Schweig Langsdorf, 1918–)

866 *Zebras*, 1942
Oil on masonite
17$\frac{1}{4}$ x 21$\frac{3}{8}$ in. (43.8 x 54.3 cm.)
Signed and dated at lower right: Martyl '42
John Lambert Fund, 1943.10

Mary Townsend Mason (Mrs. William Clarke Mason, née Stuard, 1886–1964)

867 *Splendor Falls*, 1935
Oil on canvas
21 x 30$\frac{5}{16}$ in. (53.3 x 77 cm.)
Signed and dated at lower left: MARY T. MASON 35
Gift of the artist, 1936.13

868 *Still Life with Fruit*, ca. 1921
Oil on canvas
26$\frac{3}{16}$ x 30$\frac{1}{8}$ in. (66.5 x 76.5 cm.)
Signed at lower right: Mary T Mason.
John Lambert Fund, 1922.11

Jack Massey (b. 1925)

869 *Boy with Shadow on Wall*
Oil on canvas
12 x 16$\frac{3}{16}$ in. (30.5 x 41.1 cm.)
Gift of James P. and Ruth Marshall Magill, 1957.15.23

Henry Elis Mattson (1887–1971)

870 *Self-Portrait*, 1948
Oil on canvas
24$\frac{1}{16}$ x 20 in. (61.1 x 50.8 cm.)
Signed at upper right: Mattson
Joseph E. Temple Fund, 1950.11

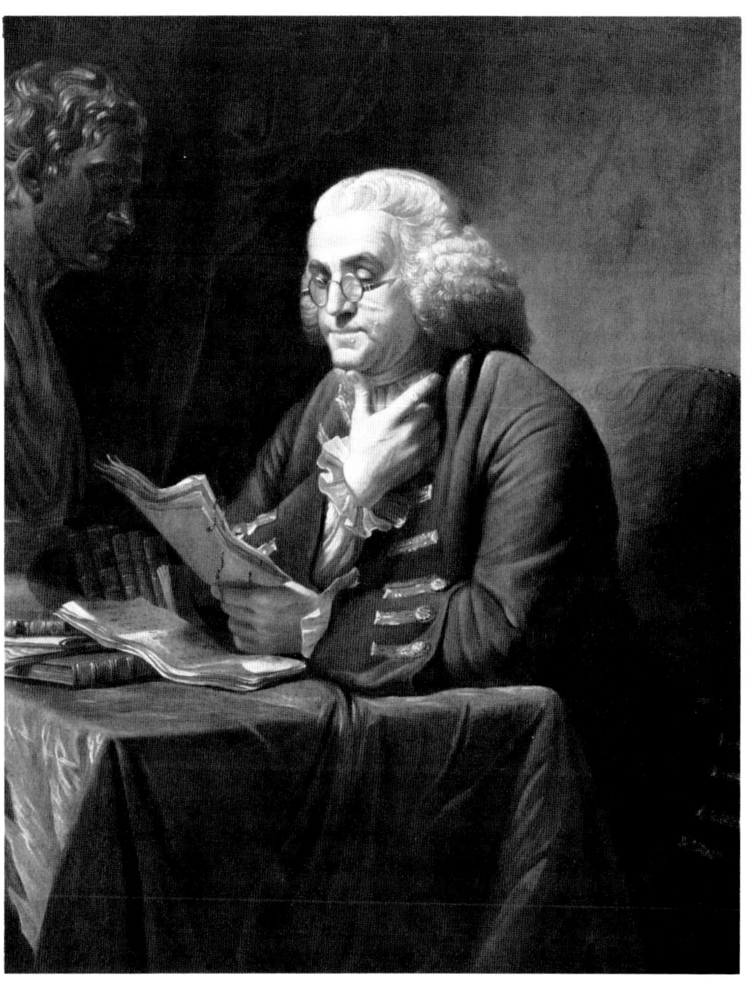
863

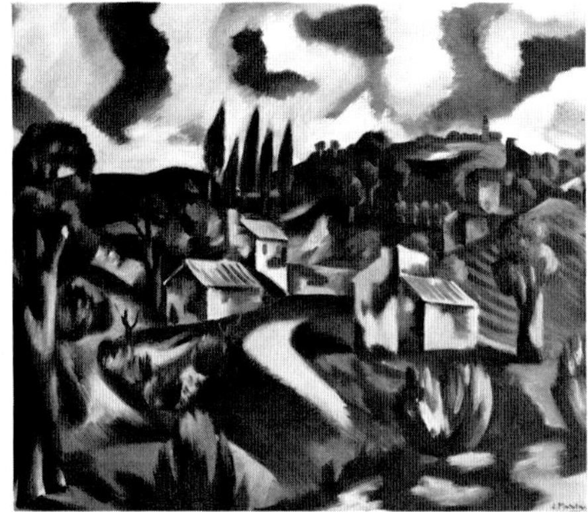

871

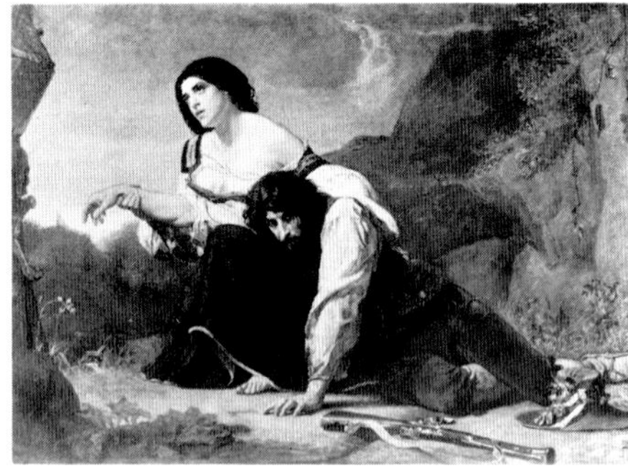

873

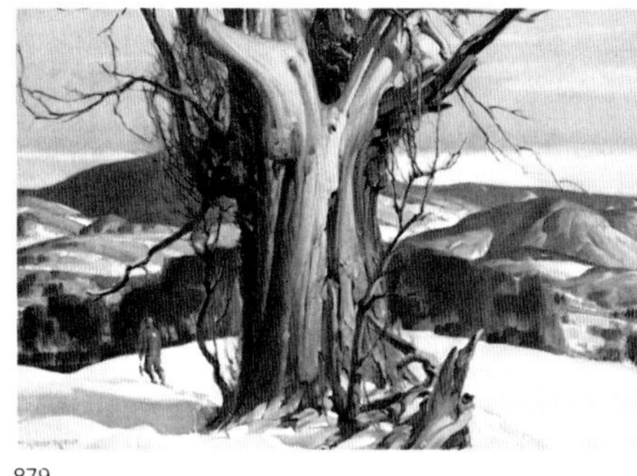

879

Jan Matulka (1890–1972)

871 *October Cloud*, ca. 1929
Oil on canvas
28 15/16 x 33 13/16 in. (73.5 x 85.9 cm.)
Signed at lower right: J. Matulka
John Lambert Fund, 1930.3

Alfred H. Maurer (1868–1932)

872 *Vase of Flowers*, ca. 1926
Oil and egg tempera on paper, mounted on canvas
30 1/16 x 20 1/16 in. (76.4 x 51 cm.)
Signed at upper right: A.H. Maurer
Gift of Carl Zigrosser, 1955.13.4

Edward Harrison May, Jr. (1824–1887)

873 *Dying Brigand*, 1855
Oil on canvas
64 x 90 in. (162.6 x 228.6 cm.)
Signed and dated at lower left: May./1855.
Pennsylvania Academy purchase, by subscription, 1857.3

Nancy Maybin
See Nancy Maybin Ferguson.

George Willoughby Maynard (1843–1923)

874 *Sappho*, ca. 1888
Oil on canvas
24 1/16 x 20 1/8 in. (61.1 x 51.1 cm.)
Signed at lower right: [M]aynard
Joseph E. Temple Fund, 1889.3

Michael Mayor (b. 1884)

875 *Sodom*, 1959
Oil on canvas
70 1/16 x 51 1/8 in. (178 x 129.9 cm.)
Signed at lower left and on back: Michael/Mayor
Gift of the artist, 1960.8

Thomas Francis Meehan (1923–)

876 *Pigeonry*, 1948
Oil on canvas
49 1/8 x 44 1/8 in. (124.8 x 112.1 cm.)
Signed at lower left: thos.
John Lambert Fund, 1949.9

877 *Still Life—Gaillardias in Coffee Pot*, 1952
Oil on canvas
24 x 16 1/16 in. (61 x 40.8 cm.)
Signed at lower left: thos.
Gift of James P. and Ruth Marshall Magill, 1957.15.24

Peggy Meid. *See* Peggy Meid Todd.

Gari Melchers (1860–1932)

878 *Skaters*, early 1890s
Oil on canvas
43 3/16 x 27 7/16 in. (109.7 x 69.7 cm.)
Signed at lower center: Gari Melchers-
Joseph E. Temple Fund, 1901.1

Arthur Meltzer (1893–)

879 *Trapper's Trail*, ca. 1936
Oil on canvas
22 x 32 1/16 in. (55.9 x 81.4 cm.)
Signed at lower left: -Arthur Meltzer
Joseph E. Temple Fund, 1937.4

Sigmund Menkes (1896–)

880 *Figure in Space*, 1949
Oil on canvas
49 x 37 in. (124.5 x 94 cm.)
Signed at upper left: Menkes
Joseph E. Temple Fund, 1951.12

881 *Woman in Pink Dressing Room*, 1926
Oil on canvas
45 13/16 x 35 3/16 in. (116.4 x 89.4 cm.)
Signed at lower right: Menkes; signed, dated, and inscribed on back: Menkes/1926./XI./fait à Sanary
Gift of Bernard Davis, 1950.20.2

Anna Lea Merritt (1844–1930)

882 *Piping Shepherd*, 1896
Oil on wood
26 1/8 x 21 5/8 in. (66.4 x 54.9 cm.)
Signed and dated at lower right: ALM [monogram]/1896
Henry D. Gilpin Fund, 1899.2

Stanley Merz (1941–)

883 *Friday Mornin's Edge*, 1975
Acrylic on canvas
66 x 50 1/4 in. (167.6 x 127.6 cm.)
Signed at lower right: MERZ; signed on canvas folded over stretcher: S.Merz
Inscribed, signed, and dated on stretcher: 50 x 66 ACRYLIC Stan Merz 1975
Pennsylvania Academy Purchase Prize from the 1975 Annual Fellowship Exhibition, 1975.8

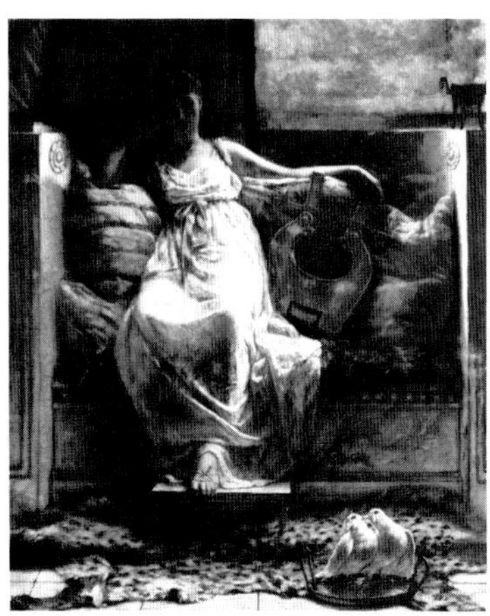

874

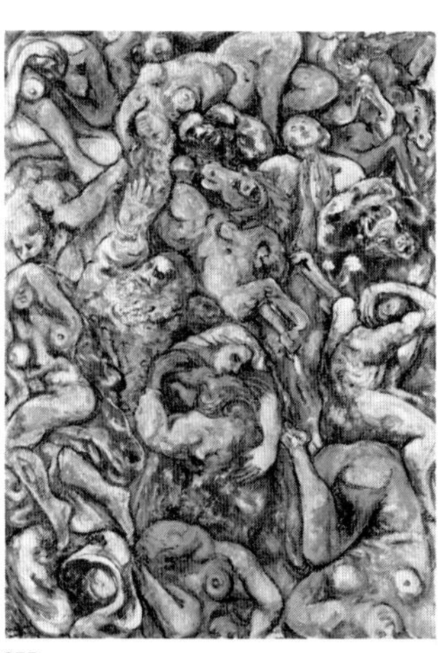

875

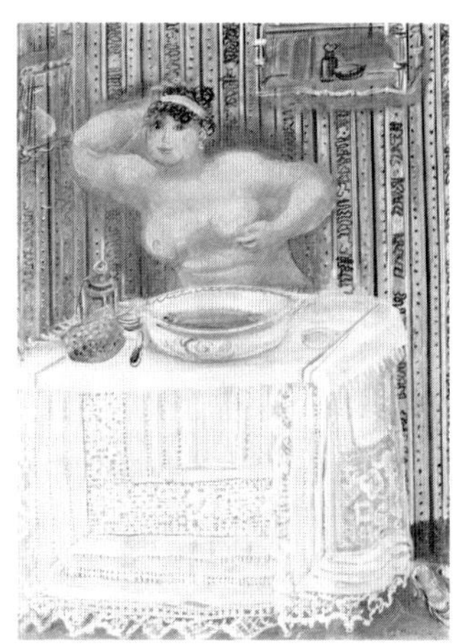

881

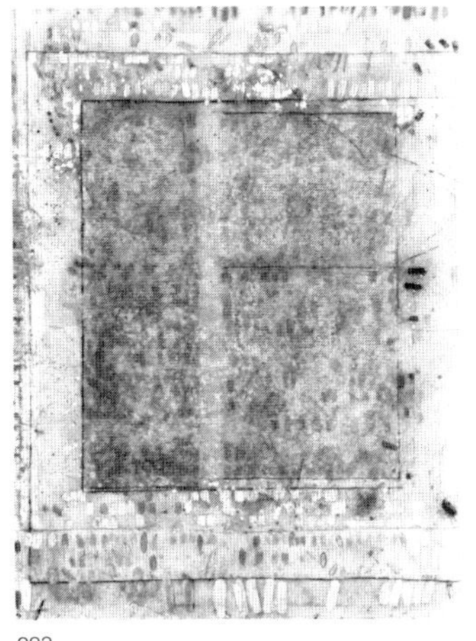

883

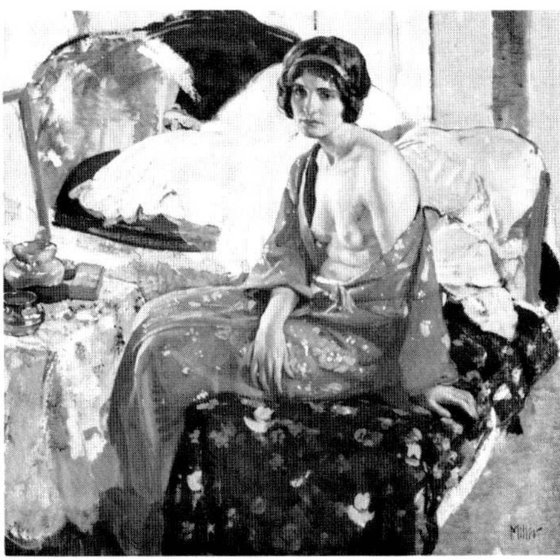

888

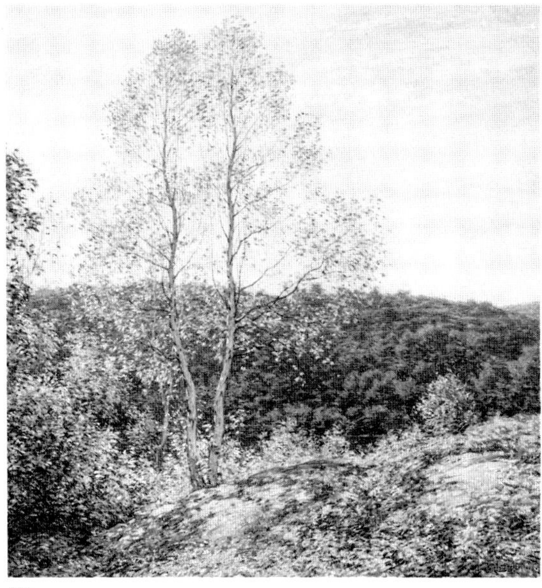

885

Hubert Mesibov (1916–)

884 *Subway*, 1951
Oil and egg tempera on masonite
36 x 48 in. (91.4 x 121.9 cm.)
Signed and dated at lower right: Mesibov 1951
John Lambert Fund, 1952.8

Willard L. Metcalf (1858–1925)

885 *The Twin Birches*, 1908
Oil on canvas
40⅛ x 39 in. (101.9 x 99.1 cm.)
Signed and dated at lower right: W.L.METCALF. 1908.
Joseph E. Temple Fund, 1909.4

Mildred Bunting Miller (b. 1892)

886 *Descending Night*, ca. 1922
Oil on canvas
25$^{3}/_{16}$ x 30$^{7}/_{16}$ in. (64 x 77.3 cm.)
Signed at lower right: M Miller
John Lambert Fund, 1923.7

Peter Miller (Mrs. C. Earle Miller, 1915–)

887 *Dragonfly, Snake, and Turtle*, 1968
Oil on linen
54 x 42 in. (137.2 x 106.7 cm.)
Signed and inscribed on back: Peter Miller/ DRAGONFLY, SNAKE AND TURTLE
Henry D. Gilpin Fund, 1969.14

Richard E. Miller (1875–1943)

888 *The Boudoir*, by 1937
Oil on canvas
34¼ x 36$^{1}/_{16}$ in. (87 x 91.6 cm.)
Signed at lower right: Miller
Gift of Mrs. Alfred G. B. Steel, 1937.14

889 *Arthur Burdett Frost* (1851–1928), ca. 1911
Oil on canvas
39½ x 32 in. (100.3 x 81.3 cm.)
Signed at lower right: Miller
Gift of Arthur Burdett Frost, 1912.11

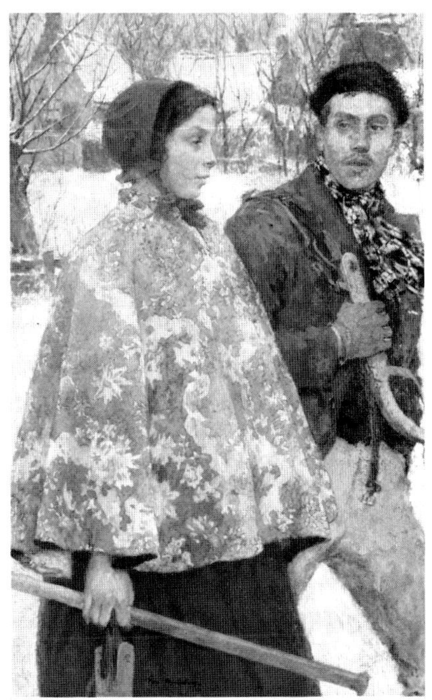

878

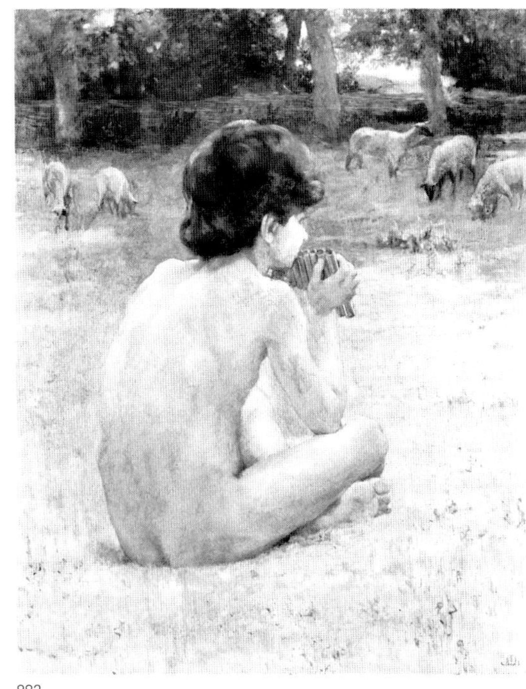

882

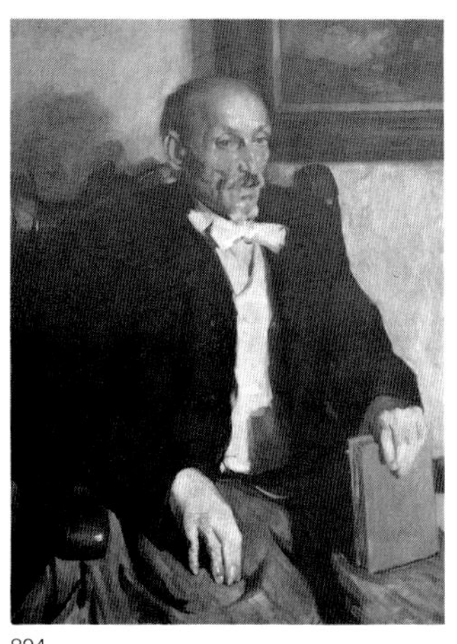

894

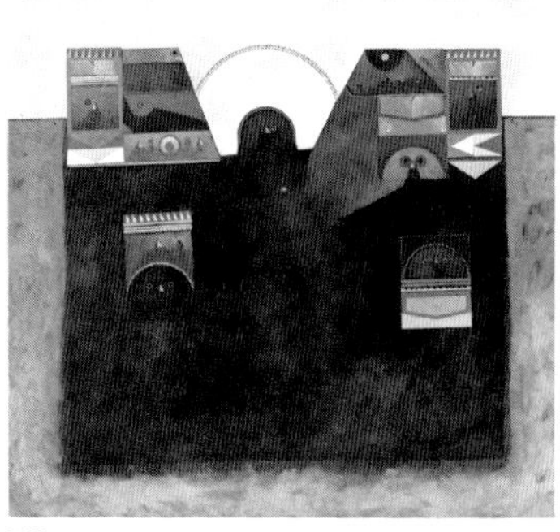

899

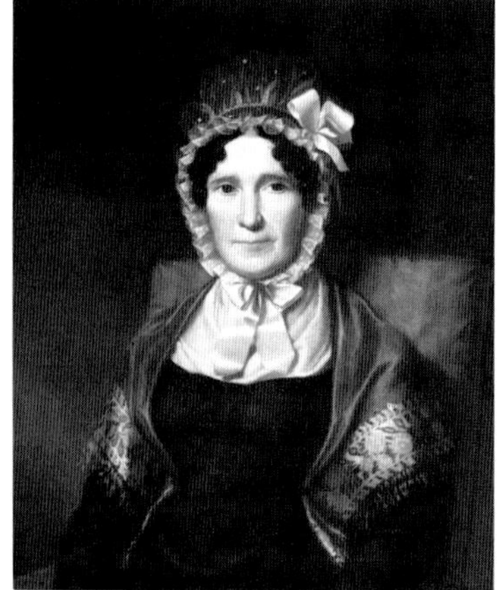

901

William Henry Miller (1854–1928)

890 *Self-Portrait*, 1926
Oil on canvas
30⅛ x 25¹⁄₁₆ in. (75.6 x 63.7 cm.)
Inscribed, signed, and dated on back: SELFPORTRAIT/Wm. H. Miller/1926
Gift of Henry A. Dubbs in accordance with the wishes of the artist, 1928.11

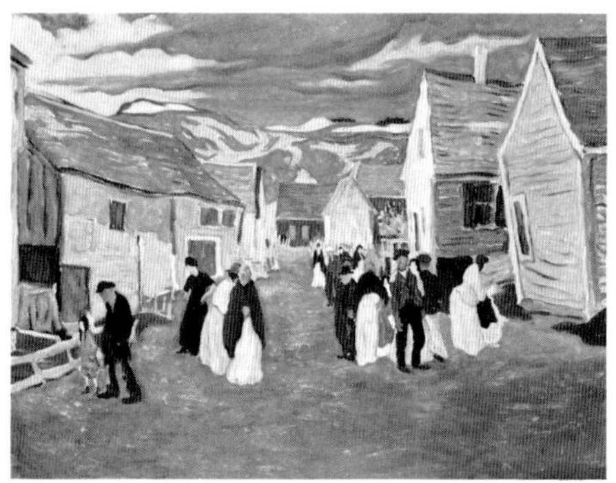

892

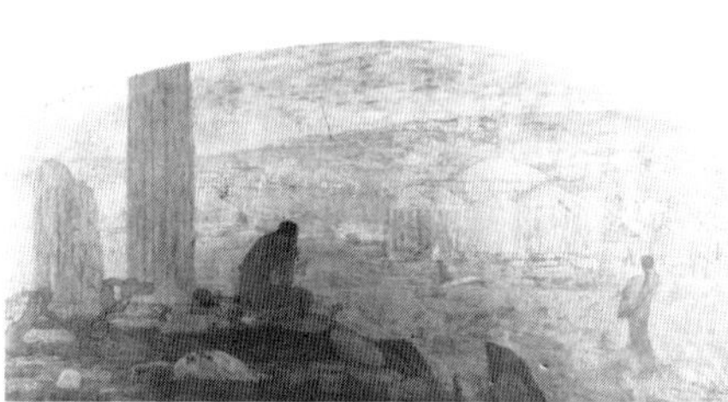

896

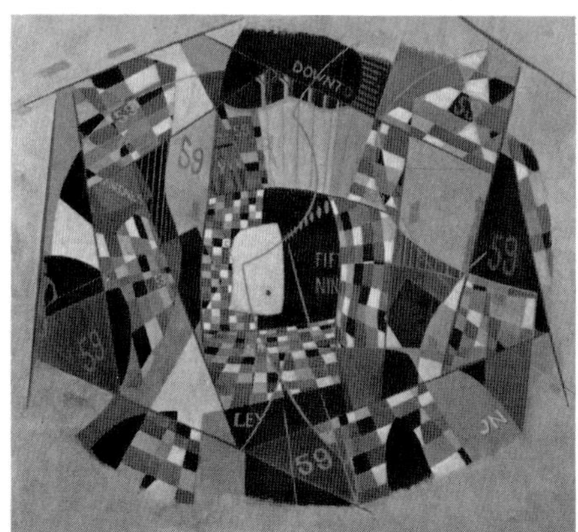

900

Gladys Amy Mock (ca. 1891–1976)

891 *The Spring*, ca. 1924
Oil on canvas
17¼ x 13¹⁵⁄₁₆ in. (43.8 x 35.4 cm.)
Signed at lower right: G.A. Mock
John Lambert Fund, 1925.6

Ross E. Moffett (1888–1971)

892 *A Provincetown Street*, 1916
Oil on canvas
36¼ x 46¼ in. (92.1 x 117.5 cm.)
Signed and dated at lower right: ROSS. E. MOFFETT: 16
John Lambert Fund, 1917.6

Maurice Molarsky (1885–1950)

893 *The Connoisseur* (Eugene Costello), by 1923
Oil on canvas
54¼ x 52¼ in. (137.8 x 132.7 cm.)
Gift of Mrs. Maurice Molarsky, 1958.23

894 *My Father*, 1907
Oil on canvas, mounted on wood
39⁷⁄₁₆ x 28¹³⁄₁₆ in. (100.2 x 73.2 cm.)
Signed and dated at upper left: M. Molarsky/ —/1907
Collections Fund, 1951.24

Hans Moller (1905–)

895 *Decoy*, 1951
Oil on canvas
29¹⁵⁄₁₆ x 39⅞ in. (76 x 101.3 cm.)
Signed and dated at lower right: Moller-51
Annotated on stretcher: "DECOY" HANS MOLLER 1951
John Lambert Fund, 1952.9

Gertrude Monaghan (1887–1962)

896 *Architecture*, 1912
Oil on canvas
Approx. 80 x 167 in. (203 x 424 cm.)
Dated and signed at lower right: 1912/ GMONAGHAN
Commissioned by the Pennsylvania Academy, 1912.16.4

John Moore (1941–)

897 *Summer*, 1972
Oil on canvas
89¾ x 75⅛ in. (228 x 190.8 cm.)
Inscribed, signed, and dated on stretcher: OIL ON CANVAS SUMMER 75x85 [*sic*] JOHN MOORE 1972
Gift of the American Academy of Arts and Letters (The Childe Hassam Fund), 1973.4

Thomas Moran (1837–1926)

898 *Venice*, 1887
Oil on canvas
20⁵⁄₁₆ x 30¹⁄₁₆ in. (51.6 x 76.4 cm.)
Signed and dated at lower left: TMORAN.[initials in monogram]/1887.
Gift of Mrs. Edward H. Coates (The Edward H. Coates Memorial Collection), 1923.9.3

Clarence Morgan (1950–)

899 *The Moon Also Rises*, 1975
Acrylic on canvas
52⅛ x 42 in. (132.4 x 106.7 cm.)
Gift of the artist in memory of Ethel Ashton, 1986.8

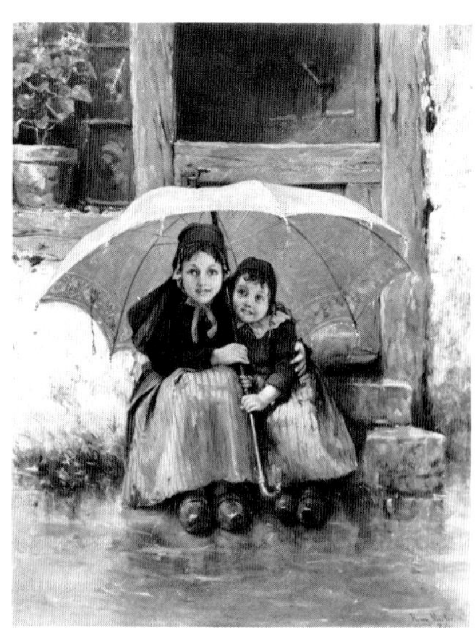

902

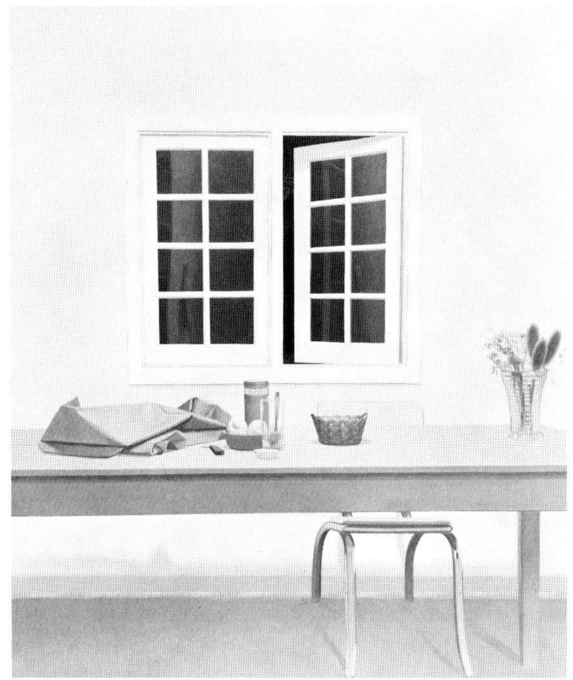

897

903

George L. K. Morris (1905–1975)

900 *IRT*, 1939–53
Oil on canvas
66¼ x 75¼ in. (168.3 x 191.1 cm.)
Signed at lower right: Morris; signed, dated, and inscribed on back: George L. K. Morris/ 1939–53/IRT
Joseph E. Temple Fund, 1954.13

Attributed to **Samuel F. B. Morse** (1791–1872)

901 *Unidentified Woman* (formerly *Dolley Madison*)
Oil on canvas
30³⁄₁₆ x 25¼ in. (76.7 x 64.1 cm.)
Gift of Mrs. John Frederick Lewis (The John Frederick Lewis Memorial Collection), 1933.10.47

Henry Mosler (1841–1920)

902 *The Rainy Day*, ca. 1880
Oil on canvas
36½ x 29⅛ in. (92.7 x 74 cm.)
Signed and inscribed at lower right: Henry Mosler./Paris.
Gift of Joseph E. Temple, 1884.1.1

Robert Motherwell (1915–)

903 *Black in Hiding*, 1976
Acrylic, paper, and canvas on canvas
72 x 24 in. (182.9 x 61 cm.)
Signed and dated at upper left: Motherwell/ 9 March 76
Annotated on cardboard backing: "Black in Hiding"/1976
Funds provided by the National Endowment for the Arts and Sponsors of the Fine Arts Ball and Discotheque, 1978.3

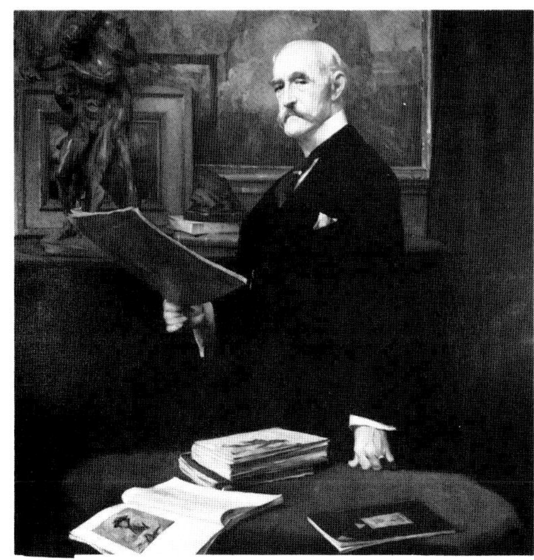

893

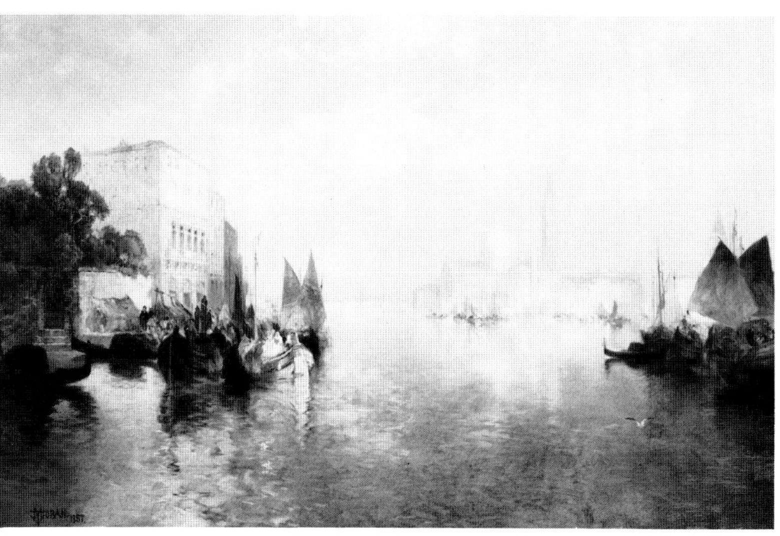

898

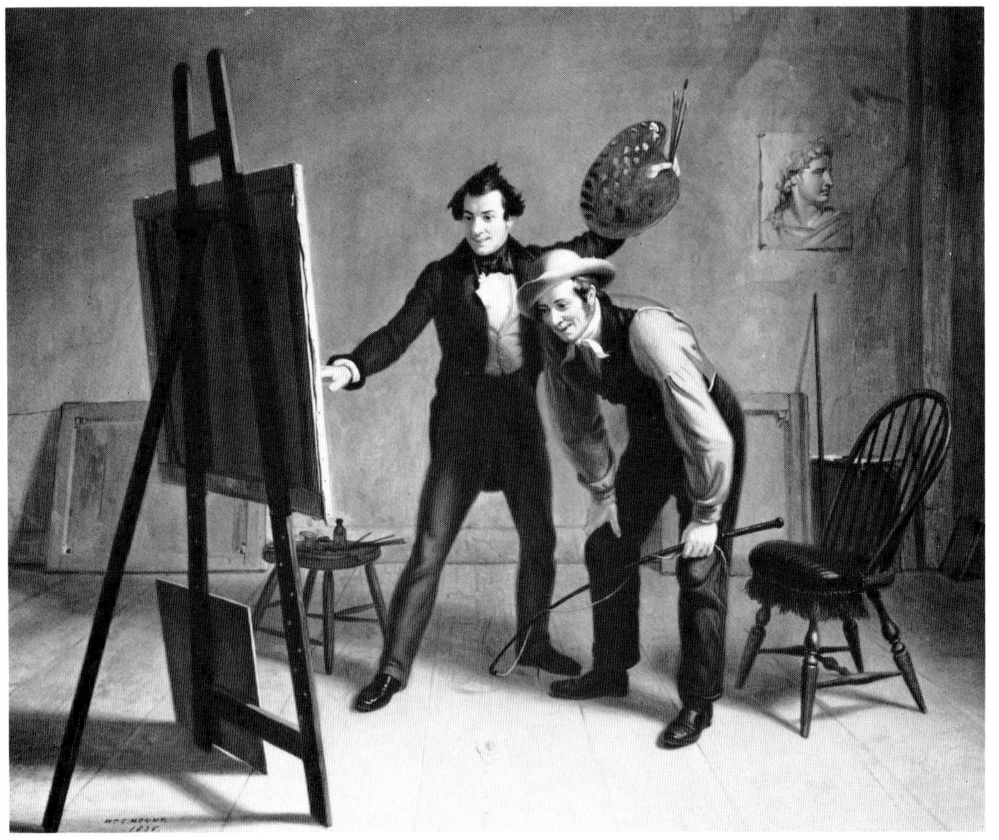

905

William Sidney Mount (1807–1868)

904 *Landscape with Figures*, 1851
Oil on canvas
19⅛ x 28¼ in. (48.6 x 71.8 cm.)
Signed and dated at lower right: WM. S. MOUNT/ NOV. 26th 1851
Source unknown, 1944.23

905 *The Painter's Triumph*, 1838
Oil on wood
23⁹⁄₁₆ x 19½ in. (59.8 x 49.5 cm.)
Signed and dated at lower left: Wm. S. MOUNT./ 1838.
Bequest of Henry C. Carey (The Carey Collection), 1879.8.18

906 *Self-Portrait*, 1854
Oil on canvas
24⅛ x 20⅛ in. (61.3 x 51.1 cm.)
Inscribed and dated on back (before lining): Portrait of Wm. S. Mount No. A/Painted by Himself-/Sept. 1854
Gift of John Frederick Lewis, 1920.10.3

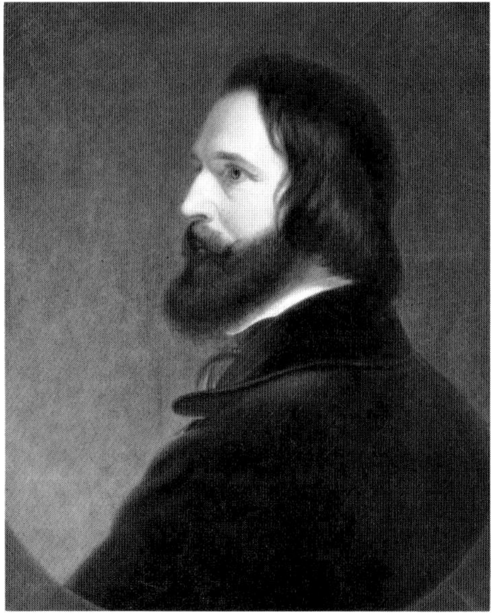

906

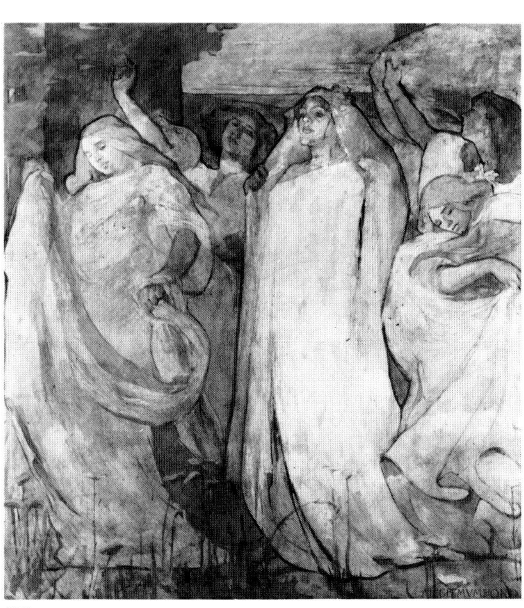

907

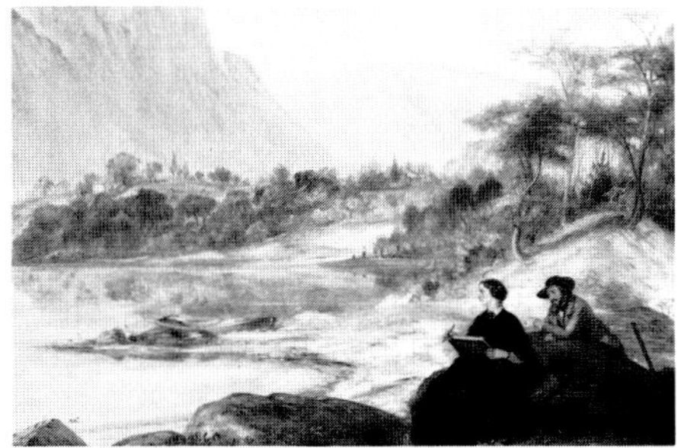

904

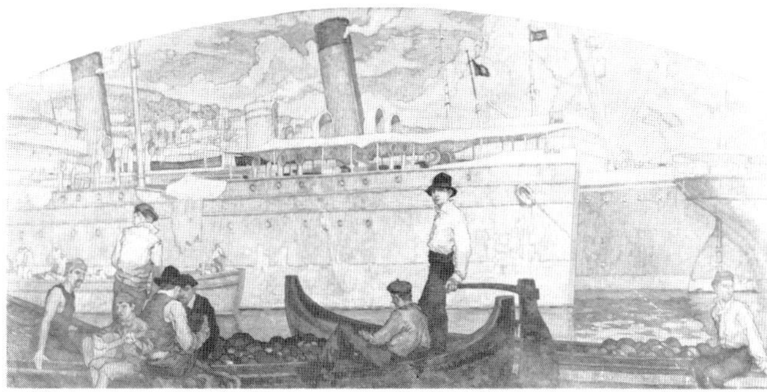

909

Alice Turner Mumford (Mrs. Stewart Colin, 1875–1950)

907 *Adagio* (formerly *Procession*), 1896–97
Oil on canvas
Approx. 78 x 73 in. (198 x 185 cm.)
Signed at lower right: ALICE MUMFORD
Commissioned by the Pennsylvania Academy, 1897.9.5

Walter Tandy Murch (1907–1967)

908 *Self-Portrait*, 1940
Oil on composition board
14¼ x 12½ in. (36.2 x 31.8 cm.)
Signed at lower right: Murch; signed and inscribed on back: Walter Tandy Murch/456 Riverside Dr./N.Y.C.
John Lambert Fund, 1946.8

Rowley W. Murphy (1891–1975)

909 *Commerce*, ca. 1912
Oil on canvas
Approx. 80 x 167 in. (203 x 424 cm.)
Commissioned by the Pennsylvania Academy, 1912.16.5

Barbara C. Myers (1934–)

910 *Behind the Scenes*, 1974
Acrylic on linen
50 x 52 in. (127 x 132.1 cm.)
Signed and dated at lower center: barbara c. myers '74
Gift of Max H. Cohen in the names of Max H. Herman and Sylvan M. Cohen, 1975.2

Naoto Nakagawa (1944–)

911 *Untitled (Butter Wouldn't Melt in Your Mouth)*, 1970
Acrylic on canvas
90 x 144 in. (288.6 x 365.8 cm.)
Inscribed, signed, and dated on back: "UNTITLED"/NAKAGAWA/1970
Gift of Dr. Milton Brutten, 1984.41

Robert Natkin (1930–)

912 *Redding View*, 1972
Acrylic on canvas
41 x 36 in. (104.1 x 91.4 cm.)
Gift of Mr. and Mrs. Jack Bershad, 1986.53

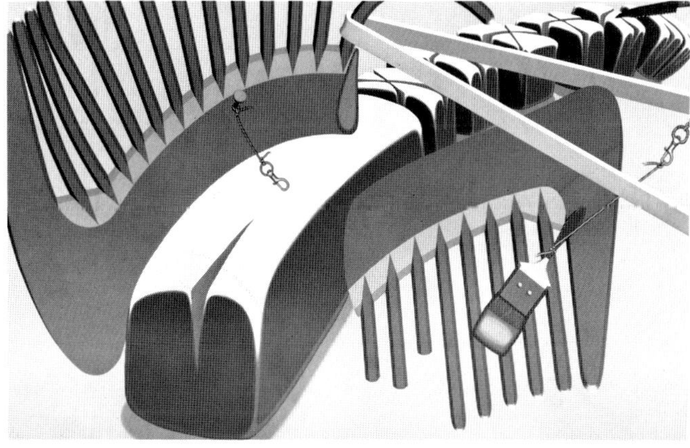

911

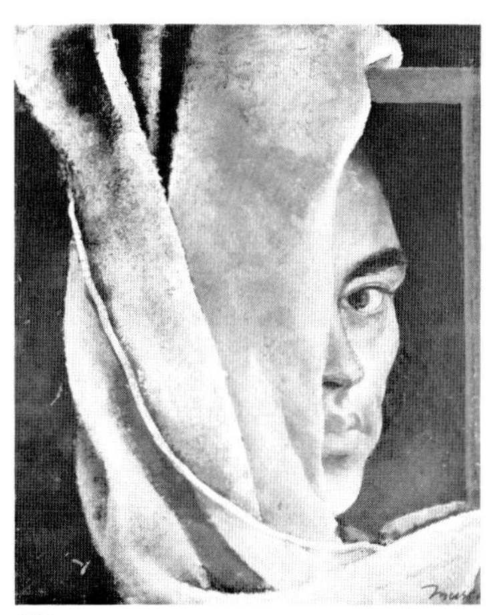

908

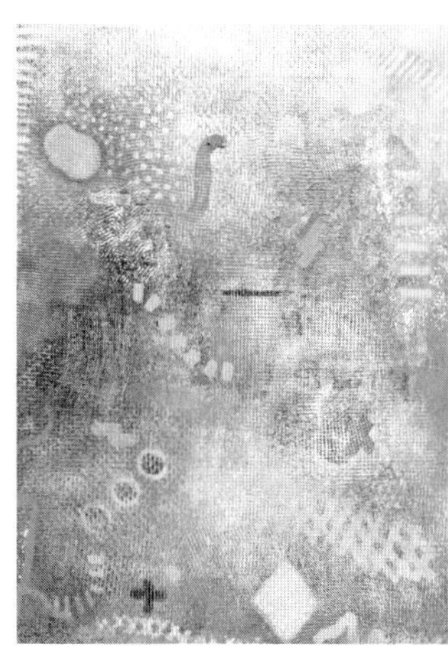

912

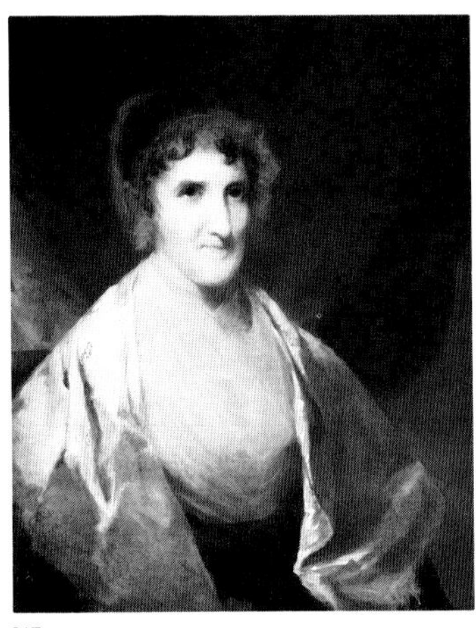

917

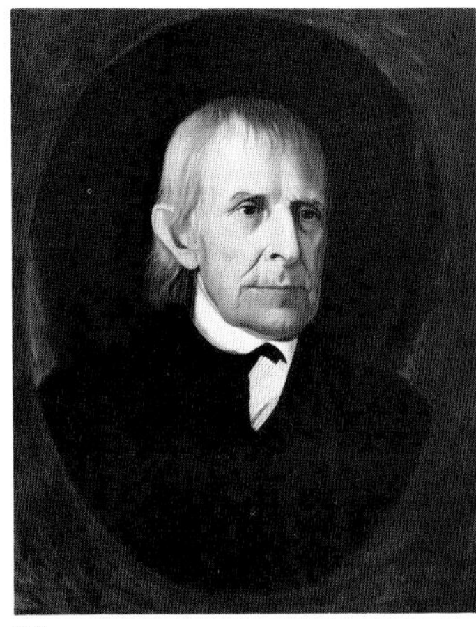

918

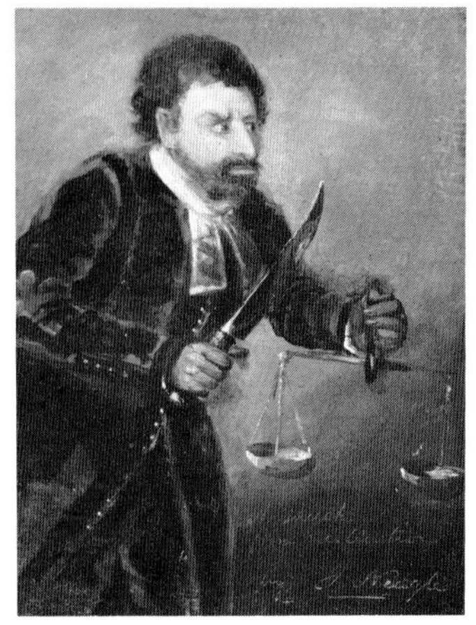

921

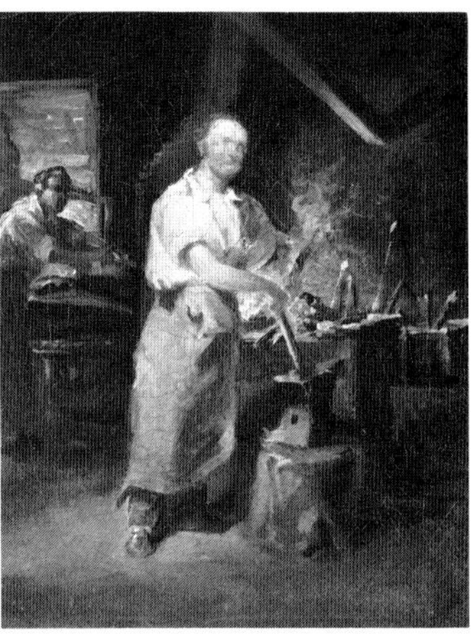

929

John Neagle (1796–1865)

913 *Matilda Washington Dawson*, 1829
Oil on canvas
56⅜ x 40⅞ in. (143.2 x 103.8 cm.)
Signed and dated at lower center: J.Neagle/1829.
Bequest of General Joseph Ripley Chandler Ward, 1931.14

914 *General Henry Dearborn* (1751–1829) (after Gilbert Stuart, 1811–12)
Oil on canvas
20⅞ x 17 in. (53 x 43.2 cm.)
Gift of Mrs. John Frederick Lewis (The John Frederick Lewis Memorial Collection), 1933.10.48

915 *Levi Dickson*, 1834
Oil on canvas
30 x 24¾ in. (76.2 x 62.9 cm.)
Annotated on back (before lining): Painted by JhnNeagle./Dec 24-1834.
Gift of Mrs. John Frederick Lewis (The John Frederick Lewis Memorial Collection), 1933.10.49

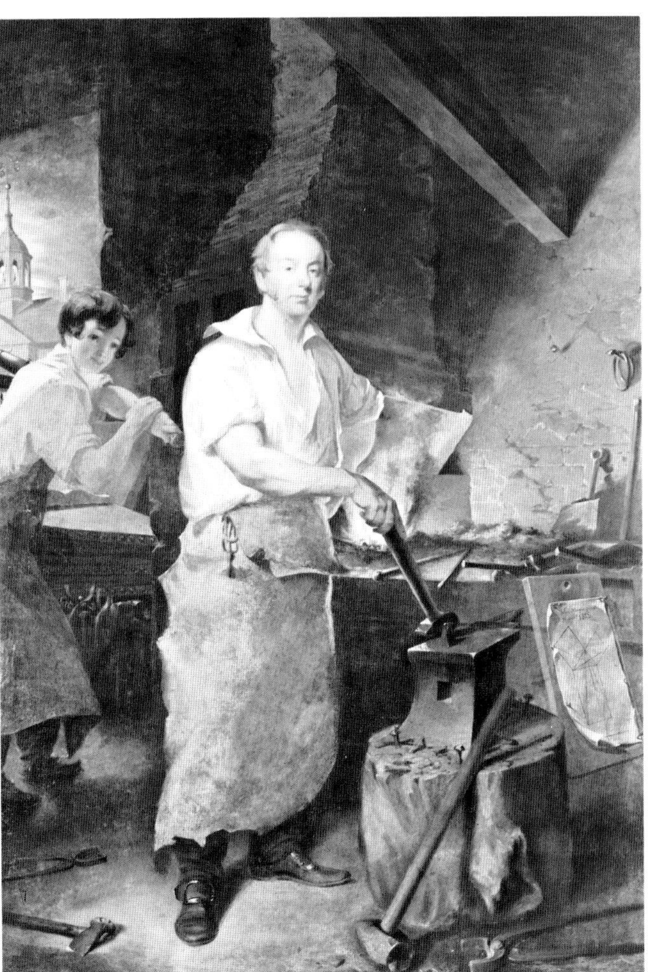

924

916 *Clayton Earl* (d. 1834), 1832
Oil on canvas
30¼ x 25 in. (76.8 x 63.5 cm.)
Signed and dated at lower left: J. Neagle 1832
Bequest of Harrison Earl, 1894.6.5

917 *Mrs. Clayton Earl* (née Cornelia Harrison, d. 1838), probably 1832
Oil on canvas
30$\frac{1}{16}$ x 24⅞ in. (76.4 x 63.2 cm.)
Bequest of Harrison Earl, 1894.6.6

918 *Adam Eckfeldt* (1769–1852), ca. 1845
Oil on canvas
24$\frac{3}{16}$ x 19$\frac{15}{16}$ in. (61.4 x 50.6 cm.)
Gift of Mrs. John Frederick Lewis (The John Frederick Lewis Memorial Collection), 1933.10.50

919 *Thomas Hilson as Tyke* (1784–1834), 1826
Oil on canvas
27$\frac{1}{16}$ x 22$\frac{1}{16}$ in. (68.7 x 56 cm.)
Gift of John Frederick Lewis, 1923.8.3

920 *Anna Gibbon Johnson* (later Mrs. Ferdinand Wakeman Hubbell, 1809–1895), 1828
Oil on canvas
45⅝ x 33¾ in. (115.9 x 85.7 cm.)
Signed and dated at left center: J.Neagle./1828.
Bequest of Helena Hubbell, 1929.7

921 *Edmund Kean as Shylock* (1787–1833), by 1821
Oil on wood
9$\frac{7}{16}$ x 7¼ in. (24 x 18.4 cm.)
Inscribed and signed at lower right: A sketch/from recollection/by J. Neagle; annotated on back: Edmund Kean as Shylock./Shy: A sentence! come/prepare. Act 4th/A rapid sketch from recollection/by John Neagle in early life./Presented by the Artist to/his old Schoolmate & Friend/Charles Durang Esq:/January 1st 1855.
Gift of the Misses Fredonia and Naomi Durang, 1922.3

922 *Harriet Hendrickson Locke*, 1851
Oil on canvas
20$\frac{3}{16}$ x 17 in. (51.3 x 43.2 cm.)
Annotated on back (before lining): Original portrait of Harriet Locke/painted by John Neagle, June 6th 1851/Philade
Bequest of Annie Putnam O'Brien, 1957.14

923 *Edward Lownes* (1793–1834), 1834
Oil on canvas
30⅛ x 25$\frac{3}{16}$ in. (76.5 x 64 cm.)

Annotated on back (before lining): Edward Lownes Aged 40 Years/by John Neagle/June 1834/Philad-a/Died 9-18-1834/at 41 Years 8 months 4 days
Gift of Mrs. George T. Macpherson, Jr., 1952.2

924 *Pat Lyon at the Forge* (1779–1829), 1829
Oil on canvas
$94\frac{1}{2} \times 68\frac{1}{2}$ in. (240 x 174 cm.)
Signed, inscribed, and dated at right center: John Neagle pinxt/Philada 1829.
Gift of the Lyon family, 1842.1
See also cat. no. 929.

925 *William Charles Macready as Macbeth*, 1827
Oil on canvas
$29\frac{7}{8} \times 24\frac{15}{16}$ in. (75.9 x 63.3 cm.)
Gift of John Frederick Lewis, 1932.13.3

926 *Judge Archibald Randall* (1797–1846), 1830
Oil on canvas
$29\frac{15}{16} \times 24\frac{15}{16}$ in. (76 x 63.3 cm.)
Signed and dated at lower left: J. N. 1830
Gift of Susan W. Randall, 1922.5.1

927 *William Crook Rudman* (1829–1861), 1845
Oil on canvas
$30\frac{3}{16} \times 25\frac{1}{4}$ in. (76.7 x 64.1 cm.)
Inscribed, signed, and dated on back: Wm C. Rudman./by Jno Neagle/1845
Gift of John Frederick Lewis, 1923.8.4

928 *The Studious Artist* (Thomas Birch, 1779–1851), 1836
Oil on canvas
$30\frac{1}{8} \times 25\frac{1}{16}$ in. (76.5 x 63.7 cm.)
Signed at lower right: J. Neagle 18[36]; annotated on back (before lining): Portrait of Thomas Birch, painted by John Neagle in 1836
Gift of John Frederick Lewis, 1922.1.3

929 *Study for "Pat Lyon at the Forge,"* ca. 1826
Oil on canvas
$9\frac{1}{2} \times 7\frac{13}{16}$ in. (24.1 x 19.8 cm.)
Inscribed on back (before lining): The Original study/in colors by Neagle/for the large picture/ of Pat: Lyon the/Blacksmith./A rapid sketch for arrangement & general effect./Philada Penna; annotated on back: The above is my/fathers/ handwriting./Jan.28/97. Garrett C. Neagle.
Gift of John Lambert, Jr., 1897.2.1
See also cat. no. 924.

930 *John William Wallace* (1815–1884)
Oil on canvas
30 x 25 in. (76.2 x 63.5 cm.), oval
Gift of Mrs. John Frederick Lewis (The John Frederick Lewis Memorial Collection), 1933.10.53

931 *John Galloway Whilldin* (1791–1824)
Oil on canvas
$29\frac{15}{16} \times 25\frac{1}{16}$ in. (76 x 63.7 cm.)
Gift of A. Adèle Leach, 1945.15.1

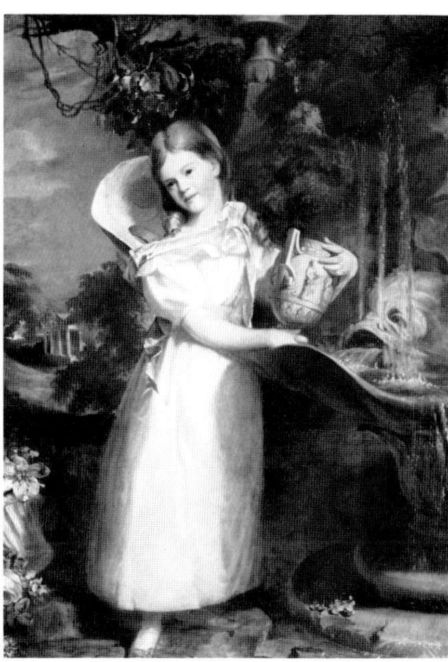
913

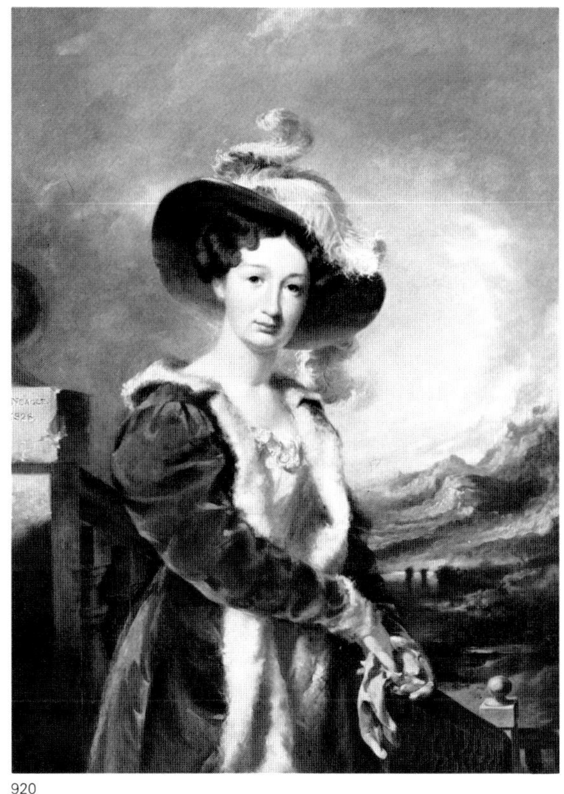

920

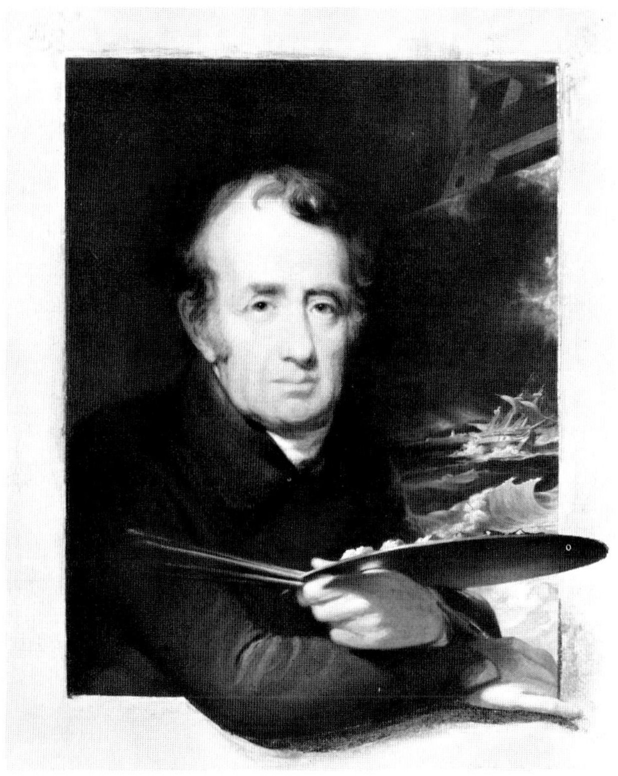
928

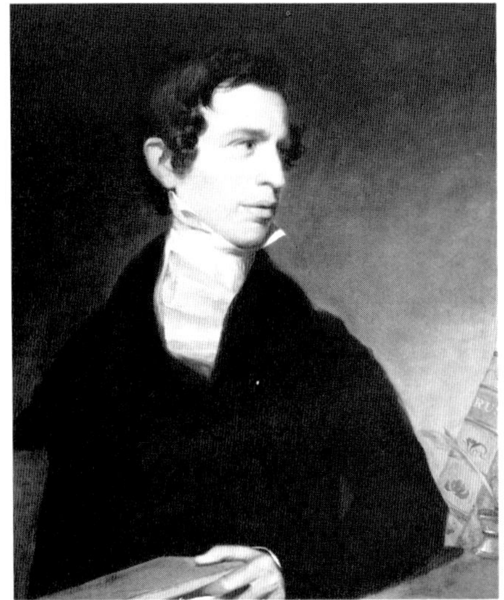
932

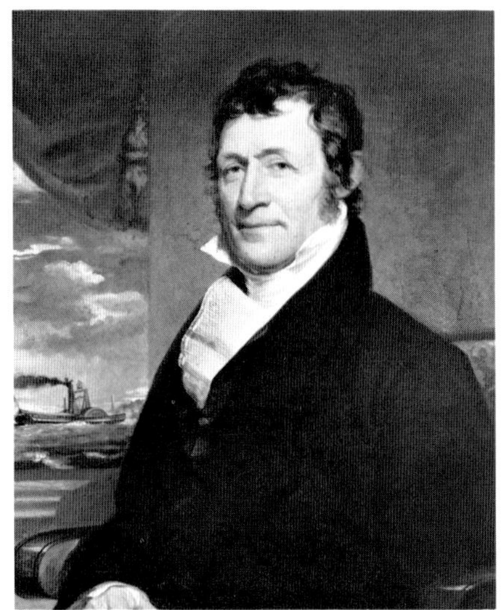
933

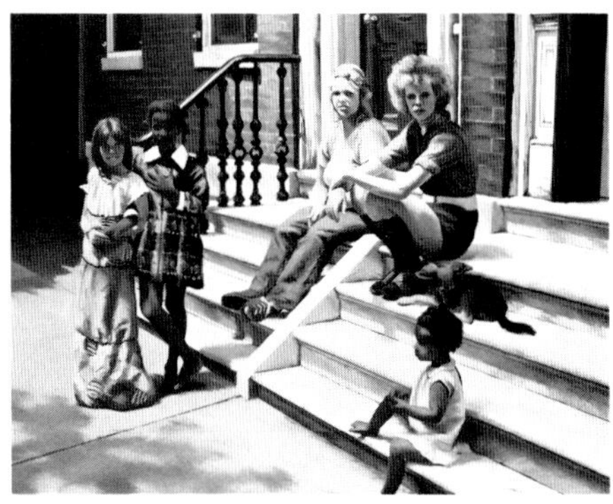
937

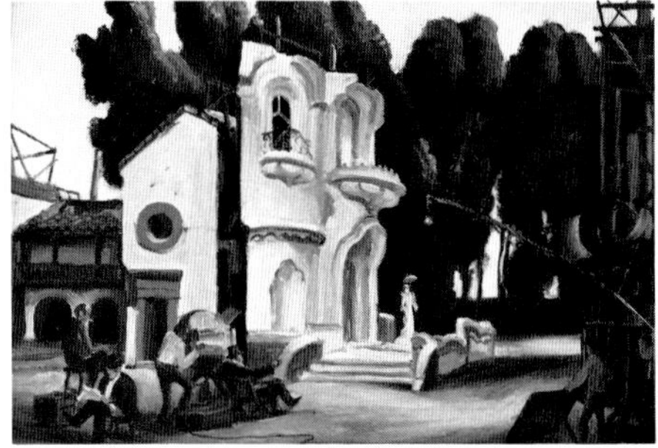
939

932 *John Galloway Whilldin with Book*
Oil on canvas
30 x 25$\frac{1}{16}$ in. (76.2 x 63.7 cm.)
Gift of A. Adèle Leach, 1945.15.2

933 *Captain Wilmon Whilldin* (1773–1852), ca. 1823
Oil on canvas
29$\frac{7}{8}$ x 24$\frac{7}{8}$ in. (75.9 x 63.2 cm.)
Gift of A. Adèle Leach, 1945.15.4

934 *Mrs. Wilmon Whilldin* (née Mary Galloway, 1776–1815), ca. 1800
Oil on canvas
30 x 25$\frac{3}{16}$ in. (76.2 x 64 cm.)
Gift of A. Adèle Leach, 1945.15.3

See also miniature, cat. no. 1643.

Attributed to **John Neagle**

935 *Captain Selah Strong* (?) (1737–1815), possibly 1817
Oil on canvas
29$\frac{15}{16}$ x 24$\frac{15}{16}$ in. (76 x 63.3 cm.)
Annotated on back: Jno. Neagle 1817
Gift of Mrs. John Frederick Lewis (The John Frederick Lewis Memorial Collection), 1933.10.51

936 *Unidentified Man*
Oil on wood
26$\frac{13}{16}$ x 22$\frac{1}{4}$ in. (68.1 x 56.5 cm.)
Gift of Mrs. John Frederick Lewis (The John Frederick Lewis Memorial Collection), 1933.10.52

Edith Neff (1943–)

937 *Girls on the Stoop*, 1971–72
Oil on canvas
53$\frac{11}{16}$ x 66 in. (136.4 x 167.6 cm.)
Signed on back: Neff
Gift of the friends of Earth Art '73, 1973.8

William Nell

938 *Green Landscape*, ca. 1919
Oil on canvas
29$\frac{7}{8}$ x 24 in. (75.9 x 61 cm.)
John Lambert Fund, 1920.8

Warren Newcombe (b. 1894)

939 *Garbo on "Anna Karenina" Set*, 1935
Oil on canvas
21 x 30$\frac{1}{8}$ in. (53.3 x 76.5 cm.)
Signed and dated at lower left: NEWCOMBE 1935
Annotated on stretcher: Garbo-Kerenina [*sic*] set/M. G. M. Warren Newcombe March 1935
John Lambert Fund, 1937.5

Vernon Kiehl Newswanger (1900–1980)

940 *Still Life with Carrots*, 1935–36
Oil on canvas
26$\frac{1}{16}$ x 31$\frac{3}{16}$ in. (66.2 x 79.2 cm.)
Inscribed, signed, and dated on back: Still Life/ with Carrots/by/Vernon Newswanger/ 1935–36
John Lambert Fund, 1936.14

Burr H. Nicholls (1848–1915)

941 *Sunlight Effect*, 1881–82
Oil on canvas
51$\frac{13}{16}$ x 41$\frac{13}{16}$ in. (131.6 x 106.2 cm.)
Signed and dated at lower left: Burr H. Nicholls/ 1881–2
Gift of Joseph E. Temple, 1883.2

Chris Nissen (1949–)

942 *Delaware Avenue*, 1980
Oil on canvas

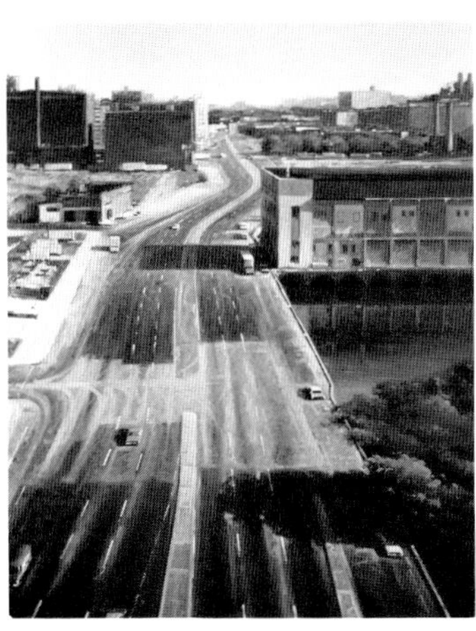
942

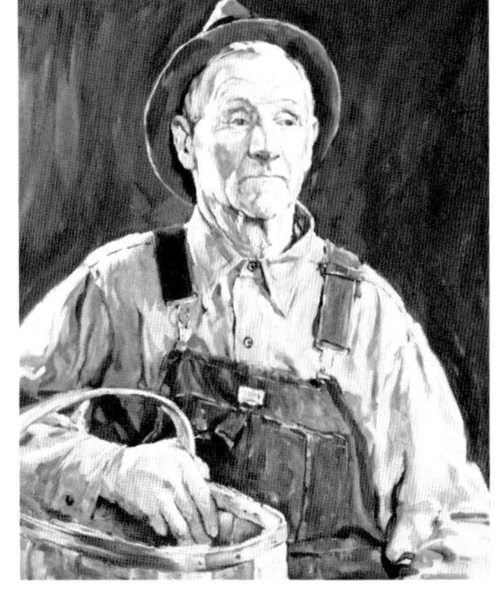
943

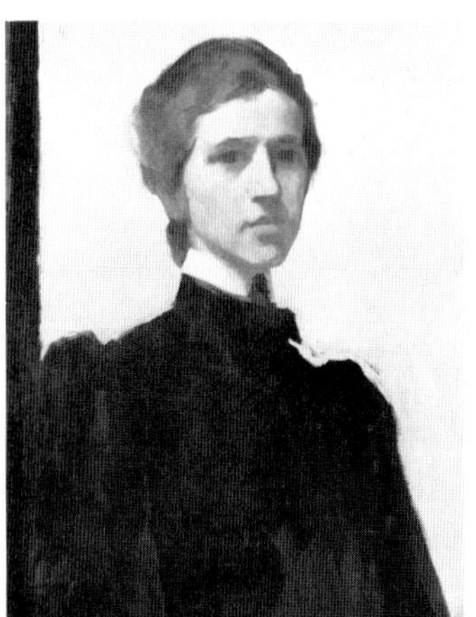
948

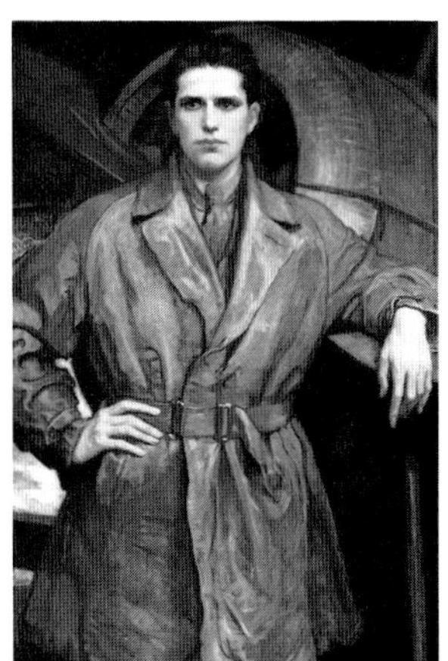
950

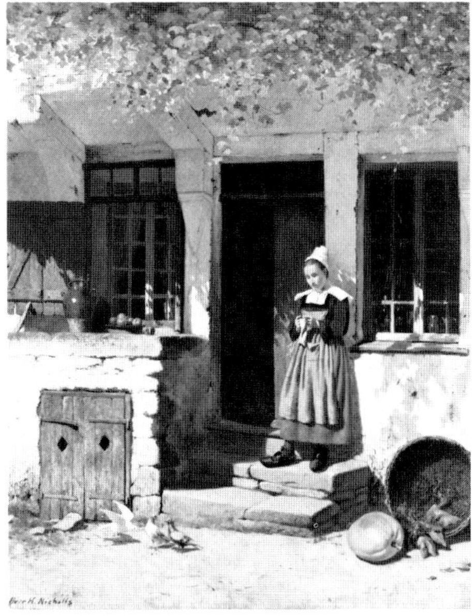

941

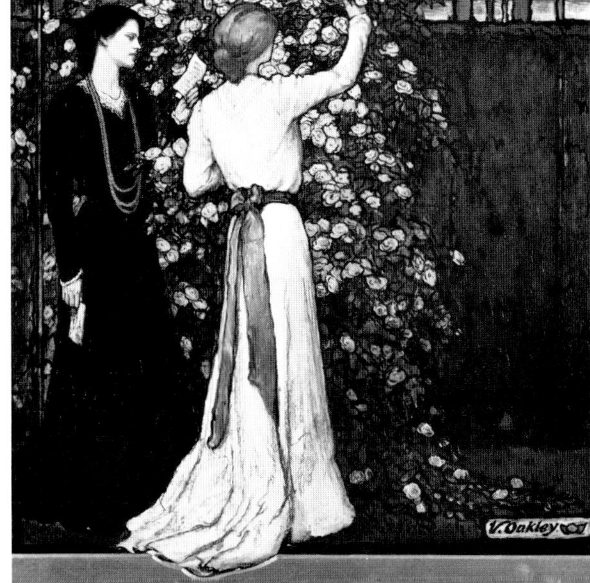

946

$66\frac{1}{8}$ x $54\frac{1}{4}$ in. (168 x 137.8 cm.)
Signed, dated, and inscribed on back: Chris Nissen/9/80 "Delaware Avenue"
Pennsylvania Academy Purchase Prize from the 1981 Annual Fellowship Exhibition, 1981.20

Roy Cleveland Nuse (1885–1975)

943 *Neighbor Blevins* (Milliard Filmore Blevins, 1870–1951), 1938
Oil on canvas
30 x $25\frac{1}{16}$ in. (76.2 x 63.7 cm.)
Signed and dated at lower left: RN. [monogram]/ '38.
Henry D. Gilpin Fund, 1939.10

944 *Robert Byers* (1877–1961), 1950
Oil on canvas
$24\frac{1}{16}$ x 22 in. (61.1 x 55.9 cm.)
Signed and dated at lower left: RN. [monogram]/ '50.
Gift of the artist, 1950.25

945 *Loughlin Morgan* (1872–1947), 1942
Oil on canvas
24 x 22 in. (61 x 55.9 cm.)
Signed and dated at lower left: RN. [monogram]/ '42.
Gift of the artist, 1942.18

Violet Oakley (1874–1961)

946 *June* (cover illustration for *Everybody's Magazine* 6, June 1902)
Oil, charcoal, and graphite on composition board
$16\frac{3}{16}$ x $17\frac{1}{16}$ in. (41.1 x 43.3 cm.)
Signed at lower right: V.Oakley.
Henry D. Gilpin Fund, 1903.4

947 *Mary Townsend Mason* (1886–1964), ca. 1920
Oil on canvas
30 x 25 in. (76.2 x 63.5 cm.)
Signed twice, at upper and lower left: Violet Oakley-; inscribed and signed on back: Portrait of/Mary Townsend Mason/by/Violet Oakley/Cogslea/St. George's Road/ Philadelphia
Gift of Edith Emerson, 1974.25

948 *Self-Portrait: The Artist in Mourning for Her Father*, ca. 1900
Oil on canvas
25 x $20\frac{1}{16}$ in. (63.5 x 51 cm.)
Gift of the Violet Oakley Memorial Foundation, 1983.10.1

949 *Tragic Muse* (Mrs. Edward H. Coates, 1850–1929), 1912
Oil on canvas
$29\frac{15}{16}$ x $24\frac{15}{16}$ in. (76 x 63.3 cm.)
Signed and dated at upper right: V. Oakley-/1912
Gift of Mrs. Edward H. Coates (The Edward H. Coates Memorial Collection), 1923.9.4

950 *Henry Howard Houston Woodward* (1896–1918), 1921
Oil on canvas
53 x 35 in. (134.6 x 88.9 cm.)
Signed and dated at lower right: Violet Oakley./ 1921; inscribed on back: henry howard houston Woodward/February 27th 1896— April 1st-1918/Lafayette Flying Corps- Pilote, Spad 94
Gift of Dr. and Mrs. George Woodward, 1924.10

Georgia O'Keeffe (1887–1986)

951 *Coxcomb*, 1931
Oil on canvas
20 x 17 in. (50.8 x 43.2 cm.)
Partial gift and bequest of Mrs. Bernice McIlhenny Wintersteen, 1977.24.2

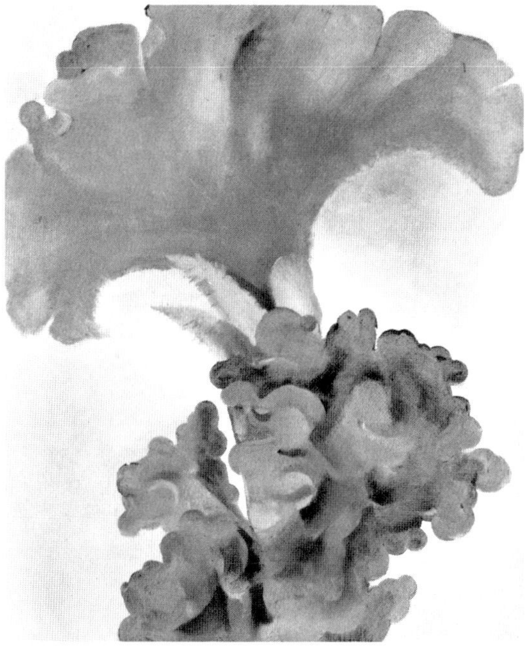

951

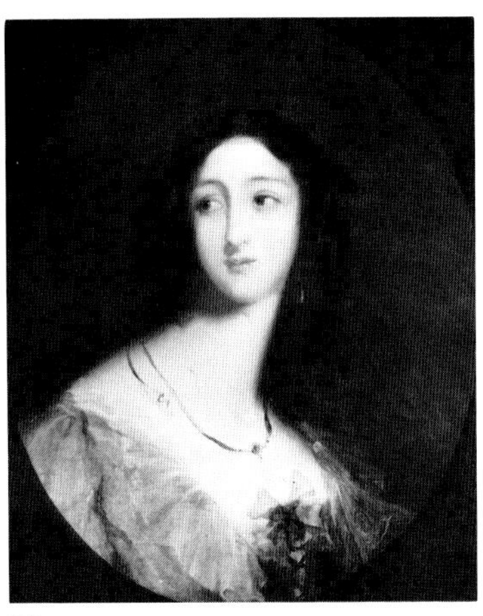
955

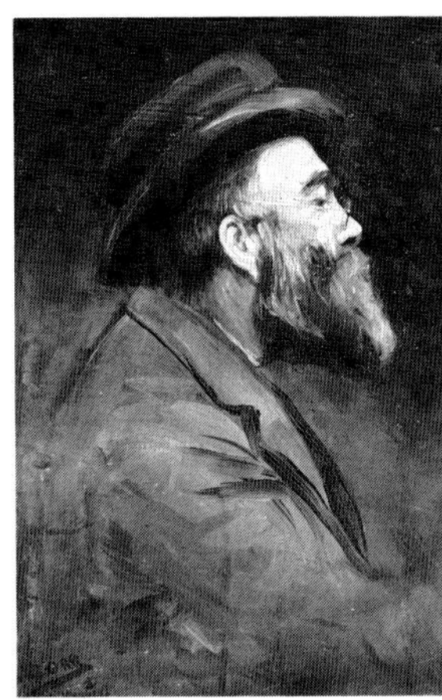
956

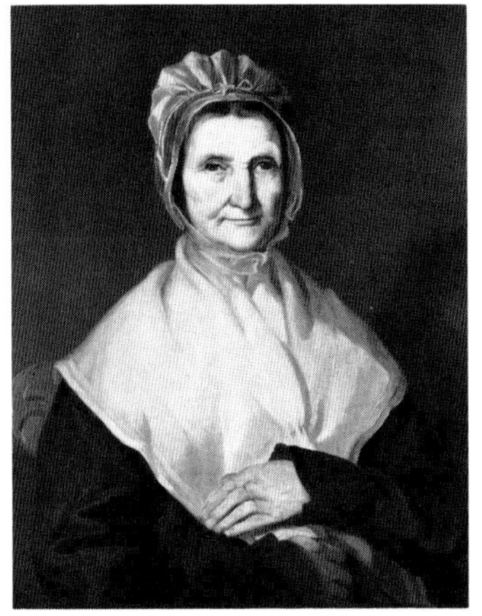
960

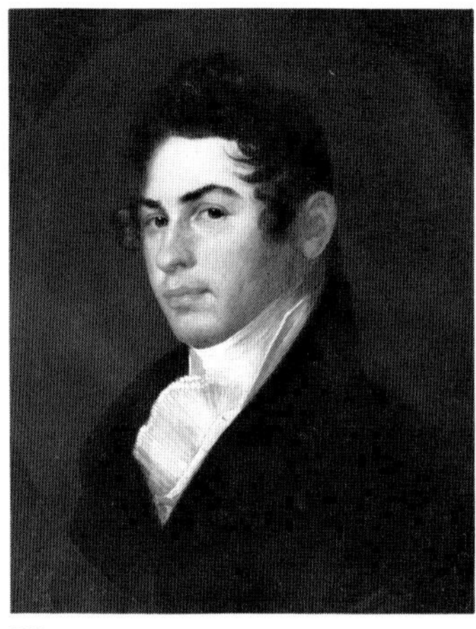
965

Jules Olitski (1922–)

952 *Purple Mekle Lippis of Beauty Mouth–2,* 1972
Acrylic on canvas
80 x 59 in. (203.2 x 149.9 cm.)
Inscribed, signed, and dated on back: Purple Mekle Lippis of/Beauty Mouth - 2/Jules Olitski/1972/Acrylic W. B.
Gift of Mr. and Mrs. J. Welles Henderson, 1984.42

Helen Omansky. *See* Helen Omansky Gross.

Leon Omwake, Jr. (1946–)

953 *Stancil Viqiv,* 1971
Acrylic with glitter on canvas
54¾ x 60⅞ in. (139.1 x 154.6 cm.)
Signed, dated, and inscribed on back: Omwake–'71/"Dec Viqive" [crossed out]/"Stancil Viqiv"
Director's Fund, 1972.2

John Opie (English, 1761–1807)

954 *Gil Blas Securing the Cook in the Robber's Cave,* ca. 1804
Oil on canvas
90¼ x 54 in. (229.2 x 137.2 cm.)
Gift of Paul Beck, Jr., 1842.2.2
See also copy by Sully, cat. no. 1328.

Joseph Biays Ord (1805–1865)

955 *Unidentified Woman,* 1834
Oil on canvas
30¼ x 25³⁄₁₆ in. (76.8 x 64 cm.)
Signed and dated at lower right: J. B. Ord/1834.
Henry D. Gilpin Fund, 1943.14

G. F. Orr

956 *Charles Lewis Fussell* (1840–1909), 1890
Oil on canvas
7⁷⁄₁₆ x 5¼ in. (18.9 x 13.3 cm.)
Signed and dated at lower left: G. F. ORR/[N]ov. 2/90
Gift of the T. Carrick Jordan Fund through Bertram L. O'Neill, Henry S. McNeil, and Mrs. Edward B. Leisenring, Jr., 1973.12.59

Elizabeth Osborne (1936–)

957 *West End Pond,* 1973
Acrylic on canvas
56¾ x 65 in. (144.1 x 165.1 cm.)
Signed and dated on back: OSBORNE '73
Signed, inscribed, and dated on stretcher: OSBORNE ACRYLIC 1973 "WEST END POND" 58 x 66
Funds provided by the National Endowment for the Arts, Pennsylvania Academy Women's Committee, and an anonymous donor, 1974.2

958 *Woman with Red,* 1962
Oil on canvas
63⅛ x 46 in. (160.3 x 116.8 cm.)
Signed at upper left: OSBORNE
Gift of the Ford Foundation, 1964.1.6

Arthur Osver (1912–)

959 *The Majestic Tenement,* 1946
Oil on canvas
46¼ x 38¾ in. (117.5 x 98.4 cm.)
Signed and dated at lower right: Osver/1946
Joseph E. Temple Fund, 1947.8

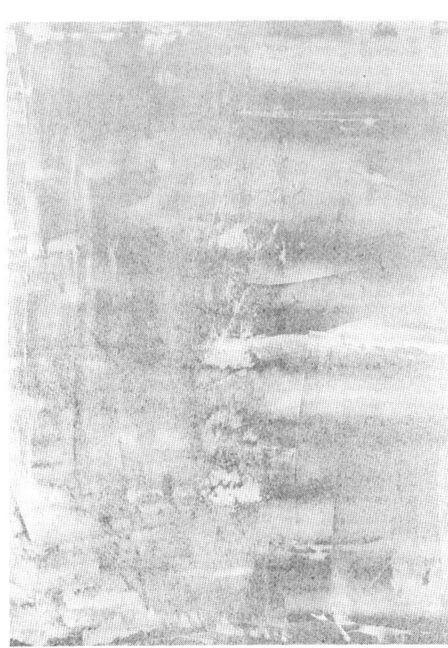

952

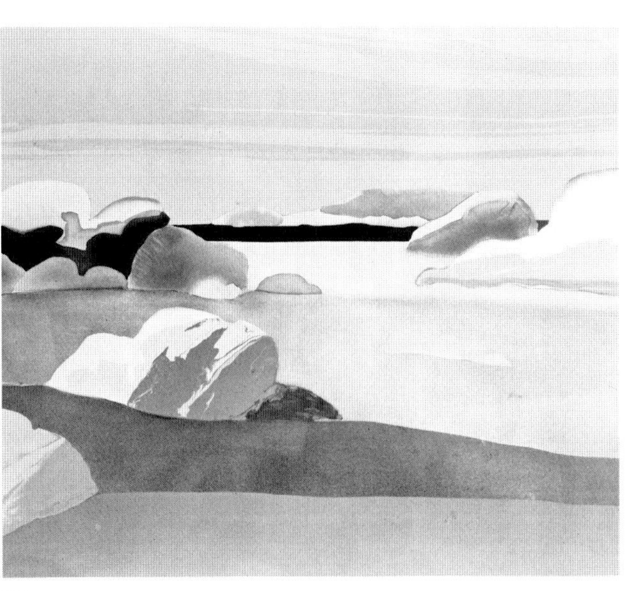
957

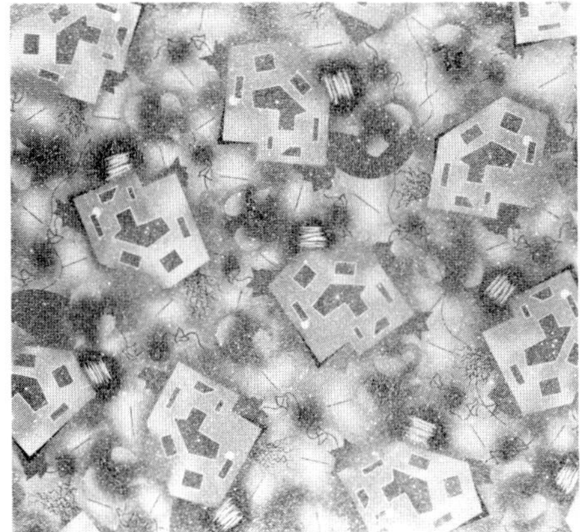

953

Bass Otis (1784–1861)

960 *Mrs. Acuff*
Oil on canvas, mounted on wood
29 15/16 x 24 7/8 in. (76 x 63.2 cm.)
Signed at lower left (by artist?): JBO
Gift of Mrs. John Frederick Lewis (The John Frederick Lewis Memorial Collection), 1933.10.54

961 *Pollard E. Birkhead*, possibly 1855
Oil on canvas
30 1/16 x 25 1/8 in. (76.4 x 63.8 cm.)
Said to be inscribed on back (before lining): B. Otis pinxt/Jan. 1855
Bequest of Ella Kintzing Birkhead, 1901.4.3

962 *Mrs. Elijah Griffiths*, 1823
Oil on canvas
30 3/16 x 25 1/8 in. (76.7 x 63.8 cm.)
Gift of Marguerite A. Keasbey, 1957.21.1

963 *Interior of a Smithy*, by 1815
Oil on canvas
50 5/8 x 80 1/2 in. (128.6 x 204.5 cm.)
Gift of the artist, 1845.2

964 *Alexander Lawson* (1773–1846), by 1824
Oil on canvas
30 x 25 1/16 in. (76.2 x 63.7 cm.)
Bequest of Mrs. Mary Lawson Birkhead, 1898.12

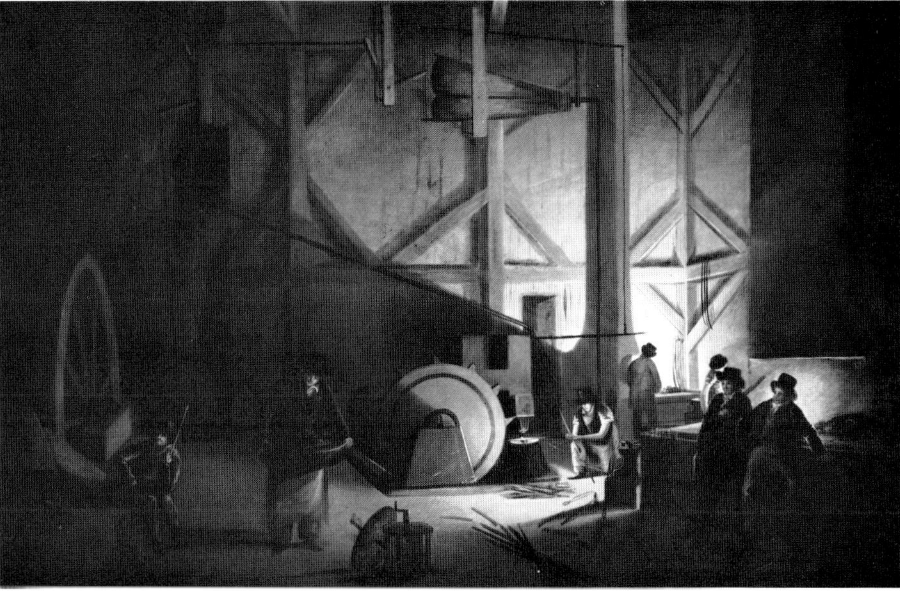

963

965 *John Neagle* (1796–1865), ca. 1815
Oil on wood
22 x 18 in. (55.9 x 45.7 cm.)
Annotated on back: Original portrait/by B. Otis/of/John Neagle/at the age of 19 years
Gift of Garrett C. Neagle, 1944.24

966 *Angelina Snyder Palethorp* (d. 1879)
Oil on canvas
30 1/16 x 25 1/16 in. (76.4 x 63.7 cm.)
Bequest of Henry B. Palethorp, 1913.15.1

967 *John Harrison Palethorp* (ca. 1798–1860)
Oil on canvas
30 1/16 x 25 1/16 in. (76.4 x 63.7 cm.)
Bequest of Henry B. Palethorp, 1913.15.2

968 *Captain Steel, U.S.N.*
Oil on canvas
30 1/2 x 25 in. (77.5 x 63.5 cm.)
Gift of Mrs. John Frederick Lewis (The John Frederick Lewis Memorial Collection), 1933.10.55

Josephine M. Page (b. 1890)

969 *Still Life*, ca. 1919
Oil on canvas, mounted on plywood
26 1/4 x 30 1/4 in. (66.7 x 76.8 cm.)
Signed at lower left: J. Page
John Lambert Fund, 1920.9

William Page (1811–1885)

970 *Mother and Child*, ca. 1835
Oil on canvas
48 3/4 x 36 5/8 in. (123.8 x 93 cm.)
Bequest of Mrs. Sarah Harrison (The Joseph Harrison, Jr. Collection), 1912.14.1

971 *The Young Merchants*, 1842
Oil on canvas
42 1/8 x 36 1/4 in. (107 x 92.1 cm.)
Signed on torn poster at upper left: W.Pa[ge]/18[?]
Bequest of Henry C. Carey (The Carey Collection), 1879.8.19

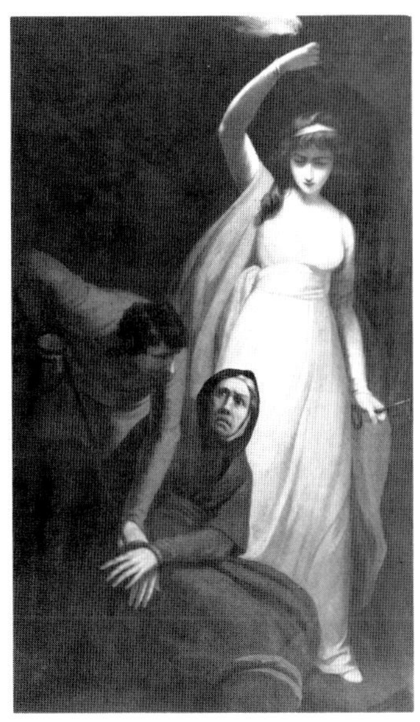

954

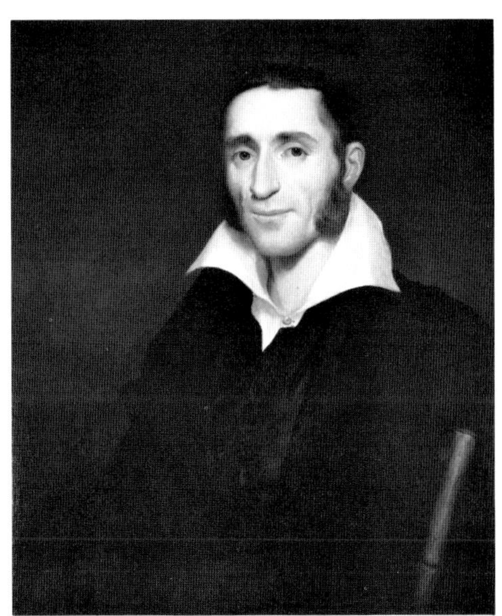

964

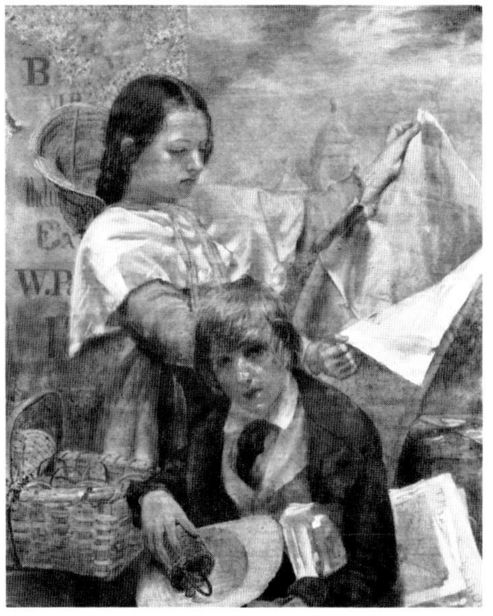

971

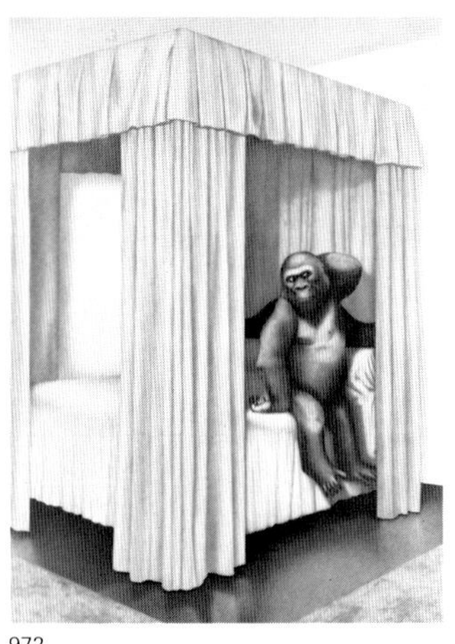

972

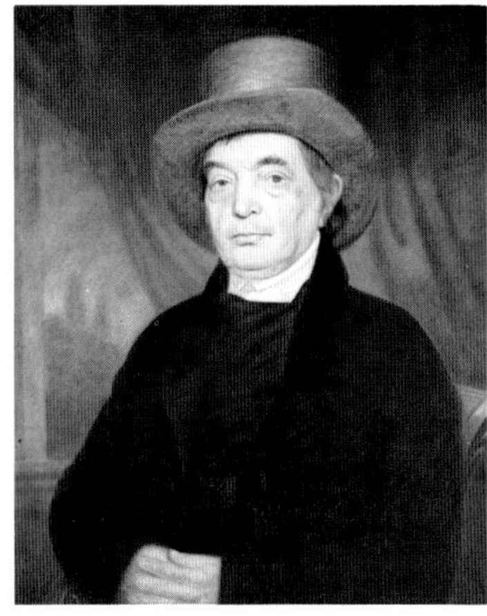

976

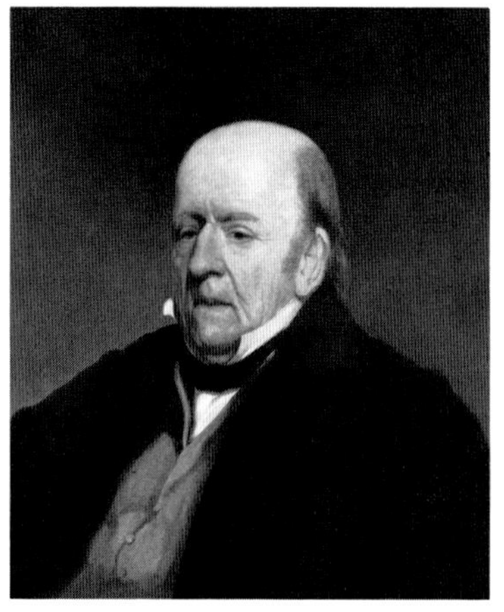

977

Tommy Dale Palmore (1945–)

972 *I Think We're Alone Now*, 1971
Acrylic on canvas
$96\frac{3}{4}$ x $72\frac{1}{2}$ in. (245.7 x 184.2 cm.)
Gift of Gaye Cooper, 1973.22

Henry Boller Pancoast, Jr. (1876–1962)

973 *November Afternoon*, by 1906
Oil on canvas
$24\frac{1}{4}$ x 30 in. (61.6 x 76.2 cm.)
Signed at lower left: Pancoast
Gift of Bertha Schwacke, 1937.15.3

Morris Hall Pancoast (1877–1963)

974 *The Pennsy Train Shed*, ca. 1917
Oil on canvas
28 x 32 in. (71.1 x 81.3 cm.)
Signed at lower right: Morris Hall Pancoast
John Lambert Fund, 1918.11

Frederick Papsdorf (b. 1887)

975 *Fresh Fruit*, 1944
Oil on canvas
$16\frac{1}{8}$ x $20\frac{1}{16}$ in. (41 x 51 cm.)
Signed and dated at lower right: PAPSDORF/44.
John Lambert Fund, 1946.9

John Paradise (1783–1833)

976 *Philip Arcularius* (ca. 1750–1824/25), ca. 1810
Oil on canvas
$29\frac{7}{8}$ x $23\frac{3}{4}$ in. (75.9 x 60.3 cm.)
Gift of John Frederick Lewis, Jr., 1952.3.1

Attributed to **John Paradise**

977 *Unidentified Man*
Oil on canvas
$24\frac{3}{16}$ x $19\frac{15}{16}$ in. (61.4 x 50.6 cm.)
Gift of John Frederick Lewis, 1923.8.5

M. S. Parker (active 1830–1846)

978 *W. C. Anderson*, 1830
Oil on canvas
$20\frac{1}{16}$ x 17 in. (51 x 43.2 cm.)
Annotated on back (before lining): Portrait of/W. C. Anderson/of Pitts.../ Painted by/M. S. Parker/1830
Source unknown, 1942.28

Maxfield Parrish (1870–1966)

979 *Princess Parizade Bringing Home the Singing Tree*, 1906
Oil on composition board
$20\frac{1}{16}$ x $16\frac{1}{16}$ in. (51 x 40.8 cm.)
Signed at lower left: M. P.; inscribed and dated on back: "The Oaks."/Windsor. Vermont./ February of 1906./Arabian Night's Entertainments./"The Story of the two Sisters who were jealous of/their Younger Sister."/ "Princess Parizade bringing home the singing tree."
Gift of Mrs. Francis P. Garvan, 1977.20

Katharine Patton (1866–1941)

980 *The Maple Woods*, ca. 1917
Oil on canvas
30 x 24 in. (76.2 x 61 cm.)
Signed at lower right: KATHARINE PATTON-
John Lambert Fund, 1918.12

William McGregor Paxton (1896–1941)

981 *Girl Sweeping*, 1912
Oil on canvas
$40\frac{1}{4}$ x $30\frac{3}{8}$ in. (102.2 x 77.2 cm.)
Signed and dated at upper left: PAXTON/1912/©
Joseph E. Temple Fund, 1912.4

Henry W. Peacock (1926–)

982 *The Hex Sign*, 1949
Oil on canvas
34 x 22 in. (86.4 x 55.9 cm.)
Signed and dated at lower right: Henry W. Peacock 1949
John Lambert Fund, 1950.12

Anna Claypoole Peale.
See cat. nos. 1644–45

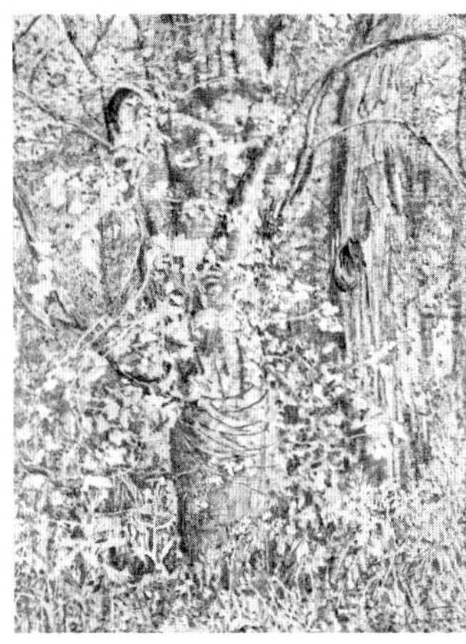

980

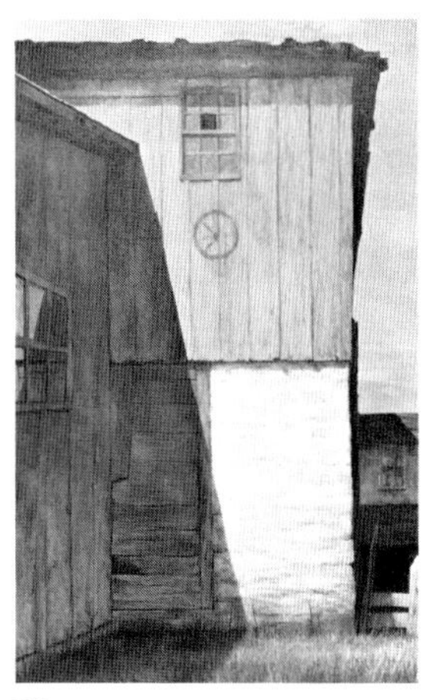

982

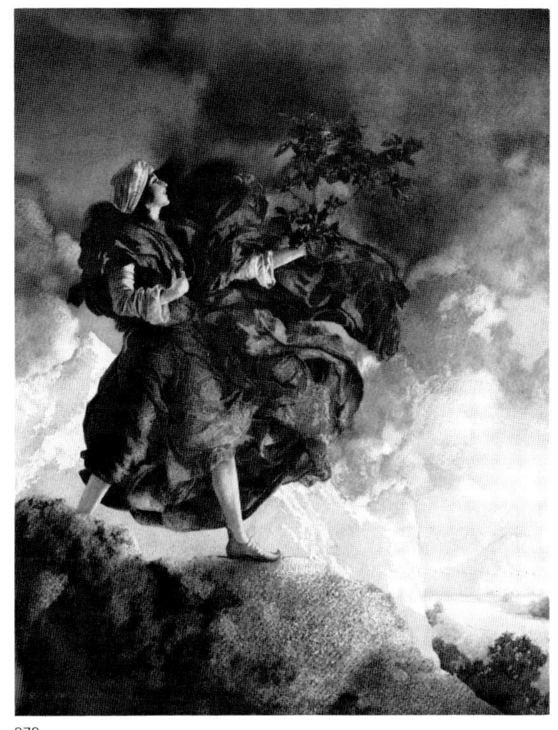
979

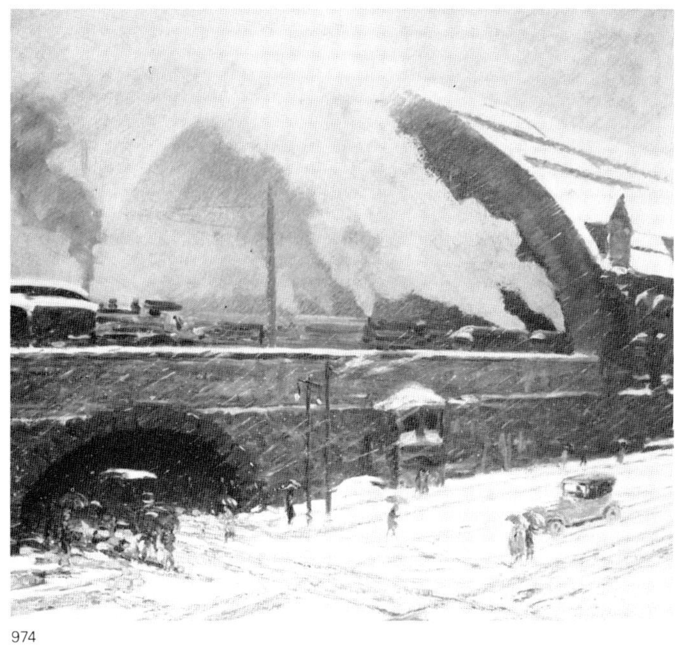
974

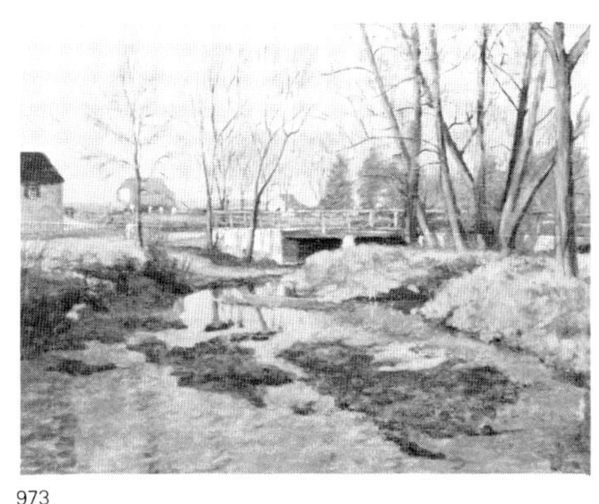
973

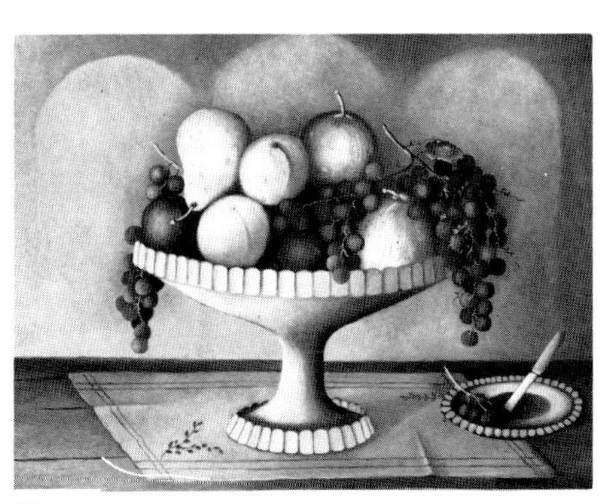
975

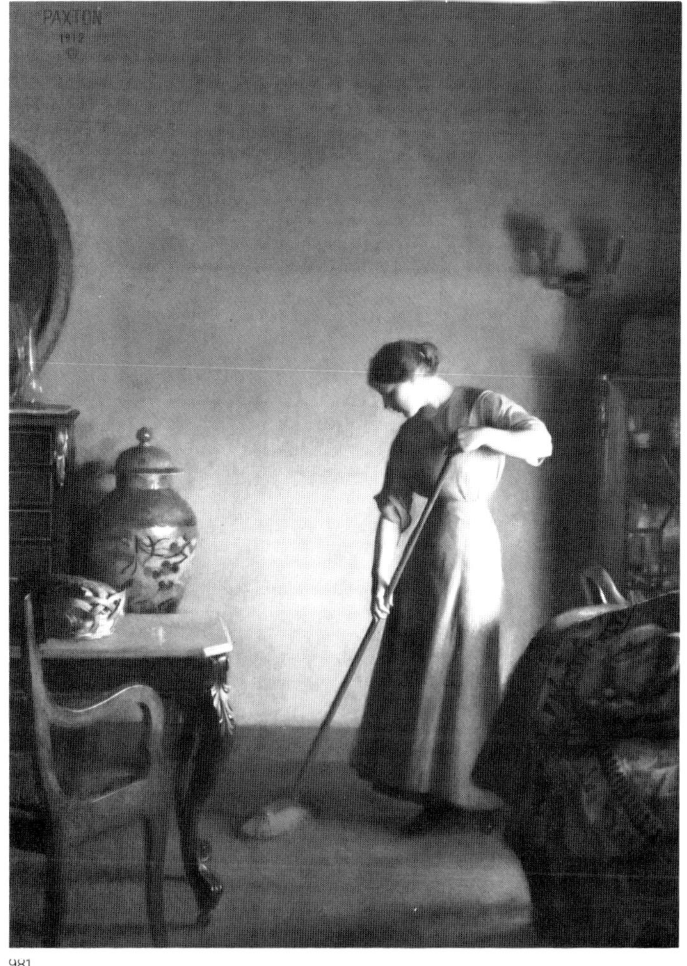

981

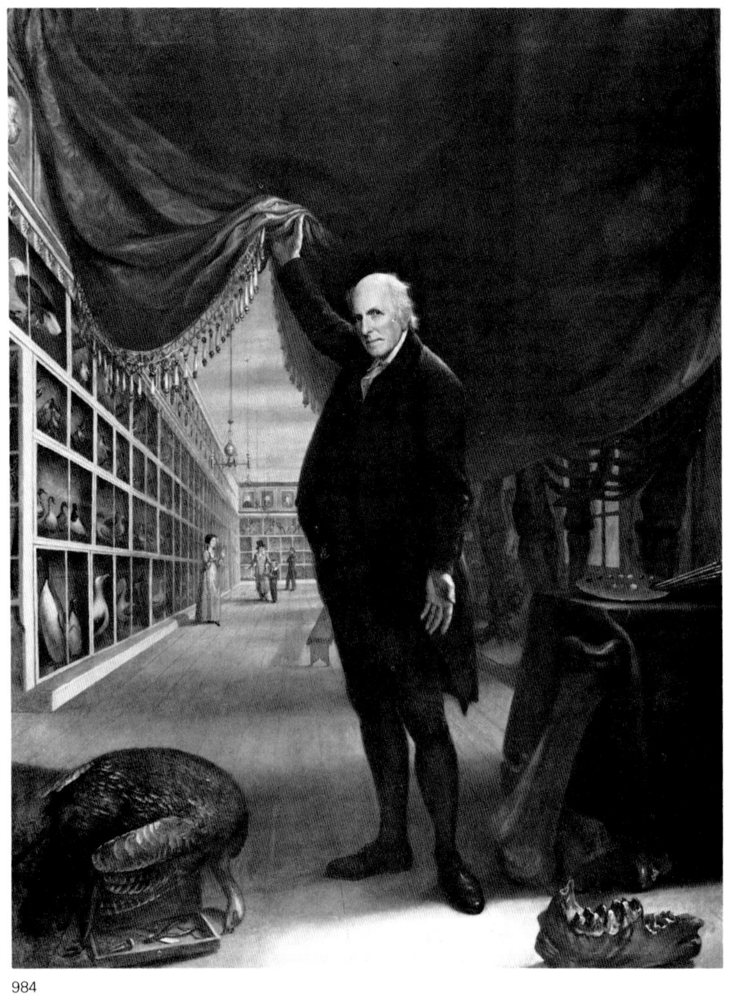
984

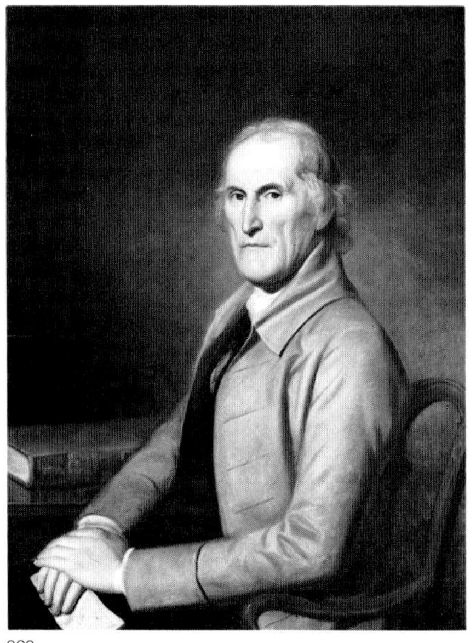
989

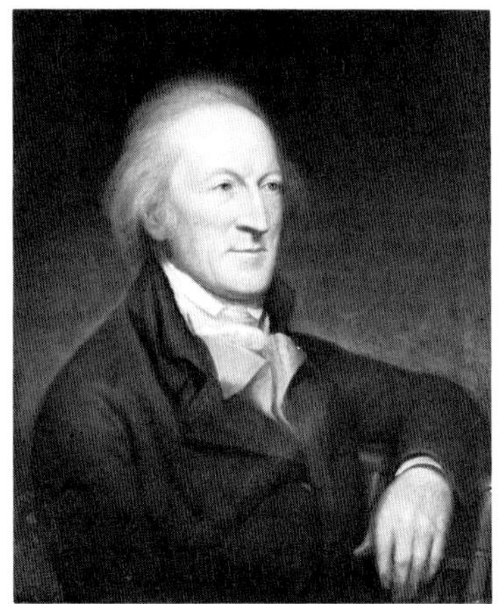
987

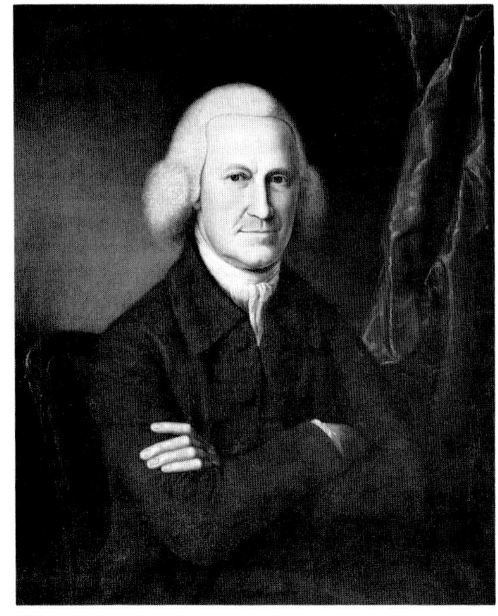
985

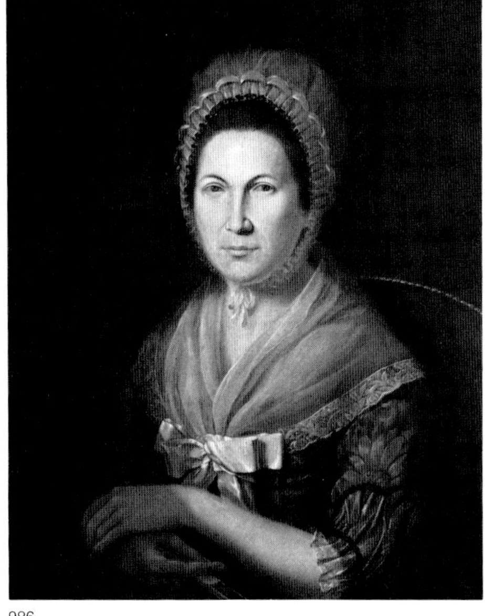
986

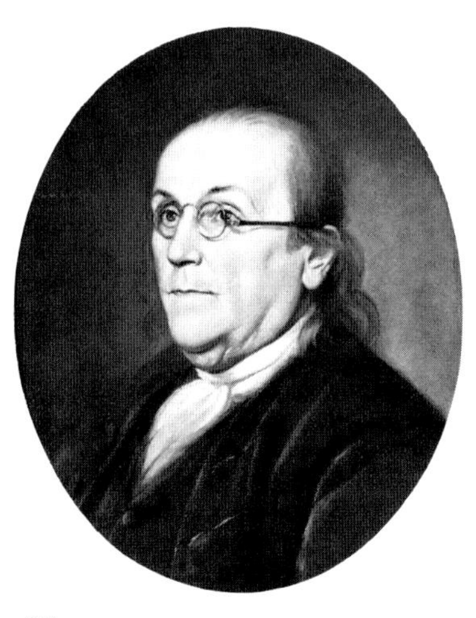
988

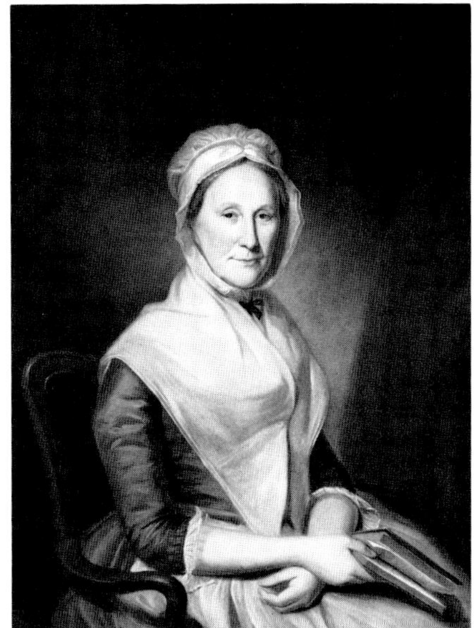

990

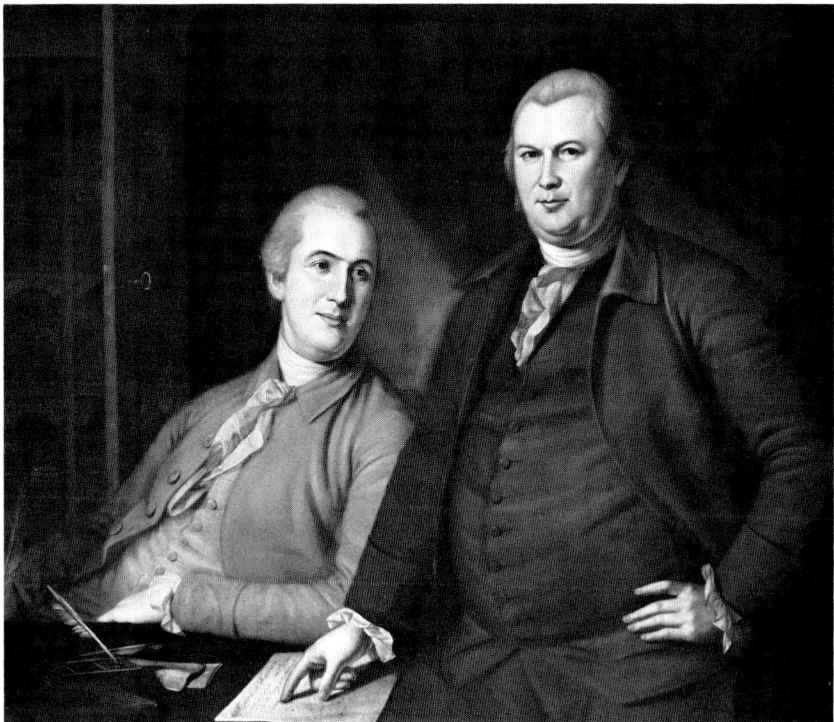

991

Charles Willson Peale (1741–1827)

983 *Captain Robert Allen* (ca. 1761–1821), ca. 1795
Oil on canvas, mounted on wood
30³⁄₁₆ x 25 in. (76.7 x 63.5 cm.)
Gift of Mrs. John Frederick Lewis (The John Frederick Lewis Memorial Collection), 1933.10.56

984 *The Artist in His Museum*, 1822
Oil on canvas
103¾ x 79⅞ in. (263.5 x 202.9 cm.)
Inscribed on fish: With this article the/Museum commenced/June 1784./Presented by Mr. R. Patterson
Gift of Mrs. Sarah Harrison (The Joseph Harrison, Jr. Collection), 1878.1.2

985 *James Claypoole* (1720–1784), ca. 1783
Oil on canvas
30⅛ x 25¹⁄₁₆ in. (76.5 x 63.7 cm.)
Henry D. Gilpin Fund, 1915.2.1

986 *Mary Chambers Claypoole*, ca. 1783
Oil on canvas
30 x 25 in. (76.2 x 63.5 cm.)
Henry D. Gilpin Fund, 1915.2.2

987 *George Clymer* (1739–1813), 1807, retouched 1810
Oil on canvas
27⅛ x 22⅛ in. (68.9 x 56.2 cm.)
Gift of the artist, 1809.2

988 *Benjamin Franklin* (1706–1790), 1785
Oil on canvas
23⅛ x 19¹⁄₁₆ in. (58.7 x 48.4 cm.), oval
Bequest of Mrs. Sarah Harrison (The Joseph Harrison, Jr. Collection), 1912.14.2

989 *James Latimer* (1720–1807), 1788–89
Oil on canvas
36 x 27¼ in. (91.4 x 69.2 cm.)
Bequest of Robert Cathcart Latimer, 1974.18.2

990 *Sarah Geddes Latimer* (1727–1813), 1788–89
Oil on canvas
36 x 27¼ in. (91.4 x 69.2 cm.)
Bequest of Robert Cathcart Latimer, 1974.18.1

991 *Gouverneur Morris and Robert Morris* (1752–1816; 1734–1806), 1783
Oil on canvas
43½ x 51¾ in. (110.5 x 131.4 cm.)
Signed and dated at lower left: C. W Peale pinxt 1783/1783
Bequest of Richard Ashhurst, 1969.20.1

992 *Noah and His Ark*, 1819
(after Charles Catton)
Oil on canvas
40¼ x 50¼ in. (102.2 x 127.6 cm.)
Collections Fund, 1951.22

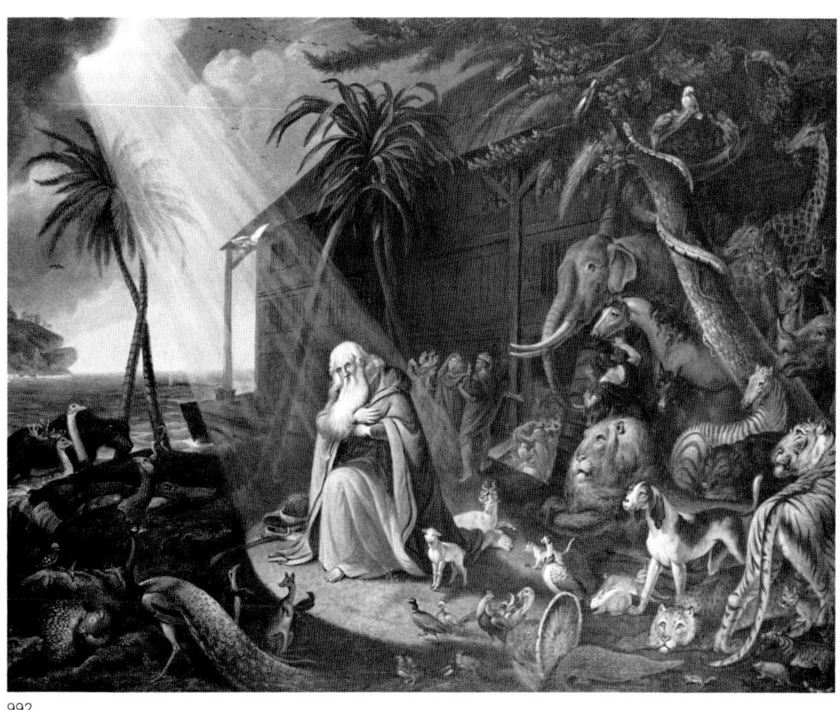

992

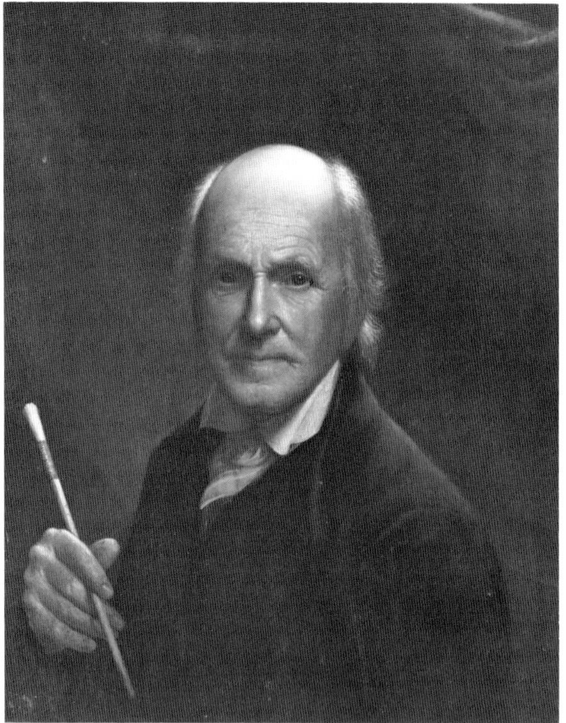
993

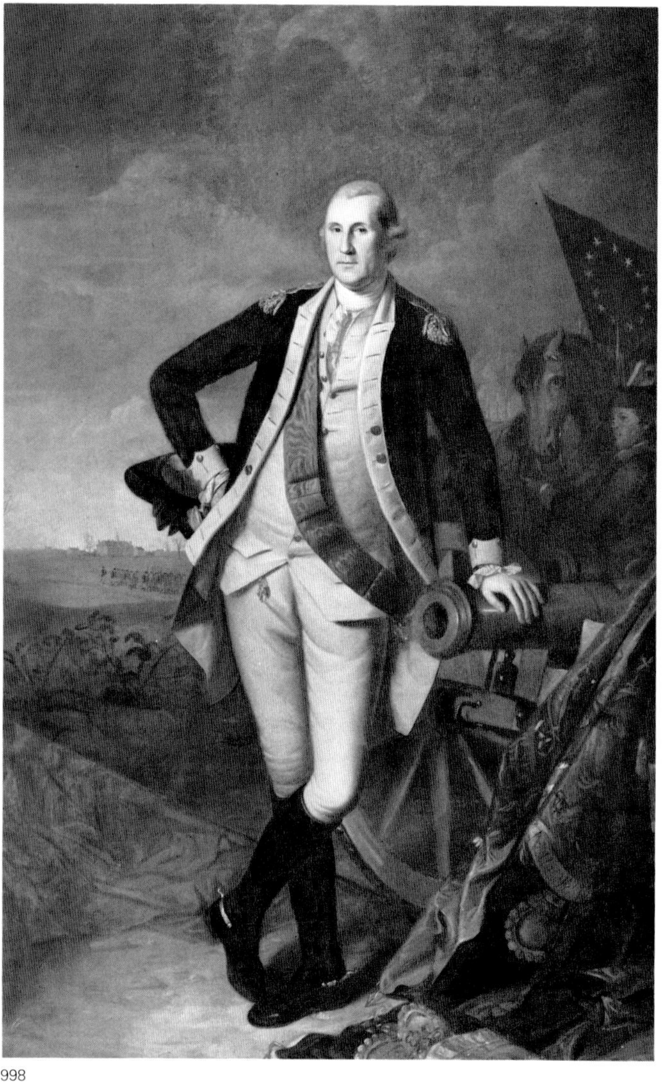
998

993 *Self-Portrait in the Character of a Painter,* 1824
Oil on canvas
26¼ x 22⅛ in. (66.7 x 56.2 cm.)
Gift of the artist (probably in 1824), 1845.5

994 *Self-Portrait with Spectacles,* ca. 1804
Oil on canvas, mounted on wood
26$\frac{3}{16}$ x 22$\frac{5}{16}$ in. (66.5 x 56.7 cm.)
Henry D. Gilpin Fund, 1939.18

995 *Baron Frederick William von Steuben* (1730–1794), 1780
Oil on canvas
29$\frac{15}{16}$ x 24$\frac{15}{16}$ in. (76 x 63.3 cm.)
Deposited by Mrs. Maria L. M. Peters, 1881.1

996 *John Vaughan* (1756–1841), ca. 1810
Oil on canvas
29⅝ x 24⅝ in. (75.2 x 62.5 cm.)
Gift of Mrs. John Frederick Lewis (The John Frederick Lewis Memorial Collection), 1933.10.58

997 *George Washington* (1732–1799), 1787
Oil on canvas
24 x 19⅛ in. (61 x 48.6 cm.)
Bequest of Mrs. Sarah Harrison (The Joseph Harrison, Jr. Collection), 1912.14.3

998 *George Washington at Princeton,* 1779
Oil on canvas
93 x 58½ in. (236.2 x 148.6 cm.)
Gift of Maria McKean Allen and Phebe Warren Downes through the bequest of their mother, Elizabeth Wharton McKean, 1943.16.2

999 *Unidentified Man*
Oil on canvas
28 x 24⅛ in. (71.1 x 61.3 cm.)
Gift of Mrs. John Frederick Lewis (The John Frederick Lewis Memorial Collection), 1933.10.57

Harriet Cany Peale (Mrs. Rembrandt Peale, 1800–1869)

1000 *Rembrandt Peale* (1778–1860), 1848 (after Rembrandt Peale, ca. 1845; *see* cat. no. 1029)
Oil on canvas, mounted on wood
20⅞ x 16⅞ in. (53 x 42.9 cm.)
Signed and dated at lower right: H.C.Peale./ 1848.
Gift of Mrs. Marta Dannenbaum McKinley and Mrs. Dorothy Dannenbaum Rudolph in memory of their parents, Dorothy Beach Dannenbaum and Walter Dannenbaum, 1983.12

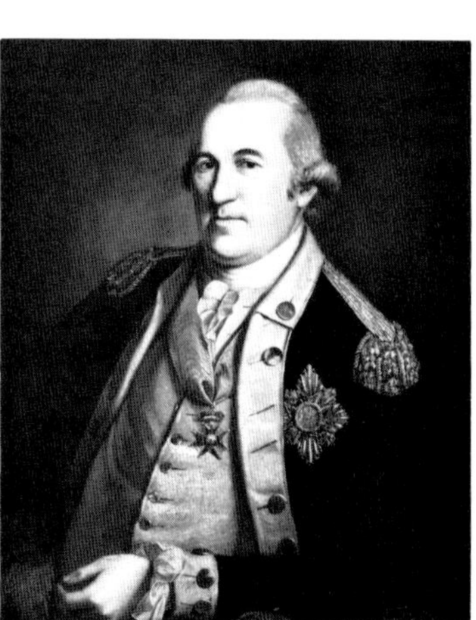
995

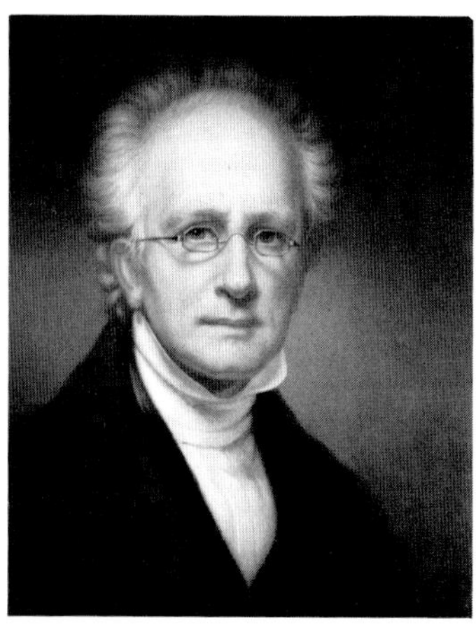
1000

James Peale (1749–1831)

1001 *The Artist and His Family*, 1795
Oil on canvas
31¼ x 32¾ in. (79.4 x 83.2 cm.)
Signed and dated at lower right: Jas. Peale 1795
Gift of John Frederick Lewis, 1922.1.1

1002 *Elizabeth Claypoole* (1751–1836), ca. 1805
Oil on canvas
24¹⁄₁₆ x 20⅛ in. (61.1 x 51.1 cm.), oval
Bequest of Mrs. John Frederick Lewis, 1939.17.4

1003 *Anna Maria Hodkinson* (1790–1876), 1800
Oil on canvas
15³⁄₁₆ x 11¹³⁄₁₆ in. (38.6 x 30 cm.)
Signed and dated at lower right: I P/1800
Gift of Mrs. Robert H. Lanning, 1916.11

1004 *Abraham Kintzing* (1763–1835), 1798
Oil on canvas
29¹⁵⁄₁₆ x 25⅛ in. (76 x 63.8 cm.)
Signed and dated at lower left: IP/1798
Bequest of Ella Kintzing Birkhead, 1901.4.1

1005 *Mrs. Abraham Kintzing* (1764–1804), 1798
Oil on canvas
29¹⁵⁄₁₆ x 25¹⁄₁₆ in. (76 x 63.7 cm.)
Signed and dated at lower left: I.P./1798
Bequest of Ella Kintzing Birkhead, 1901.4.2

1006 *Clementine Antoinette Martin* (Mrs. William Martin, 1770–1855), 1814
Oil on canvas
29⅛ x 24¹⁄₁₆ in. (74 x 61.1 cm.)
Signed and dated at lower right: IP/1814
Gift of Mrs. Elizabeth Runk Kayan and B.F. Dewees Runk, 1970.28.3

1007 *William Martin*, probably 1814
Oil on canvas
29¼ x 24¹⁄₁₆ in. (74.3 x 61.1 cm.)
Gift of Mrs. Elizabeth Runk Kayan and B.F. Dewees Runk, 1970.28.4

1008 *Anna and Margaretta Peale* (1791–1878; 1795–1882), ca. 1805
Oil on canvas
29 x 24 in. (73.7 x 61 cm.)
Pennsylvania Academy purchase, 1902.5

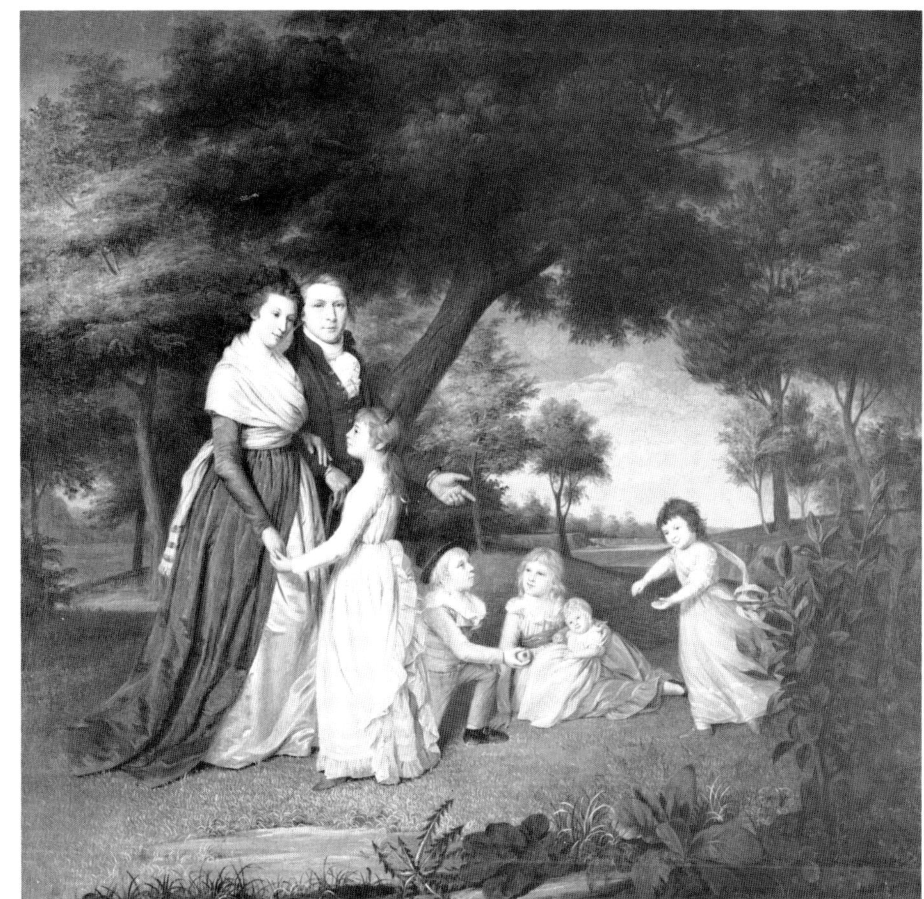
1001

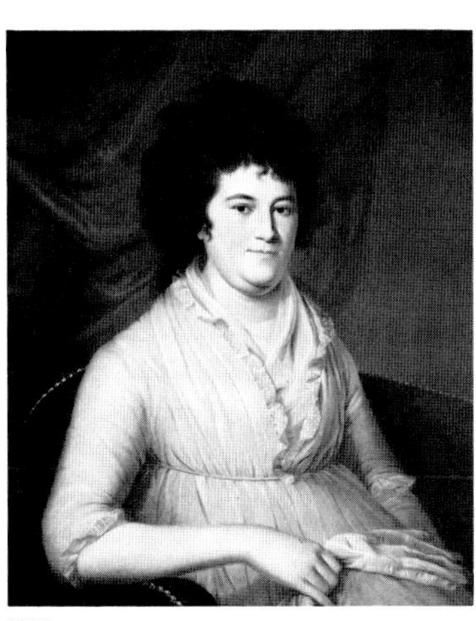
1005

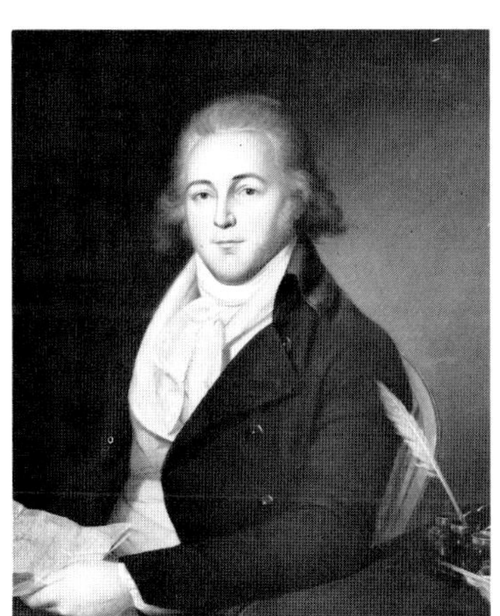
1004

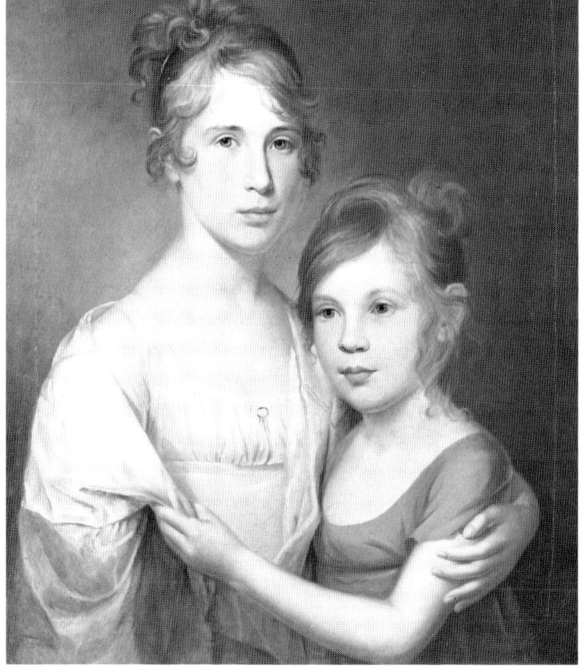
1008

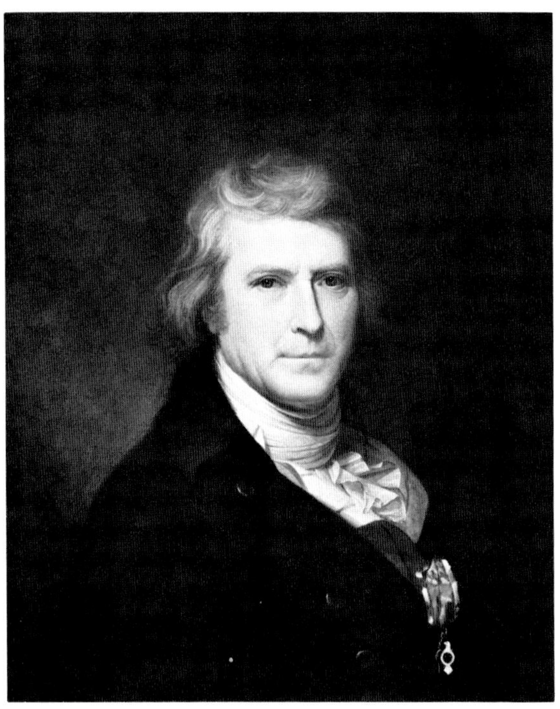
1010

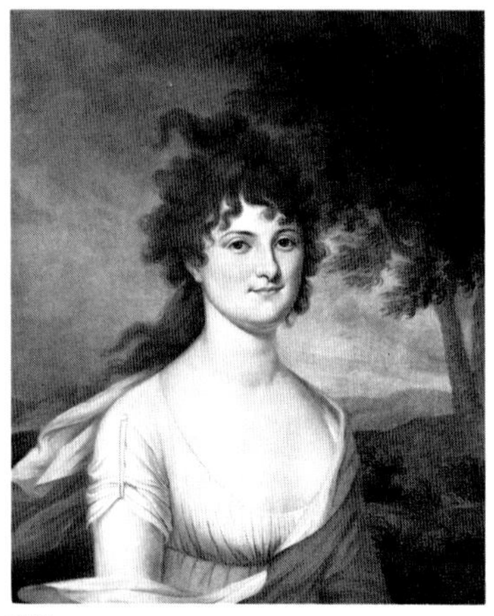
1013

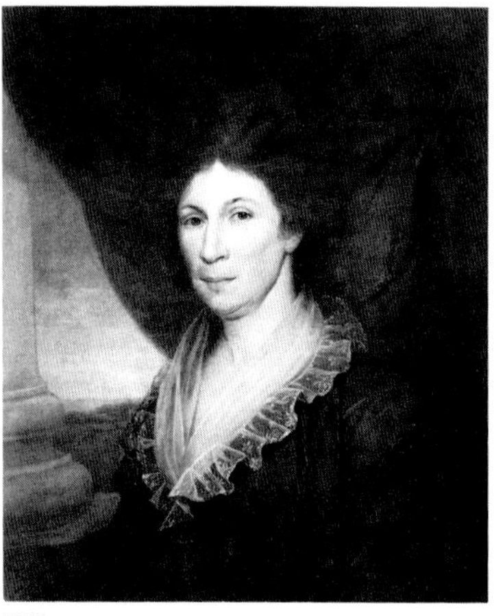
1009

1009 *Mrs. James Peale* (née Mary Claypoole, 1753–1829), ca. 1805
Oil on canvas, mounted on masonite
28 x 23 7/16 in. (71.1 x 59.5 cm.)
Henry D. Gilpin Fund, 1915.2.4

1010 *Self-Portrait*, ca. 1805
Oil on canvas
28 1/8 x 23 5/8 in. (71.4 x 60 cm.)
Henry D. Gilpin Fund, 1915.2.3

1011 *Still Life #1*, 1827
Oil on canvas
20 1/16 x 26 5/8 in. (51 x 67.6 cm.)
Annotated on back: Painted by James Peale/in the 75th year of his age..1827
Source unknown, 1847.6

1012 *Still Life #2*, 1821
Oil on wood
18 x 26 7/16 in. (45.7 x 67.2 cm.)
Signed and dated at lower left: Jas. Peale 1821.
Henry D. Gilpin Fund, 1915.8

1013 *Unidentified Woman*, 1802
Oil on canvas
29 x 24 1/16 in. (73.7 x 61.1 cm.)
Signed and dated at lower right: I Peale/1802
Source unknown, 1944.27

See also miniatures, cat. nos. 1646–47.

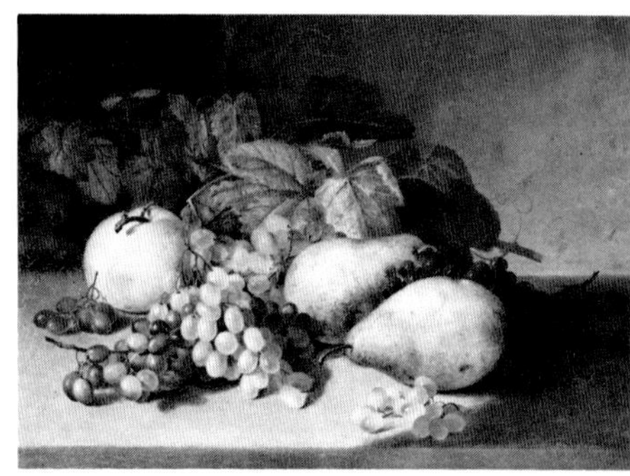
1011

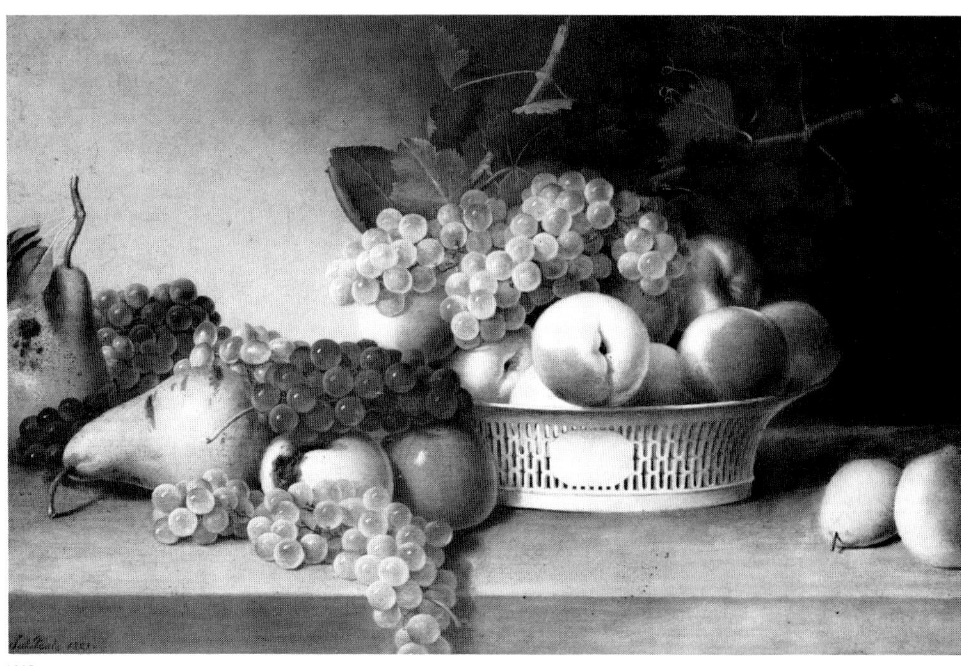
1012

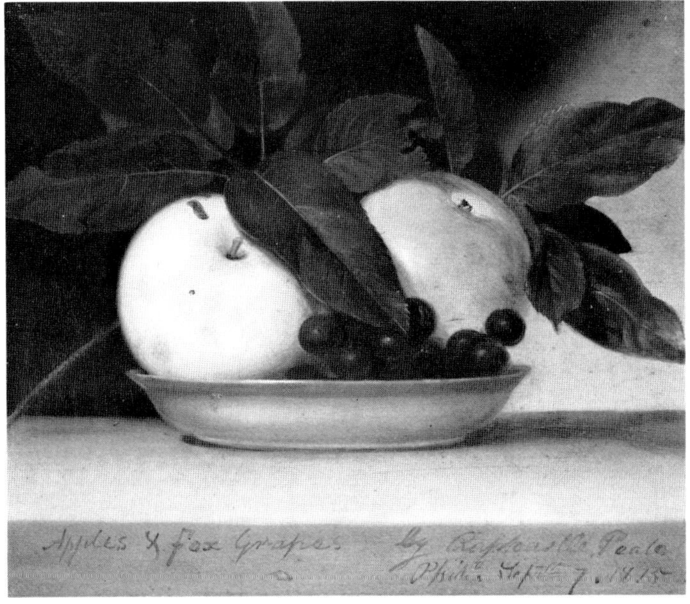
1015

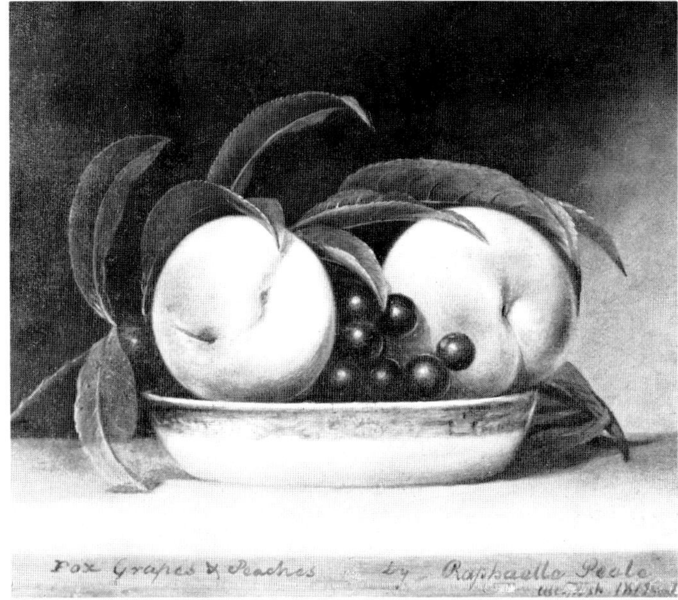
1016

Margaretta Angelica Peale (1795–1882)

1014 *Strawberries and Cherries*
Oil on canvas
10$\frac{1}{16}$ x 12$\frac{1}{8}$ in. (25.6 x 30.8 cm.)
Source unknown, 1924.11

Raphaelle Peale (1774–1825)

1015 *Apples and Fox Grapes*, 1815
Oil on wood
9$\frac{11}{16}$ x 11$\frac{7}{16}$ in. (24.6 x 29.1 cm.)
Inscribed, signed, and dated across bottom: Apples x Fox Grapes by Raphaelle Peale/Phila Septr 7. 1815
Source unknown (probably Pennsylvania Academy purchase, 1817), 1847.9

1016 *Fox Grapes and Peaches*, 1815
Oil on wood
9$\frac{11}{16}$ x 11$\frac{7}{16}$ in. (24.6 x 29.1 cm.)
Inscribed, signed, and dated across bottom: Fox Grapes x Peaches by Raphaelle Peale/August 1815
Source unknown (probably Pennsylvania Academy purchase, 1817), 1845.6

Rembrandt Peale (1778–1860)

1017 *Ella Hollenback Bicking* (later Mrs. Louis Emory, 1837–1932), 1842
Oil on wood
29 x 36 in. (73.7 x 91.4 cm.)
Inscribed, signed, and dated on back: Ella Bicking-/Rembrandt Peale Pinxit./1842.
Bequest of Mrs. Henry H. Pease through Pauline T. Pease, 1979.7.2

1018 *Mary Ann Roset Bicking* (later Mrs. William Brisbane, 1829–1894), 1844
Oil on canvas, mounted on masonite
20 x 24 in. (50.8 x 61 cm.)
Bequest of Mrs. Henry H. Pease through Pauline T. Pease, 1979.7.1

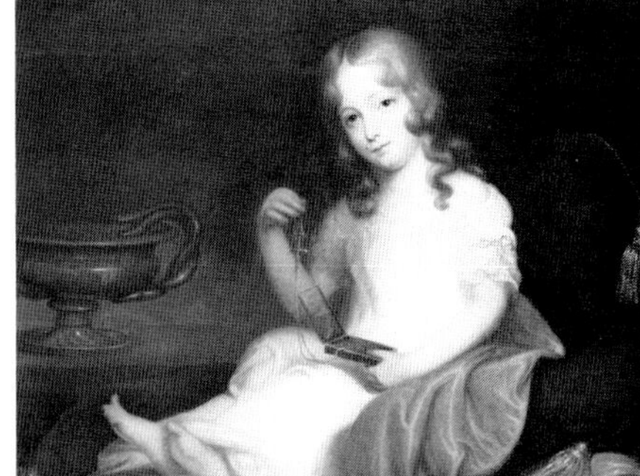
1017

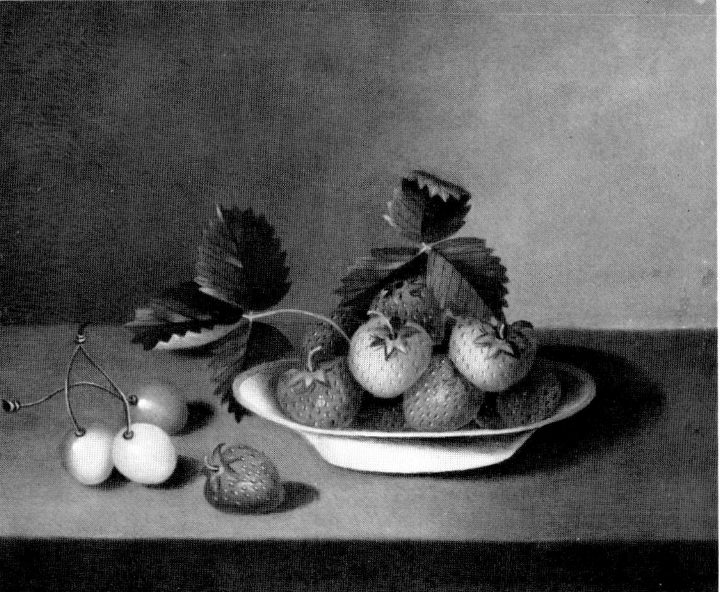
1014

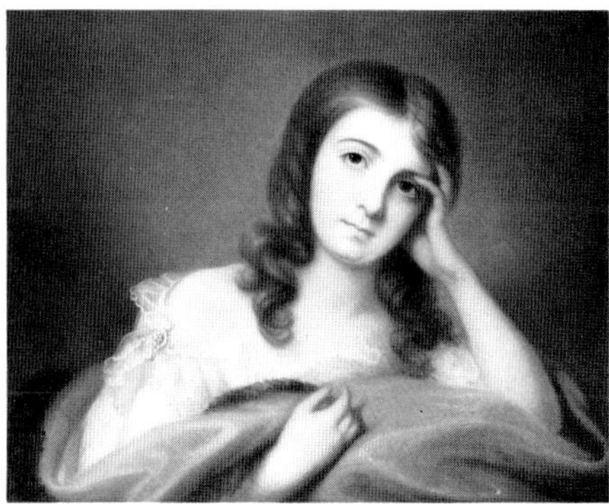
1018

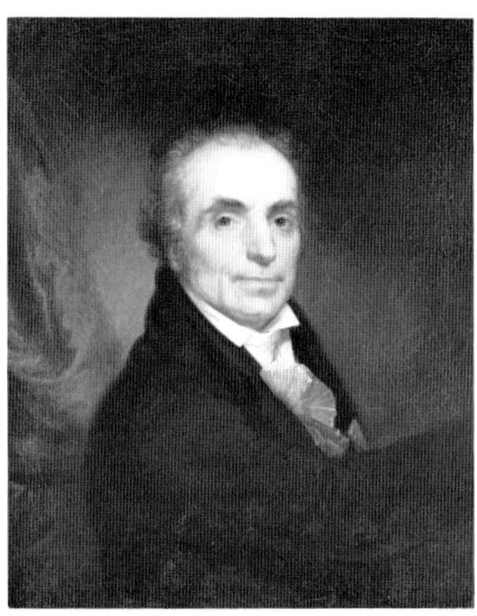
1023

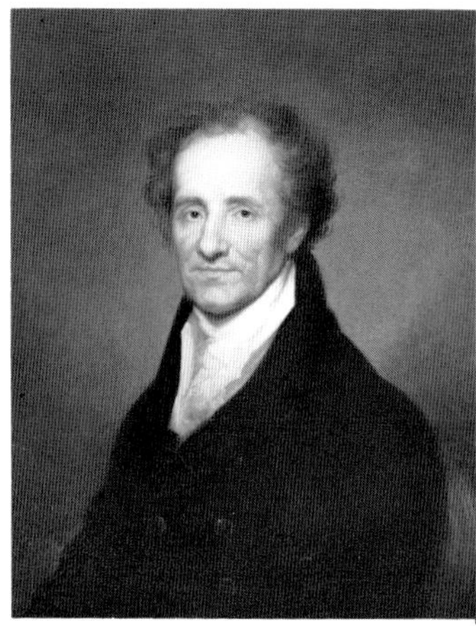
1021

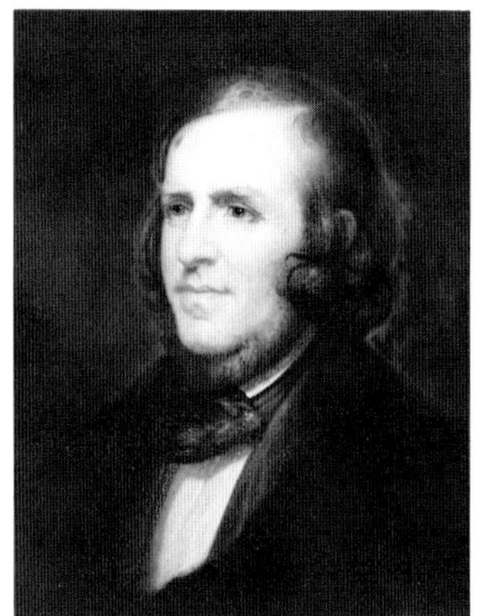
1025

1019 *Presley Blakiston* (1741–1819), ca. 1814
Oil on canvas
30 x 25 in. (76.2 x 63.5 cm.)
Gift of J. Forsyth Alexander in memory of his mother, Edith F. Alexander, 1985.45

1020 *Jacques Louis David* (1748–1825), 1810
Oil on canvas
28½ x 23 in. (72.4 x 58.4 cm.)
General Fund, 1854.1.1

1021 *Dominique Vivant Denon* (1747–1825), 1808
Oil on canvas
28½ x 23³⁄₁₆ in. (72.4 x 58.9 cm.)
General Fund, 1854.1.2

1022 *Emmaline Fox* (1803–1882), ca. 1830
Oil on canvas
30¹⁄₁₆ x 25 in. (76.4 x 63.5 cm.)
Gift of Mrs. John Large Fox, 1969.31

1023 *Jean Antoine Houdon* (1741–1826), 1808
Oil on canvas
28⁷⁄₁₆ x 23 in. (72.2 x 58.4 cm.)
General Fund, 1854.1.3

1024 *Andrew Caldwell Mitchell*, ca. 1806
Oil on canvas
27¹⁄₁₆ x 22³⁄₁₆ in. (68.7 x 56.4 cm.)
Henry D. Gilpin Fund, 1931.12

1025 *Benjamin Franklin Peale* (1795–1870), 1849
Oil on canvas
21¹⁄₁₆ x 17³⁄₁₆ in. (53.5 x 43.7 cm.)
Signed at left center: R.P.
Gift of the Baldwin Locomotive Works, 1925.11.2

1026 *Judge Richard Peters of Belmont* (1744–1828), ca. 1810
Oil on wood
8¹⁵⁄₁₆ x 7¹⁄₃₂ in. (22.7 x 17.8 cm.)
Gift of Mr. and Mrs. John White Field, 1887.1.6

1027 *Richard Peters, Jr.* (1780–1848), ca. 1810
Oil on canvas
30³⁄₁₆ x 25⅛ in. (76.7 x 63.8 cm.)
Bequest of Mrs. John White Field, 1902.6

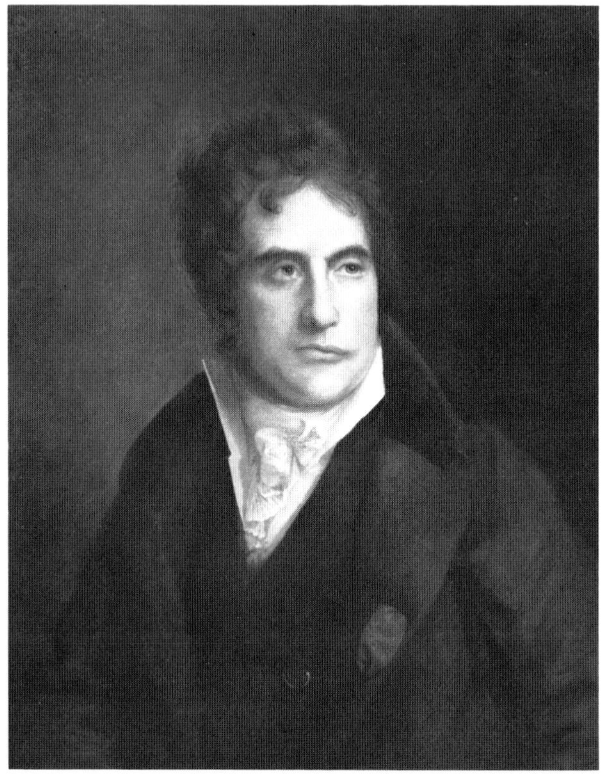
1020

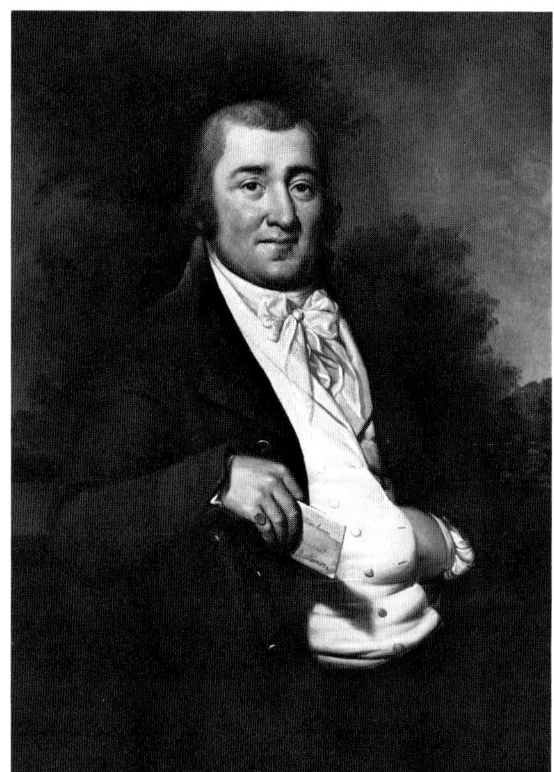
1028

1028 *William Raborg* (1740–1822), 1797
Oil on canvas
36⅛ x 27⅛ in. (91.8 x 68.9 cm.)
Signed and dated at lower right: REMBRANDT/ PEALE. pinxt/1797; inscribed on letter held by sitter: [W]illiam Raborg/Merchant/Baltimore
Gift of Brigadier General and Mrs. Edgar R. Owens, 1973.6

1029 *Self-Portrait*, ca. 1845
Oil on paper, mounted on canvas
20¾ x 16¹⁵⁄₁₆ in. (52.7 x 43 cm.)
Bequest of Mrs. Rembrandt Peale, 1869.1
See also copy, cat. no. 1000.

1030 *Hon. Edward Tilghman* (1750–1815), 1809
Oil on canvas
28¹⁵⁄₁₆ x 23½ in. (73.5 x 59.7 cm.)
Gift of Mrs. John Frederick Lewis (The John Frederick Lewis Memorial Collection), 1933.10.62

1031 *Chief Justice William Tilghman* (1756–1827), ca. 1819
Oil on canvas
30 x 25¹⁄₁₆ in. (76.2 x 63.7 cm.)
Gift of Mrs. John Frederick Lewis (The John Frederick Lewis Memorial Collection), 1933.10.63

1032 *George Washington* (1732–1799)
(after Gilbert Stuart's Athenaeum portrait, 1796)
Oil on canvas
30 x 25 in. (76.2 x 63.5 cm.)
Henry D. Gilpin Fund, 1916.13

1033 *George Washington*
(after Gilbert Stuart's Athenaeum portrait)
Oil on canvas
29 x 23¹⁵⁄₁₆ in. (73.7 x 60.8 cm.)
Gift of Mrs. John Frederick Lewis (The John Frederick Lewis Memorial Collection), 1933.10.66

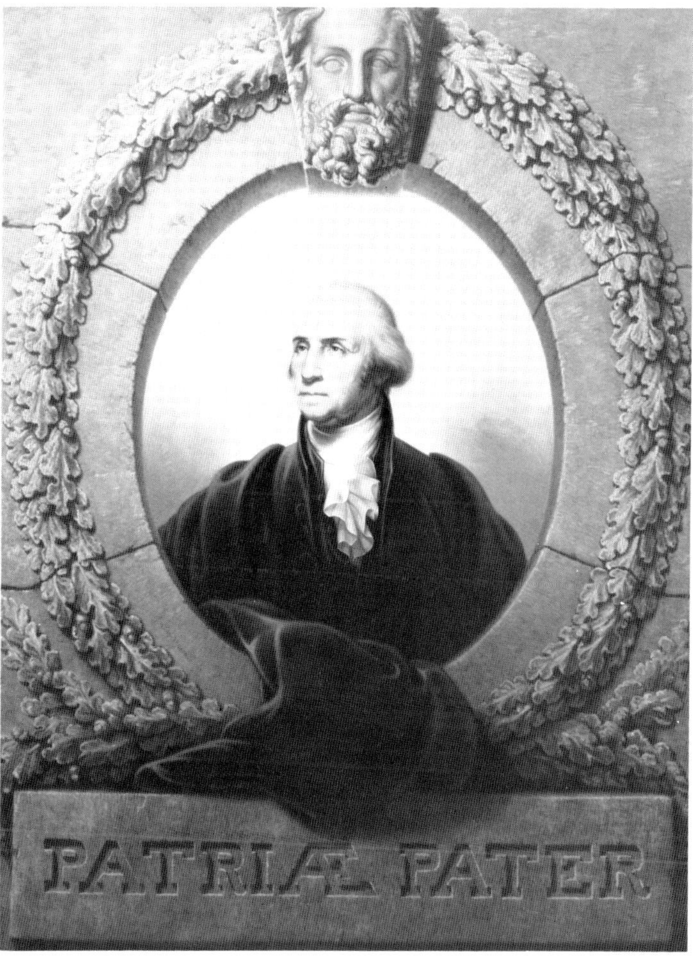

1035

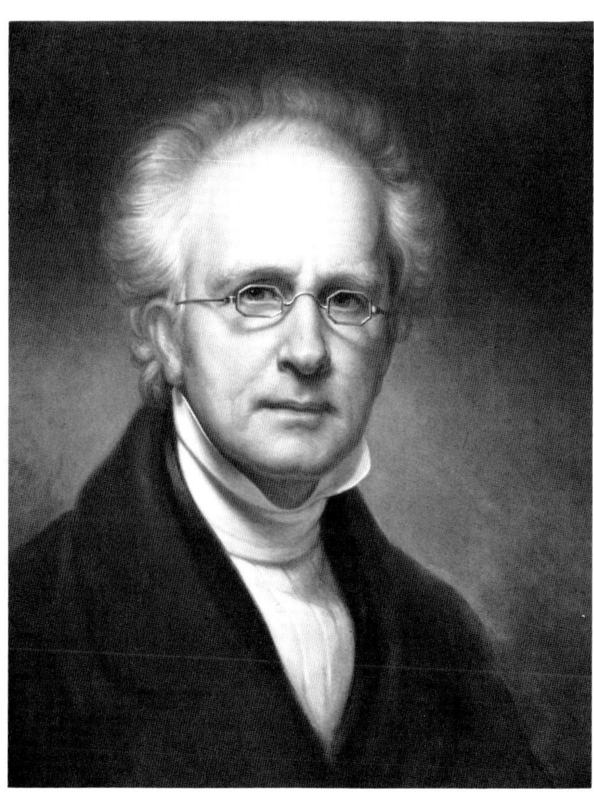
1029

1034 *George Washington*
(after Gilbert Stuart's Vaughan portrait, 1795)
Oil on canvas
30⅛ x 25¼ in. (76.5 x 64.1 cm.)
Bequest of Maude Harrison Gibbs through Sarah Gibbs McClure, George F. Gibbs, Jr., and Maurine Montgomery Gibbs, 1974.21

1035 *George Washington, Patriae Pater*, ca. 1824
Oil on canvas
72¼ x 54¼ in. (183.5 x 137.8 cm.)
Signed at lower left: Rembrandt Peale
Bequest of Mrs. Sarah Harrison (The Joseph Harrison, Jr. Collection), 1912.14.4

See also palette, cat. no. 1623.

Attributed to **Rembrandt Peale**

1036 *George Washington*
(after Gilbert Stuart's Athenaeum portrait)
Oil on canvas
29⅞ x 23¹³⁄₁₆ in. (75.9 x 60.5 cm.)
Gift of Mrs. John Frederick Lewis (The John Frederick Lewis Memorial Collection), 1933.10.65

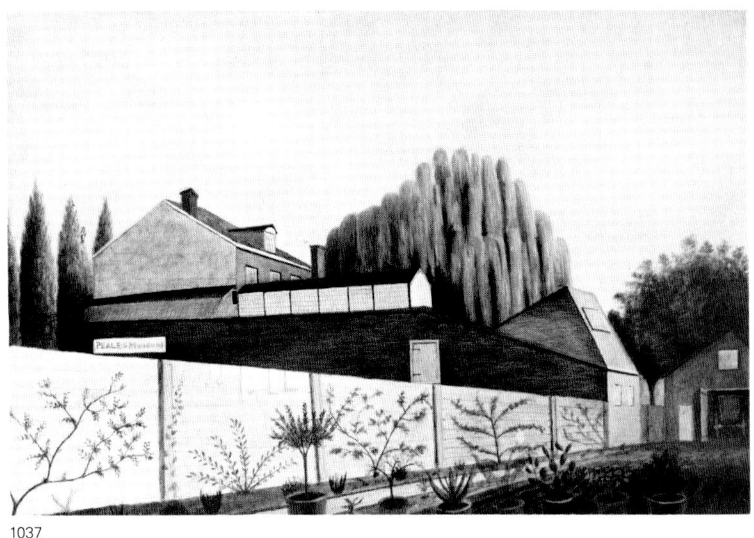
1037

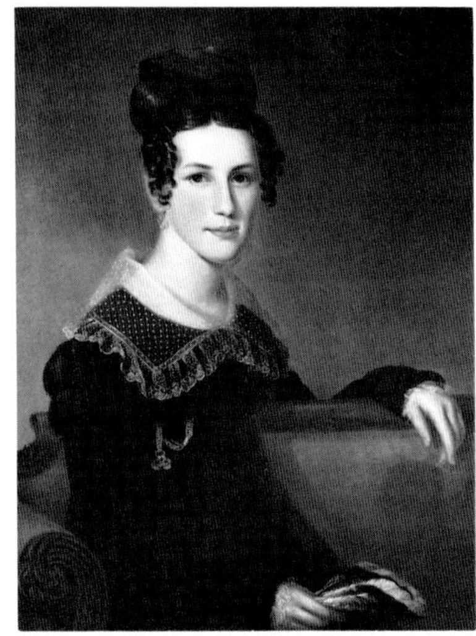
1038

Rubens Peale (1784–1865)

1037 *The Old Museum*, 1858–60
Oil on tin
14 1/16 x 20 1/16 in. (35.7 x 51 cm.)
Inscribed on sign at lower left: PEALES MUSEUM
Bequest of Charles Coleman Sellers, 1980.9

Sarah Miriam Peale (1800–1885)

1038 *Anna Maria Smyth* (later Mrs. Matthew James Burnside, d. 1848), 1821
Oil on canvas
35 15/16 x 27 7/16 in. (91.3 x 69.7 cm.)
Signed and dated at lower right: Sarah M. Peale/ 1821
Gift of Mrs. John Frederick Lewis (The John Frederic Lewis Memorial Collection), 1933.10.67

Charles Sprague Pearce (1851–1914)

1039 *Fantasie*, ca. 1882
Oil on canvas
41 5/8 x 30 in. (105.7 x 76.2 cm.)
Signed and inscribed at lower right: Charles Sprague Pearce CSP [initials in monogram within triangle] - Paris.
Gift of Joseph E. Temple, 1884.1.2

Philip Pearlstein (1924–)

1040 *Two Female Models on Hammock and Floor*, 1974
Oil on canvas
72 x 72 in. (182.9 x 182.9 cm.)
Signed and dated at lower left: PEARLSTEIN 74 ©
Gift of Betsy and Frank Goodyear, Jr., 1983.21

Henry Pearson (1914–)

1041 *Median (Part I)*, 1966
Acrylic on canvas
73 1/8 x 76 1/8 in. (185.7 x 193.4 cm.)
Signed and inscribed on canvas folded over stretcher: Henry Pearson - TRIPTYCH (PART I)
Gift of Will Barnet, 1975.7a

1042 *Median (Part II)*, 1966
Acrylic on canvas
73 1/8 x 76 in. (185.7 x 193 cm.)
Dated, signed, and inscribed on canvas folded over stretcher: 1966/Henry Pearson - TRIPTYCH (PART II)/MEDIAN
Inscribed and dated on stretcher: MEDIAN (TRIPTYCH) #6 - 1966/LIQUITEX
Gift of Will Barnet, 1975.7b

1043 *Median (Part III)*, 1966
Acrylic on canvas
73 1/8 x 73 1/8 in. (185.7 x 185.7 cm.)
Signed and inscribed on canvas folded over stretcher: Henry Pearson - TRIPTYCH - (PART III)
Gift of Will Barnet, 1975.7c

Joseph T. Pearson, Jr. (1876–1951)

1044 *Emily*, by 1906
Oil on canvas
44 1/8 x 33 3/4 in. (112.1 x 85.7 cm.)
Joseph E. Temple Fund, 1942.13

1045 *In Vain* (also called *Crucifixion*)
Oil on wood
64 3/4 x 37 3/4 in. (164.5 x 95.9 cm.)
Gift of the artist's family, 1952.15.1

1046 *Winter*, by 1917
Oil on canvas
61 x 73 in. (154.9 x 185.4 cm.)
Signed at lower left: P.
Gift of the artist's family, 1952.15.2

Mrs. Joseph T. Pearson, Jr.
See Alice Kent Stoddard.

David G. Pease (1932–)

1047 *Firecracker over Vilas*, 1958
Oil and collage on masonite
48 x 36 in. (121.9 x 91.4 cm.)
John Lambert Fund, 1960.10

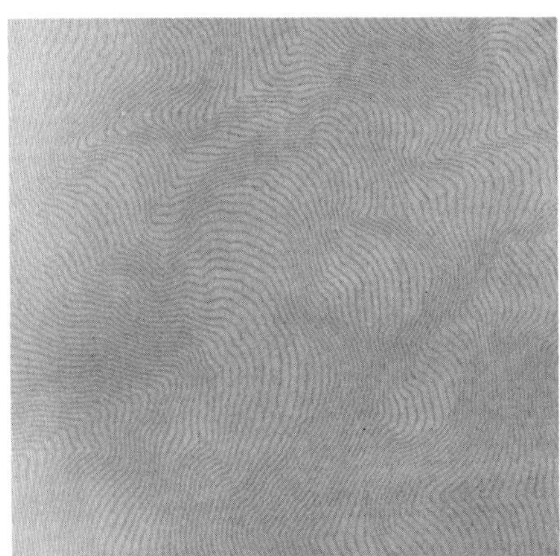
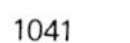
1041

1042

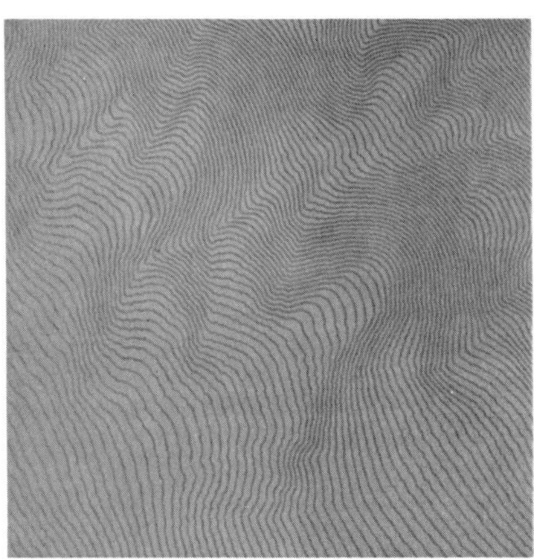
1043

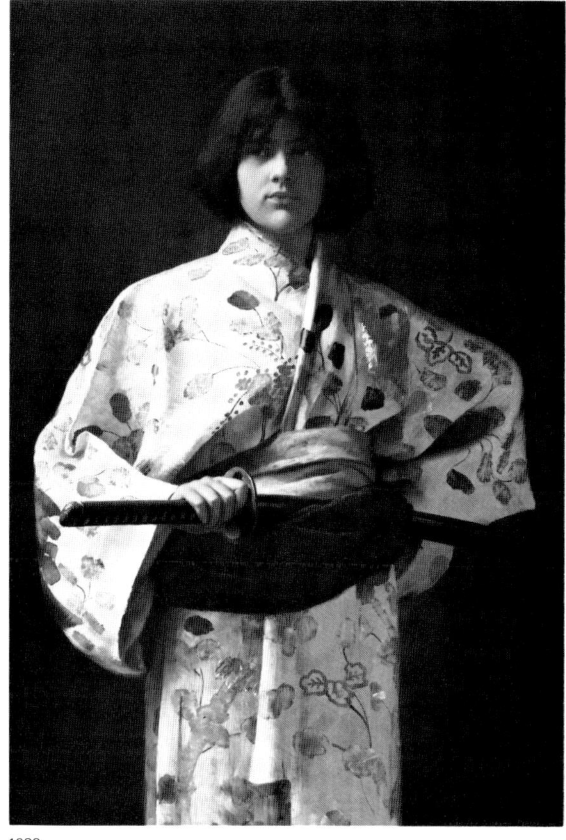

1039

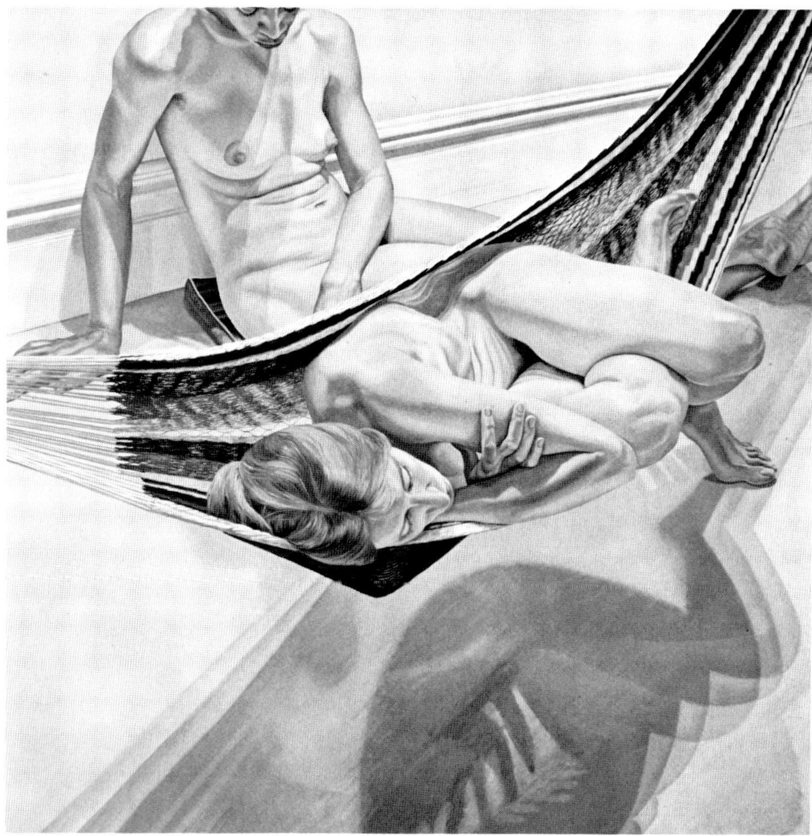

1040

Natalie Peck (b. 1886)

1048 *Storm Clouds*, ca. 1915
Oil on canvas
19¼ x 23¹³⁄₁₆ in. (48.9 x 60.5 cm.)
John Lambert Fund, 1916.6

Waldo Peirce (1884–1970)

1049 *Spring in Monsey*, 1937
Oil on canvas
32⅛ x 46 in. (81.6 x 116.8 cm.)
Signed and dated at lower right: WP '37.
John Lambert Fund, 1939.11

Guy Pène du Bois. *See* du Bois.

Gabor Peterdi (1915–)

1050 *Desert I*, 1961
Oil on canvas
50⅛ x 60¼ in. (127.3 x 153 cm.)
Signed and dated at lower left: Peterdi 61; signed, dated, and inscribed on back: PETERDI/ 1961/50 x 60/DESERT I
Joseph E. Temple Fund, 1962.9

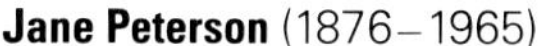

Jane Peterson (1876–1965)

1051 *Spring Bouquet*
Oil on canvas
40¹⁄₁₆ x 30 in. (101.8 x 76.2 cm.)
Signed at upper left: JANE PETERSON.
Gift of Martin Horwitz, 1976.22

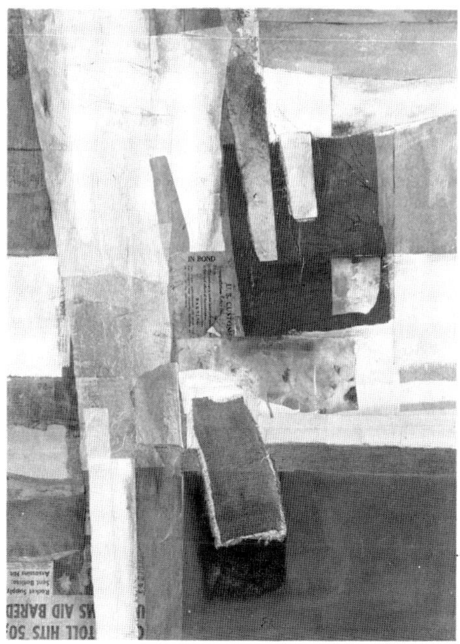

1047

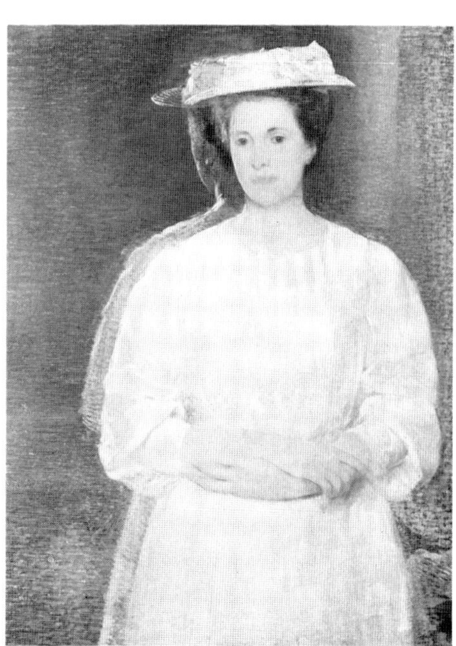

1044

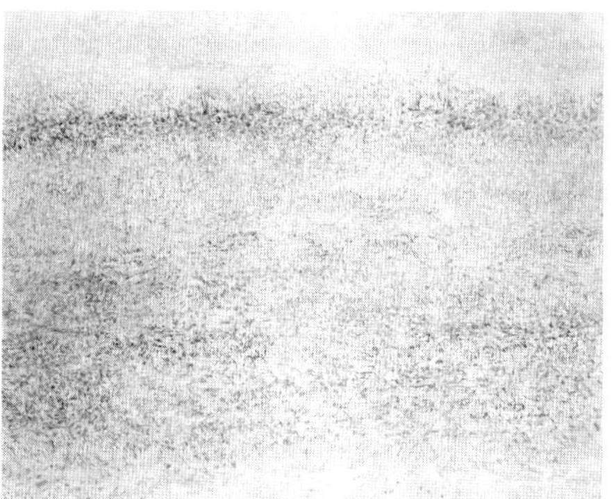

1050

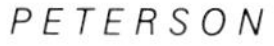

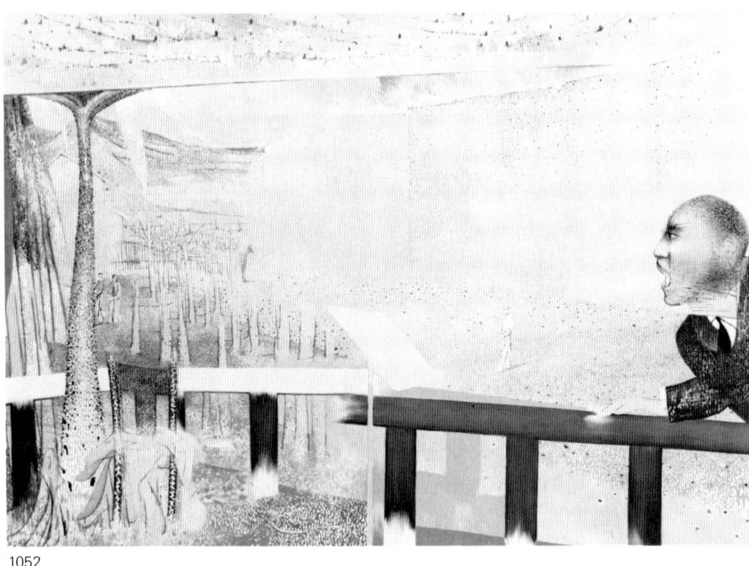
1052

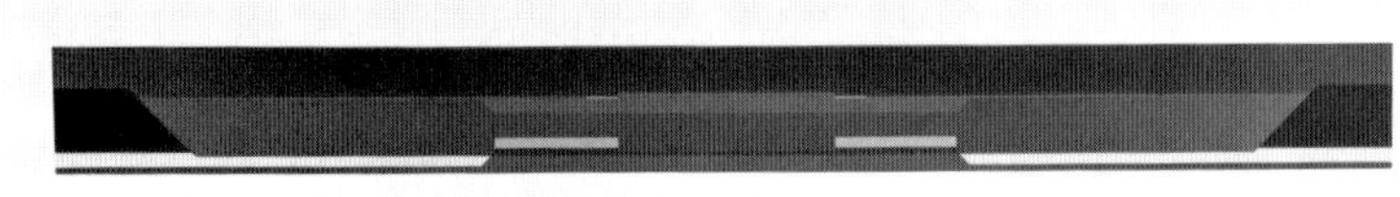
1055

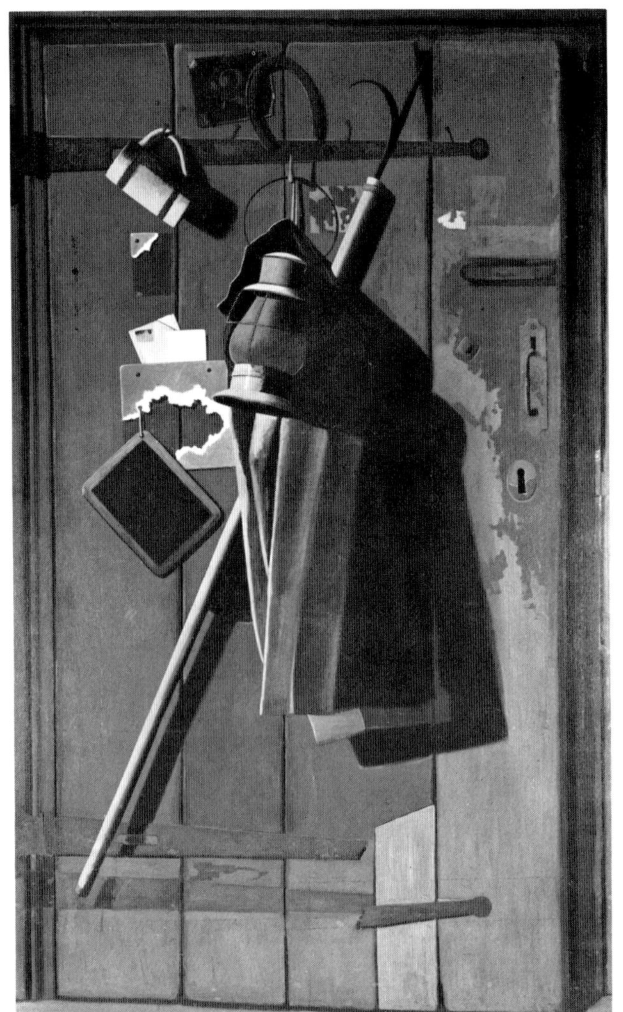
1054

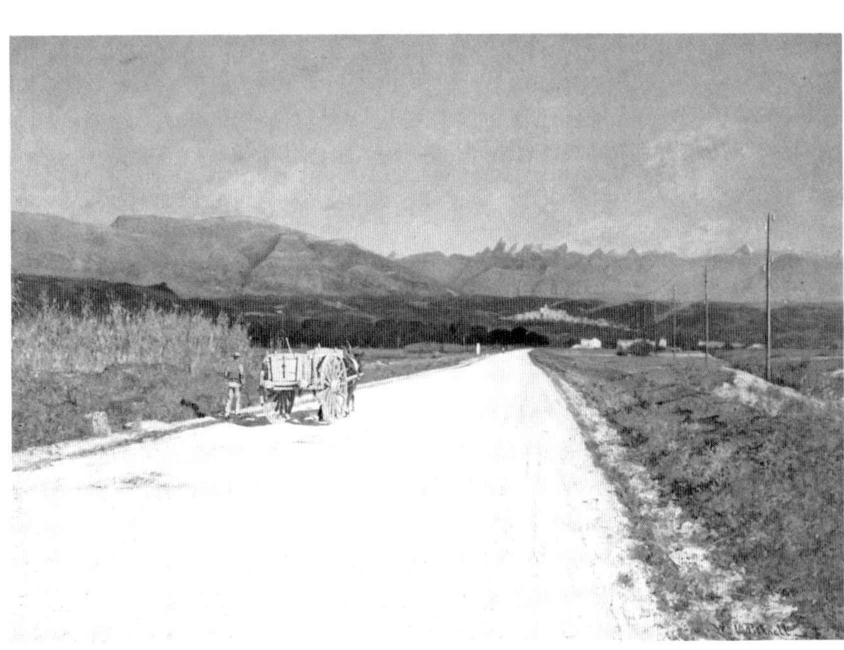
1058

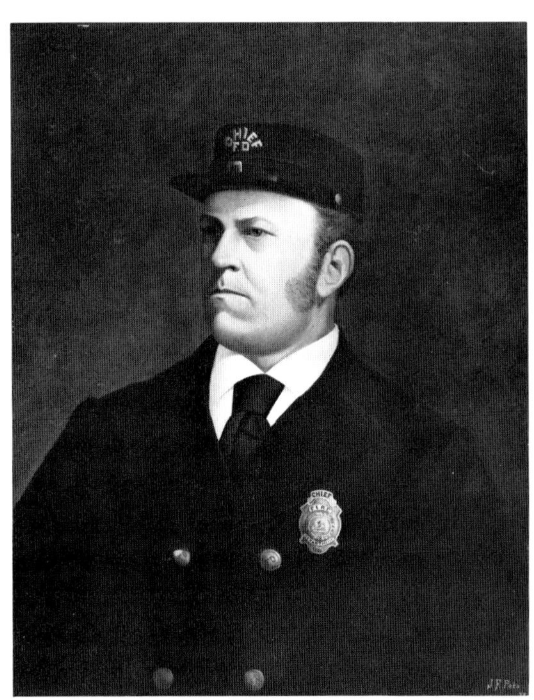

1053

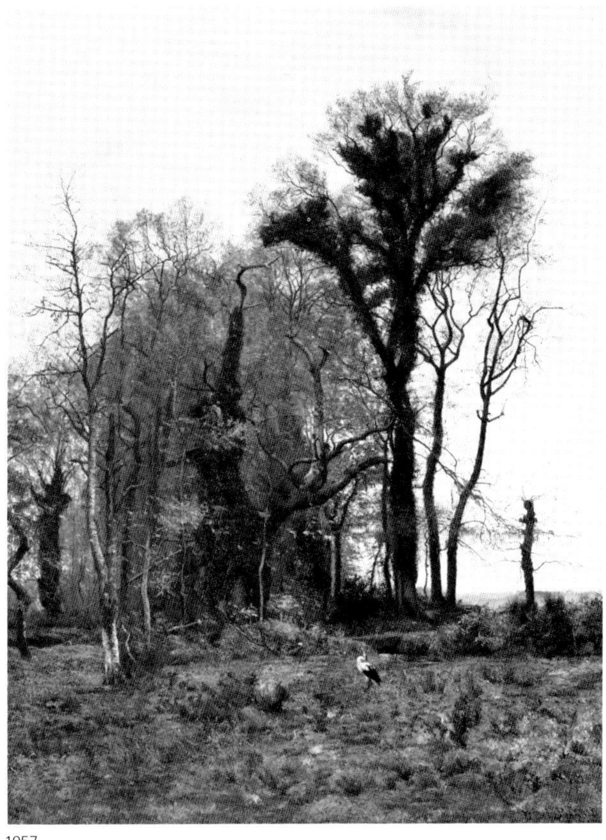
1057

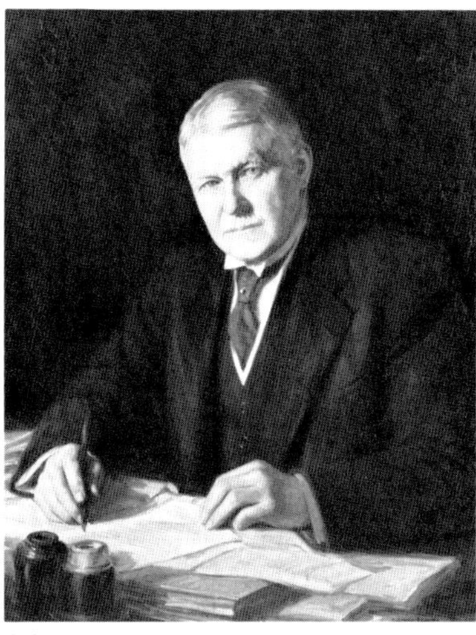
1056

Philippe A. Peticolas. *See* cat. no. 1648.

Irving Petlin (1934–)

1052 *The Disappeared*, 1985
Oil on canvas
78 x 108 in. (198.1 x 274.3 cm.)
Signed, inscribed, and dated on back: I. Petlin/ N.Y. 1985
Lewis S. Ware Fund and the Leo Model Foundation, 1986.6

John F. Peto (1854–1907)

1053 *The First Fire Chief of Philadelphia: Portrait of the Artist's Father* (Thomas H. Peto, d. 1895), 1878
Oil on canvas
31¼ x 25³⁄₁₆ in. (79.4 x 64 cm.)
Signed and dated at lower right: J.F. Peto/78
Gift of the Barra Foundation, 1983.13

1054 *The Fish House Door*, 1890s
Oil on canvas
63⅛ x 40⅛ in. (160.3 x 101.9 cm.)
Collections Fund, 1958.15

John J. H. Phillips (1949–)

1055 *Host*, 1975
Acrylic on canvas
30½ x 110⅛ in. (77.5 x 279.7 cm.)
Signed, dated, and inscribed on back: JJH PHILLIPS 1275 "Host"
Gift of Frederick McBrien, 1977.21

Samuel George Phillips (1890–1965)

1056 *John Frederick Lewis* (1860–1932), 1935
Oil on canvas
35 x 28¹⁵⁄₁₆ in. (88.9 x 73.5 cm.)
Signed and dated at lower right: S. George Phillips./1935
Gift of John Frederick Lewis, Jr., 1935.14

William L. Picknell (1853–1897)

1057 *On the Borders of the Marsh*, 1880
Oil on canvas
79 x 59½ in. (200.7 x 151.1 cm.)
Signed and dated at lower right: Wm. L. Picknell./1880.
Gift of Joseph E. Temple, 1881.2

1058 *Road to Nice*, 1896
Oil on canvas
58¼ x 84¼ in. (148 x 211.4 cm.)
Signed at lower right: Wm L. Picknell
Bequest of Gertrude Flagg, 1906.5

Robert Edge Pine (1730–1788)

1059 *General Henry Lee* (1756–1818), ca. 1784
Oil on canvas
24 x 19½ in. (61 x 49.5 cm.)
Gift of Mrs. John Frederick Lewis (The John Frederick Lewis Memorial Collection), 1933.10.68

Angelo Pinto (1908–)

1060 *Amusement Park*, ca. 1935
Oil on canvas
30 x 50⅛ in. (76.2 x 127.3 cm.)
Signed at lower right: Angelo Pinto
John Lambert Fund, 1936.15

Biagio Pinto (1911–)

1061 *Landscape*, ca. 1931
Oil on canvas
16 x 20 in. (40.6 x 50.8 cm.)
Signed at lower left: Biagio Pinto
John Lambert Fund, 1932.10

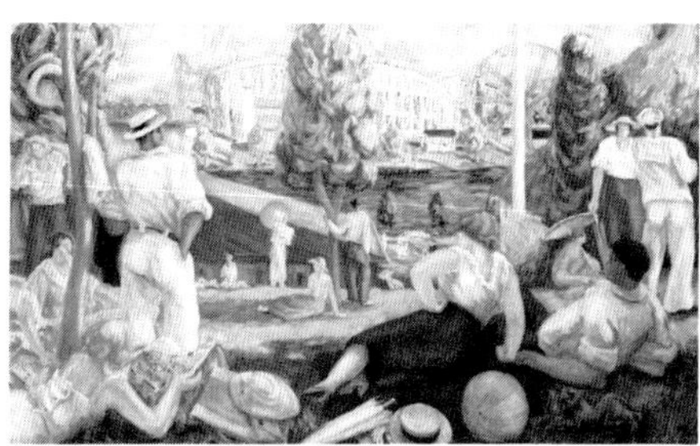
1060

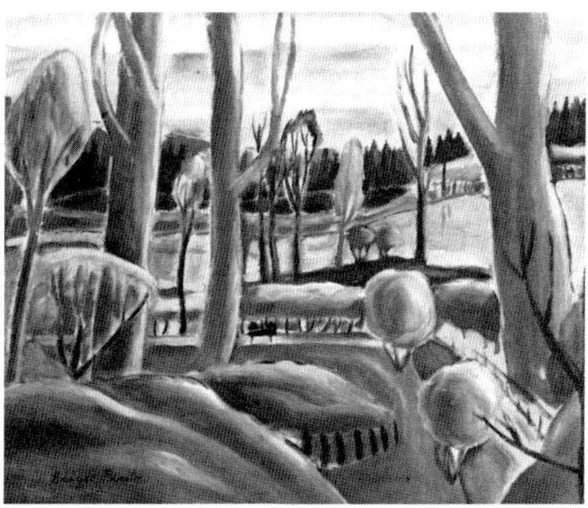
1061

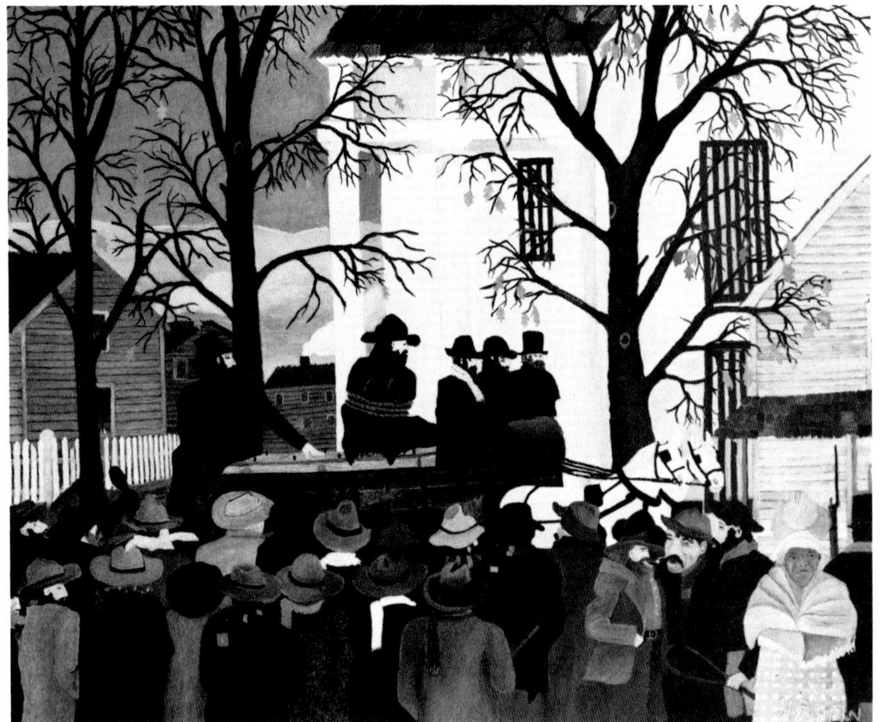

1065

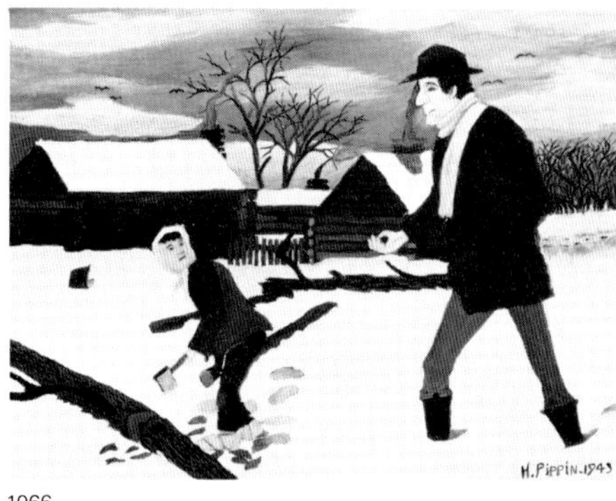

1066

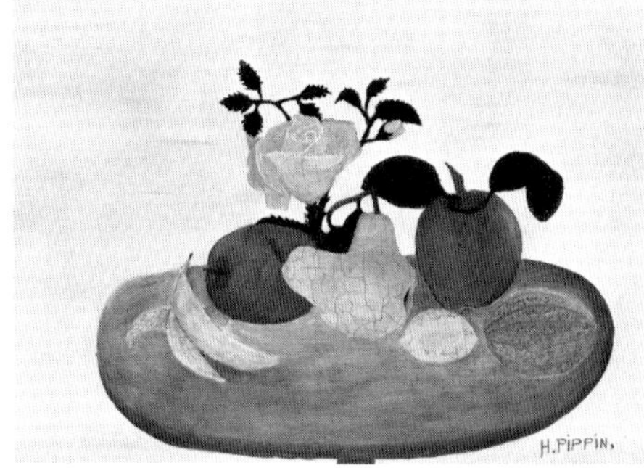

1070

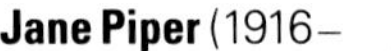

Jane Piper (1916–)

1062 *Flowers toward Landscape*, 1973
Acrylic on canvas
$40\frac{1}{8}$ x 59 in. (101.9 x 149.9 cm.)
Signed at lower right: Jane Piper
Anonymous gift, 1974.33

1063 *Study in Red*, 1953
Oil on masonite
$39\frac{7}{8}$ x 32 in. (101.3 x 81.3 cm.)
Signed at lower right: Jane Piper; and on back: JANE PIPER
John Lambert Fund, 1954.12

Horace Pippin (1888–1946)

1064 *Giant Daffodils*, 1940
Oil on canvas board
$13\frac{15}{16}$ x 10 in. (35.4 x 25.4 cm.)
Signed and dated at lower right: H. PIPPIN./1940
Bequest of David J. Grossman in honor of Mr. and Mrs. Charles S. Grossman and Mr. and Mrs. Meyer Speiser, 1979.1.2

1065 *John Brown Going to His Hanging*, 1942
Oil on canvas
$24\frac{1}{8}$ x $30\frac{1}{4}$ in. (61.3 x 76.8 cm.)
Signed at lower right: H. Pippin
John Lambert Fund, 1943.11

1066 *Abe Lincoln, the Good Samaritan*, 1943
Oil on canvas board
9 x 12 in. (22.9 x 30.5 cm.)
Signed and dated at lower right: H. PIPPIN. 1943
Bequest of David J. Grossman in honor of Mr. and Mrs. Charles S. Grossman and Mr. and Mrs. Meyer Speiser, 1979.1.5

1067 *Maple Sugaring*, 1941
Oil on burnt wood
$6\frac{7}{16}$ x $11\frac{15}{16}$ in. (16.4 x 30.3 cm.)
Signed and dated at lower right: H. PIPPIN;/1941.
Bequest of David J. Grossman in honor of Mr. and Mrs. Charles S. Grossman and Mr. and Mrs. Meyer Speiser, 1979.1.6

1068 *The Moose*, 1945
Oil on canvas
$18\frac{1}{8}$ x $22\frac{13}{16}$ in. (46 x 57.9 cm.)
Dated and signed at lower right: 1945./H.PIPPIN. AUG 26.
Bequest of David J. Grossman in honor of Mr. and Mrs. Charles S. Grossman and Mr. and Mrs. Meyer Speiser, 1979.1.7

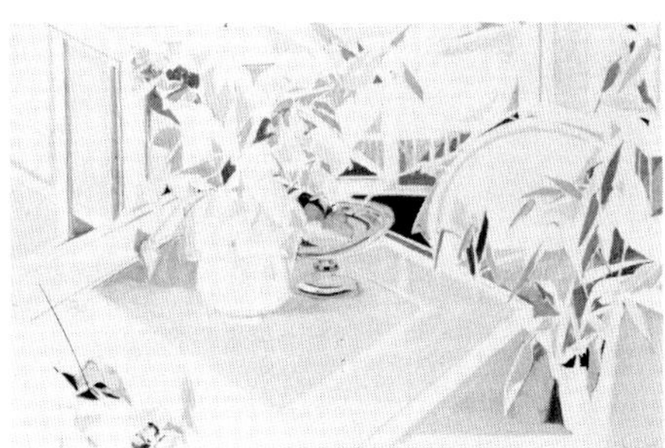

1062

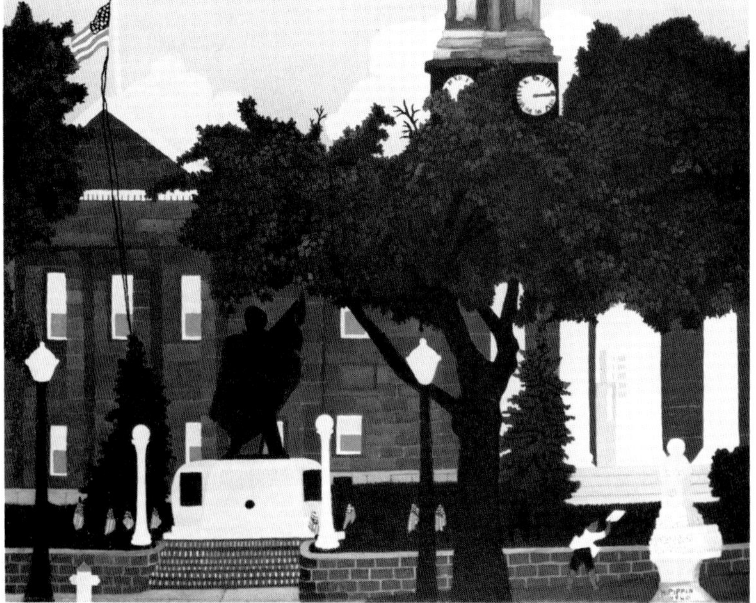

1071

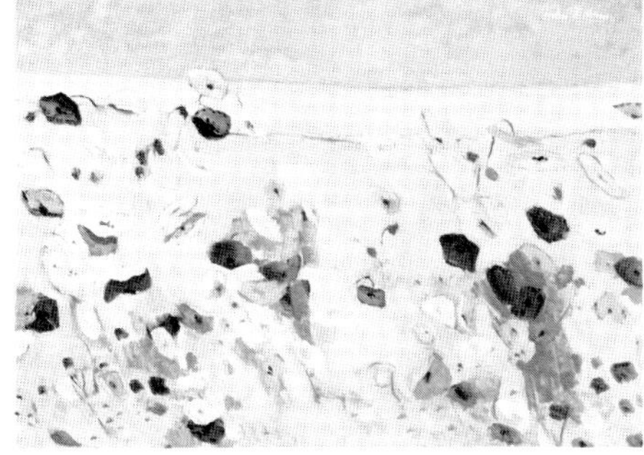
1074

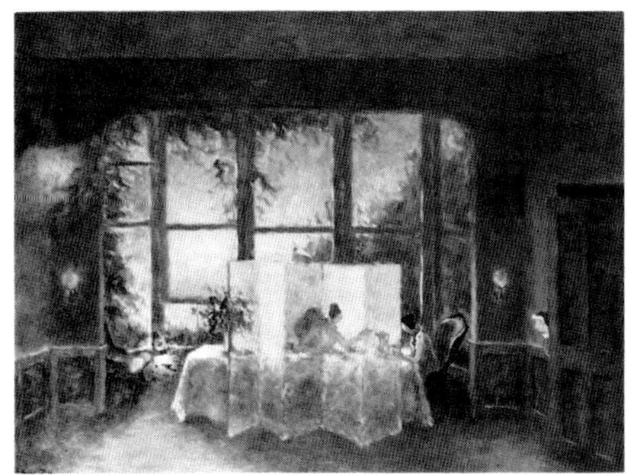
1075

1069 *Pink Cyclamen*, 1941
Oil on canvas board
10 x 14 in. (25.4 x 35.6 cm.)
Signed and dated at lower right: H.PIPPIN./1941
Bequest of David J. Grossman in honor of Mr. and Mrs. Charles S. Grossman and Mr. and Mrs. Meyer Speiser, 1979.1.4

1070 *The Warped Table*, 1940
Oil on canvas board
11 13/16 x 16 in. (30 x 40.6 cm.)
Signed at lower right: H.PIPPIN,
Bequest of David J. Grossman in honor of Mr. and Mrs. Charles S. Grossman and Mr. and Mrs. Meyer Speiser, 1979.1.1

1071 *West Chester Court House*, 1940
Oil on canvas board
22 x 28 in. (55.9 x 71.1 cm.)
Signed and dated at lower right: H. PIPPIN/1940
Bequest of David J. Grossman in honor of Mr. and Mrs. Charles S. Grossman and Mr. and Mrs. Meyer Speiser, 1979.1.3

Hobson Pittman (1899 or 1900–1972)

1072 *Anniversary (The Return)*, 1955
Oil on masonite
30 x 39⅞ in. (76.2 x 101.3 cm.)
Gift of the artist, 1967.1

1073 *Dressing Table and Roses*
Oil on canvas
36 x 48 in. (91.4 x 121.9 cm.)
Signed at upper right: Hobson Pittman
Bequest of the artist, 1972.18.3

1074 *Garden with Poppies*, ca. 1968
Oil on cardboard
29⅜ x 41½ in. (74.6 x 105.4 cm.)
Signed at upper right: Hobson Pittman
Bequest of the artist, 1972.18.5

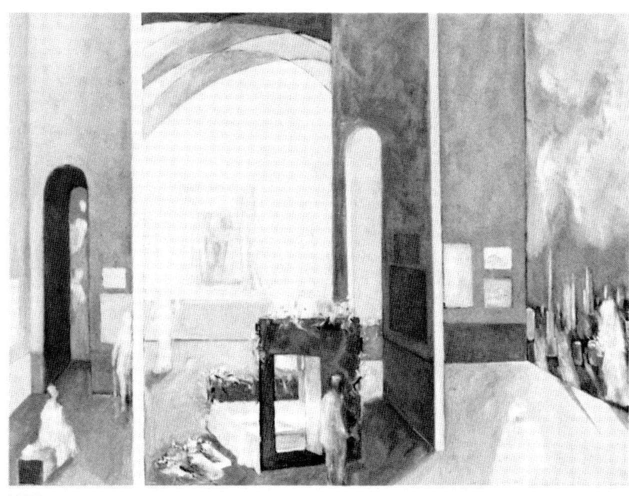
1072

1075 *The Gossips*, 1940–41
Oil on canvas
30⅜ x 40¼ in. (77.2 x 102.2 cm.)
Signed at lower left: Hobson Pittman
Gift of William S. Wassell, 1952.21

1076 *Interior with Three Ladies*
Oil on cardboard
29¾ x 42 in. (75.6 x 106.7 cm.)
Bequest of the artist, 1972.18.8

1077 *Mirror, Mirror, No. 1*
Oil on canvas
54 x 72 in. (137.2 x 182.9 cm.)
Signed and inscribed at upper right: Hobson Pittman/Mirror, Mirror
Bequest of the artist, 1972.18.1

1078 *Mirror, Mirror, No. 2*
Oil on canvas
53¾ x 71¾ in. (136.5 x 182.2 cm.)
Bequest of the artist, 1972.18.2

1079 *Morning Paper, No. 2*, 1952–53
Oil on masonite
13 1/16 x 26⅛ in. (33.2 x 66.4 cm.)
Signed at upper left: Hobson Pittman
John Lambert Fund, 1953.19

1080 *Narcissus and Seashells*
Oil on cardboard
30 x 42 in. (76.2 x 106.7 cm.)
Signed at upper left: Hobson Pittman
Bequest of the artist, 1972.18.6

1081 *Pansies in a White Vase*
Oil on masonite
13½ x 14 in. (34.3 x 35.6 cm.)
Signed at lower right: Hobson Pittman
Bequest of the artist, 1972.18.12

1082 *Poppies on a Windowsill*
Oil on cardboard
42 x 29¾ in. (106.7 x 75.6 cm.)
Signed at upper left: Hobson Pittman
Bequest of the artist, 1972.18.7

1083 *Reflected Interior*, probably 1954
Oil on canvas
30½ x 40 in. (77.5 x 101.6 cm.)
Signed at upper right: Hobson Pittman
Gift of James P. and Ruth Marshall Magill, 1957.15.27

1084 *Roses in a Green Vase*
Oil on masonite
13 15/16 x 15 in. (35.4 x 38.1 cm.)
Signed at upper left: Hobson Pittman
Bequest of the artist, 1972.18.11

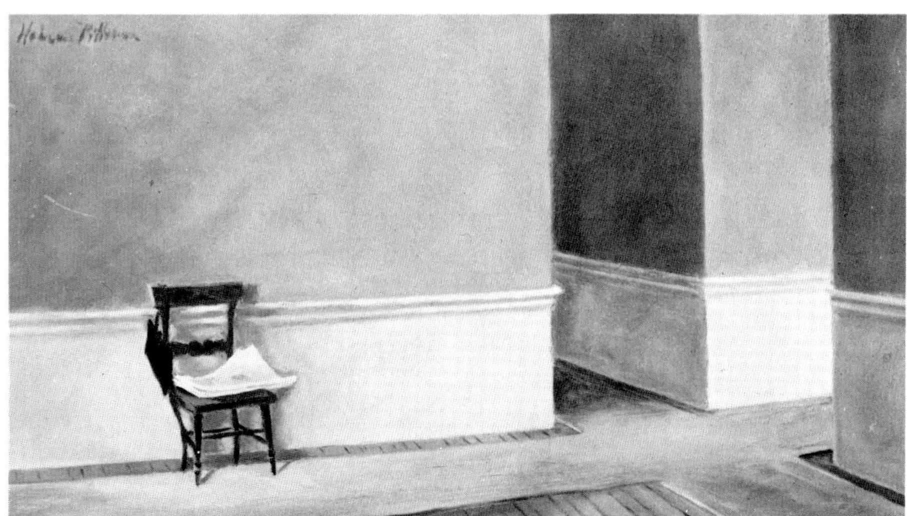
1079

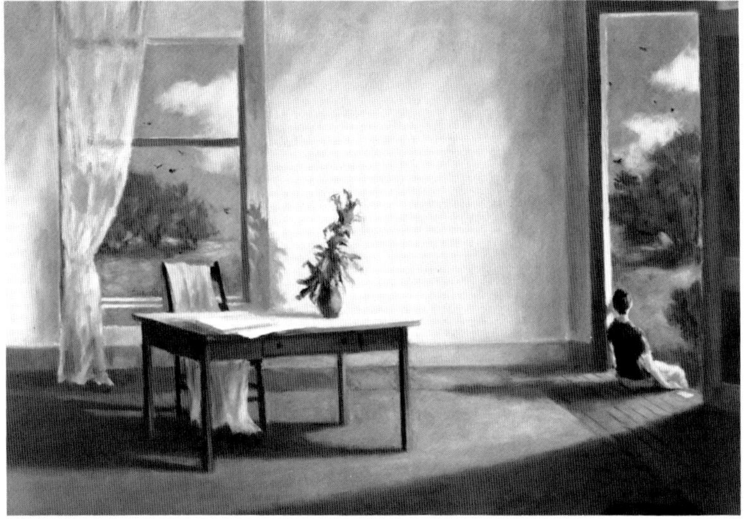

1086

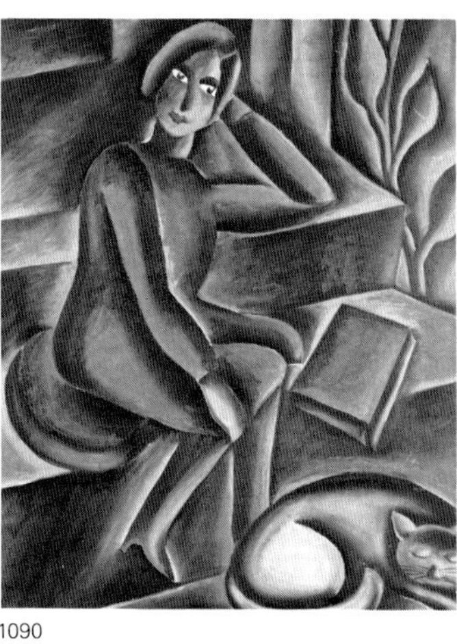

1090

1085 *The Solarium*
Oil on masonite
20 x 11 9/16 in. (50.8 x 29.4 cm.)
Signed at lower left: Hobson Pittman
Bequest of Elizabeth Dewan Reese, 1974.26

1086 *The Spinster*, ca. 1938
Oil on canvas
19 5/16 x 27 3/8 in. (49.1 x 69.5 cm.)
Signed at lower right: Hobson Pittman
Henry D. Gilpin Fund, 1939.12

1087 *Study for "The Pool,"* ca. 1965
Oil on cardboard
33 15/16 x 43 15/16 in. (86.2 x 111.6 cm.)
Signed at upper left: Hobson Pittman
Bequest of the artist, 1972.18.4

1088 *Two Vases of Roses and Seashells*
Oil on cardboard
29 15/16 x 42 1/8 in. (76 x 107 cm.)
Bequest of the artist, 1972.18.9

1089 *White Lady with Screens*
Oil on cardboard
29 7/8 x 42 in. (75.9 x 106.7 cm.)
Bequest of the artist, 1972.18.10

1090 *Woman with Cat*, 1923
Oil on canvas
20 1/8 x 16 1/4 in. (51.1 x 41.3 cm.)
Signed at upper left: Pittman
Gift of the artist, 1960.17

Henry C. Pitz (1895–1976)

1091 *Dress Rehearsal Interlude*, by 1963
Oil and acrylic on canvas
30 1/16 x 40 1/16 in. (76.4 x 101.8 cm.)
Signed at lower right: Henry C Pitz
Gift of Clarence Morris, 1963.2

Eleanor Plaisted
See Eleanor Plaisted Abbott.

Charles Peale Polk (1767–1822)

1092 *Jean Baptiste Donatien de Vimeur, Comte de Rochambeau* (1725–1807), 1783
(after Charles Willson Peale, 1782)
Oil on paper, mounted on canvas
25 x 19 in. (63.5 x 48.3 cm.), oval
Annotated on lined canvas on back: Rochambeau/Pinxt/Peale Polk/1778./COPIED FROM BACK/OF THE ORIGINAL.
Gift of Mrs. John Frederick Lewis (The John Frederick Lewis Memorial Collection), 1933.10.69

1093 *George Washington* (1732–1799), 1783
(after Charles Willson Peale, 1782)
Oil on paper, mounted on canvas
20 3/4 x 16 1/4 in. (52.7 x 41.3 cm.), oval
Signed and dated on back: Charles/Polk - pinxt/ May 1783–

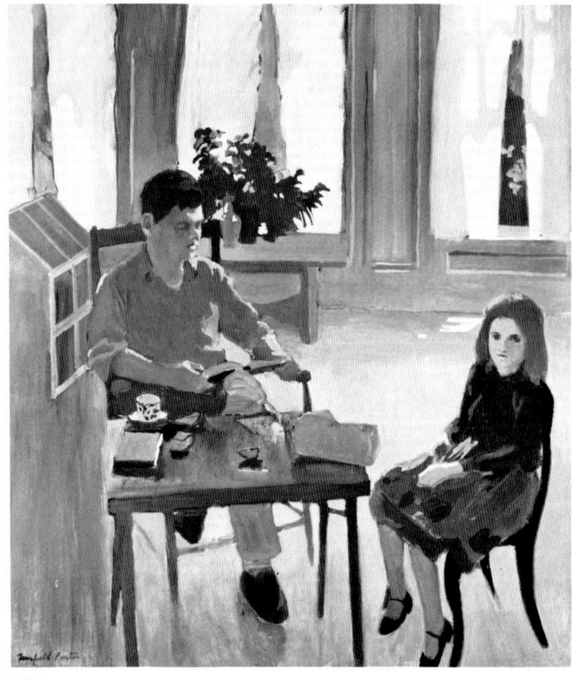

1097

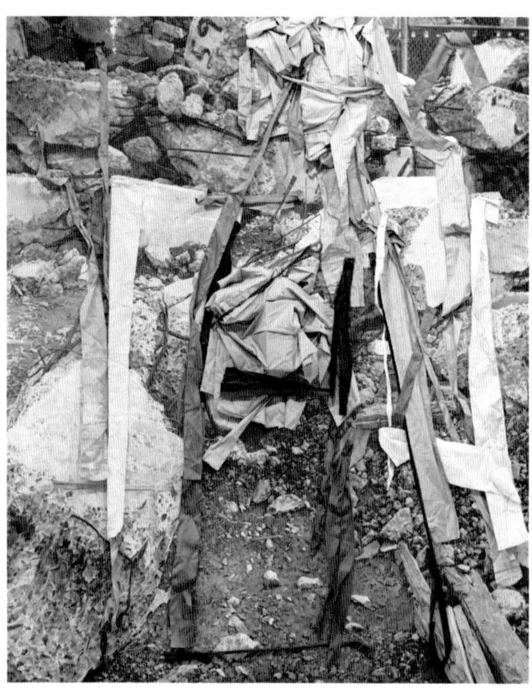

1100

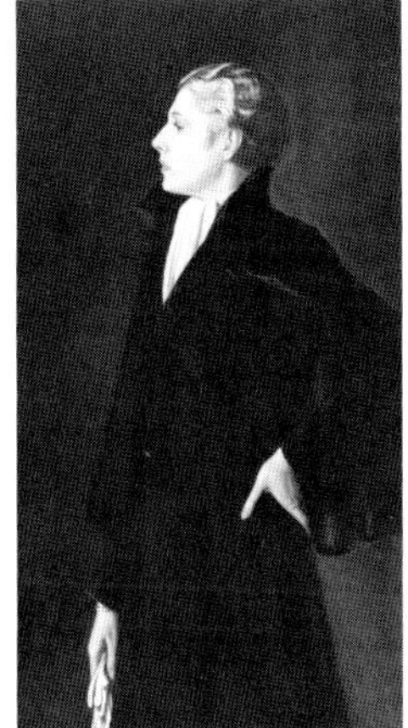
1094

1101

Gift of Mrs. John Frederick Lewis (The John Frederick Lewis Memorial Collection), 1933.10.70

Abram Poole (1883–1961)

1094 *Greta Kemble Cooper*, ca. 1929
Oil on canvas
47¼ x 26⅛ in. (120 x 66.4 cm.)
Signed and inscribed on back: A Poole/134 E. 47/ N.Y.C./"Greta Kemble Cooper"
Joseph E. Temple Fund, 1930.4

Henry Varnum Poor (1888–1970)

1095 *Still Life—Grape Leaves*, ca. 1943
Oil on canvas
20 x 29 15/16 in. (50.8 x 76 cm.)
Signed at lower left: HVPoor
Joseph E. Temple Fund, 1944.5

Doris Lucile Porter (Mrs. Donald J. McLean, b. 1898)

1096 *Still Life*, ca. 1932
Oil on canvas
22 x 24 in. (55.9 x 61 cm.)
John Lambert Fund, 1933.5

Fairfield Porter (1907–1975)

1097 *Jimmy and Liz* (James Schuyler and Elizabeth Porter), ca. 1963
Oil on canvas
45 x 40⅛ in. (114.3 x 101.9 cm.)
Signed at lower left: Fairfield Porter
Inscribed, dated, and signed on stretcher (partially erased): Blue Spruce oil/Jimmy & Liz 45" x 40" oil/about/1963 ? Fairfield Porter
Henry D. Gilpin Fund, 1980.15

1098 *Under the Elms*, 1971–72
Oil on canvas
62 5/16 x 46¼ in. (158.3 x 117.5 cm.)
Signed and dated twice, at lower right: Fairfield Porter 71–72
Inscribed, dated, and signed on stretcher: 62" x 46" Under the Elms-oil-1972 [written over "1"]-Fairfield Porter
Gift of Mrs. Fairfield Porter, 1981.15

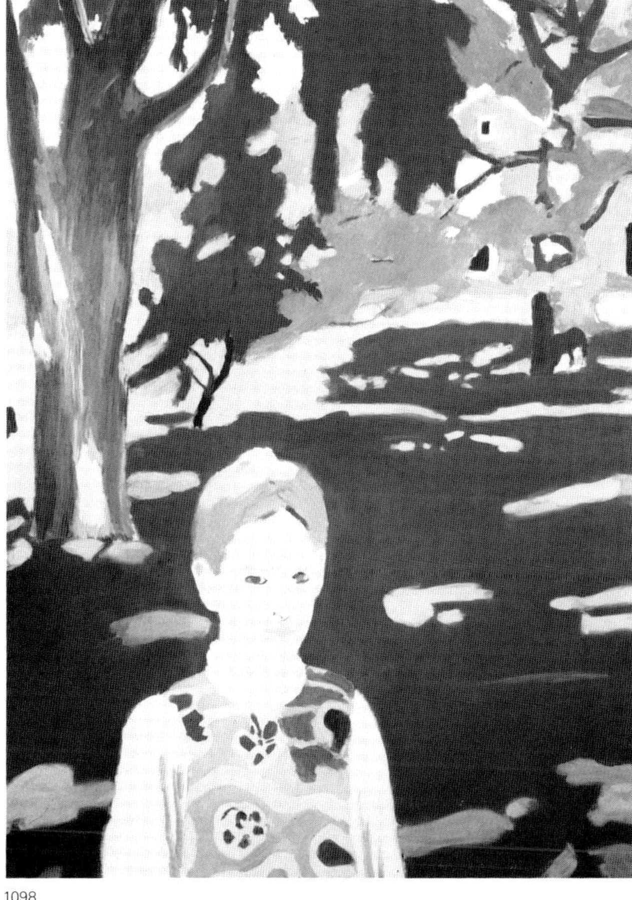
1098

Katherine Porter (1941–)

1099 *Shipwreck in the Stars*, 1984
Oil on linen, mounted on wood
39 x 81 in. (99.1 x 205.7 cm.)
Anonymous fund and the Pennsylvania Academy Art Fund, 1984.32

Stephen Posen (1939–)

1100 *Variations on a Millstone*, 1976
Oil on canvas
86⅜ x 68⅛ in. (219.4 x 173 cm.)
Signed and dated at lower right: © S.P. 1976; and on back: ©1976/STEPHEN/POSEN/Stephen/ Posen

Funds provided by the National Endowment for the Arts, Charles E. Merrill Trust, and Crag Burn Fund, 1976.14.1

May Audubon Post (d. 1929)

1101 *Old Fisherman and His Grandson*
Oil on canvas
39 11/16 x 28 15/16 in. (100.8 x 73.7 cm.)
Signed at lower right: MAPost; and on back: May A Post
Gift of the Fellowship of the Pennsylvania Academy, 1931.8

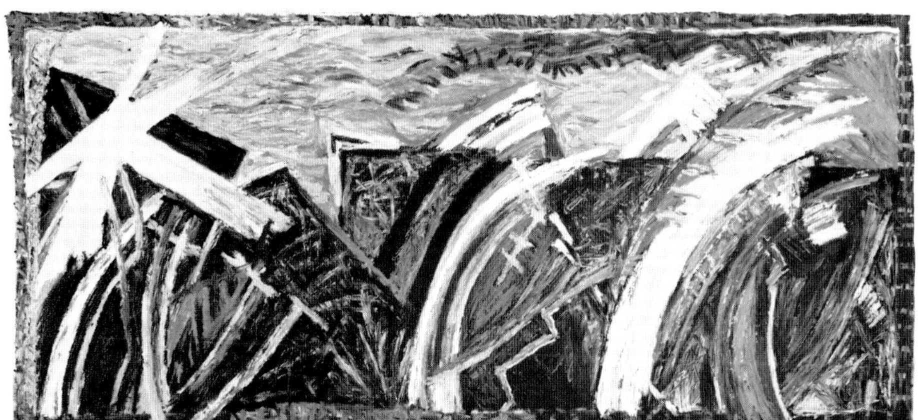
1099

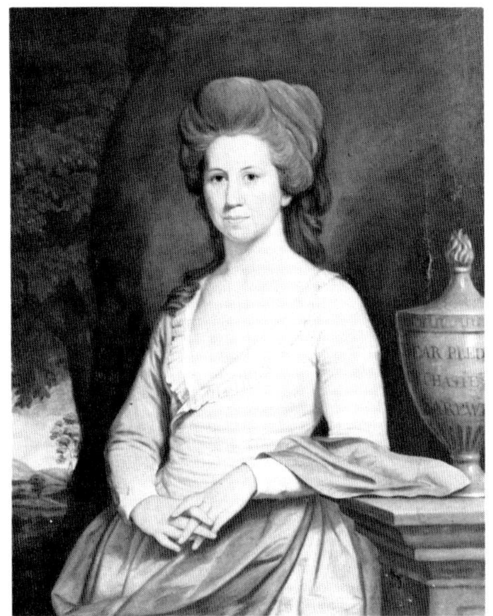
1103

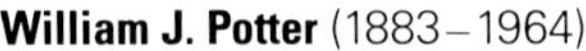

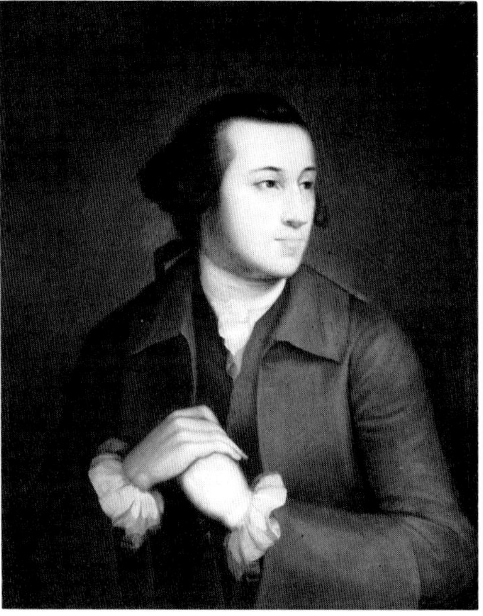
1104

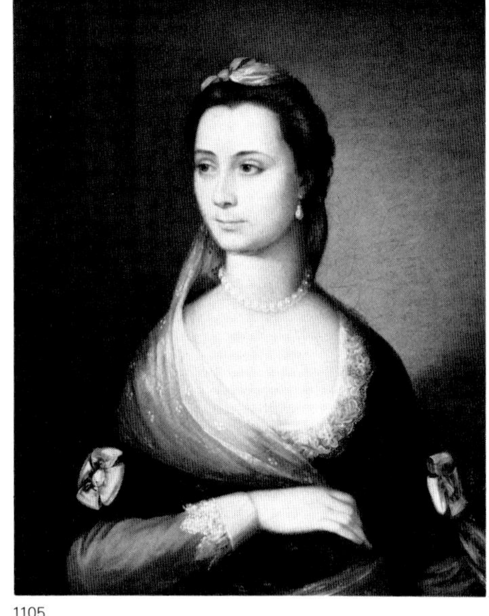
1105

William J. Potter (1883–1964)

1102 *Flowers in Blue Jug*, 1964
Oil on canvas
$24\frac{1}{16}$ x $20\frac{1}{16}$ in. (61.1 x 51 cm.)
Signed at lower right: WJPOTTER
Gift of Mrs. William J. Potter, 1965.6

Matthew Pratt (1734–1805)

1103 *Mrs. Samuel Powel* (née Elizabeth Willing, 1742–1830), ca. 1793
Oil on canvas
$39\frac{3}{16}$ x $32\frac{1}{16}$ in. (99.5 x 81.4 cm.)
Henry D. Gilpin Fund, 1912.12

1104 *Benjamin West* (1738–1820), 1765
Oil on canvas
$30\frac{1}{4}$ x $25\frac{1}{8}$ in. (76.8 x 63.8 cm.)
Gift of Mrs. Rosalie V. Tiers Jackson, 1892.3.1

1105 *Mrs. Benjamin West* (née Elizabeth Shewell, 1741–1814), ca. 1765
Oil on canvas
$30\frac{3}{16}$ x $25\frac{1}{4}$ in. (76.7 x 64.1 cm.)
Gift of Mrs. Rosalie V. Tiers Jackson, 1892.3.2

Charles Prendergast (1863–1948)

1106 *North Shore*, 1939
Oil and graphite on gessoed masonite
26 x 28 in. (66 x 71.1 cm.)
Signed and dated at lower right: C Prendergast 1939 [incised in paint]
Gift of Margot Newman Stickley in memory of her parents, Philip and Helene S. Newman, 1987.18.4

Maurice B. Prendergast (1858–1924)

1107 *Bathers in a Cove*, 1916
Oil on canvas
$20\frac{3}{8}$ x $26\frac{1}{2}$ in. (51.8 x 67.3 cm.)
Signed at lower left: Prendergast
John S. Phillips bequest, by exchange (acquired from the Philadelphia Museum of Art), 1985.18

Esther Estelle Pressoir (b. 1906)

1108 *Still Life*, ca. 1926
Oil on composition board
$23\frac{3}{4}$ x $19\frac{5}{8}$ in. (60.3 x 49.8 cm.)
Signed at lower left: ESTHER PRESSOIR
John Lambert Fund, 1927.6

Sara Provan (b. 1917)

1109 *Delicacies*, 1949–50
Oil on canvas
$18\frac{3}{16}$ x $17\frac{3}{4}$ in. (46.2 x 45.1 cm.)
Signed at lower right and twice on back: Provan
John Lambert Fund, 1952.10

Cora Gibson Purviance (1904–1967)

1110 *The China Cup*, ca. 1941
Oil on canvas
$26\frac{1}{16}$ x $21\frac{3}{4}$ in. (66.2 x 55.2 cm.)
Signed at lower right: Purviance
John Lambert Fund, 1942.8

Leo Quanchi (1892–1974)

1111 *World Poem*, 1952
Oil and casein on canvas
$12\frac{1}{8}$ x $28\frac{1}{16}$ in. (30.8 x 71.3 cm.)

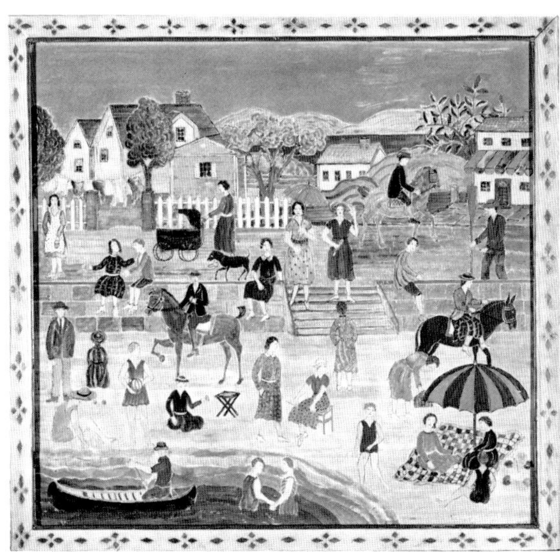
1106

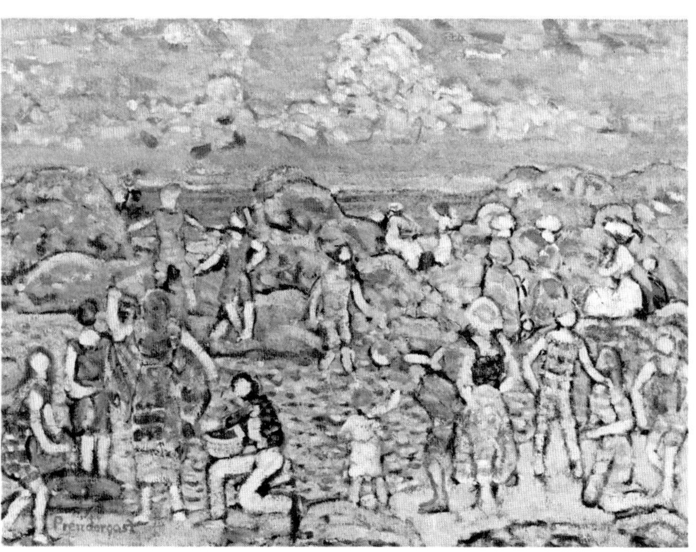

1107

Signed at lower right: Quanchi
John Lambert Fund, 1953.5

Edmund Quincy (1903–)

1112 *Sargeant Street*, ca. 1936
Oil on linen
19 11/16 x 24 in. (50 x 61 cm.)
Signed at lower left: Quincy
John Lambert Fund, 1937.6

Lazar Raditz (1887–1958)

1113 *Self-Portrait*, 1910
Oil on canvas
30 3/8 x 25 5/16 in. (77.2 x 64.3 cm.)
Signed and dated at upper left: Lazar Raditz/1910
Gift of the artist, 1918.13

Steve Raffo (1912–)

1114 *La Casa de Dios*, 1947
Oil on canvas, mounted on masonite
28 x 38 in. (71.1 x 96.5 cm.)
Signed at lower right: Raffo; dated on canvas folded over masonite: 5/47–8/47
Inscribed and signed on labels on frame: Title:/ LA CASA DE DIOS Steve RAFFO
John Lambert Fund, 1948.9

Henry Ashbury Rand (1886–1961)

1115 *Snow Shadows*, 1914
Oil on canvas
19 15/16 x 24 in. (50.6 x 61 cm.)
Signed and dated at lower right: Henry A Rand 1914
John Lambert Fund, 1915.5

Henry Ward Ranger (1858–1916)

1116 *Near Noank*, 1903
Oil on wood
11 13/16 x 16 in. (30 x 40.6 cm.)
Signed and dated at lower left: H W Ranger/1903
Gift of Seymour Adelman, 1955.14

1117 *Sheep Pasture*, 1900
Oil on canvas
28 1/8 x 36 in. (71.4 x 91.4 cm.)
Signed and dated at lower left: H W Ranger 1900.
Joseph E. Temple Fund, 1901.2

Kathryn K. Rank

1118 *Applebutter Time*, 1949
Oil on canvas
21 7/8 x 15 15/16 in. (55.6 x 40.5 cm.)
Signed at lower left: KATHRYN K. RANK; inscribed, signed, and dated on back: "APPLEBUTTER TIME" by Kathryn K. Rank. 1949
John Lambert Fund, 1950.13

Abraham Rattner (1895–1978)

1119 *The French Flag*, ca. 1928
Oil on canvas
32 x 25 11/16 in. (81.3 x 65.2 cm.)
John Lambert Fund, 1929.4

1120 *Kiosk*, 1944
Oil on canvas
39 1/8 x 31 3/4 in. (99.4 x 80.6 cm.)
Signed at lower right: Rattner
Gift of Benjamin Tepper, 1953.23

1121 *The Round Table*, 1945
Oil on canvas
32 1/16 x 25 11/16 in. (81.4 x 65.2 cm.)
Signed at lower left: Rattner; and on back: AR
Joseph E. Temple Fund, 1946.10

Thomas Buchanan Read (1822–1872)

1122 *The Flight of the Arrow*, 1868
Oil on canvas
36 x 27 3/4 in. (91.4 x 70.5 cm.)
Signed, inscribed, and dated at lower right: T.Buchanan Read/Rome 1868; inscribed, signed, and dated on back (before lining): The Flight of the Arrow/painted by T. Buchanan Read/Rome 1868.
Gift of the children of A. D. Jessup, 1881.3

1123 *Joseph Harrison, Jr.* (1810–1874), 1860
Oil on canvas
51 x 41 1/4 in. (129.5 x 104.8 cm.)
Signed and dated at lower right: T.Buchanan Read/1860
Gift of Leland Harrison, 1953.11.1

Walter Redding (1902–1972)

1124 *Painting Table #1*, 1955
Oil on canvas
33 15/16 x 24 1/16 in. (86.2 x 61.1 cm.)
Signed at lower left: Redding; signed and inscribed on back: WALTER REDDING/PAINTING TABLE #1
Gift of Benjamin D. Bernstein, 1959.10.4

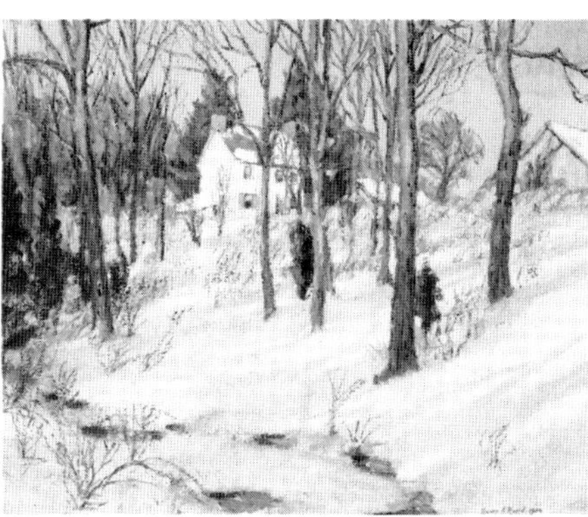
1115

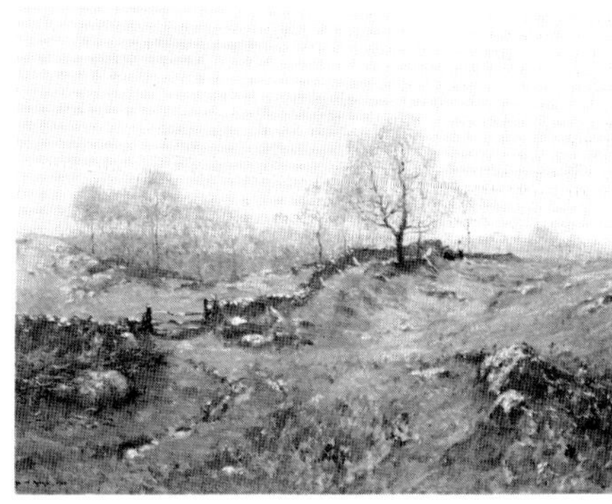
1117

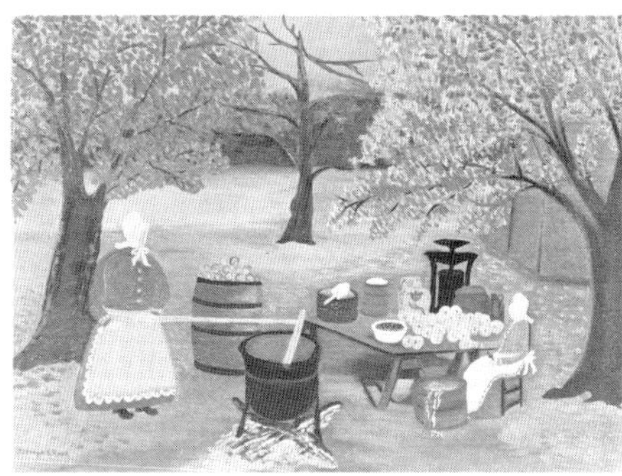
1118

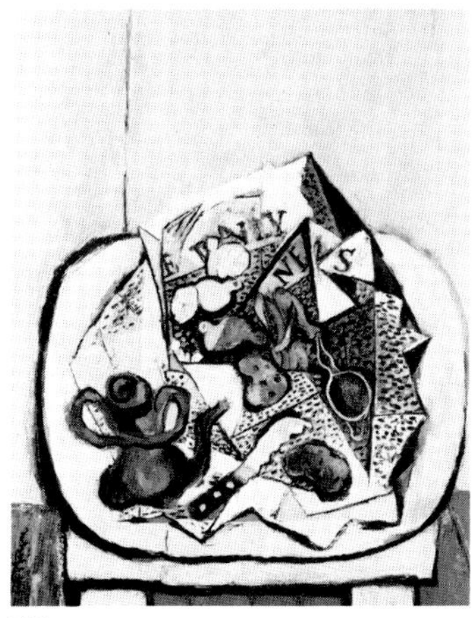
1121

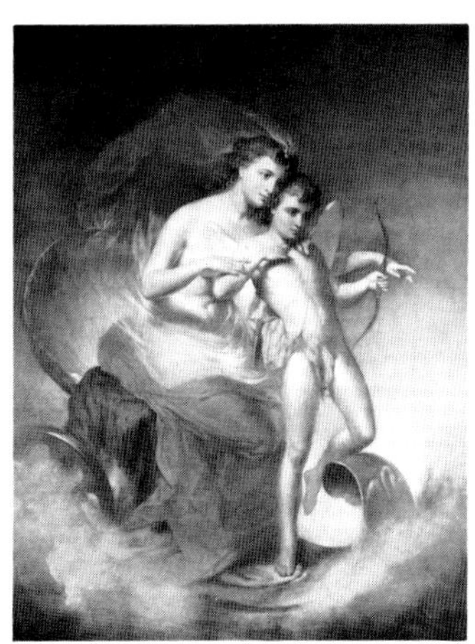
1122

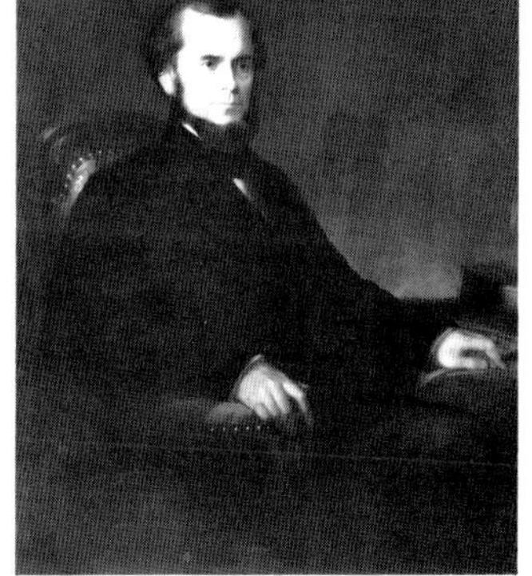
1123

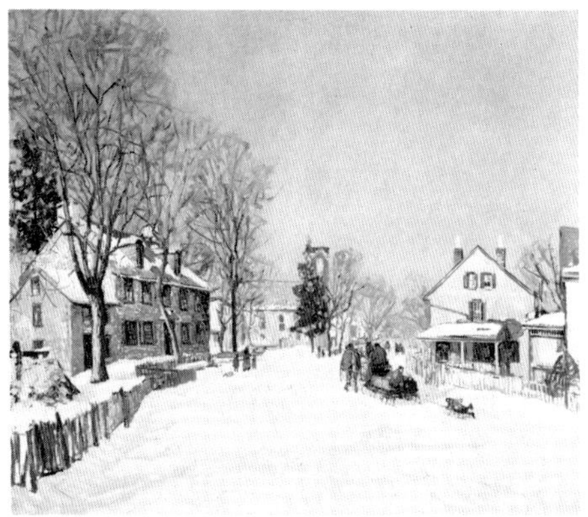
1125

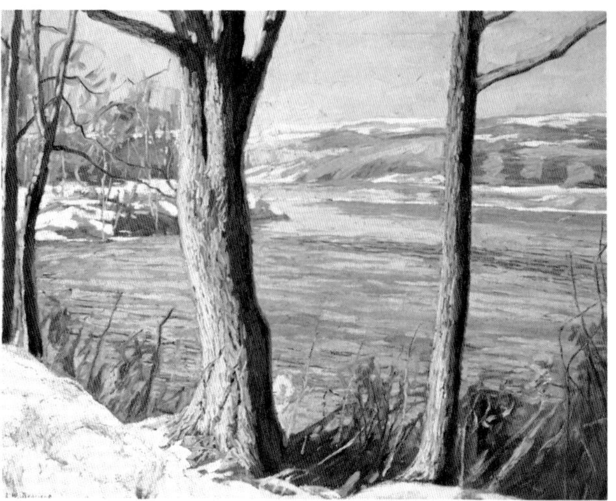
1126

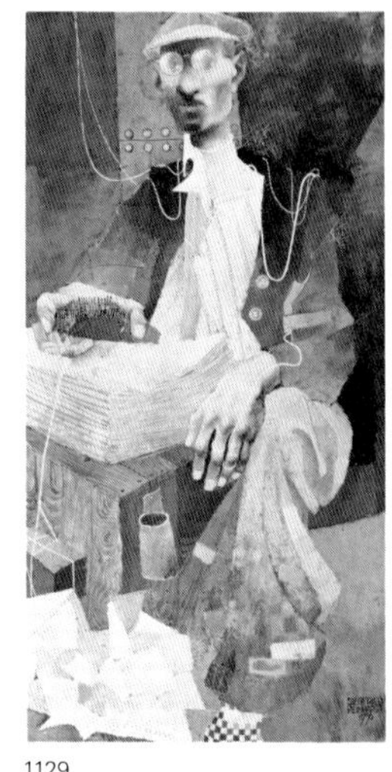
1129

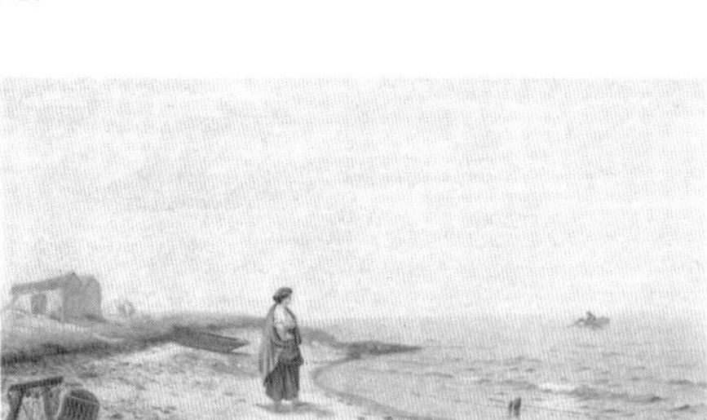
1127

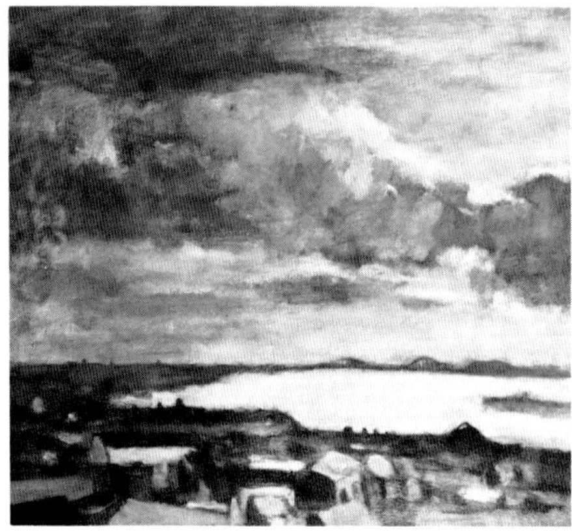
1130

Edward W. Redfield (1869–1965)

1125 *New Hope*, ca. 1926
Oil on canvas
50⅛ x 56⅛ in. (127.3 x 142.6 cm.)
Signed at lower left: EW.REDFIELD
Joseph E. Temple Fund, 1927.7

1126 *The Old Elm*, 1906
Oil on canvas
32¼ x 40⅜ in. (81.9 x 102.6 cm.)
Signed and dated at lower left: E W Redfield/ 1906
Joseph E. Temple Fund, 1907.2

Frank K. M. Rehn (1848–1914)

1127 *A Scene on the Jersey Coast*, 1881
Oil on canvas
20¼ x 36 in. (51.4 x 91.4 cm.)
Signed and dated at lower right: F.K.M.Rehn 1881
Given in memory of Thomas de Quartel Richardson and Agnes A. C. Richardson by their children, 1935.15

John William Reilly (1929–1968)

1128 *Antique Shops, Pine Street, Philadelphia*, by 1957
Oil on canvas
28 x 39$^{15}/_{16}$ in. (71.1 x 101.4 cm.)
Gift of James P. and Ruth Marshall Magill, 1957.15.29

Siegfried Gerhard Reinhardt (b. 1925)

1129 *The Newsboy* (formerly *Newsman*), 1950
Encaustic on masonite
27$^{13}/_{16}$ x 15¾ in. (70.6 x 40 cm.)
Signed and dated at lower right: SIEGFRIED/ REINHARDT/1950
Annotated on frame: "The News Boy"
Gift of Dr. and Mrs. Matthew T. Moore in memory of Julius Bloch, 1966.13

Seymour Remenick (1923–)

1130 *Delaware River from Bridge*, 1953
Oil on canvas
19$^{15}/_{16}$ x 22 in. (50.6 x 55.9 cm.)
Signed at lower center: REMENICK
Gift of Benjamin D. Bernstein, 1959.10.3

William Trost Richards (1833–1905)

1131 *The Beach at Tenby, Wales*, ca. 1885
Oil on canvas
35$^{1}/_{16}$ x 26$^{3}/_{16}$ in. (89.1 x 66.5 cm.)
Signed at lower right: Wm. T. Richards.
Gift of Dr. Bernard J. Ronis, 1979.14

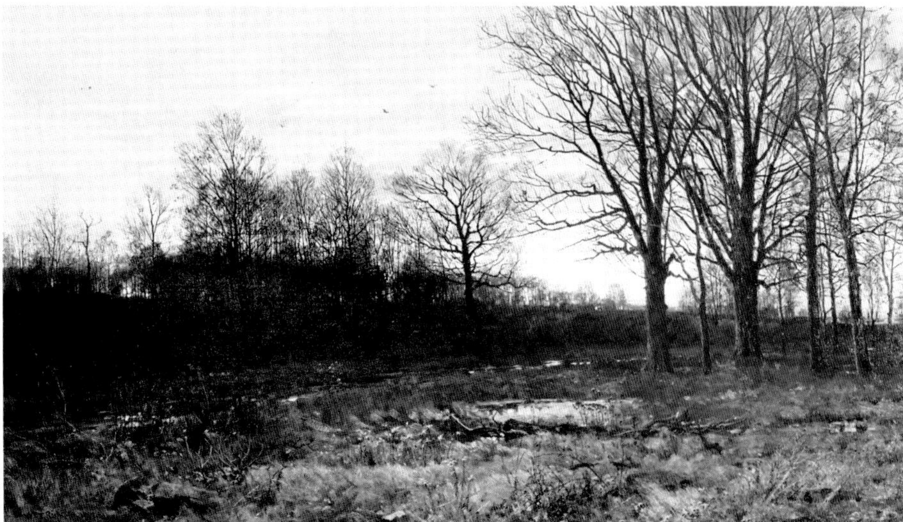
1133

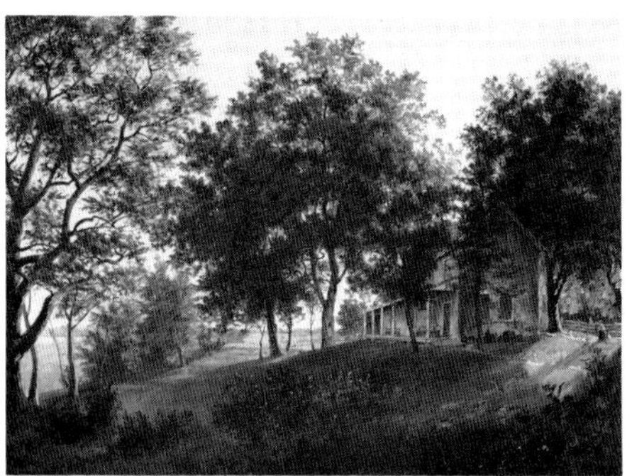
1138

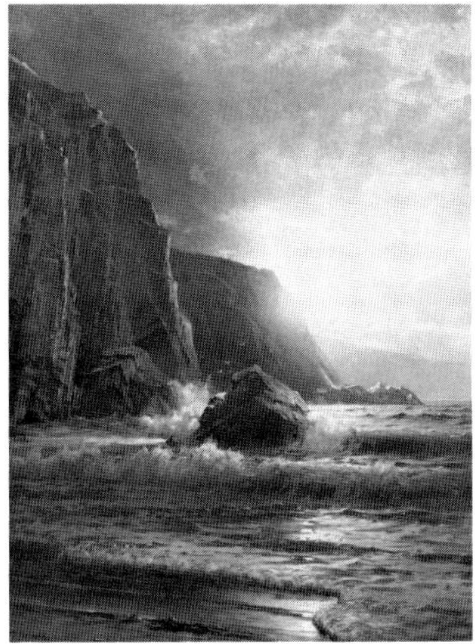
1131

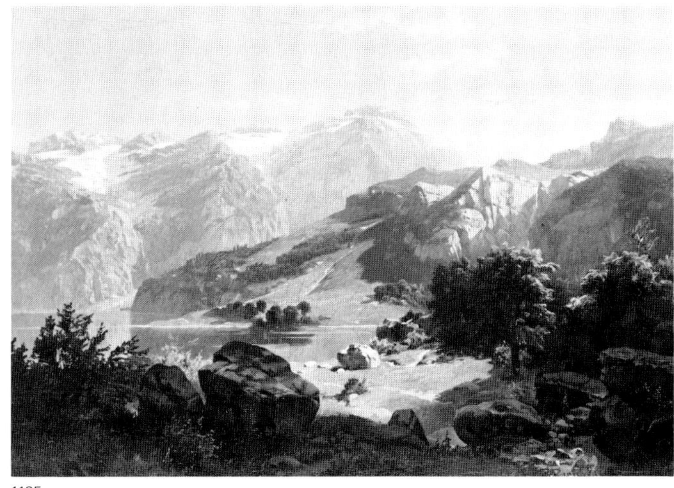
1135

1132 *The Bell Buoy, Newport, Rhode Island*, 1891
Oil on canvas
40 7/16 x 72 1/4 in. (102.7 x 183.5 cm.)
Signed and dated at lower left: Wm. T. Richards. 91.
Joseph E. Temple Fund, 1891.9

1133 *February*, 1887
Oil on canvas, mounted on wood
40 1/4 x 72 in. (102.2 x 182.9 cm.)
Signed and dated at lower left: Wm T. Richards. 1887.
Gift of Mrs. Edward H. Coates (The Edward H. Coates Memorial Collection), 1923.9.5

1134 *Horsehead, Conanicut Island* (sketch)
Oil on canvas board
10 x 19 15/16 in. (25.4 x 50.6 cm.)
Source unknown, 1954.2.1

1135 *A Mountain Lake*, ca. 1855
Oil on canvas
17 x 12 1/8 in. (43.2 x 30.8 cm.)
Signed and inscribed at lower right: Wm T. Richards Phila
Gift of Mr. and Mrs. Evan Randolph, 1974.31

1136 *Old Ocean's Gray and Melancholy Waste*, 1885
Oil on canvas
40 3/4 x 72 1/4 in. (103.5 x 183.5 cm.)
Signed and dated at lower right: Wm.T.Richards. 1885.
Gift of Mrs. Edward H. Coates (The Edward H. Coates Memorial Collection), 1923.9.6

1137 *Orkney Islands* (sketch), ca. 1892
Oil on cardboard
9 3/4 x 15 3/4 in. (24.8 x 40 cm.)
Source unknown, 1954.2.2

1138 *Paschall Homestead at Gibson's Point, Philadelphia*, 1857
Oil on canvas
18 1/4 x 24 3/8 in. (46.4 x 61.9 cm.)
Signed at lower left: WM. T. RICHARDS-; inscribed and dated at lower right: PHIL. 1857
Gift of Ann Paschall, 1931.11

1139 *Seacoast*, 1900
Oil on canvas
20 x 30 in. (50.8 x 76.2 cm.)
Signed and dated at lower left: Wm. T. Richards. 1900
Gift of Mr. and Mrs. Morris L. Weisberg, 1986.50.4

1140 *Shipwreck*, 1872
Oil on canvas
24 x 42 in. (61 x 106.7 cm.)
Signed and dated at lower right: Wm. T. Richards, 1872
Annotated on original panel in stretcher: Sept. 2nd 1870 Atlantic City. N. J., William T. Richards Phila., Feby. 1872
Gift of Henry R. Pemberton, 1961.2

1141 *Sunset* (sketch)
Oil on canvas
10 1/4 x 18 1/8 in. (26 x 46 cm.)
Source unknown, 1954.2.3

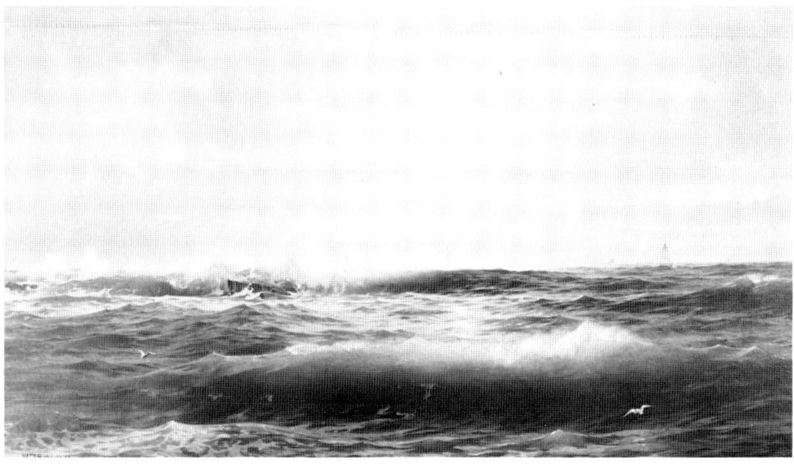
1132

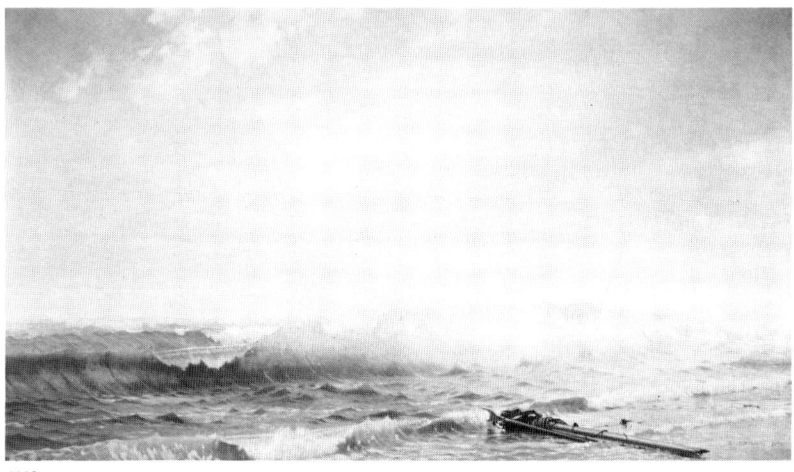
1140

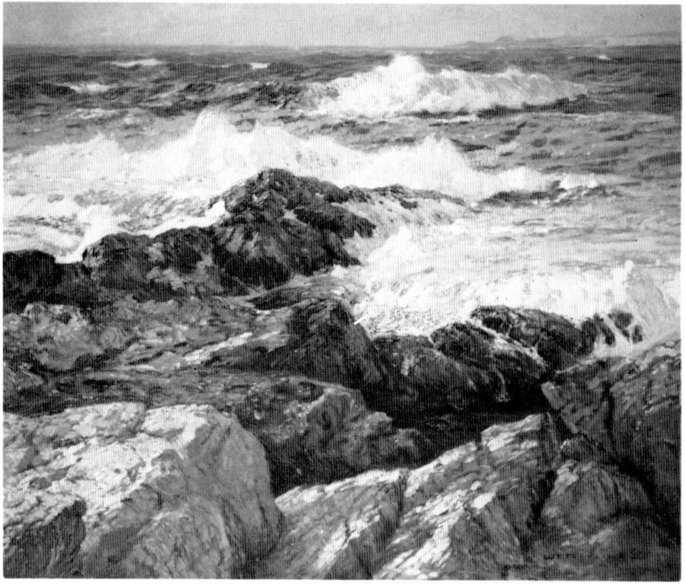
1144

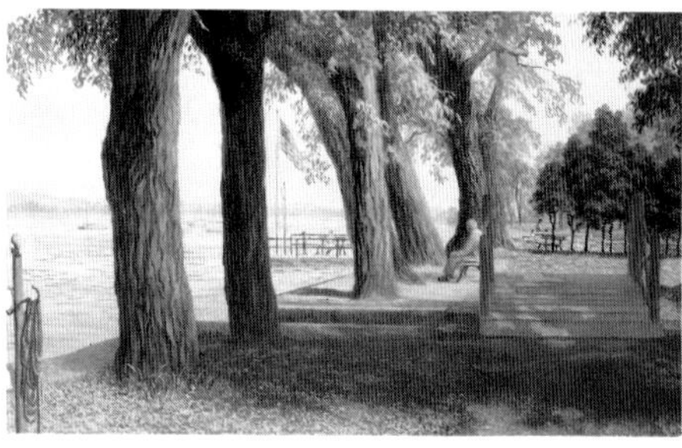
1142

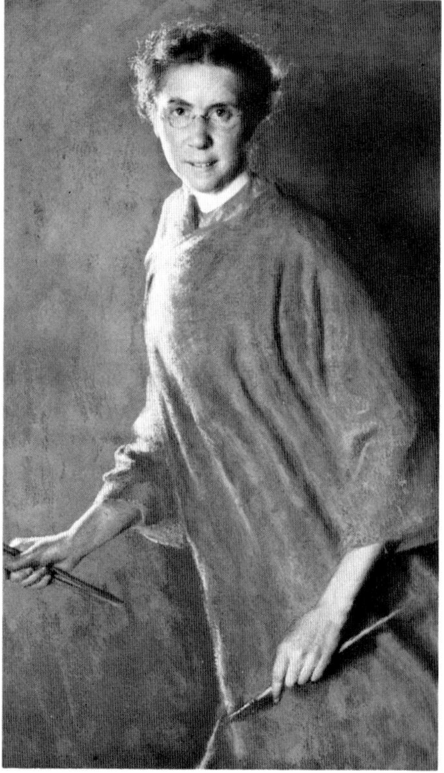
1143

Constance Coleman Richardson
(Mrs. Edgar P. Richardson, 1905–)

1142 *Fourth of July*, 1944
Oil on gessoed masonite
$14\frac{1}{16}$ x $22\frac{1}{16}$ in. (35.7 x 56 cm.)
Signed and dated at lower left: C. C RICHARDSON/ 1944; inscribed and signed on back: The Fourth of July/Constance Richardson
John Lambert Fund, 1945.10

Margaret Foster Richardson (1881–ca. 1945)

1143 *A Motion Picture* (self-portrait), 1912
Oil on canvas
$40\frac{3}{8}$ x $23\frac{1}{8}$ in. (102.6 x 58.7 cm.)
Signed and dated on back: Margaret F./ Richardson/1912
Henry D. Gilpin Fund, 1913.13

Alice Riddle. *See* Alice Riddle Kindler.

William Ritschel (1864–1949)

1144 *Rocks and Breakers, California*, 1913
Oil on canvas
50 x $60\frac{3}{16}$ in. (127 x 152.9 cm.)
Signed and dated at lower right: Wm RITSCHEL/ 1913.
Joseph E. Temple Fund, 1914.10

Alice T. Roberts (1876–1955)

1145 *Fruit and Flowers*
Oil on canvas
$29\frac{15}{16}$ x $29\frac{15}{16}$ in. (76 x 76 cm.)
Signed at lower right: A.T.ROBERTS.
Gift of George B. Roberts, 1955.10.1

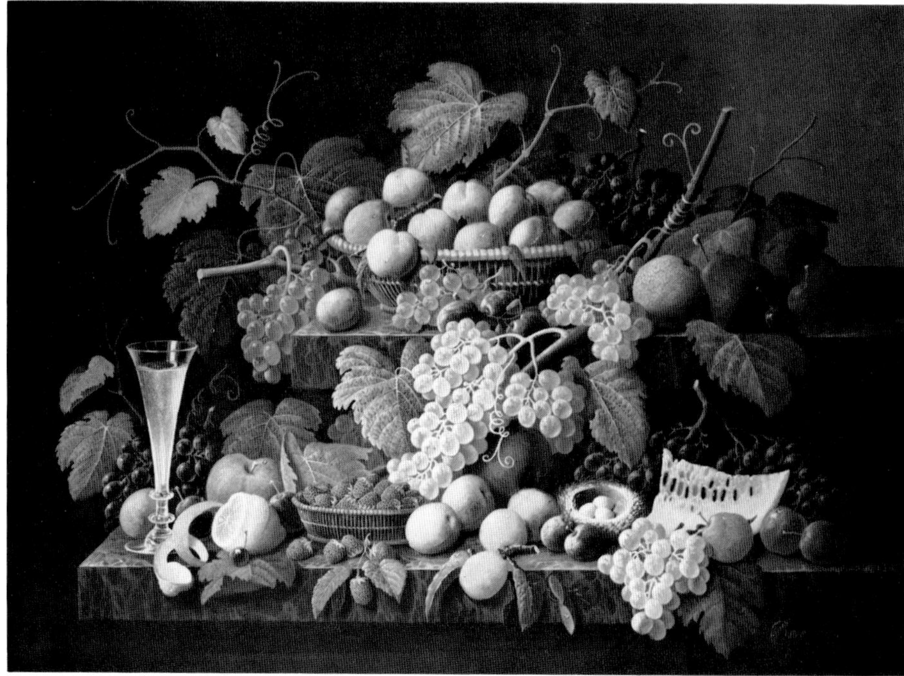

1151

1146 *Henry McCarter* (1864–1942), ca. 1930
Oil on canvas
27 x $22\frac{1}{16}$ in. (68.6 x 56 cm.)
Signed at lower left: ALICE.T.ROBERTS.
Gift of George B. Roberts, 1955.10.2

1147 *Still Life with Apples*
Oil on canvas
$19\frac{7}{8}$ x $25\frac{1}{8}$ in. (50.5 x 63.8 cm.)
Gift of George B. Roberts, by exchange, 1955.10.3

Elizabeth Wentworth Roberts (1871–1927)

1148 *The Boy with the Violin*, 1901
Oil on canvas
$24\frac{3}{16}$ x $16\frac{1}{8}$ in. (61.4 x 41 cm.)
Signed and dated at upper right: EWRoberts/ 1901–
Gift of the artist, 1906.4

Theodore Robinson (1852–1896)

1149 *Girl at Piano*, ca. 1887
Oil on canvas
$21\frac{3}{4}$ x $18\frac{1}{16}$ in. (55.2 x 45.9 cm.)

Signed at lower left: Th Robinson
Henry D. Gilpin Fund, 1898.7

1150 *Port Ben, Delaware and Hudson Canal,* 1893
Oil on canvas
28¼ x 32¼ in. (71.8 x 81.9 cm.)
Signed and dated at lower right: Th Robinson '93
Gift of the Society of American Artists as a memorial to Theodore Robinson, 1900.5

Severin Roesen (1815/16–1872 or after)

1151 *Still Life with Fruit,* ca. 1855
Oil on canvas
30⅛ x 40⅛ in. (76.5 x 101.9 cm.)
Signed at lower right: SRoesen [initials in monogram]
Gift of William C. Williamson, by exchange, and Henry S. McNeil and the Henry D. Gilpin Fund, 1976.4

Warren Rohrer (1927–)

1152 *Pasture Scape,* 1968
Oil on canvas
39⅞ x 44⁵⁄₁₆ in. (101.3 x 112.6 cm.)
Signed at lower right: ROHRER
Inscribed and signed on stretcher: "SHADED COW" WARREN ROHRER
John Lambert Fund, 1968.14

1153 *Planting Two,* 1973
Oil on canvas
66⅛ x 66¼ in. (168 x 168.3 cm.)
Inscribed, dated, and signed on canvas folded over stretcher: PLANTING TWO 1973 W. Rohrer
Gift of Mrs. Suzanne McBrien, 1979.13

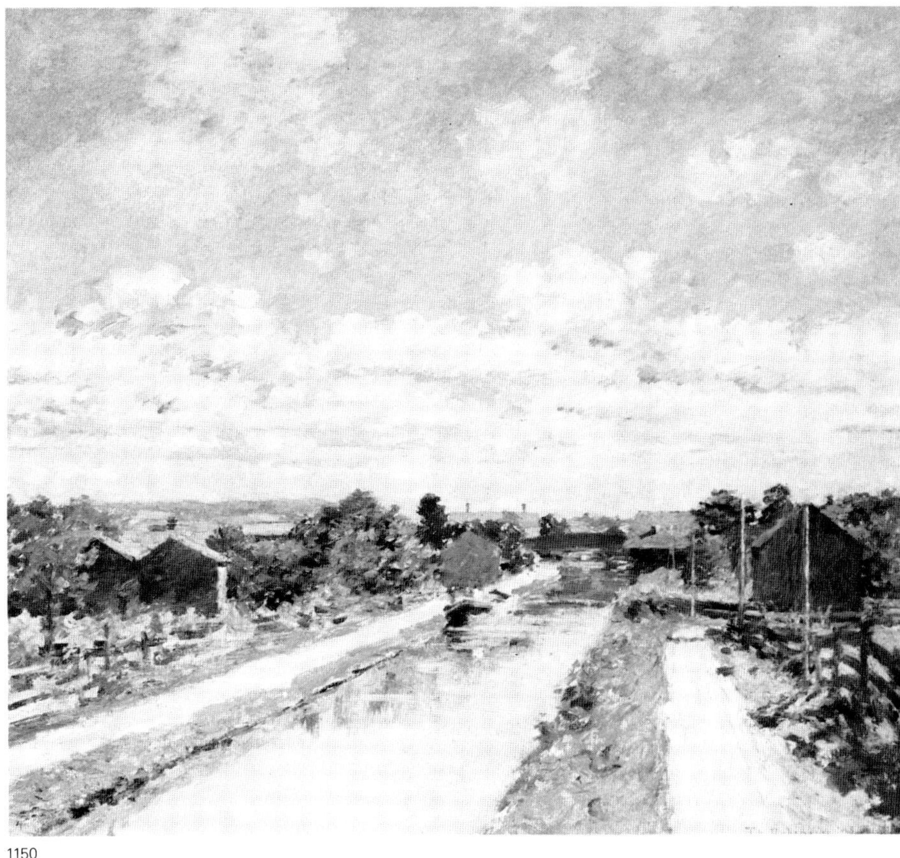
1150

Umberto Romano (1905–1982)

1154 *Ecce Homo,* 1947
Oil on canvas
40 x 28½ in. (101.6 x 72.4 cm.)
Signed at lower right: Umberto Romano
Annotated on stretcher: Umberto Romano/title/ "Ecce Homo"
Gift of Dr. and Mrs. Abraham J. Rosenfeld in honor of their son, Richard, 1953.17

Edward Francis Rook (1870–1960)

1155 *Deserted Street, Moonlight,* ca. 1897
Oil on canvas
18³⁄₁₆ x 21¾ in. (46.2 x 55.2 cm.)
Signed at lower right: EFRook
Henry D. Gilpin Fund, 1898.5

Albert Rosenthal (1863–1939)

1156 *Joseph A. Dugan* (1766–1845), 1915 (after Thomas Sully, 1810)
Oil on canvas
36⅛ x 29¼ in. (91.8 x 74.3 cm.)
Signed, dated, and inscribed on back: Copied by Albert Rosenthal, 1915/From the Original by T.Sully 1810/Owned by Herbert T.A. Pratt Esq./ New York
Gift of the artist, 1916.2

1157 *Max Rosenthal* (1833–1918), 1899
Oil on canvas
40 x 50 in. (101.6 x 127 cm.)
Signed and dated at lower left: Albert Rosenthal/ 1899–
Bequest of the artist, 1940.12.2

1158 *Self-Portrait,* 1923
Oil on canvas
30¹⁄₁₆ x 24¹⁵⁄₁₆ in. (76.4 x 63.3 cm.)
Signed and dated at upper left: Albert Rosenthal. 1923
Bequest of the artist, 1940.12.3

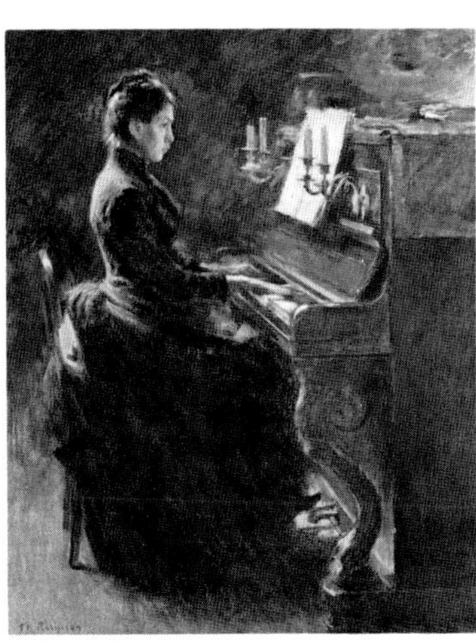
1149

1153

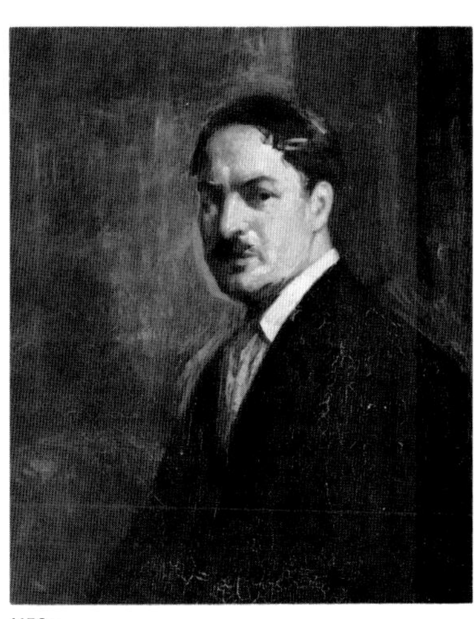
1158

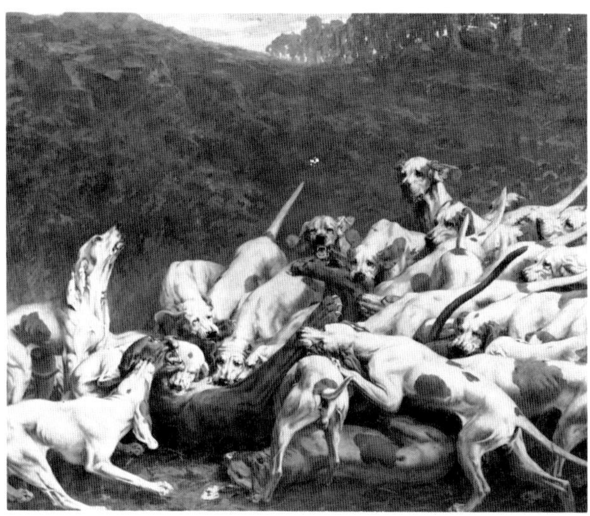
1159

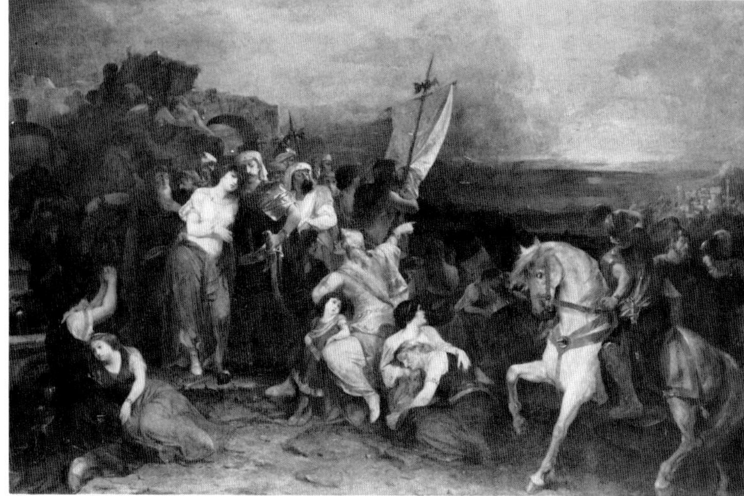
1165

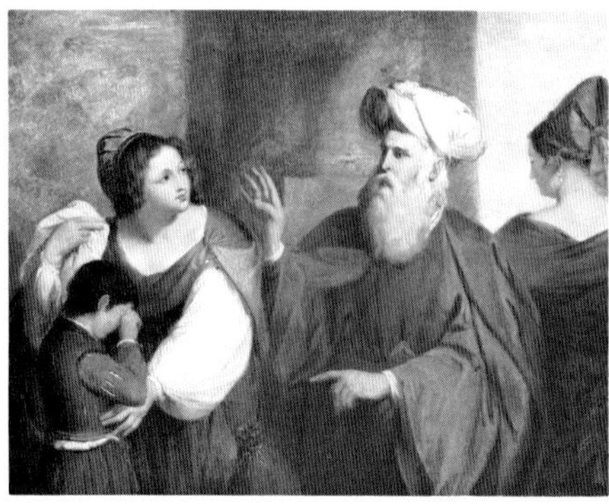
1160

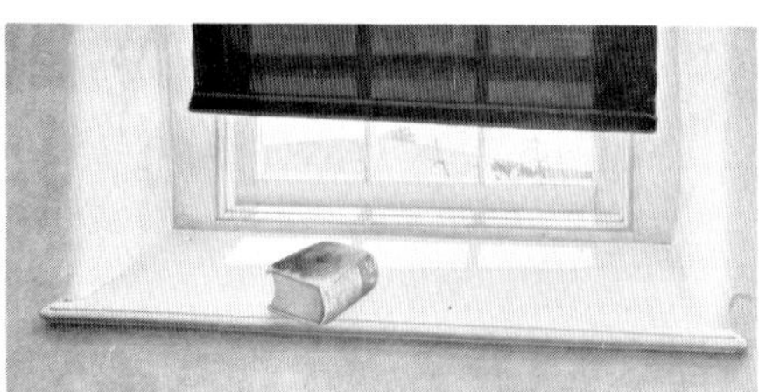
1175

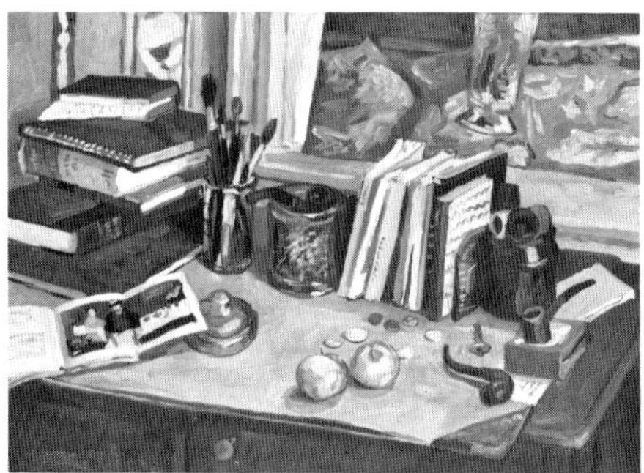
1180

Percival Leonard Rosseau (1859–1937)

1159 *Taking of a Panther in Texas*, 1905
Oil on canvas
93½ x 112¼ in. (237.5 x 285.1 cm.)
Signed and dated at lower left: Rosseau/1905
Gift of Mrs. Leon B. Rosseau and Francis V. Rosseau, 1980.17

Peter Frederick Rothermel (1812–1895)

1160 *Abraham Casting Out Hagar and Ishmael*, by 1845
Oil on canvas
20^{1}/16 x 25^{5}/16 in. (51 x 64.3 cm.)
Gift of Mr. and Mrs. Gordon H. B. Bretschneider, 1975.6

1161 *The Bather*, 1865
Oil on canvas
16¾ x 10^{9}/16 in. (42.5 x 26.8 cm.)
Signed and dated at lower left: P F Rothermel/ 1865
Bequest of Henry C. Gibson, 1892.6.74

1162 *Desdemona*, by 1866
Oil on canvas
11^{3}/16 x 8^{1}/16 in. (28.4 x 20.5 cm.)
Bequest of Henry C. Gibson, 1892.6.75

1163 *De Soto Raising the Cross on the Banks of the Mississippi*, 1851
Oil on canvas
40 x 50 in. (101.6 x 127 cm.)
Signed on canvas folded over stretcher: [Ro]thermel
Henry C. Gibson Fund, 1987.31

1164 *Four Kneeling Figures in Historical Costume*
Oil on canvas
12½ x 15⅞ in. (31.8 x 40.3 cm.)
Gift of Saul and Ellin Lapp, 1983.20.19

1165 *The Last Sigh of the Moor*, 1864
Oil on canvas
47^{15}/16 x 72 in. (121.8 x 182.9 cm.)
Signed and dated at lower left: P F Rothermel. 1864
Gift of Caroline Gibson Taitt, 1910.2.6

1166 *Man in Historical Costume*
Oil on canvas
12⅝ x 9 in. (32.1 x 22.9 cm.)
Gift of Saul and Ellin Lapp, 1984.24.25

1167 *State House on the Day of the Battle of Germantown*, 1862
Oil on canvas
34½ x 47½ in. (87.6 x 120.7 cm.)
Signed and dated at lower right: P F Rothermel/ 1862
Bequest of Henry C. Gibson, 1892.6.76

1168 *Study for Head of a Martyr*, 1862
Oil on canvas
20 x 17 in. (50.8 x 43.2 cm.)
Signed and dated at right center: P.F.Rothermel/ 1862; inscribed, signed, and dated on back: Study for Head of a/martyr/P.F.Rothermel,/ 1862
Gift of Caroline Gibson Taitt, 1910.2.7

1169 *Thou Art the Man*, 1884
Oil on canvas
50 x 62¼ in. (127 x 158.1 cm.)
Signed and dated at lower left: Rothermel/1884
Gift of Craig Heberton, 1922.9.2

1170 *The Virtuoso* (formerly *Portrait of Mr. McDowell*), 1852
Oil on canvas
30½ x 25¼ in. (77.5 x 64.1 cm.)
Signed and inscribed at lower left: P.F. Rothermel/Philadelphia/USA
Gift of Peter Frederick Rothermel, 1981.12

1171 *Unidentified Woman*
Oil on canvas
30^{3}/16 x 25 in. (76.7 x 63.7 cm.)
Bequest of Josephine A. Natt, 1935.3.1

1172 *Unidentified Woman*
Oil on canvas
27^{3}/16 x 23^{5}/16 in. (69.1 x 59.2 cm.)
Gift of Peter Frederick Rothermel, 1982.1

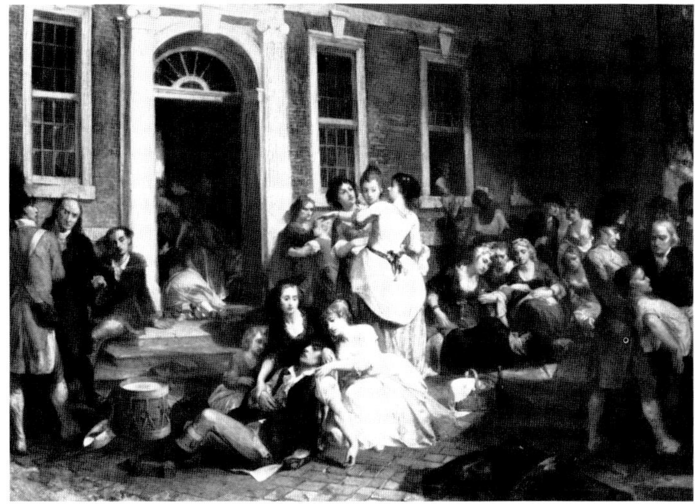

1167

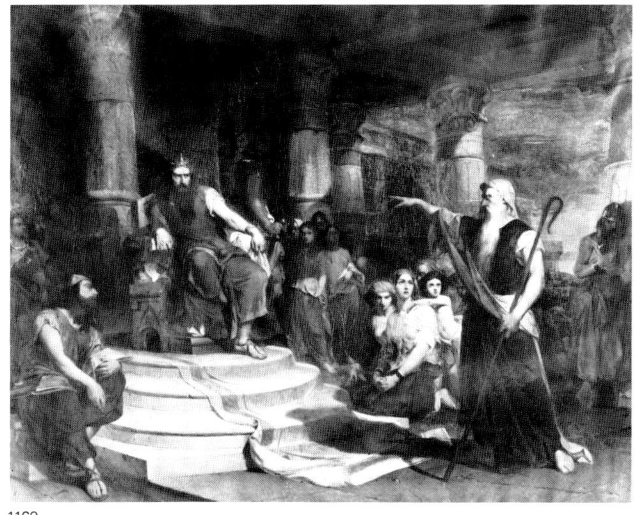

1169

Henry L. Rothman (b. 1918)

1173 *Hilah;* on back, *Unidentified Woman*, ca. 1938
Oil on canvas
21¾ x 17 15/16 in. (55.2 x 45.6 cm.)
John Lambert Fund, 1939.14

Tom Rowlands (1925–)

1174 *Black Tide*, ca. 1961
Oil on canvas
60 x 72 in. (152.4 x 182.9 cm.)
John Lambert Fund, 1962.10

Barclay Rubincam (b. 1920)

1175 *I Believe*, 1955
Oil on gessoed masonite
19 15/16 x 39 15/16 in. (50.6 x 101.4 cm.)
Signed and dated at lower right: Barclay Rubincam/1955
John Lambert Fund, 1958.17

George Gordon Russell (1932–1985)

1176 *Architectural Study*, 1952
Oil on canvas
30¼ x 36 3/16 in. (76.8 x 91.9 cm.)
John Lambert Fund, 1953.12

1177 *Birdland*, 1967–69
Oil on canvas
68 x 57⅛ in. (172.7 x 145.1 cm.)
Gift of the Louis Comfort Tiffany Foundation, 1969.19

Chauncey F. Ryder (1868–1949)

1178 *C. C. C. Camp*, ca. 1935
Oil on canvas
45¼ x 60 3/16 in. (114.9 x 152.9 cm.)
Signed at lower right: Ch—y/F. Ryder
Joseph E. Temple Fund, 1936.18

Raphael Sabatini (1898–1985)

1179 *Juggler*, ca. 1931
Oil on canvas
38¼ x 18 1/16 in. (97.2 x 45.9 cm.)
Signed at lower right: Sabatini
John Lambert Fund, 1932.11

S. Hilbert Sabin (1935–)

1180 *Art Collector's Desk*, by 1957
Oil on canvas
28 x 40 in. (71.1 x 101.6 cm.)
Gift of James P. and Ruth Marshall Magill, 1957.15.51

1181 *Still Life: Lemon on Silver Plate*
Oil on canvas
12 x 22 1/16 in. (30.5 x 56 cm.)
Signed at upper right: Sabin
Gift of James P. and Ruth Marshall Magill, 1957.15.30

Lawrence Saint (1885–1961)

1182 *Self-Portrait*, 1921
Oil on canvas board
12⅝ x 11 in. (32.1 x 27.9 cm.)
Signed and dated at lower left: LAWRENCE SAINT 1921
Gift of the artist, 1948.10

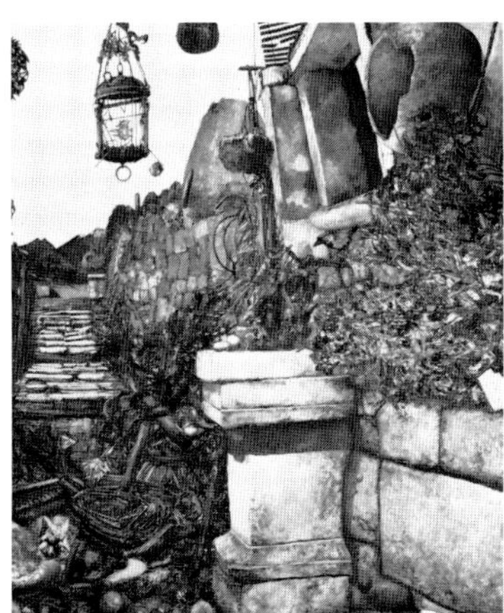

1177

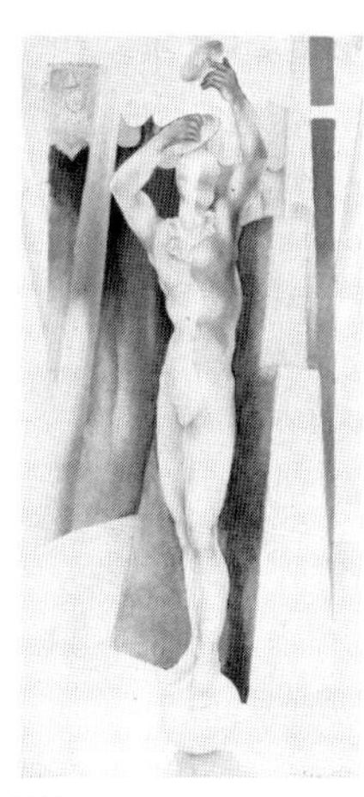

1179

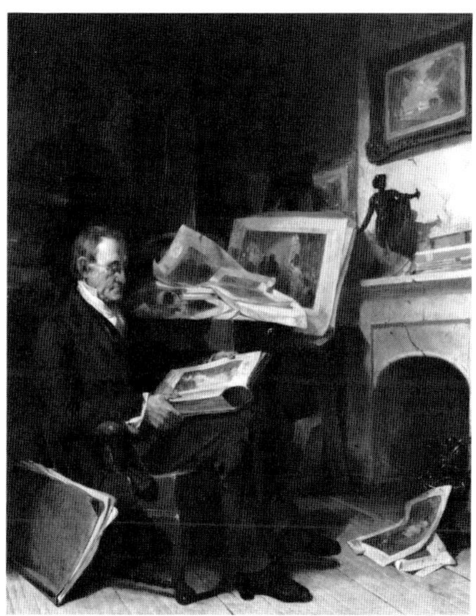

1170

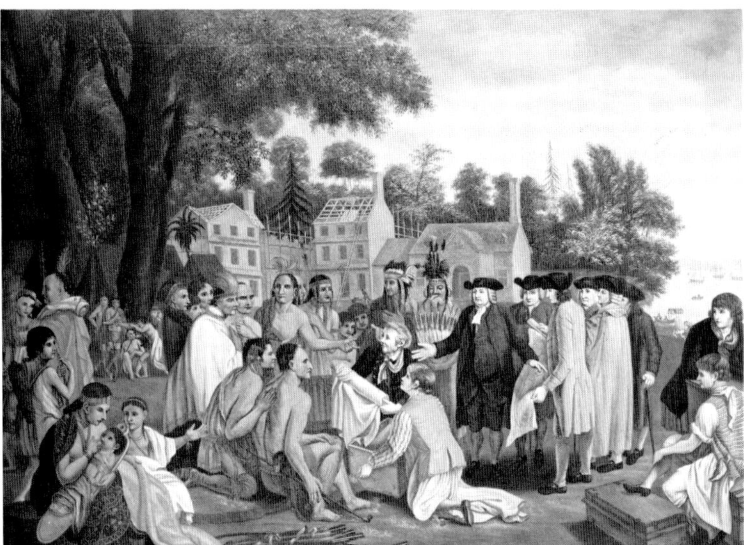
1191

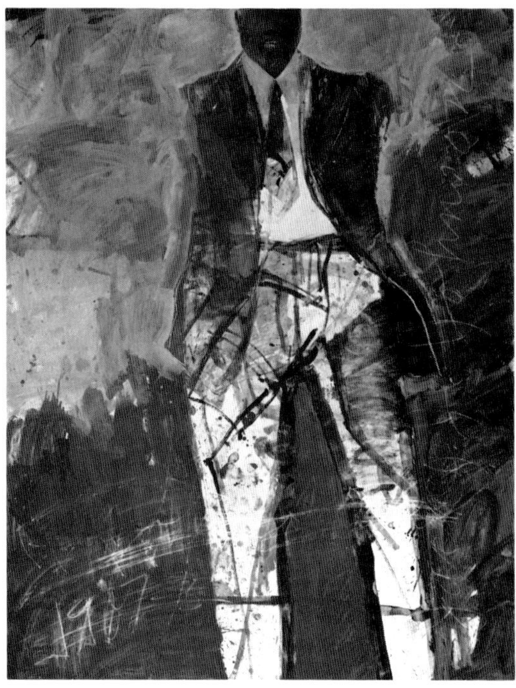
1189

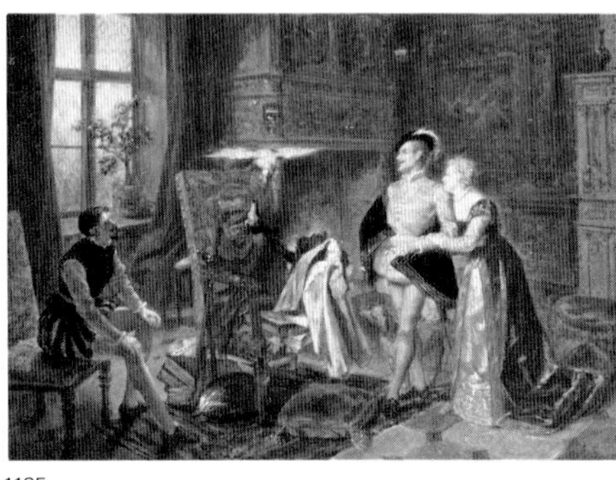
1185

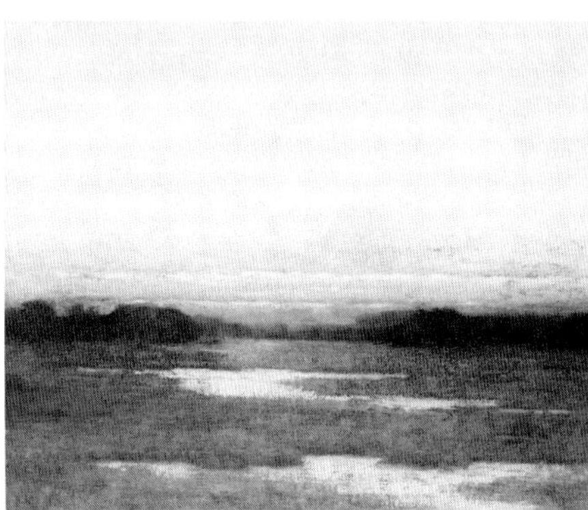
1186

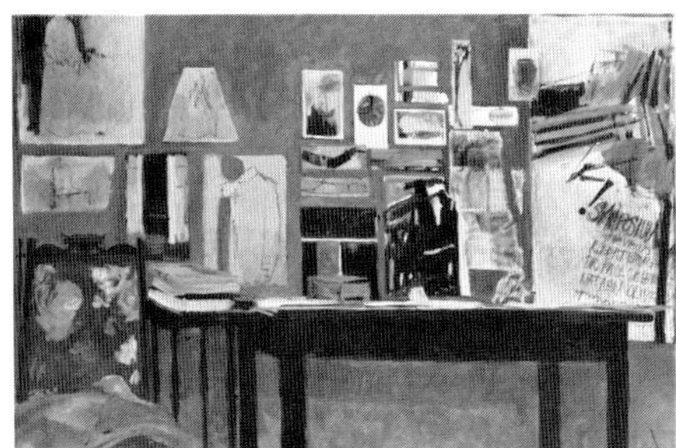
1188

Henry Sargent (1770–1845)

1183 *General Benjamin Lincoln* (1733–1810), ca. 1806
Oil on wood
17 x 15½ in. (43.2 x 39.4 cm.)
Gift of Mrs. John Frederick Lewis (The John Frederick Lewis Memorial Collection), 1933.10.71

John Singer Sargent (1856–1925)

1184 *Mr. and Mrs. John White Field* (1815–1887; 1820–1902), 1882
Oil on canvas
44⅞ x 32 in. (114 x 81.3 cm.)
Signed, inscribed, and dated at upper right: John S. Sargent. Paris 1882
Gift of Mr. and Mrs. John White Field, 1891.10

Emily Sartain (1841–1927)

1185 *Untitled* (possibly *The Expectancy*), 1887
Oil on wood
16¹⁄₁₆ x 22³⁄₁₆ in. (40.8 x 56.4 cm.)
Signed at lower right: E. Sartain
Gift of Dr. James F. Adams, 1976.19

William Sartain (1843–1924)

1186 *Solitude*, by 1892
Oil on canvas
20⅛ x 24¹⁄₁₆ in. (51.1 x 61.1 cm.)
Signed at lower right: W. SARTAIN.
Gift of Mrs. James Mapes Dodge in accordance with the wishes of the artist, 1931.13.1

1187 *The Young Musician*, by 1882
Oil on canvas
18 x 14¹³⁄₁₆ in. (45.7 x 37.6 cm.)
Signed at lower right: Wm SARTAIN; signed and inscribed on back (before lining): W.SARTAIN./THE YOUNG MUSICIAN/no. 110/15 x 18. W. Sartain/ Young Musician
Gift of Mrs. James Mapes Dodge in accordance with the wishes of the artist, 1931.13.2

Raymond Saunders (1934–)

1188 *La Chambre*, 1961
Oil on canvas
42¼ x 64¼ in. (107.3 x 163.2 cm.)
Signed at lower right: Saunders
John Lambert Fund, 1962.11

1189 *Jack Johnson*, 1971
Oil on canvas
82⅜ x 63⅝ in. (209.2 x 161.6 cm.)
Inscribed from lower to upper right: Jack J. J. Johnson
Funds provided by the National Endowment for the Arts, Pennsylvania Academy Women's Committee, and an anonymous donor, 1974.9.1

Edward Savage (1761–1817)

1190 *Major William Popham* (1752–1848), ca. 1800
Oil on canvas
30¾ x 24⅝ in. (78.1 x 62.5 cm.)
Annotated on lining: Major William Popham/

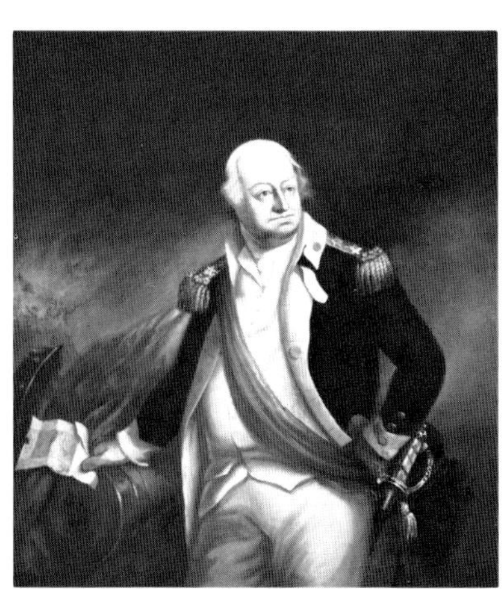
1183

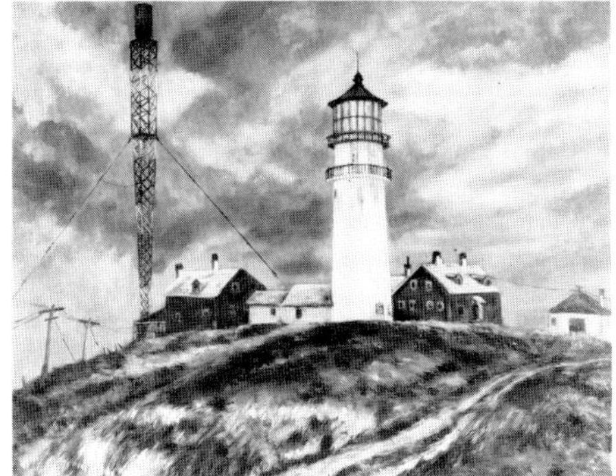

1192

Born Sept 19, 1752–1 Died 1847[*sic*]; and in another hand: Age 96/7th President/ Cincinnatti [*sic*] Society
Gift of Mr. and Mrs. Charles P. Hidden, 1961.11

1191 *William Penn's Treaty with the Indians*, ca. 1800
(after John Hall's 1775 engraving after Benjamin West, 1771–72; *see* cat. no. 1481)
Oil on canvas
38 5/16 x 52 3/16 in. (97.3 x 132.6 cm.)
Gift of the Philadelphia Electric Company, 1976.5

Helen Alton Sawyer (Mrs. Jerry Farnsworth, 1900–)

1192 *Sailors Take Warning*, ca. 1939
Oil on canvas
28 x 36 1/16 in. (71.1 x 91.6 cm.)
Signed at lower left: Helen Sawyer; and on back: Helen SAWYER
Signed and inscribed on stretcher: Helen Sawyer/"Sailors Take Warning."
John Lambert Fund, 1940.6

Saul Schary (1904–1978)

1193 *Portrait of E. R.*, 1932
Oil on canvas
35 1/16 x 25 in. (89.1 x 63.5 cm.)
Signed and dated at upper left: Schary '32
John Lambert Fund, 1933.6

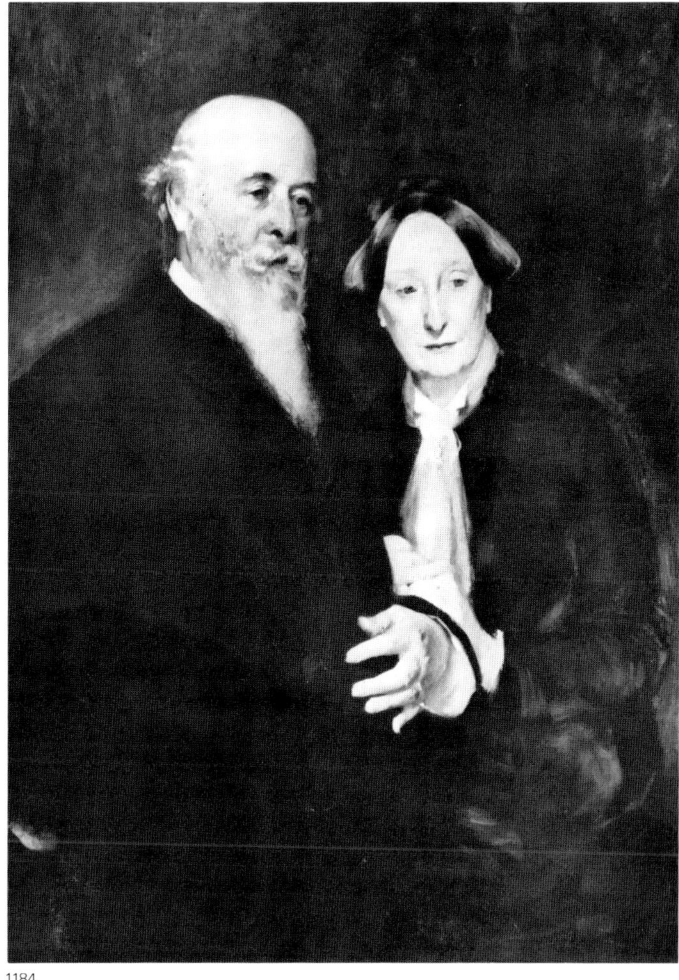

1184

Alice Schille (1869–1955)

1194 *Coffee Drinkers, Holland*
Oil on cardboard
8 5/8 x 10 9/16 in. (21.9 x 26.8 cm.)
Inscribed on back: Coffee Drinkers/Holland
Gift of Vera White, 1960.18.4

Carl H. Schmolze (1823–1859)

1195 *Washington Sitting for His Portrait to Gilbert Stuart*, 1858
Oil on canvas
50 3/4 x 40 1/2 in. (128.9 x 102.9 cm.)
Signed, inscribed, and dated at lower right: C.H Schmolze/Philadelphia 1858.
Gift of Mrs. John Frederick Lewis (The John Frederick Lewis Memorial Collection), 1933.10.72

Henry E. Schnakenberg (1892–1970)

1196 *Still Life*, ca. 1924
Oil on canvas
24 1/16 x 24 1/16 in. (61.1 x 61.1 cm.)
Signed at lower right: H.E.Schnakenberg
John Lambert Fund, 1925.7

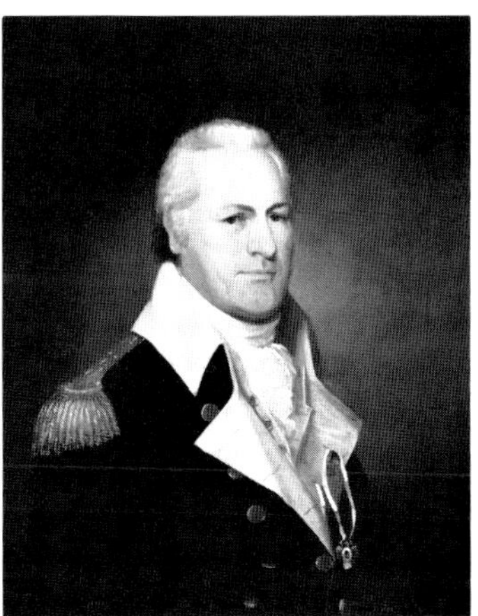

1190

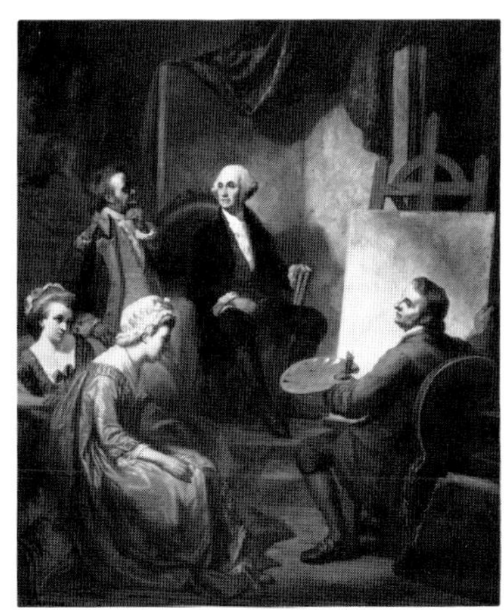

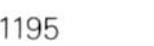

1195

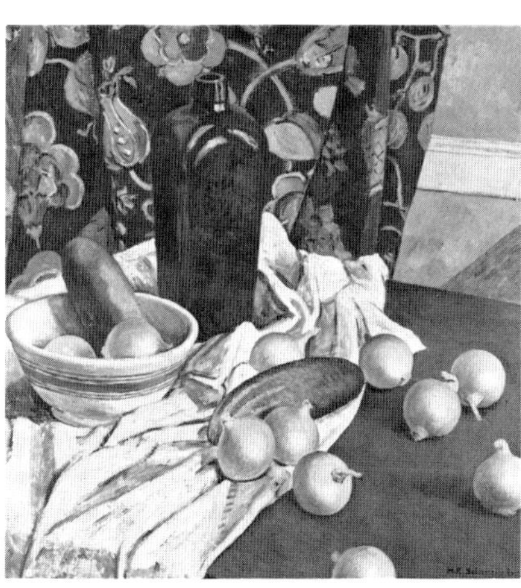

1196

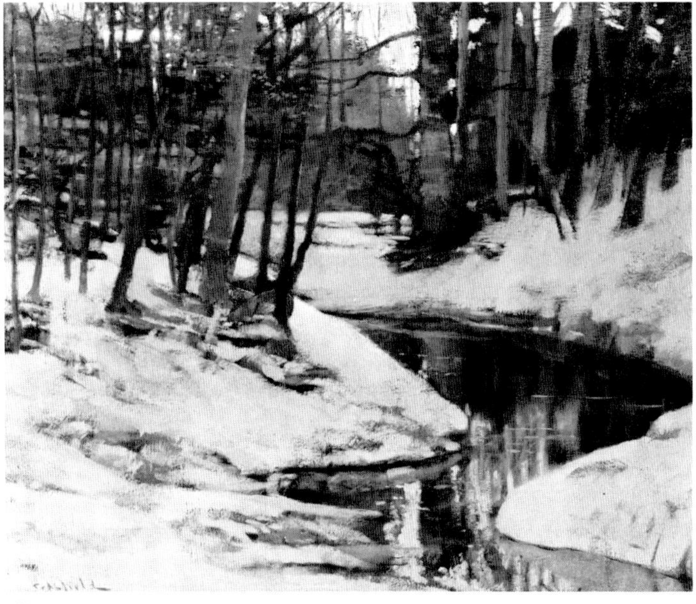

1197

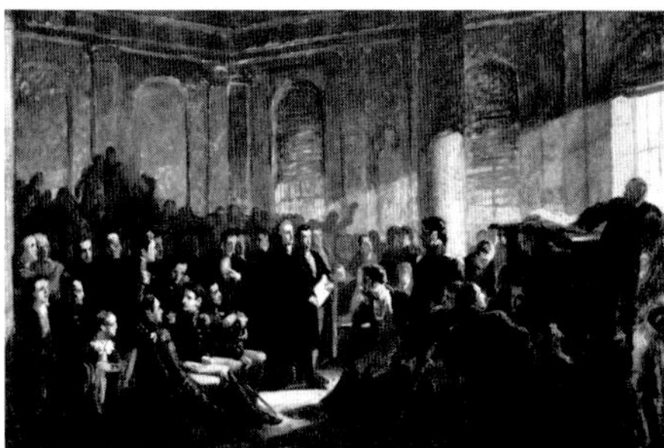

1200

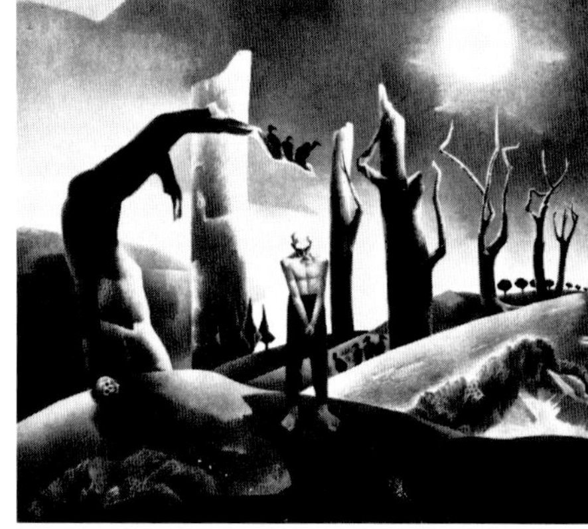

1201

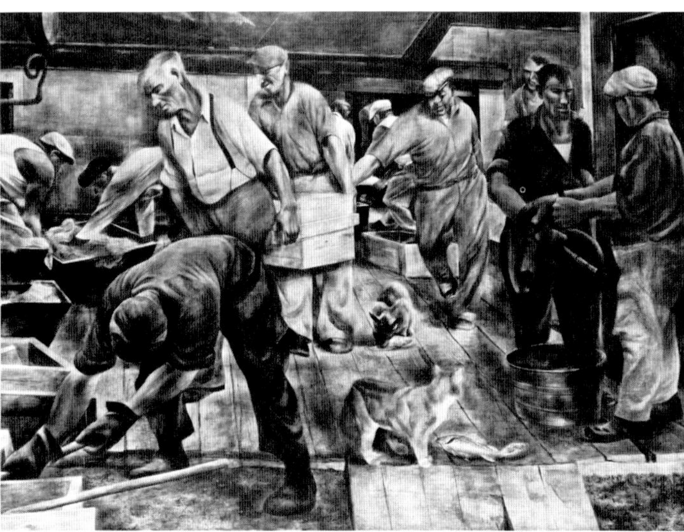

1208

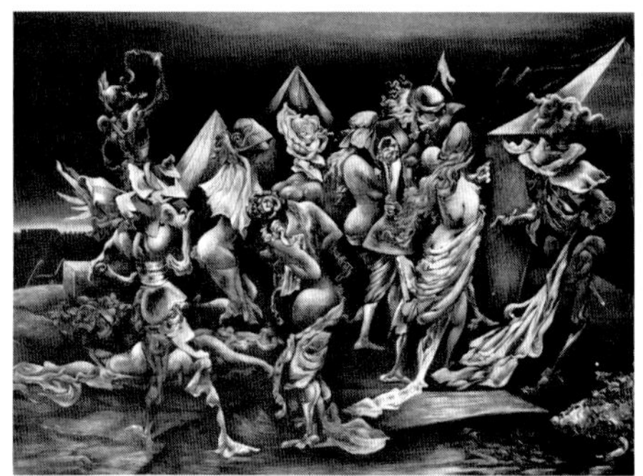

1206

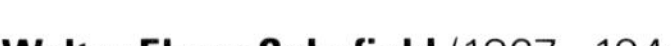

Walter Elmer Schofield (1867–1944)

1197 *Winter*, 1899
Oil on canvas
29 1/2 x 36 in. (74.9 x 91.4 cm.)
Signed at lower left: Schofield
Henry D. Gilpin Fund, 1899.3

William K. Schulhoff (1898–1943)

1198 *Figure Composition*, ca. 1929
Oil on canvas
30 1/16 x 36 1/16 in. (76.4 x 91.6 cm.)
John Lambert Fund, 1930.5

Christian Schussele (1824–1879)

1199 *Old Man*
Oil on composition board
10 x 7 15/16 in. (25.4 x 20.2 cm.)
Gift of John Frederick Lewis, 1922.1.4

1200 *Study for "The Trial of General Jackson before Judge Hall,"* ca. 1858
Oil on canvas
20 1/2 x 30 1/8 in. (52.1 x 76.5 cm.)
Collections Fund, 1957.16

William S. Schwartz (1896–1977)

1201 *De Profundis*, 1947
Oil on canvas
36 1/16 x 40 1/8 in. (91.6 x 101.9 cm.)
Signed at lower right: WILLIAM S.SCHWARTZ; inscribed and signed on back: "DE PROFUNDIS" 513/BY/WILLIAM S. SCHWARTZ
Gift of the artist, 1967.11.1

1202 *Scene in Sheboygan*, 1940
Oil on canvas
30 x 36 in. (76.2 x 91.4 cm.)
Signed at lower left: WILLIAM S.SCHWARTZ
Inscribed, signed, and dated on stretcher: "AN

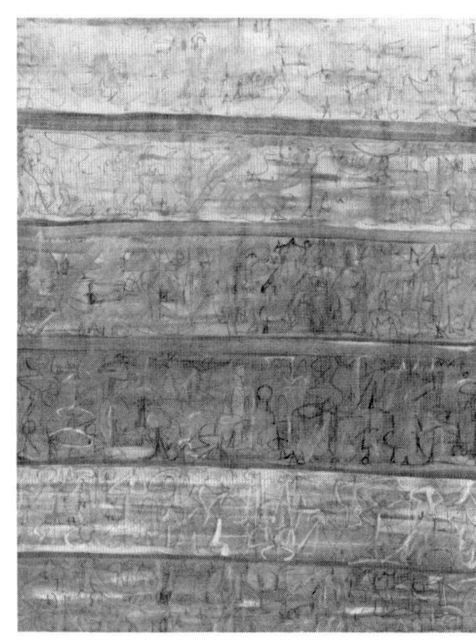

1205

INTERSECTION [overlapped by] SCENE IN SHEBOYGAN"/BY/WILLIAM S. SCHWARTZ/ PAI #426–40
Gift of the artist, 1951.25

1203 *Symphonic Forms #43*, 1960
Oil on canvas
35 15/16 x 29 15/16 in. (91.3 x 76 cm.)
Signed at lower right: WILLIAM S. SCHWARTZ; inscribed and signed on back: SYMPHONIC FORMS #43/BY WILLIAM S. SCHWARTZ
Inscribed and signed on stretcher: SYMPHONIC FORMS #43 ARRANGEMENT/BY WILLIAM. S SCHWARTZ/ #636 TO MOTHER
Gift of the artist, 1967.11.2

1204 *To-morrow, To-morrow, and To-morrow*, 1945
Oil on canvas
36 x 40 in. (91.4 x 101.6 cm.)
Signed at lower left: WILLIAM-S-SCHWARTZ; inscribed and signed on back: "TO-MORROW TO-MORROW AND TO-MORROW"/BY/ WILLIAM S. SCHWARTZ #491
Gift of the artist, 1967.11.3

Sonia Sekula (1918–1963)

1205 *The Rains*, 1949
Oil and graphite on canvas
46 1/8 x 36 in. (117.1 x 91.4 cm.)
Signed and dated at lower right: Sekula49; inscribed, dated, and signed on back: "The Rains"/(remembering Uruapan)/1949/ Sokula
Gift of the Betty Parsons Foundation, 1985.47

Kurt Seligmann (1900–1962)

1206 *The Virtue of Alexander*, 1947
Oil on canvas
34 15/16 x 47 7/8 in. (88.7 x 121.6 cm.)
Signed and dated at lower left: Seligmann 1947
Joseph E. Temple Fund, 1949.10

Charles Semser (1922–)

1207 *Dock Street*, 1947
Oil on canvas
18 1/4 x 24 in. (46.4 x 61 cm.)
Signed and dated at left center: Semser 47; and on back: Semser
John Lambert Fund, 1948.11

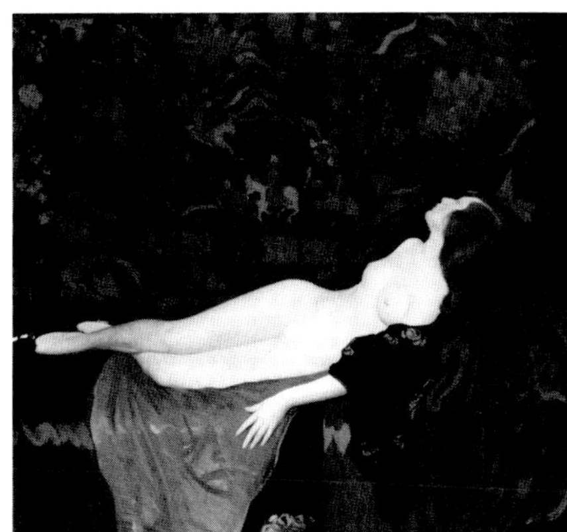

1213

Zoltan L. Sepeshy (1898–1974)

1208 *Olsen's Men*, 1948
Egg tempera on masonite
33 x 45 in. (83.8 x 114.3 cm.)
Signed at lower left: Z Sepeshy; inscribed and signed on back: "OLSEN'S MEN"/Tempera./ ZOLTAN SEPESHY
Collections Fund, 1950.23.2

Albert B. Serwazi (1905–)

1209 *Red Table Cover*, 1940
Oil on canvas
37 1/4 x 52 1/8 in. (94.6 x 132.4 cm.)
Signed at lower right: Serwazi
Annotated on stretcher: 1940
Joseph E. Temple Fund, 1941.7

1210 *Violin with Hat*, 1936
Oil on canvas
24 x 32 1/8 in. (61 x 81.6 cm.)
Signed and dated at lower right: Serwazi/36
John Lambert Fund, 1937.7

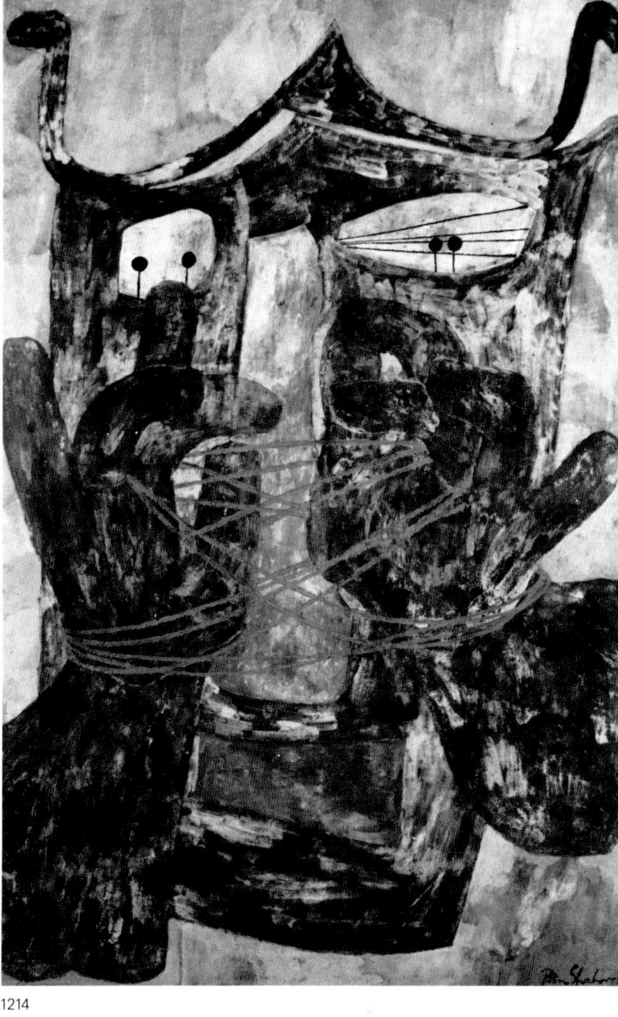

1214

Helen Fleck Seyffert (Mrs. Leopold Seyffert, 1887–1947)

1211 *Landscape*, ca. 1916
Oil on canvas
25 x 30 in. (63.5 x 76.2 cm.)
John Lambert Fund, 1917.7

Leopold Seyffert (1887–1956)

1212 *James Montgomery Beck* (1861–1936), 1919
Oil on canvas
29 15/16 x 24 15/16 in. (76 x 63.3 cm.)
Signed and dated at lower right: Leopold Seyffert/1919
Gift of Mrs. James Montgomery Beck, 1943.18

1213 *Lacquer Screen*, ca. 1917
Oil on canvas
54 3/16 x 60 in. (137.6 x 152.4 cm.)
Joseph E. Temple Fund, 1918.5

Ben Shahn (1898–1969)

1214 *Cat's Cradle in Blue*, ca. 1959
Egg tempera on composition board
39 3/4 x 25 3/4 in. (101 x 65.4 cm.)
Signed at lower right: Ben Shahn
Joseph E. Temple Fund, 1960.11

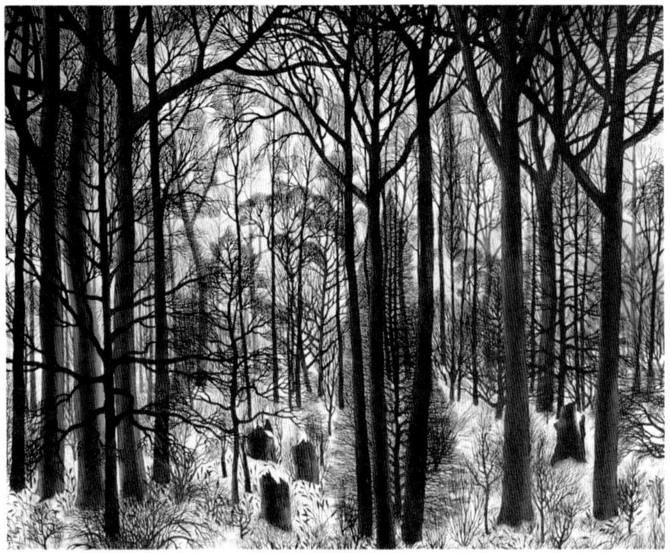
1216

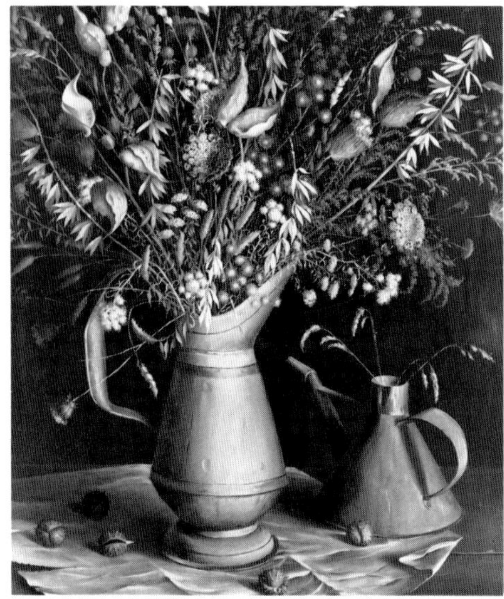
1217

John Sharp (b. 1911)

1215 *The Kite*, ca. 1952
Oil on masonite
24 x 20 in. (61 x 50.8 cm.)
Signed at lower right: J.Sharp -
John Lambert Fund, 1953.13

1216 *Spring Snow*, 1946
Oil on canvas
24 15/16 x 31 in. (63.3 x 78.7 cm.)
John Lambert Fund, 1947.9

1217 *Winter Bouquet*, 1948
Oil on canvas
28 1/16 x 24 1/16 in. (71.3 x 61.1 cm.)
Signed and dated at lower right: J.SHARP..48
Inscribed on stretcher: WINTER BOUQUET
Gift of Mr. and Mrs. Meyer P. Potamkin, 1984.40

Attributed to **James Sharples, Sr.** (ca. 1751–1811)

1218 *John Adams* (1735–1826)
Oil on wood
13 15/16 x 11 7/8 in. (35.4 x 30.2 cm.)
Gift of Mrs. John Frederick Lewis (The John Frederick Lewis Memorial Collection), 1933.10.73

1219 *Self-Portrait* (?)
Oil on copper
10 1/8 x 8 in. (25.7 x 20.3 cm.), oval
Gift of John Frederick Lewis, 1931.10.1

Joshua Shaw (1770/76–1860)

1220 *Landscape with Farmhouse and Castle*, ca. 1818
Oil on canvas
15 1/4 x 21 1/2 in. (38.7 x 54.6 cm.)
Bequest of Henry C. Carey (The Carey Collection), 1879.8.21

1221 *Landscape with Watermill*, ca. 1818
Oil on canvas
15 1/4 x 21 3/4 in. (38.7 x 55.2 cm.)
Bequest of Henry C. Carey (The Carey Collection), 1879.8.20

Francis W. Sheafer

1222 *Euterpe* (formerly *Music*), 1896–97
Oil on canvas
Approx. 77 1/4 x 43 1/2 in. (196 x 110 cm.)
Signed at lower left: F.W./SHEA-/FER
Commissioned by the Pennsylvania Academy, 1897.9.9

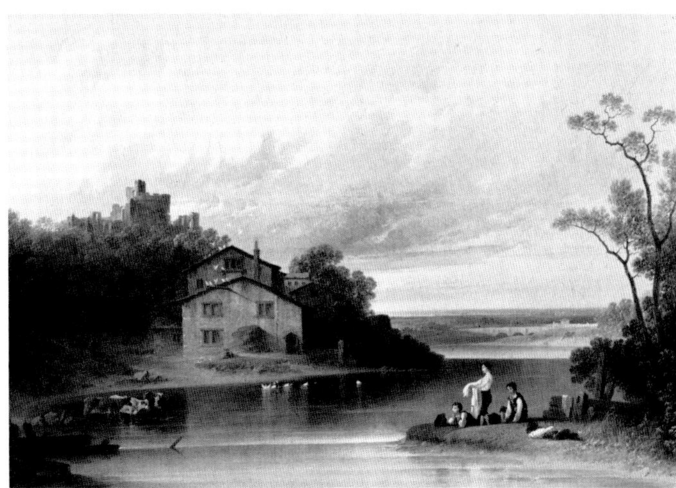
1220

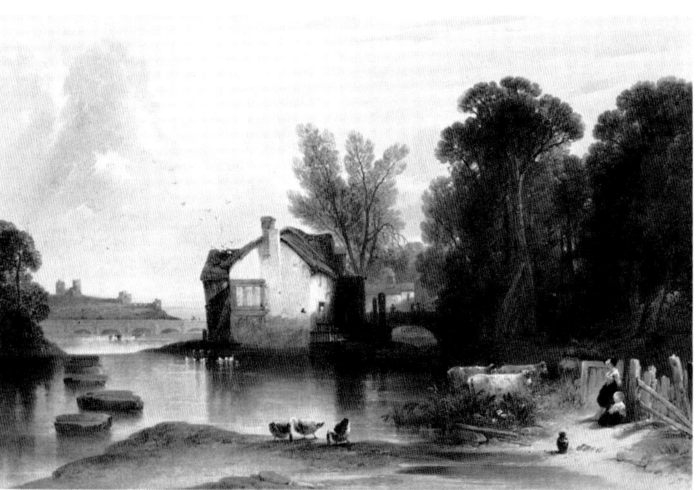
1221

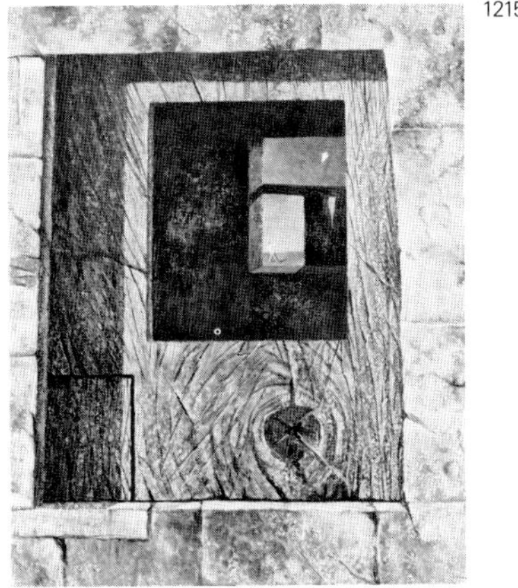
1215

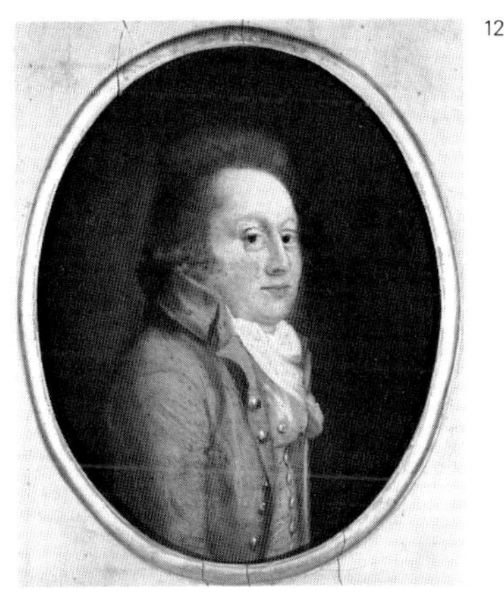
1219

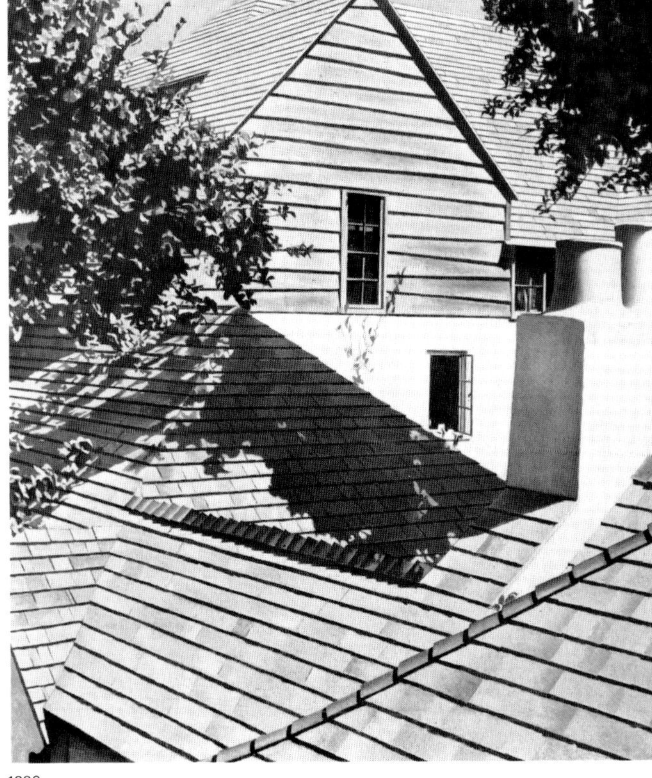
1226

1223 *Sacred Music* (formerly *Adoration of Literature*), 1896–97
Oil on canvas
Approx. 78 x 156 in. (198 x 396 cm.)
Signed at lower right: F. W. SHEAFER.
Commissioned by the Pennsylvania Academy, 1897.9.7

1224 *The Senses (Hearing and Touch)*, 1896–97
Oil on canvas
Approx. 77½ x 28 in. (196 x 71 cm.)
Signed at lower right: F. W. SHEAFER; inscribed across top: HEARING/TOUCH
Commissioned by the Pennsylvania Academy, 1897.9.8

1225 *The Senses (Taste, Sight, and Smell)*, 1896–97
Oil on canvas
Approx. 77½ x 50½ in. (196 x 128 cm.)
Signed at lower left: F.W./SHEA-/FER; inscribed across top: TASTE/SIGHT/SMELL
Commissioned by the Pennsylvania Academy, 1897.9.10

Charles Sheeler (1883–1965)

1226 *Clapboards*, 1936
Oil on canvas
21⅛ x 19¼ in. (53.7 x 48.9 cm.)
Signed and dated at lower right: Sheeler—1936.
Gift of W. Griffin Gribbel, R. Sturgis Ingersoll, John Frederick Lewis, Jr., William Clarke Mason, Henry T. McIlhenny, Lessing J. Rosenwald, Alfred G. B. Steel, Mrs. George F. Tyler, William L. Van Alen, and Joseph E. Widener, 1939.19

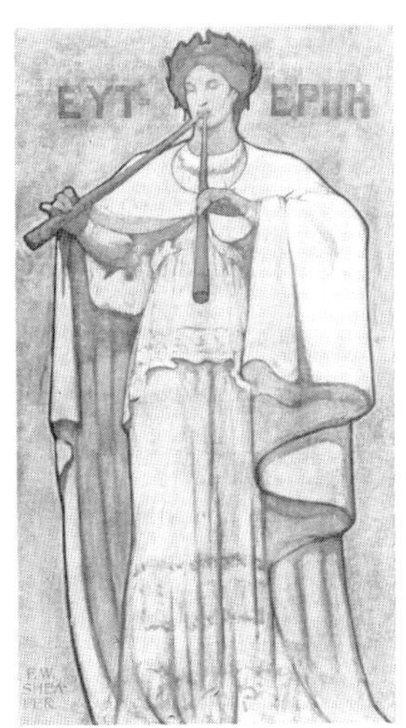

1222

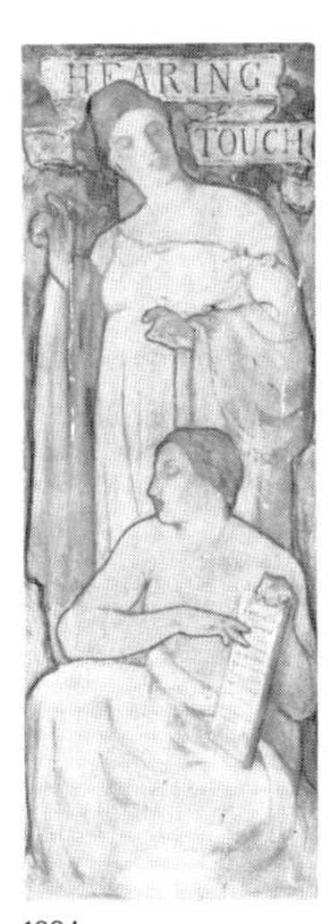

1224

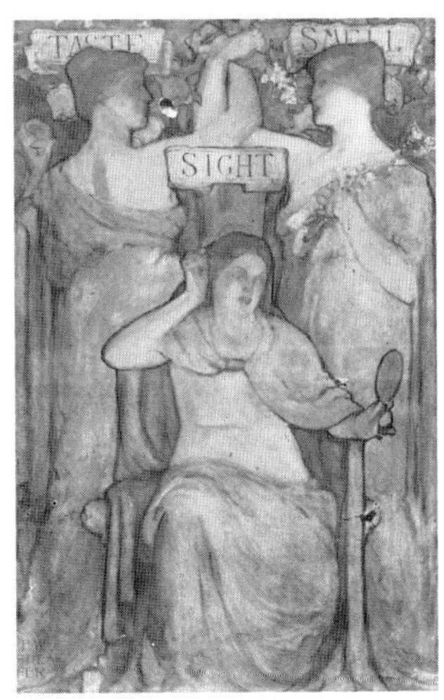

1225

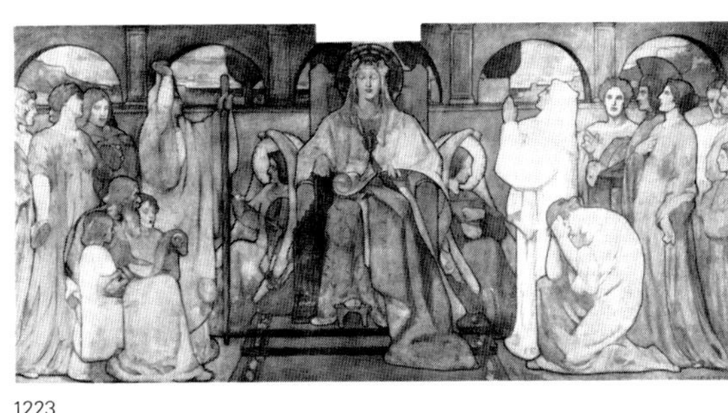
1223

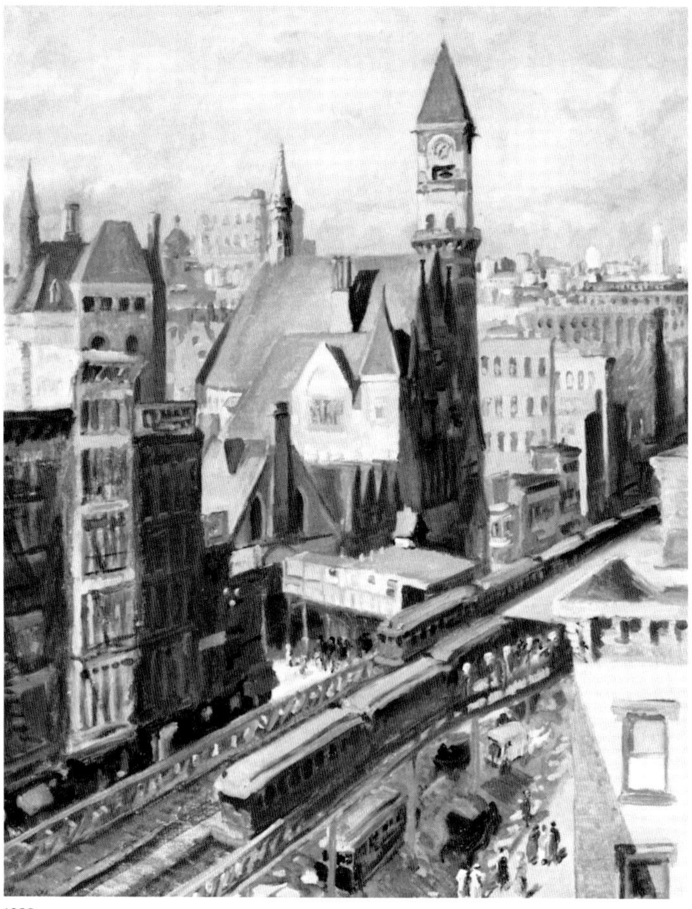
1233

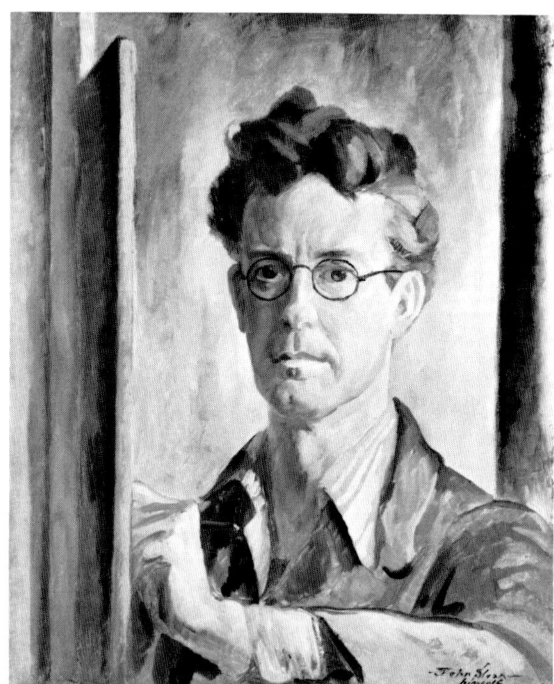
1235

Everett Shinn (1876–1953)

1227 *Strong Man, Clown, and Dancer*
Oil on canvas board
9 15/16 x 7 7/8 in. (25.2 x 20 cm.)
Signed at lower left: E SHINN
Collections Fund, 1956.13

Henry Colton Shumway
See cat. nos. 1649–50.

S. I. Sigfus

1228 *Fisherman*, ca. 1929
Oil on canvas
20 x 26 3/16 in. (50.8 x 66.5 cm.)
Signed at lower right: Sigfus
John Lambert Fund, 1930.6

Ellen Chisholm Sinclair (b. 1907)

1229 *Lake*, ca. 1933
Oil on canvas
28 x 34 in. (71.1 x 86.4 cm.)
Signed at lower right: Ellen C. Sinclair
John Lambert Fund, 1934.10

Clyde Singer (1908–)

1230 *Bill*, 1935
Oil on cardboard
68 x 31 3/4 in. (172.7 x 80.6 cm.)
Signed and dated at lower right: SINGER/JUN 1935
John Lambert Fund, 1936.16

William H. Singer, Jr. (1868–1943)

1231 *Fantastic North*, 1932
Oil on canvas
41 1/2 x 39 1/2 in. (105.4 x 100.3 cm.)
Signed and dated at lower left: W.H.SINGER.JR/ –1932–
Joseph E. Temple Fund, 1937.8

John Sloan (1871–1951)

1232 *Dramatic Music* (formerly *The Opera*), 1896–97
Oil on canvas
78 x 103 in. (198.1 x 261.6 cm.)
Signed at lower left: JOHN SLOAN
Commissioned by the Pennsylvania Academy, 1897.9.11

1233 *Jefferson Market*, 1917, retouched 1922
Oil on canvas
32 x 26 1/8 in. (81.3 x 66.4 cm.)
Signed at lower left: -JohnSloan-; inscribed on back: 6 AVE JEFFERSON M/JEFFERSON MARKET 19[?]
Henry D. Gilpin Fund, 1944.10

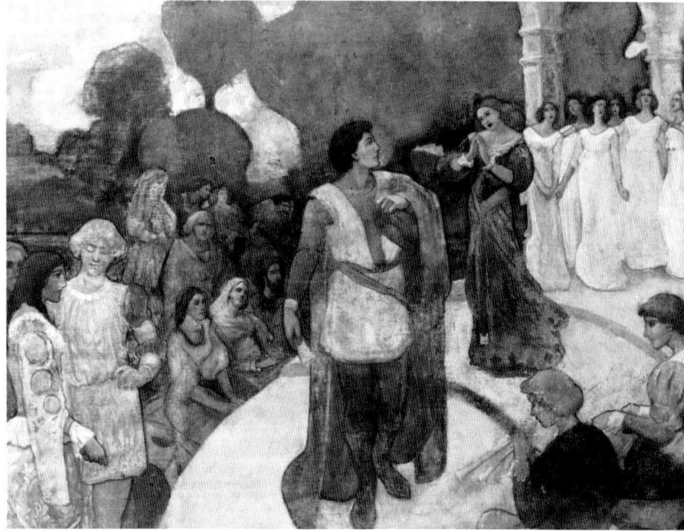
1232

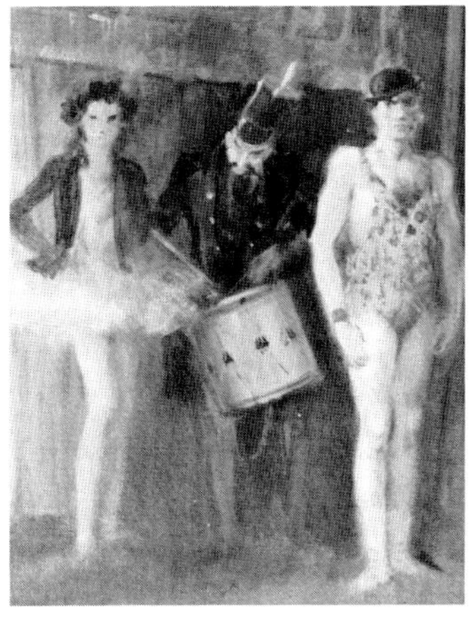
1227

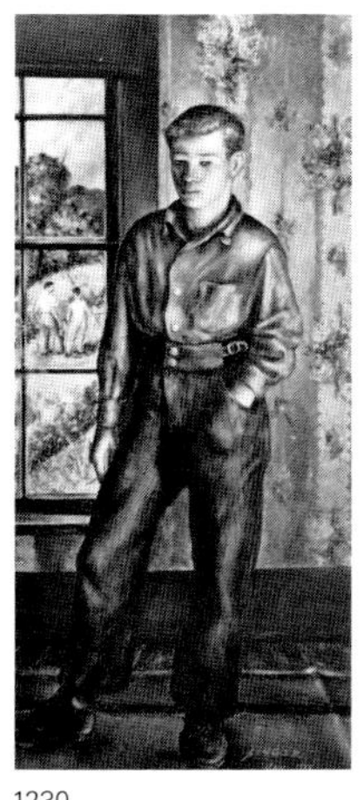
1230

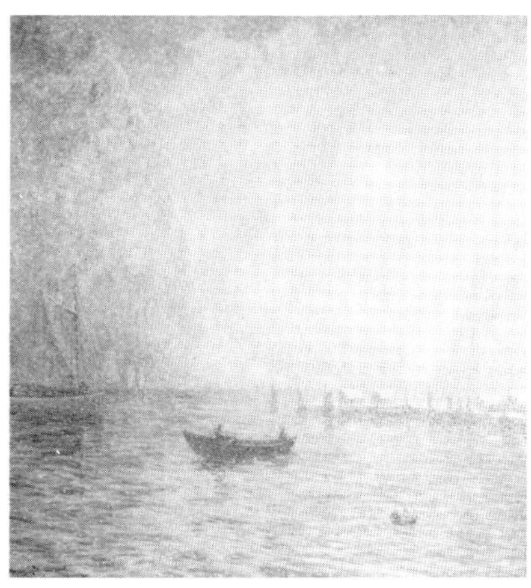
1231

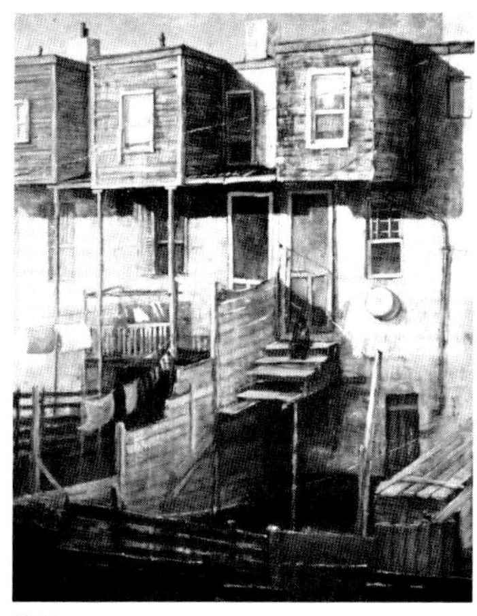
1237

1234 *Mary Kerr*, 1902
Oil on canvas
27 x 22 in. (68.6 x 55.9 cm.)
Signed and dated at lower left: John/Sloan/'02
Gift of Helen Farr Sloan, 1987.23

1235 *Self-Portrait*, 1917–22
Oil on canvas
24⅛ x 20 in. (61.3 x 50.8 cm.)
Signed and inscribed at lower right: -John Sloan-/ himself
Gift of Helen Farr Sloan, 1973.15

1236 *Horace L. Traubel* (1858–1919), 1916
Oil on canvas
32 x 26 in. (81.3 x 66 cm.)
Inscribed, signed, and dated at lower right: HORACE TRAUBEL/John Sloan-16
Gift of Helen Farr Sloan, 1977.14

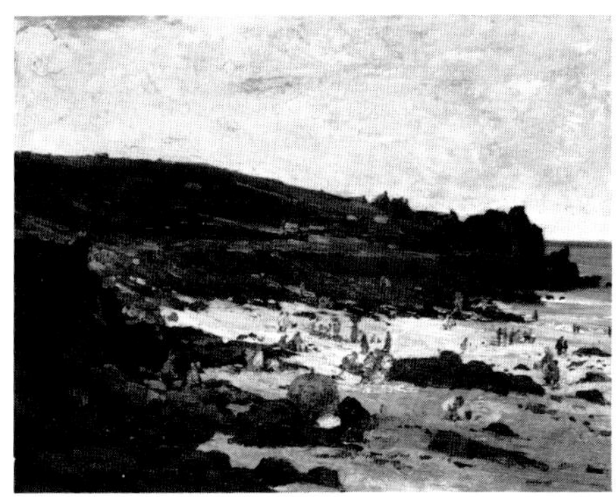
1239

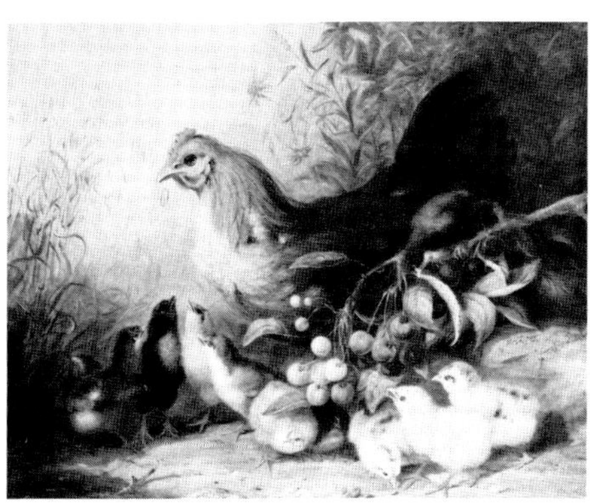
1243

Louis B. Sloan (1932–)

1237 *Backyards*, 1955
Oil on canvas
44 x 36 in. (111.8 x 91.4 cm.)
Signed and dated at lower right: SLOAN/55
Gift of Louis C. Sunstein, 1955.8.3

1238 *Gathering Storm over Philadelphia*, ca. 1961
Oil on canvas
38 x 46¼ in. (96.5 x 117.5 cm.)
Signed at lower right: SLOAN
John Lambert Fund, 1962.12

Marianna Sloan (1875–1954)

1239 *A Rocky Beach*, ca. 1914
Oil on canvas
26³⁄₁₆ x 33³⁄₁₆ in. (66.5 x 84.3 cm.)
Signed at lower right: MARIANNA SLOAN
John Lambert Fund, 1915.6

Anita Miller Smith (b. 1893)

1240 *Houses in the Dunes*, ca. 1918
Oil on canvas
22¹⁄₁₆ x 26 in. (56 x 66 cm.)
Signed at lower right: Anita M.S.
John Lambert Fund, 1919.5

Howard Everett Smith (1885–1970)

1241 *The Captain's Widow*, ca. 1930
Oil on canvas
40¼ x 32⅛ in. (102.2 x 81.6 cm.)
Signed at lower left: Howard E Smith
Joseph E. Temple Fund, 1931.7

James P. Smith. *See* cat. nos. 1651–53.

Jessie Willcox Smith (1863–1935)

1242 *Bonnie as a Young Girl* (Bernice McIlhenny, later Mrs. John Wintersteen, 1900–1986), ca. 1910
Oil on canvas
40⅛ x 28³⁄₁₆ in. (101.9 x 71.6 cm.)
Signed at lower left: JESSIE WILLCOX SMITH
Bequest of Mrs. Bernice McIlhenny Wintersteen, 1986.31.2

Mary Smith (1842–1878)

1243 *Picking Cherries*, 1872
Oil on canvas
20¹⁄₁₆ x 23³⁄₁₆ in. (51 x 58.9 cm.)
Signed and dated at lower right: Mary Smith/ 1872
Gift of Russell Smith, 1878.3

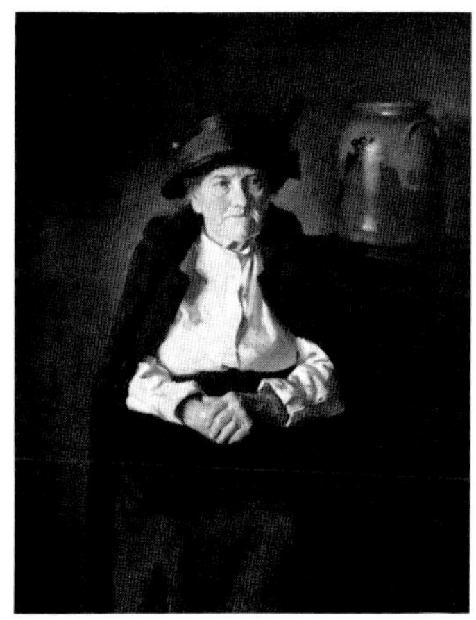
1241

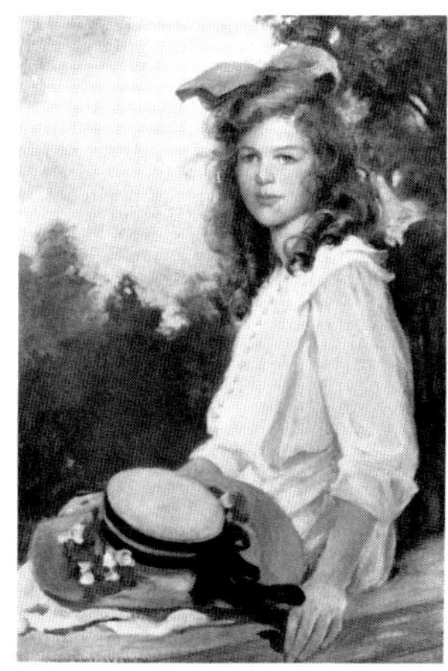
1242

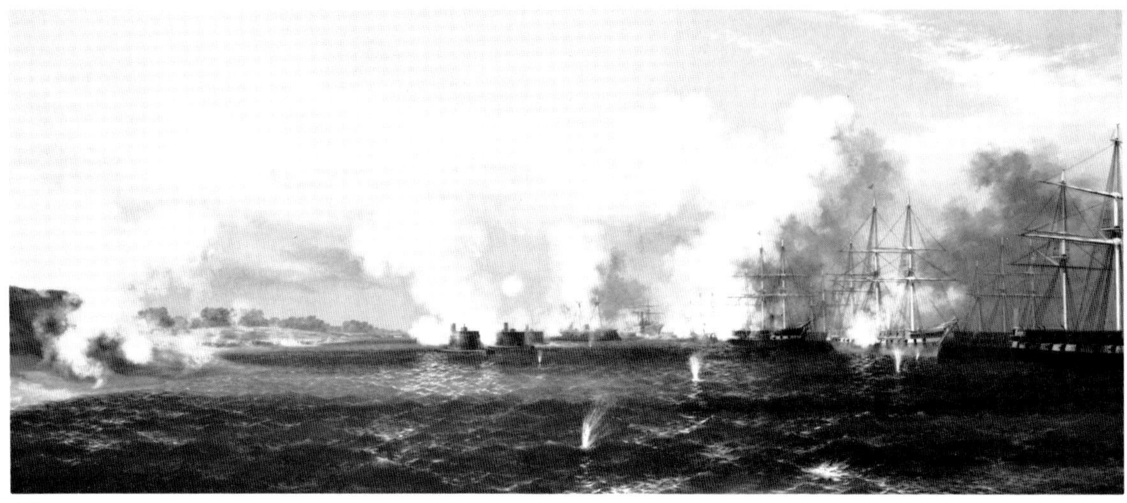
1249

Russell Smith (1812–1896)

1244 *Chew House, Germantown*, 1843
Oil on wood
16 13/16 x 24 in. (42.7 x 61 cm.)
Signed and dated at lower left: Russell Smith 1843
Gift of the artist, 1845.4

1245 *Landscape with Windmill*, probably 1886
Oil on canvas, mounted on academy board
11 15/16 x 17 13/16 in. (30.3 x 45.2 cm.)
Signed at lower right: RS
Annotated on back: Sketch for a Scene/Russell Smith/1886
Bequest of Mary Shiras, 1982.15.1

1246 *Mahonoy Mountain on the Susquehanna River*, 1840
Oil on canvas
41 1/8 x 50 5/8 in. (104.4 x 128.6 cm.)
Signed and dated at lower right: WT. Russell Smith/1840; inscribed on back: [map with "walls of Athens" and other site identifications]
Gift of R. Alexander Montgomery, 1979.9

1247 *Pennypack*, 1889
Oil on canvas
12 1/16 x 18 in. (30.6 x 45.7 cm.)
Signed and dated at lower left: RS./89; inscribed, signed, and dated on back: Pennypack./Russell Smith 1889.
Bequest of Mary Shiras, 1982.15.2

1248 *Unidentified Woman*
Oil on wood
28 x 23 3/4 in. (71.1 x 60.3 cm.)
Bequest of Mary Shiras, 1982.15.3

Xanthus Smith (1838–1929)

1249 *Final Assault upon Fort Fisher, North Carolina*, 1872–73
Oil on canvas
56 x 123 1/2 in. (142.2 x 313.7 cm.)
Signed and dated at lower right: Xanthus Smith/1873; inscribed, signed, and dated on back: Final assault upon Fort Fisher N.C./Painted for Jos.Harrison Jr. Esq-/By Xanthus Smith/1872–3.
Gift of Mrs. Sarah Harrison (The Joseph Harrison, Jr. Collection), 1878.1.6

William Snaith (1908–1974)

1250 *Cathedral Architect*, 1950
Oil on masonite
36 x 30 in. (91.4 x 76.2 cm.)

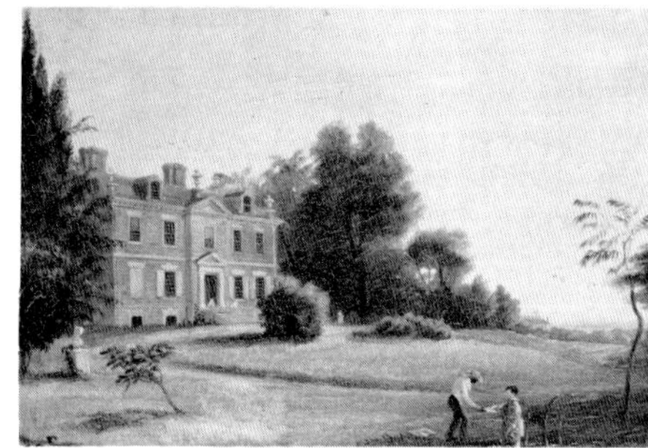
1244

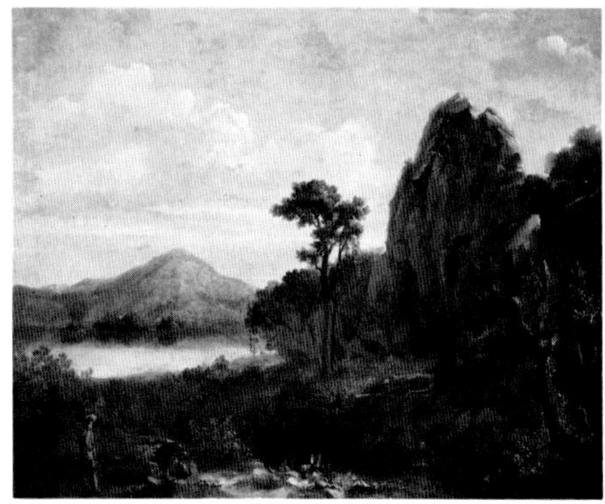
1246

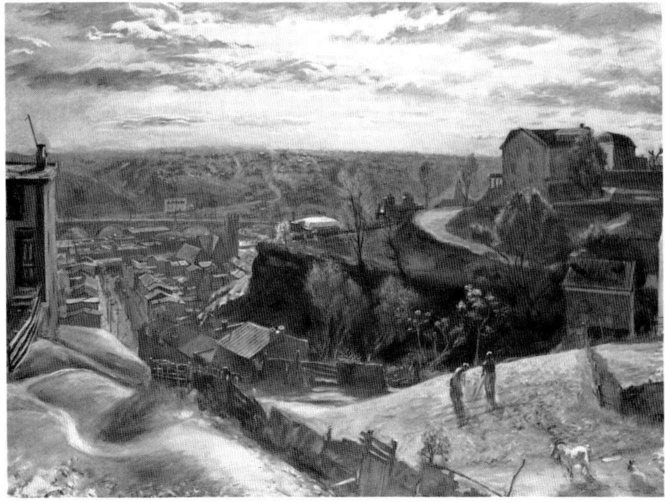
1261

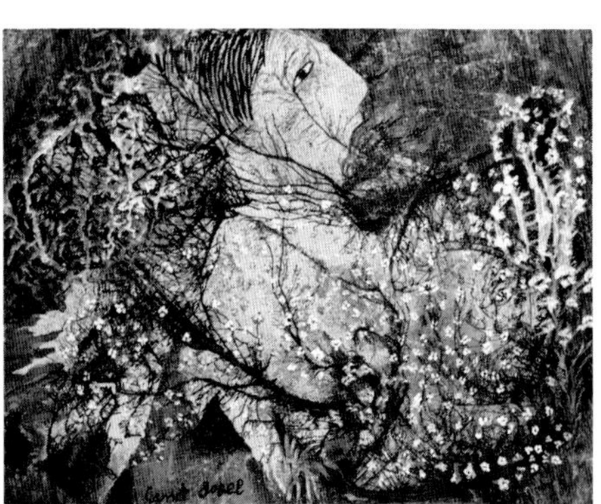
1252

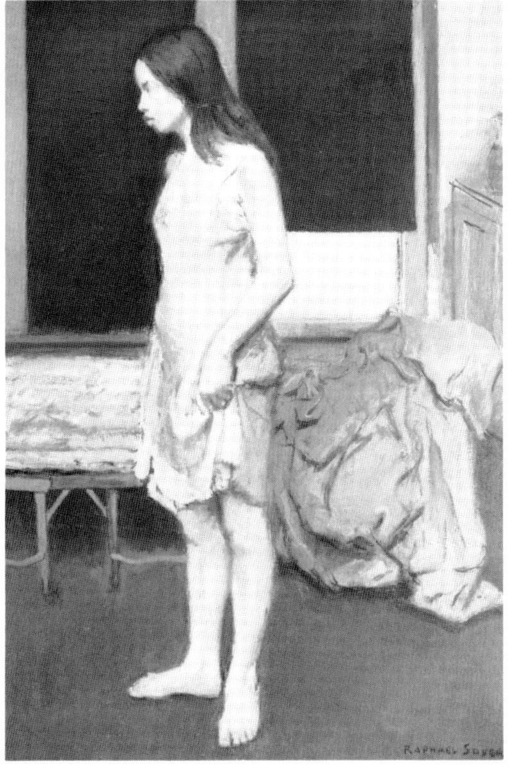
1253

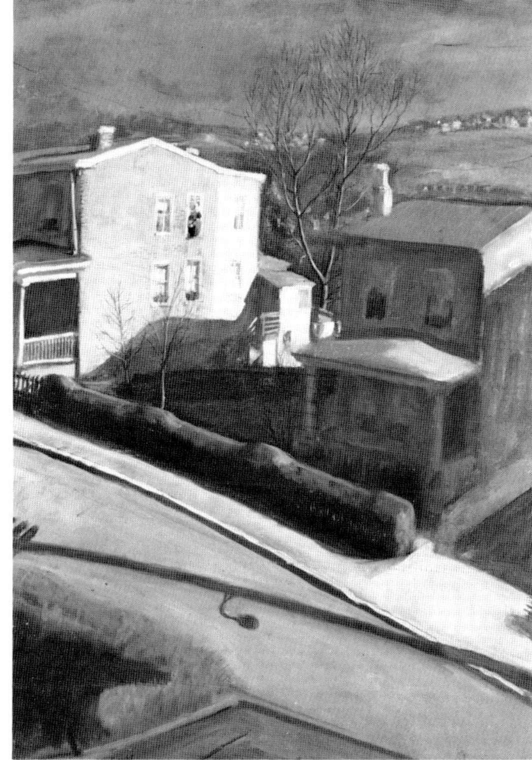
1260

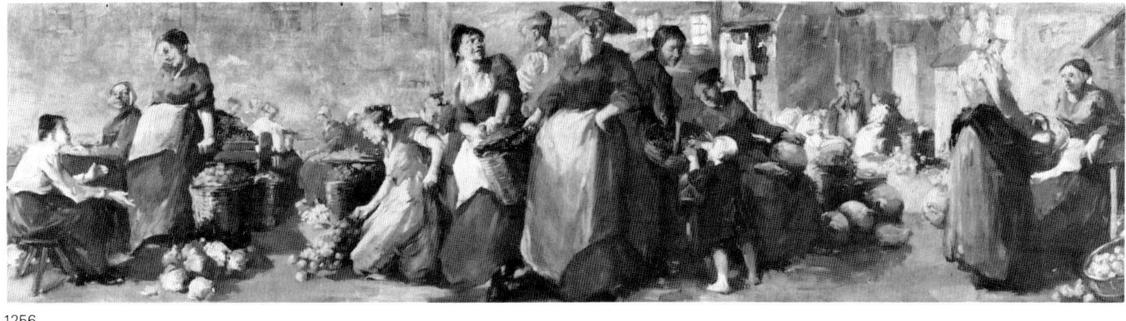
1256

Signed and dated at lower left: Snaith/50
John Lambert Fund, 1951.13

Henry B. Snell (1858–1943)

1251 *A Moonlight Night*
Oil on cardboard
11½ x 13½ in. (29.2 x 34.3 cm.)
Signed at lower left: Hry B Snell
Gift of friends of the artist, 1947.13

Janet Sobel (b. 1894)

1252 *Invasion Day*, 1944
Oil on canvas
22¹⁄₁₆ x 28 in. (56 x 71.1 cm.)
Signed at lower left: Janet Sobel
John Lambert Fund, 1945.11

Raphael Soyer (1899–1987)

1253 *Disorder*, 1947
Oil on canvas
36¹⁄₁₆ x 25 in. (91.6 x 63.5 cm.)
Signed at lower right: RAPHAEL SOYER
Henry D. Gilpin Fund, 1948.12

Marie Haughton Spaeth (1883–1937)

1254 *Apennine Village*, ca. 1913
Oil on canvas
27 x 26¹⁄₁₆ in. (68.6 x 66.2 cm.)
John Lambert Fund, 1914.11

Elizabeth Sparhawk-Jones (1885–1968)

1255 *Injustice*, 1944
Watercolor on primed linen, mounted on masonite
39⁹⁄₁₆ x 20³⁄₁₆ in. (100.5 x 51.3 cm.)
Signed at lower left: ESJ
John Lambert Fund, 1948.20

1256 *The Market*, by 1909
Oil on canvas
35 x 133 in. (88.9 x 337.8 cm.)
Source unknown, 1909.10

1257 *Woman with Fish*, 1936 or 1937
Oil on canvas
18³⁄₁₆ x 15 in. (46.2 x 38.1 cm.)
Signed at lower left: E. S-J
Gift of Mrs. Thomas E. Drake (The Margaretta S. Hinchman Collection), 1955.15.13

Francis Speight (1896–)

1258 *Glendale*, by 1937
Oil on canvas
31⅞ x 42¹⁄₁₆ in. (81 x 106.8 cm.)
Gift of Mrs. Alfred G. B. Steel, 1953.14

1259 *Highland Avenue, Manayunk*, 1956
Oil on canvas
20¹⁄₁₆ x 26 in. (51 x 66 cm.)
Signed and dated at lower left: F. Speight/'56
Gift of James P. and Ruth Marshall Magill, 1957.15.31

1260 *Late Afternoon*, 1931
Oil on canvas
30³⁄₁₆ x 22⅛ in. (76.7 x 56.2 cm.)
Signed at lower left: Francis Speight
John Lambert Fund, 1943.15

1261 *Schuylkill Valley Town*, 1940
Oil on canvas
40¼ x 54⅛ in. (102.2 x 137.5 cm.)
Signed at lower left: Francis Speight
Joseph E. Temple Fund, 1942.11

Mrs. Francis Speight. *See* Sarah Blakeslee.

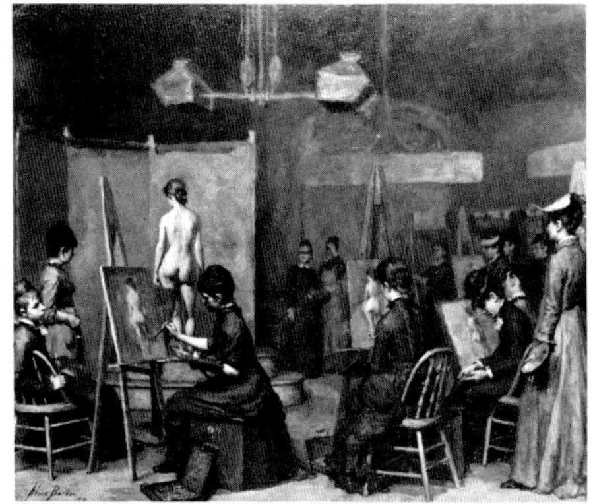

1265

1266

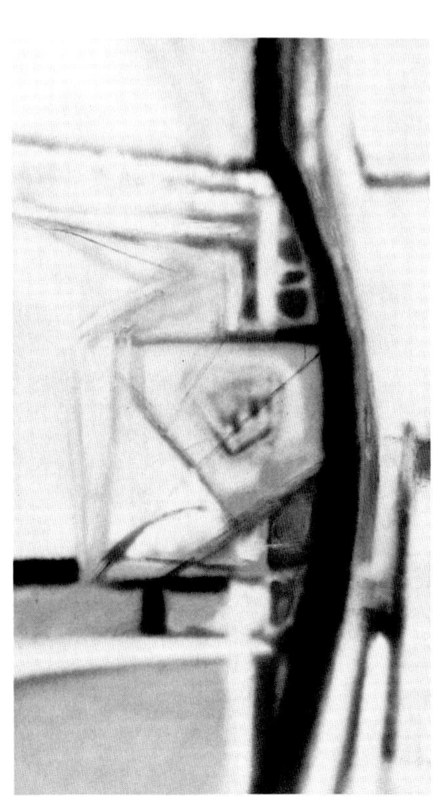

1267

Benton M. Spruance (1904–1967)

1262 *Jeweler's Window*, 1948
Oil on canvas
$23\frac{15}{16}$ x 30 in. (60.8 x 76.2 cm.)
Signed at lower right: BS
Joseph E. Temple Fund, 1949.11

Everett F. Spruce (1908–)

1263 *Austin Hills*, 1945
Oil on composition board
16 x 20 in. (40.6 x 50.8 cm.)
Signed at lower right: ESPRUCE; signed, inscribed, and dated on back: EVERETT SPRUCE/AUSTIN HILLS/OIL 1945/16 x 20 16 x 20
John Lambert Fund, 1948.13

Richard M. Staigg. *See* cat. no. 1654.

Julian Stanczak (1928–)

1264 *Interlocking Shadows*, 1965
Acrylic on canvas
$53\frac{3}{4}$ x $72\frac{3}{4}$ in. (136.5 x 184.8 cm.)
Signed, dated, and inscribed on stretcher: 9410 JULIAN STANCZAK 1965/"INTERLOCKING SHADOWS"
John Lambert Fund, 1966.6

Mrs. William Staughton. *See* Anna Claypoole Peale, cat. nos. 1644–45.

Alice Barber Stephens (Mrs. Charles H. Stephens, 1858–1932)

1265 *The Women's Life Class* (illustration for William C. Brownell, "The Art Schools of Philadelphia," *Scribner's Monthly* 18, Sept. 1879, pp. 737–50), ca. 1879
Oil on cardboard (grisaille)
12 x 14 in. (30.5 x 35.6 cm.)
Signed and dated at lower left: Alice Barber/'79
Gift of the artist, 1879.2

Charles H. Stephens (ca. 1855–1931)

1266 *Anatomical Lecture by Dr. William Williams Keen* (illustration for William C. Brownell, "The Art Schools of Philadelphia," *Scribner's Monthly* 18, Sept. 1879, pp. 737–50), ca. 1879
Oil on cardboard (grisaille)
$8\frac{5}{8}$ x 11 in. (21.9 x 27.9 cm.)
Gift of the artist, 1879.6

Hedda Sterne (1916–)

1267 *Roads, No. 6*, 1956
Oil on canvas
$86\frac{1}{8}$ x $50\frac{1}{8}$ in. (218.8 x 127.3 cm.)
Signed at lower right: HeddaSterne
John Lambert Fund, 1960.13

Maurice Sterne (1878–1957)

1268 *Misty Day*, 1951
Oil on masonite
$32\frac{3}{8}$ x $45\frac{1}{2}$ in. (82.2 x 115.6 cm.)
Signed and dated at lower left: Sterne/51
Bequest of Vera Segal Sterne, 1966.9

Florine Stettheimer (1871–1944)

1269 *Picnic at Bedford Hills*, 1918
Oil on canvas
$40\frac{5}{16}$ x $50\frac{1}{4}$ in. (102.4 x 127.6 cm.)
Signed at lower left: FS [monogram]; inscribed and dated on pot: SUMME[R]/1918; inscribed on umbrellas: FLORINE; ETTIE; CATHIE
Gift of Ettie Stettheimer, 1950.21

A. Brockie Stevenson (1919–)

1270 *Black Crows*, 1947
Oil over egg tempera on masonite
$23\frac{13}{16}$ x 40 in. (60.5 x 101.6 cm.)
Signed and dated at lower right and on back: A. Brockie Stevenson/1947
John Lambert Fund, 1948.14

Ethelyn Cosby Stewart (b. 1900)

1271 *Magnolias*, 1934
Oil on canvas, mounted on canvas board
$19\frac{7}{8}$ x $15\frac{13}{16}$ in. (50.5 x 40.2 cm.)
Signed and dated at lower right: Ethelyn C. Stewart 1934
Joseph E. Temple Fund, 1936.19

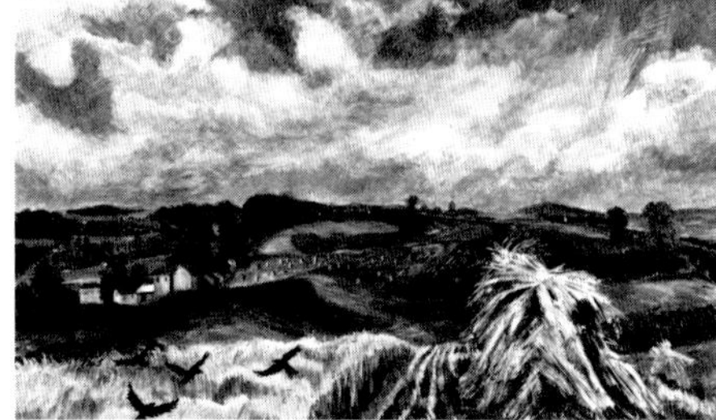

1270

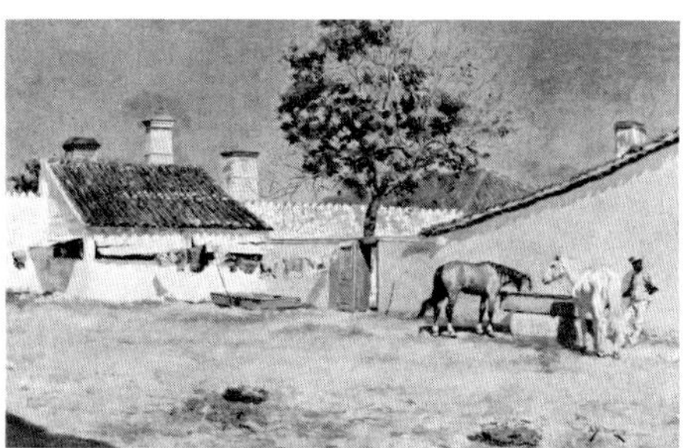

1272

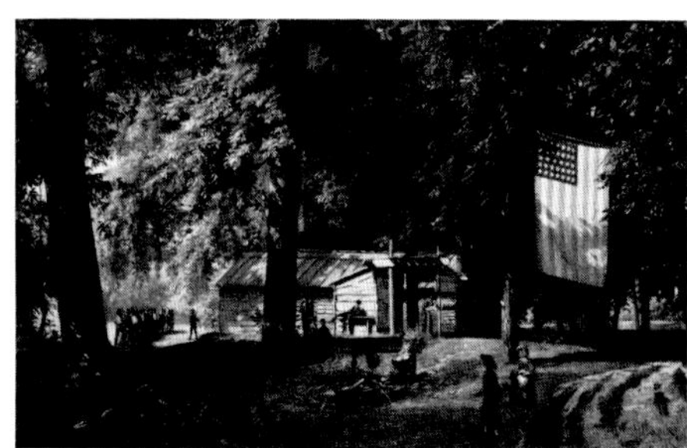

1273

Julius L. Stewart (1855–1920)

1272 *Horse Trough on Cuban Plantation*, 1876
Oil on wood
9 3/16 x 13 13/16 in. (23.3 x 35.1 cm.)
Signed and dated at lower right: JLStewart. 76.
Gift of Mrs. Ellen P. Broleman in accordance with the wishes of her brother Robert Ralston Stewart, 1919.9.4

Attributed to **William James Stillman** (1828–1901)

1273 *Union Soldiers in Camp*, ca. 1861
Oil on canvas
12 9/16 x 20 in. (31.9 x 50.8 cm.)
Gift of Mr. and Mrs. Edward Kesler, 1975.20.8

Alice Kent Stoddard (Mrs. Joseph T. Pearson, Jr., 1885–1976)

1274 *Polly* (Mrs. H. Lea Hudson), by 1928
Oil on canvas
54 x 44 1/8 in. (137.2 x 112.1 cm.)
Signed at upper left: A. K. STODDARD
Gift of Mrs. H. Lea Hudson, 1966.1

1275 *Elizabeth Sparhawk-Jones* (1885–1968), ca. 1910
Oil on canvas
27 x 20 1/16 in. (68.6 x 51 cm.)
Henry D. Gilpin Fund, 1911.4

Julian Story (1857–1919)

1276 *Marie Charlotte Corday* (1768–1793), 1889
Oil on canvas
99 x 79 in. (251.5 x 200.7 cm.)
Signed and dated at lower right: Julian Story 89
Gift of Mrs. Julian Story, 1946.15

1277 *Harriet Hare McClelland*, probably 1893
Oil on canvas
74 1/8 x 56 1/4 in. (188.3 x 142.9 cm.)
Signed, inscribed, and dated at lower left: Julian Story/Paris 189[3]
Gift of Mrs. Mary Hall White, 1982.14

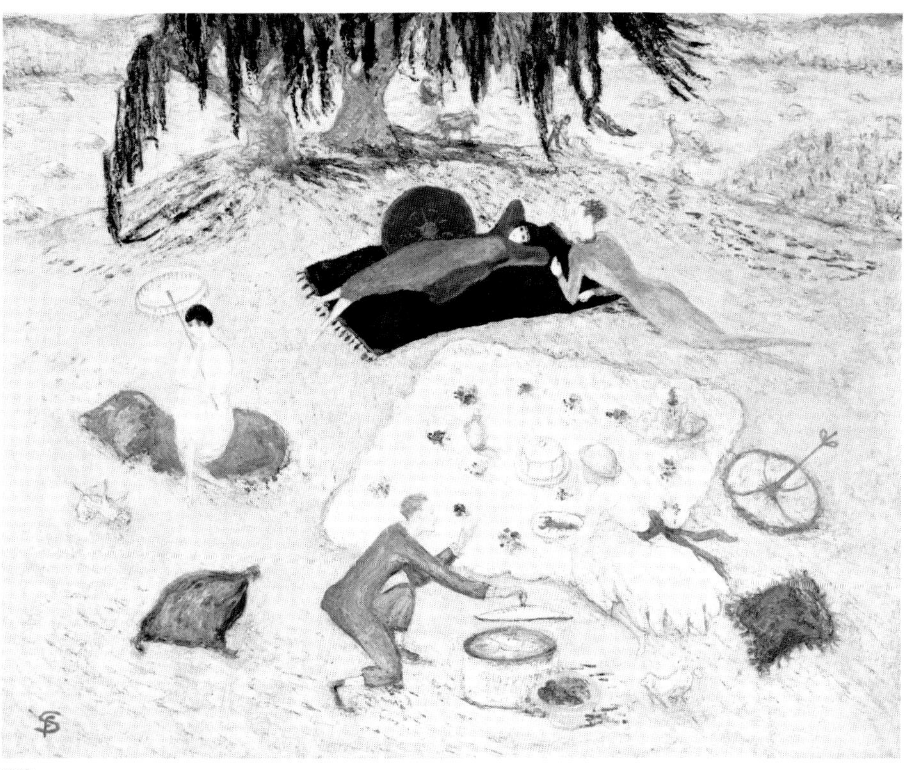

1269

Robert Street (1796–1865)

1278 *Joseph Bonaparte* (1768–1844), 1834
Oil on canvas, mounted on plywood
29 15/16 x 25 1/16 in. (76 x 63.7 cm.)
Signed and dated at upper left: BY R.STREET/1834
Gift of Mrs. John Frederick Lewis (The John Frederick Lewis Memorial Collection), 1933.10.75

1279 *George Washington* (1732–1799) (after Gilbert Stuart)
Oil on canvas
30 3/16 x 25 1/4 in. (76.7 x 64.1 cm.)
Gift of Mrs. John Frederick Lewis (The John Frederick Lewis Memorial Collection), 1933.10.76

Alf Jorgen Stromsted (b. 1898)

1280 *Sanctuary*, 1942
Oil on canvas
18 3/16 x 24 1/16 in. (46.2 x 61.1 cm.)
Signed and dated at lower left: Stromsted/42
John Lambert Fund, 1944.6

Laura D. Stroud. *See* Laura D. S. Ladd.

Mary Stuard. *See* Mary Townsend Mason.

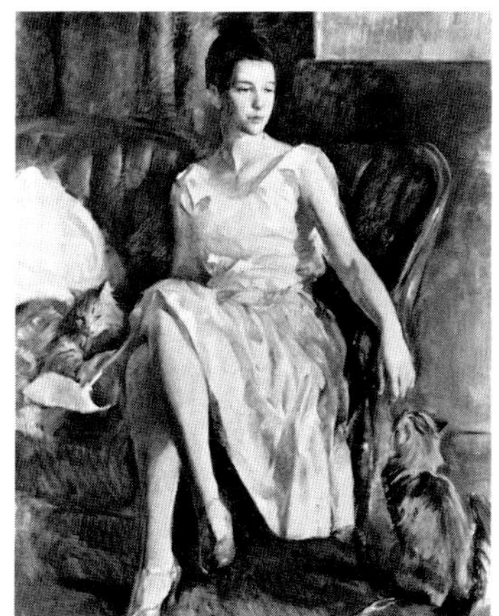

1274

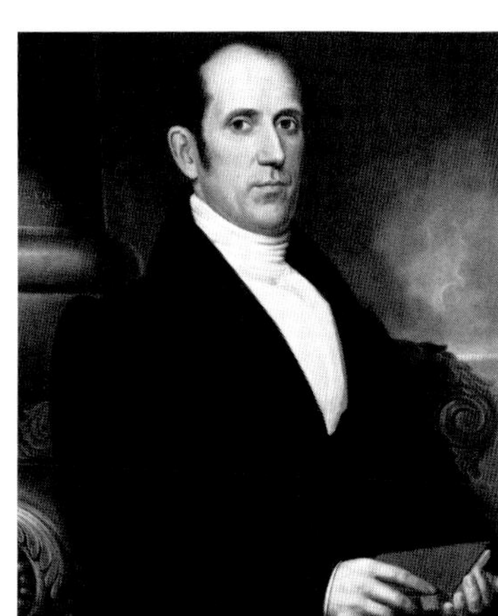

1278

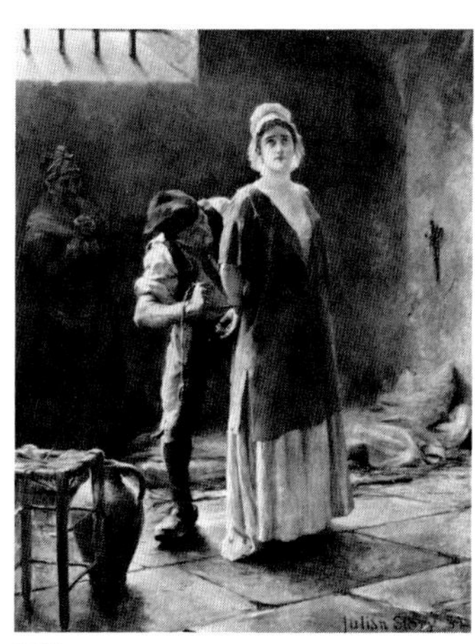

1276

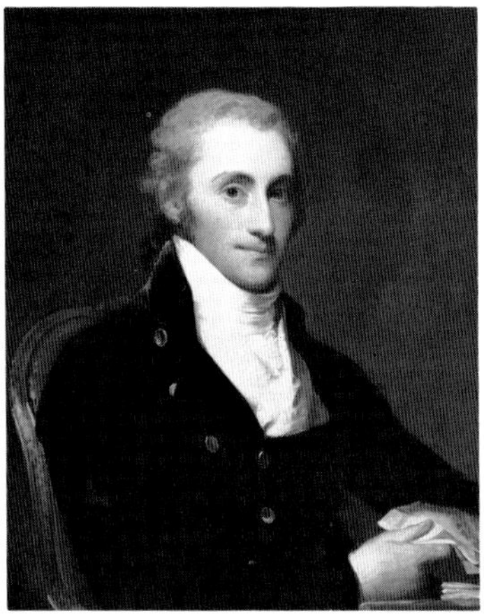

1289

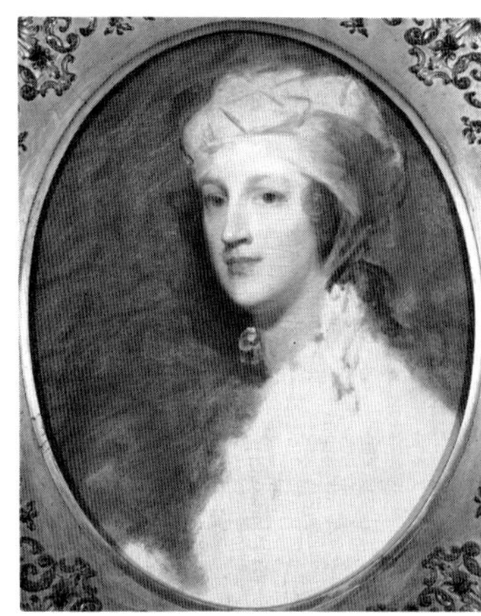

1284

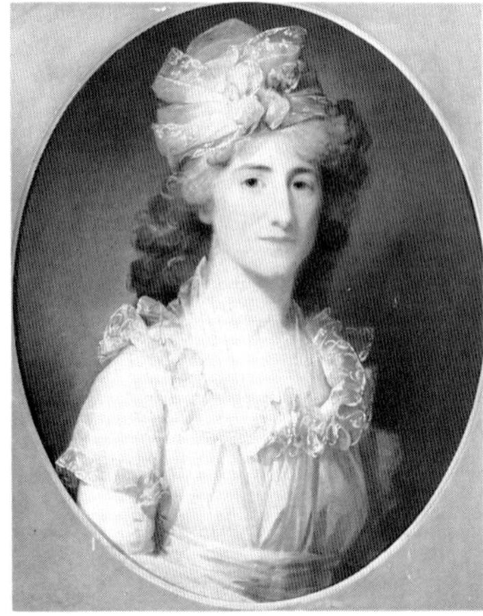

1293

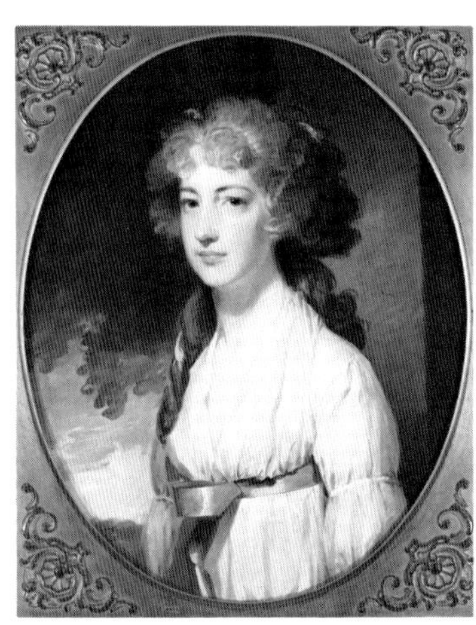

1285

Gilbert Stuart (1755–1828)

1281 *Ann Penn Allen* (later Mrs. James Greenleaf, 1769–1851), ca. 1795
Oil on canvas
29 x 24 in. (73.7 x 61 cm.)
Bequest of Mrs. Mary W. F. Howe in memory of her father, J. Gillingham Fell, 1924.6

1282 *Captain Joseph Anthony* (1738–1798), ca. 1795
Oil on canvas
$29\frac{15}{16}$ x $25\frac{1}{16}$ in. (76 x 63.7 cm.)
Bequest of Oliver Wolcott Gibbs, 1909.11

1283 *Admiral Sir Henry Lorraine Baker* (1787–1859), 1817
Oil on wood
$25\frac{15}{16}$ x $21\frac{1}{4}$ in. (65.9 x 54 cm.)
Gift of the Reverend Alfred Langdon Elwyn, by exchange, 1891.11

1284 *Mrs. Samuel Blodget* (née Rebecca Smith, 1772–1837), ca. 1798
Oil on canvas
$27\frac{1}{2}$ x $23\frac{1}{4}$ in. (69.9 x 59.1 cm.)
Bequest of Henry C. Carey (The Carey Collection), 1879.8.23

1285 *Elizabeth Beale Bordley* (1777–1863), ca. 1797
Oil on canvas
$29\frac{1}{4}$ x 24 in. (74.3 x 61 cm.)
Bequest of Elizabeth Mifflin, 1886.2

1286 *Alexander James Dallas* (1759–1817), ca. 1800
Oil on canvas
$28\frac{15}{16}$ x $23\frac{7}{8}$ in. (73.5 x 60.6 cm.)
Annual Membership Fund, 1900.3

1287 *Dr. John Fothergill* (1712–1780), 1781
Oil on canvas
$35\frac{5}{8}$ x $27\frac{3}{4}$ in. (90.5 x 70.5 cm.)
Signed at lower right: G. Stuar[t]
Annual Membership Fund, 1903.5

1288 *Colonel Isaac Franks* (1759–1822), 1802
Oil on canvas
$29\frac{1}{8}$ x $24\frac{1}{16}$ in. (74 x 61.1 cm.)
Bequest of Henry C. Gibson, 1892.6.86

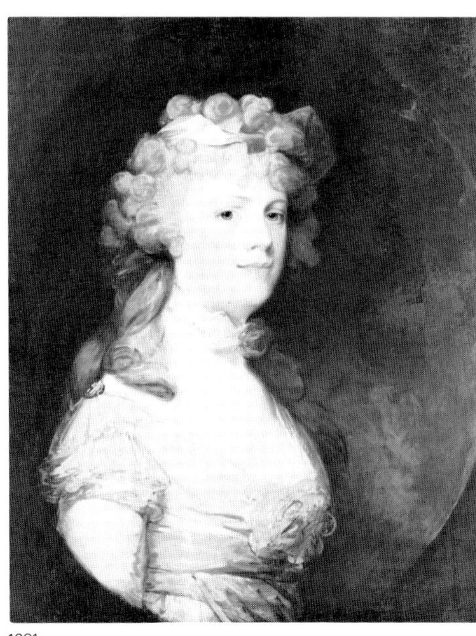

1281

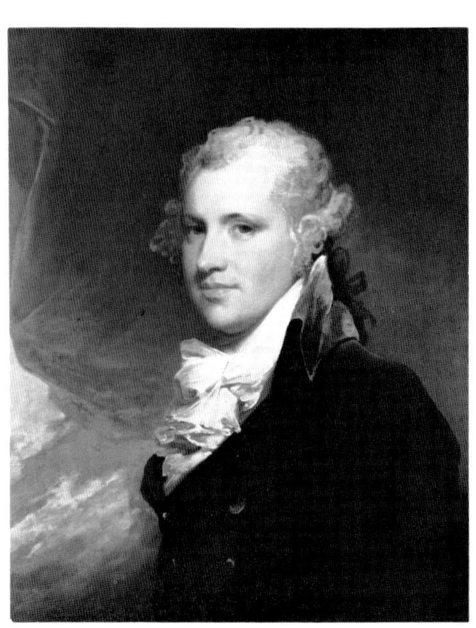

1291

1289 *Samuel Gatliff* (d. 1806), ca. 1800
Oil on canvas
29³⁄₁₆ x 24⅛ in. (74.1 x 61.3 cm.)
Bequest of Dr. Ferdinand Campbell Stewart, 1899.9.1

1290 *Mrs. Samuel Gatliff and Daughter Elizabeth* (Mrs. Gatliff, 1779–1853), ca. 1798
Oil on canvas
29¼ x 24 in. (74.3 x 61 cm.)
Bequest of Dr. Ferdinand Campbell Stewart, 1899.9.2

1291 *James Greenleaf* (1765–1843), 1795
Oil on canvas
29 x 24 in. (73.7 x 61 cm.)
Deposited by J. Rush Ritter on behalf of the Livingston family, 1883.3

1292 *Samuel Griffin* (1750–1810), ca. 1800
Oil on canvas
29 x 24 in. (73.7 x 61 cm.)
Bequest of Dr. Ferdinand Campbell Stewart, 1899.9.3

1293 *Mrs. William Jackson* (née Elizabeth Willing, 1768–1858), ca. 1798
Oil on canvas
29⁵⁄₁₆ x 24¼ in. (74.5 x 61.6 cm.)
Bequest of Ann Willing Jackson, 1876.2.1

1294 *Mrs. James Madison* (née Dorothea "Dolley" Payne, 1768–1849), 1804
Oil on canvas
29 x 24 in. (73.7 x 61 cm.)
Harrison Earl Fund, 1899.7.1

1295 *Peter Meircken* (1766–1822), 1798
Oil on canvas
28¹⁵⁄₁₆ x 23¹⁵⁄₁₆ in. (73.5 x 60.8 cm.)
Henry D. Gilpin Fund, 1918.6.1

1296 *Mrs. Peter Meircken* (née Maria Snowden, 1777–1840), 1798
Oil on canvas
29 x 24 in. (73.7 x 61 cm.)
Henry D. Gilpin Fund, 1918.6.2

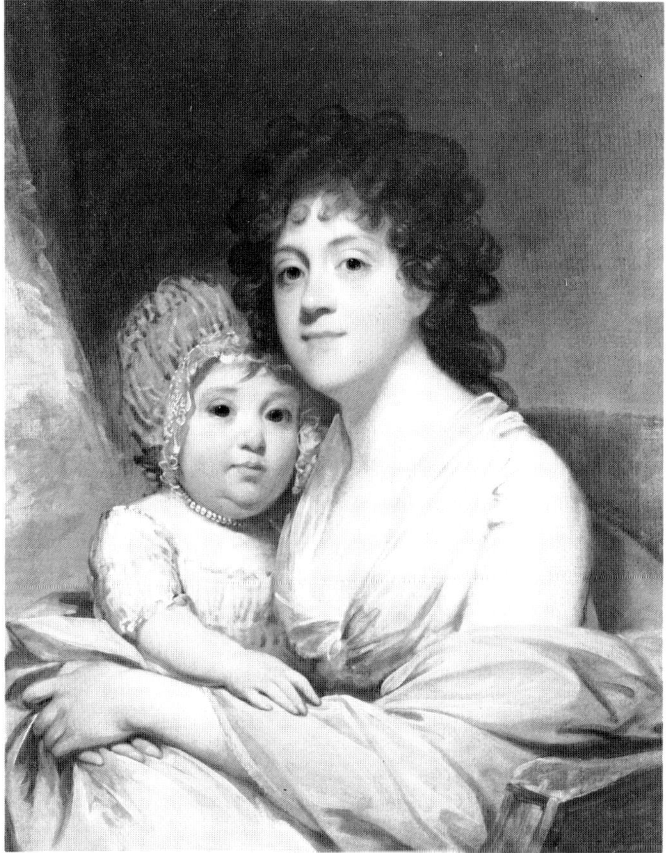
1290

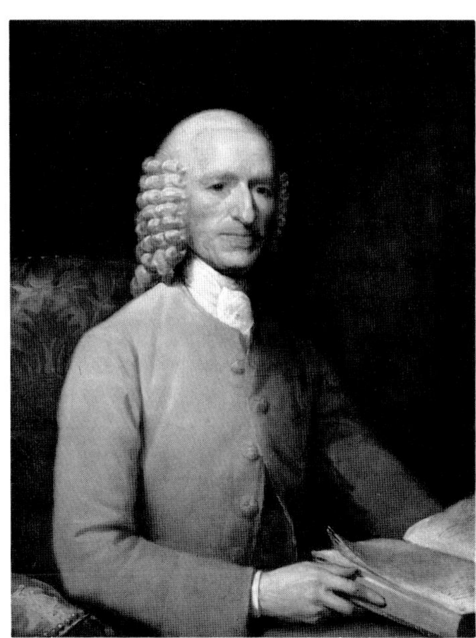
1287

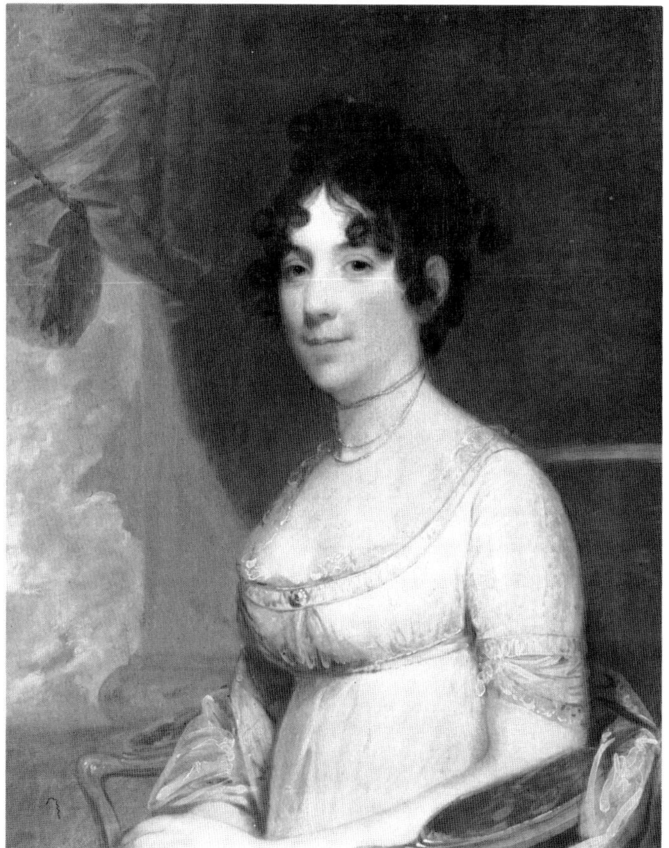
1294

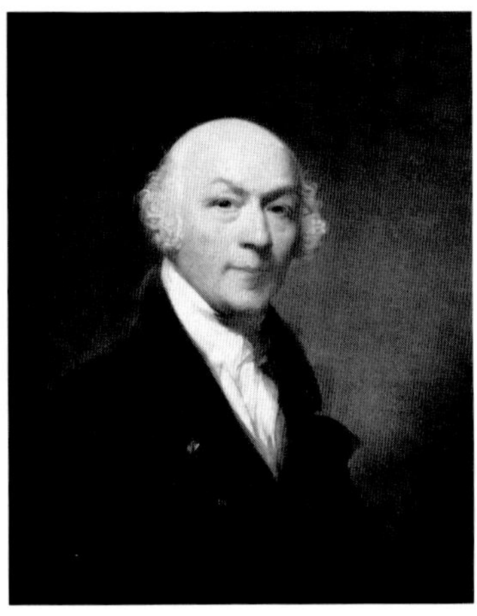
1298

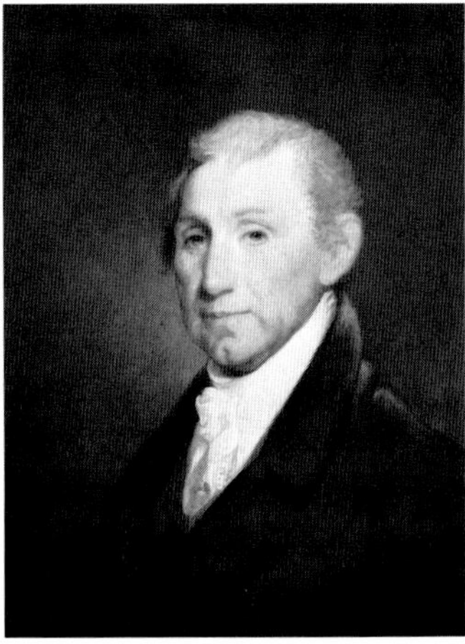
1297

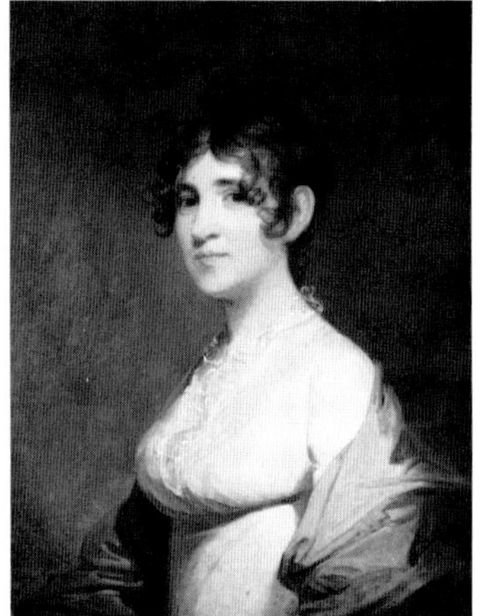
1299

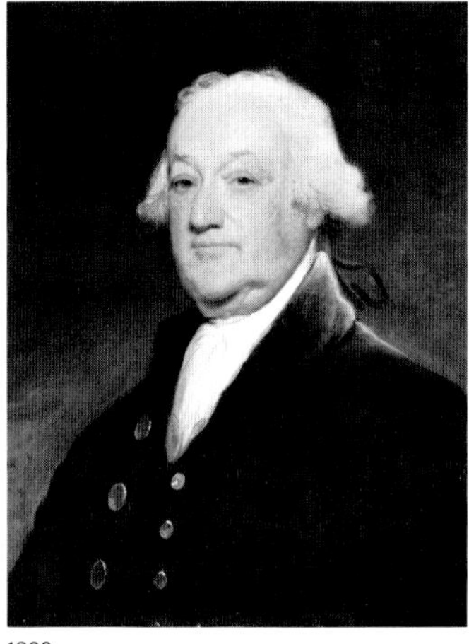
1300

1297 *James Monroe* (1758–1831), 1817
Oil on wood
26⅝ x 21½ in. (67.6 x 54.6 cm.)
Pennsylvania Academy purchase, 1900.4

1298 *William Montgomery* (1752–1831), 1807
Oil on canvas
29 x 24³⁄₁₆ in. (73.7 x 61.4 cm.)
Bequest of Annie M. Wilcox, 1932.12.2

1299 *Mrs. William Montgomery* (née Rachel Harvey), 1807
Oil on canvas
29 x 24⅛ in. (73.7 x 61.3 cm.)
Bequest of Annie M. Wilcox, 1932.12.1

1300 *Colonel John Nixon* (1735–1808), 1800
Oil on canvas
29 x 24 in. (73.7 x 61 cm.)
Bequest of Henry Cramond, 1887.5

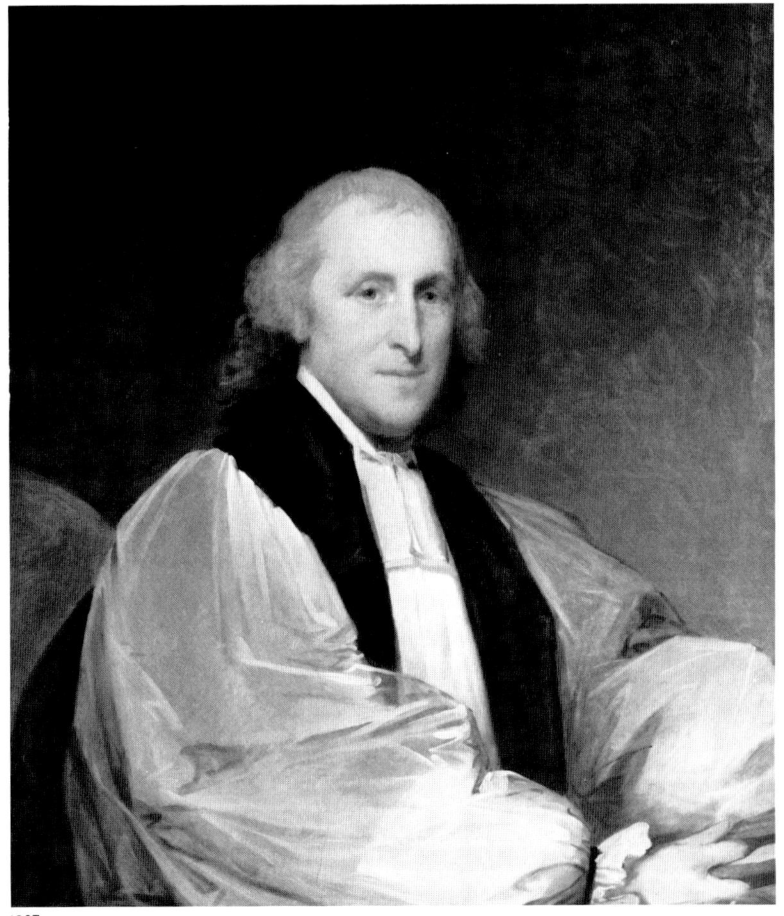
1307

1301 *George Plumstead* (1765–1805), 1800
Oil on canvas
29¼ x 24¼ in. (74.3 x 61.6 cm.)
Bequest of Helen Ross Scheetz, 1891.12.1

1302 *Mrs. George Plumstead* (née Anna Helena Amelia Ross, 1776–1846), 1800
Oil on canvas
29⅜ x 24³⁄₁₆ in. (74.6 x 61.4 cm.)
Bequest of Helen Ross Scheetz, 1891.12.2

1303 *George Reignold*
Oil on wood
29 x 23⁹⁄₁₆ in. (73.7 x 59.8 cm.)
Harrison Earl Fund, 1898.8

1304 *Constantine François Volney, Count of Chasseboeuf* (1757–1820), ca. 1795
Oil on canvas
29¹⁄₁₆ x 23¹⁄₁₆ in. (73.8 x 58.6 cm.)
Gift of Mrs. Thomas Bayard, 1922.8

1305 *George Washington* (1732–1799) (Athenaeum-type portrait), after 1796
Oil on canvas
29½ x 24½ in. (74.9 x 62.2 cm.)
Bequest of Paul Beck, Jr., 1845.3.2

1306 *George Washington (The Lansdowne Portrait)*, 1796
Oil on canvas
96 x 60 in. (243.8 x 152.4 cm.)
Signed and dated at lower left: G. Stuart/1796
Bequest of William Bingham, 1811.2

1307 *Bishop William White* (1748–1836), ca. 1795
Oil on canvas
36 x 31 in. (91.4 x 78.7 cm.)
Bequest of William White, 1913.11.3

1308 *Abigail Willing* (later Mrs. Richard Peters, Jr., 1777–1841), ca. 1803
Oil on canvas
28½ x 24½ in. (72.4 x 62.2 cm.)
Gift of Mr. and Mrs. John White Field, 1887.1.8

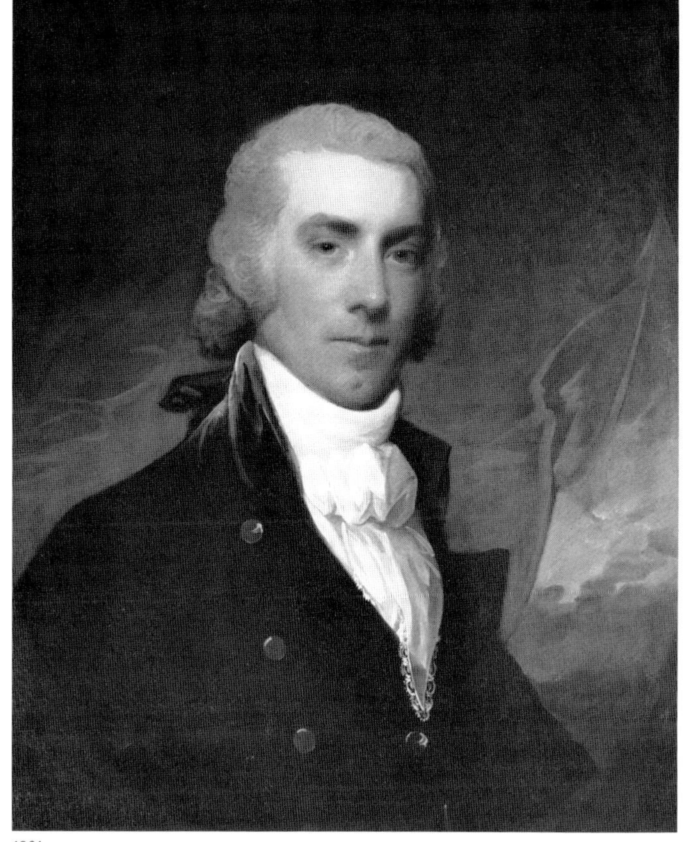
1301

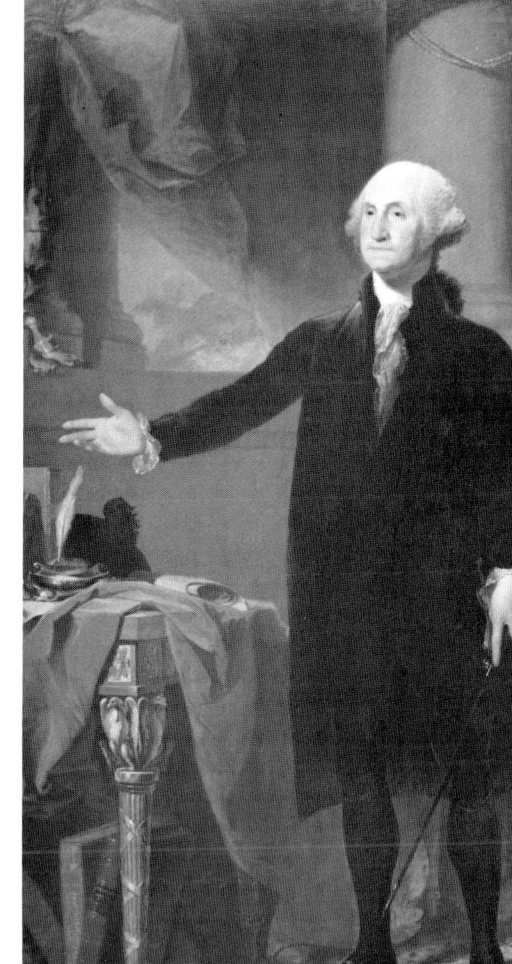
1306

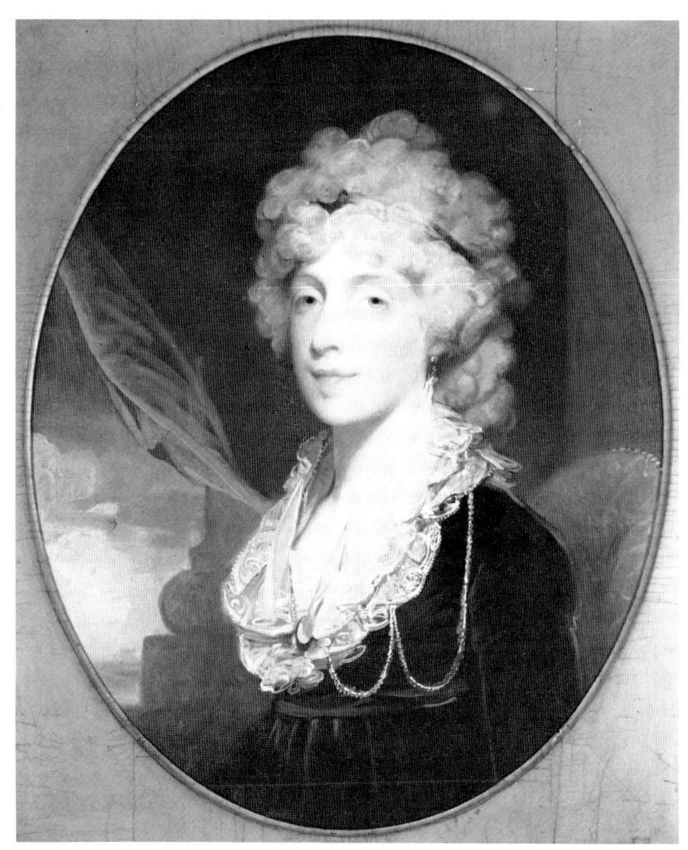
1302

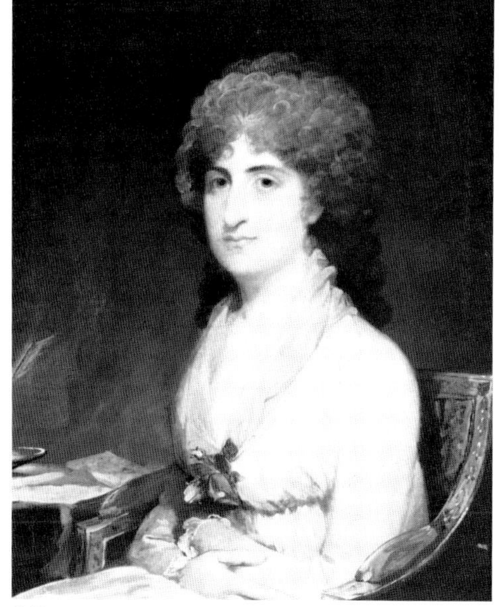
1308

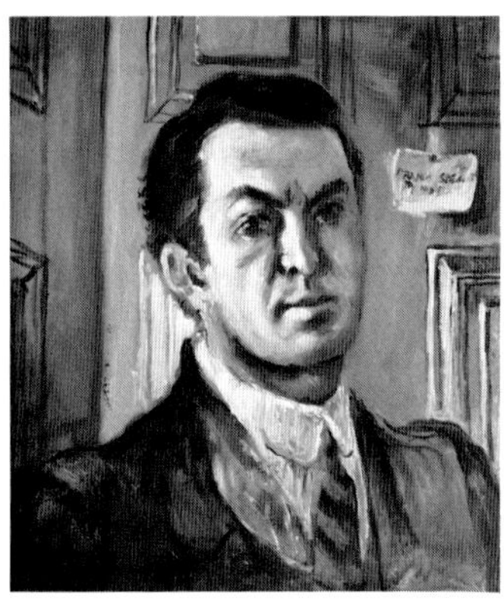

1311

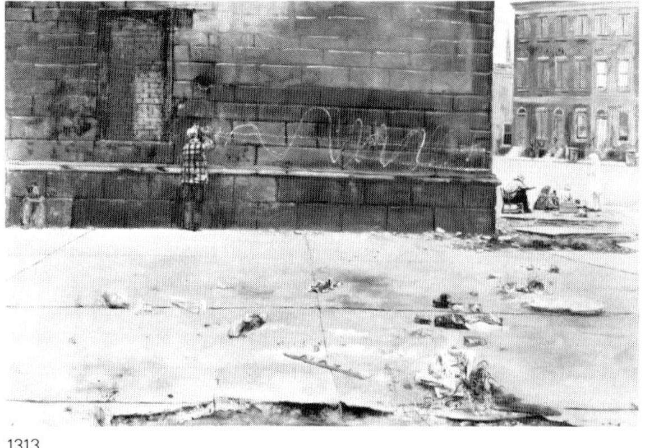

1313

Walter Stuempfig (1914–1970)

1309 *Return at Six*, ca. 1934
Oil on canvas
29 3/8 x 36 1/4 in. (74.6 x 92.1 cm.)
Signed at lower right: W. Stuempfig
John Lambert Fund, 1935.9

1310 *Serenade*, by 1943
Oil on canvas
35 5/8 x 42 1/4 in. (90.5 x 107.3 cm.)
Signed at lower right: STUEMPFIG
Gift of Mrs. R. Kirk Askew, 1978.20

1311 *Sketch of Francis Speight* (1896–), ca. 1950
Oil on canvas
21 1/8 x 18 1/4 in. (53.7 x 46.4 cm.)
Inscribed at upper right: FRANCIS SPEIGHT/BY HIS F[RIEND]
Gift of Francis Speight, 1977.12

1312 *Sturgeon*
Oil on canvas
18 x 14 in. (45.7 x 35.6 cm.)
Signed at lower right: STUEMPFIG
Gift of Dr. and Mrs. Emile Gordon Stoloff, 1972.5

1313 *The Wall*, 1946
Oil on canvas
31 5/16 x 48 1/4 in. (79.5 x 122.6 cm.)
Signed and dated at lower right: STUEMPFIG 1946
Joseph E. Temple Fund, 1947.10

Jane Cooper Sully
See Jane Cooper Sully Darley.

Thomas Sully (1783–1872)

1314 *The Reverend James B. Abercrombie* (1758–1841), 1810
Oil on canvas
29 x 36 3/16 in. (73.7 x 91.9 cm.)
Bequest of Eleanor C. A. Jackson, 1964.13

1315 *Lewis Richard Ashhurst* (1806–1874), 1833
Oil on canvas
30 3/8 x 24 7/8 in. (77.2 x 63.2 cm.)
Signed and dated at lower right: TS.1833.
Bequest of Richard Ashhurst, 1969.20.2

1316 *Major Thomas Biddle* (1790–1831), 1818
Oil on canvas
36 1/2 x 28 1/16 in. (92.7 x 71.3 cm.)
Bequest of Ann E. Biddle, 1925.8

1317 *The Reverend Robert Blackwell* (1748–1831), 1853
Oil on canvas
29 3/16 x 24 1/8 in. (74.1 x 61.3 cm.)
Inscribed, signed, and dated on back (before lining): Revd Robert Blackwell./TS–1853/ From a miniature
Bequest of Mrs. Willing Spencer, 1963.5.1

1318 *Henry C. Budd* (1849–1921), 1856–57
Oil on canvas, mounted on cardboard
23 15/16 x 19 15/16 in. (60.8 x 50.6 cm.), oval
Bequest of Ida Budd, 1935.2.2

1319 *Ida Budd*, 1857
Oil on canvas, mounted on cardboard
24 3/8 x 19 13/16 in. (61.9 x 50.3 cm.), oval
Bequest of Ida Budd, 1935.2.3

1320 *Susan Campbell* (d. 1846), 1842
Oil on millboard
24 x 19 15/16 in. (61 x 50.6 cm.)
Signed and dated at lower right: TS. 1842
Gift of Mrs. John Frederick Lewis through her son, John Frederick Lewis, Jr., 1938.13.1

1321 *Edward L. Carey* (1806–1845), 1859
Oil on canvas
30 1/4 x 25 1/4 in. (76.8 x 64.1 cm.)
Signed, dated, and inscribed on back: TS 1859/ March. Copy no 3
Gift of Maria Carey, 1859.1

1322 *Child Reposing*, 1859
Oil on academy board
12 9/16 x 10 1/16 in. (31.9 x 25.6 cm.)
Signed and dated at lower left: TS 1859
Bequest of Henry C. Gibson, 1892.6.87

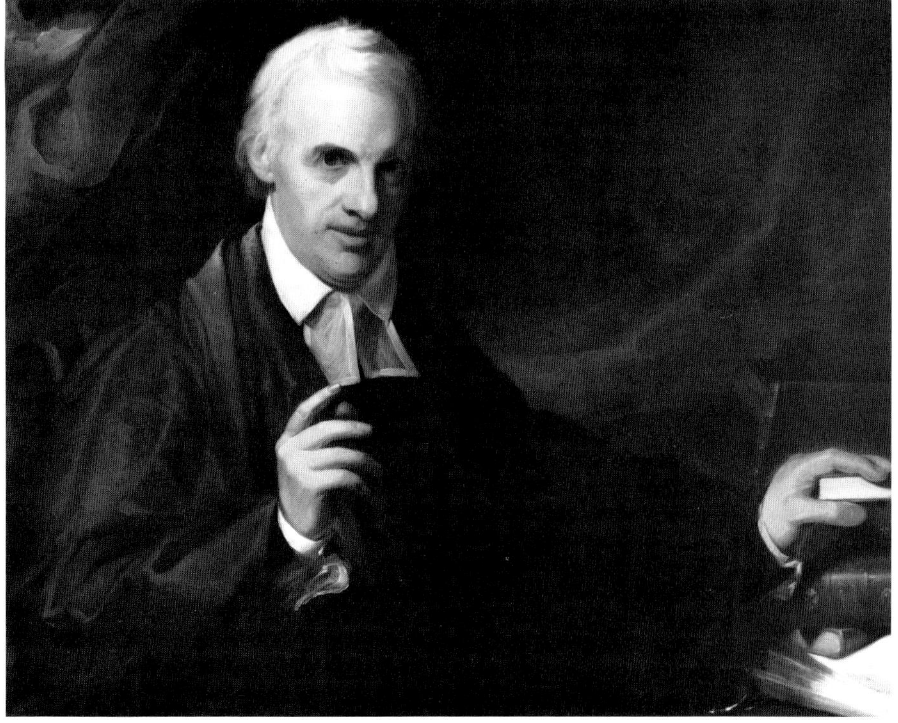

1314

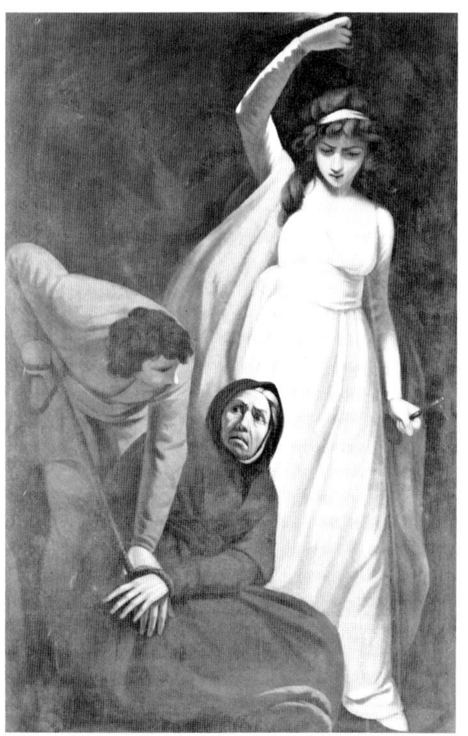

1328

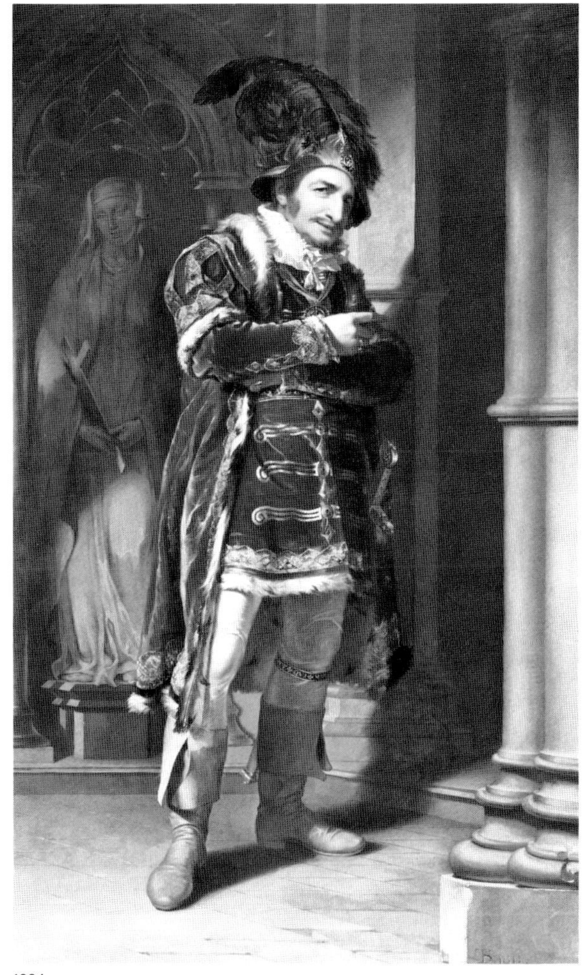
1324

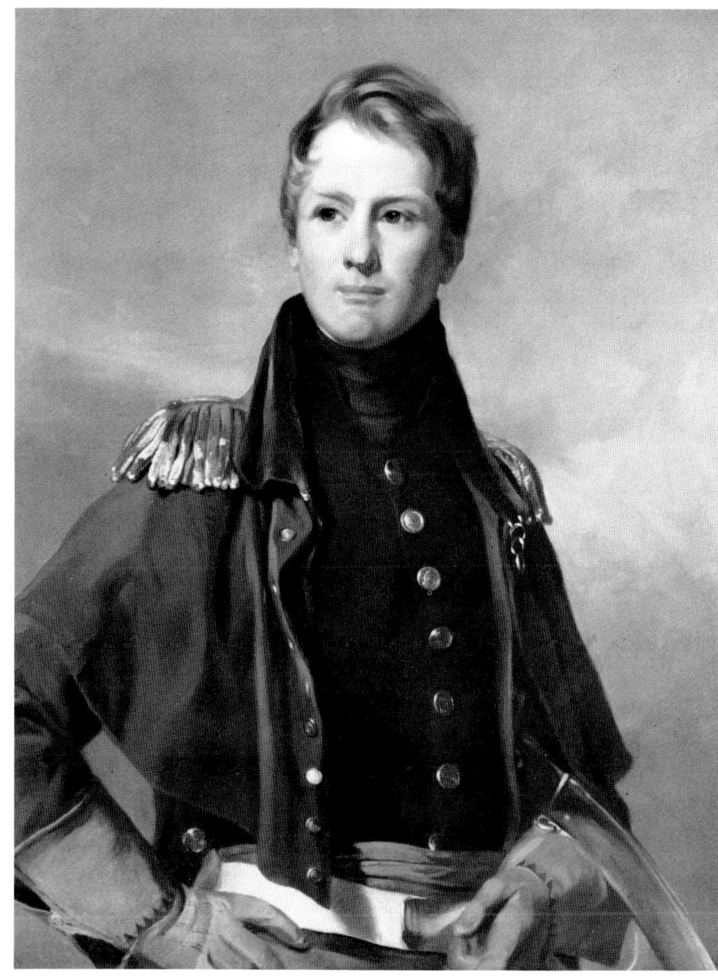
1316

1323 *Child with Dog and Flowers*, 1828
Oil on canvas
32⁵⁄₁₆ x 38⁵⁄₁₆ in. (82.1 x 97.3 cm.)
Signed and dated at lower center: TS 1828
Bequest of Mrs. Anna R. Aspinwall, 1842.3

1324 *George Frederick Cooke as Richard III* (1756–1812), 1811–12
Oil on canvas
94⅞ x 60½ in. (241 x 153.7 cm.)
Signed and dated at lower right: TS. [monogram] 1811.
Gift of friends and admirers of the artist, 1812.1

1325 *Abbie Ann Cope* (Mrs. Caleb Cope, 1804–1845), 1837
Oil on canvas
36⁷⁄₁₆ x 28¼ in. (92.6 x 71.8 cm.)
Signed and dated at lower left: TS/1837.
Bequest of Elizabeth Yarnall Maguire, 1980.18

1326 *Benjamin Cross* (1786–1857), 1866
Oil on canvas
30 x 24⅞ in. (76.2 x 63.2 cm.)
Signed and dated on back: TS 1866
Gift of Augustus T. Cross, 1925.13

1327 *Colonel Gideon Fairman* (1774–1827), 1824
Oil on wood
9¾ x 7⅞ in. (24.8 x 20 cm.)
Bequest of Cephas G. Childs, 1871.1.2

1328 *Gil Blas Securing the Cook in the Robber's Cave*, 1812
(after John Opie, ca. 1804; *see* cat. no. 954)
Oil on canvas
83¾ x 53¹³⁄₁₆ in. (212.7 x 136.7 cm.)
Pennsylvania Academy purchase, 1855.2

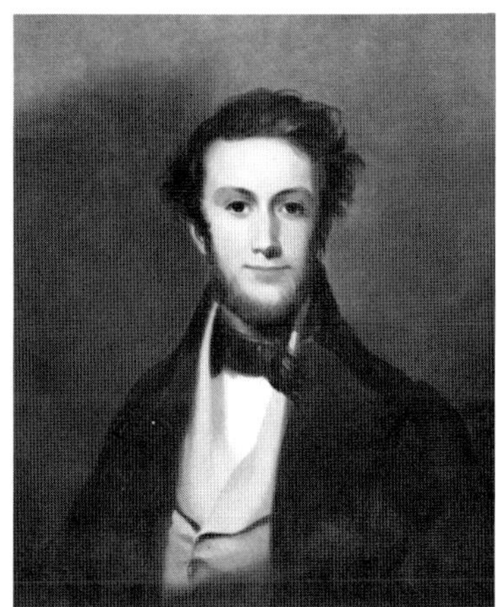
1321

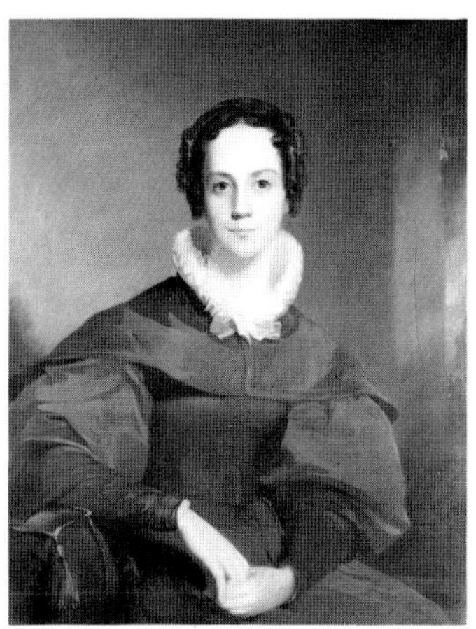
1325

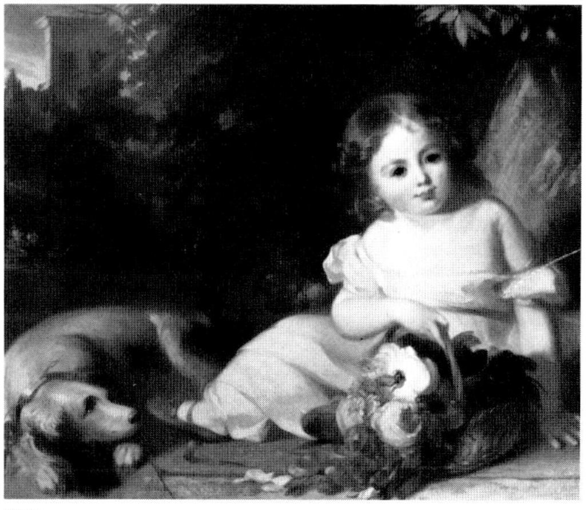
1323

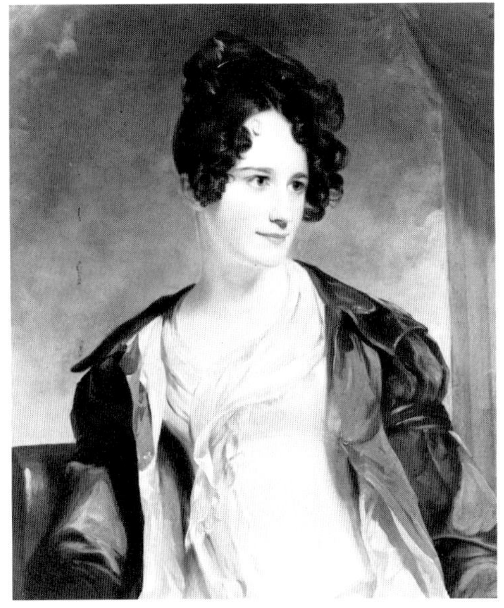

1332

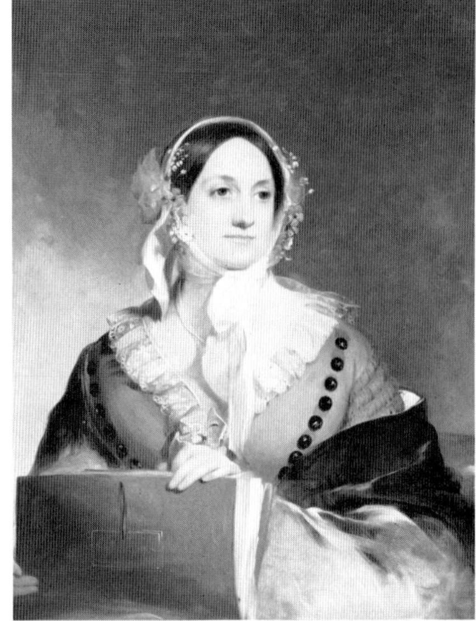

1338

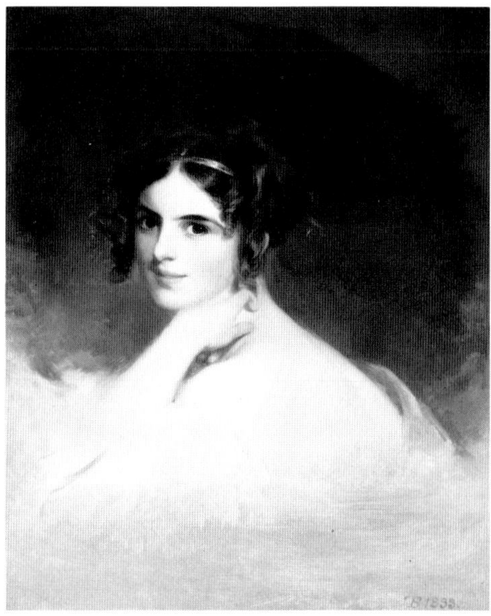

1335

1329 *Dr. Elijah Griffiths* (1765–1847), 1808
Oil on canvas
29¼ x 24½ in. (74.3 x 62.2 cm.)
Gift of Marguerite A. Keasbey, 1957.21.2

1330 *Isaac Hazlehurst* (1808–1891), 1838
Oil on canvas
30⅛ x 25³⁄₁₆ in. (76.5 x 64 cm.)
Signed and dated at lower right: TS. 1838
Gift of Mrs. John Frederick Lewis (The John Frederick Lewis Memorial Collection), 1933.10.78

1331 *Mary Hazlehurst* (later Mrs. Lewis Richard Ashhurst, 1806–1890), 1831
Oil on canvas
30⁷⁄₁₆ x 25¼ in. (77.3 x 64.1 cm.)
Signed and dated at upper left: TS 1831
Bequest of Richard Ashhurst, 1969.20.3

1332 *Mary McKean Hoffman* (1797–1882), 1821
Oil on canvas
30 x 25 in. (76.2 x 63.5 cm.)
Signed and dated at upper right: TS. 1821.
Bequest of Fredericka Mary Kerr, 1942.12.1

1333 *Elizabeth Willing Jackson* (1803–1821), 1822
Oil on canvas
30¹⁄₁₆ x 25⅛ in. (76.4 x 63.8 cm.)
Signed and dated at upper right: TS. 1822
Bequest of Ann Willing Jackson, 1876.2.2

1334 *Charles Kemble as Fazio* (1775–1854), 1833
Oil on canvas
30³⁄₁₆ x 25⅛ in. (76.7 x 63.8 cm.)
Signed and dated at lower center: TS 1833
Gift of Mrs. John Ford, 1843.1.1

1335 *Frances Anne Kemble as Beatrice* (1809–1893), 1833
Oil on canvas
30 x 25 in. (76.2 x 63.5 cm.)
Signed and dated at lower right: TS 1833.
Bequest of Henry C. Carey (The Carey Collection), 1879.8.24

1336 *Frances Anne Kemble as Bianca*, 1833
Oil on canvas
30⅛ x 25³⁄₁₆ in. (76.5 x 64 cm.)
Signed and dated at lower right: TS. 1833
Gift of Mrs. John Ford, 1843.1.2

1337 *Frances Anne Kemble as Isabella in "Measure for Measure,"* 1836
Oil on canvas
36¼ x 28⅜ in. (92.1 x 72.1 cm.)
Inscribed, signed, and dated on back: "Isabella"/from Shakspeare's play of/"Measure for Measure"/TS 1836/Novem r
Bequest of Henry C. Carey (The Carey Collection), 1879.8.25

1338 *Eliza Leslie* (1787–1858), 1844
Oil on canvas
36 x 28 in. (91.4 x 71.1 cm.)
Pennsylvania Academy purchase, 1861.1

1339 *Emma and Adelaide Leslie*, 1855
Oil on canvas
25 x 30 in. (63.5 x 76.2 cm.)
Inscribed, signed, and dated on back (before lining): E x A Leslie/T Sully/copied from my original/TS 1855
Bequest of Gertrude Leslie, 1908.3.1

1340 *Gertrude Leslie* (Mrs. Thomas Jefferson Leslie), 1829
Oil on wood
18⅞ x 14¹¹⁄₁₆ in. (47.9 x 37.3 cm.)
Signed and dated at lower right: TS 1829
Bequest of Gertrude Leslie, 1908.3.2

1341 *Mrs. Samuel Neave Lewis and Her Daughter Martha*, 1811
Oil on canvas
30 x 25 in. (76.2 x 63.5 cm.)
Signed at lower left: TS
Bequest of Lydia Lewis Waln, 1972.13

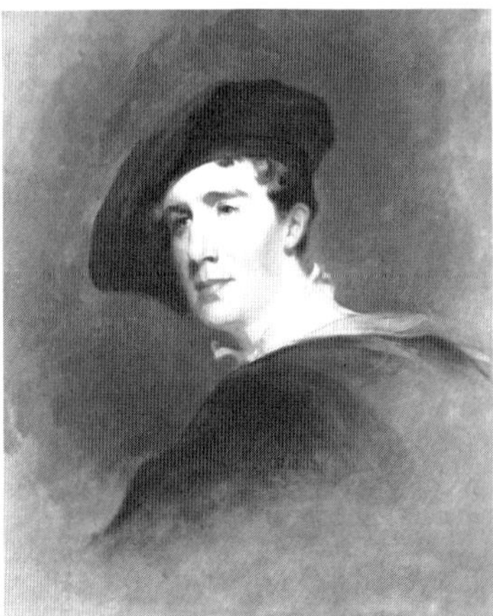

1334

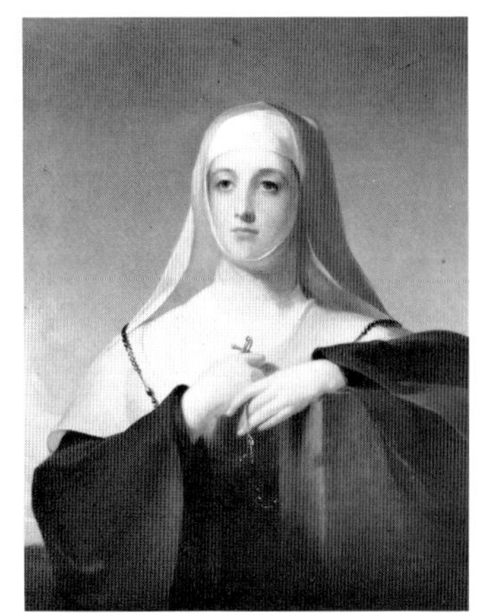

1337

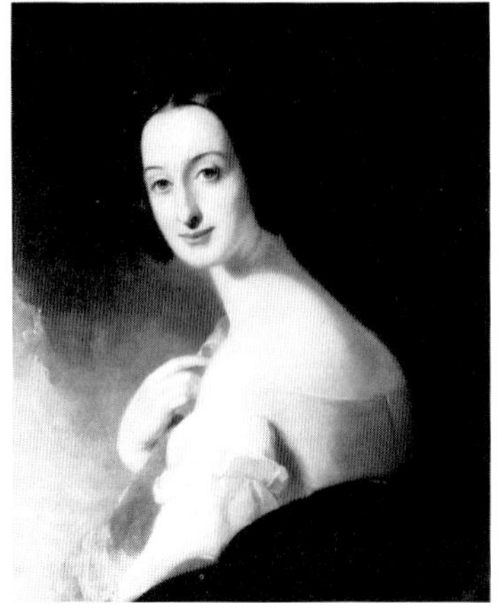

1346

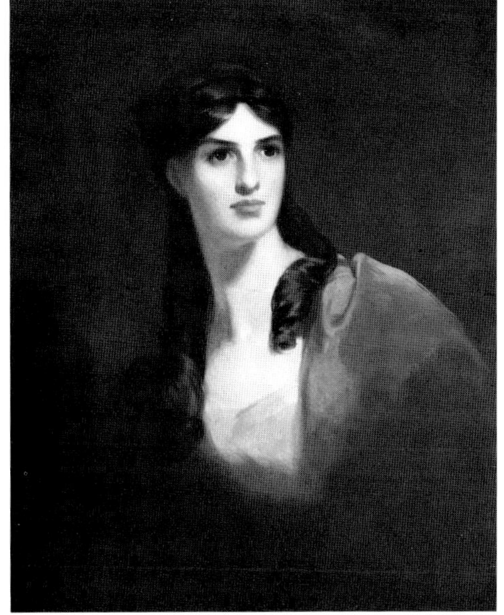
1336

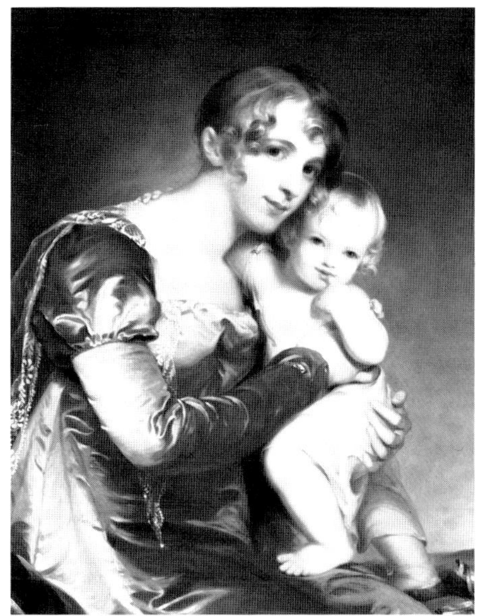
1341

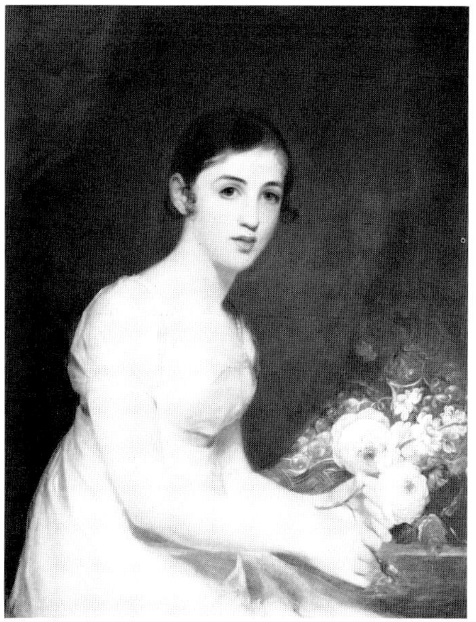
1345

1342 *Richard McCunney* (d. 1857), 1825
Oil on canvas
26¹¹⁄₁₆ x 21⅞ in. (67.8 x 55.6 cm.)
Signed and dated on back: TS 1825
Gift of Mrs. John Frederick Lewis (The John Frederick Lewis Memorial Collection), 1933.10.79

1343 *Hon. John McLean* (1785–1861), 1831
Oil on wood
20 x 16⁷⁄₁₆ in. (50.8 x 41.8 cm.)
Signed and dated at lower right: TS 1831
Source unknown, 1880.3

1344 *Margaret O'Neill* (Mrs. Thomas O'Neill), 1866
Oil on canvas
30⅛ x 25¹⁄₁₆ in. (76.5 x 63.7 cm.)
Signed and dated on back: TS 1866/February
Gift of Edward O'Neill, 1922.4

1345 *Margaret Sarah Page* (1797–1879), 1810
Oil on wood
32¹⁄₁₆ x 25¹⁄₁₆ in. (81.4 x 63.7 cm.)
Gift of Thomas C. and Horace T. Potts, 1921.7

1346 *Eliza Willing Spring Peters* (later Mrs. John White Field, 1820–1902), 1841
Oil on canvas
30⅛ x 24¹³⁄₁₆ in. (76.5 x 63 cm.)
Signed and dated on back: TS 1841.
Gift of Mrs. John White Field, 1890.2

1347 *Mrs. Mary Forde Poore* (1804–1892), ca. 1820
Oil on canvas
30 x 25⅛ in. (76.2 x 63.8 cm.), oval
Bequest of Mrs. Sallie Forde Morris, 1946.13

1348 *James Potter* (1793–1862), 1849
Oil on canvas
30¹⁄₁₆ x 24⅝ in. (76.4 x 62.5 cm.)
Gift of James P. Polk in memory of Anna Warren Ingersoll, 1980.29

1349 *James Ross* (1762–1847), 1813
Oil on canvas
50½ x 40 in. (128.3 x 101.6 cm.)
Commissioned by the Pennsylvania Academy, 1814.1

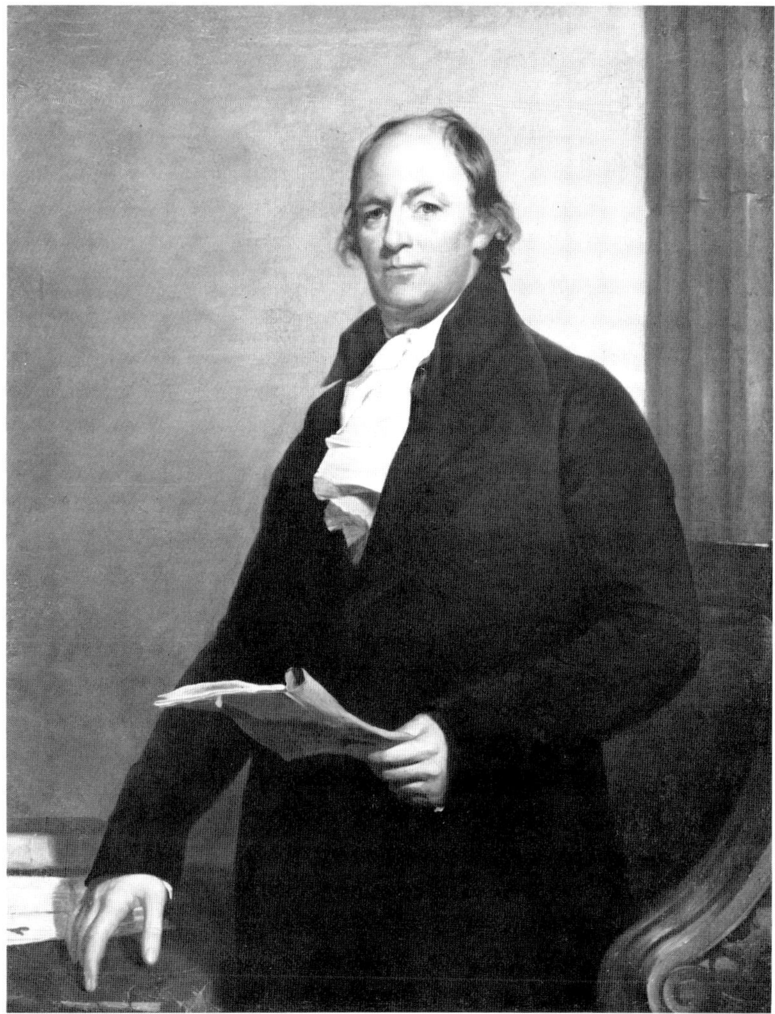
1349

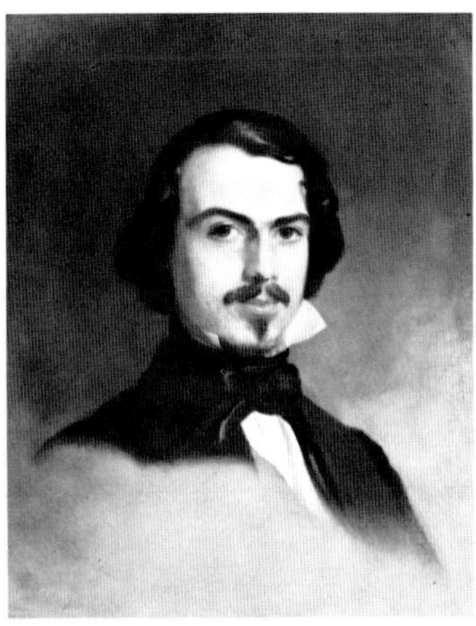
1351

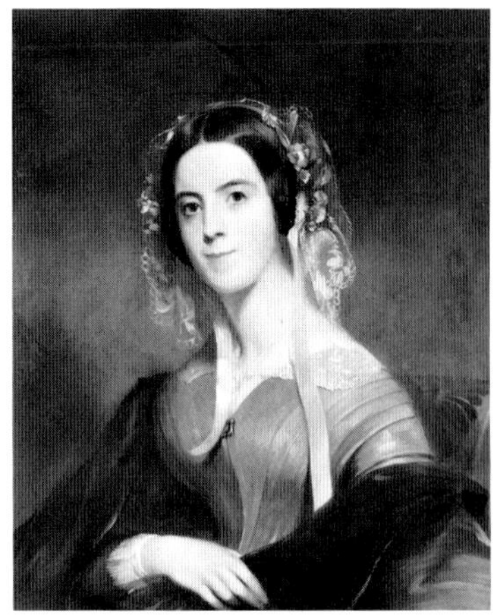
1350

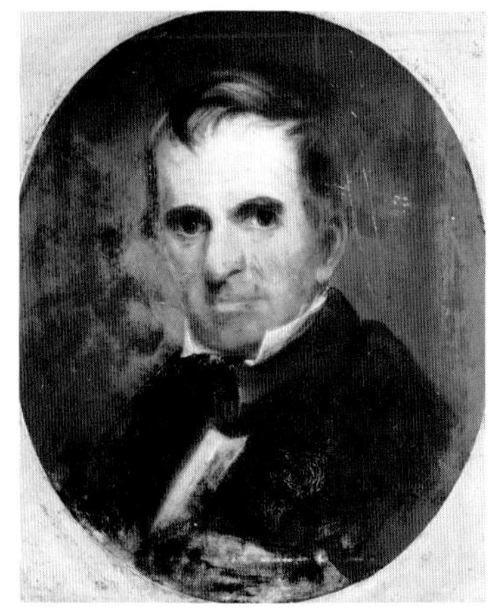
1352

1350 *Mrs. John Sartain* (née Susannah Longman Swaine), 1843
Oil on canvas
30 x 25 3/16 in. (76.2 x 64 cm.)
Signed and dated on back: TS 1843
Bequest of Dr. Paul J. Sartain, 1945.18.2

1351 *Samuel Sartain* (1830–1906), 1852
Oil on canvas
24 x 20 in. (61 x 50.8 cm.)
Signed and dated on back: TS 1852
Gift of Harriet Sartain, 1953.18

1352 *Self-Portrait*, 1834
Oil on canvas
18 x 15 1/8 in. (45.7 x 38.4 cm.)
Inscribed, signed, and dated on back: Portrait of/ Thos. Sully/by himself./(1834)
Gift of John Frederick Lewis, 1909.6

1353 *Dugald Stewart* (1753–1828), 1824
(after Sir Henry Raeburn)
Oil on canvas
28 15/16 x 23 15/16 in. (73.5 x 60.8 cm.)
Gift of Mrs. John Frederick Lewis (The John Frederick Lewis Memorial Collection), 1933.10.80

1354 *Thomas Wilcocks Sully, Jr.* (1811–1847)
Oil on canvas
25 3/4 x 22 in. (65.4 x 55.9 cm.)
Henry D. Gilpin Fund, 1913.10

1355 *Tribute Money*, 1813–14
(after Peter Paul Rubens, ca. 1611)
Oil on canvas
59 7/8 x 75 1/2 in. (152.1 x 191.8 cm.)
Gift of the artist, 1815.1

1356 *Mrs. John Bradford Wallace* (1778–1849), 1839
Oil on canvas
30 x 24 15/16 in. (76.2 x 63.3 cm.)
Signed and dated on back: TS 1839
Bequest of Mrs. Willing Spencer, 1963.5.2

1357 *Benjamin West* (1738–1820), 1864
(after Charles R. Leslie, after Sir Thomas Lawrence, ca. 1820)
Oil on canvas
58 5/8 x 48 1/4 in. (148.9 x 122.6 cm.)
Pennsylvania Academy purchase, 1864.1

See also palettes, cat. nos. 1624–26, and *Dancing Doll*, cat. no. 1679.

Attributed to **Thomas Sully**

1358 *Unidentified Girl*
(after Rembrandt)
Oil on canvas
30 3/16 x 25 in. (76.7 x 63.5 cm.)
Gift of Mrs. Annesley R. Govett, 1917.2

Thomas Wilcocks Sully, Jr. (1811–1847)

1359 *John Swift* (1790–1873), 1845
Oil on canvas
30 x 25 in. (76.2 x 63.5 cm.)
Signed and dated on back: T. Sully Jr. Pinxit/Nov. 9. 1845
Gift of John B. Swift, 1925.1

Robert S. Susan (1888–1957)

1360 *The Golden Screen*, 1920
Oil on canvas
55 x 41 1/4 in. (139.7 x 104.7 cm.)
Signed and dated at lower right: Robert Susan —/1920
Joseph E. Temple Fund, 1921.8

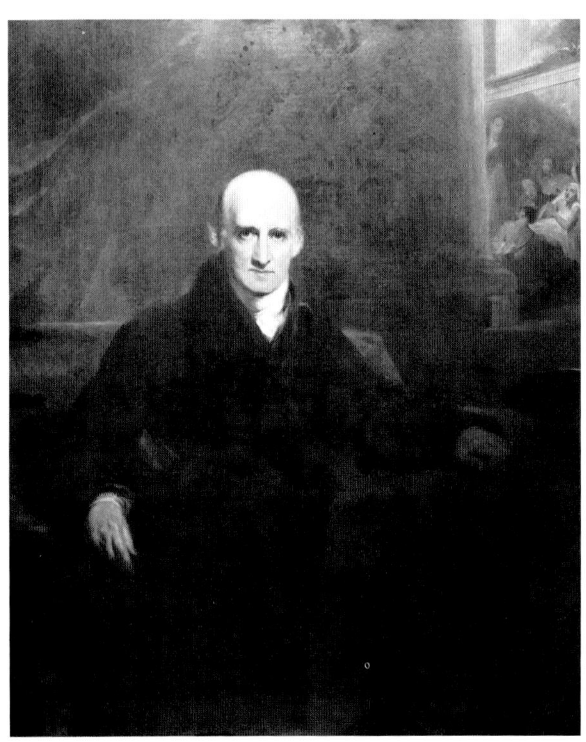
1357

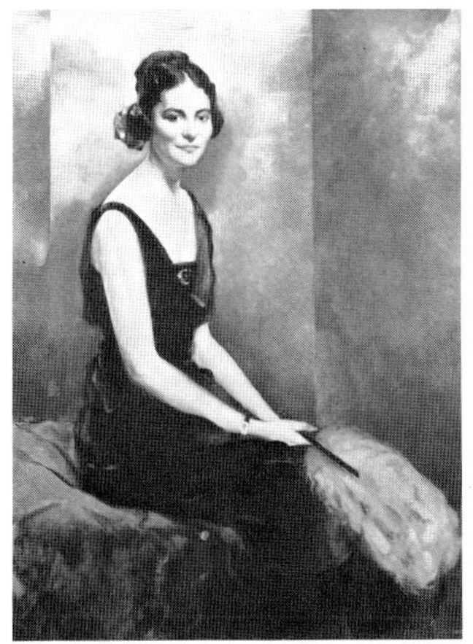
1360

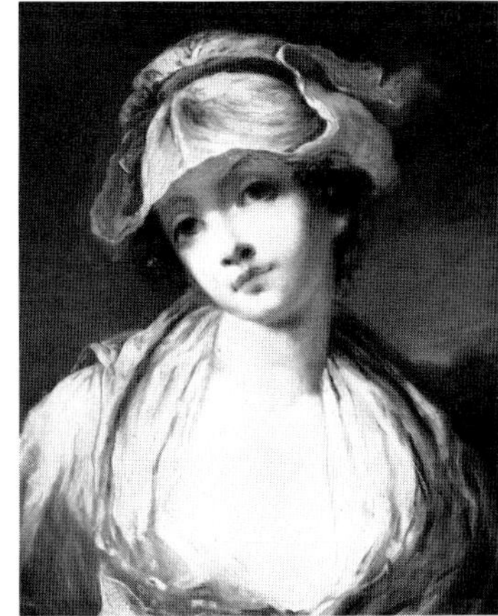
1362

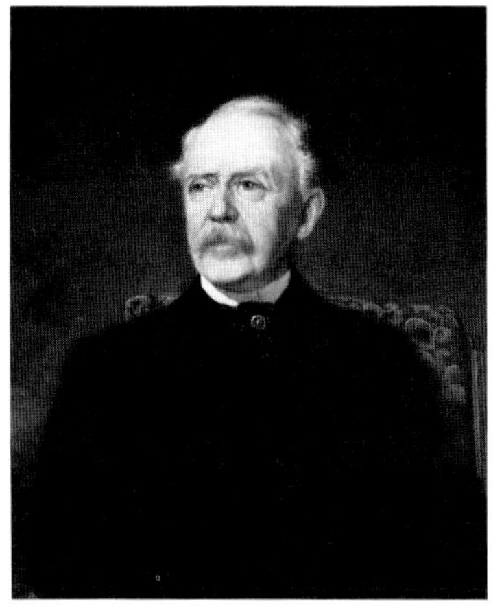
1363

Faye Swengel (Mrs. Bernard Badura, 1904–)

1361 *Tillie and Kittens*, by 1940
Oil on wood
18⅜ x 22⁵⁄₁₆ in. (46.7 x 56.7 cm.)
Signed at lower left: fayeSwengel; inscribed and signed on back: Tillie and kittens./faye Swengel.../New Hope Lumberville Pa. [crossed out]
Gift of the Fellowship of the Pennsylvania Academy, 1940.10.2

O. L. Swire

1362 *Head of a Girl*
Oil on canvas
22⅛ x 18⅛ in. (56.2 x 46 cm.)
Signed at lower left: O.LS[w]ire.
Gift of Caroline Gibson Taitt, 1910.2.10

James B. Sword (1839–1915)

1363 *Newbold Hough Trotter* (1827–1898), 1893
Oil on canvas
30 x 25 in. (76.2 x 63.5 cm.)
Signed at lower right: J.B.Sword; inscribed, signed, and dated on back: Newbold. H. Trotter./Painted by/J.B.Sword/1893
Gift of John Frederick Lewis, 1920.10.1

Yves Tanguy (1900–1955)

1364 *Suites Illimitées*, 1951
Oil on canvas
39¹⁄₁₆ x 32³⁄₁₆ in. (99.2 x 81.8 cm.)
Signed and dated at lower right: YVES TANGUY 51; inscribed on back: "SUITES ILLIMITEES"
Henry D. Gilpin Fund, 1953.6

Henry O. Tanner (1859–1937)

1365 *Nicodemus*, 1899
Oil on canvas
33¹¹⁄₁₆ x 39½ in. (85.6 x 100.3 cm.)
Signed, inscribed, and dated at lower left: H.O. TANNER/JERUSALEM 1899
Joseph E. Temple Fund, 1900.1

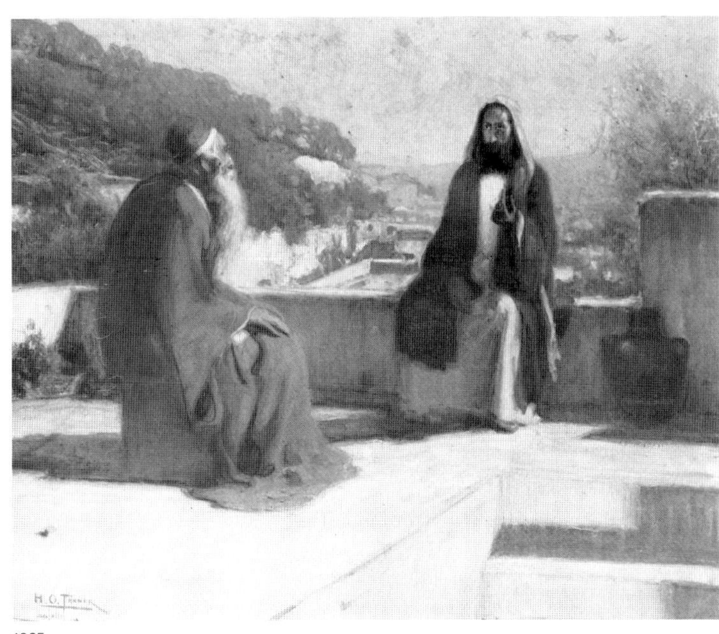
1365

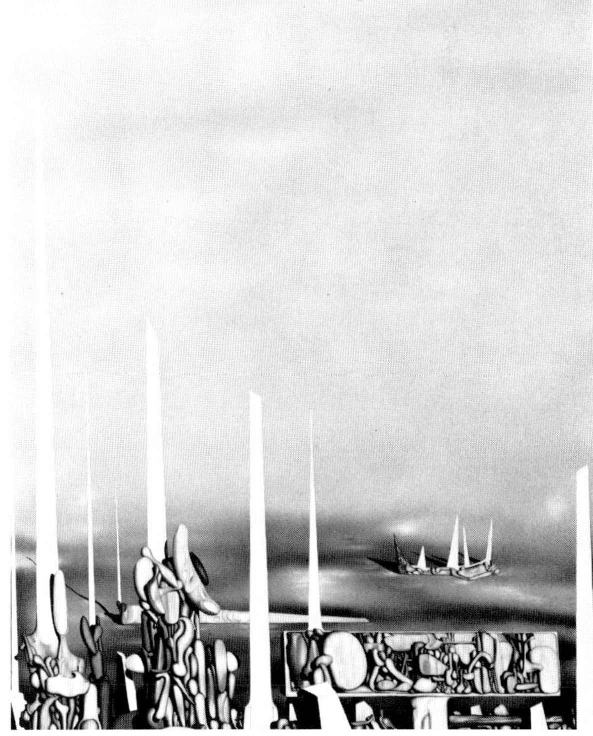
1364

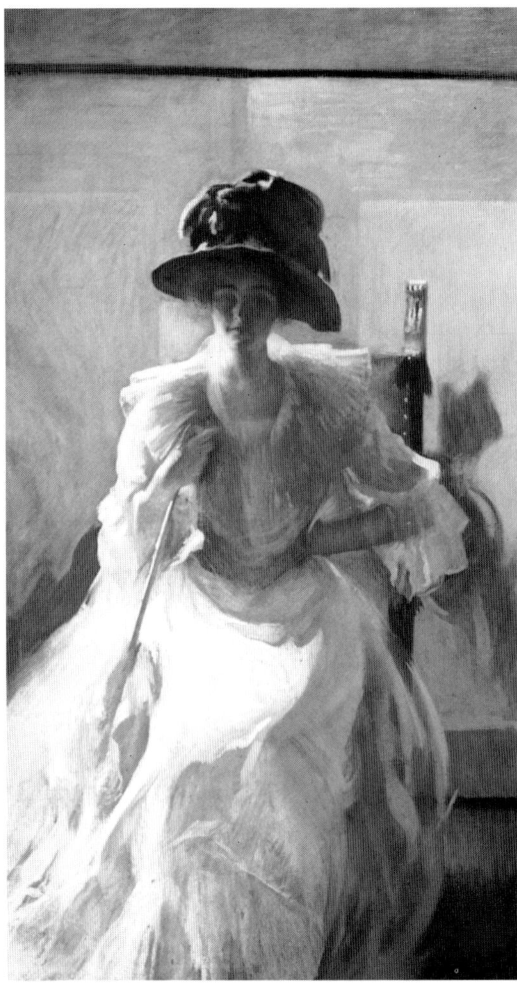

1367

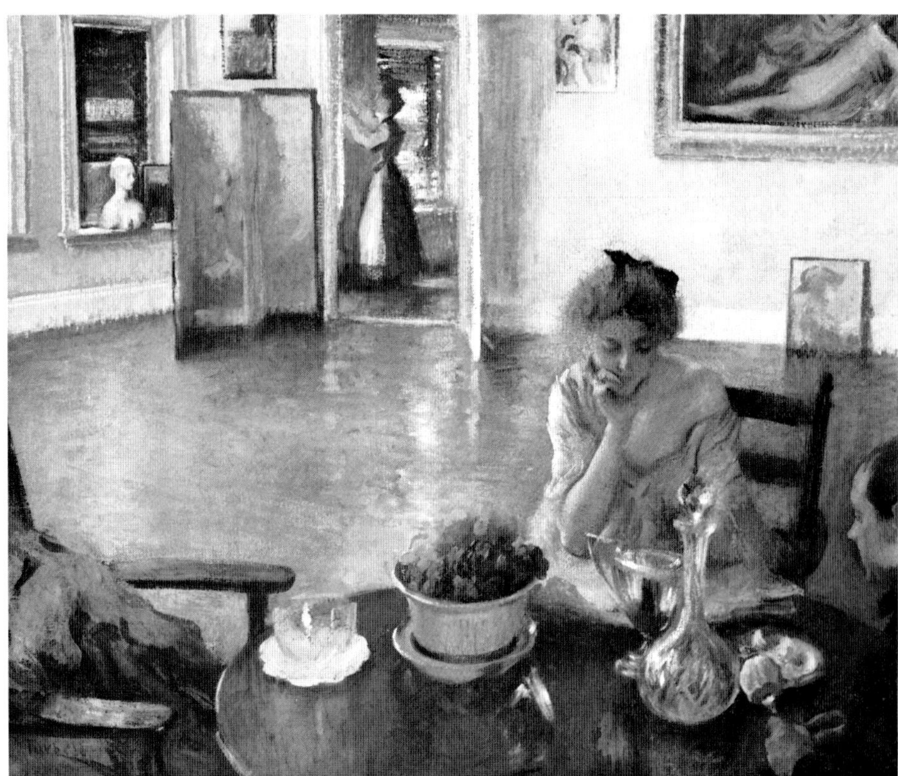

1366

Edmund C. Tarbell (1862–1938)

1366 *The Breakfast Room*, ca. 1903
Oil on canvas
25 x 30 in. (63.5 x 76.2 cm.)
Signed at lower left: Tarbell
Gift of Clement B. Newbold, 1973.25.3

1367 *The Golden Screen*, ca. 1898
Oil on canvas
77½ x 43¼ in. (196.9 x 109.9 cm.)
Signed at lower right: Tarbell
Joseph E. Temple Fund, 1899.4

Emily Drayton Taylor. *See* cat. no. 1655.

Frank W. Taylor (1874–1921)

1368 *Classical Music* (formerly *Music*), 1896–97
Oil on canvas
Approx. 78 x 156 in. (198 x 396 cm.)
Signed at lower right: F. W. TAYLOR
Commissioned by the Pennsylvania Academy, 1897.9.12

Jeanne Taylor (1912–)

1369 *Woman in Red Vest*, 1953
Oil on canvas
30 x 20 in. (76.2 x 50.8 cm.)
Signed and dated at lower left: Jeanne Taylor 53
John Lambert Fund, 1954.15

Ralph Taylor (1896–1978)

1370 *Center City Construction*, 1964
Oil on canvas
30⅛ x 30⅛ in. (76.5 x 76.5 cm.)
Annotated on stretcher: Ralph Taylor
Gift of Mrs. Ralph Taylor, 1980.12

1371 *The Studio*, ca. 1921
Oil on canvas
36 x 36 in. (91.4 x 91.4 cm.)
John Lambert Fund, 1922.14

Esther Kee Temple. *See* Esther Kee.

William G. Temple (1909–1984)

1372 *Pears*, ca. 1935
Oil on canvas
22¼ x 28⅛ in. (56.5 x 71.4 cm.)
John Lambert Fund, 1936.17

Polly Thayer (1904–)

1373 *Portrait of Diana*, ca. 1934
Oil on canvas
21 x 17¹⁄₁₆ in. (53.3 x 43.3 cm.)
Signed at upper right: Thayer
John Lambert Fund, 1935.10

Attributed to **Jeremiah Theus** (1716–1774)

1374 *Unidentified Man*, by mid-1750s
Oil on canvas
14⅝ x 12¹⁄₁₆ in. (37.2 x 30.6 cm.)
Collections Fund, 1954.16

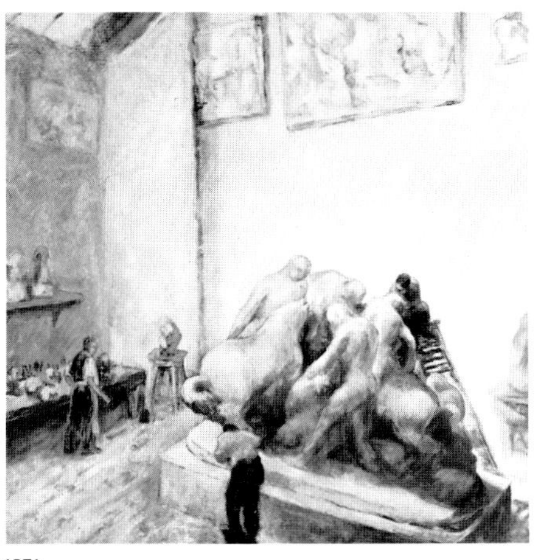
1371

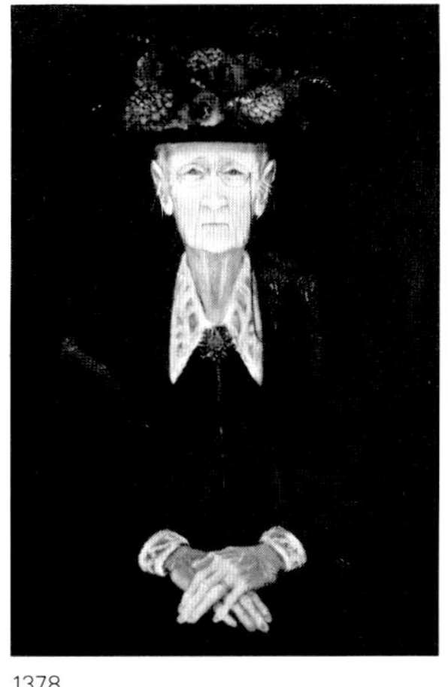
1378

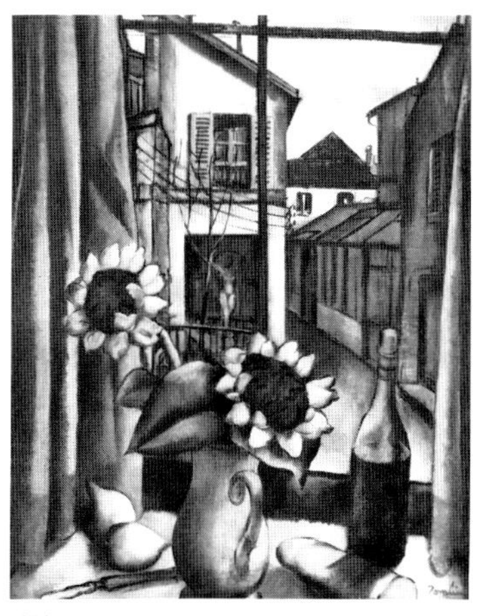
1379

William Thoeny (1888–1949)

1375 *Arrival in New York*, ca. 1943
Oil on canvas
48 x 61 in. (121.9 x 154.9 cm.)
Signed at upper right: W.Thöny
Signed and inscribed on stretcher: W. THÖNY : ARRIVÉE À NEW YORK
Joseph E. Temple Fund, 1944.34

Byron Thomas (1902–1978)

1376 *Pine Trees*, 1946
Oil on canvas
40⅛ x 28½ in. (101.9 x 72.4 cm.)
Signed at lower right: Byron Thomas
Joseph E. Temple Fund, 1948.15

Mark Tobey (1890–1976)

1377 *Last Supper*, 1949
Egg tempera on paper, mounted on masonite
20⅜ x 26⅛ in. (51.8 x 66.4 cm.)
Signed and dated at lower right: Tobey '49; inscribed on back: Last Supper
John Lambert Fund, 1951.14

Peggy Meid Todd (1925–)

1378 *Esther at Easter*, 1947
Oil on masonite
33$\frac{11}{16}$ x 23¾ in. (85.6 x 60.3 cm.)
Signed at lower right: P. Meid
John Lambert Fund, 1948.8

Bradley Walker Tomlin (1899–1953)

1379 *Studio Window*, ca. 1928
Oil on canvas
39 x 32⅛ in. (99.1 x 81.6 cm.)
Signed at lower right: Tomlin; and on back: TOMLIN
John Lambert Fund, 1929.5

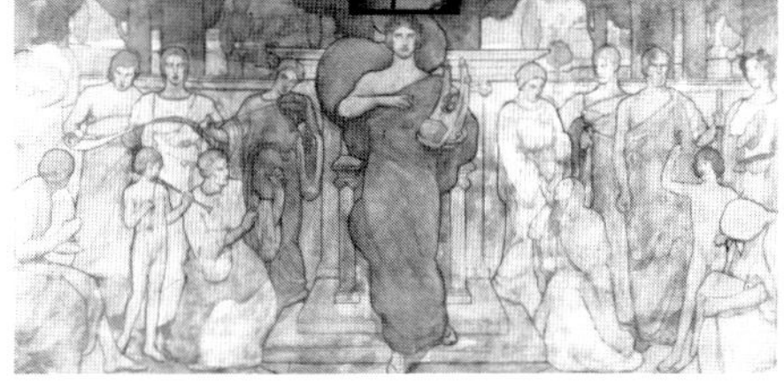
1368

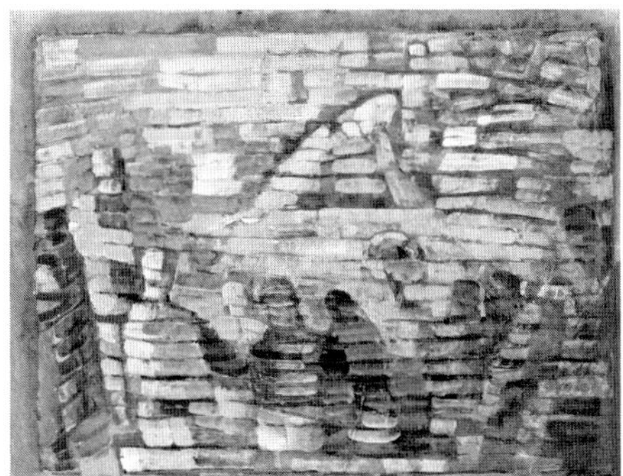
1377

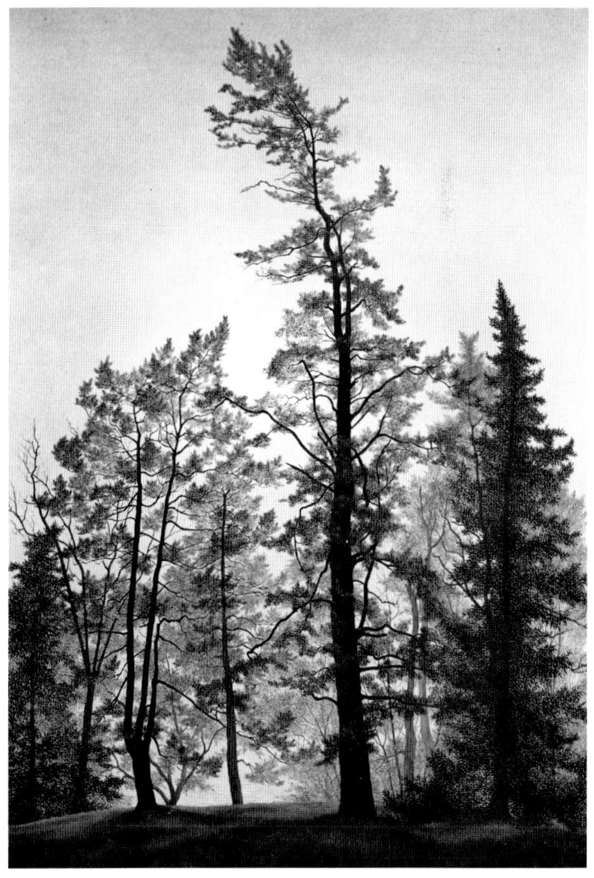
1376

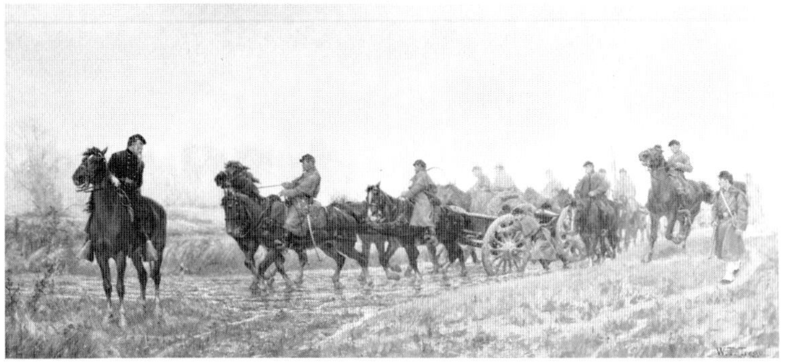

1380

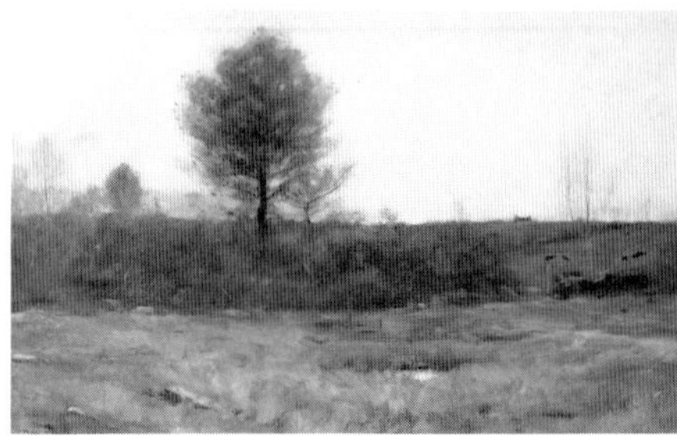

1385

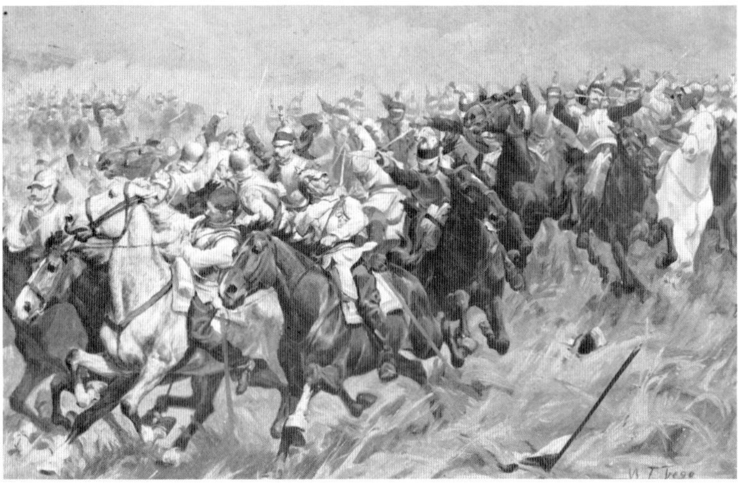

1381

William B. T. Trego (1859–1909)

1380 *Battery of Light Artillery en Route*, 1882
Oil on canvas
30⅛ x 64⅛ in. (76.5 x 162.9 cm.)
Signed, inscribed, and dated at lower right: W. T. Trego./Philada 1882
Gift of Fairman Rogers, 1883.4

1381 *Cavalry Sketch*
Oil on canvas
15¹⁄₁₆ x 24 in. (38.3 x 61 cm.)
Signed at lower right: W.T.Trego
Gift of Edward H. Coates, 1921.12.2

Newbold Hough Trotter (1827–1898)

1382 *The Meadow in Spring*, 1871
Oil on canvas
30 x 45¼ in. (76.2 x 114.9 cm.)
Signed and dated at lower right: N.H.Trotter/1871
Gift of Mrs. J. Maurice Gray, 1962.23.2

Attributed to **John Trumbull** (1756–1843)

1383 *Commodore Stephen Decatur* (?) (1779–1820)
Oil on canvas
30 x 25 in. (76.2 x 63.5 cm.)
Gift of Mrs. John Frederick Lewis (The John Frederick Lewis Memorial Collection), 1933.10.81

1384 *David Rittenhouse* (1732–1796)
Oil on canvas
24⅛ x 20⁵⁄₁₆ in. (61.3 x 51.6 cm.)
Henry D. Gilpin Fund, 1915.7

Dwight W. Tryon (1849–1925)

1385 *Evening*, 1886
Oil on canvas
16 x 24¹⁄₁₆ in. (40.6 x 61.1 cm.)
Signed and dated at lower left: D.W.TRYON. 1886
Henry D. Gilpin Fund, 1899.5

Nahum Tschacbasov (1899–1984)

1386 *The Clown*, 1948
Oil on masonite
44 x 27 in. (111.8 x 68.6 cm.)
Signed and dated at lower left: Tschacbasov 48-
Anonymous gift, 1950.24

John H. Twachtman (1853–1902)

1387 *Flowers*, by 1907
Oil on canvas
30¼ x 25 in. (76.8 x 63.5 cm.)
Gift of Mrs. Edward H. Coates (The Edward H. Coates Memorial Collection), 1923.9.7

1388 *Sailing in the Mist*, 1890s
Oil on canvas
30³⁄₁₆ x 30⅛ in. (76.7 x 76.5 cm.)
Signed at lower left: J H. Twachtman-
Joseph E. Temple Fund, 1906.1

Jack Tworkov (1900–1982)

1389 *Indian Red Series #2*, 1979
Oil on canvas
72 x 72 in. (182.9 x 182.9 cm.)
Signed and dated on back: Tworkov/79
Gift of Rachel Tworkov, 1987.24

Carroll Tyson, Jr. (1878–1956)

1390 *Western Mountain, Mount Desert*, 1944
Oil on canvas
30 x 36 in. (76.2 x 91.4 cm.)
Signed and dated at lower right: Carroll Tyson–1944–
Joseph E. Temple Fund, 1945.12

Walter Ufer (1876–1936)

1391 *Artist and Model* (self-portrait), ca. 1920
Oil on canvas
30 x 25 in. (76.2 x 63.5 cm.)
Signed at lower right: WUfer
Joseph E. Temple Fund, 1921.9

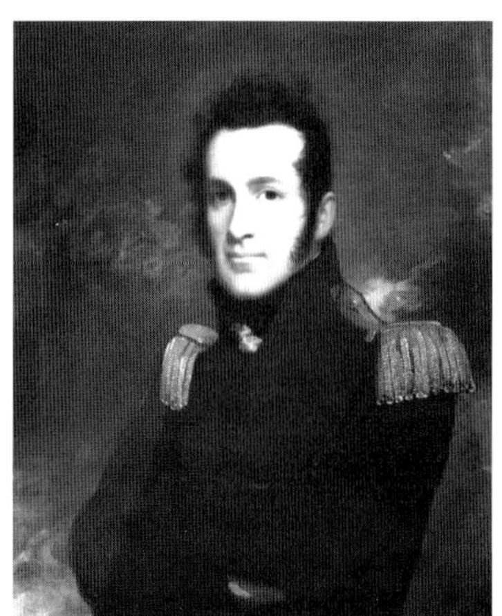

1383

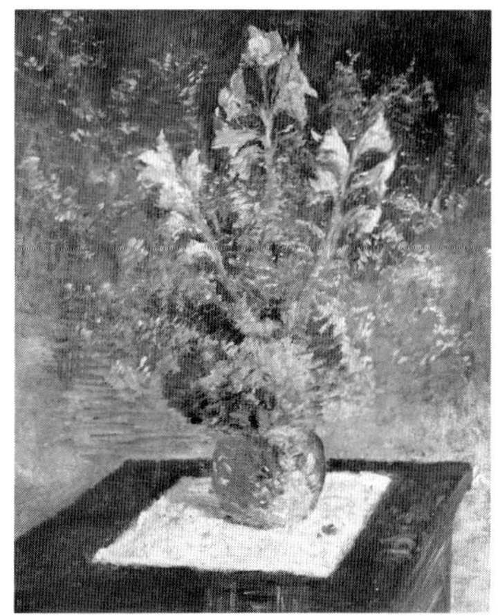

1387

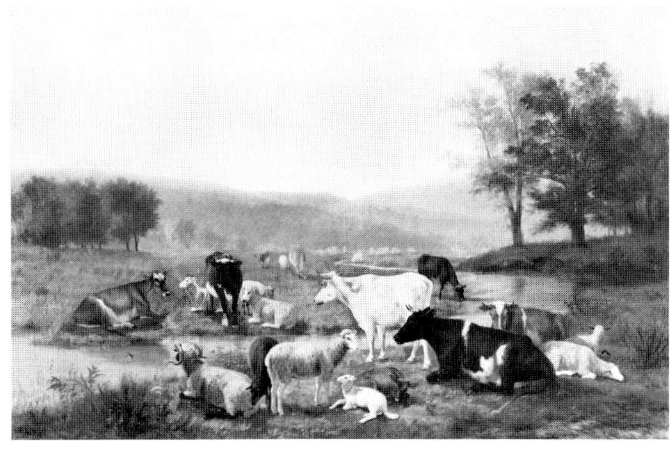

1382

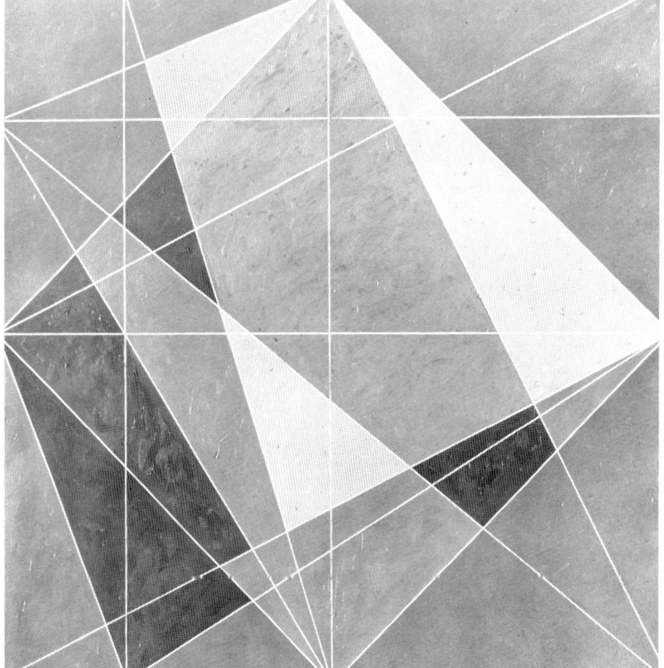

1389

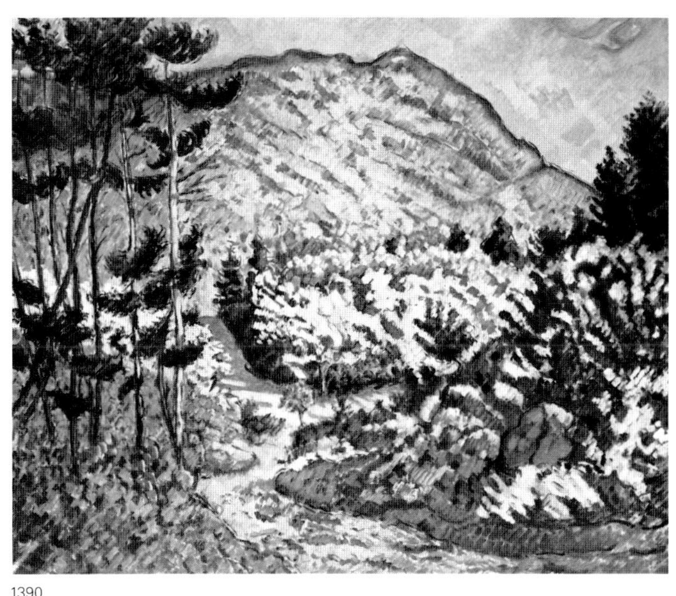

1390

1388

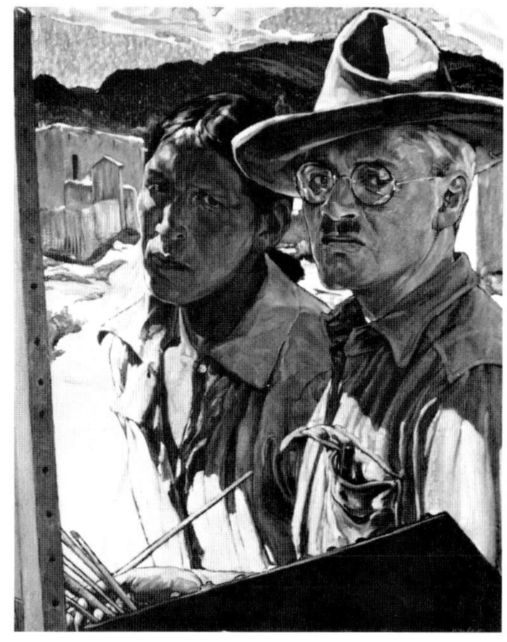

1391

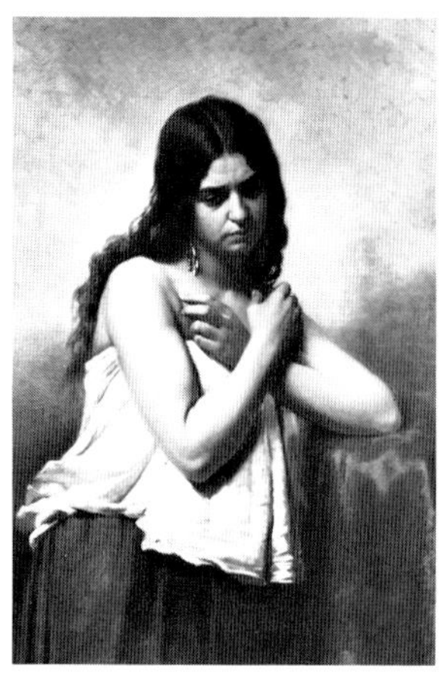

1395

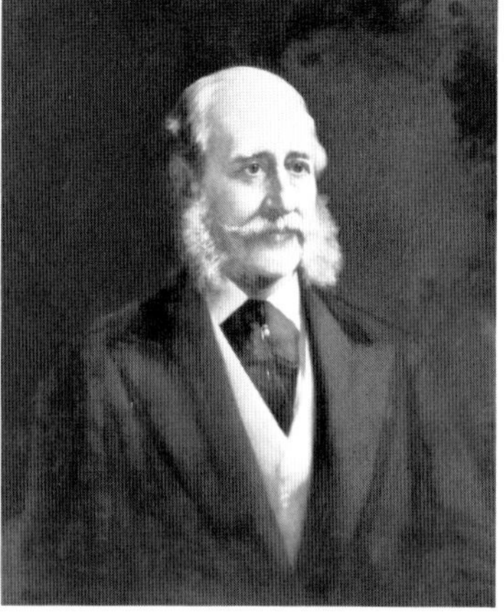

1396

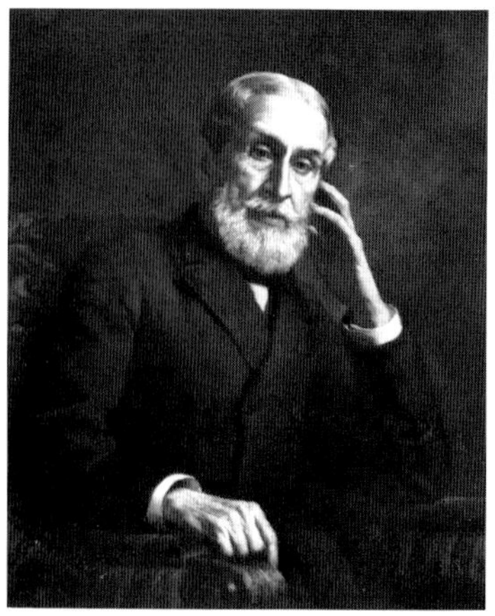

1393

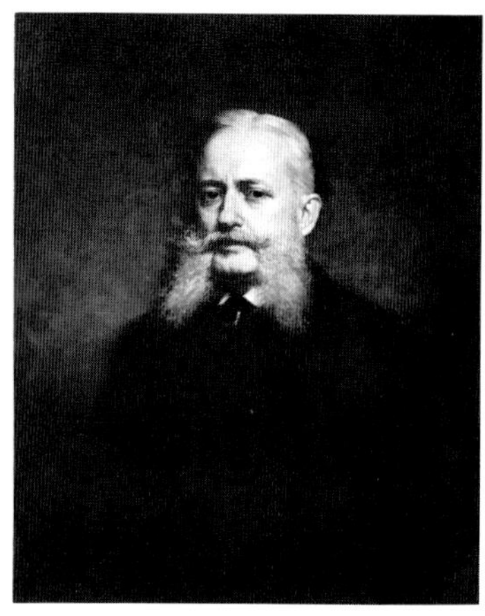

1392

Bernhard Uhle (1847–1930)

1392 *Henry C. Gibson* (1830–1891), 1891
Oil on canvas
34 x 27⅛ in. (86.4 x 68.9 cm.)
Signed and dated at lower right: B.Uhle./1891.
Bequest of Henry C. Gibson, 1892.6.90

1393 *George S. Pepper* (1808–1890), ca. 1890
Oil on canvas
34⅛ x 28¼ in. (86.7 x 71.8 cm.)
Signed at upper left: B.Uhle. pxt.
Gift of George S. Pepper, 1890.3

1394 *Self-Portrait*, 1878
Oil on canvas
27¼ x 22$\frac{15}{16}$ in. (69.2 x 58.3 cm.)
Signed and dated at lower right: B.Uhle/ Pxt. 1878
Gift of Dr. Henry Leffman, 1924.8

1395 *A Spanish Gypsy*
Oil on canvas
44¼ x 30¼ in. (112.4 x 76.8 cm.)
Gift of Mrs. Frederick W. Koepnick, 1984.12

1396 *Joseph E. Temple* (1811–1886), ca. 1885
Oil on canvas, mounted on wood
30 x 25¼ in. (76.2 x 64.1 cm.)
Gift of Joseph E. Temple, 1886.3

Alice G. Uhlmann (b. 1912)

1397 *American Community;* on back, *Portrait Sketch*, 1940
Oil on canvas
22⅛ x 35$\frac{15}{16}$ in. (56.2 x 91.3 cm.)
Signed and dated at lower right: A.G. Uhlmann '40
John Lambert Fund, 1941.8

Edward Ulreich (b. 1889)

1398 *Music*, probably 1912
Oil on canvas
Approx. 80 x 167 in. (203 x 424 cm.)
Signed and dated at lower right: Ed Ulreich./ 191[2]
Commissioned by the Pennsylvania Academy, 1912.16.6

James Robert Valerio (1938–)

1399 *Elizabeth's Visit* (Elizabeth Meyers), 1981
Oil on canvas
92⅛ x 100$\frac{5}{16}$ in. (234 x 254.8 cm.)
Gift of David N. Pincus, 1985.66

John Vanderlyn (1775–1852)

1400 *Ariadne Asleep on the Island of Naxos*, 1809–14
Oil on canvas
68½ x 87 in. (1/4 x 221 cm.)
Signed, inscribed, and dated at lower left: J. Vanderlyn fect/Parisiis 1814
Gift of Mrs. Sarah Harrison (The Joseph Harrison, Jr. Collection), 1878.1.11

Dorothy Van Loan (1904–)

1401 *Synthesis*, ca. 1933
Oil on canvas
35$\frac{15}{16}$ x 30 in. (91.3 x 76.2 cm.)
Signed at lower right and on back: Van Loan
John Lambert Fund, 1934.11

Paulette Van Roekens (1896–1988)

1402 *Treat 'Em Rough*, 1918
Oil on canvas
25⅛ x 30 in. (63.8 x 76.2 cm.)
Signed at lower right: PAULETTE VAN ROEKEN[S]
John Lambert Fund, 1919.6

Theodore van Soelen (1890–1964)

1403 *Summer Morning* (formerly *Along the River*), ca. 1915
Oil on canvas
36 x 34 in. (91.4 x 86.4 cm.)
Signed at lower left: Theo. van Soelen
John Lambert Fund, 1916.7

Margit Varga (1908–)

1404 *Going Fishing*, 1944
Oil on parchment
24 x 19$\frac{15}{16}$ in. (61 x 50.6 cm.)
Signed and dated at lower right: Varga/44
John Lambert Fund, 1946.14

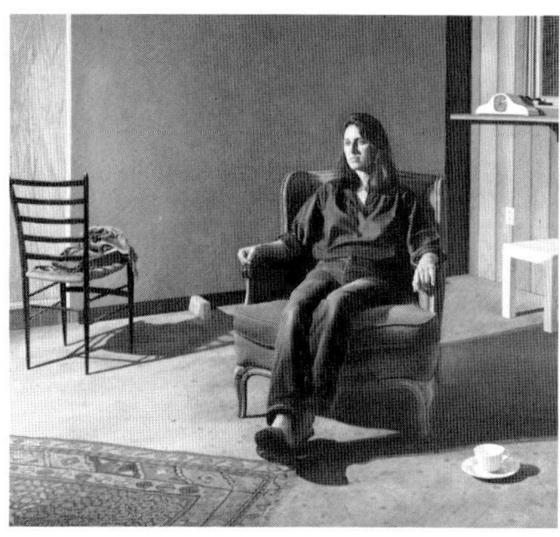

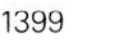

1399

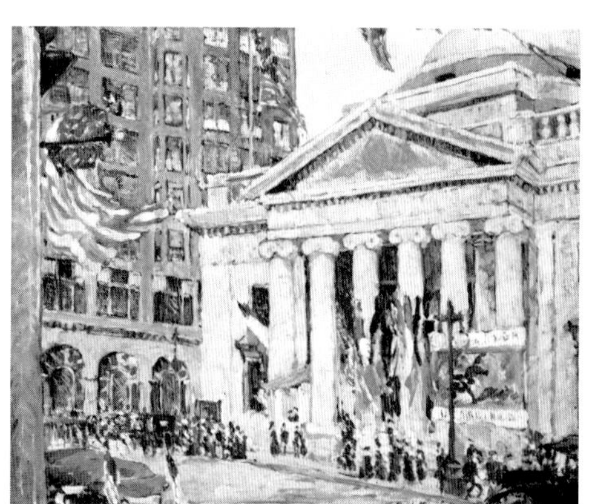

1402

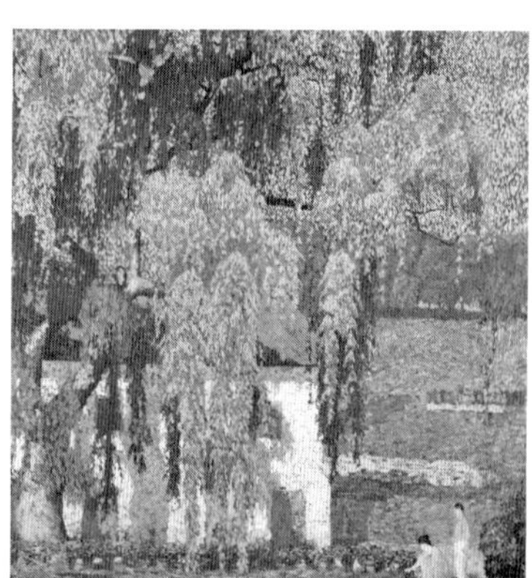

1403

Nicholas Vasilieff (1892–1970)

1405 *Still Life with Green Bowl*, 1953
Oil on canvas
36$\frac{1}{16}$ x 48 in. (91.6 x 121.9 cm.)
Signed and dated at lower right: N. Vasilieff 1953
John Lambert Fund, 1954.17

Elihu Vedder (1836–1923)

1406 *Girl with Bundle*, 1870
Oil on paper, mounted on masonite
8 x 4 in. (20.3 x 10.2 cm.)
Gift of the American Academy of Arts and Letters (The Childe Hassam Fund), 1957.19

1407 *The Sphinx, Egypt*, 1890
Oil on canvas
20$\frac{1}{8}$ x 14$\frac{3}{4}$ in. (51.1 x 37.5 cm.)
Signed twice, at lower left and left center: Elihu Vedder
Bequest of Edgar P. Richardson, 1985.44

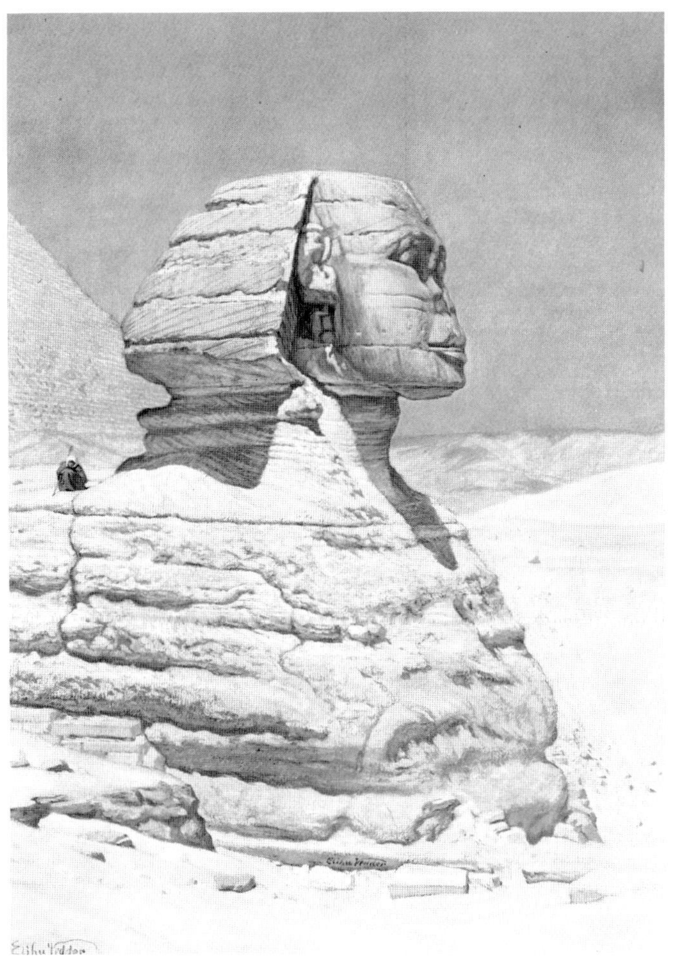

1407

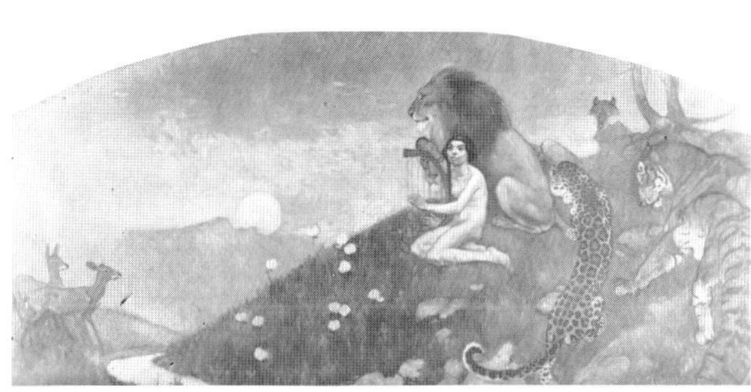

1398

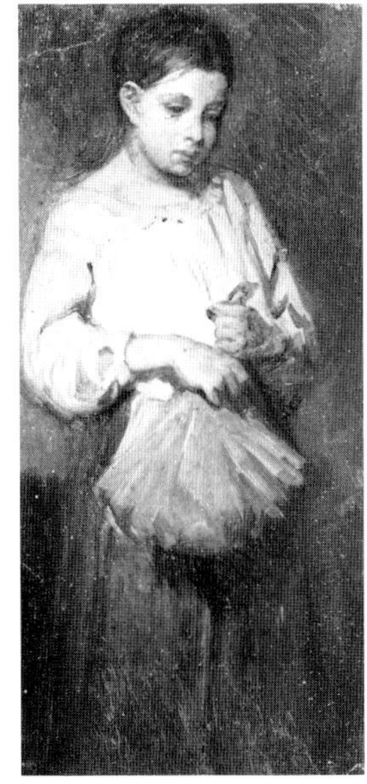

1406

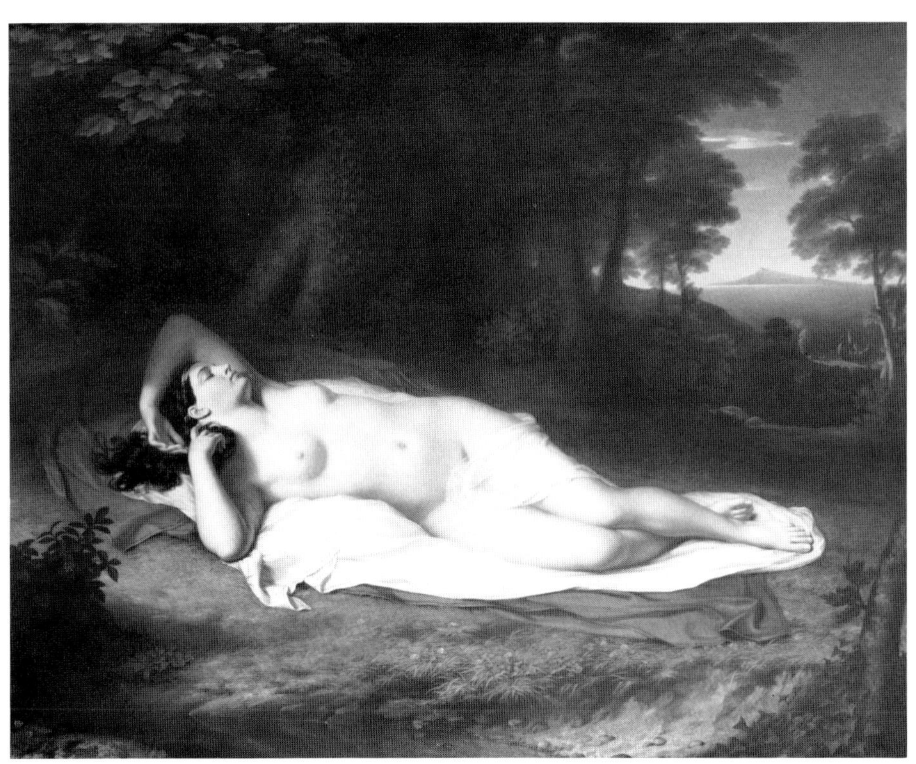

1400

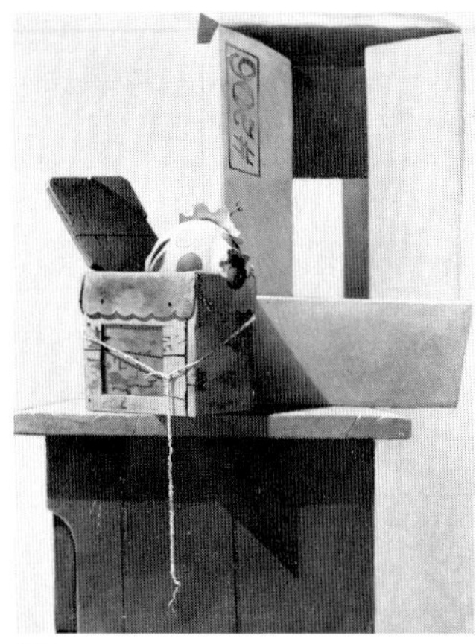
1408

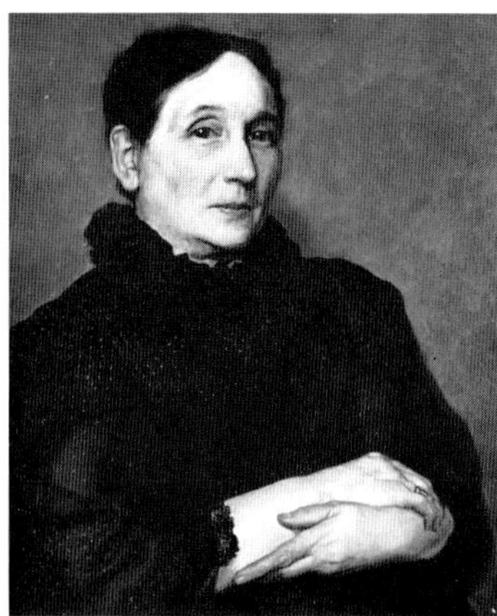
1410

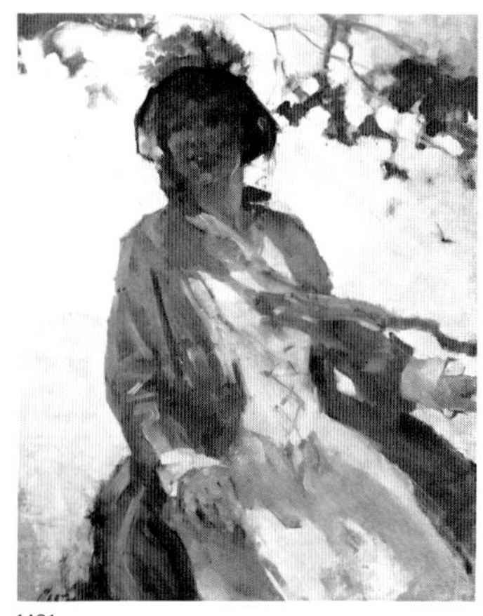
1421

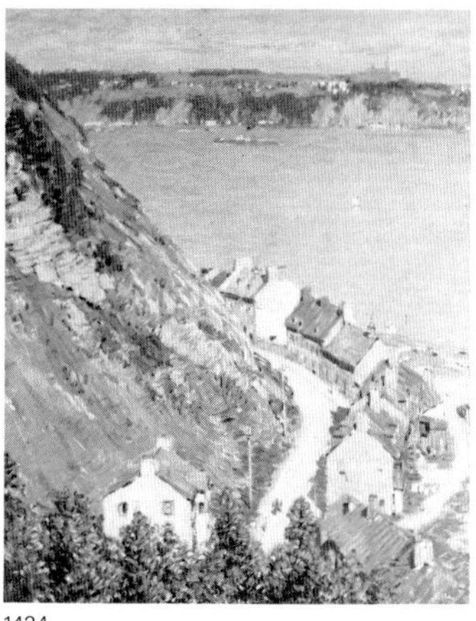
1424

Charles Vinson (1927–1978)

1408 *Box Number Two-O-Six*, 1952
Oil on canvas
28 1/16 x 22 1/16 in. (71.3 x 56 cm.)
Signed and dated at lower right: VINSON 52; inscribed at upper center: #206
John Lambert Fund, 1953.7

Denis A. Volozon (active 1799–1819)

1409 *Homer Reciting His Poems in the City of Argos*, by 1811
Oil on canvas
32 1/2 x 41 1/4 in. (82.6 x 104.8 cm.)
Source unknown, 1834.1

Francis von der Lancken (1872–1950)

1410 *My Mother*, ca. 1936
Oil on canvas
13 x 10 15/16 in. (33 x 27.8 cm.)
Signed at lower right: -F.von der Lancken-
Henry D. Gilpin Fund, 1937.13

Robert W. Vonnoh (1858–1933)

1411 *Edward H. Coates* (1846–1921), 1893
Oil on canvas
50 1/8 x 40 1/8 in. (127.3 x 101.9 cm.)
Signed, inscribed, and dated at lower left: Vonnoh/Phila/1893-
Gift of Mrs. Edward H. Coates (The Edward H. Coates Memorial Collection), 1923.9.9

1412 *Companion of the Studio*, 1888
Oil on canvas
51 1/4 x 36 1/4 in. (130.2 x 92.1 cm.)
Signed, inscribed, and dated at lower left: Robt. W.Vonnoh/Paris 1888
Joseph E. Temple Fund, 1891.14

1413 *Dr. Silas Weir Mitchell* (1829–1912), 1918
Oil on canvas
29 x 36 in. (73.7 x 91.4 cm.)
Signed and dated at lower right: Vonnoh—1918.
Gift of Edward H. Coates, 1918.15

1414 *November*, 1890
Oil on canvas
32 x 39 3/8 in. (81.3 x 100 cm.)
Signed and dated at lower left: R.W.Vonnoh 1890.
Joseph E. Temple Fund, 1894.5

1415 *Nude*, ca. 1896
Oil on canvas
16 x 12 15/16 in. (40.6 x 32.9 cm.)
Signed at lower right and on back: Vonnoh
Gift of Mrs. Edward H. Coates (The Edward H. Coates Memorial Collection), 1923.9.10

1416 *Self-Portrait*, 1901
Oil on canvas
24 x 18 1/16 in. (61 x 45.9 cm.)
Signed and dated at lower right: Vonnoh 1901
Henry D. Gilpin Fund, 1911.5

Vaclav Vytlacil (1892–1984)

1417 *Images of Pompeii*, 1951
Oil over egg tempera on canvas
72 3/8 x 56 1/4 in. (183.8 x 142.9 cm.)
Signed and dated at lower center: Vaclav Vytlacil 1951
Joseph E. Temple Fund, 1953.8

Fred Wagner (1864–1940)

1418 *Addingham Winter*, ca. 1911
Oil on canvas
32 x 36 in. (81.3 x 91.4 cm.)
Signed at lower right: F. Wagner
Joseph E. Temple Fund, 1912.6

1419 *Broad Street Station, Spring*, ca. 1919
Oil on canvas, mounted on masonite
36 x 36 in. (91.4 x 91.4 cm.)
Signed at lower right: F.WAGNER
Gift of Mr. and Mrs. Edward H. DaCosta, 1972.21

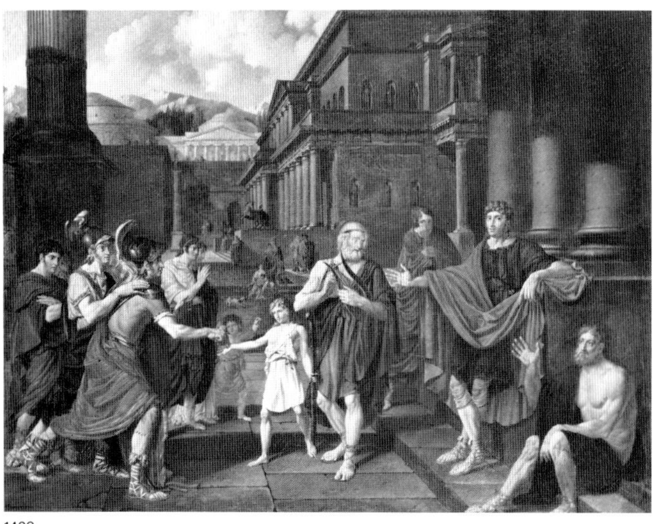
1409

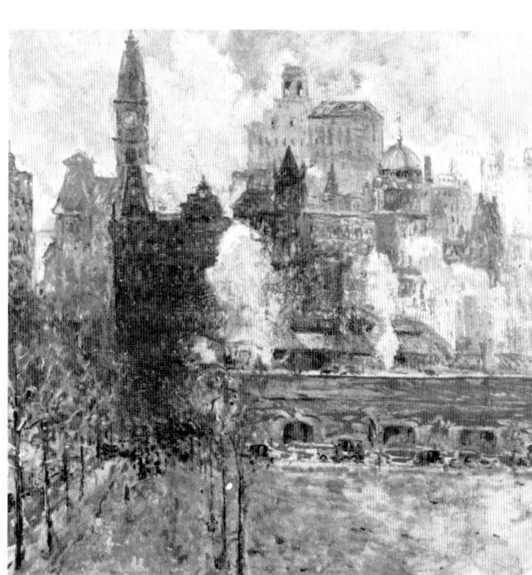
1419

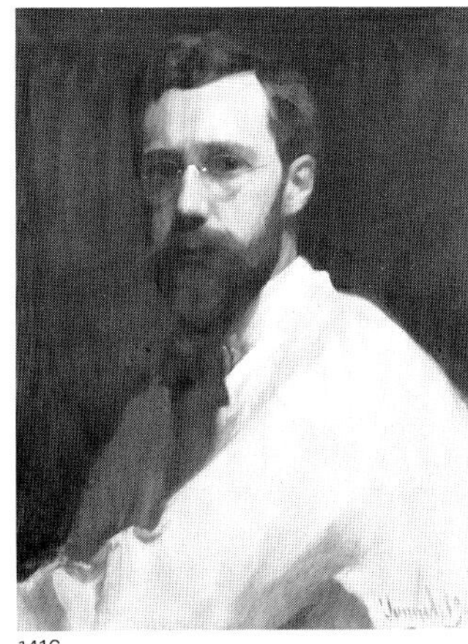
1416

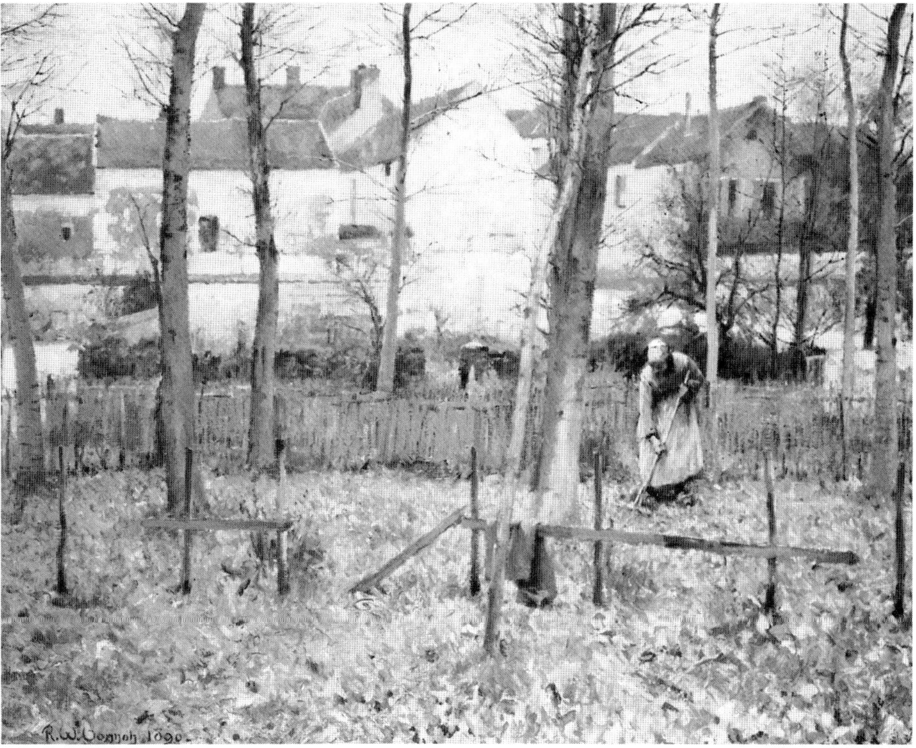
1414

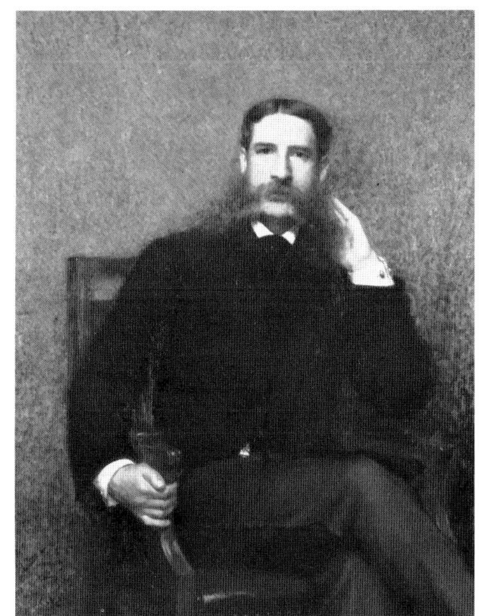
1411

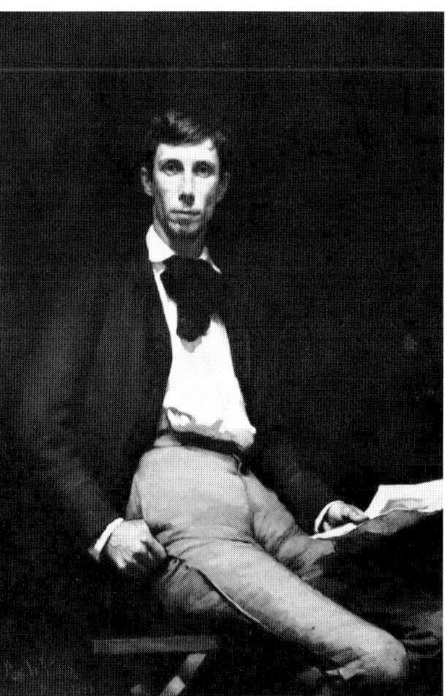
1412

Mary Wyman Wallace (1857–1896)

1420 *John S. Phillips* (1800–1876), 1882
Oil on canvas
30 x 24 in. (76.2 x 61 cm.)
Signed and dated at upper right: M.W. WALLACE./1882
Pennsylvania Academy purchase, 1905.1

Martha Walter (1875–1976)

1421 *Dorothy Lee Bell*, ca. 1915
Oil on canvas
40¼ x 32 in. (102.2 x 81.3 cm.)
Signed at lower left: Martha Walter
Joseph E. Temple Fund, 1916.8

Nina B. Ward (1885–1944)

1422 *Elizabeth*, 1913
Oil on canvas
35 x 29¹⁵⁄₁₆ in. (88.9 x 76 cm.)
Signed and dated at lower right: Nina B. Ward./ 1913; signed twice on back: N.B. Ward; and inscribed: Composition
Gift of John Frederick Lewis, 1923.8.18

Everett L. Warner (1877–1963)

1423 *Gloucester*
Oil on canvas board
6¼ x 9⁷⁄₁₆ in. (15.9 x 24 cm.)
Signed at lower left: E.L.WARNER
Gift of Vera White, 1956.3.3

1424 *Quebec*, ca. 1913
Oil on canvas
40 x 32⅛ in. (101.6 x 81.6 cm.)
Signed at lower right: EVERETT WARNER/ QUEBEC
Joseph E. Temple Fund, 1914.12

Howard Warshaw (1920–1977)

1425 *Wooden Horses*, 1956
Oil and Vynalite on canvas
48 x 96 in. (121.9 x 243.8 cm.)
John Lambert Fund, 1958.18

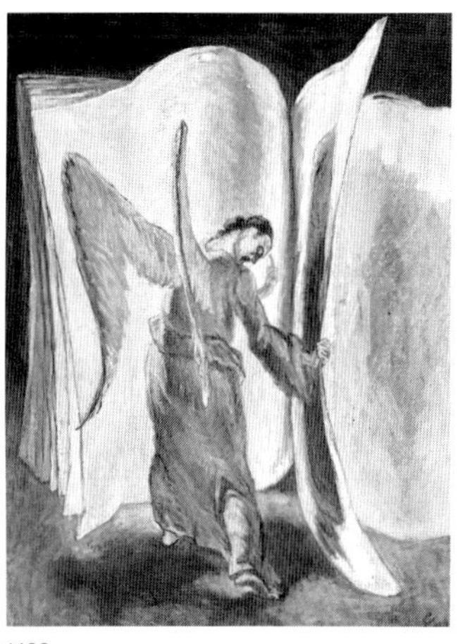
1428

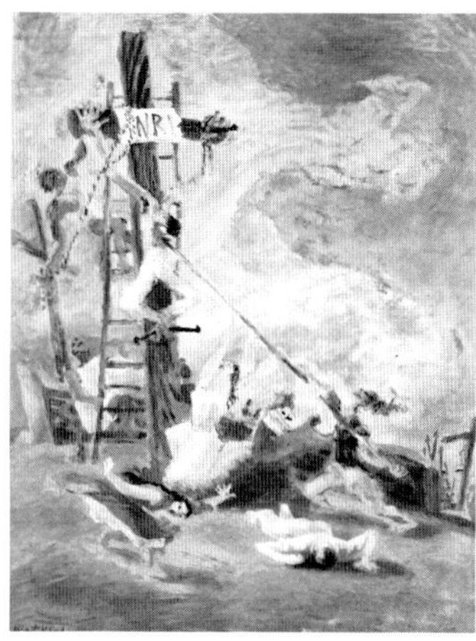
1429

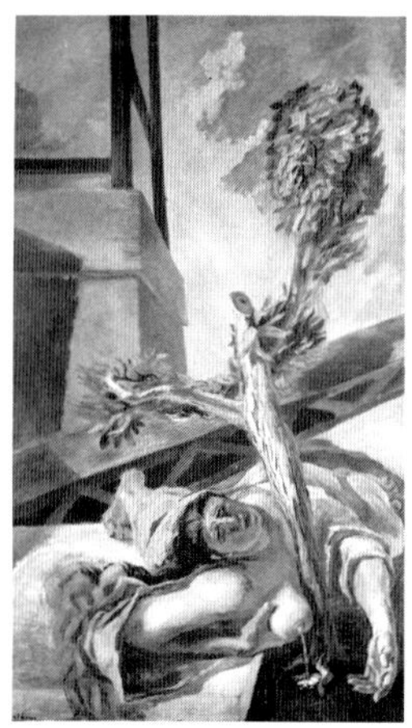
1433

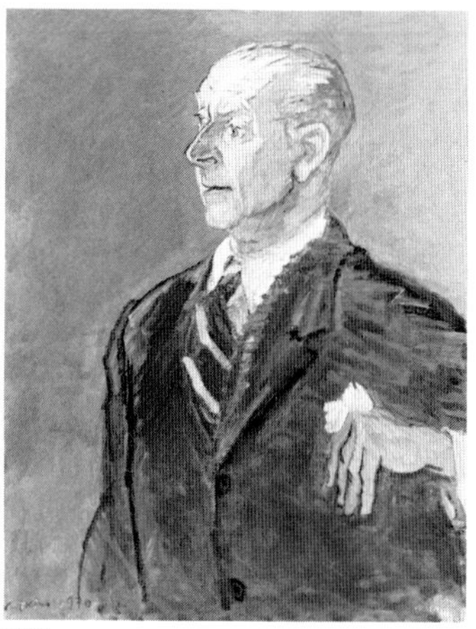
1430

Elizabeth Fisher Washington (1871–1953)

1426 *View near Chester Springs*, 1917
Oil on canvas
42 1/16 x 44 1/4 in. (106.8 x 112.4 cm.)
Signed and dated at lower left: E.F.WASHINGTON/ 1917; inscribed on back: Chester/Springs
Bequest of J. Mitchell Elliot, 1952.22.3

Franklin C. Watkins (1894–1972)

1427 *Angel Descending*
Oil on canvas
42 1/8 x 33 13/16 in. (107 x 85.9 cm.)
Signed at lower left: F.W.; inscribed and signed on back: Angel Descending/F.C.WATKINS
Bequest of David J. Grossman in honor of Mr. and Mrs. Charles S. Grossman and Mr. and Mrs. Meyer Speiser, 1979.1.8

1428 *Angel Turning a Page in the Book*, 1944
Oil on canvas
25 1/16 x 19 1/16 in. (63.7 x 48.4 cm.)
Signed at lower right: F.W.; inscribed on back: Angel Turning/a Page/in the Book
Gift of Mrs. Herbert Cameron Morris in memory of Ruth Kathryn and Emily Millward Morris, 1975.22

1429 *Crucifixion*, 1931
Oil on canvas
28 1/8 x 22 1/16 in. (71.4 x 56 cm.)
Signed at lower left: Watkins
Gift of Harry G. Sundheim, Jr., 1958.25.2

1430 *Joseph T. Fraser, Jr.* (1898–), 1970
Oil on canvas
29 3/8 x 23 11/16 in. (74.6 x 60.2 cm.)
Signed and dated at lower left: Watkins 1970
Commissioned by the Pennsylvania Academy, 1970.32

1431 *R. Sturgis Ingersoll* (1891–1973), 1938
Oil on canvas
23 x 24 in. (58.4 x 61 cm.)
Signed and dated twice, at lower left and right: F.W./38
Bequest of R. Sturgis Ingersoll, 1973.21

1432 *Negro*, ca. 1930
Oil on canvas
34 1/16 x 22 in. (86.5 x 55.9 cm.)
Signed at lower left: Watkins
John Lambert Fund, 1931.9

1433 *Nourishment*, 1931
Oil on canvas
84 1/2 x 48 3/4 in. (214.6 x 123.8 cm.)
Signed at lower left: Watkins
Bequest of Anna Warren Ingersoll, 1980.26

1434 *Portrait of Lucky*, 1959
Oil on canvas
33 3/4 x 23 1/4 in. (85.7 x 59.1 cm.)
Signed at lower left: Watkins
Gift of Mrs. John Wintersteen, 1973.28

1435 *Roman Garden (Lawrence Roberts's Garden in Rome)*, 1954
Oil on canvas
22 1/4 x 29 7/8 in. (56.5 x 75.9 cm.)
Signed at lower left: Watkins
Gift of James P. and Ruth Marshall Magill, 1957.15.42

1436 *Seascape*
Oil on canvas
16 1/8 x 16 1/8 in. (41 x 41 cm.)
Signed at lower left: F.W
Gift of James P. and Ruth Marshall Magill, 1957.15.43

1437 *John Frederick Steinman* (1884–1980)
Oil on canvas
40 x 32 1/16 in. (101.6 x 81.4 cm.)
Signed at lower left: F.W.
Bequest of Shirley Watkins Steinman, 1981.8.2

1438 *Still Life: Anemones*, 1964
Oil on canvas
30 1/4 x 25 1/4 in. (76.8 x 64.1 cm.)
Signed and dated at upper right: Watkins/64
Gift of Mrs. Roy F. Larson in memory of her husband, 1978.15

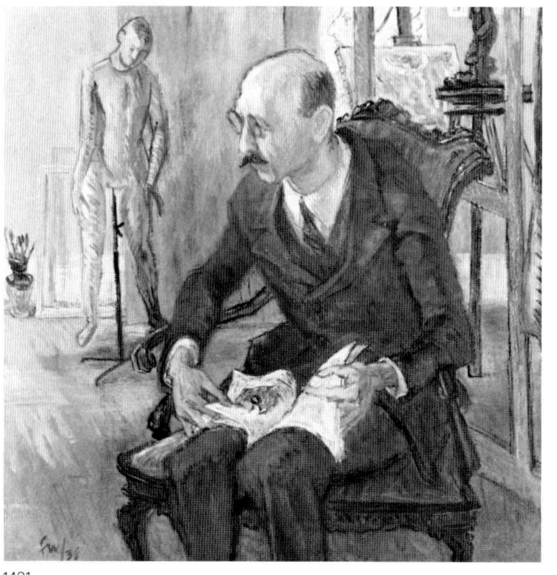
1431

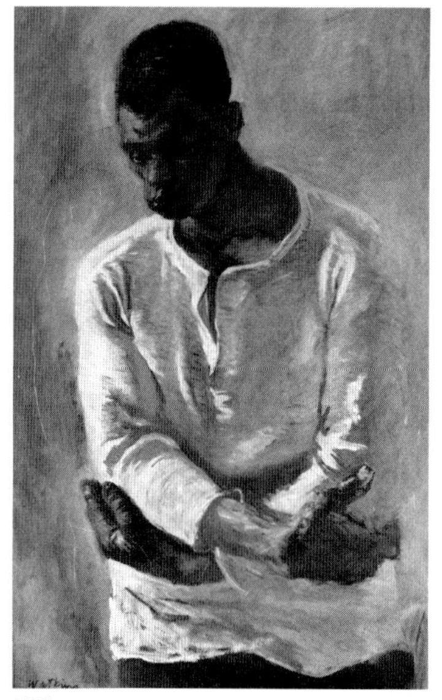
1432

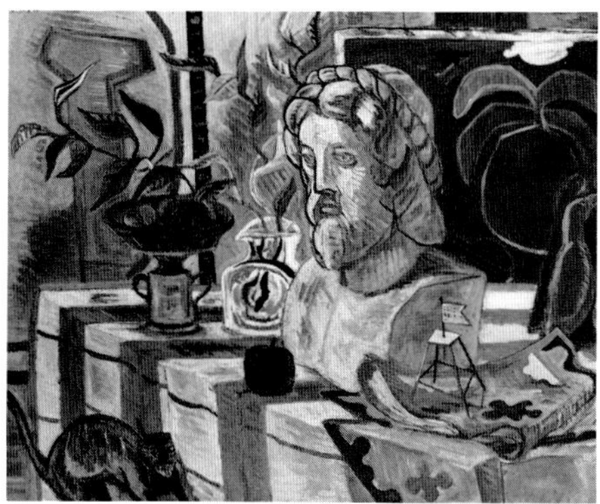
1439

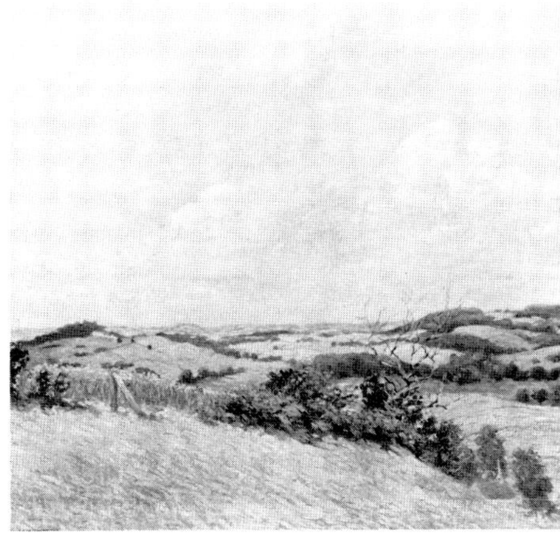
1426

1439 *Still Life: Classical Head, Cat, and China Parrot*, 1960
Oil on canvas
34 x 42 in. (86.4 x 106.7 cm.)
Signed at upper left: Watkins
Bequest of David J. Grossman in honor of Mr. and Mrs. Charles S. Grossman and Mr. and Mrs. Meyer Speiser, 1979.1.9

1440 *Still Life: Fruit #2*, 1954
Oil on canvas
12 x 22⅛ in. (30.5 x 56.2 cm.)
Signed at upper left: F.W.
Gift of James P. and Ruth Marshall Magill, 1957.15.44

1441 *Still Life: Red Flowers*, 1960
Oil on canvas
36⅜ x 30³⁄₁₆ in. (92.4 x 76.7 cm.)
Signed at lower left: Watkins
Bequest of David J. Grossman in honor of Mr. and Mrs. Charles S. Grossman and Mr. and Mrs. Meyer Speiser, 1979.1.10

1442 *Still Life with Bird Cage*, 1955
Oil on canvas
36¼ x 54 in. (92.1 x 137.2 cm.)
Signed at lower left: Watkins
Gift of James P. and Ruth Marshall Magill, 1957.15.45

1443 *Still Life with Cat on Sideboard and Birds in Sky*, 1971
Oil on canvas
27³⁄₁₆ x 35⁷⁄₁₆ in. (69.1 x 90 cm.)
Signed and dated at lower left: Watkins/71
Bequest of Shirley Watkins Steinman, 1981.8.5

1444 *Still Life with Skulls on Table*
Oil on canvas
21¹⁄₁₆ x 28 in. (53.5 x 71.1 cm.)
Signed at upper left: Watkins
Bequest of Shirley Watkins Steinman, 1981.8.6

1445 *Summer Scene*, 1950
Oil on canvas
32 x 48 in. (81.3 x 121.9 cm.)
Signed at lower right: Watkins; signed and dated on back: F. Watkins 1950
Henry D. Gilpin Fund, 1951.15

1446 *Sunny Morning*, 1956
Oil on canvas
30¹⁄₁₆ x 34 in. (76.4 x 86.4 cm.)
Signed at lower left: Watkins
Bequest of Shirley Watkins Steinman, 1981.8.3

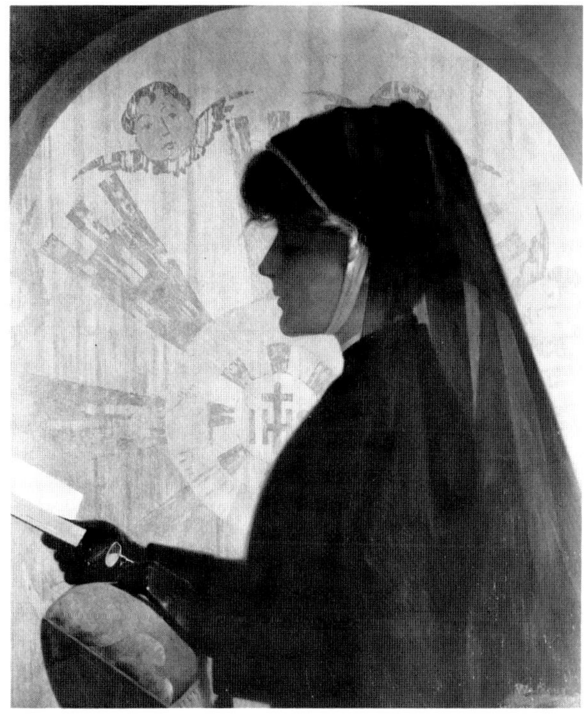
1447

Harry W. Watrous (1857–1940)

1447 *Devotion*, by 1924
Oil on canvas
27⅞ x 24 in. (70.8 x 61 cm.)
Signed and inscribed at right: Watrous/ Copyright/By Harry W. Watrous
Gift of Russell C. Graef in memory of his wife, Jennie M. Graef, 1956.16

Myer Wattman (ca. 1911–1936)

1448 *Landscape*, ca. 1932
Oil on canvas
38 x 30 in. (96.5 x 76.2 cm.)
John Lambert Fund, 1933.7

William Clothier Watts (1868–1961)

1449 *Entrance to the Mosque, Morocco*
Oil on canvas
30 x 24 in. (76.2 x 61 cm.)
Bequest of the artist, 1961.12

Frederick J. Waugh (1861–1940)

1450 *The Blue Gulf Stream*, ca. 1913
Oil on canvas
52⅛ x 68³⁄₁₆ in. (132.4 x 173.2 cm.)
Signed at lower right: Waugh
Joseph E. Temple Fund, 1914.13

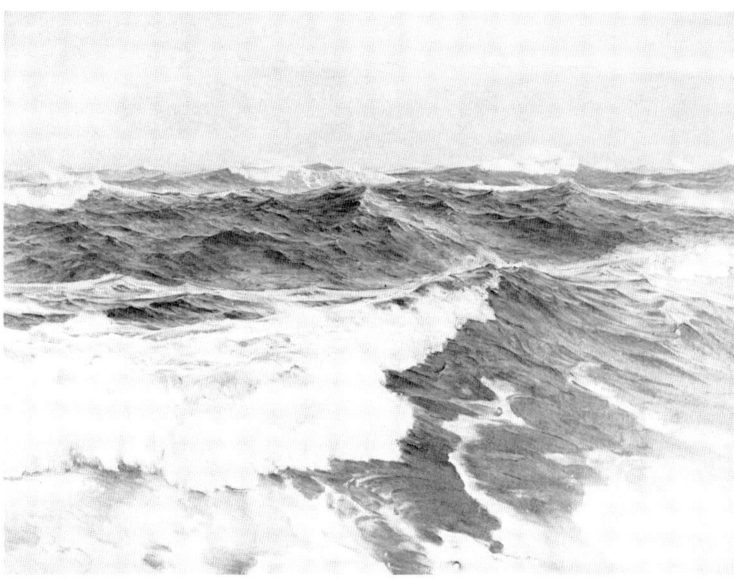
1450

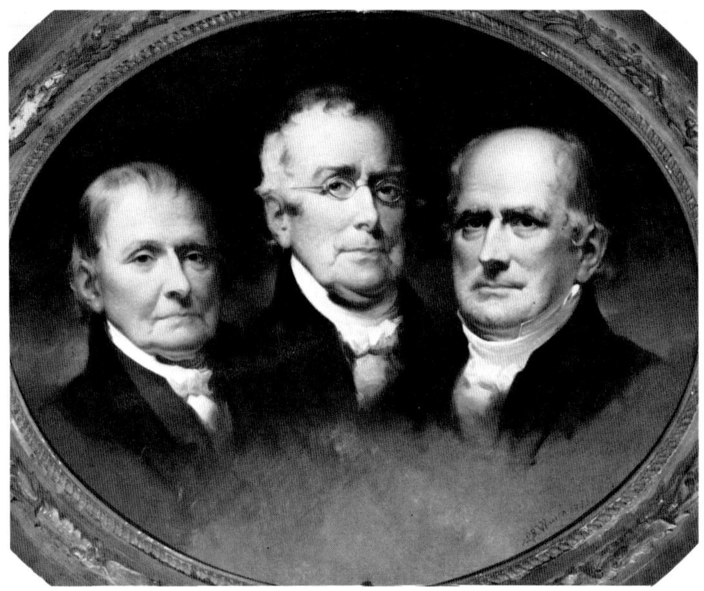
1451

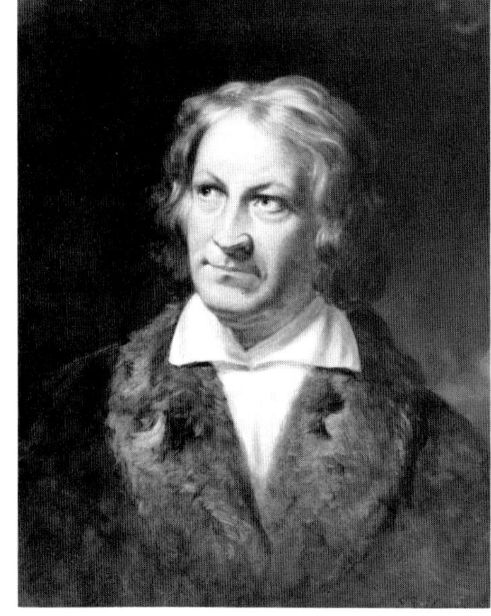
1455

Samuel Bell Waugh (1814–1885)

1451 *Cope Brothers* (Jasper, b. 1775; Thomas Pym, 1768–1854; and Israel, b. 1776), 1853
Oil on canvas
29 x 35⅝ in. (73.7 x 90.5 cm.), oval
Signed and dated at lower right: S.B.Waugh 1853.
Gift of Caleb Cope, 1876.3

1452 *Mrs. Henry D. Gilpin* (née Elizabeth Sibley, 1796–1874), by 1867
Oil on canvas
36⅞ x 31 in. (93.7 x 78.7 cm.)
Gift of Mrs. Henry D. Gilpin, 1867.2

1453 *Joseph R. Ingersoll* (1786–1868), 1868
Oil on canvas
30¼ x 25¼ in. (76.8 x 64.1 cm.)
Signed and dated at lower left: S B Waugh.1868.
Bequest of Mrs. Kirk B. Wells, 1898.6

1454 *Abraham Lincoln* (1809–1865), 1863
Oil on canvas
27¼ x 22⅛ in. (69.2 x 56.2 cm.)
Signed and dated at lower right: S.B.Waugh 1863.
Bequest of C. Cresson Wistar, 1917.10

1455 *Bertel Thorwaldsen* (1770–1844)
Oil on canvas
29⅛ x 24⅛ in. (74 x 61.3 cm.)
Signed at lower right: S.B.Waugh.
Gift of Mrs. C. Schillard-Smith, 1927.9

Carl Weber (1850–1921)

1456 *Study of Plants*
Oil on canvas
7⁹⁄₁₆ x 14⁷⁄₁₆ in. (19.2 x 36.7 cm.)
Signed at lower left: Carl Weber
Gift of Mr. and Mrs. Theodore T. Newbold, 1980.30

Max Weber (1881–1961)

1457 *The Fallen Tree*, 1942
Oil on canvas
30⅛ x 36 in. (76.5 x 91.4 cm.)
Signed and dated at lower right: MAX WEBER 1942
Collections Fund, 1950.23.3

Paul Weber (1823–1916)

1458 *Landscape: Evening*, 1856
Oil on canvas
60¼ x 86 in. (153 x 218.4 cm.)
Signed and dated at lower right: Paul Weber/ 1856.
Pennsylvania Academy purchase, by subscription, 1857.1

Edwin Lord Weeks (1849–1903)

1459 *The Three Beggars of Cordova*, ca. 1891
Oil on canvas
66 x 98½ in. (167.6 x 250.2 cm.)
Signed at lower left: E.L.WEEKS.
Gift of Charles W. Wharton, 1892.5

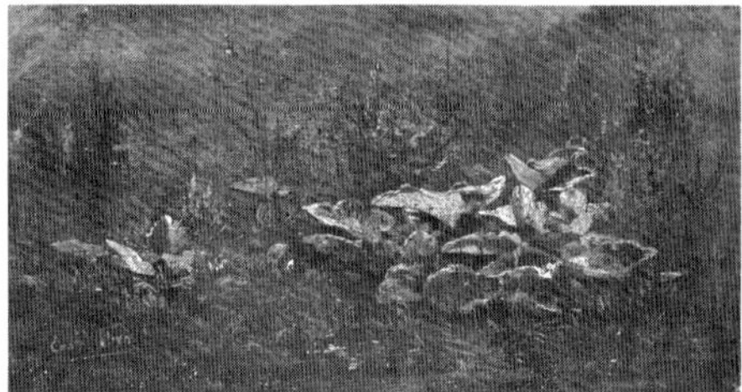
1456

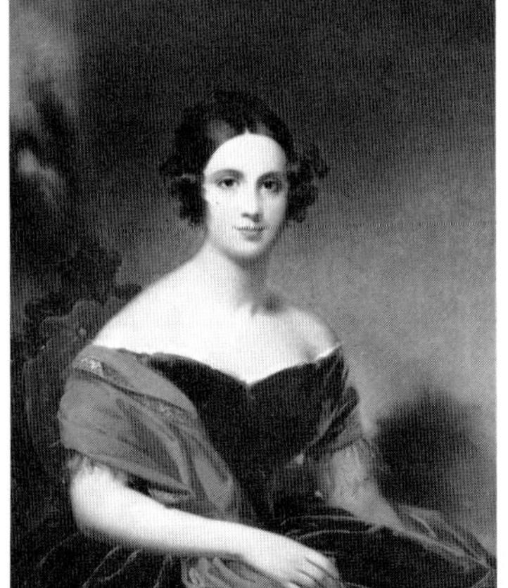
1452

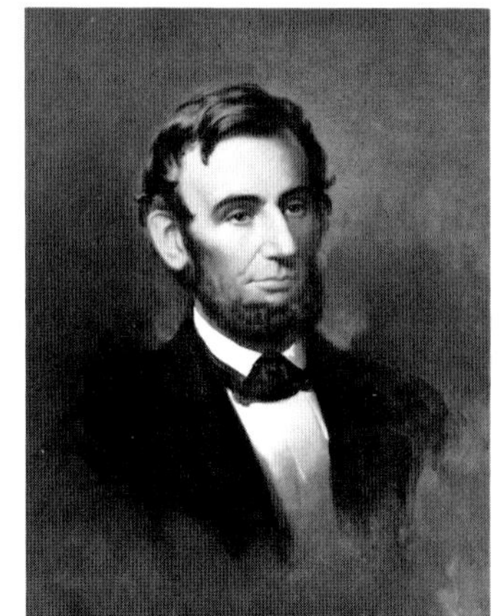
1454

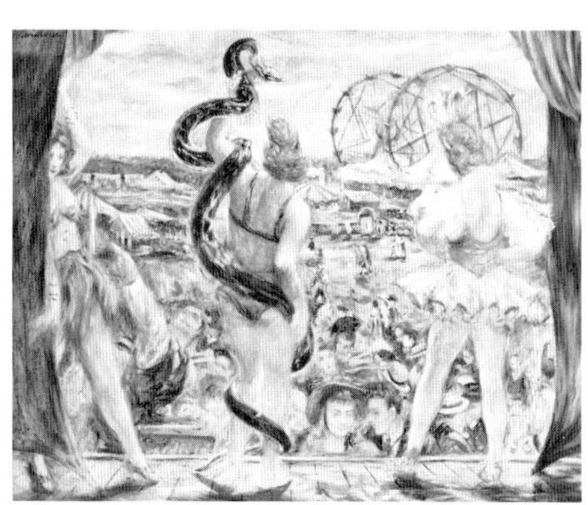
1461

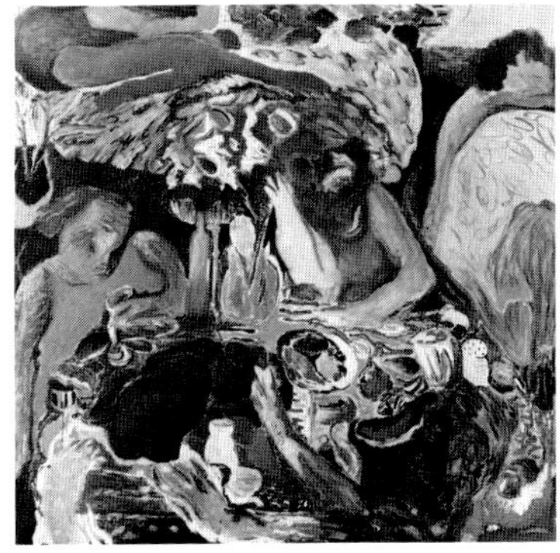
1463

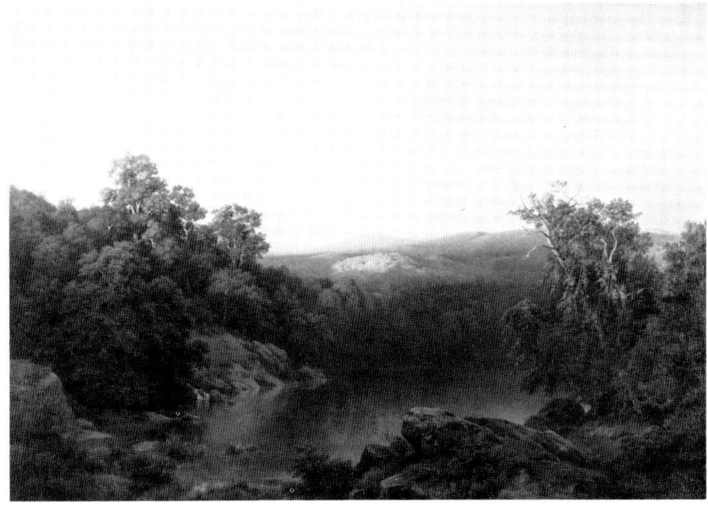
1458

Doris Kunzie Weidner (Mrs. Roswell Weidner, 1910–)

1460 *The River*, ca. 1939
Oil on canvas
28¹⁄₁₆ x 32 in. (71.3 x 81.3 cm.)
Signed at upper right: Doris Kunzie
John Lambert Fund, 1940.5

Roswell Weidner (1911–)

1461 *The County Fair*, 1938
Oil on canvas
24¹⁵⁄₁₆ x 30³⁄₈ in. (63.3 x 77.2 cm.)
Signed at upper left: Weidner
John Lambert Fund, 1940.7

1462 *Portrait of Dorcas Combing Her Hair* (Doris Kunzie Weidner), 1949
Oil over egg tempera on masonite
22¹⁵⁄₁₆ x 28¹⁄₁₆ in. (58.3 x 71.3 cm.)
Signed and dated at lower left: R Weidner 49
Gift of the artist, 1960.21

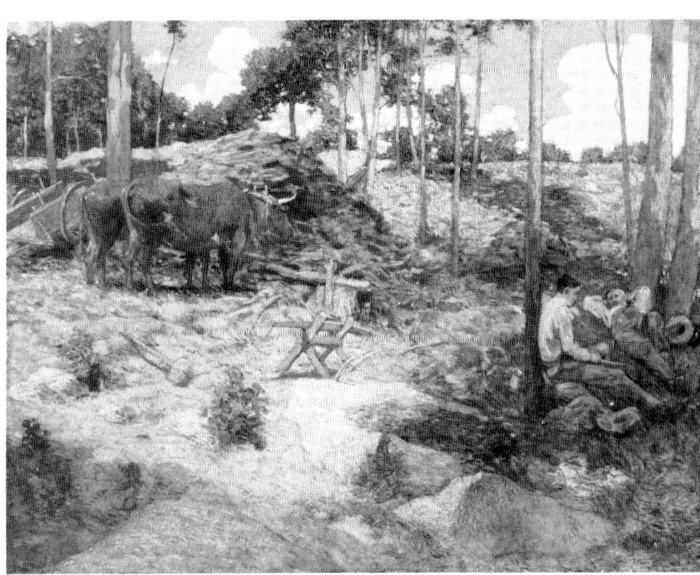
1465

Joyce Weinstein (1931–)

1463 *Figures in an Interior*, 1953
Oil on canvas
50 x 50 in. (127 x 127 cm.)
Signed and dated at lower left: J. Weinstein '53
John Lambert Fund, 1954.18

Howard Weinstone (1928–)

1464 *Six Bathers, Pink Beach*, 1971
Acrylic on canvas
50¹⁄₈ x 72¹⁄₈ in. (127.3 x 183.2 cm.)
Inscribed, signed, and dated on back: SIX BATHERS, PINK BEACH/ACRYLIC/Howard Weinstone 1971
Gift of Mr. and Mrs. Alan Salke, 1972.23

J. Alden Weir (1852–1919)

1465 *Midday Rest in New England*, 1897
Oil on canvas
39⁵⁄₈ x 50³⁄₈ in. (100.6 x 128 cm.)
Signed, dated, and inscribed at lower right: J. Alden Weir—1897./Branchville. Conn.
Gift of Isaac H. Clothier, Edward H. Coates, Dr. Francis W. Lewis, Robert C. Ogden, and Joseph G. Rosengarten, 1898.9

Hugh Weiss (1925–)

1466 *Café, Rue d'Alesia*, 1949
Oil on canvas
31¹³⁄₁₆ x 23⁹⁄₁₆ in. (80.8 x 59.8 cm.)
Signed and dated at upper right: Weiss/49
John Lambert Fund, 1951.16

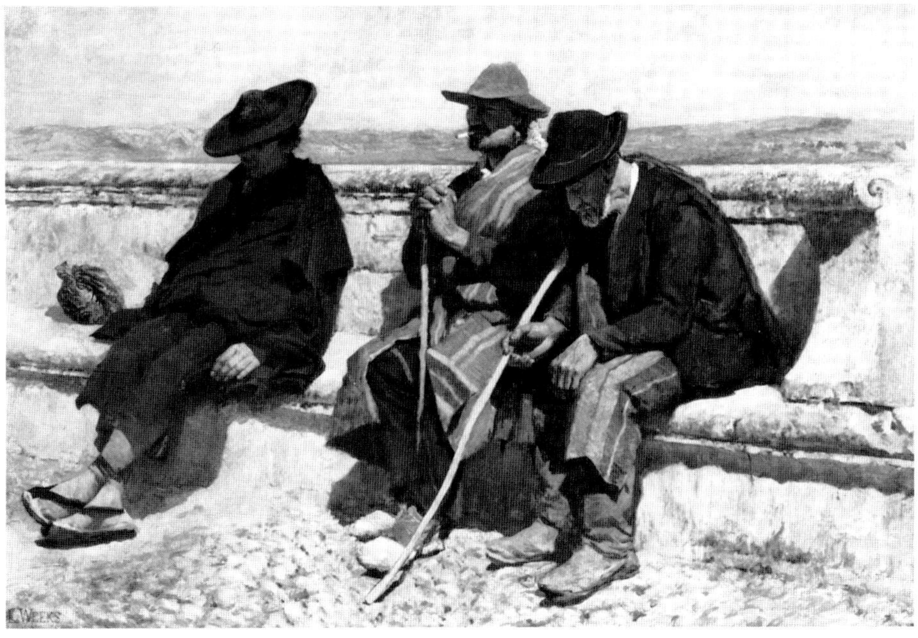
1459

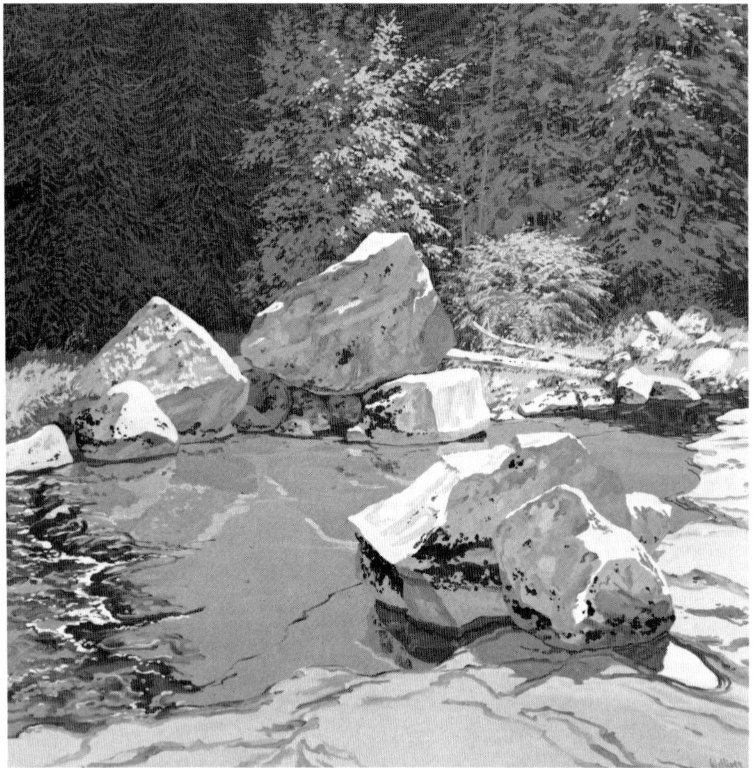
1468

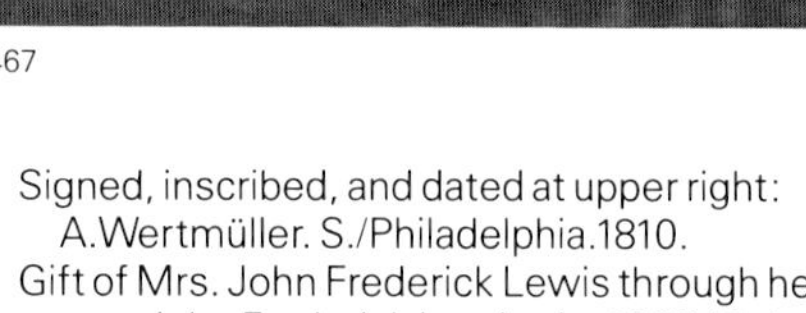
1467

Charles D. Weldon (1855–1935)

1467 *Tokens*, by 1887
Oil on canvas
45 x 28½ in. (114.3 x 72.4 cm.)
Annotated on frame: C. D. Weldon/222 W. 23 St./"Tokens" New York
Gift of Mrs. Edward H. Coates (The Edward H. Coates Memorial Collection), 1923.9.11

Neil G. Welliver (1929–)

1468 *Cedar Breaks*, 1976
Oil on canvas
96 x 96 in. (243.8 x 243.8 cm.)
Signed at lower right: Welliver
Funds provided by the National Endowment for the Arts and the Charles E. Merrill Trust, 1976.14.2

Theodore Wendel (1859–1932)

1469 *Winter at Ipswich*, ca. 1908
Oil on canvas
24⅞ x 29$^{15}/_{16}$ in. (63.2 x 76 cm.)
Joseph E. Temple Fund, 1909.5

Adolph Ulric Wertmüller (1751–1811)

1470 *Andrew Hamilton II* (1712–1747), 1810
Oil on canvas
27$^{1}/_{16}$ x 21$^{3}/_{16}$ in. (68.7 x 53.8 cm.)
Signed, inscribed, and dated at upper right: A.Wertmüller. S./Philadelphia.1810.
Gift of Mrs. John Frederick Lewis through her son, John Frederick Lewis, Jr., 1938.13.4

1471 *Mrs. Andrew Hamilton II* (d. 1803), 1810
Oil on canvas
27$^{1}/_{16}$ x 21¼ in. (68.7 x 54 cm.)
Signed, inscribed, and dated at upper left: A:Wertmüller. S./Philadelphia. 1810.
Gift of Mrs. John Frederick Lewis through her son, John Frederick Lewis, Jr., 1938.13.5

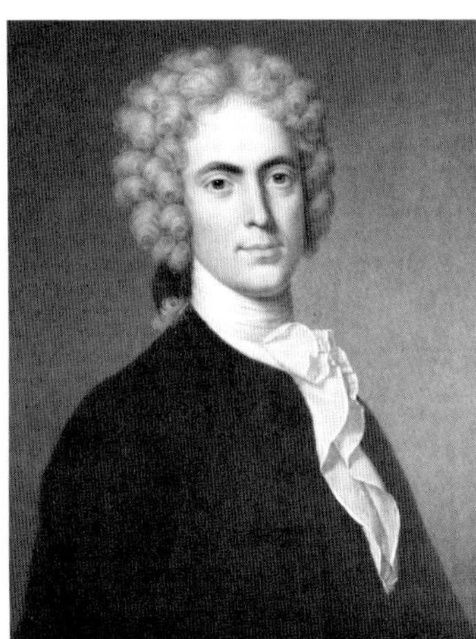
1470

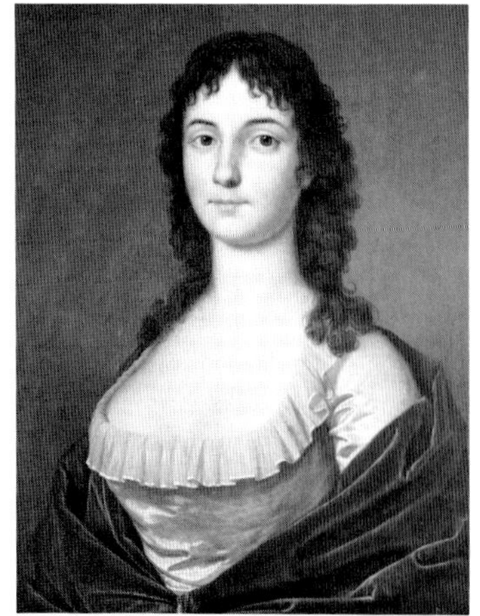
1471

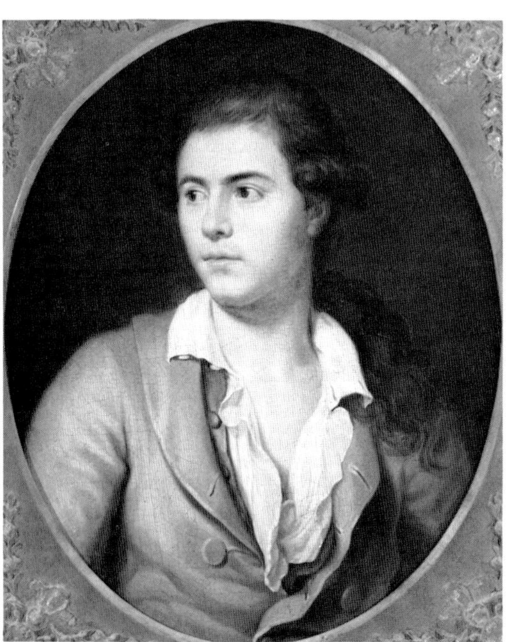
1472

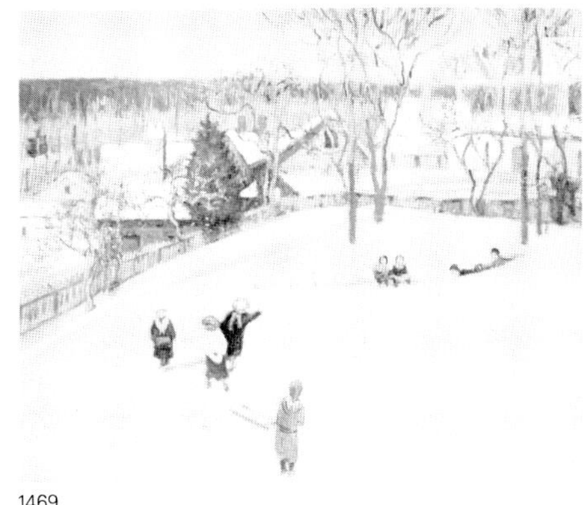
1469

1476 *The Outer Shoals*, 1967
Oil on canvas
$29^{15}/_{16}$ x 50 in. (76 x 127 cm.)
Signed at lower right: Paul Wescott
Annotated on frame: THE OUTER SHOALS— 1967
Gift of Mrs. Paul Wescott, 1972.4

Benjamin West (1738–1820)

1477 *Christ Rejected*, 1814
Oil on canvas
200 x 260 in. (508 x 660.4 cm.)
Signed and dated at lower left: Benj. West/1814
Gift of Mrs. Sarah Harrison (The Joseph Harrison, Jr. Collection), 1878.1.9

1478 *Death on the Pale Horse*, 1817
Oil on canvas
176 x 301 in. (447 x 764.5 cm.)
Signed and dated at lower right: Benj West/Octr. 10/1817
Pennsylvania Academy purchase, 1836.1

1479 *Paul and Barnabas Rejecting the Jews and Receiving the Gentiles*, ca. 1793
Oil on canvas
147 x 115 in. (373.4 x 292.1 cm.)
Gift of the City of Philadelphia, by exchange, 1848.1

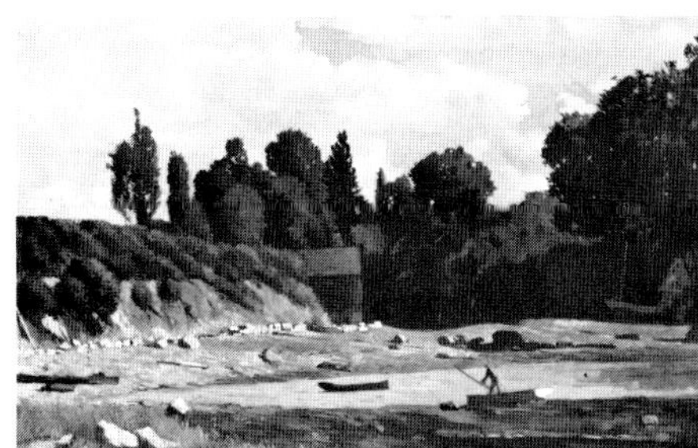
1475

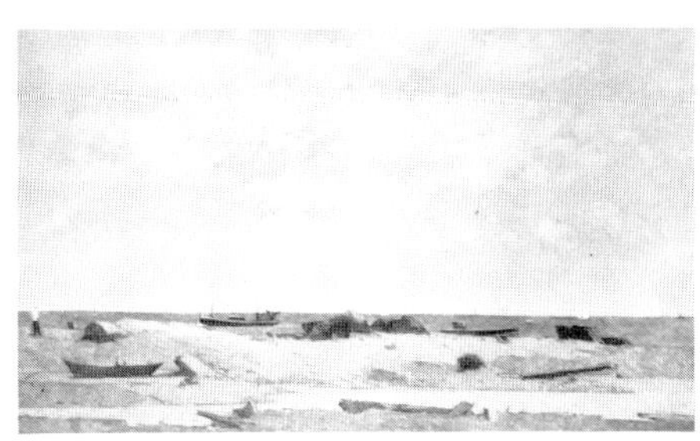
1476

1472 *Self-Portrait*, 1770s
Oil on canvas
$25\frac{1}{4}$ x $21\frac{1}{8}$ in. (64.1 x 53.7 cm.), oval
Gift of John Frederick Lewis, 1914.15

Paul Wescott (1904–1970)

1473 *Country Road, Chester Springs*, 1929
Oil on canvas
$30\frac{1}{16}$ x 36 in. (76.4 x 91.4 cm.)
Signed and dated at lower right: Paul Wescott/1929
Pennsylvania Academy purchase, 1929.6

1474 *Maine Shore*, probably 1955
Oil on canvas
$13^{15}/_{16}$ x $25\frac{1}{16}$ in. (35.4 x 63.7 cm.)
Signed at lower right: Paul Wescott
Gift of James P. and Ruth Marshall Magill, 1957.15.46

1475 *Osier's Cove*, ca. 1942
Oil on canvas
25 x 40 in. (63.5 x 101.6 cm.)
Signed at lower left: Paul Wescott
John Lambert Fund, 1943.1

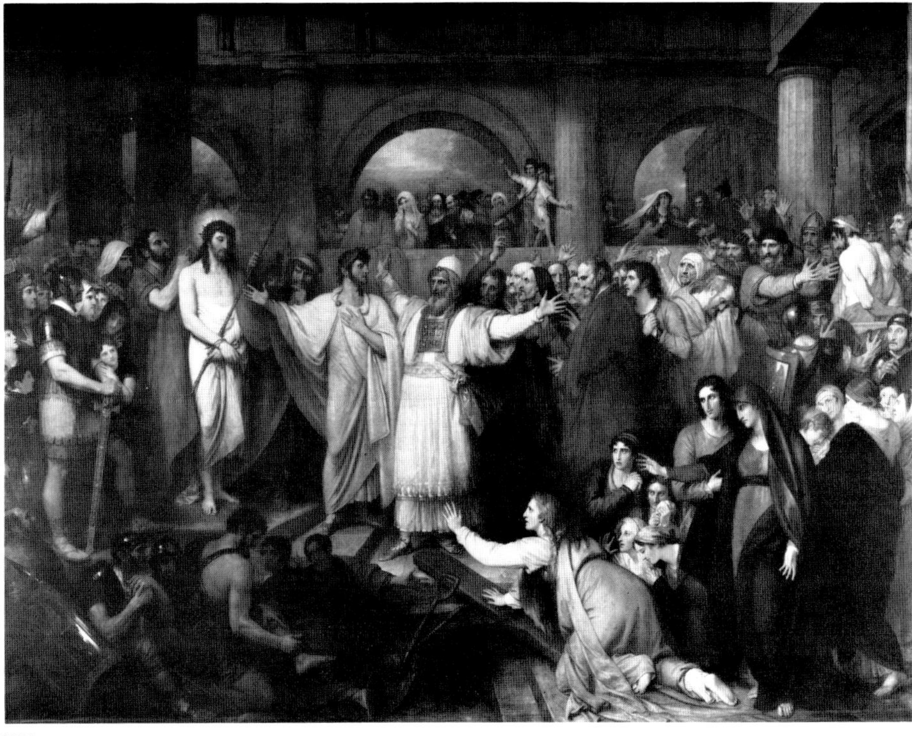
1477

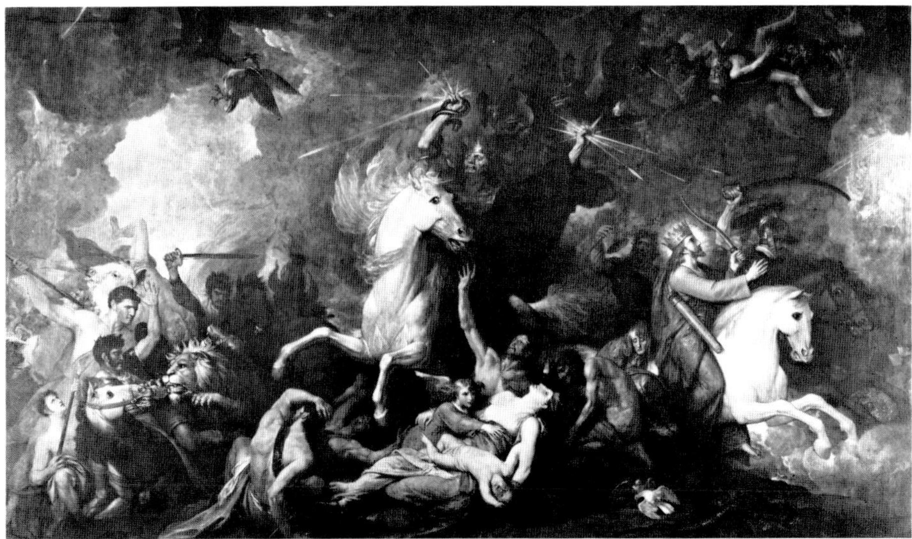
1478

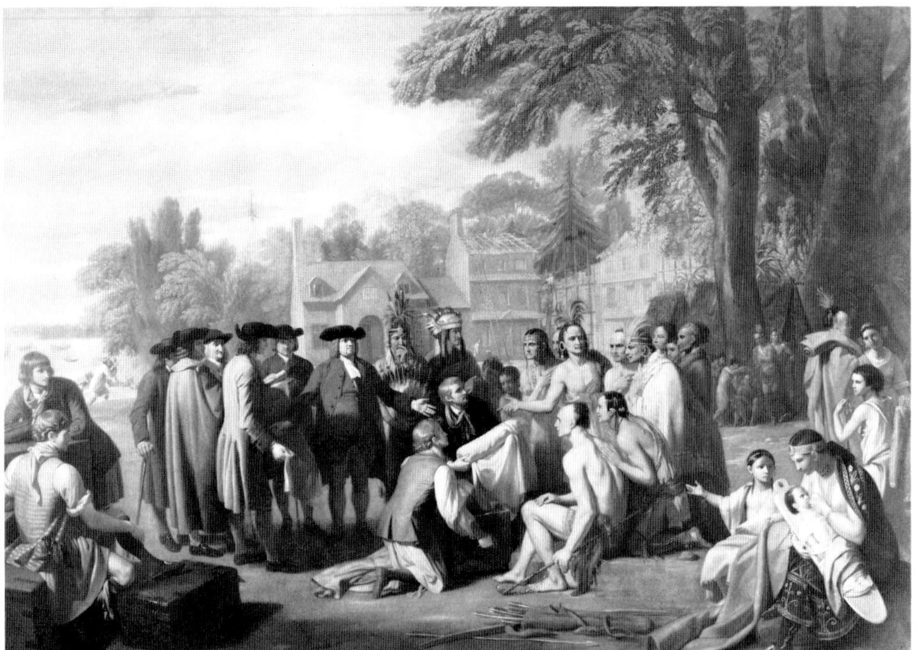

1481

1480 *Elizabeth Peel* (later Mrs. Francis Harris), ca. 1757
Oil on canvas
47⅛ x 34⅜ in. (119.7 x 87.3 cm.)
Gift of John Frederick Lewis, 1923.8.13

1481 *Penn's Treaty with the Indians*, 1771–72
Oil on canvas
75½ x 107¾ in. (191.8 x 273.7 cm.)
Signed and dated at lower left: B. West/1771
Gift of Mrs. Sarah Harrison (The Joseph Harrison, Jr. Collection), 1878.1.10
See also copy by Savage, cat. no. 1191.

1482 *Self-Portrait*, 1806
Oil on canvas
36⅛ x 28⅛ in. (91.8 x 71.4 cm.)
Signed and dated at upper right: B. West 1806
Gift of Mr. and Mrs. Henry R. Hallowell, 1964.11

Lilian Westcott. *See* Lilian Westcott Hale.

Harold Weston (1894–1972)

1483 *Peasant Kitchen*, 1926
Oil on canvas, mounted on plywood
21⅜ x 25⅝ in. (54.3 x 65.1 cm.)
Signed and dated at lower left: W26
John Lambert Fund, 1928.6

Elisha Kent Kane Wetherill (1874–1929)

1484 *Ideal Head*, 1899
Oil on canvas
12⅞ x 9⅜ in. (32.7 x 23.8 cm.)
Signed and inscribed at lower left: E K. K. Wetherill/Paris 99
Gift of Vera White, 1960.18.5

1485 *Edith Lisée*
Oil on canvas
19⅝ x 13$\frac{3}{16}$ in. (49.8 x 33.5 cm.)
Gift of Vera White, 1956.3.4

1486 *Red Sails*
Oil on canvas
7½ x 10⅝ in. (19.1 x 27 cm.)
Signed at lower left: E.K.K.Wetherill
Gift of Vera White, 1960.18.6

1487 *Seascape, No. 1*
Oil on wood
5 x 7$\frac{1}{16}$ in. (12.7 x 17.9 cm.)
Signed at lower center: E.K.K.Wetherill; inscribed and signed on back: Seascape No 1/ Kent Wetherill
Gift of Vera White, 1956.3.5

1488 *Seascape, No. 2*
Oil on canvas
6⅜ x 10$\frac{11}{16}$ in. (16.2 x 27.1 cm.)
Gift of Vera White, 1956.3.6

Vera White (Mrs. Samuel S. White III, 1889–1966)

1489 *Bermuda Flowers*
Oil on canvas
18 x 16 in. (45.7 x 40.6 cm.)
Gift of Dr. and Mrs. Samuel Sugarman, 1980.27

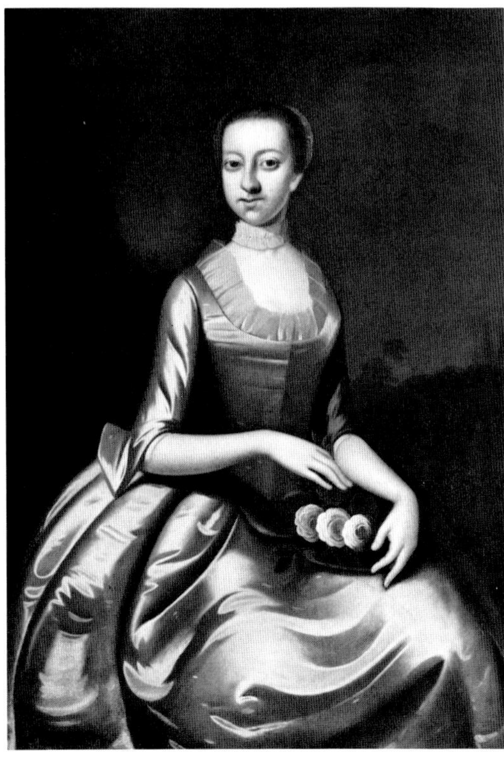

1480

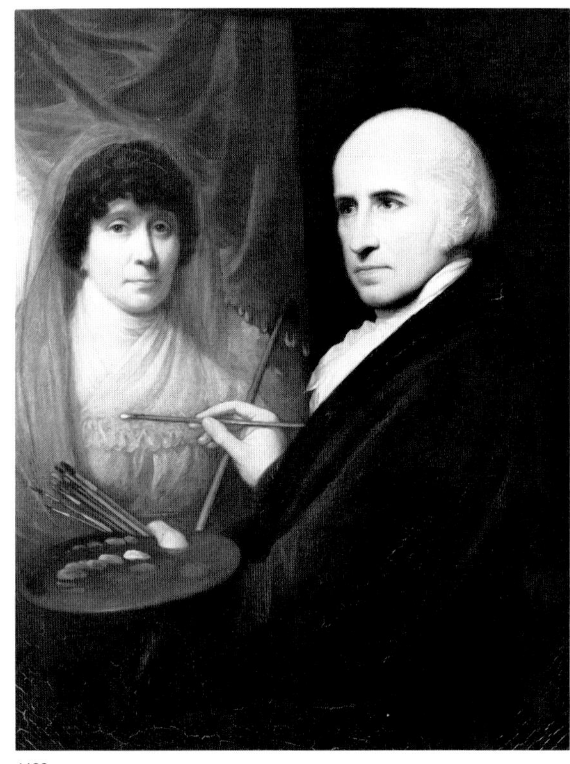

1482

Florence Standish Whiting (1888–1947)

1490 *White Flowers*, ca. 1934
Oil on canvas
24$^{15}/_{16}$ x 19$^{1}/_{8}$ in. (63.3 x 48.6 cm.)
Signed at lower right: Florence Standish Whiting
John Lambert Fund, 1935.11

Alice E. Whitten
See Alice Whitten Lindborg.

Worthington Whittredge (1820–1910)

1491 *Motive from the River Nahe*, 1854
Oil on canvas
15$^{1}/_{16}$ x 18$^{3}/_{4}$ in. (38.3 x 47.6 cm.)
Signed at lower right: T. W. Whitridge [his early spelling of surname]
Gift of Mr. and Mrs. Edward Kesler, 1975.20.2

Carleton Wiggins (1848–1932)

1492 *Early Morning*, 1887
Oil on canvas
23 x 33$^{3}/_{16}$ in. (58.4 x 84.3 cm.)
Signed and dated at lower left: CARLETON WIGGINS./1887.; inscribed and signed on back: "EARLY MORNING"/Carleton Wiggins
Gift of Mrs. Edward H. Coates (The Edward H. Coates Memorial Collection), 1923.9.12

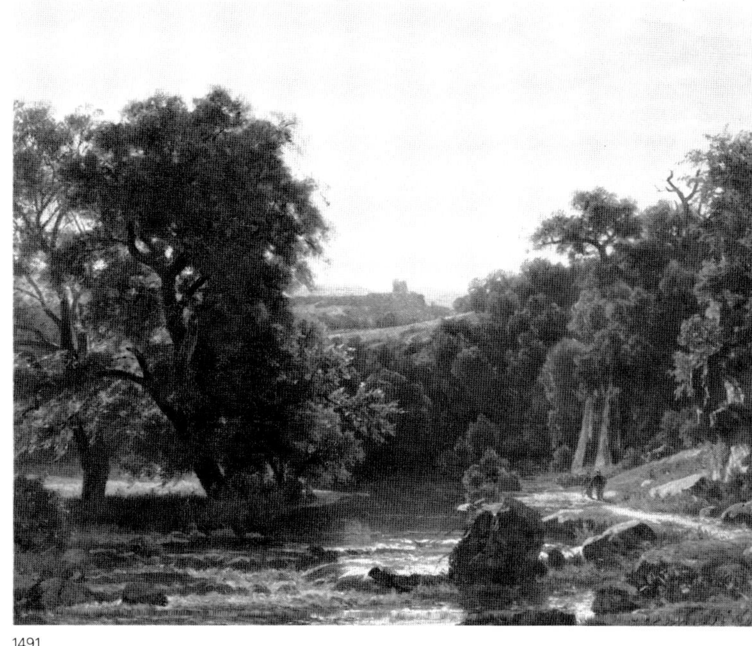

1491

John Wilde (1919–)

1493 *In the Hand*, 1957
Oil on tempered masonite
9$^{15}/_{16}$ x 13$^{7}/_{8}$ in. (25.2 x 35.2 cm.)
Signed and dated at upper right: J 1957; inscribed on back: In the Hand
John Lambert Fund, 1958.19

Max S. Wilkes (b. 1884)

1494 *Girl Resting*, 1942–43
Oil on canvas
20$^{1}/_{16}$ x 24$^{1}/_{16}$ in. (51 x 61.1 cm.)
Signed at lower right: M.S.Wilkes-
Joseph E. Temple Fund, 1949.12

Esther Williams (Mrs. Oliver H. Williams, née Baldwin, 1907–1969)

1495 *Circus Horses*, ca. 1934
Oil on canvas
29$^{7}/_{8}$ x 36$^{1}/_{16}$ in. (75.9 x 91.6 cm.)
Signed at lower right: Esther Williams; signed and inscribed on back: Esther Williams/6 West 8th St. N.Y.C.
John Lambert Fund, 1935.12

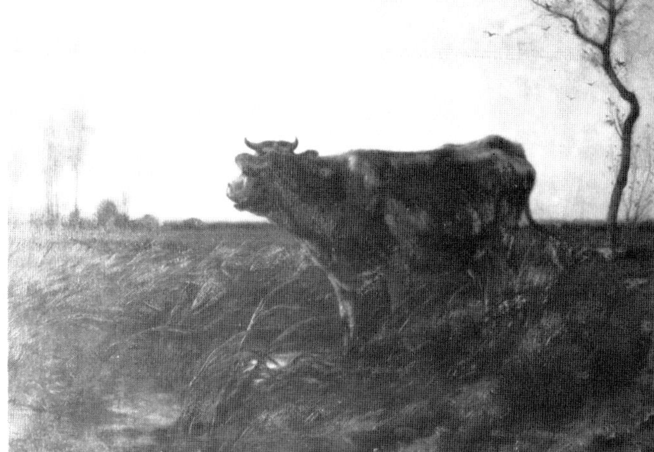

1492

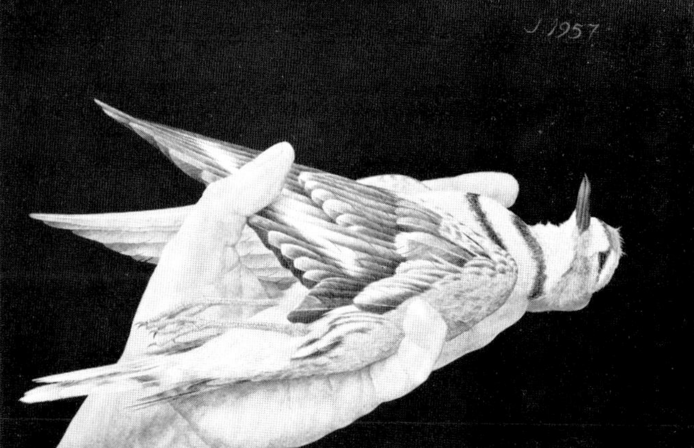

1493

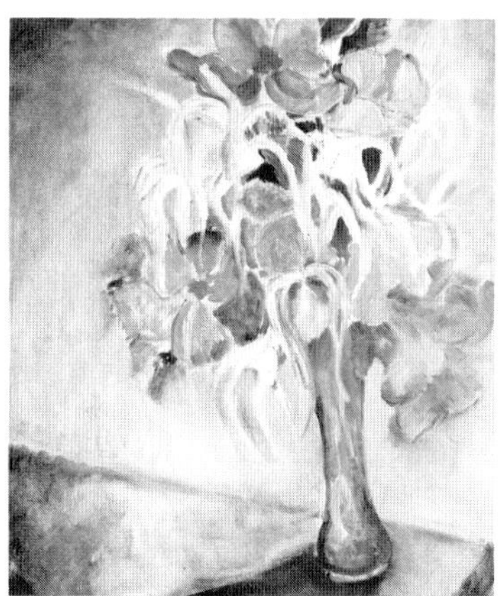

1489

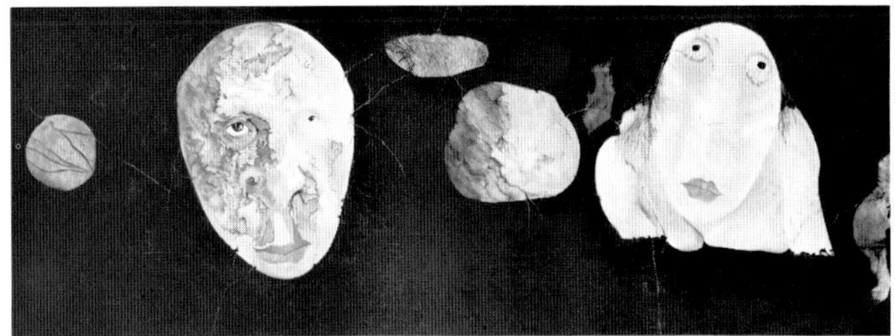
1496

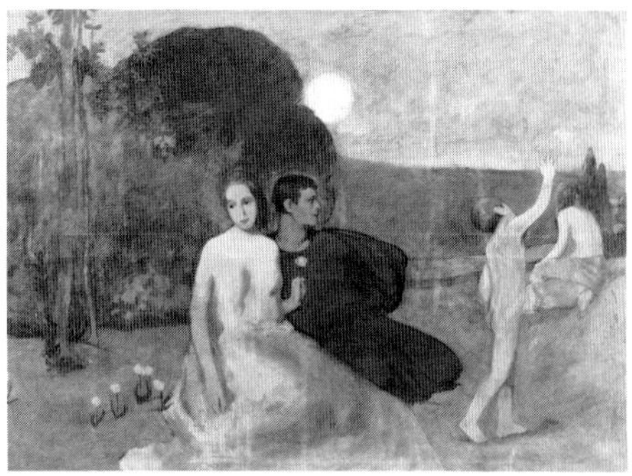
1502

Hiram D. Williams (1917–)

1496 *Metamorphosis*, 1952
Oil on masonite
19⅝ x 48 in. (49.8 x 121.9 cm.)
Signed and dated at lower left: h.d. Williams.'52
Gift of Hobson Pittman, 1962.18

Isaac L. Williams (1817–1895)

1497 *Henrietta Williamina Smith Hobart* (Mrs. Robert Enoch Hobart, Jr., 1814–1873), ca. 1844
Oil on canvas
30⅛ x 24⅞ in. (76.5 x 63.2 cm.)
Gift of Jessie Ives Rutter, 1952.18

1498 *John Neagle* (1796–1865), ca. 1890 (after a daguerreotype by Frederick de Bourg Richards, ca. 1846)
Oil on canvas
27 x 21¹⁵⁄₁₆ in. (68.6 x 55.7 cm.)
Gift of Garrett C. Neagle, 1894.7

1499 *Hon. Thaddeus Stevens* (1792–1868), 1830s
Oil on canvas
25⅞ x 20⅛ in. (65.7 x 51.1 cm.)
Inscribed and signed on back: Portrait of Hon T. Stevens/Hon T Stevens/Painted frome [*sic*] Life./Isaac. Williams.
Gift of Mrs. John Frederick Lewis (The John Frederick Lewis Memorial Collection), 1933.10.103

1500 *View in Dovedale, England*, 1866
Oil on canvas
24⅛ x 36 in. (61.3 x 91.4 cm.)
Signed, dated, and inscribed at lower left: I. L Williams/1866/Paris
Source unknown, 1879.10

Mildred Emerson Williams (b. 1892)

1501 *Skating, Central Park*, 1927
Oil on canvas
32 x 36¼ in. (81.3 x 92.1 cm.)
Signed at lower right: MILDRED E. WILLIAMS-
Signed and dated on stretcher: MILDRED E. WILLIAMS 1927
John Lambert Fund, 1928.7

Francis Vaux Wilson (1874–1938)

1502 *Poetry* (formerly *Romance*), 1896–97
Oil on canvas
Approx. 78 x 105 in. (198 x 266 cm.)
Signed at lower left: F.V.Wilson
Commissioned by the Pennsylvania Academy, 1897.9.13

J. B. Wilson

1503 *The Horse Fair*, 1867 (after Rosa Bonheur, 1853)
Oil on canvas
36½ x 76½ in. (92.7 x 194.3 cm.)
Signed and dated at lower right: J.B. Wilson 1867
Source unknown, 1972.7

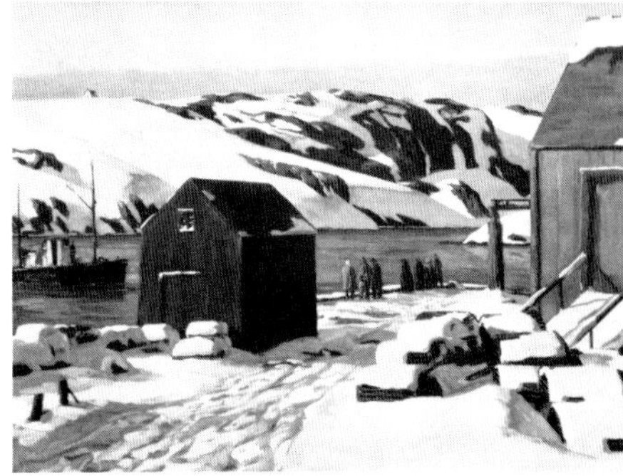
1508

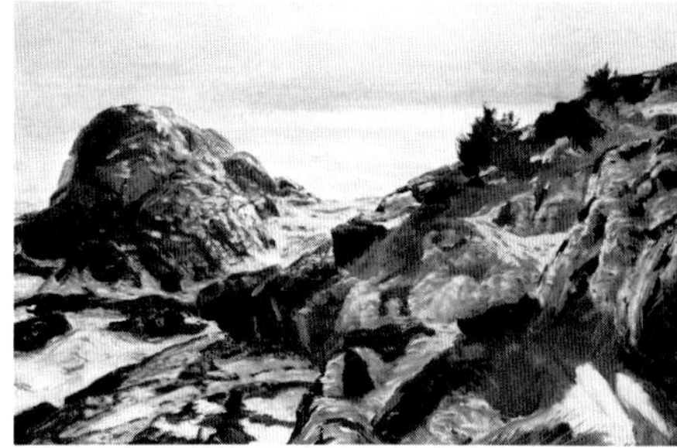
1509

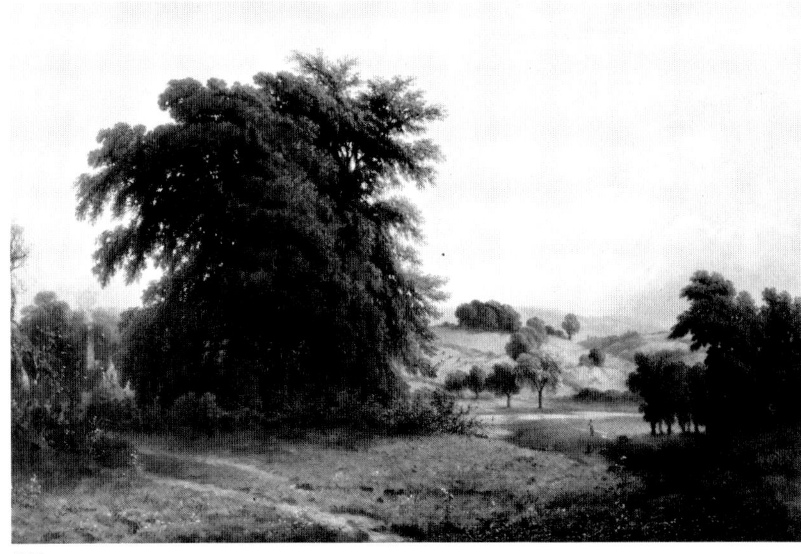
1500

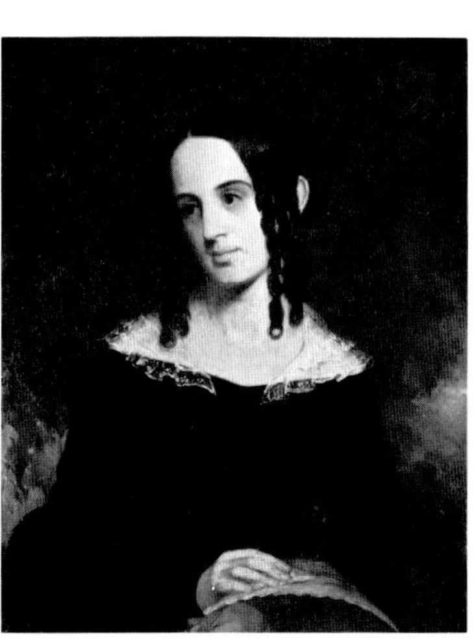
1497

Jane Wilson (1924–   )

1504 *Some of Willa's Things*, 1971
Oil on canvas
60 x 80³⁄₁₆ in. (152.4 x 203.7 cm.)
Signed at lower right: Jane Wilson
Inscribed, dated, and signed on stretcher:
SOME OF WILLA'S THINGS 1971 JANE WILSON 60 x 80 WINSOR NEWTON OPALMEDIUM—USE ONLY MATTE VARNISH
Gift of the American Academy of Arts and Letters (The Childe Hassam Fund), 1972.3

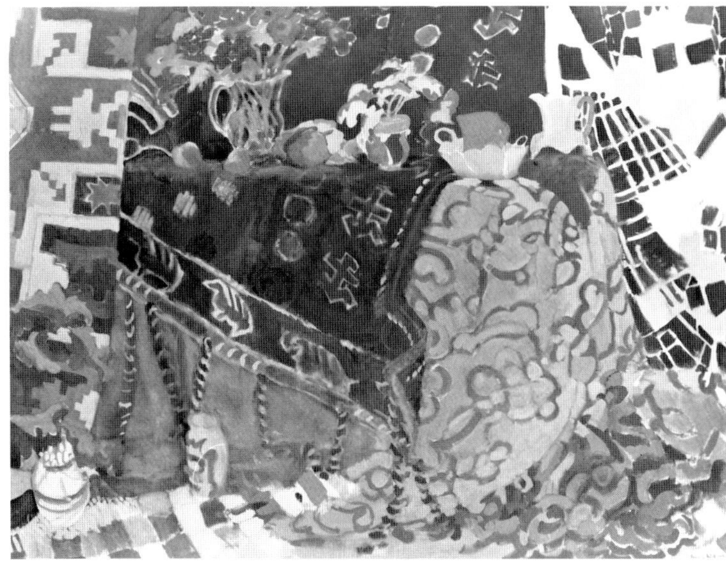
1504

Richard Wilt (1915–1981)

1505 *The Family*, 1957
Oil on canvas
42 x 30¹⁄₁₆ in. (106.7 x 76.4 cm.)
Signed and dated at upper right: Richard Wilt 1957
Gift of Harold C. Goldman, 1965.8

William E. Winner (ca. 1815–1883)

1506 *Thomas Asay Mitchell*, 1841
Oil on canvas
36 x 28¾ in. (91.4 x 73 cm.)
Inscribed, signed, and dated on back (before lining): Painted by Wm. E. Winner/Phila. Feb. 1841
Gift of Mrs. John Frederick Lewis (The John Frederick Lewis Memorial Collection), 1933.10.104

1507 *Self-Portrait*, 1873
Oil on cardboard
17³⁄₁₆ x 11½ in. (43.7 x 29.2 cm.)
Signed and dated at lower center: W E Winner. '73
Gift of John Frederick Lewis, 1931.10.2

Andrew Winter (1893–1958)

1508 *News from the Mainland*, 1934
Oil on canvas
30 x 40 in. (76.2 x 101.6 cm.)
Signed and dated at lower right: A WINTER/'34
Joseph E. Temple Fund, 1937.9

1509 *Silvery Lights, Monhegan*, 1944
Oil on canvas
24 x 36 in. (61 x 91.4 cm.)
Signed and dated at lower left: A. Winter/44
Henry D. Gilpin Fund, 1945.13

Attributed to **John Wollaston** (active 1736–1767)

1510 *Richard Peters* (1704–1776), ca. 1758
Oil on canvas
30¹⁄₁₆ x 25¹⁄₁₆ in. (76.4 x 63.7 cm.)
Gift of Mrs. Maria L. M. Peters, 1881.5

Edith Longstreth Wood (1885–1967)

1511 *Anemones*, ca. 1936
Oil on canvas
21⅛ x 18⅛ in. (53.7 x 46 cm.)
Signed at lower left: ELWood
John Lambert Fund, 1937.10

1512 *Dark Tree*
Oil on canvas board
22 x 17⅞ in. (55.9 x 45.4 cm.)
Gift of Walter Longstreth, 1967.14.1

1513 *Flowers*
Oil on canvas
28¼ x 23¼ in. (71.8 x 59.1 cm.)
Signed at lower left: EdithWood-; and on back: E. L. WOOD
Gift of Walter Longstreth, 1967.14.2

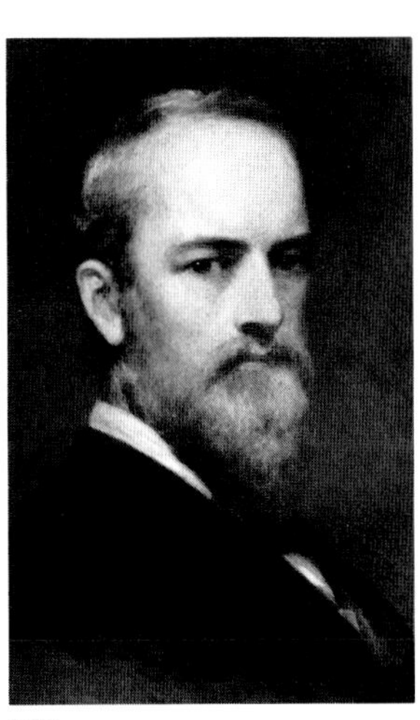
1507

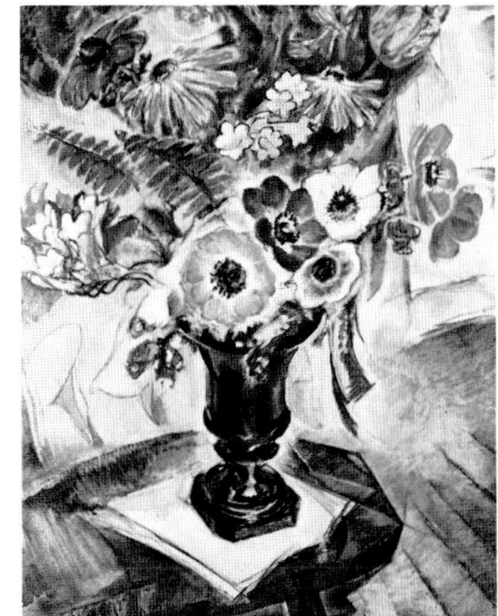
1511

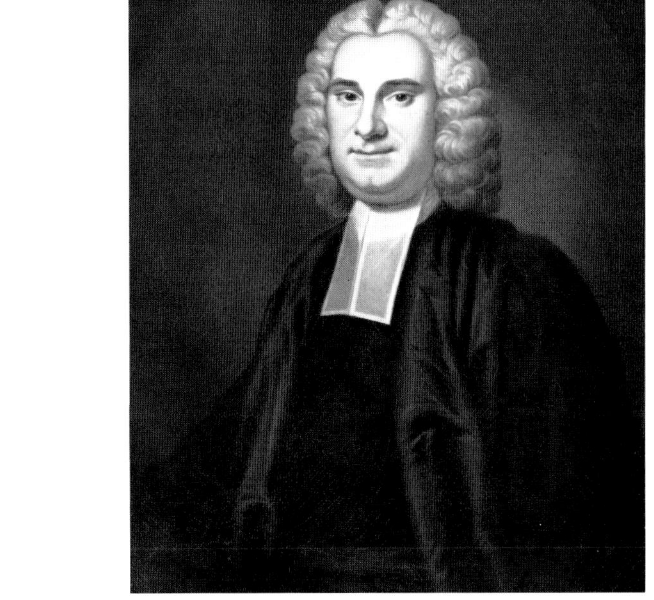
1510

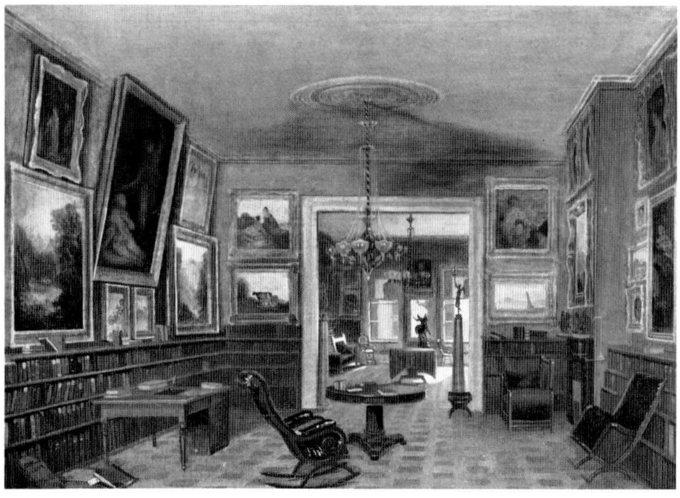

1514

1515

George Bacon Wood (1832–1910)

1514 *Interior of the Library of Henry C. Carey,* 1879
Oil on canvas
14 x 20¼ in. (35.6 x 51.4 cm.)
Signed, dated, and inscribed at lower left: GBWood/1879/Phila
Gift of the artist, 1880.1

Joseph Wood. *See* cat. no. 1656.

Attributed to **Joseph Wood** (ca. 1778–1830)

1515 *John Randolph of Roanoke* (?) (1777–1833)
Oil on canvas
30 x 24 15/16 in. (76.2 x 63.3 cm.)
Gift of Mrs. John Frederick Lewis (The John Frederick Lewis Memorial Collection), 1933.10.105

Abraham Woodside (1819–1853)

1516 *Cupid in Wine Glass*
Oil on paper, mounted on canvas
7 x 8 11/16 in. (17.8 x 22.1 cm.)
Signed at lower left: W [illegible]
Gift of the Hon. James T. Mitchell, 1908.4

Catharine Morris Wright (1899–1988)

1517 *Twilight*, 1936
Oil on linen
20 1/16 x 40⅛ in. (51 x 101.9 cm.)
Signed and dated at lower left: C. M. Wright 1936
Inscribed and signed on stretcher: "TWILIGHT" Catharine Morris Wright Ends[m]eet Farm Glenside, Pa.
John Lambert Fund, 1937.11

John Heritage Wright (b. 1914)

1518 *Pennsylvania Farmland*, ca. 1940
Oil on canvas
25 x 44 in. (63.5 x 111.8 cm.)
Signed at lower right: JOHN H. WRIGHT.
Annotated on frame: Penna. Farmland/by John H. Wright
John Lambert Fund, 1941.9

Joseph Wright (1756–1793)

1519 *The Wright Family* (Joseph and his wife, Sarah, d. 1793, with their children, Sarah, Harriet, and Joseph), 1793, unfinished
Oil on canvas
37 5/16 x 32 in. (94.8 x 81.3 cm.)
Gift of Edward S. Clarke, 1886.5

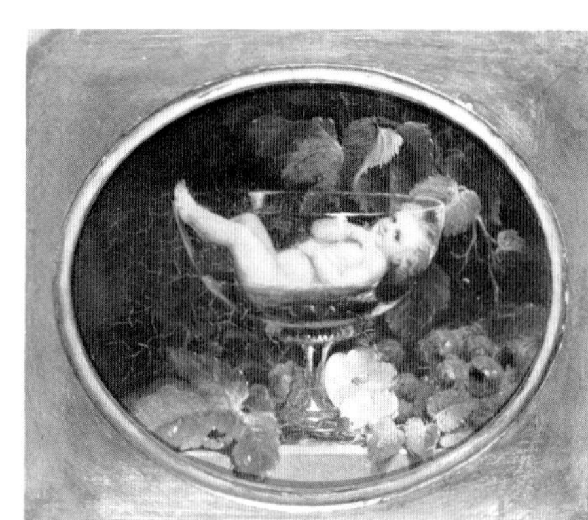

1516

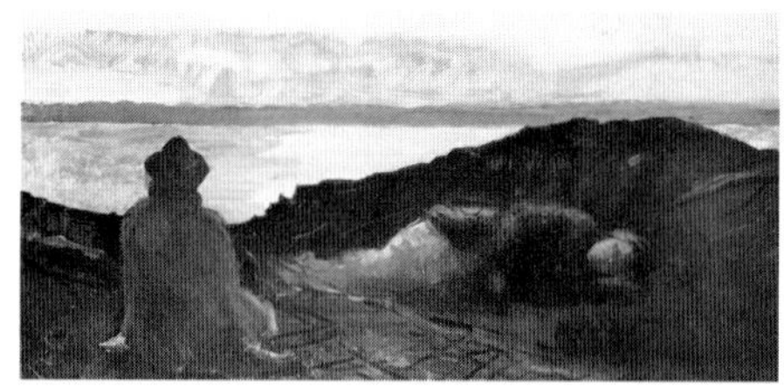

1517

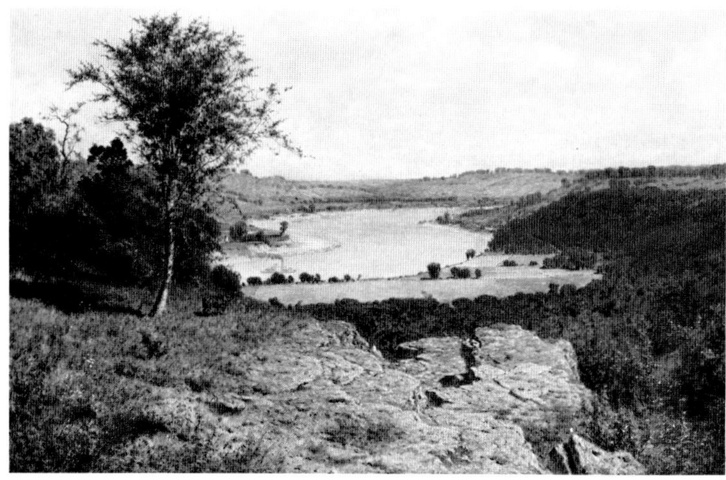

1523

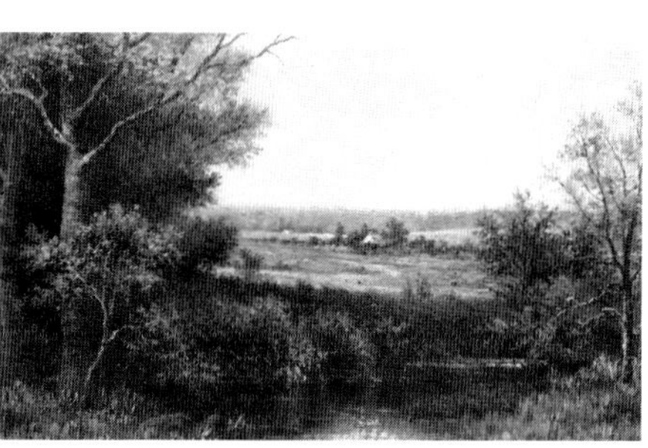

1522

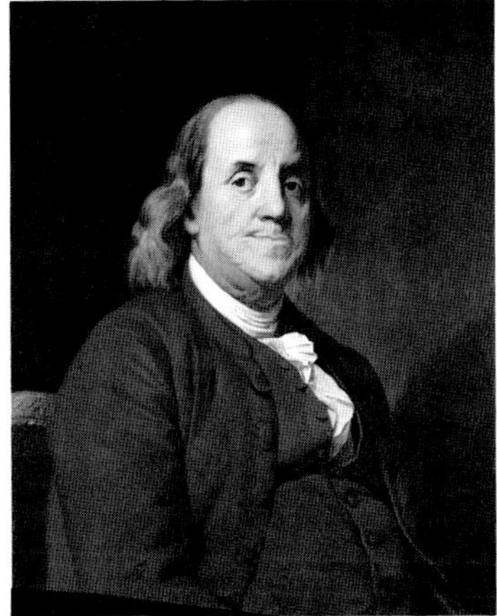

1520

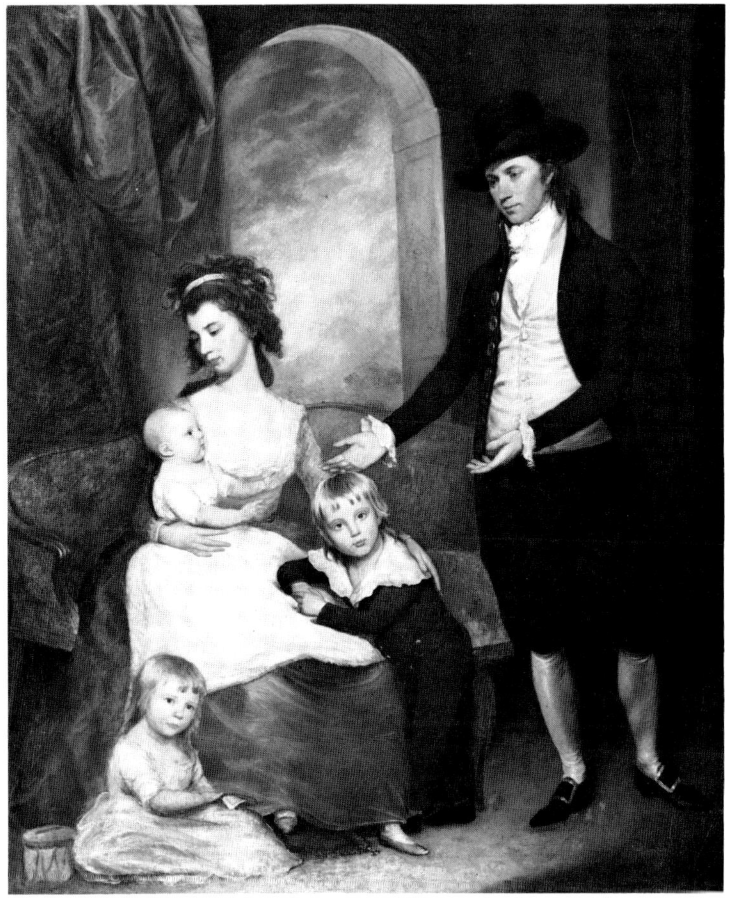

1519

Attributed to **Joseph Wright**

1520 *Benjamin Franklin* (1706–1790), after 1782
Oil on canvas
31¾ x 25$^{5}/_{16}$ in. (80.6 x 64.3 cm.)
Bequest of Mrs. Sarah Harrison (The Joseph Harrison, Jr. Collection), 1912.14.6

Rufus Wright (1832–after 1889)

1521 *William Henry Seward* (1801–1872), 1863
Oil on canvas
30⅞ x 25$^{1}/_{16}$ in. (78.4 x 63.7 cm.)
Signed at lower right: Rufus Wright; inscribed, signed, and dated on back: Wm. H Seward-/ by Rufus Wright/Nov. 1863
Gift of Mrs. John Frederick Lewis (The John Frederick Lewis Memorial Collection), 1933.10.106

Alexander H. Wyant (1836–1892)

1522 *Landscape*, 1873
Oil on canvas
8$^{5}/_{16}$ x 13⅜ in. (21.1 x 34 cm.)
Signed at lower left: A. H. Wyant
Gift of Mr. and Mrs. Edward Kesler, 1975.20.7

1523 *On the Ohio River*, 1867
Oil on canvas
22 x 34⅛ in. (55.9 x 86.7 cm.)
Signed and dated at lower right: AHWyant—67
Gift of Mrs. Robert McKay Green, 1974.24

Andrew Wyeth (1917–)

1524 *Young America*, 1950
Egg tempera on gessoed board ("Renaissance Panel")
32½ x 45$^{5}/_{16}$ in. (82.6 x 115.1 cm.)
Signed at lower left: Andrew Wyeth
Joseph E. Temple Fund, 1951.17

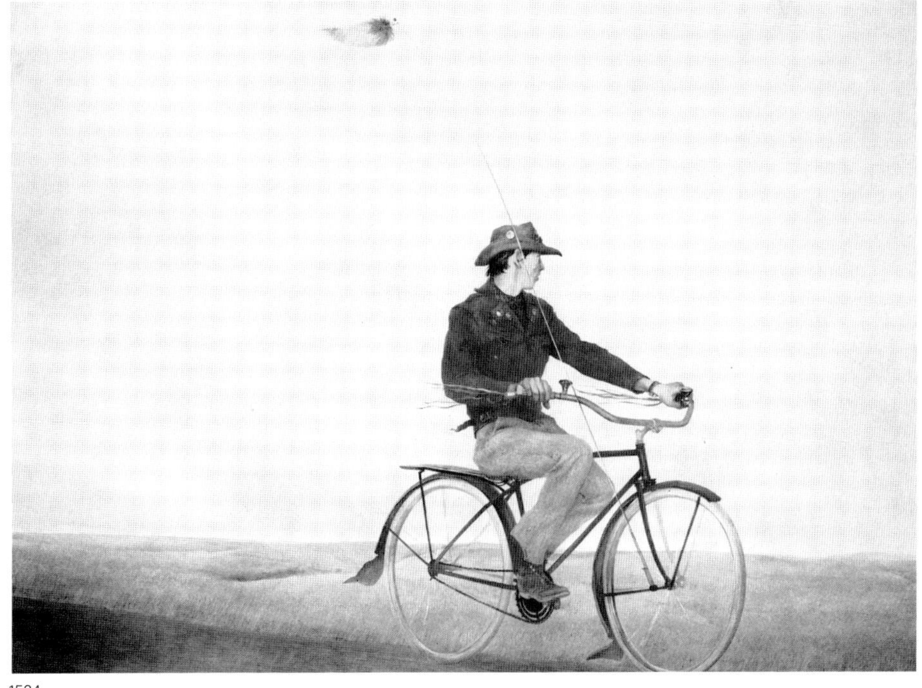

1524

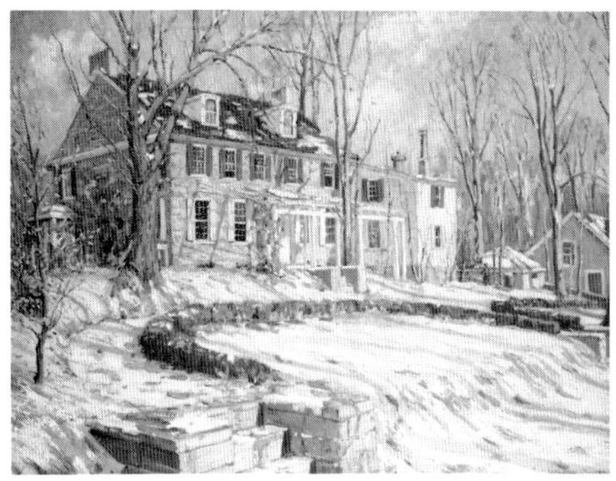

1533

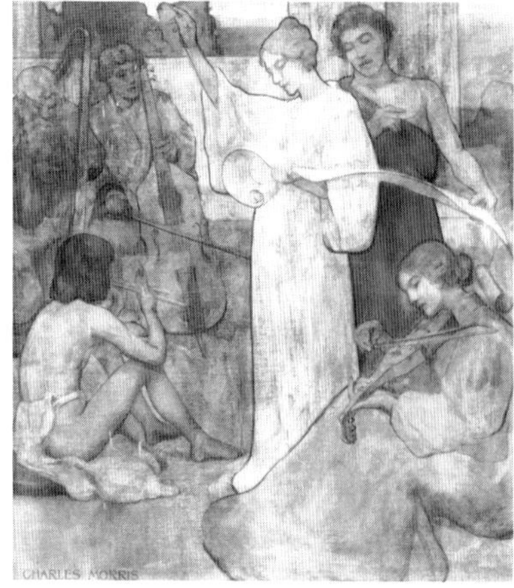
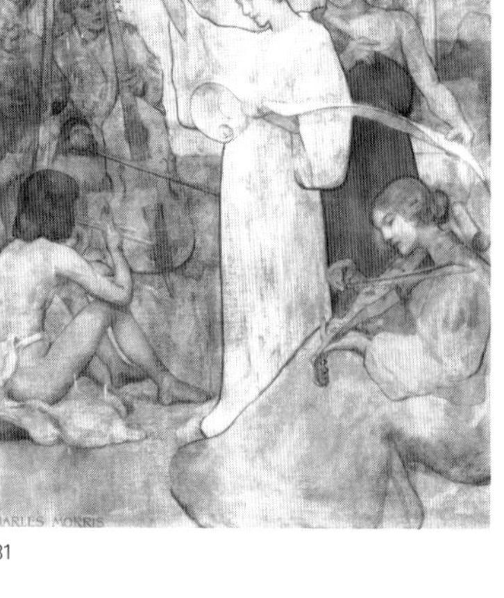

1531

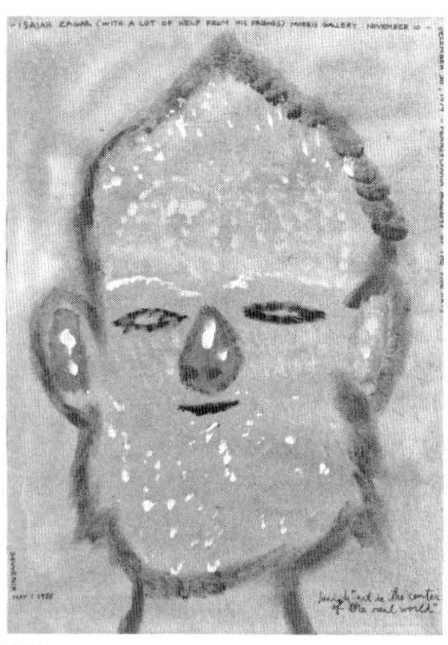

1535

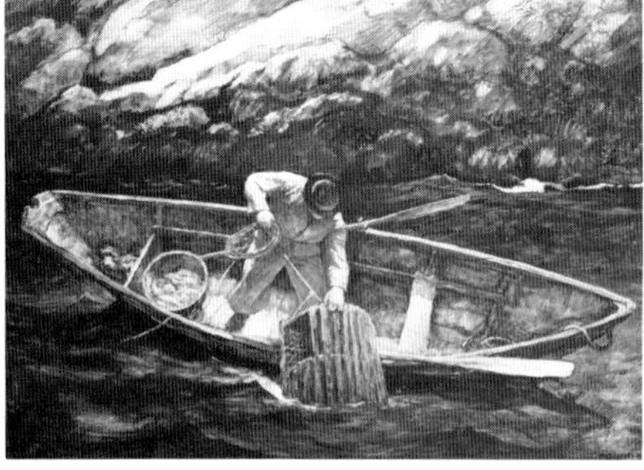

1525

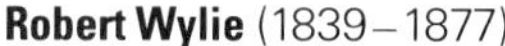
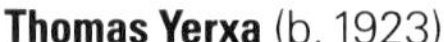
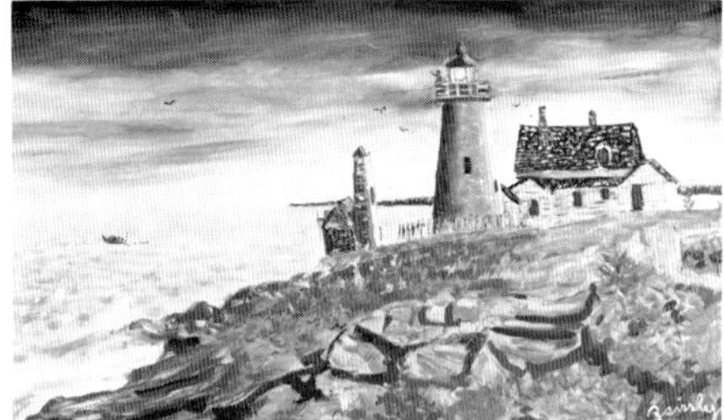

1538

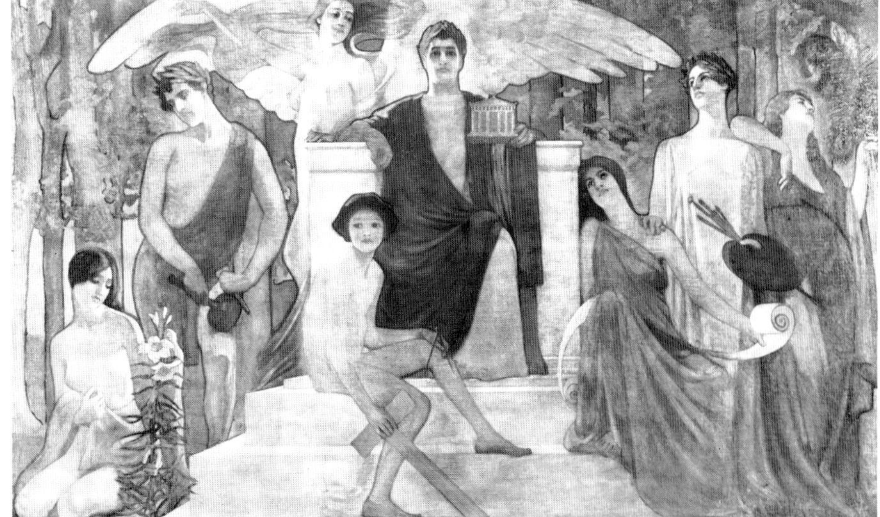

1529

N. C. Wyeth (1882–1945)

1525 *Deep Cove Lobster Man*, ca. 1938
Oil on gessoed board ("Renaissance Panel")
16¼ x 22¾ in. (41.3 x 57.8 cm.)
Signed at lower right: N.C.WYETH
Joseph E. Temple Fund, 1939.16

Robert Wylie (1839–1877)

1526 *The Postman*, 1868
Oil on canvas
46⅛ x 57¾ in. (117.2 x 146.7 cm.)
Signed at lower right: R Wylie
Gift of Desna and Herman Goldman, 1984.34

Thomas Yerxa (b. 1923)

1527 *At Midnight*, 1953
Oil on linen
16 1/16 x 25 15/16 in. (40.8 x 65.9 cm.)
Signed and dated at lower right: YERXA 53
John Lambert Fund, 1954.19

1528 *Mother and Child*, 1956
Oil on linen
26⅛ x 38⅛ in. (66.4 x 96.8 cm.)
Signed and dated at lower right: YERXA56
Gift of Mr. and Mrs. Richardson Dilworth, 1969.13

Georgie York (1872–1900)

1529 *Art* (formerly *The Arts*), 1896–97
Oil on canvas
Approx. 78 x 126 in. (198 x 320 cm.)
Signed at lower right: GEORGIE YORK
Commissioned by the Pennsylvania Academy, 1897.9.14

Arthur M. Young (1866–1943)

1530 *Steamboat, Venice*, 1932
Oil on canvas
15 x 18 1/16 in. (38.1 x 45.9 cm.)
Signed and dated at lower left: A.M.Young/1932
John Lambert Fund, 1933.8

Charles Morris Young (1869–1964)

1531 *Concerted Music* (formerly *Music*), 1896–97
Oil on canvas
Approx. 78 x 78 in. (198 x 198 cm.)
Signed at lower left: CHARLES MORRIS/YOUNG
Commissioned by the Pennsylvania Academy, 1897.9.15

1532 *Fox Hunters at White Horse*, ca. 1932
Oil on canvas
25 x 30 1/16 in. (63.5 x 76.4 cm.)
Signed at lower right: Chas Morris Young
Gift of Thomas H. Hall, Jr., 1948.17

1533 *My House in Winter*, ca. 1911
Oil on canvas
30 x 40 in. (76.2 x 101.6 cm.)
Signed at lower right: Chas.Morris Young
Gift of Walter M. Jeffords, 1948.1

1534 *Winter Morning after Snow*, 1899
Oil on canvas
22⅛ x 36⅛ in. (56.2 x 91.8 cm.)
Signed at lower right: C.Morris Young.
Henry D. Gilpin Fund, 1901.3

Isaiah Zagar (1939–)

1535 *Isaiah Zagar (with a Lot of Help from His Friends)*, 1985
Oil on canvas
29⅞ x 22 1/16 in. (75.9 x 56 cm.)
Signed and inscribed at upper left: —ISAIAH ZAGAR (WITH A LOT OF HELP FROM HIS FRIENDS) MORRIS GALLERY. NOVEMBER 10—; inscribed at upper right: DECEMBER 30, 1979—PENNSYLVANIA

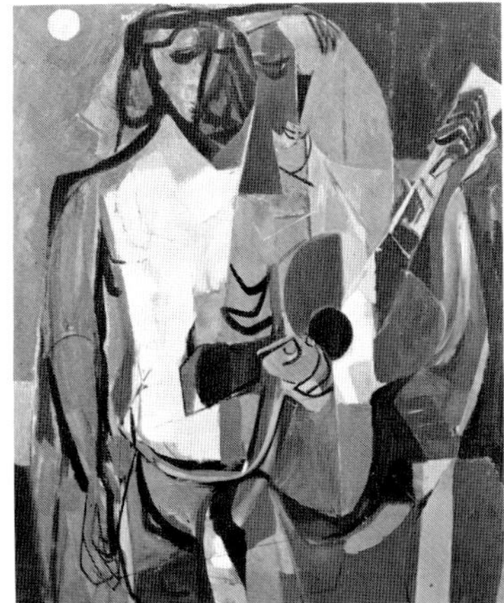
1537

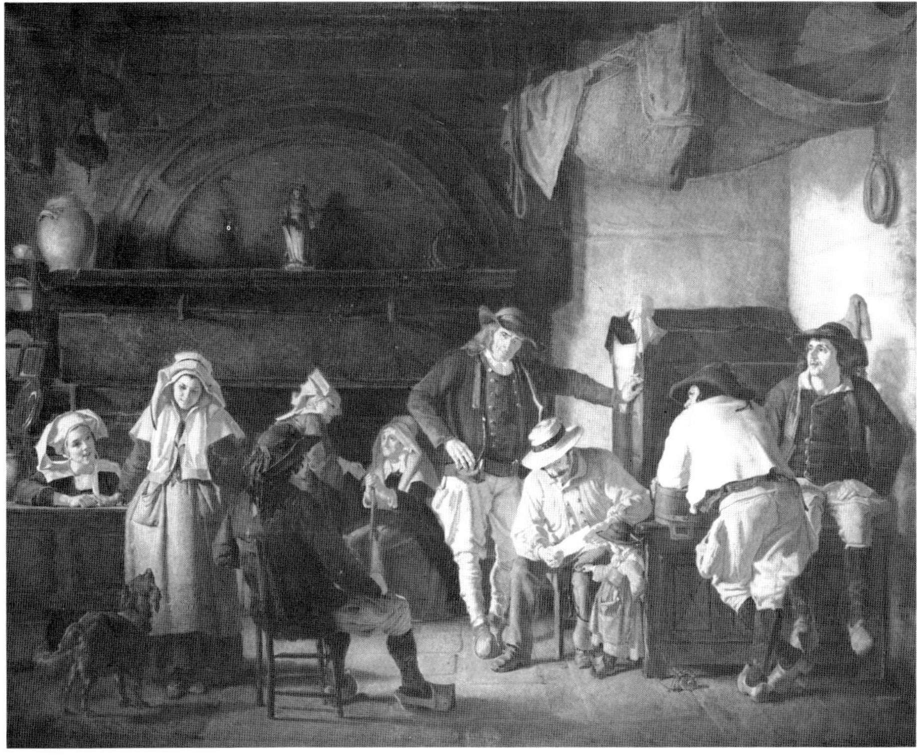
1526

ACADEMY OF THE FINE ARTS-; inscribed at lower right: Isaiah "art is the center/of the real world."; and dated at lower left: SOUVENIR/ MAY 1 1985
Gift of the artist, 1985.33

Emilie Zeckwer
See Emilie Zeckwer Dooner.

Paul W. Zimmerman (1921–)

1536 *August Garden*, 1961
Oil on masonite
48 x 56 in. (121.9 x 142.2 cm.)
Signed at lower right: P.Zimmerman; inscribed and signed on back: 48 x 56/61.2/ P.ZIMMERMAN/AUGUST GARDEN
Henry D. Gilpin Fund, 1962.14

Richard Zoellner (1908–)

1537 *Summer Evening*, 1949
Oil on canvas
36 x 29⅞ in. (91.4 x 75.9 cm.)
Signed and dated at lower right: Zoellner/49; signed and inscribed on back: RICHARD ZOELLNER/"SUMMER EVENING"
John Lambert Fund, 1951.18

Zsissly (Malvin Marr Albright, 1897–)

1538 *Summer Storm*, by 1951
Oil on canvas
27⅞ x 47⅞ in. (70.8 x 121.6 cm.)
Signed at lower right: Zsissly-
Annotated on stretcher: SUMMER STORM
Gift of John Frederick Lewis, Jr., 1951.19

Unidentified Artist
(formerly attributed to Alonzo Chappel)

1539 *John Quincy Adams* (1767–1848), mid-19th century
Oil on canvas
24 x 20 in. (61 x 50.8 cm.)
Gift of Mrs. John Frederick Lewis (The John Frederick Lewis Memorial Collection), 1933.10.5

Unidentified Artist
(formerly attributed to Henry Inman)

1540 *Artist in His Studio*
Oil on canvas
26 x 22⅛ in. (66 x 56.2 cm.)
Gift of Mrs. John Frederick Lewis (The John Frederick Lewis Memorial Collection), 1933.10.27

Unidentified Artist

1541 *Anna Warner Bailey* (?) (1758–1850), late 18th century
Oil on canvas
29⅞ x 25 in. (75.9 x 63.5 cm.)
Gift of Mrs. John Frederick Lewis (The John Frederick Lewis Memorial Collection), 1933.10.82

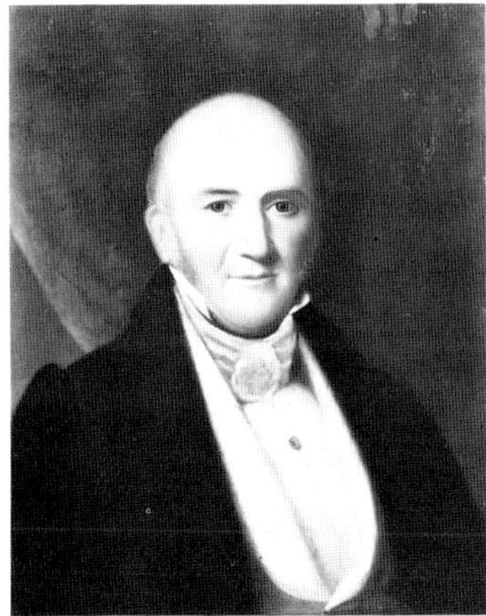
1539

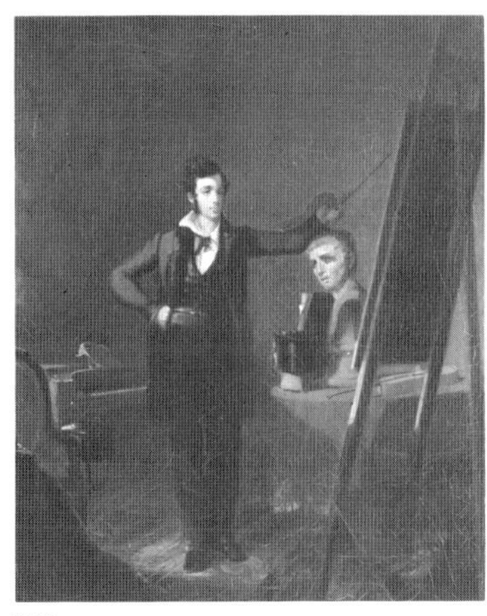
1540

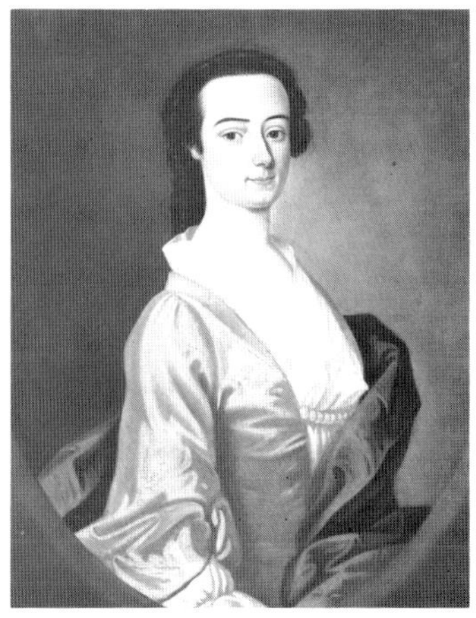
1541

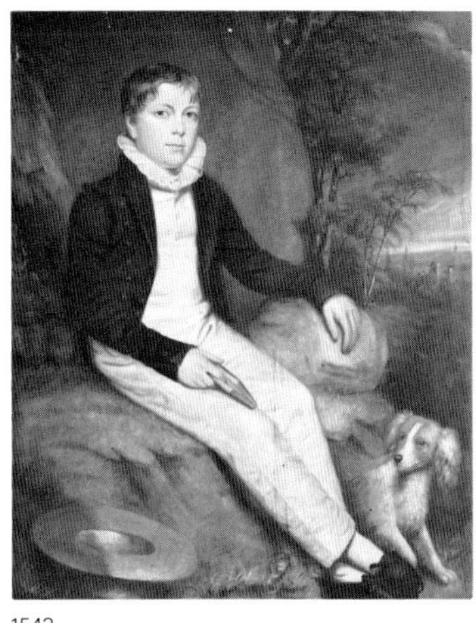

1543

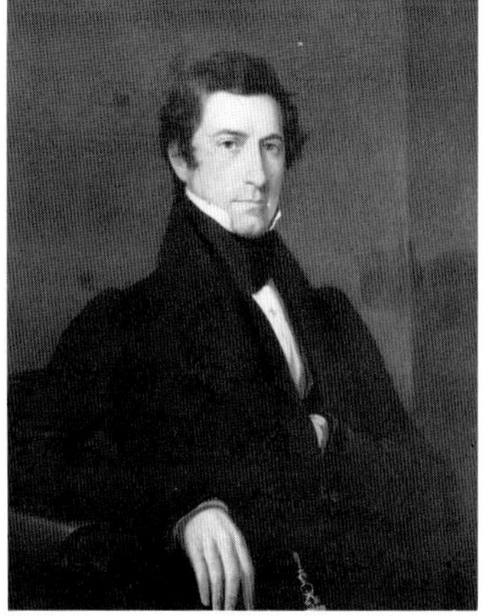

1544

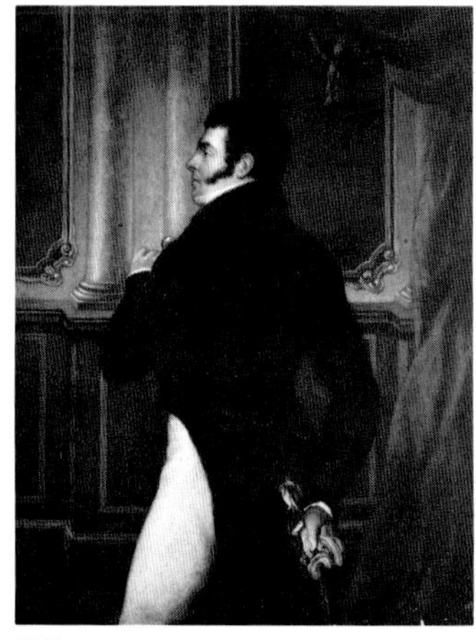

1542

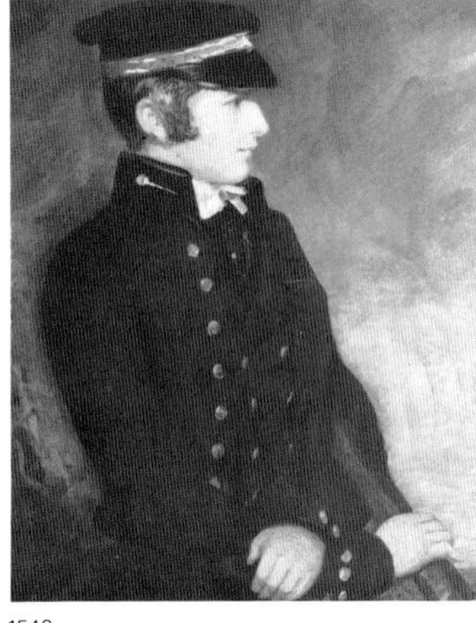

1546

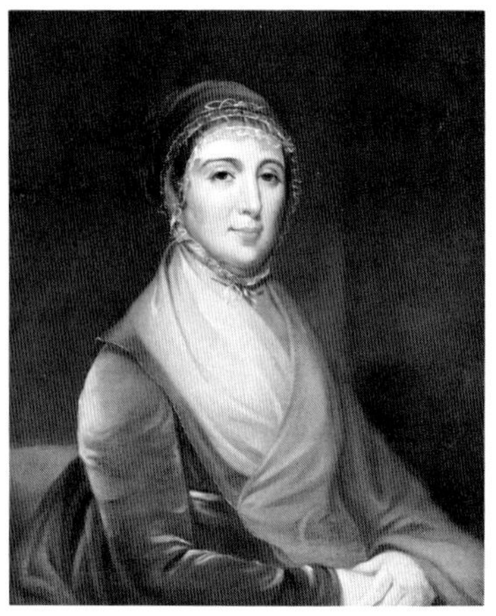

1547

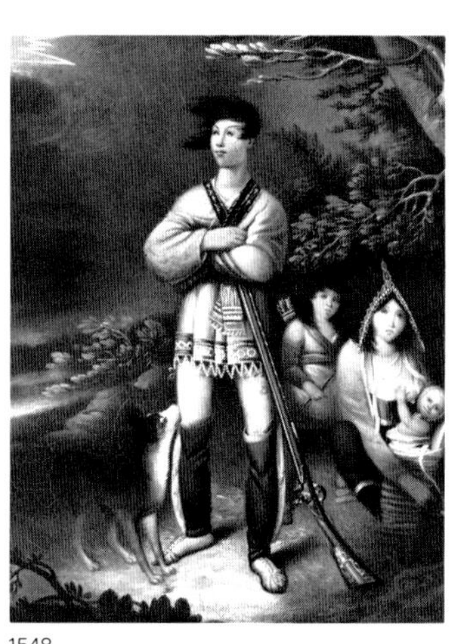

1548

Unidentified Artist
(formerly attributed to Charles C. Ingham)

1542 *Commodore William Bainbridge* (1774–1883)
Oil on canvas
24⅜ x 18$\frac{1}{16}$ in. (61.9 x 45.9 cm.)
Gift of Mrs. John Frederick Lewis (The John Frederick Lewis Memorial Collection), 1933.10.23

Unidentified Artist
(formerly attributed to Oliver S. Frazer)

1543 *Lord Bates*, early to mid-19th century
Oil on canvas
50 x 40⅛ in. (127 x 101.9 cm.)
Gift of Mrs. John Frederick Lewis (The John Frederick Lewis Memorial Collection), 1923.8.7

Unidentified Artist
(formerly attributed to Henry Inman)

1544 *Theodore Romeyn Beck* (1791–1855)
Oil on canvas
34¼ x 28¼ in. (87 x 71.8 cm.)
Gift of Mrs. John Frederick Lewis (The John Frederick Lewis Memorial Collection), 1933.10.25

Unidentified Artist

1545 *Delphine Bowen*, 19th century
Oil on canvas
24⅛ x 20 in. (61.3 x 50.8 cm.), oval
Bequest of Nannie Drill Ash, 1955.9.1

Unidentified Artist
(formerly attributed to Thomas Sully)

1546 *Boy in Uniform*, mid-19th century
Oil on canvas
29$\frac{15}{16}$ x 24⅞ in. (76 x 63.2 cm.)
Incorrectly annotated on back:
"BOY" PAINTED BY THOMAS SULLY/1839
Gift of Mrs. John Frederick Lewis (The John Frederick Lewis Memorial Collection), 1933.10.83

Unidentified Artist

1547 *Mrs. Daniel Buckley* (née Sarah Brooke, 1766–1821), early 19th century
(after Jacob Eichholtz, 1814)
Oil on canvas
30⅛ x 25$\frac{1}{16}$ in. (76.5 x 63.7 cm.)
Gift of Mrs. John Frederick Lewis (The John Frederick Lewis Memorial Collection), 1933.10.84

Unidentified Artist

1548 *Canadian Indian Family*, early 19th century
Oil on canvas
26$\frac{3}{16}$ x 9$\frac{15}{16}$ in. (66.5 x 25.2 cm.)
Falsely signed and dated at lower right:
RWW/1828
Gift of Mrs. Alfred C. Harrison, 1969.35

Unidentified Artist
(formerly attributed to James Peale)

1549 *Children of Henry Robinson*, early 19th century
Oil on canvas
30 x 25 in. (76.2 x 63.5 cm.)
Gift of John Frederick Lewis, 1923.8.6

Unidentified Artist
(formerly attributed to Rembrandt Peale)

1550 *Henry Clay* (1777–1852)
Oil on canvas
30½ x 25¼ in. (77.5 x 64.1 cm.)
Falsely signed at right center: R. Peale
Gift of Mrs. John Frederick Lewis (The John Frederick Lewis Memorial Collection), 1933.10.60

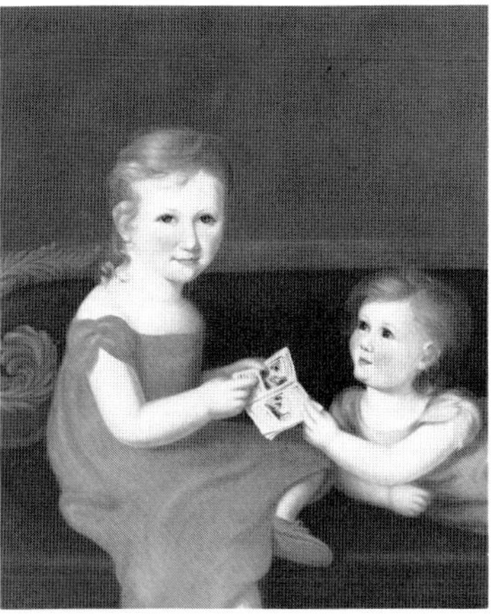

1549

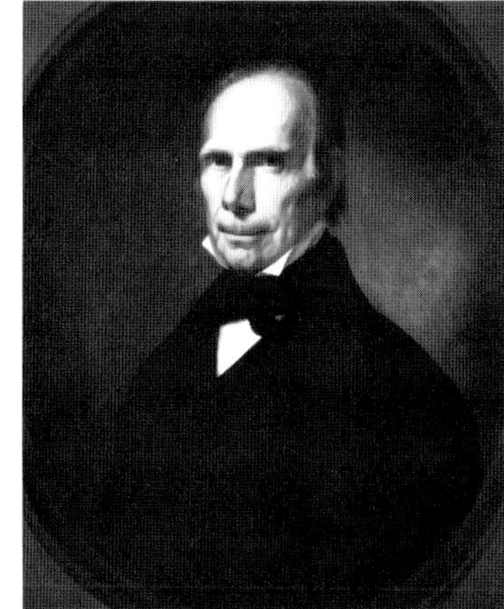

1550

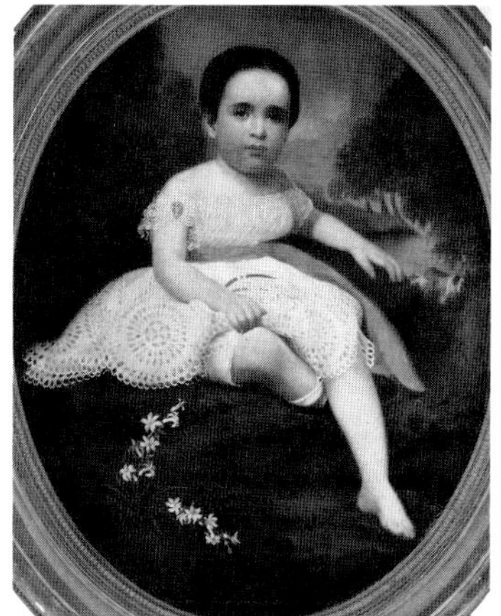

1552

Unidentified Artist
(formerly attributed to Thomas Sully)

1551 *Samuel Ewing*, early 19th century
Oil on canvas
24 1/16 x 20 1/16 in. (61.1 x 51 cm.)
Gift of Mme Marie Ester Eweig de Guzman, 1908.2

Unidentified Artist

1552 *Mrs. John Ferrell as a Child*, mid-19th century
Oil on canvas
36 x 29 in. (91.4 x 73.7 cm.), oval
Bequest of Nannie Drill Ash, 1955.9.2

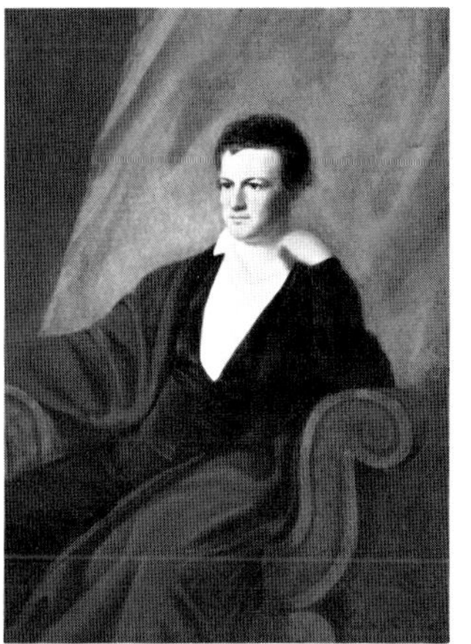

1553

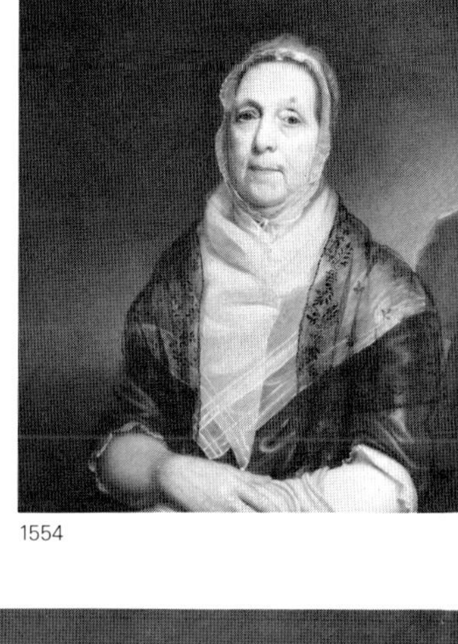

1554

Unidentified Artist
(formerly attributed to Charles C. Ingham)

1553 *Edwin Forrest* (1806–1872)
Oil on canvas
20 1/8 x 15 1/8 in. (51.1 x 38.4 cm.)
Gift of Mrs. John Frederick Lewis (The John Frederick Lewis Memorial Collection), 1933.10.24

Unidentified Artist

1554 *Eleanor Bodkin Fulford* (1738–1819), early 19th century
Oil on canvas, mounted on wood
34 x 26 1/8 in. (86.4 x 66.4 cm.)
Bequest of Mrs. Eleanor F. T. Conner, 1921.10.3

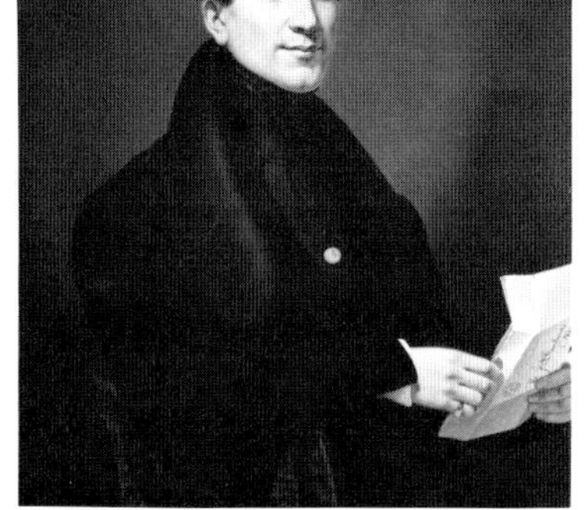

1558

1557

Unidentified Artist

1555 *Mrs. Elizabeth George* (?), early 19th century
Oil on canvas
27 x 22 in. (68.6 x 55.9 cm.), oval
Gift of Mrs. John Frederick Lewis through her son, John Frederick Lewis, Jr., 1938.13.2

Unidentified Artist
(formerly attributed to Gilbert Stuart)

1556 *William Gilmor* (1813–1890), early 19th century
Oil on canvas
29 7/8 x 23 11/16 in. (75.9 x 60.2 cm.)
Gift of John Frederick Lewis, 1932.1

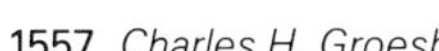

Unidentified Artist
(formerly attributed to John Vanderlyn)

1557 *Charles H. Groesbeeck*, 1835
Oil on canvas
30 7/8 x 26 7/16 in. (78.4 x 67.2 cm.)
Inscribed and dated on letter on table: Dear Brother/New York 25th July, 1835.
Gift of John Frederick Lewis, 1923.8.11

Unidentified Artist
(formerly attributed to John Vanderlyn)

1558 *John H. Groesbeeck*, ca. 1835
Oil on canvas
30 3/4 x 26 1/8 in. (78.1 x 66.4 cm.)
Inscribed on letter held by sitter: Mr. J. H. Groesbeeck/Albany N.Y./New York 25 July
Gift of Mrs. John Frederick Lewis (The John Frederick Lewis Memorial Collection), 1933.10.107

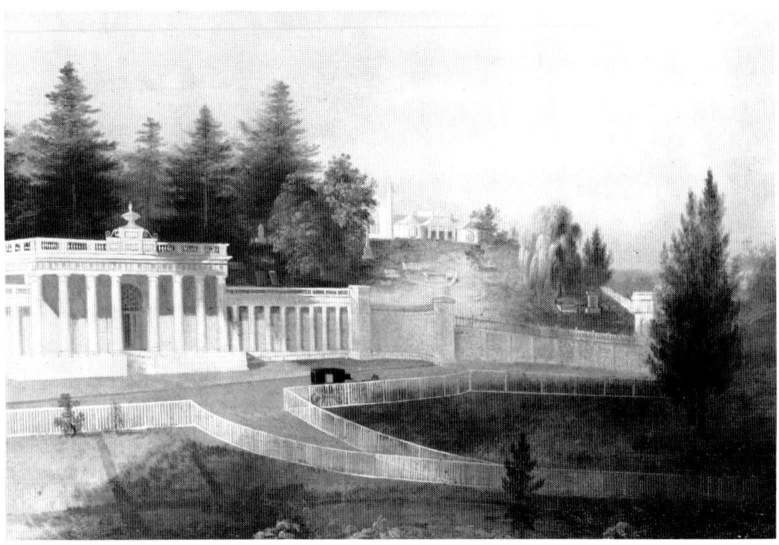
1571

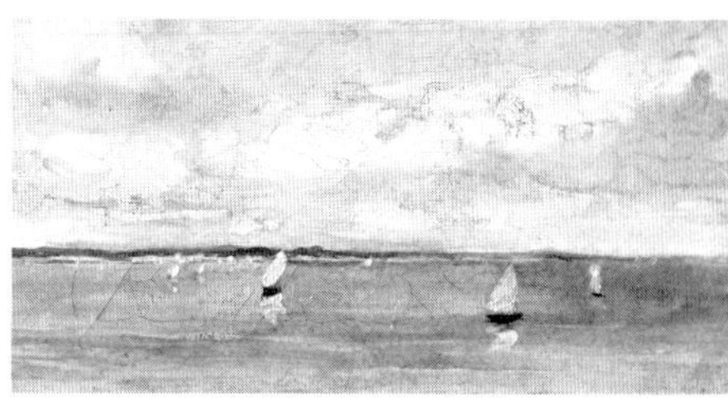
1562

Unidentified Artist
(formerly attributed to John Trumbull)

1559 *Alexander Hamilton* (1757–1804), early 19th century
Oil on canvas
25 x 21³⁄₁₆ in. (63.5 x 53.8 cm.)
Gift of Mrs. John Frederick Lewis (The John Frederick Lewis Memorial Collection), 1933.10.86

Unidentified Artist
(formerly attributed to John Singleton Copley)

1560 *John Hancock* (?) (1737–1793), mid-18th century
Oil on canvas
29⅞ x 24¹¹⁄₁₆ in. (75.9 x 62.7 cm.)
Gift of Mrs. John Frederick Lewis (The John Frederick Lewis Memorial Collection), 1933.10.87

Unidentified Artist
(formerly attributed to Thomas Buchanan Read)

1561 *Sarah Poulterer Harrison* (1817–1906), ca. 1850
Oil on canvas
50⅛ x 40⅜ in. (127.3 x 102.6 cm.)
Gift of Leland Harrison, 1953.11.2

Unidentified Artist
(formerly attributed to James McNeill Whistler)

1562 *Honfleur*, late 19th century
(after James McNeill Whistler)
Oil on canvas
7⅛ x 13¹⁄₁₆ in. (18.1 x 33.2 cm.)
Incorrectly annotated on stretcher: Honfleur, par Whistler, Drouet X.Z.
Bequest of J. Mitchell Elliot, 1952.22.4

Unidentified Artist
(formerly attributed to Ralph Blakelock)

1563 *Indian Camp, Sunset*, late 19th to early 20th century
Oil on canvas
30⅛ x 25⅛ in. (76.5 x 63.8 cm.)
Falsely signed at lower right in arrow: R.A. Blakelock
Bequest of J. Mitchell Elliot, 1952.22.1

Unidentified Artist
(formerly attributed to Rembrandt Peale)

1564 *Andrew Jackson* (?) (1767–1845), early to mid-19th century
Oil on wood
30 x 24⁷⁄₁₆ in. (76.2 x 62.1 cm.)
Gift of Mrs. John Frederick Lewis (The John Frederick Lewis Memorial Collection), 1933.10.88

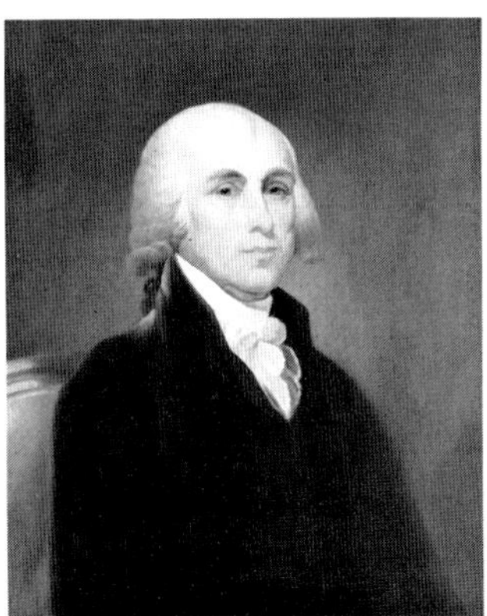
1572

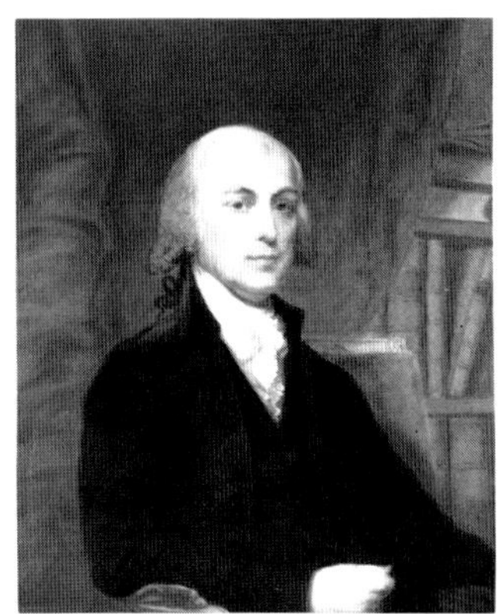
1573

Unidentified Artist
(formerly attributed to Asher B. Durand)

1565 *Thomas Jefferson* (1743–1826), 19th century
(after Gilbert Stuart, 1805–7)
Oil on canvas
27 x 22 in. (68.6 x 55.9 cm.)
Bequest of Mrs. John Frederick Lewis, 1939.17.1

Unidentified Artist
(formerly attributed to John Wesley Jarvis)

1566 *Thomas Jefferson*
Oil on canvas
30 x 25⅛ in. (76.2 x 63.8 cm.)
Gift of Mrs. John Frederick Lewis (The John Frederick Lewis Memorial Collection), 1933.10.30

Unidentified Artist
(formerly attributed to Charles Willson Peale)

1567 *Francis Scott Key* (1779–1843), 19th century
Oil on canvas
30¹⁄₁₆ x 25 ¹⁄₁₆ in. (76.4 x 63.7 cm.)
Pennsylvania Academy purchase, 1906.2

Unidentified Artist
(formerly attributed to Ezra Ames)

1568 *Marquis de Lafayette* (1757–1834), 19th century
Oil on wood
23 x 20 in. (58.4 x 50.8 cm.)
Falsely signed and dated on back: Ezra Ames/ 1824
Gift of Mrs. John Frederick Lewis (The John Frederick Lewis Memorial Collection), 1933.10.89

Unidentified Artist
(formerly attributed to Charles Bird King)

1569 *Marquis de Lafayette*, mid-19th century
Oil on canvas
30 x 25¼ in. (76.2 x 64.1 cm.)
Gift of Mrs. John Frederick Lewis (The John Frederick Lewis Memorial Collection), 1933.10.39

Unidentified Artist
(formerly attributed to George Inness)

1570 *Landscape*, late 19th to early 20th century
Oil on canvas
18 x 14 in. (45.7 x 35.6 cm.)
Falsely signed at lower left: -G-Inness-
Pennsylvania Academy purchase, 1945.22

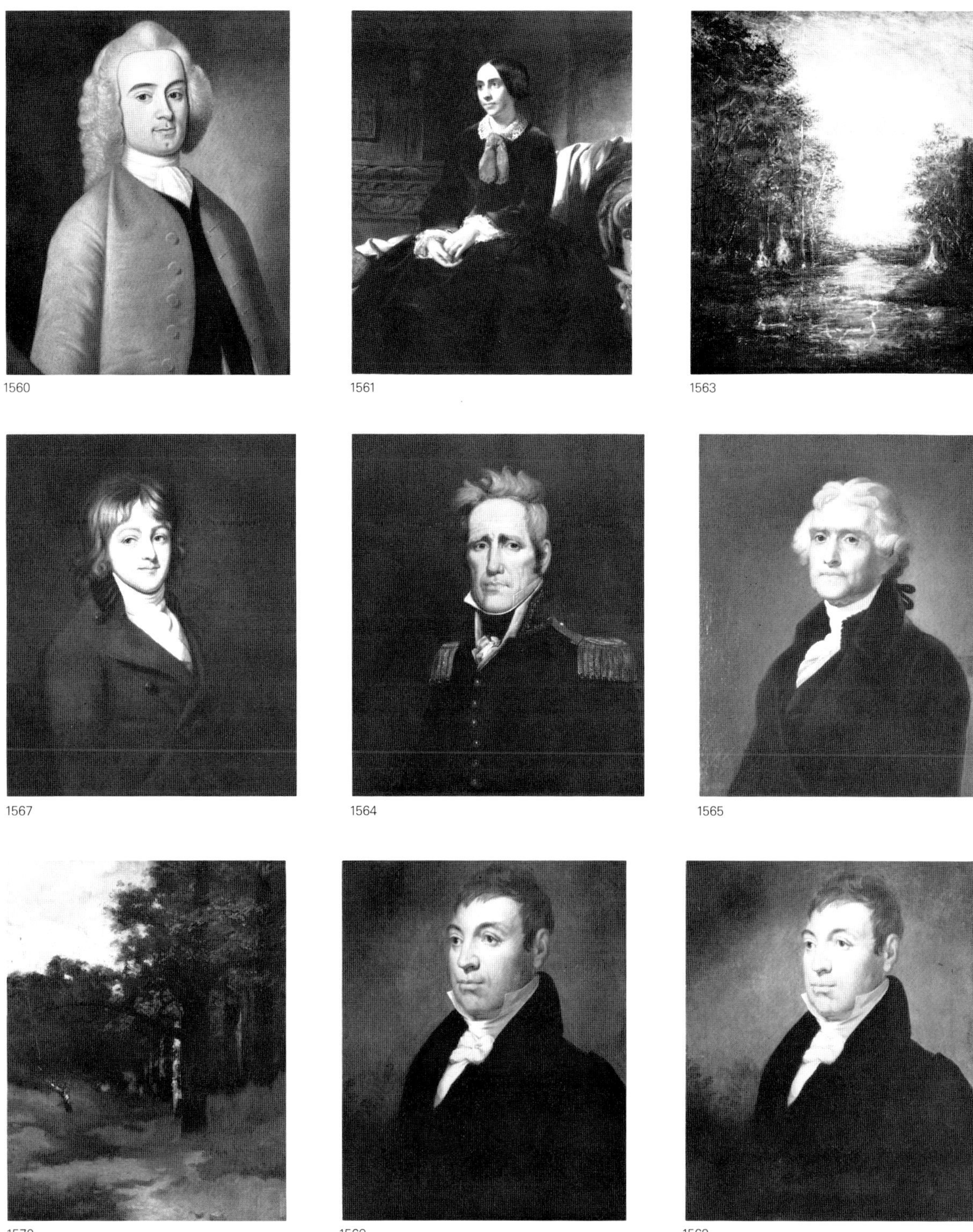

1560 1561 1563

1567 1564 1565

1570 1568 1569

Unidentified Artist

1571 *Laurel Hill Cemetery Gate, Philadelphia,* ca. 1840
Oil on canvas
16 x 24⅛ in. (40.6 x 61.3 cm.)
Gift of Mrs. Edgar P. Richardson, 1986.29.5

Unidentified Artist
(formerly attributed to Asher B. Durand)

1572 *James Madison* (1751–1836), 19th century
(after Gilbert Stuart)
Oil on canvas
27 x 22 in. (68.6 x 55.9 cm.)
Bequest of Mrs. John Frederick Lewis, 1939.17.2

Unidentified Artist
(formerly attributed to Gilbert Stuart)

1573 *James Madison*, 19th century
(after Gilbert Stuart)
Oil on canvas
30 x 25 in. (76.2 x 63.5 cm.)
Harrison Earl Fund, 1899.7.2

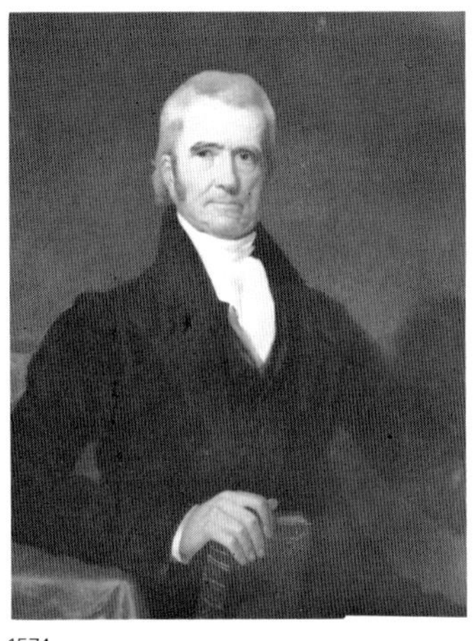

1574

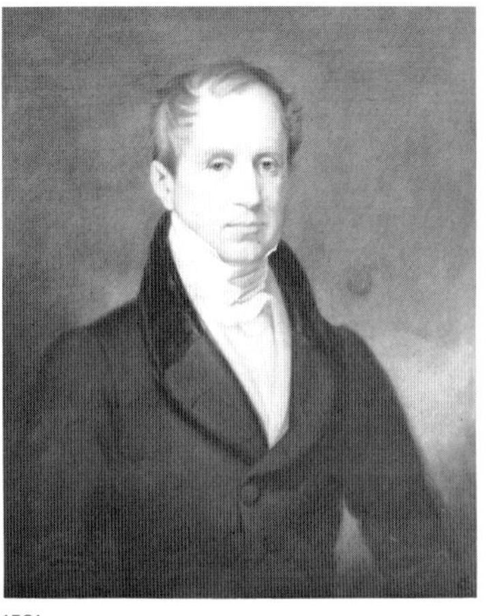

1581

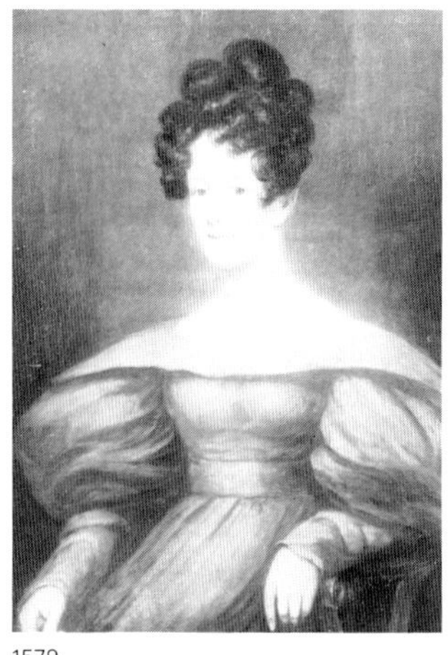

1579

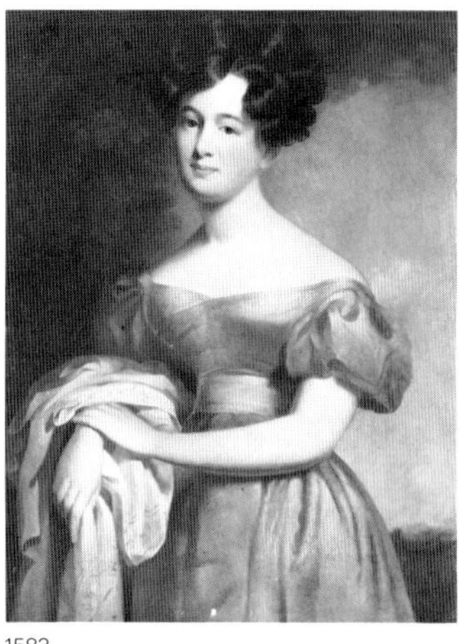

1583

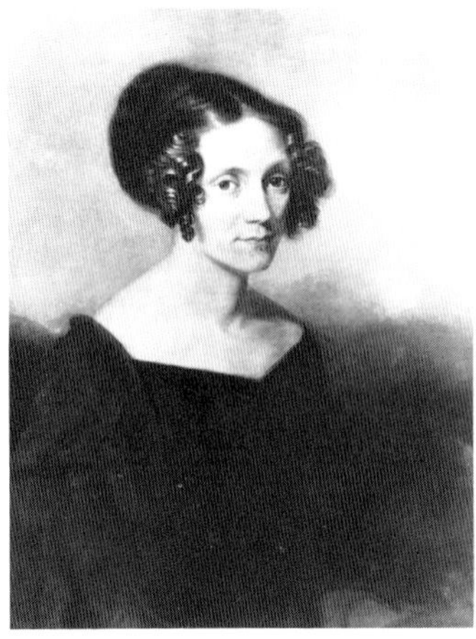

1582

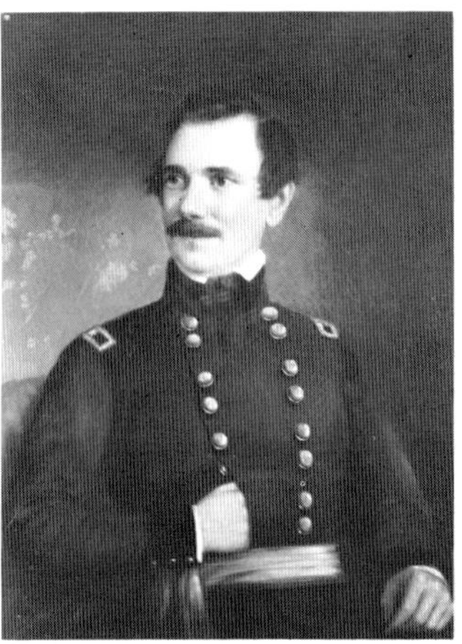

1585

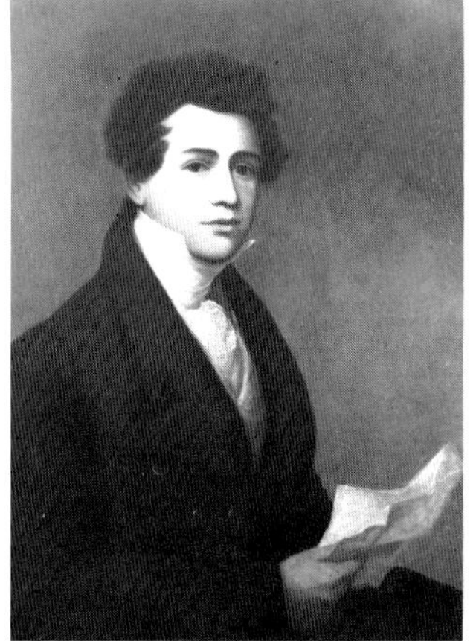

1587

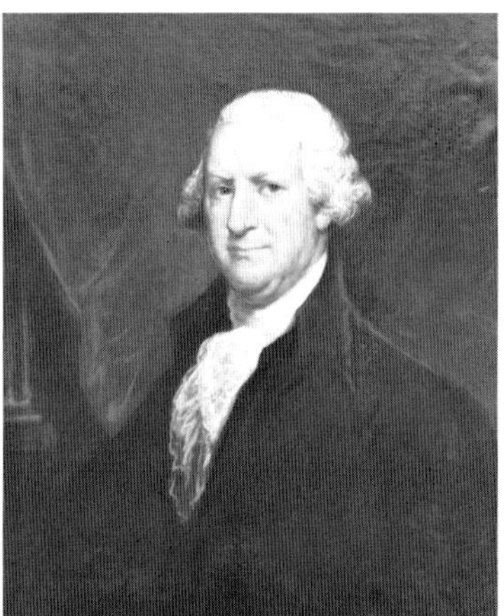

1586

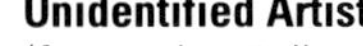

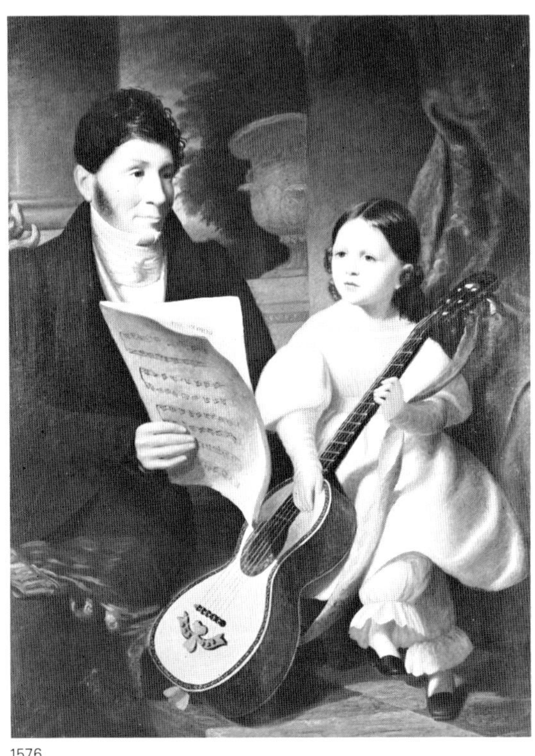

1576

Unidentified Artist
(formerly attributed to Henry Inman)

1574 *Chief Justice John Marshall* (1755–1835)
(after Henry Inman, 1831)
Oil on canvas
$36\frac{7}{16} \times 29\frac{1}{4}$ in. (92.6 x 74.3 cm.)
Gift of Mrs. John Frederick Lewis (The John Frederick Lewis Memorial Collection), 1933.10.26

Unidentified Artist

1575 *Thomas Mifflin* (1744–1800), 19th century
Oil on canvas, mounted on cardboard
$27\frac{5}{16} \times 20\frac{5}{8}$ in. (69.4 x 52.4 cm.)
Gift of John Frederick Lewis, 1932.13.10

Unidentified Artist
(formerly attributed to Rembrandt Peale)

1576 *The Music Master*, ca. 1835
Oil on canvas
48 x 36 in. (121.9 x 91.4 cm.)
Gift of Mrs. John Frederick Lewis (The John Frederick Lewis Memorial Collection), 1933.10.90

Unidentified Artist

1577 *Niagara Falls*, ca. 1845
Oil on canvas

23 1/2 x 37 3/8 in. (59.7 x 94.9 cm.)
Gift of Mr. and Mrs. J. Welles Henderson, 1976.24.1

Unidentified Artist

1578 *Edward Pacnog*, early to mid-19th century
Oil on canvas
30 1/16 x 24 15/16 in. (76.4 x 63.3 cm.)
Gift of Mrs. John Frederick Lewis (The John Frederick Lewis Memorial Collection), 1933.10.91

Unidentified Artist
(formerly attributed to Thomas Sully)

1579 *Elizabeth Patterson* (Mme Jerome Bonaparte, 1785–1879), ca. 1830
Oil on wood
35 5/8 x 25 3/4 in. (90.5 x 65.4 cm.)
Gift of Mrs. John Frederick Lewis (The John Frederick Lewis Memorial Collection), 1933.10.92

Unidentified Artist
(formerly attributed to Benjamin West)

1580 *Lydia Peel*, mid-18th century
Oil on canvas
35 1/4 x 28 1/16 in. (89.5 x 71.3 cm.)
Gift of John Frederick Lewis, 1923.8.9

Unidentified Artist
(formerly attributed to Charles Bird King)

1581 *John Holmes Prentiss* (1784–1861), early 19th century
Oil on canvas
29 7/8 x 24 15/16 in. (75.9 x 63.3 cm.)
Gift of Mrs. John Frederick Lewis (The John Frederick Lewis Memorial Collection), 1933.10.40

Unidentified Artist
(formerly attributed to John Neagle)

1582 *Mrs. Archibald Randall*, 1830s
Oil on canvas
29 7/8 x 25 3/16 in. (75.9 x 64 cm.)
Gift of Susan W. Randall, 1922.5.3

Unidentified Artist

1583 *Mrs. Alexander Reynolds*, ca. 1845
Oil on canvas
36 x 28 in. (91.4 x 71.1 cm.)
Bequest of Nannie Drill Ash in memory of her husband Gordon Monges Ash, 1955.9.3

Unidentified Artist (possibly European)

1584 *Dolly Shepherd* (?), ca. 1815
Oil on canvas
33 5/8 x 26 1/2 in. (85.4 x 67.3 cm.)
Gift of John Frederick Lewis, 1923.8.10

Unidentified Artist
(formerly attributed to George Catlin)

1585 *General James Shields* (1806–1879), mid-19th century
Oil on canvas
36 1/8 x 29 1/16 in. (91.8 x 73.8 cm.)
Incorrectly annotated on back (before lining): Gen. James Shields/George Catlin pinx.
Gift of Mrs. John Frederick Lewis (The John Frederick Lewis Memorial Collection), 1933.10.4

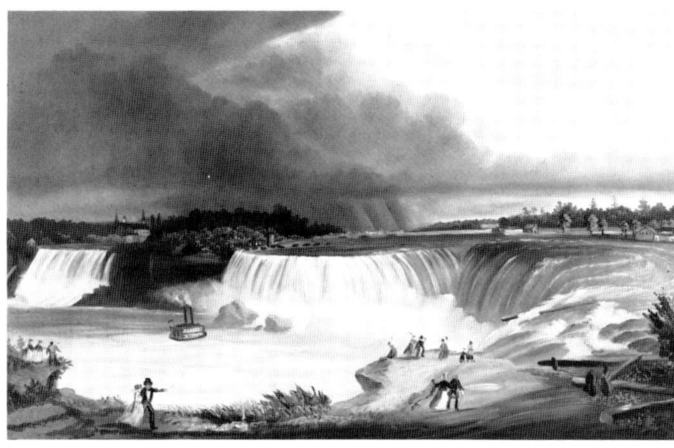

1577

Unidentified Artist

1586 *Chief Justice Edward Shippen* (1729–1806), early 19th century
(after Gilbert Stuart, 1803)
Oil on canvas
30 x 25 1/4 in. (76.2 x 64.1 cm.)
Gift of Mrs. John Frederick Lewis (The John Frederick Lewis Memorial Collection), 1933.10.93

Unidentified Artist
(formerly attributed to Rembrandt Peale)

1587 *Nathaniel Smith* (1762–1822)
Oil on canvas
30 1/4 x 25 1/8 in. (76.8 x 63.8 cm.)
Gift of Mrs. John Frederick Lewis (The John Frederick Lewis Memorial Collection), 1933.10.61

Unidentified Artist
(formerly attributed to John Trumbull)

1588 *Baron Friedrich Wilhelm von Steuben* (1730–1794)
Oil on canvas
30 1/4 x 25 in. (76.8 x 63.5 cm.)
Inscribed on back: Baron von Steuben
Gift of Mrs. John Frederick Lewis (The John Frederick Lewis Memorial Collection), 1933.10.94

Unidentified Artist

1589 *Still Life with Flowers*, early 20th century
Oil on cardboard
16 7/16 x 12 5/16 in. (41.8 x 31.3 cm.)
Source unknown, 1944.30

Unidentified Artist

1590 *Still Life with Lettuce and Beets*, 19th century
Oil on canvas, mounted on cardboard
17 3/8 x 24 3/16 in. (44.1 x 61.4 cm.)
Source unknown, 1944.25

Unidentified Artist

1591 *Still Life with Pumpkin*, 19th century
Oil on canvas, mounted on cardboard
17 5/16 x 24 1/4 in. (44 x 61.6 cm.)
Source unknown, 1944.26

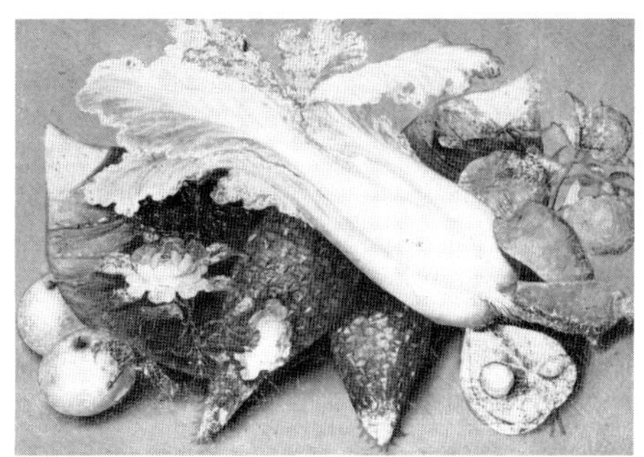

1590

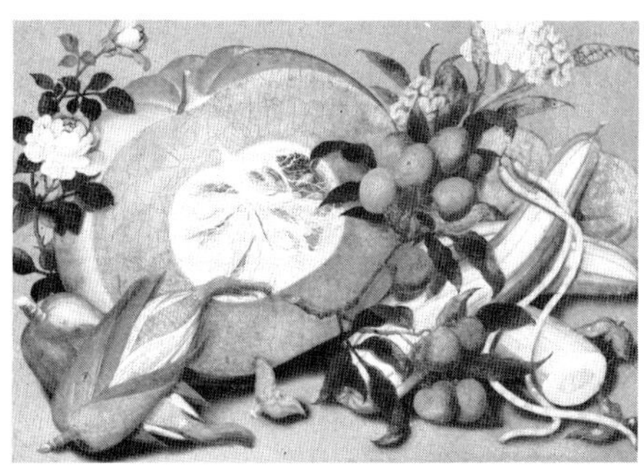

1591

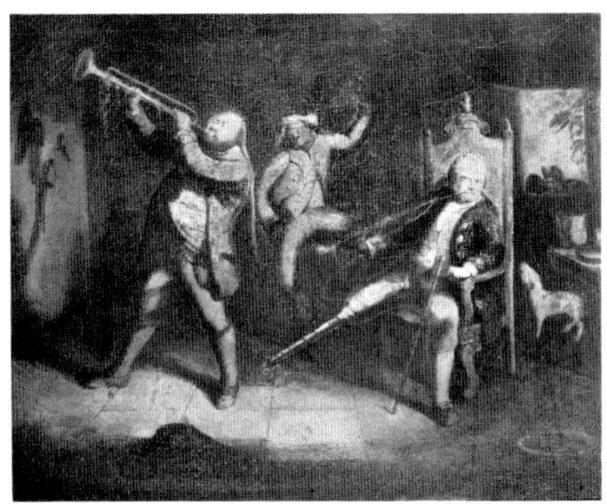

1592

Unidentified Artist
(formerly attributed to John Quidor)

1592 *The Trumpeter and Peter Stuyvesant*
Oil on canvas
$26\frac{15}{16}$ x 34¾ in. (68.4 x 88.3 cm.)
Gift of John Frederick Lewis, Jr., 1952.3.3

Unidentified Artist
(formerly attributed to Gilbert Stuart)

1593 *Baron von Seeger*, early 19th century
Oil on wood
$30\frac{1}{16}$ x 24¾ in. (76.4 x 62.9 cm.)
Gift of John H. McFadden, 1912.13.1

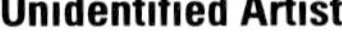

Unidentified Artist
(formerly attributed to Gilbert Stuart)

1594 *Baroness von Seeger*, early 19th century
Oil on canvas
$30\frac{3}{16}$ x 25⅛ in. (76.7 x 63.8 cm.)
Gift of John H. McFadden, 1912.13.2

Unidentified Artist

1595 *George Washington* (1732–1799), 19th century
(after Gilbert Stuart's Athenaeum portrait, 1796)
Oil on canvas
28¾ x 24¼ in. (73 x 61.6 cm.)
Bequest of Mrs. John Frederick Lewis, 1939.17.6

Unidentified Artist
(formerly attributed to John Wollaston)

1596 *Martha Washington* (1731–1802), mid-18th century
(after John Wollaston, 1757)
Oil on canvas
$27\frac{1}{16}$ x 22 in. (68.7 x 55.9 cm.)
Gift of John Frederick Lewis, 1923.8.14

Unidentified Artist
(formerly attributed to Rembrandt Peale)

1597 *Martha Washington*, probably early 19th century
(after Gilbert Stuart, 1796)
Oil on canvas
30⅛ x 25 in. (76.5 x 63.5 cm.)
Bequest of Mrs. John Frederick Lewis, 1939.17.7

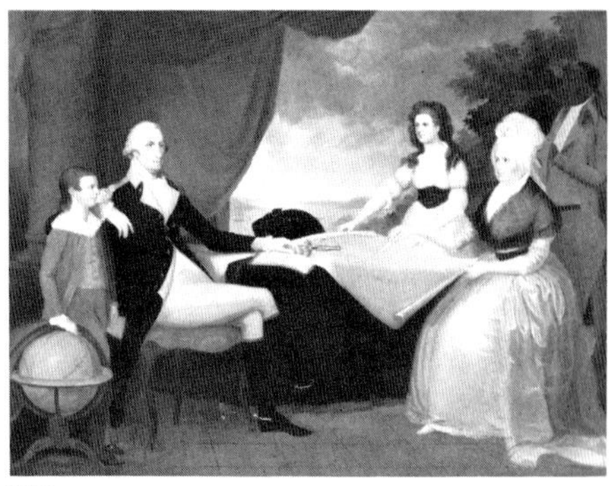

1598

Unidentified Artist

1598 *Washington Family at Mount Vernon #1*, early 19th century
(after Edward Savage, 1796)
Oil on canvas
$29\frac{1}{16}$ x 36¼ in. (73.8 x 92.1 cm.)
Gift of Mrs. John Frederick Lewis (The John Frederick Lewis Memorial Collection), 1933.10.101

Unidentified Artist

1599 *Washington Family at Mount Vernon #2*, early 19th century
(after Edward Savage, 1796)
Oil on canvas
28 x 36 in. (71.1 x 91.4 cm.)
Bequest of Mrs. John Frederick Lewis, 1939.17.5

Unidentified Artist
(formerly attributed to James Peale)

1600 *The Washington Grays in Camp*
Oil on canvas
$29\frac{15}{16}$ x 25 in. (76 x 63.5 cm.)
Gift of Mrs. John Frederick Lewis (The John Frederick Lewis Memorial Collection), 1933.10.59

Unidentified Artist

1601 *Hon. Joseph Watson*, early 19th century
Oil on wood
25⅞ x $21\frac{15}{16}$ in. (65.7 x 55.7 cm.)
Gift of Mrs. John Frederick Lewis (The John Frederick Lewis Memorial Collection), 1933.10.102

Unidentified Artist
(formerly attributed to Rembrandt Peale)

1602 *Joseph Whitfield* (1809–1877), early 19th century
Oil on canvas
20⅛ x 16 in. (51.1 x 40.6 cm.)
Gift of J. E. Harper, 1923.13

Unidentified Artist

1603 *Unidentified Girl*, mid-19th century
Oil on canvas
20⅛ x 17 in. (51.1 x 43.2 cm.)
Bequest of Josephine A. Natt, 1935.3.2

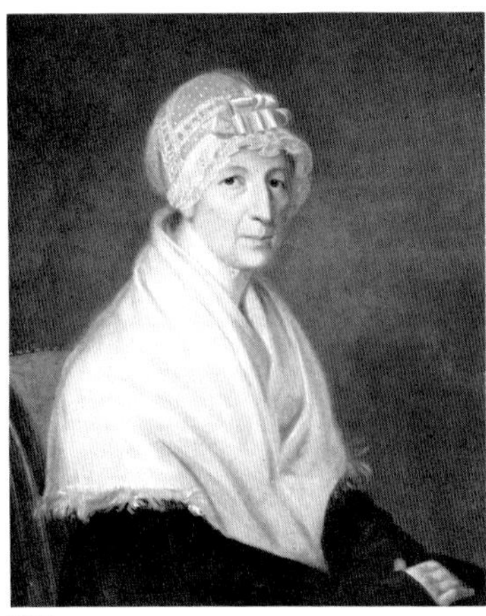

1594

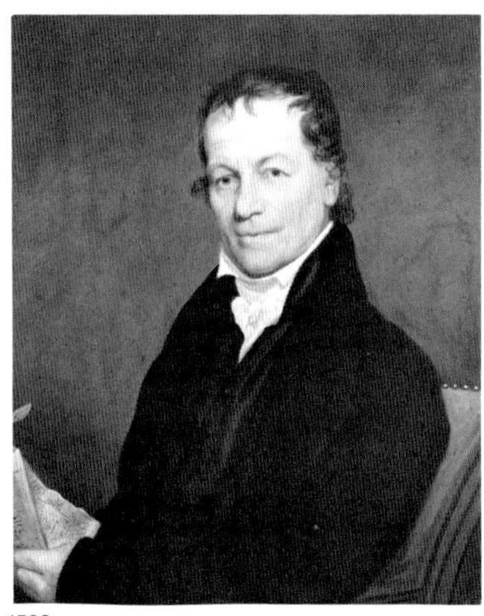

1593

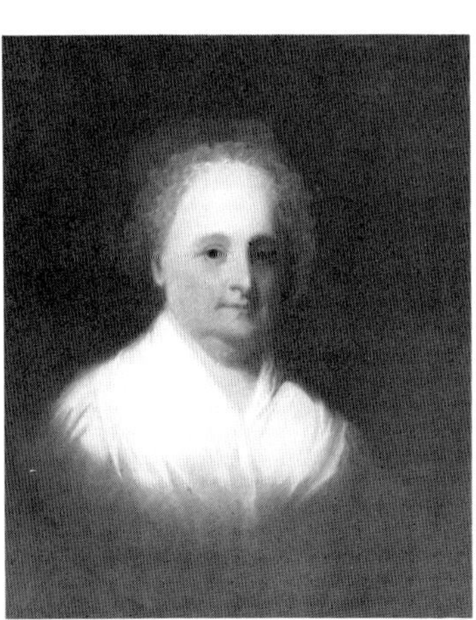

1597

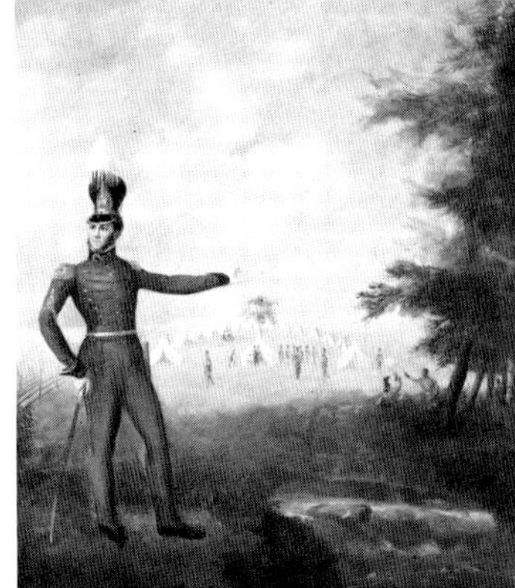

1600

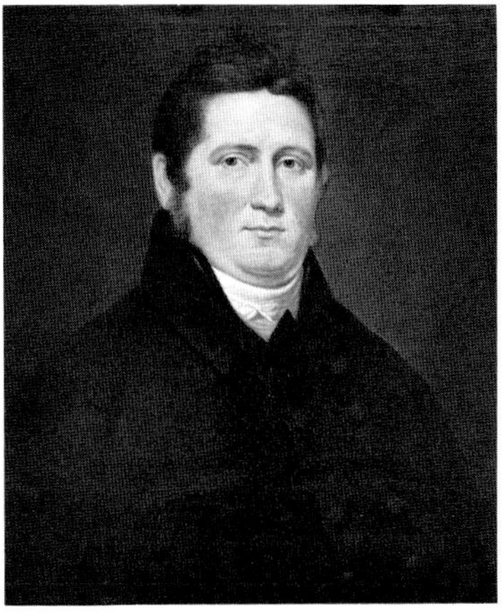
1601

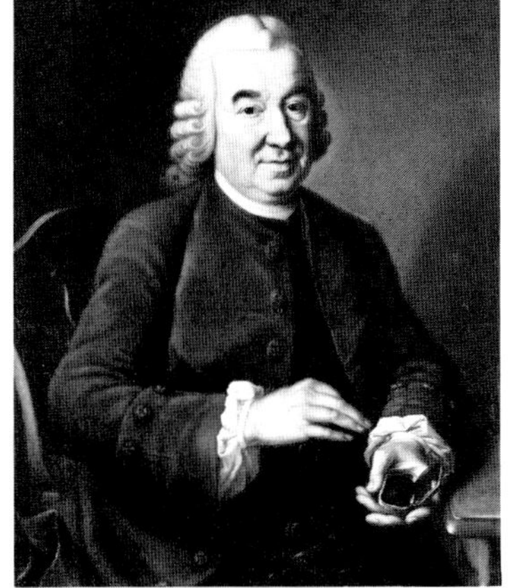
1611

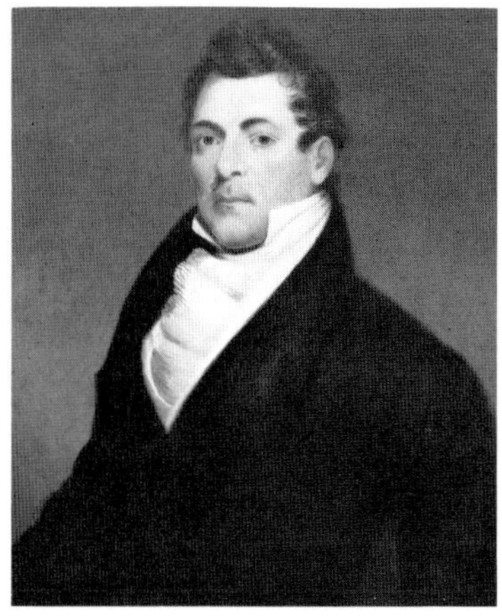
1605

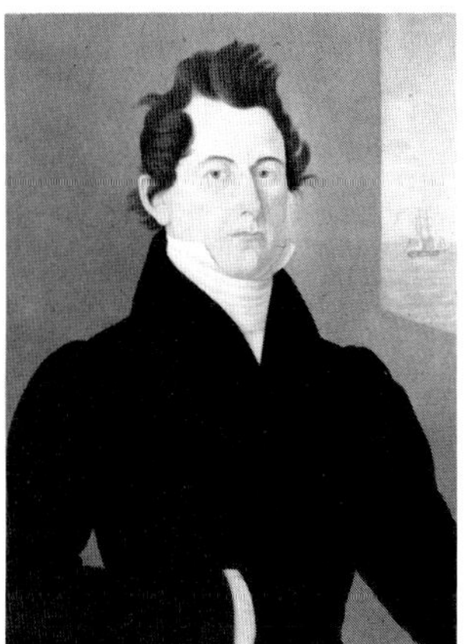
1614

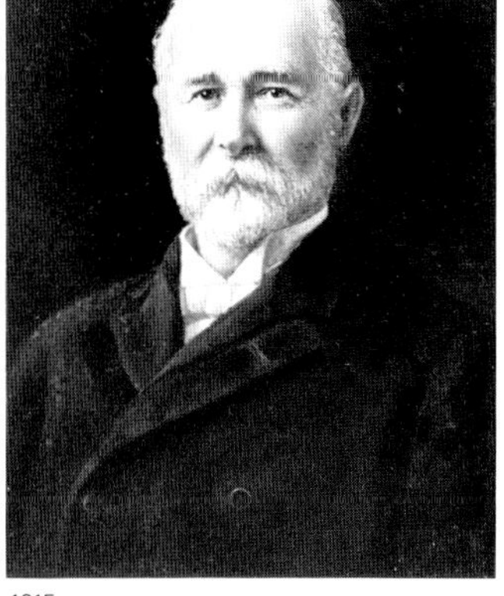
1615

Unidentified Artist
(formerly attributed to John Vanderlyn)

1604 *Unidentified Man* (formerly *John James Audubon*), early 19th century
Oil on canvas
19 15/16 x 16 5/16 in. (50.6 x 41.4 cm.)
Gift of Mrs. John Frederick Lewis (The John Frederick Lewis Memorial Collection), 1933.10.99

Unidentified Artist
(formerly attributed to Robert Fulton)

1605 *Unidentified Man* (formerly *Robert Fulton*), early 19th century
Oil on canvas, mounted on masonite
30 1/8 x 25 1/8 in. (76.5 x 63.8 cm.)
Gift of Alfred G. B. Steel, 1947.16

Unidentified Artist
(formerly attributed to Washington Allston)

1606 *Unidentified Man* (formerly *Andrew Jackson*), early 19th century
Oil on canvas
29 5/16 x 23 1/16 in. (74.5 x 58.6 cm.)
Gift of Mrs. John Frederick Lewis (The John Frederick Lewis Memorial Collection), 1933.10.98

Unidentified Artist
(formerly attributed to Bass Otis)

1607 *Unidentified Man* (formerly *Thomas Jefferson*), ca. 1825
Oil on canvas
36 x 30 1/4 in. (91.4 x 76.8 cm.)
Gift of Mrs. John Frederick Lewis (The John Frederick Lewis Memorial Collection), 1933.10.96

Unidentified Artist
(formerly attributed to John Neagle)

1608 *Unidentified Man* (formerly *William N. Johnson*), early 19th century
Oil on canvas
29 1/2 x 25 in. (74.9 x 63.5 cm.)
Inscribed on book: MR DOM MARTIN/[?]/[?]
Gift of Mrs. John Frederick Lewis (The John Frederick Lewis Memorial Collection), 1933.10.95

Unidentified Artist
(formerly attributed to John Wesley Jarvis)

1609 *Unidentified Man* (formerly *Thomas MacDonough, USN*), mid-19th century
Oil on canvas
30 3/16 x 23 7/8 in. (76.7 x 60.6 cm.)
Gift of Mrs. John Frederick Lewis (The John Frederick Lewis Memorial Collection), 1933.10.31

Unidentified Artist
(formerly attributed to John Trumbull)

1610 *Unidentified Man* (formerly *Benjamin West*), early to mid-19th century
Oil on canvas
36 3/16 x 28 3/16 in. (91.9 x 71.6 cm.)
Gift of Mrs. John Frederick Lewis (The John Frederick Lewis Memorial Collection), 1933.10.97

Unidentified Artist (possibly English)

1611 *Unidentified Man*, mid-18th century
Oil on canvas
33 7/8 x 28 15/16 in. (86 x 73.5 cm.)
Gift of Mrs. John Frederick Lewis (The John Frederick Lewis Memorial Collection), 1933.10.100

Unidentified Artist

1612 *Unidentified Man*, late 18th century
Oil on canvas
30 x 24 13/16 in. (76.2 x 63 cm.)
Gift of John Frederick Lewis, 1932.13.4

Unidentified Artist

1613 *Unidentified Man*, early 19th century
Oil on canvas
22 1/2 x 17 7/8 in. (57.2 x 45.4 cm.)
Gift of John Frederick Lewis, 1932.13.5

Unidentified Artist

1614 *Unidentified Man*, early 19th century
Oil on canvas
30 7/16 x 22 1/8 in. (77.3 x 56.2 cm.)
Gift of John Frederick Lewis, 1932.13.6

Unidentified Artist

1615 *Unidentified Man*, late 19th to early 20th century
Oil on cardboard
5 1/4 x 3 7/8 in. (13.3 x 9.8 cm.)
Source unknown, 1970.13

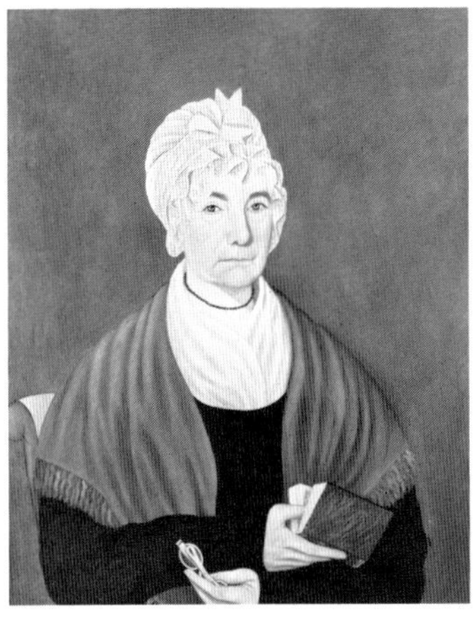
1616

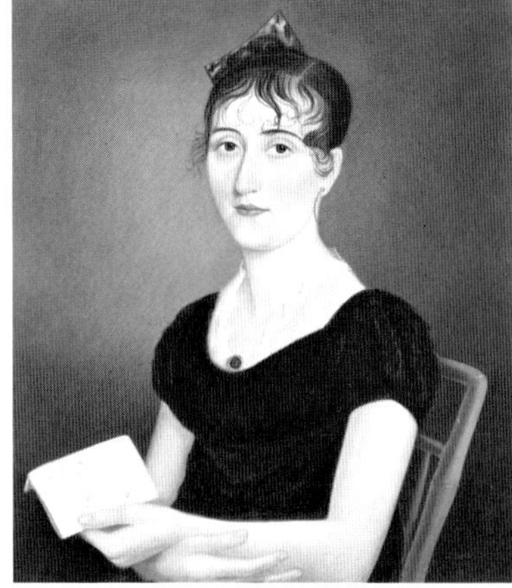
1617

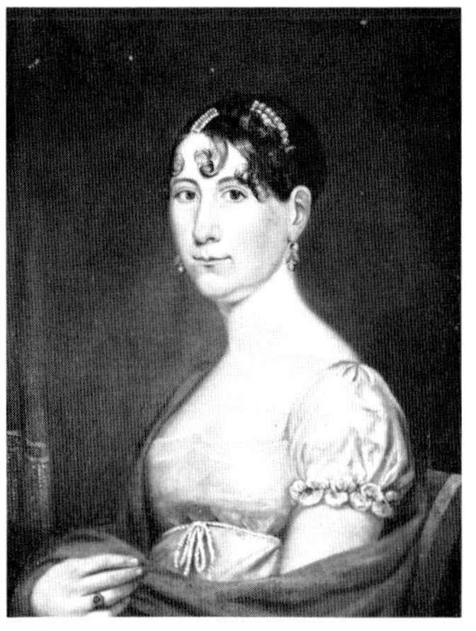
1618

Unidentified Artist

1616 *Unidentified Woman*, late 18th to early 19th century
Oil on canvas
33⅛ x 27 in. (84.1 x 68.6 cm.)
Bequest of David J. Grossman in honor of Mr. and Mrs. Charles S. Grossman and Mr. and Mrs. Meyer Speiser, 1979.1.11

Unidentified Artist
(formerly attributed to Bass Otis)

1617 *Unidentified Woman*, ca. 1815
Oil on canvas
26 x 22¹⁵⁄₁₆ in. (66 x 58.3 cm.)
Inscribed on letter: M.E.Tay [?]/Philadelphia; inscribed on sitter's brooch: ETH [monogram]
Gift of John Frederick Lewis, 1932.13.8

Unidentified Artist

1618 *Unidentified Woman*, ca. 1815
Oil on canvas, mounted on cardboard
24½ x 19 in. (62.2 x 48.3 cm.)
Source unknown, 1944.31

Unidentified Artist
(formerly attributed to Ezra Ames)

1619 *Unidentified Woman*, early to mid-19th century
Oil on canvas
34¹⁄₁₆ x 27 in. (86.5 x 68.6 cm.)
Gift of John Frederick Lewis, 1923.8.8

Unidentified Artist

1620 *Unidentified Woman*, mid-19th century
Oil on canvas
29⅞ x 25¹⁄₁₆ in. (75.9 x 63.7 cm.)
Gift of John Frederick Lewis, 1932.13.9

Unidentified Artist
(formerly attributed to Thomas Sully)

1621 *Unidentified Woman*, mid-19th century
Oil on canvas
25¹⁄₁₆ x 21¹⁄₁₆ in. (63.7 x 53.5 cm.)
Gift of Mrs. John Frederick Lewis through her son, John Frederick Lewis, Jr., 1938.13.3

Palettes

William Merritt Chase (1849–1916)

1622 *Palette*
Oil on wood
15½ x 23¹⁵⁄₁₆ in. (39.4 x 60.8 cm.)
Gift of Mary Townsend Mason, 1960.19

Rembrandt Peale (1778–1860)

1623 *Palette*
Oil on paper
9⅞ x 7⁷⁄₁₆ in. (25.1 x 18.9 cm.)
Annotated on back: Palette used by Rembrandt Peale./Presented by Mrs Peale to Eliza J. Haldeman/1865.
Gift of Guy K. Haldeman, 1955.2

Thomas Sully (1783–1872)

1624 *Palette*, 1832
Oil on paper
14¼ x 8⁷⁄₁₆ in. (36.2 x 21.4 cm.)
Annotated: Thos Sullys Palette. 1832; and in another hand: The Penna Academy of Fine Arts/from Charles Henry Hart/May 1896
Gift of Charles Henry Hart, 1896.5.1
See also verso, cat. no. 1626.

1625 *Palette*, 1852
Oil on paper
4¹³⁄₁₆ x 7⁵⁄₁₆ in. (12.2 x 18.6 cm.)
Dated: April 7th 1852.
Annotated: Palette for Portraits–Thomas Sully–1852; and on back: Thomas Sully's palette of color for Portraits/given to Samuel Sartain May 1852/during sittings for portrait
Gift of Mr. and Mrs. Arthur Meltzer, 1959.15

1626 *Replica of Gilbert Stuart's Palette*
Oil on paper
14¼ x 8⁷⁄₁₆ in. (36.2 x 21.4 cm.)
Gift of Charles Henry Hart, 1896.5.2
See also recto, cat. no. 1624.

Miniatures

Anna Margaretta Archambault (1856–1956)

1627 *Clara Agnes Clark*, 1919
Watercolor on ivory
3 x 2⁷⁄₁₆ in. (7.6 x 6.2 cm.), oval
Signed and dated at right center: ARCHAMBAULT 1919
Engraved on case: CLARA AGNES CLARK/ 1919
Gift of Mrs. Edgar White, 1962.15.1

1628 *Mrs. William Ives Rutter* (née Sarah May Hobart), 1914
Watercolor on ivory
3⁵⁄₁₆ x 2⁷⁄₁₆ in. (8.4 x 6.2 cm.), oval
Signed and dated at right center: Archambault. 1914
Bequest of Helen Burr Smith, 1981.11

1629 *James C. Wignall*, 1900
Watercolor on ivory
3⁵⁄₁₆ x 2⁹⁄₁₆ in. (8.4 x 6.5 cm.), oval
Gift of Mrs. Edgar White, 1962.15.2

1630 *Mary Ann Wignall*, 1920
Watercolor on ivory
3¼ x 2½ in. (8.3 x 6.4 cm.), oval
Signed and dated at upper right: A.M. ARCHAMBAULT. 1920
Engraved on case: MARY ANN WIGNALL/1920
Gift of Mrs. Edgar White, 1962.15.3

William Russell Birch (1755–1834)

1631 *Falls of Niagara*, by 1827
Enamel on copper
2½ x 2¼ in. (6.4 x 5.7 cm.)
Signed at lower left: W.B.
Inscribed on back: This wild oblique sketch/from the corner of the falls/of Niagara/taken by - Ranagal from the spot/and painted by me Wm./Birch gives in my opinion/a greater idea of its mag/nitude then [*sic*] the front/view where the distance/necessary loses its immen/sity.
Bequest of Eliza Howard Burd, 1860.1

1632 *Venus*, ca. 1810
Enamel on copper
1⅞ x 1⁹⁄₁₆ in. (4.7 x 4 cm.), oval
Signed and dated at lower left: WB/[?] 9
Gift of John M. Staney, 1869.4

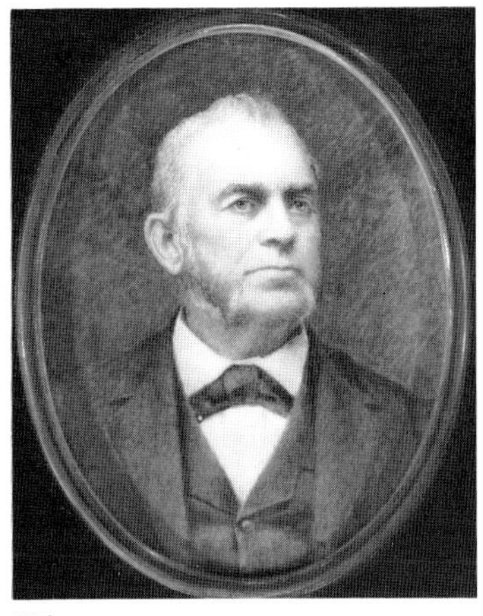
1629

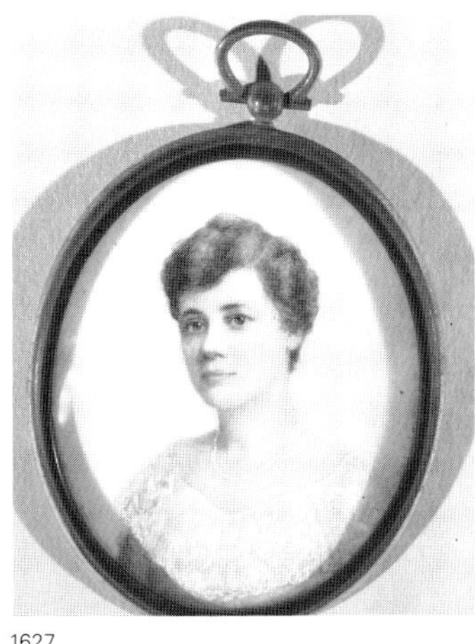
1627

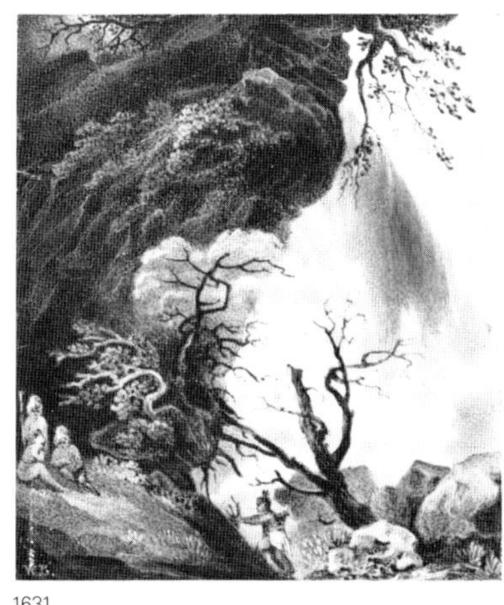
1631

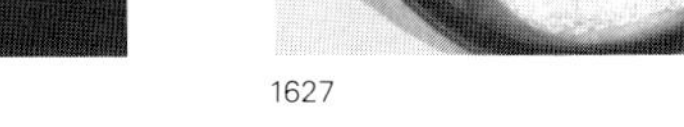

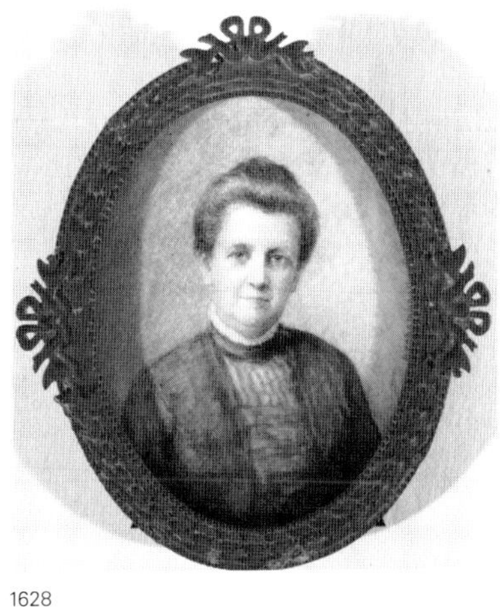
1628

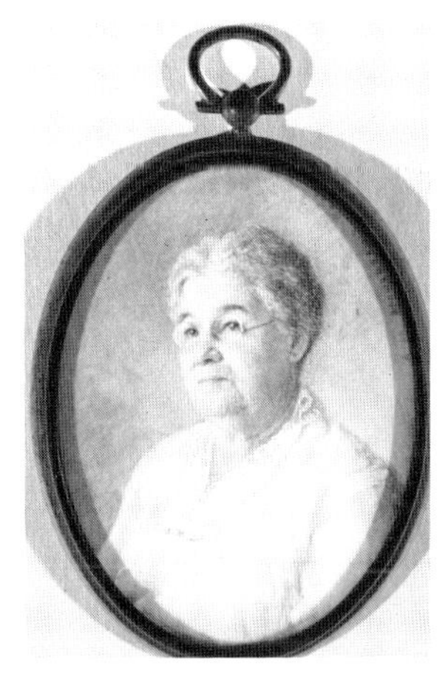
1630

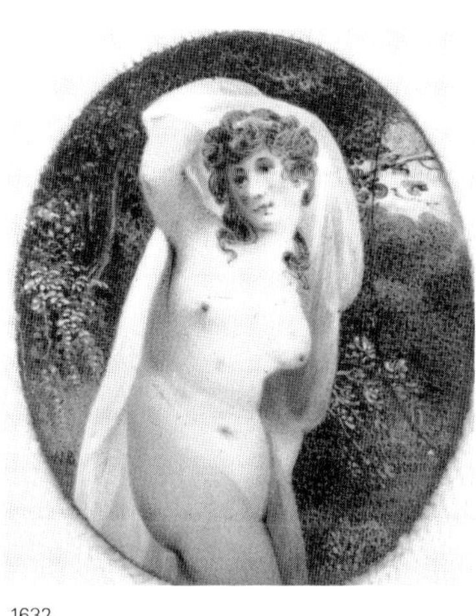
1632

Charles Van Dyck Brown (1848–1892)

1633 *John Henry Brown* (1818–1891), 1891
Watercolor on ivory
4⅝ x 3⅜ in. (11.8 x 8.6 cm.), oval
Signed and dated at right center: C.V.B. 91
Gift of Mrs. J. Howard Brown, 1948.21.1

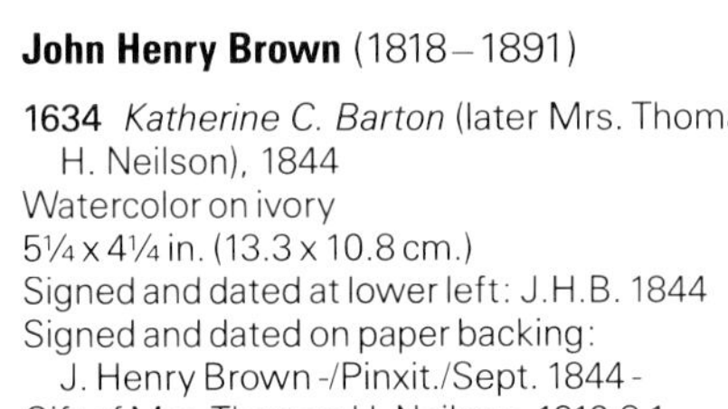

John Henry Brown (1818–1891)

1634 *Katherine C. Barton* (later Mrs. Thomas H. Neilson), 1844
Watercolor on ivory
5¼ x 4¼ in. (13.3 x 10.8 cm.)
Signed and dated at lower left: J.H.B. 1844
Signed and dated on paper backing: J. Henry Brown -/Pinxit./Sept. 1844 -
Gift of Mrs. Thomas H. Neilson, 1912.8.1

1635 *Lord George Gordon Byron* (1788–1824), ca. 1810
Watercolor on ivory
3 13/16 x 2 15/16 in. (9.7 x 7.5 cm.)
Gift of Mrs. J. Howard Brown, 1948.21.2

1636 *The Harpist*, 1842
Watercolor on ivory
3¾ x 3⅛ in. (9.5 x 7.9 cm.)
Signed and dated at lower center: J.H. Brown. Pinxit./April. –1842.
Gift of Mrs. J. Howard Brown, 1949.15.1

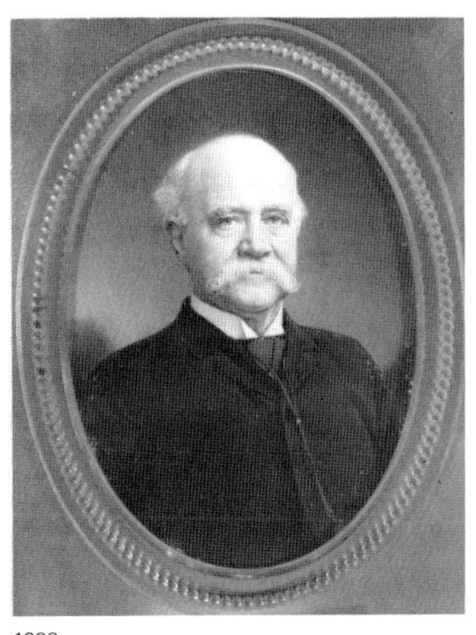
1633

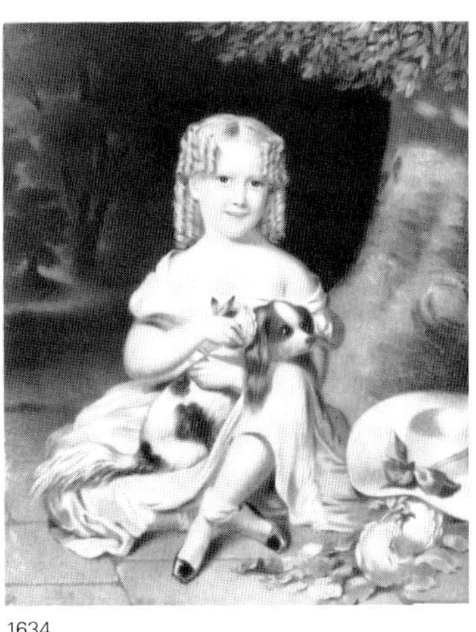
1634

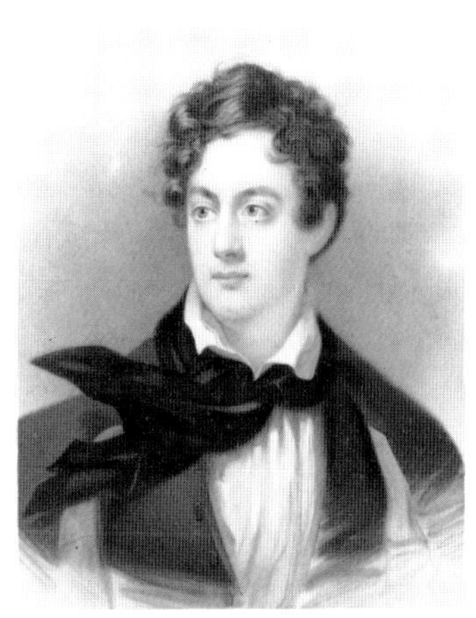
1635

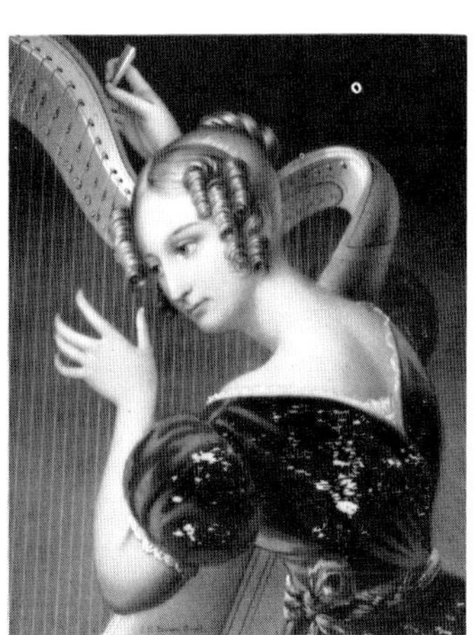
1636

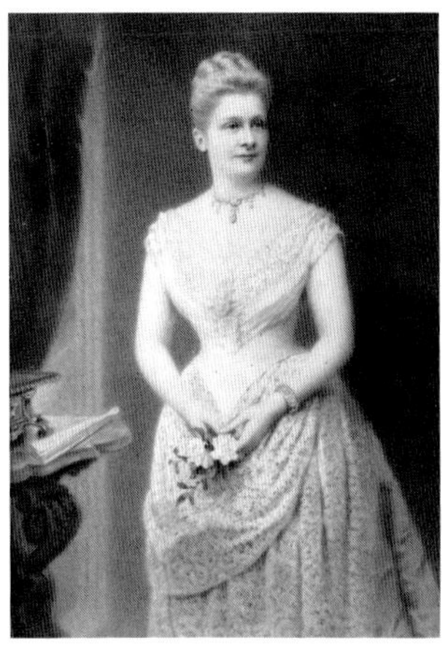
1637

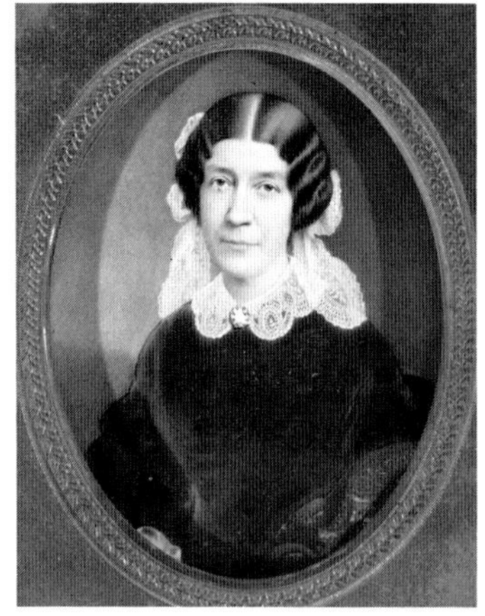
1638

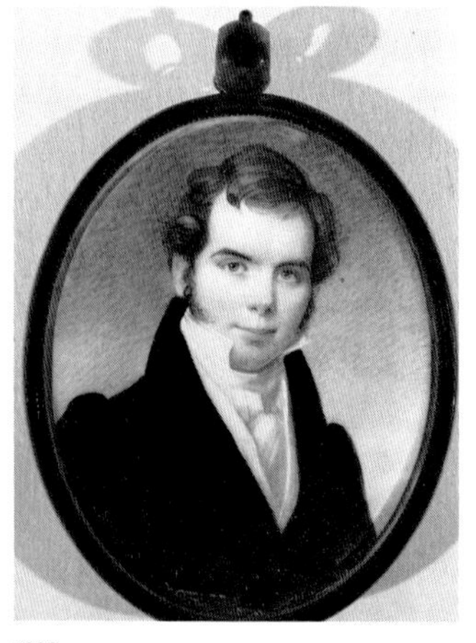
1639

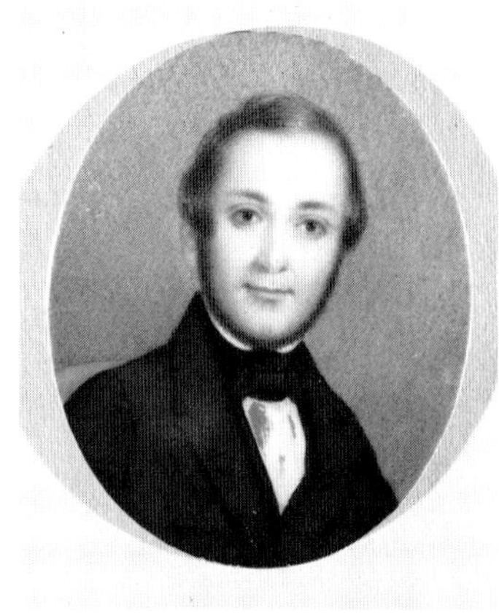
1640

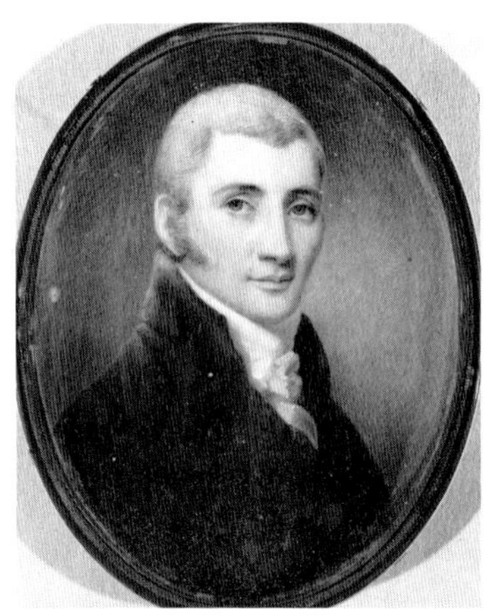
1641

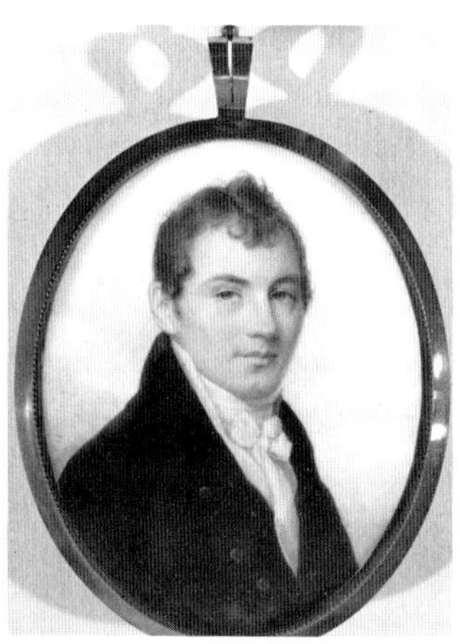
1642

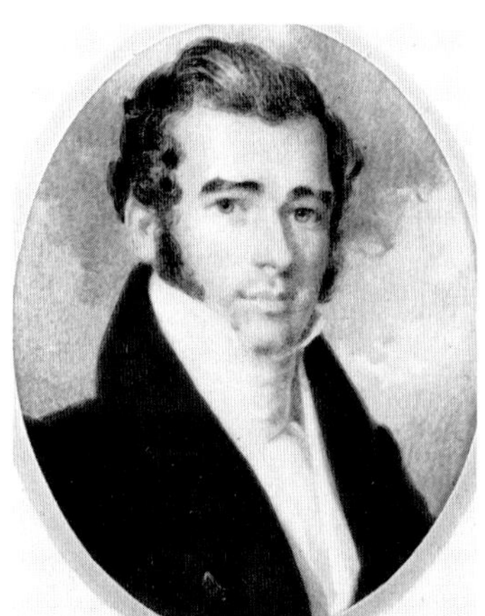
1643

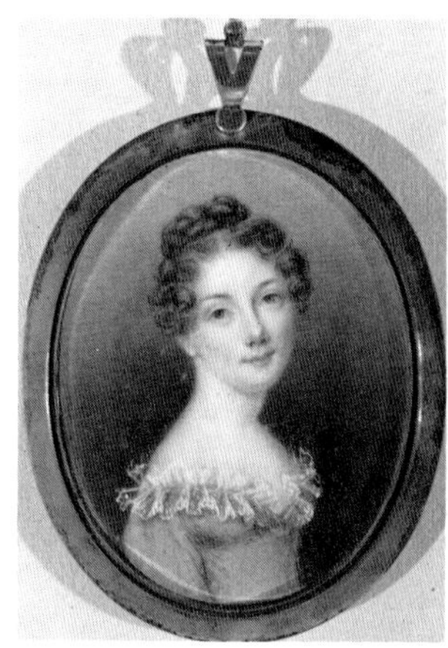
1644

1637 *Mrs. John Le Conte*, 1888
Watercolor on ivory
5¼ x 3⅞ in. (13.3 x 9.8 cm.)
Signed and dated at lower right:
J. Henry Brown. 1888.
Gift of Mrs. Robert Le Conte, 1925.12

1638 *Unidentified Woman*, 1861
Watercolor on ivory
4¹¹⁄₁₆ x 3½ in. (11.9 x 8.9 cm.), oval
Signed and dated at lower left:
J. Hy. Brown. 1861.
Gift of Mrs. J. Howard Brown, 1949.15.2

Daniel Dickinson (b. 1795)

1639 *Jacob Bennett*, ca. 1820
Watercolor on ivory
2¹³⁄₁₆ x 2³⁄₁₆ in. (7.1 x 5.6 cm.), oval
Bequest of Marian Bennett, 1929.8

Eliot Gregory

1640 *Self-Portrait*, 1844
Watercolor on ivory
2⁵⁄₁₆ x 1⅞ in. (5.9 x 4.7 cm.), oval
Annotated on paper backing: A likeness of/
E. Gregory/Painted by himself/in Philadelphia/
January 1844
Gift of Herman Deigendesch, 1915.10

Edward Greene Malbone (1777–1807)

1641 *Asher Marx*, 1803
Watercolor on ivory
2¾ x 2⅛ in. (7 x 5.4 cm.), oval
Gift of Frank Marx Etting, 1886.1.1

1642 *Joseph Marx*, 1806
Watercolor on ivory
3 x 2⅜ in. (7.6 x 6 cm.), oval
Gift of Frank Marx Etting, 1886.1.2

John Neagle (1796–1865)

1643 *J. Edgar Thomson* (1808–1874), ca. 1830
Watercolor on ivory
2½ x 1¹⁵⁄₁₆ in. (6.4 x 4.9 cm.), oval
Bequest of Edgar L. Thomson, 1913.17

Anna Claypoole Peale (Mrs. William Staughton, 1791–1878)

1644 *Madame Lallemand*, 1810s
Watercolor on ivory
1⅞ x 1½ in. (4.7 x 3.8 cm.), oval
Signed and dated at lower right: Anna C./Peale/
181[?] [incised]
Engraved on case: Madame Lallemand/Anna
C. Peale/Pinxt
Gift of Charles Hare Hutchinson, 1898.10

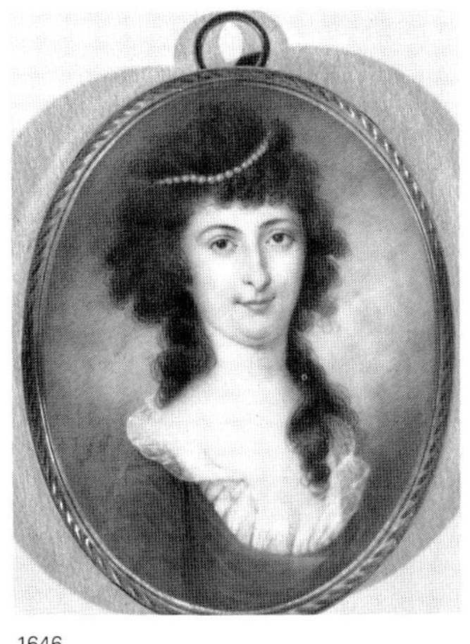
1646

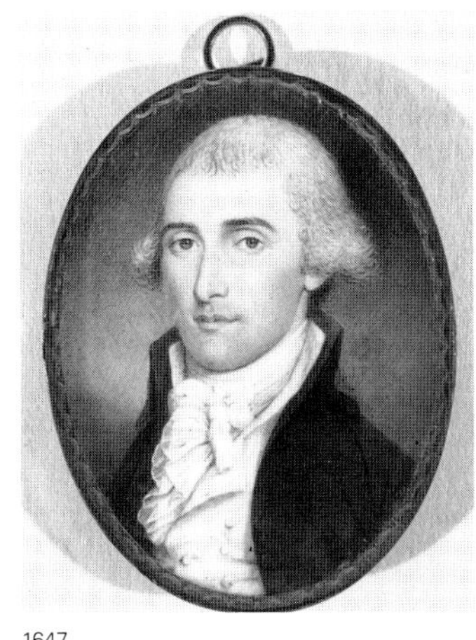
1647

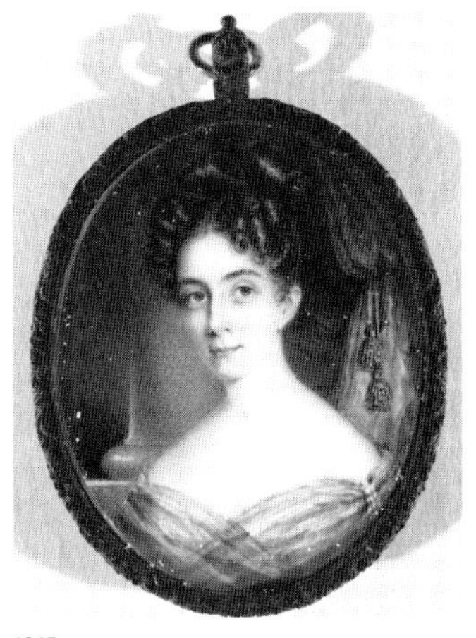
1645

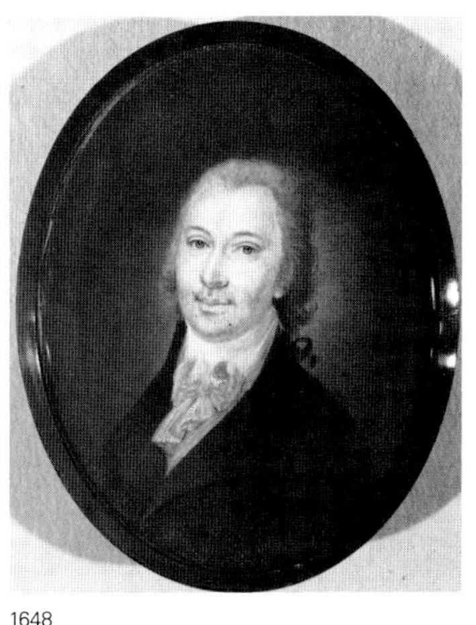
1648

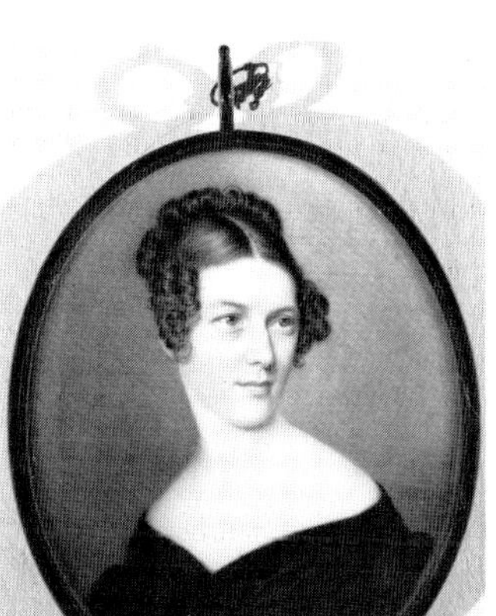
1651

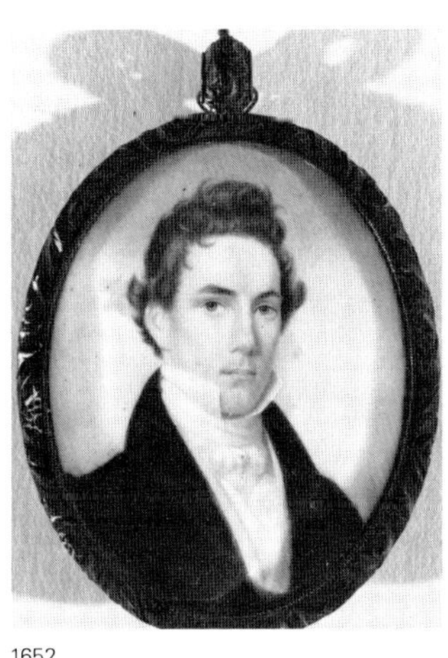
1652

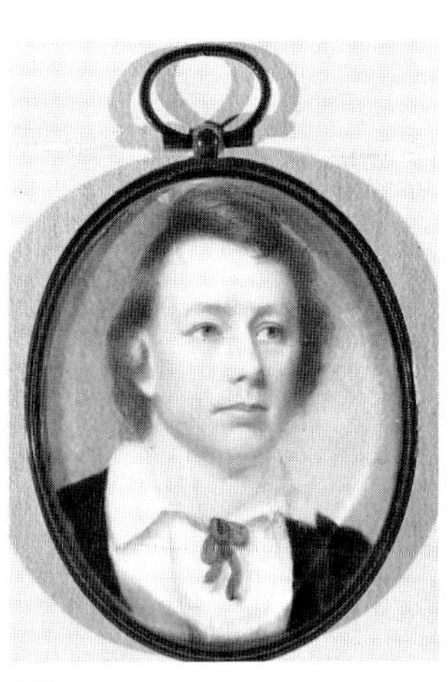
1649

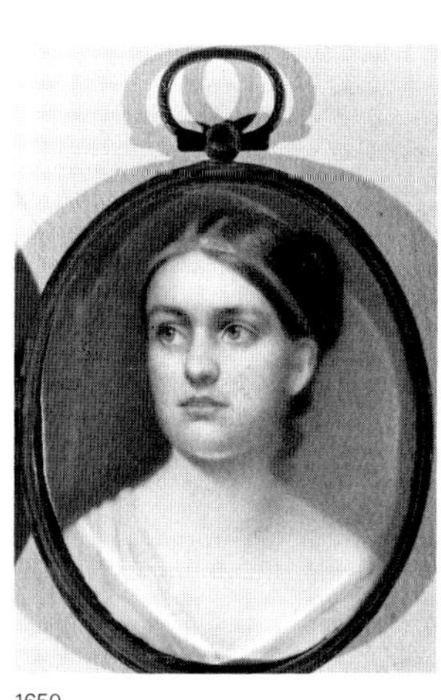
1650

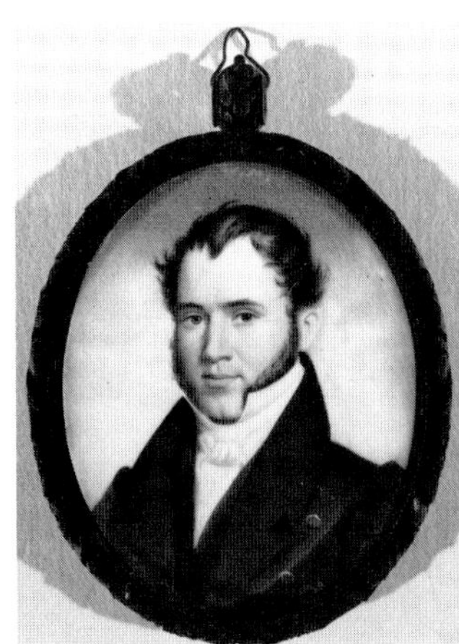
1653

Attributed to **Anna Claypoole Peale**

1645 *Elizabeth Kinsey Brick*, 1840
Watercolor on ivory
2⅝ x 2¹⁄₁₆ in. (6.7 x 5.2 cm.), oval
Engraved on case: JR & EKB/1840
Gift of Sarah Fitzwater, 1935.13a
See also verso, cat. no. 1657.

James Peale (1749–1831)

1646 *Frances Gratz Etting* (b. 1771), 1794
Watercolor on ivory
2⅜ x 1⁹⁄₁₆ in. (6 x 4 cm.), oval
Signed and dated at lower left: IP/1794
Gift of Frank Marx Etting, 1886.1.4

1647 *Reuben Etting* (1762–1848), 1794
Watercolor on ivory
2⁷⁄₁₆ x 1¹³⁄₁₆ in. (6.2 x 4.6 cm.), oval
Signed and dated at right center: IP/1794
Gift of Frank Marx Etting, 1886.1.5

Philippe A. Peticolas (1760–1843)

1648 *Unidentified Man*, 1799
Watercolor on ivory
2¹³⁄₁₆ x 2⅜ in. (7.1 x 6 cm.), oval
Signed and dated at lower left: P Peticolas/1799
Gift of Frank Marx Etting, 1886.1.6

Henry Colton Shumway (1807–1884)

1649 *John Frazee* (1790–1852), ca. 1833
Watercolor on ivory
2⁷⁄₁₆ x 1¹⁵⁄₁₆ in. (6.2 x 7.5 cm.), oval
Gift of Ada Blanche Belknap, 1934.13.2

1650 *Mrs. John Frazee* (née Lydia Place, b. ca. 1816), ca. 1833
Watercolor on ivory
2⁷⁄₁₆ x 2 in. (6.2 x 5 cm.), oval
Gift of Ada Blanche Belknap, 1934.13.1

James P. Smith (1803–1888)

1651 *Elizabeth C. Barton*, ca. 1835
Watercolor on ivory
2⅝ x 2³⁄₁₆ in. (6.7 x 5.6 cm.), oval
Gift of Mrs. Thomas H. Neilson, 1912.8.2

1652 *Charles Lindell Rowand* (1810–1872), ca. 1830
Watercolor on ivory
2⅜ x 1⅞ in. (6 x 4.7 cm.), oval
Gift of C. Monteith Gilpin, 1937.16

1653 *George W. Wood*
Watercolor on ivory
2⅜ x 1⅞ in. (6 x 4.7 cm.), oval
Bequest of Marian Bennett, 1929.10

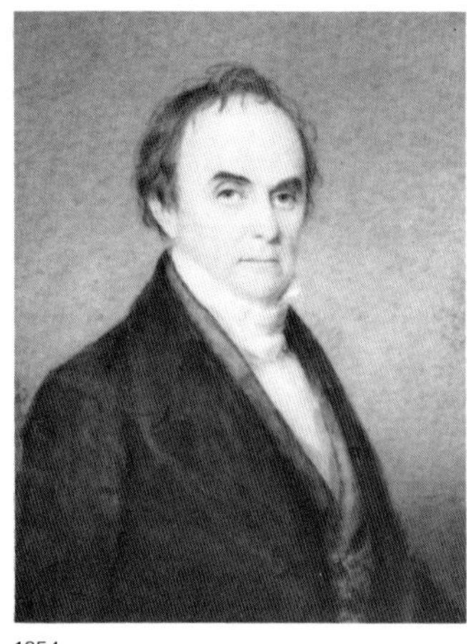
1654

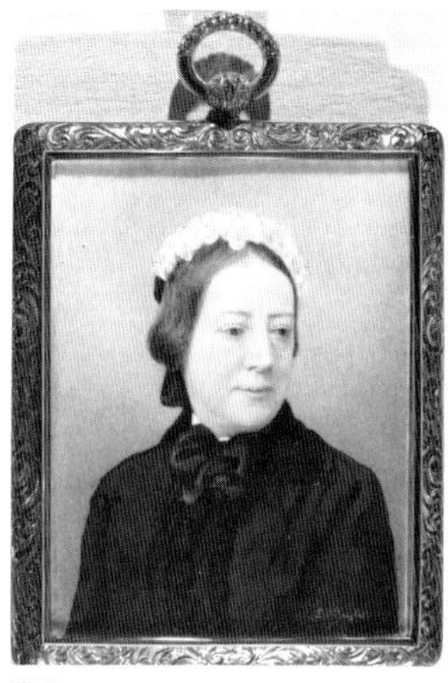
1655

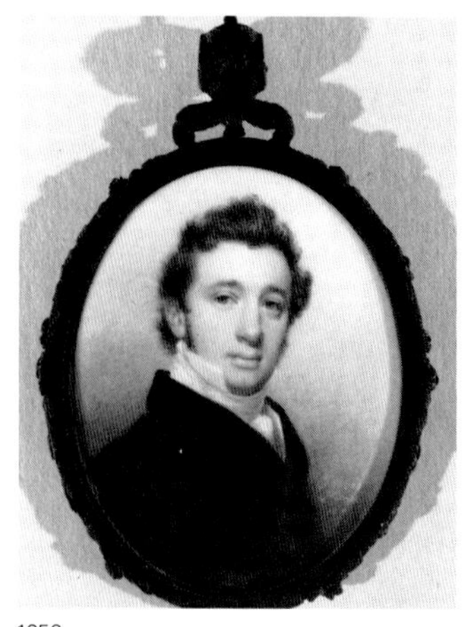
1656

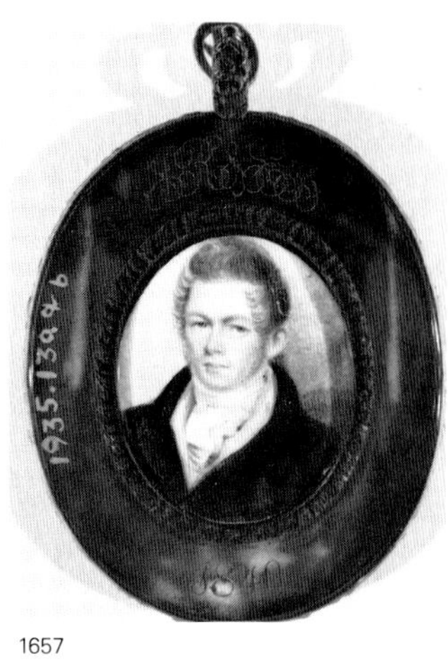
1657

1660

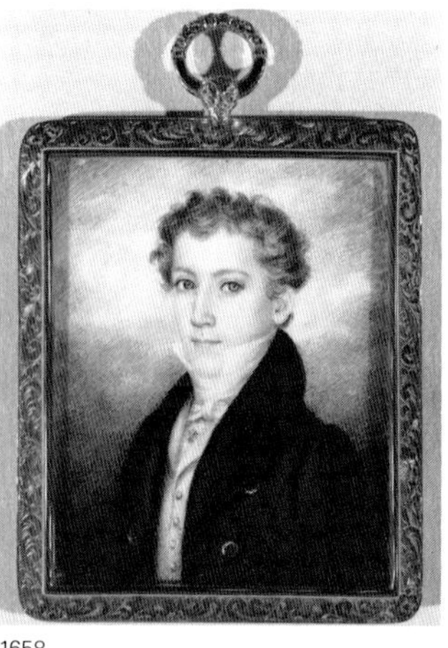
1658

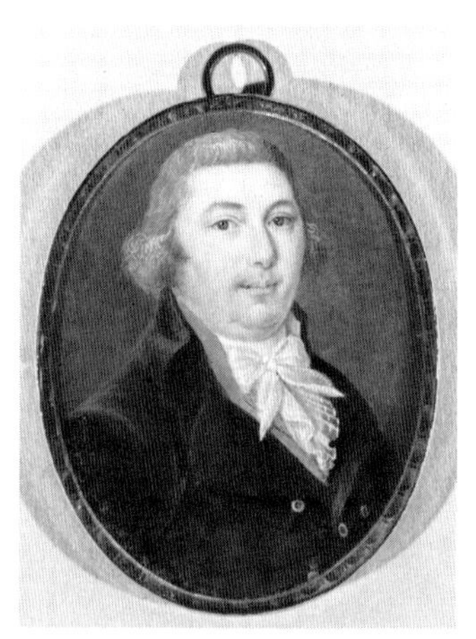
1661

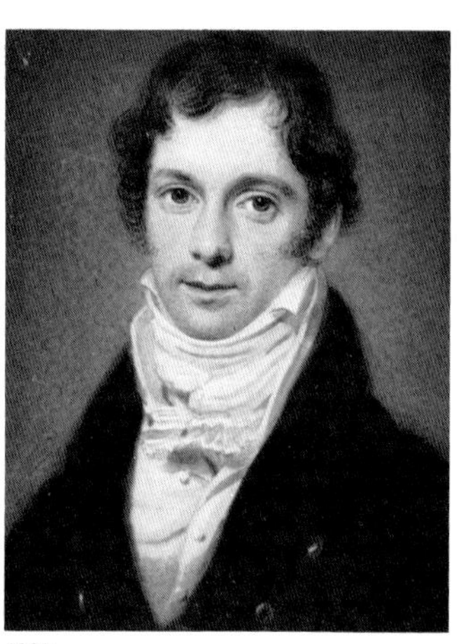
1662

Richard M. Staigg (1817–1881)

1654 *Daniel Washington Webster* (1782–1852), 1844
Watercolor on ivory
$4\frac{15}{16}$ x $3\frac{7}{8}$ in. (12.5 x 9.8 cm.)
Signed and dated at lower right: R.M. Staigg/ 1844
Annotated on paper backing: Daniel Webster/ original miniature painted/from life by Richard M. Staigg/Washington 1844; and in another hand: Purchased from the widow of the artist. Jany 30. 1892/by Alexander Biddle/and presented by him to/the Penna. Acad. of Fine Arts
Gift of Alexander Biddle, 1892.4

Emily Drayton Taylor (Mrs. J. Madison Taylor, 1860–1952)

1655 *Mrs. Charles Wallace Brooke* (née Elizabeth Tilghman Rawle, 1818–1897), 1894
Watercolor on ivory
$2\frac{3}{8}$ x $1\frac{13}{16}$ in. (6 x 4.6 cm.)
Signed and dated at lower right: E.D Taylor./ 1894.
Engraved on case: Mrs. Charles Wallace Brooke,/Elizabeth Tilghman Rawle./ Philadelphia./1818–1897.
Bequest of William Brooke Rawle, 1927.12.3

Joseph Wood (ca. 1778–1830)

1656 *Samuel Etting*, 1819
Watercolor on ivory
$2\frac{3}{8}$ x $1\frac{13}{16}$ in. (6 x 4.6 cm.), oval
Signed and dated at lower right: J Wood/Pinx./ 1819
Gift of Sarah Miris Hayes Goodrich, 1919.8

Unidentified Artist

1657 *John R. Brick*, 1840
Watercolor on ivory
$1\frac{9}{16}$ x $1\frac{5}{16}$ in. (4 x 3.3 cm.), oval
Engraved on case: JR & EKB/1840
Gift of Sarah Fitzwater, 1935.13b
See also recto, cat. no. 1645.

Unidentified Artist

1658 *Charles Wallace Brooke* (1813–1849), ca. 1830
Watercolor on ivory
$2\frac{1}{16}$ x $1\frac{11}{16}$ in. (5.2 x 4.3 cm.)
Engraved on case: Charles Wallace Brooke./ Philadelphia./1813–1849.
Bequest of William Brooke Rawle, 1927.12.4

Unidentified Artist

1659 *Danaë*, ca. 1810
Watercolor on ivory
$1\frac{9}{16}$ x $2\frac{3}{4}$ in. (4 x 7 cm.), oval
Gift of Caroline Wood Stretch, 1947.17

Unidentified Artist
(formerly attributed to Benjamin Trott)

1660 *Solomon Etting* (1764–1847), ca. 1810
Watercolor on ivory
$2\frac{11}{16}$ x $2\frac{1}{4}$ in. (6.8 x 5.7 cm.), oval
Gift of Frank Marx Etting, 1886.1.8

Unidentified Artist

1661 *Conrad Laub* (1751–1807), ca. 1800
Watercolor on ivory
2 x $1\frac{9}{16}$ in. (5 x 4 cm.), oval
Engraved on case: Conrad Laub./Born–1751./ Died–1807.
Gift of Elizabeth P. Frank, 1975.24

Unidentified Artist

1662 *Jacob C. Levy* (b. 1788), ca. 1820
Watercolor on ivory
$2\frac{15}{16}$ x $2\frac{1}{4}$ in. (7.5 x 5.7 cm.)
Bequest of Emma Repplier Witmer, 1972.8.1

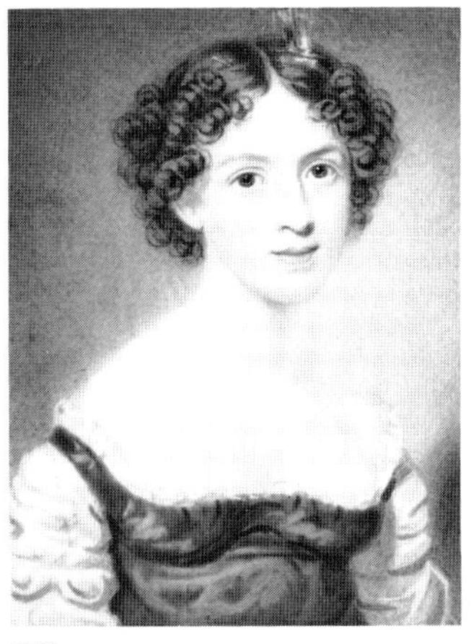
1663

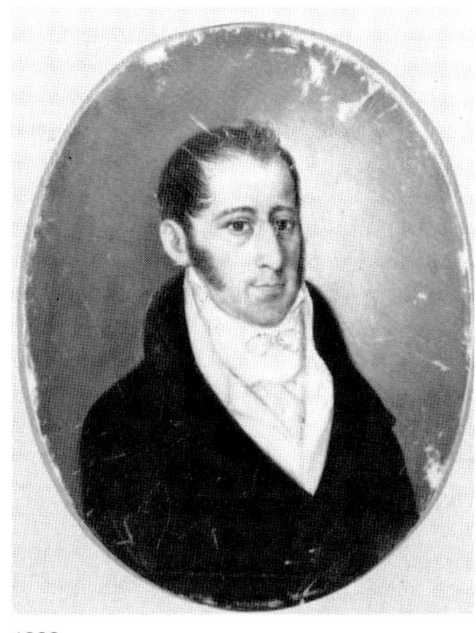
1666

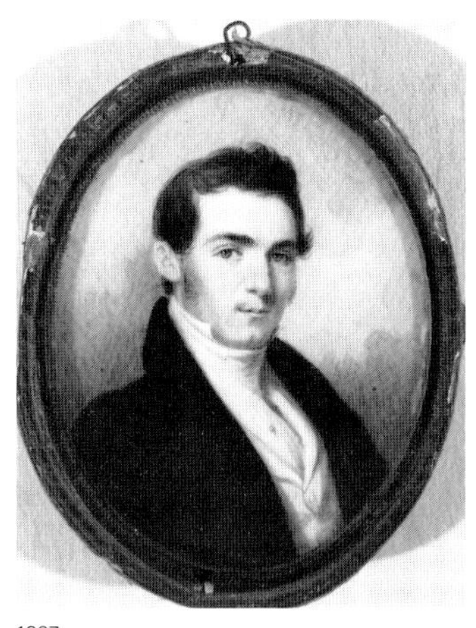
1667

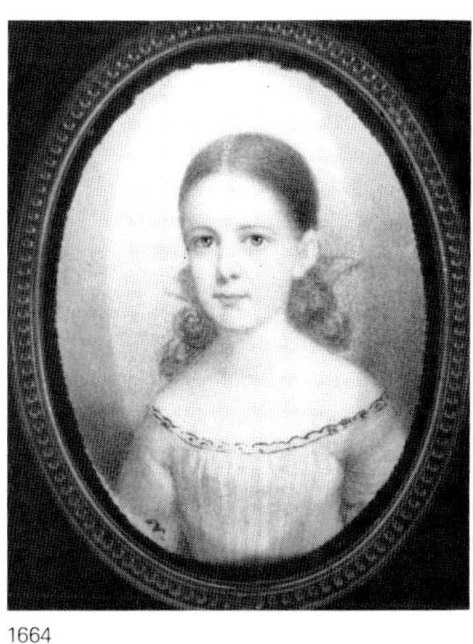
1664

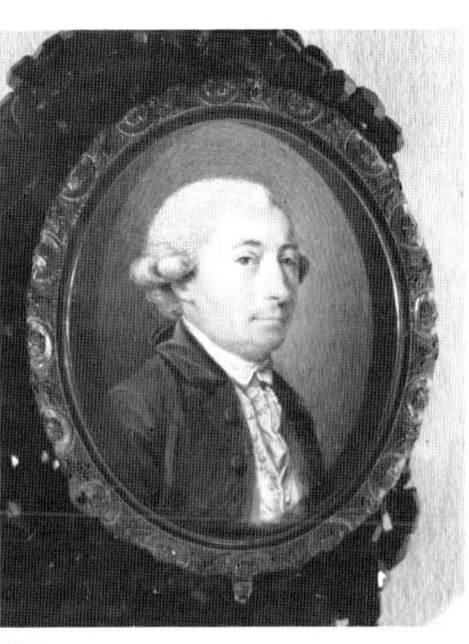
1669

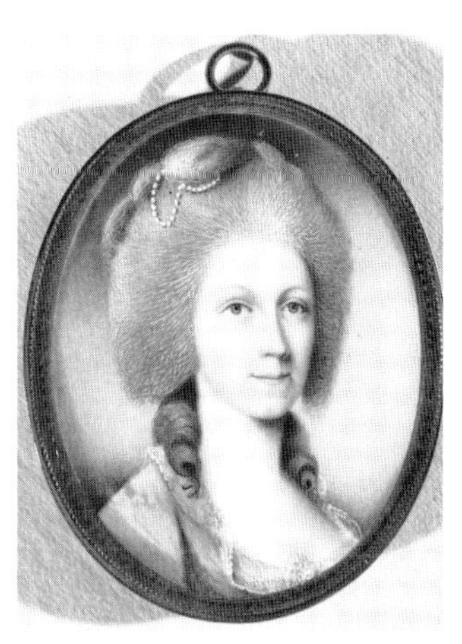
1668

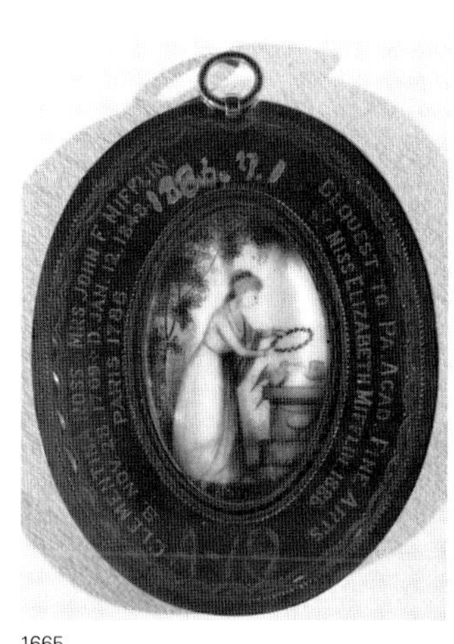
1665

Unidentified Artist

1663 *Mrs. Jacob C. Levy* (née Fanny Yates, 1797–1892), ca. 1820
Watercolor on ivory
3 x $2\frac{1}{4}$ in. (7.6 x 5.7 cm.)
Bequest of Emma Repplier Witmer, 1972.8.2

Unidentified Artist

1664 *Ellen Jane Lewis* (later Mrs. J. E. Coonan, 1838–1930), ca. 1848
Watercolor on ivory
$1\frac{7}{8}$ x $1\frac{3}{4}$ in. (4.7 x 4.4 cm.)
Gift of J. E. Coonan in memory of his wife, 1946.1

Unidentified Artist

1665 *Memorial Scene*
Watercolor on ivory
$1\frac{1}{8}$ x $\frac{3}{4}$ in. (2.9 x 1.9 cm.), oval
Case: 2 x $1\frac{11}{16}$ in. (5 x 4.3 cm.)
Bequest of Elizabeth Mifflin, 1886.4.1b
See also recto, cat. no. 1668.

Unidentified Artist

1666 *Dr. Emmanuel Phillips*, ca. 1820
Watercolor on ivory
$3\frac{1}{8}$ x $2\frac{7}{16}$ in. (7.9 x 6.2 cm.), oval
Gift of J. Bunford Samuel, 1914.16

Unidentified Artist

1667 *Judge Archibald Randall* (1797–1846), ca. 1820
Watercolor on ivory
$1\frac{15}{16}$ x $2\frac{3}{8}$ in. (4.9 x 6 cm.), oval
Gift of Susan W. Randall, 1922.5.2

Unidentified Artist

1668 *Clementina Ross* (Mrs. John F. Mifflin, 1769–1848), 1786
(after Robert Fulton)
Watercolor on ivory
$1\frac{7}{8}$ x $1\frac{1}{2}$ in. (4.7 x 3.7 cm.), oval
Engraved on case: CLEMENTINA ROSS. MRS JOHN F. MIFFLIN./B. Nov. 28. 1769 D. JAN. 12. 1848/ PARIS 1786/Bequest to Pa. Acad. Fine Arts/by Miss Elizabeth Mifflin, 1886
Bequest of Elizabeth Mifflin, 1886.4.1a
See also verso, cat. no. 1665.

Unidentified Artist

1669 *John Ross* (1729–1800), 1786
Watercolor on ivory
$1\frac{9}{16}$ x $1\frac{5}{16}$ in. (4 x 3.3 cm.), oval
Engraved on case: JOHN ROSS./B JAN. 29.1729/ D. MARCH 1800/PARIS 1786/Bequest to Pa. Acad. Fine Arts/By Miss Elizabeth Mifflin/1886
Bequest of Elizabeth Mifflin, 1886.4.2

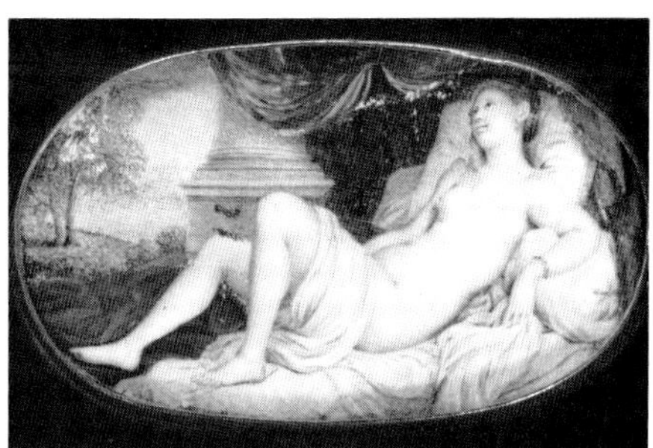
1659

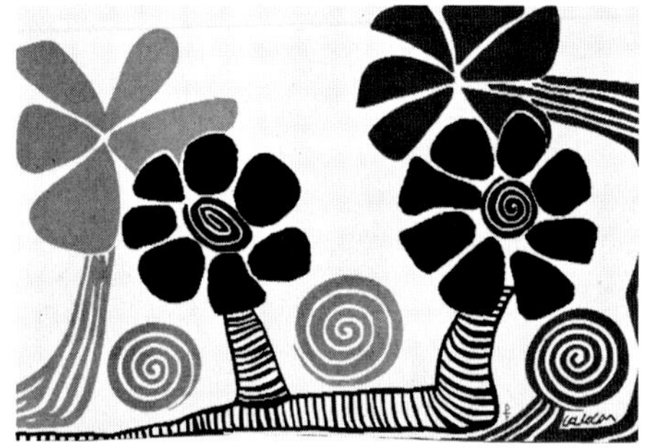
1670

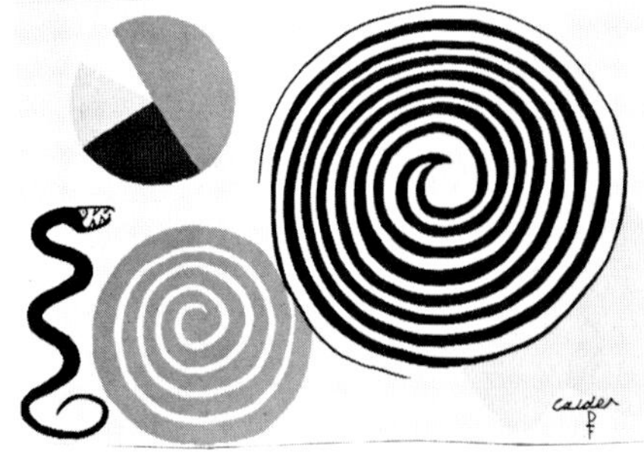
1671

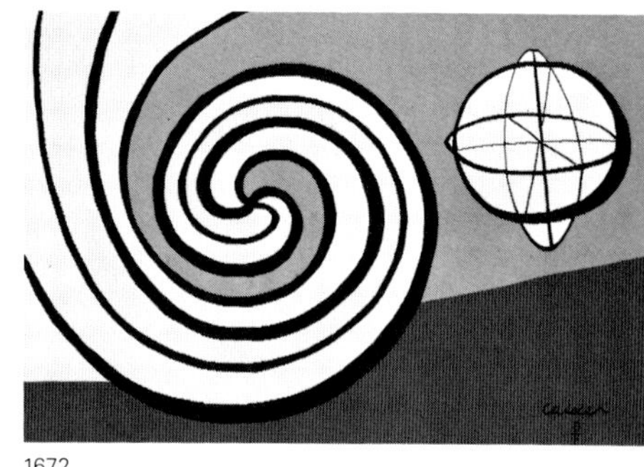
1672

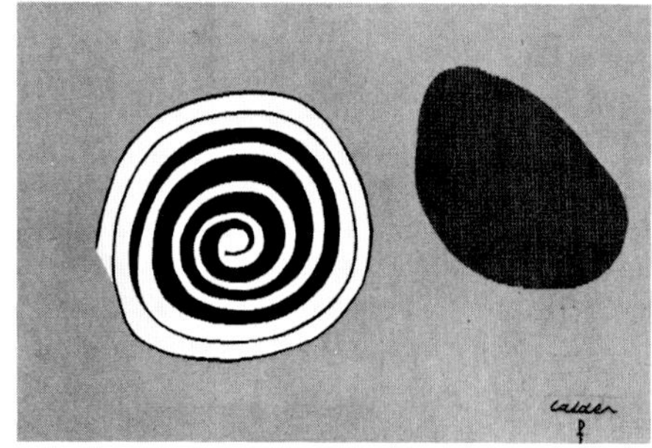
1673

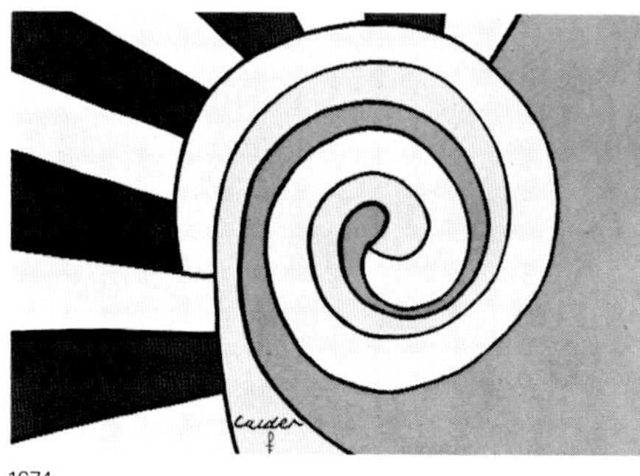
1674

1675

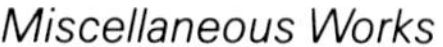
Miscellaneous Works

Alexander Calder (1898–1976)

The Bicentennial Tapestries:

1670 *Les Palmiers (The Palms)*, 1975
Wool
40½ x 59 in. (102.9 x 149.9 cm.)
Signed at lower right: Calder/P/F
Gift of Mr. and Mrs. Philip Berman, 1976.12.6

1671 *La Poire, le fromage, et le serpent (The Pear, the Cheese, and the Serpent)*, 1975
Wool
40½ x 59 in. (102.9 x 149.9 cm.)
Signed at lower right: Calder/P/F
Gift of Mr. and Mrs. Philip Berman, 1976.12.5

1672 *Le Sphère et les spirales (The Sphere and the Spirals)*, 1975
Wool
40½ x 59 in. (102.9 x 149.9 cm.)
Signed at lower right: Calder/P/F
Gift of Mr. and Mrs. Philip Berman, 1976.12.4

1673 *La Tache bleue (The Blue Blob)*, 1975
Wool
40½ x 59 in. (102.9 x 149.9 cm.)
Signed at lower right: Calder/P/F
Gift of Mr. and Mrs. Philip Berman, 1976.12.3

1674 *Trois Spirales (Three Spirals)*, 1975
Wool
40½ x 59 in. (102.9 x 149.9 cm.)
Signed at lower center: Calder/P/F
Gift of Mr. and Mrs. Philip Berman, 1976.12.2

1675 *Les Vagues (The Waves)*, 1975
Wool
40½ x 59 in. (102.9 x 149.9 cm.)
Signed at lower right: Calder/P/F
Gift of Mr. and Mrs. Philip Berman, 1976.12.1

Judy Chicago (1939–)

1676 *Creation of the World*, 1980–81
Design by Judy Chicago, embroidered by Pamela Nesbit
8 x 16 in. (20.3 x 40.6 cm.)
Gift of Through the Flower Corporation, 1985.2

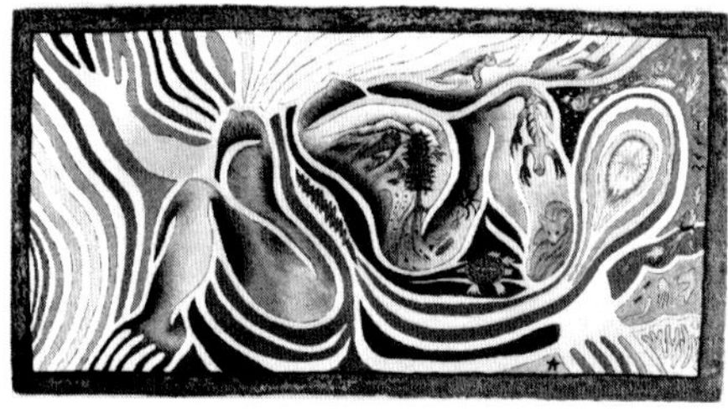
1676

John La Farge (1835–1910)

1677 *Curtain Design* (stained-glass window from Thomas E. Grover House, Canton, Mass.), ca. 1884
Opalescent stained glass, lead came, and wood sash
39½ x 27¾ in. (100.3 x 70.5 cm.)
Gift of Mr. and Mrs. Theodore T. Newbold in memory of Louis I. Kahn, 1976.7.2

1678 *Hollyhocks and Morning Glories* (stained-glass window from Thomas E. Grover House, Canton, Mass.), ca. 1884
Opalescent stained glass, lead came, and wood sash
39½ x 27¾ in. (100.3 x 70.5 cm.)
Gift of Mr. and Mrs. Theodore T. Newbold in memory of Louis I. Kahn, 1976.7.1

Thomas Sully (1783–1872)

1679 *Dancing Doll*
Oil on paper with cloth, cloth flowers, and sequins
14½ x 9½ in. (36.8 x 24.1 cm.)
Gift of Marion Lummis, 1924.9

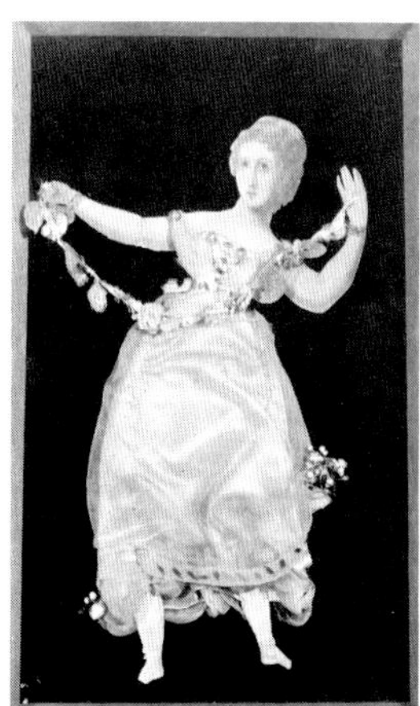

1679

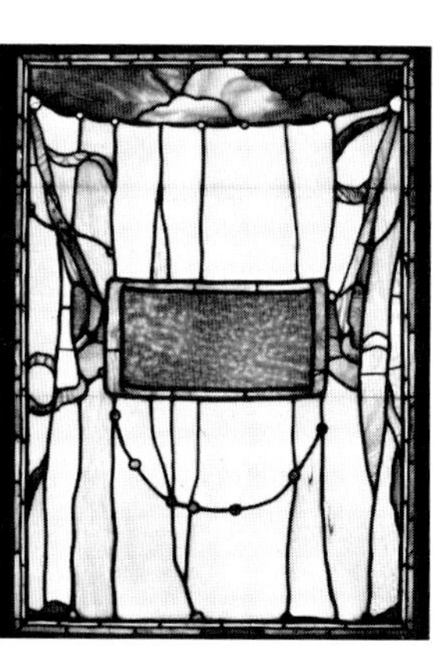
1677

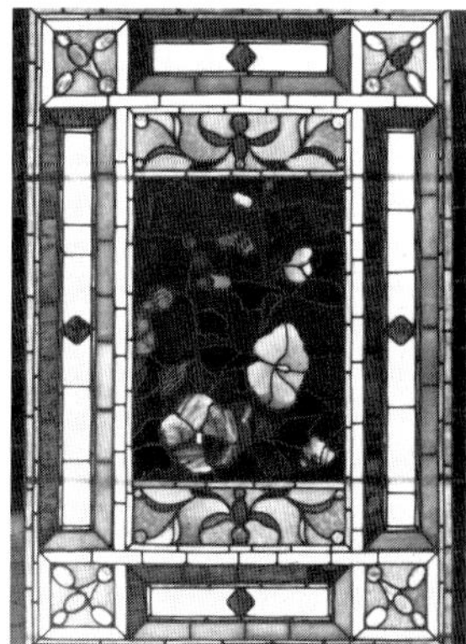
1678

Looking Back on Two Centuries of Collecting

The Pennsylvania Academy of the Fine Arts traces its history to mid-1805, when the founders acquired the land for its first building. The cornerstone was quickly laid, and an application for a charter was drawn up and signed by seventy-two prominent Philadelphians, including the artists Charles Willson Peale, his son Rembrandt, and William Rush. The charter was granted on March 28, 1806; and in the spring the Pennsylvania Academy opened to the public at Tenth and Chestnut streets. The board of directors sought advice on teaching from the eminent painter Benjamin West. He was then president of the Royal Academy in London and was acting as mentor to the many fledgling American artists who visited his studio. West recommended that students draw from casts of antique sculpture, and the Academy duly ordered such casts from Paris. In addition to their use in the School, these objects formed the beginning of the permanent collection.

The first paintings acquired for the collection were by European artists and, like the sculptures, were intended to serve as models for the art students. The first American painting to enter the collection was probably a portrait of the Academy's first president, George Clymer, painted and presented by Charles Willson Peale in 1809. Two years later, when the annual exhibitions were established, the Academy bought Gilbert Stuart's *George Washington (The Lansdowne Portrait)*, and thus began its long tradition of acquiring paintings from the annuals.

In 1805, Benjamin West had been chosen by the Pennsylvania Academy to be its first honorary member. Twenty-four artists, including Thomas Sully, became the first elected academicians in 1812. The board of directors initially stipulated that each new academician donate to the Academy "a specimen of his talents," but the requirement does not seem to have been put into effect. The only such donation was made by Sully, who gave his *Tribute Money,* a copy after Rubens.

The growth of the paintings collection was slow during most of the nineteenth century. Joseph Allen Smith became the first major donor when he gave his collection of European art in 1812. Two years later, the board of directors appointed a committee specifically to acquire American art, but funds were limited. Nevertheless, important American paintings were gradually acquired by gift and purchase. It was a major coup in 1816 when the Academy bought Washington Allston's early masterpiece *The Dead Man Restored to Life by Touching the Bones of the Prophet Elisha.* Sent from London where Allston was then living, the painting was the Academy's first acquisition of an American work in the popular style of monumental history and religious painting. Forty-six subscribers donated money toward the purchase price, but the Academy had to mortgage its building to make up the full amount. Charles R. Leslie's *The Murder of Rutland by Lord Clifford* was donated in 1831 by the artist's family. (Leslie's European studies had been subsidized by the Academy.)

In 1836 the building was mortgaged again in order to buy Benjamin West's *Death on the Pale Horse.* John Neagle's *Pat Lyon at the Forge* was given by the Lyon family in 1842, and in the same year Paul Beck, Jr., donated John Lewis Krimmel's *Country Wedding, Bishop White Officiating.* Three years later, the Academy bought Krimmel's *Fourth of July in Centre Square* from the Beck estate. Thomas Birch's *Fairmount Water Works,* depicting a new Philadelphia landmark designed by Frederick Graff, was bequeathed in 1845 by Charles Graff, the architect's brother. In 1854, three noteworthy portraits painted in Paris by Rembrandt Peale were purchased: *Jacques Louis David, Jean Antoine Houdon,* and *Dominique Vivant Denon.*

Two fires caused major setbacks in the nineteenth century. The first, an 1845 arson, destroyed the cast collection and a number of European paintings. Fortunately, West's *Death on the Pale Horse* was heroically saved by firemen who had to cut it from its stretcher. The second fire, in 1886, took a toll of forty-nine paintings and damaged seven others. Although the losses were substantial, the Academy recovered from both disasters and prospered. The School was growing rapidly, and the Academy commissioned the architectural firm of Frank Furness and George Hewitt to design a new building. It was built at the corner of Broad and Cherry streets and opened in 1876 during the nation's centennial celebration. The building, which the Academy still occupies, has been acclaimed an architectural masterpiece.

In the last decade of the nineteenth and first decade of the twentieth centuries, the collection was greatly expanded through the determined efforts of the Academy's president, Edward H. Coates, and its managing director, Harrison S. Morris. Through the Joseph E. Temple Fund alone, twenty-four paintings of exceptional quality were acquired. They included Cecilia Beaux's *New England Woman,* George de Forest Brush's *Mother and Child,* William Merritt Chase's *Portrait of Mrs. C. (Lady with a White Shawl),* Frank Duveneck's *The Turkish Page,* Thomas Eakins's *The Cello Player,* Alexander Harrison's *The Wave,* Childe Hassam's *Cat Boats, Newport,* Winslow Homer's *Fox Hunt,* Henry O. Tanner's *Nicodemus,* Edmund C. Tarbell's *The Golden Screen,* and John H. Twachtman's *Sailing in the Mist.* Among the acquisitions through the Henry D. Gilpin Fund during those years were William Morris Hunt's *Study for "The Flight of Night"* and Charles C. Curran's *A Breezy Day.* In 1891, Daniel Ridgway Knight's *Hailing the Ferry* was given by John H. Converse, a member of the board of directors. An important gift from Edward H. Coates's own collection was given in his memory by his wife in 1923; the paintings included Thomas Hovenden's beautiful *Peonies*, Thomas Moran's *Venice*, and William Trost Richards's *February.*

The Gilpin, John Lambert, and Temple funds have provided important acquisitions during the twentieth century. Through the Gilpin fund, for example, came works by Isabel Bishop, Reginald Marsh, and Raphael Soyer, and, more recently, Fairfield Porter and Richard Diebenkorn. Edward Hopper's *Apartment Houses* and two paintings by Stuart Davis, *Table with Pipe* and *Letter and His Ecol*, were acquired through the Lambert fund. The Temple fund made possible the purchase of *North River* by George Bellows, *Ultra-Marine* by Stuart Davis, *Clown with Folded Arms* by Walt Kuhn, and *Young America* by Andrew Wyeth.

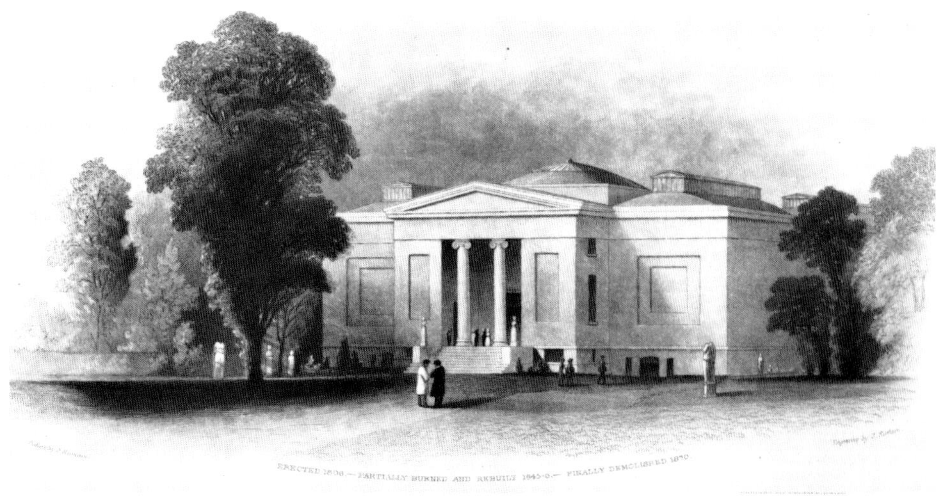

Pennsylvania Academy's second building, designed by Richard Gilpin and located at Tenth and Chestnut streets, 1847-70. Mezzotint, engraving, and etching by John Sartain, after 1870, after a drawing by James Hamilton (Pennsylvania Academy of the Fine Arts, Dr. Paul J. Sartain bequest)

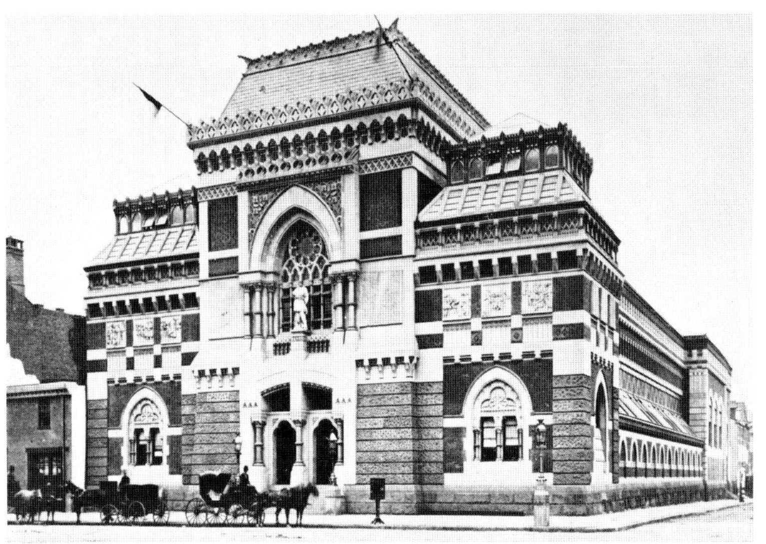

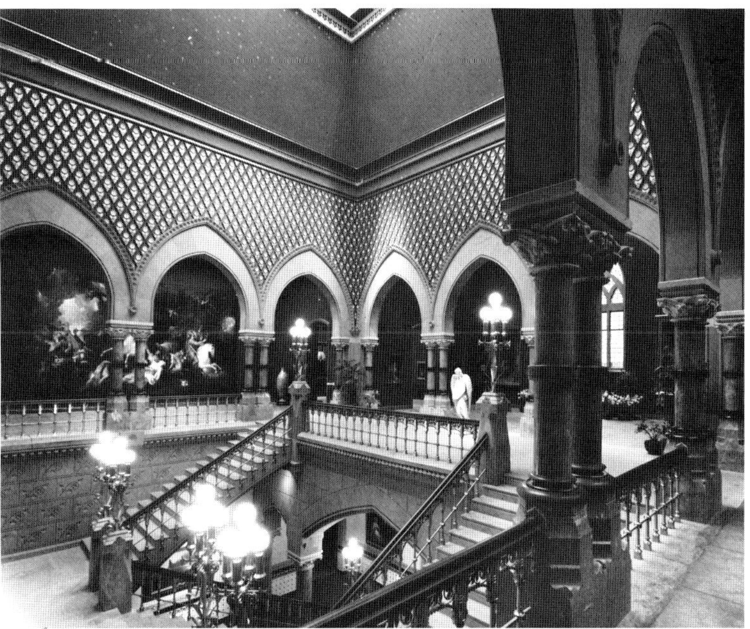

Pennsylvania Academy's present main building, designed by Frank Furness and George Hewitt and located at Broad and Cherry streets. Facade, ca. 1876 (top), and Grand Stairhall (both photos from archives of Pennsylvania Academy)

In the 1980s, the Pennsylvania Academy has acquired works by major contemporary painters, including Gregory Amenoff's *Gordian Knot II*, William Bailey's *Monte Migiana Still Life,* Red Grooms's *A Room in Connecticut*, Alex Katz's *Night*, Philip Pearlstein's *Two Female Models on Hammock and Floor*, and Irving Petlin's *The Disappeared*.

The collection has always had a special relationship with the School–the students learning from the art in the collection and the Museum buying outstanding faculty and student art for the collection. Three groups of paintings, however, bear a particular historical significance. The first is a series of grisaille paintings commissioned to illustrate William C. Brownell's "The Art Schools of Philadelphia (with Illustrations by the Pupils)," which appeared in the September 1879 issue of *Scribner's Monthly.* The Academy and especially Thomas Eakins's teaching methods were discussed. Ten monochrome paintings by students were reproduced by wood engraving as illustrations. Six of these small, informative works remain in the paintings collection: Thomas P. Anshutz's *Dissecting Room*, Walter M. Dunk's *Men's Life Class*, Charles Lewis Fussell's *Academy Students Dissecting a Horse*, James P. Kelly's *The Modeling Class*, Alice Barber Stephens's *The Women's Life Class*, and Charles H. Stephens's *Anatomical Lecture by Dr. William Williams Kean.*

In 1896–97, a series of murals was made for the lecture room (now the Hamilton Auditorium) by older students and artists connected with the School. Henry Thouron, an instructor, supervised the project; and the board of directors paid the students' expenses. There were thirteen panels on the arts and sciences (*Allegro* by Eleanor Plaisted Abbott; *Pastoral Music* by William J. Edmondson; *Science* by William J. Glackens; *Military Music* by Frederick W. Gruger; *Adagio* by Alice Turner Mumford; *Sacred Music, The Senses (Hearing and Touch)*, and *The Senses (Taste, Sight, and Smell)* by Francis W. Sheafer; *Dramatic Music* by John Sloan; *Classical Music* by Frank W. Taylor; *Poetry* by Francis Vaux Wilson; *Art* by Georgie York; and *Concerted Music* by Charles Morris Young). Eight other panels, depicting the Muses, were painted; only two still exist, *Clio* by William J. Edmondson and *Euterpe* by Francis W. Sheafer. A panel by Maxfield Parrish to cover the proscenium arch and a series of sculptures in high relief by students in the modeling classes were planned but never carried out. In 1911, the board of directors approved another group of murals by students for the corridor of the School. Chosen by competition, the designs were executed under the direction of Henry Pearson, an instructor in composition. Six works were completed by 1912 (*Agriculture* by Julius T. Block, *Landscape Painting* by Burton R. Keeler, *Poetry* by Gertrude A. Lambert, *Architecture* by Gertrude Monaghan, *Commerce* by Rowley W. Murphy, and *Music* by Edward Ulreich). A seventh was added in 1924: *Harvest Evening* by Frank Baisden. These murals deserve special attention as examples of a once popular form of American art, brought to its peak in many government buildings during the 1930s through the WPA projects of the New Deal.

The permanent collection contains a substantial number of works by past and present Academy faculty and students. Recently received, for example, was a gift of more than 4,000 objects (paintings, books, drawings, and pastels) from the estate of Violet Oakley, a prominent Philadelphia artist and much-loved teacher at the Academy. Quite a few former students have, after becoming established, donated or bequeathed paintings to the Academy. More often, however, the works were acquired from Academy exhibitions in which they had been judged so outstanding as to merit purchase prizes. The paintings collection also bears the names of the many Academy presidents and members of the board of directors who generously donated funds and works of art. As a grace note, the collection contains portraits of some of these people who did so much to shape it–the artists Charles Willson Peale, Violet Oakley, and Henry Thouron, such collectors as the Carey brothers, Joseph E. Temple, and Bernice McIlhenny (later Mrs. John Wintersteen), and the Academy administrators Edward H. Coates, Harrison S. Morris, and Joseph T. Fraser, Jr.–to name only a few. Their likenesses make up the Academy's own "family portraits."

INDEX

Numbers refer to entries rather than pages.

I

J

K

Q

R

T

U

V

W